D1481717

BENJAMIN FRANKLIN

Benjamin Franklin

REPRESENTATIVE SELECTIONS, WITH
INTRODUCTION, BIBLIOGRAPHY, AND NOTES

BY

CHESTER E. JORGENSON

AND

FRANK LUTHER MOTT

Revised Edition

American Century Series

ⓌHILL AND WANG — NEW YORK

The bibliography in this American Century Series edition of
Benjamin Franklin has been revised and brought up to date.
The original edition was published in the American Writers
Series, under the general editorship of Harry Hayden Clark.

PREFACE

Benjamin Franklin's reputation in America has been singularly distorted by the neglect of his works other than his *Autobiography* and his most utilitarian aphorisms. If America has contented herself with appraising him as "the earliest incarnation of 'David Harum,'" as "the first high-priest of the religion of efficiency," as "the first Rotarian," it may be that this aspect of Franklin is all that an America plagued by growing pains, by peopling and mechanizing three thousand miles of frontier, has been able to see. That facet of Franklin's mind and mien which allowed Carlyle to describe him as "the Father of all Yankees" was appreciated by Sinclair Lewis's George F. Babbitt: "Once in a while I just naturally sit back and size up this Solid American Citizen, with a whale of a lot of satisfaction." But this is not the Franklin of "imperturbable common-sense" honored by Matthew Arnold as "the very incarnation of sanity and clear-sense, a man the most considerable . . . whom America has yet produced." Nor is this the Franklin who emerges from his collected works (and the opinions of his notable contemporaries) as an economist, political theorist, educator, journalist, scientific deist, and disinterested scientist. If he wrote little that is narrowly belles-lettres, he need not be ashamed of his voluminous correspondence, in an age which saw the fruition of the epistolary art. The Franklin found in his collected and uncollected writings is, as the following Introduction may suggest, not the Franklin who too commonly is synchronized exclusively with the wisdom and wit of *Poor Richard*.

Since the present interpretation of the growth of Franklin's mind, with stress upon its essential unity in the light of scientific deism, tempered by his debt to Puritanism, classicism, and neo-classicism, may seem somewhat novel, the editors have felt it desirable to document their interpretation with considerable fullness. It is hoped that the reader will withhold judgment as to the validity of this interpretation until the documentary

v

evidence has been fully considered in its genetic significance, and that he will feel able to incline to other interpretations only in proportion as they can be equally supported by other evidence. The present interpretation is also supported by the Selections following—the fullest collection hitherto available in one volume—which offer, the editors believe, the essential materials for a reasonable acquaintance with the growth of Franklin's mind, from youth to old age, in its comprehensive interests—educational, literary, journalistic, economic, political, scientific, humanitarian, and religious.

With the exception of the selections from the *Autobiography*, the works are arranged in approximate chronological order, hence inviting a necessarily genetic study of Franklin's mind. The *Dissertation on Liberty and Necessity, Pleasure and Pain*, never before printed in an edition of Franklin's works or in a book of selections, is here printed from the London edition of 1725, retaining his peculiarities of italics, capitalization, and punctuation. Attention is also drawn to the photographically reproduced complete text of *Poor Richard Improved* (1753), graciously furnished by the late William Smith Mason. *The Way to Wealth* is from an exact reprint made by Mr. Mason, and with his permission here reproduced. One of the editors is grateful for the privilege of consulting Mr. Mason's magnificent collection of Franklin correspondence (original MSS), especially the Franklin-Galloway and Franklin-Jonathan Shipley (Bishop of St. Asaph) unpublished correspondence. With Mr. Mason's generous permission the editors reproduce fragments of this correspondence in the Introduction.

The bulk of the selections have been printed from the latest, standard edition, *The Writings of Benjamin Franklin*, collected and edited with a Life and Introduction by Albert Henry Smyth (10 vols., 1905-1907). For permission to use this material the editors are grateful to The Macmillan Company, publishers. The editors are indebted to the late Dr. Max Farrand, Director of the Henry E. Huntington Library, for permission to reprint part of Franklin's MS version of the *Autobiography*.

The work of the editors has been vastly eased by Beata

Preface

Prochnow Jorgenson's assistance in typing and proofreading. They are extremely grateful to Professor Harry Hayden Clark for incisive suggestions and valuable editorial assistance.

Although our knowledge of Dr. B. Franklin as man and mind has been deepened by the scholarship of the past quarter century, we are not aware that the added facts oblige us to change our interpretations of 1936. Of the many additions to the original bibliography, the most important is the projected Yale University edition of forty volumes, *The Papers of Benjamin Franklin*, edited by Professor Leonard W. Labaree and his associates. But until the Yale edition is completed, the student of Franklin will still be dependent on the collections arranged by Sparks, Bigelow, and Smyth.

C. E. J.
F. L. M.

CONTENTS

INTRODUCTION
    I. Franklin's Milieu: The Age of Enlightenment, xiii
    II. Franklin's Theories of Education, xxxii
    III. Franklin's Literary Theory and Practice, xlvi
    IV. Franklin as Printer and Journalist, lvii
    V. Franklin's Economic Views, lxiv
    VI. Franklin's Political Theories, lxxxii
    VII. Franklin as Scientist and Deist, cx

CHRONOLOGICAL TABLE, cxlii

SELECTED BIBLIOGRAPHY
    I. Works, cli
    II. Collections and Reprints, cliv
    III. Biographies, clvi
    IV. Biographical and Critical Studies, clix
    V. The Age of Franklin, clxxvi
    VI. Bibliographies and Check Lists, clxxxvii

SELECTIONS
    From the Autobiography, 3
    Dogood Papers, No. I (1722), 96
    Dogood Papers, No. IV (1722), 98
    Dogood Papers, No. V (1722), 102
    Dogood Papers, No. VII (1722), 105
    Dogood Papers, No. XII (1722), 109
    Editorial Preface to the *New England Courant* (1723), 111
    A Dissertation on Liberty and Necessity, Pleasure and Pain (1725), 114
    Rules for a Club Established for Mutual Improvement (1728), 128
    Articles of Belief and Acts of Religion (1728), 130
    The Busy-Body, No. 1 (1728/9), 137
    The Busy-Body, No. 2 (1728/9), 139
    The Busy-Body, No. 3 (1728/9), 141
    The Busy-Body, No. 4 (1728/9), 145
    Preface to the *Pennsylvania Gazette* (1729), 150
    A Dialogue between Philocles and Horatio (1730), 152
    A Second Dialogue between Philocles and Horatio (1730), 156
    A Witch Trial at Mount Holly (1730), 161
    An Apology for Printers (1731), 163
    Preface to *Poor Richard* (1733), 169
    A Meditation on a Quart Mugg (1733), 170
    Preface to *Poor Richard* (1734), 172

ix

Preface to *Poor Richard* (1735), 174

Hints for Those That Would Be Rich (1736), 176

To Josiah Franklin (April 13, 1738), 177

Preface to *Poor Richard* (1739), 179

A Proposal for Promoting Useful Knowledge among the British Plantations in America (1743), 180

Shavers and Trimmers (1743), 183

To the Publick (1743), 186

Preface to Logan's Translation of "Cato Major" (1743/4), 187

To John Franklin, at Boston (March 10, 1745), 188

Preface to *Poor Richard* (1746), 189

The Speech of Polly Baker (1747), 190

Preface to *Poor Richard* (1747), 193

To Peter Collinson (August 14, 1747), 194

Preface to *Poor Richard Improved* (1748), 195

Advice to a Young Tradesman (1748), 196

To George Whitefield (July 6, 1749), 198

Proposals Relating to the Education of Youth in Pensilvania (1749), 199

Idea of the English School (1751), 206

To Cadwallader Colden Esq., at New York (1751), 213

Exporting of Felons to the Colonies (1751), 214

Observations Concerning the Increase of Mankind, Peopling of Countries, Etc. (1751), 216

To Peter Collinson (October 19, 1752), 223

Poor Richard Improved (1753)—facsimile reproduction, 225

To Joseph Huey (June 6, 1753), 261

Three Letters to Governor Shirley (1754), 263

To Miss Catherine Ray, at Block Island (March 4, 1755), 270

To Peter Collinson (August 25, 1755), 272

To Miss Catherine Ray (September 11, 1755), 274

To Miss Catherine Ray (October 16, 1755), 277

To Mrs. Jane Mecom (February 12, 1756), 278

To Miss E. Hubbard (February 23, 1756), 278

To Rev. George Whitefield (July 2, 1756), 279

The Way to Wealth (1758), 280

To Hugh Roberts (September 16, 1758), 289

To Mrs. Jane Mecom (September 16, 1758), 291

To Lord Kames (May 3, 1760), 293

To Miss Mary Stevenson (June 11, 1760), 295

To Mrs. Deborah Franklin (June 27, 1760), 298

To Jared Ingersoll (December 11, 1762), 300

To Miss Mary Stevenson (March 25, 1763), 301

To John Fothergill, M.D. (March 14, 1764), 304

To Sarah Franklin (November 8, 1764), 307

From A Narrative of the Late Massacres in Lancaster County (1764), 308

To the Editor of a Newspaper (May 20, 1765), 315

To Lord Kames (June 2, 1765), 318

Letter Concerning the Gratitude of America (January 6, 1766), 321

To Lord Kames (April 11, 1767), 325

To Miss Mary Stevenson (September 14, 1767), 330

On the Labouring Poor (1768), 336

To Dupont de Nemours (July 28, 1768), 340

To John Alleyne (August 9, 1768), 341

To the Printer of the *London Chronicle* (August 18, 1768), 343

Positions to be Examined, Concerning National Wealth (1769), 345

To Miss Mary Stevenson (September 2, 1769), 347

To Joseph Priestley (September 19, 1772), 348

To Miss Georgiana Shipley (September 26, 1772), 349

To Peter Franklin (undated), 351

On the Price of Corn, and Management of the Poor (undated), 355

An Edict by the King of Prussia (1773), 358

Rules by Which a Great Empire May Be Reduced to a Small One
     (1773), 363

To William Franklin (October 6, 1773), 371

Preface to "An Abridgment of the Book of Common Prayer" (1773),
     374

A Parable against Persecution, 379

A Parable on Brotherly Love, 380

To William Strahan (July 5, 1775), 381

To Joseph Priestley (July 7, 1775), 382

To a Friend in England (October 3, 1775), 383

To Lord Howe (July 30, 1776), 384

The Sale of the Hessians (1777), 387

Model of a Letter of Recommendation (April 2, 1777), 389

To ——— (October 4, 1777), 390

To David Hartley (October 14, 1777), 390

A Dialogue between Britain, France, Spain, Holland, Saxony and
     America, 394

To Charles de Weissenstein (July 1, 1778), 397

The Ephemera (1778), 402

To Richard Bache (June 2, 1779), 404

Morals of Chess (1779), 406

To Benjamin Vaughan (November 9, 1779), 410

The Whistle (1779), 412

The Lord's Prayer (1779?), 414

The Levée (1779?), 417

Proposed New Version of the Bible (1779?), 419

To Joseph Priestley (February 8, 1780), 420

To George Washington (March 5, 1780), 421

To Miss Georgiana Shipley (October 8, 1780), 422

To Richard Price (October 9, 1780), 423

Dialogue between Franklin and the Gout (1780), 424

The Handsome and Deformed Leg (1780?), 430

To Miss Georgiana Shipley (undated), 432

To David Hartley (December 15, 1781), 434

Supplement to the Boston *Independent Chronicle* (1782), 434

To John Thornton (May 8, 1782), 443

To Joseph Priestley (June 7, 1782), 443

To Jonathan Shipley (June 10, 1782), 445

To James Hutton (July 7, 1782), 447

To Sir Joseph Banks (September 9, 1782), 448

Information to Those Who Would Remove to America (1782?), 449

Apologue (1783?), 458

To Sir Joseph Banks (July 27, 1783), 459

To Mrs. Sarah Bache (January 26, 1784), 460

An Economical Project (1784?), 466

To Samuel Mather (May 12, 1784), 471

To Benjamin Vaughan (July 26, 1784), 472

To George Whately (May 23, 1785), 479

To John Bard and Mrs. Bard (November 14, 1785), 481

To Jonathan Shipley (February 24, 1786), 481

To ————— (July 3, 1786?), 484

Speech in the Convention; On the Subject of Salaries (1787), 486

Motion for Prayers in the Convention (1787), 489

Speech in the Convention at the Conclusion of Its Deliberations (1787), 491

To the Editors of the *Pennsylvania Gazette* (1788), 493

To Rev. John Lathrop (May 31, 1788), 496

To the Editor of the *Federal Gazette* (1788?), 496

To Charles Carroll (May 25, 1789), 500

An Account of the Supremest Court of Judicature in Pennsylvania, viz. the Court of the Press (1789), 501

An Address to the Public (1789), 505

To David Hartley (December 4, 1789), 506

To Ezra Stiles (March 9, 1790), 507

On the Slave-Trade (1790), 510

Remarks Concerning the Savages of North America, 513

An Arabian Tale, 519

A Petition of the Left Hand (date unknown), 520

Some Good Whig Principles (date unknown), 521

The Art of Procuring Pleasant Dreams, 523

NOTES, 529

INTRODUCTION

I. FRANKLIN'S MILIEU: THE AGE OF ENLIGHTENMENT

Benjamin Franklin's reputation, according to John Adams, "was more universal than that of Leibnitz or Newton, Frederick or Voltaire, and his character more beloved and esteemed than any or all of them." [1] The historical critic recognizes increasingly that Adams was not thinking idly when he doubted whether Franklin's panegyrical and international reputation could ever be explained without doing "a complete history of the philosophy and politics of the eighteenth century." Adams conceived that an explication of Franklin's mind and activities integrated with the thought patterns of the epoch which fathered him "would be one of the most important that ever was written; much more interesting to this and future ages than the 'Decline and Fall of the Roman Empire.'" And such a historical and critical colossus is still among the works hoped for but yet unborn. Too often, even in the scholarly mind, Franklin has become a symbol, and it may be confessed, not a winged one, of the self-made man, of New-World practicality, of the successful tradesman, of the Sage of *Poor Richard* with his penny-saving economy and frugality. In short, the Franklin legend fails to transcend an allegory of the success of the *doer* in an America allegedly materialistic, uncreative, and unimaginative.

It is the purpose of this essay to show that Franklin, the American Voltaire,—always reasonable if not intuitive, encyclopedic if not sublimely profound, humane if not saintly,—is best explained with reference to the Age of Enlightenment, of which he was the completest colonial representative. Due atten-

[1] *The Works of John Adams*, ed. by C. F. Adams (Boston, 1856), I, 660.

tion will, however, be paid to other factors. And therefore it is necessary to begin with a brief survey of the pattern of ideas of the age to which he was responsive. Not without reason does one critic name him as "the most complete representative of his century that any nation can point to." [2]

When Voltaire, "the patriarch of the *philosophes*," in 1726 took refuge in England, he at once discovered minds and an attitude toward human experience which were to prove the seminal factors of the Age of Enlightenment. He found that Englishmen had acclaimed Bacon "the father of experimental philosophy," and that Newton, "the destroyer of the Cartesian system," was "as the Hercules of fabulous story, to whom the ignorant ascribed all the feats of ancient heroes." Voltaire then paused to praise Locke, who "destroyed innate ideas," Locke, than whom "no man ever had a more judicious or more methodical genius, or was a more acute logician." Bacon, Newton, and Locke brooded over the currents of eighteenth-century thought and were formative factors of much that is most characteristic of the Enlightenment.

To Bacon was given the honor of having distinguished between the fantasies of old wives' tales and the certainty of empiricism. Moved by the ghost of Bacon, the Royal Society had for its purpose, according to Hooke, "To improve the knowledge of naturall things, and all useful Arts, Manufactures, Mechanick practises, Engynes and Inventions by Experiments." [3] The zeal for experiment was equaled only by its miscellaneousness. Cheese making, the eclipses of comets, and the intestines

[2] W. P. Trent, "Benjamin Franklin," *McClure's Magazine*, VIII, 273 (Jan., 1897).

[3] Cited in C. R. Weld's *History of the Royal Society* (London, 1848), I, 146. For Baconian influence see I, 57 f. See also Edwin Greenlaw, "The New Science and English Literature in the Seventeenth Century," *Johns Hopkins Alumni Magazine*, XIII, 331–59 (1925). Of dominant tendencies he stresses (a) a "new realism, or sense of fact and reliance on observation and experiment"; (b) the disregard for authority in favor of free inquiry; and (c) the development of faith in progress, inspiring men to improve their worldly condition.

of gnats were alike the objects of telescopic or microscopic
scrutiny. The full implication of Baconian empiricism came to
fruition in Newton, who in 1672 was elected a Fellow of the
Royal Society. Bacon was not the least of those giants upon
whose shoulders Newton stood. To the experimental tradition
of Kepler, Brahe, Harvey, Copernicus, Galileo, and Bacon,
Newton joined the mathematical genius of Descartes; and as
a result became "as thoroughgoing an empiricist as he was a
consummate mathematician," for whom there was "no *a priori*
certainty." [4] At this time it is enough to note of Newtonianism,
that for the incomparable physicist "science was composed of
laws stating the mathematical behaviour of nature solely—laws
clearly deducible from phenomena and exactly verifiable in
phenomena—everything further is to be swept out of science,
which thus becomes a body of absolutely certain truth about
the doings of the physical world." [5] The pattern of ideas known
as Newtonianism may be summarized as embracing a belief in
(1) a universe governed by immutable natural laws, (2) which
laws constitute a sublimely harmonious system, (3) reflecting a
benevolent and all-wise Geometrician; (4) thus man desires to
effect a correspondingly harmonious inner heaven; (5) and feels
assured of the plausibility of an immortal life. Newton was a
believer in scriptural revelation. It is ironical that through his
cosmological system, mathematically demonstrable, he lent re-

---

[4] E. A. Burtt, *The Metaphysical Foundations of Modern Physical Science*,
208. Newtonianism as a method and a philosophy has been ably examined
by recent scholars. See, for examples, C. Becker, *The Declaration of Independence*, especially chap. II, and *The Heavenly City of the Eighteenth-
Century Philosophers;* and in Bibliography, pp. cli ff., below, W. M. Horton
(chap. II); C. S. Duncan; H. Drennon; L. Bloch; E. Halévy. See also
Isabel St. John Bliss, "Young's *Night Thoughts* in Relation to Contemporary Christian Apologetics," *Publications of the Modern Language Association*, XLIX, 37–70 (March, 1934); J. H. Randall, *The Making of the
Modern Mind* (Boston, 1926), chap. X ff.; H. H. Clark, "An Historical
Interpretation of Thomas Paine's Religion," *University of California
Chronicle*, XXXV, 56–87 (Jan., 1933), and "Toward a Reinterpretation
of Thomas Paine," *American Literature*, V, 133–45 (May, 1933).

[5] Burtt, *op. cit.* 223.

inforcement to deism, the most destructive intellectual solvent of the authority of the altar.

Deists, as defined by their contemporary, Ephraim Chambers (in his *Cyclopædia* . . . , London, 1728), are those "whose distinguishing character it is, not to profess any particular form, or system of religion; but only to acknowledge the existence of a God, without rendering him any external worship, or service. The Deists hold, that, considering the multiplicity of religions, the numerous pretences to revelation, and the precarious arguments generally advanced in proof thereof; the best and surest way is, to return to the simplicity of nature, and the belief of one God, which is the only truth agreed to by all nations." They "reject all revelations as an imposition, and believe no more than what natural light discovers to them. . . ." [6] The "simplicity of nature" signifies "the established order, and course of natural things; the series of second causes; or the laws which God has imposed on the motions impressed by him." [7] And attraction, a kind of *conatus accedendi*, is the crown, according to the eighteenth century, of the series of secondary causes. Hence, Newtonian physics became the surest ally of the deist in his quest for a religion, immutable and universal. The Newtonian progeny were legion: among them were Boyle, Keill, Desaguliers, Shaftesbury, Locke, Samuel Clarke, 'sGravesande, Boerhaave, Diderot, Trenchard and Gordon, Voltaire, Gregory, Maclaurin, Pemberton, and others. The eighteenth century echoed Fontenelle's eulogy that Newtonianism was "sublime geometry." If, as Boyle wrote, mathematical and mechanical principles were "the alphabet, in which God wrote the world," Newtonian science and empiricism were the lexicons which the deists used to read the cosmic volume in which the universal laws were inscribed. And the deists and the liberal political theorists "found the fulcrum for subverting existing institu-

[6] Article, "Deism."
[7] Article, "Nature."

tions and standards only in the laws of nature, discovered, as they supposed, by mathematicians and astronomers." [8]

Complementary to Newtonian science was the sensationalism of John Locke. Conceiving the mind as *tabula rasa*, discrediting innate ideas, Lockian psychology undermined such a theological dogma as total depravity—man's innate and inveterate malevolence—and hence was itself a kind of *tabula rasa* on which later were written the optimistic opinions of those who credited man's capacity for altruism. If it remained for the French *philosophes* to deify Reason, Locke honored it as the crowning experience of his sensational psychology. [9] Then, too, as Miss Lois Whitney has ably demonstrated, Lockian psychology "cleared the ground for either primitivism or a theory of progress." [10] In addition, his social compact theory, augmenting seventeenth-century liberalism, furnished the political theorists of the Enlightenment with "the principle of Consent" [11] in their

[8] P. Smith, *A History of Modern Culture* (New York, 1934), II, 17–8.

[9] See S. Hefelbower, *The Relation of John Locke to English Deism.*

[10] *Primitivism and the Idea of Progress in English Popular Literature of the Eighteenth Century*, 168–9: "One inference that might be drawn from the theory was that while the infant whose mind is a blank page at birth is not so well off from the primitivistic point of view as the one who comes into the world already equipped with a complete set of the laws of nature and a predisposition to obey them, he is infinitely better off than the infant whose poor little mind had been loaded with original sin by his remote ancestors. For the orthodox baby, born in sin, there is almost no hope, except in supernatural aid; but if we suppose that man's ideas are all derived, as Locke postulated, from sense-impressions, then we may conclude that all men, rich and poor, primitive and civilized, are on an equal footing intellectually at birth. Although the primitive child does not have the help of civilization in the development of his mind, neither does he have its superstitions, prejudices, and corrupting influences; and he might actually be better off than the product of civilization—at least so many a primitivist argued. But one might draw another inference from the *tabula rasa* theory. Men, however corrupt they are now, may still have a chance of regeneration if their mind is really like blank paper at birth." For eighteenth-century primitivism see also H. N. Fairchild, *The Noble Savage* (New York, 1928).

[11] H. J. Laski, *Political Thought in England from Locke to Bentham* (New York, 1920), 9. See also W. A. Dunning, *A History of Political Theories from Luther to Montesquieu;* G. S. Veitch, *Genesis of Parliamentary Reform;* and G. P. Gooch, *English Democratic Ideas in the Seventeenth Century* (2d ed., Cambridge, England, 1927).

antipathy for monarchial obscurantism. Locke has been described as the "originator of a psychology which provided democratic government with a scientific basis." [12] The full impact of Locke will be felt when philosophers deduce that if sensations and reflections are the product of outward stimuli—those of nature, society, and institutions—then to reform man one needs only to reform society and institutions, or remove to some tropical isle. We remember that the French Encyclopedists, for example, were motivated by their faith in the "indefinite malleability of human nature by education and institutions." [13]

"With the possible exception of John Locke," C. A. Moore observes, "Shaftesbury was more generally known in the mid-century than any other English philosopher." [14] Shaftesbury's a priori "virtuoso theory of benevolence" may be viewed as complementary to Locke's psychology to the extent that both have within them the implication that through education and reform man may become perfectible. Both tend to undermine social, political, and religious authoritarianism. Shaftesbury's insistence upon man's innate altruism and compassion, coupled with the deistic and rationalistic divorce between theology and morality, resulted in the dogma that the most acceptable service to God is expressed in kindness to God's other children and helped to motivate the rise of humanitarianism.

The idea of progress [15] was popularized (if not born) in the eighteenth century. It has been recently shown that not only

[12] K. Martin, *French Liberal Thought in the Eighteenth Century*, 13.
[13] See J. B. Bury, *The Idea of Progress*, chap. VIII; and J. Morley, *Diderot and the Encyclopædists*, I, 6: "The great central moral of it all was this: that human nature is good, that the world is capable of being made a desirable abiding-place, and that the evil of the world is the fruit of bad education and bad institutions."
[14] "Shaftesbury and the Ethical Poets in England, 1700-1700, *Publications of the Modern Language Association*, XXXI (N. S. XXIV), 277 (June, 1916).
[15] See Bury, *op. cit.*; Whitney, *op. cit.*; and J. Delvaille, *Essai sur l'histoire de l'idée de progrès* (Paris, 1910).

the results of scientific investigations but also Anglican defenses of revealed religion served to accelerate a belief in progress. In answer to the atheists and deists who indicted revealed religion because revelation was given so late in the growth of the human family and hence was not eternal, universal, and immutable, the Anglican apologists were forced into the position of asserting that man enjoyed a progressive ascent, that the religious education of mankind is like that of the individual. If, as the deists charged, Christ appeared rather belatedly, the apologists countered that he was sent only when the race was prepared to profit by his coming. God's revelations thus were adjusted to progressive needs and capacities.[16]

Carl Becker has suggestively dissected the Enlightenment in a series of antitheses between its credulity and its skepticism. If the eighteenth-century philosopher renounced Eden, he discovered Arcadia in distant isles and America. Rejecting the authority of the Bible and church, he accepted the authority of "nature," natural law, and reason. Although scorning metaphysics, he desired to be considered philosophical. If he denied miracles, he yet had a fond faith in the perfectibility of the species.[17]

Even as Voltaire had his liberal tendencies stoutly reinforced by contact with English rationalism and deism,[18] so were the other French *philosophes*, united in their common hatred of the Roman Catholic church, also united in their indebtedness to exponents of English liberalism, dominated by Locke and Newton. If, as Madame de Lambert wrote in 1715, Bayle more than others of his age shook "the Yoke of authority and opinion," English free thought powerfully reinforced the native French revolt against authoritarianism. After 1730 English was the

[16] R. Crane, "Anglican Apologetics and the Idea of Progress, 1699–1745," *Modern Philology*, XXXI, 273–306 (Feb., 1934), and 349–82 (May, 1934).
[17] *The Heavenly City of the Eighteenth-Century Philosophers*, 30–1.
[18] N. L. Torrey, *Voltaire and the English Deists*.

model for French thought.[19]   Nearly all of Locke's works had
been translated in France before 1700.   Voltaire's affinity for the
English mind has already been touched on.   D'Alembert comments, "When we measure the interval between a Scotus and a
Newton, or rather between the works of Scotus and those of
Newton, we must cry out with Terence, *Homo homini quid
præstat.*" [20]

Any doctrine was intensely welcome which would allow
the Frenchman to regain his natural rights curtailed by the
revocation of the Edict of Nantes, by the inequalities of a state
vitiated by privileges, by an economic structure tottering because of bankruptcy attending unsuccessful wars and the up-
keep of a Versailles with its dazzling ornaments, and by a religious program dominated by a Jesuit rather than a Gallican
church. [21]   Economic, political, and religious abuses were in-
extricably united; the spirit of revolt did not feel obliged to
discriminate between the authority of the crown and nobles and
the authority of the altar.   Graphic is Diderot's vulgar vitupera-
tion: he would draw out the entrails of a priest to strangle a king!

Let us now turn to the American backgrounds.   The bibliolatry of colonial New England is expressed in William
Bradford's resolve to study languages so that he could "see with
his own eyes the ancient oracles of God in all their native
beauty." [22]   In addition to furnishing the new Canaan with

<hr/>

[19] D. Mornet, *French Thought in the Eighteenth Century*, 50–1. Also see
his *Les sciences de la nature en France au XVIIIᵉ siècle* (Paris, 1911),
and R. L. Cru, *Diderot as a Disciple of English Thought* (New York,
1913).   See Morley, *op. cit.*, I, 31 ff., and Martin, *op. cit.*

[20] *An Account of the Destruction of the Jesuits in France* (Glasgow, 1766),
61.

[21] Consult M. Roustan, *The Pioneers of the French Revolution*, and L.
Ducros, *French Society in the Eighteenth Century.*

[22] Quoted in J. Fiske's *The Beginnings of New England*, 73.   For
the seventeenth-century New England way, see especially F. H. Foster,
A Genetic History of the New England Theology (Chicago, 1907); P. Miller,
Orthodoxy in Massachusetts, 1630–1650: A Genetic Study (Cambridge,
Mass., 1933); B. Wendell, *Cotton Mather, The Puritan Priest;* I. W. Riley,
American Philosophy: The Early Schools, 3–58 and *passim;* H. W.

ecclesiastical and political precedent, Scripture provided "not a partiall, but a perfect rule of Faith, and manners." Any dogma contravening the "ancient oracle" was a weed sown by Satan and fit only to be uprooted and thrown in the fire. The colonial seventeenth century was one which, like John Cotton, regularly sweetened its mouth "with a piece of Calvin." One need not be reminded that Calvinism was inveterately and completely antithetical to the dogma of the Enlightenment.[23] Calvinistic bibliolatry contended with "the sacred book of nature." Its wrathful though just Deity was unlike the compassionate, virtually depersonalized Deity heralded in the eighteenth century, in which the Trinity was dissolved. The redemptive Christ became the amiable philosopher. Adam's universally contagious guilt was transferred to social institutions, especially the tyrannical forms of kings and priests. Calvin's forlorn and depraved man became a creature naturally compassionate. If once man worshipped the Deity through seeking to parallel the divine laws scripturally revealed, in the eighteenth century he honored his benevolent God, who was above demanding worship, through kindnesses shown God's other children. The individual was lost in society, self-perfection gave way to humanitarianism, God to Man, theology to morality, and faith to reason. The colonial seventeenth century was politically oligarchical:

Schneider, *The Puritan Mind;* J. Haroutunian, *Piety versus Moralism;* R. and L. Boas, *Cotton Mather: Keeper of the Puritan Conscience* (New York, 1928). See Bk. V of Mather's *Magnalia,* "prose epic of New England Puritanism" (B. Wendell, *Literary History of America,* 50).

[23] Prior to the Treaty of Paris (1763) the American colonies were indebted primarily to English liberalism for ideas subversive of colonial orthodoxy. If works of Fénelon, Fontenelle, Bayle, Voltaire, and Rousseau are occasionally found in the colonies prior to 1763, these are dwarfed beside the impact of such English minds as those of Trenchard and Gordon, Collins, Wollaston, Tillotson, Boyle, Shaftesbury, Locke, and Newton. It was only in the twilight of the century that French liberalism, itself nursed on English speculation, began to impinge on the thought-life of the colonies. See H. M. Jones, *America and French Culture.* Also see L. Rosenthal, "Rousseau at Philadelphia," *Magazine of American History,* VII, 46–55. See works of Riley, Koch, Gohdes, Morais, in Bibliography, pp. cli ff., below.

when Thomas Hooker heckled Winthrop on the lack of suffrage, Winthrop with no compromise asserted that "the best
part is always the least, and of that best part the wiser part is
always the lesser." [24] If the seventeenth-century college was a
cloister for clerical education, the Enlightenment sought to
train the layman for citizenship.

With the turn of the seventeenth century several forces came
into prominence, undermining New England's Puritan heritage.
Among those relevant for our study are: the ubiquitous frontier,
and the rise of Quakerism, deism, Methodism, and science. The
impact of the frontier was neglected until Professor Turner
called attention to its existence; he writes that "the most important effect of the frontier has been in the promotion of
democracy here and in Europe. . . . It produces antipathy to
control, and particularly to any direct control. . . . The frontier
conditions prevalent in the colonies are important factors in
the explanation of the American Revolution. . . ." [25] In the
period included in our survey the frontier receded from the coast
to the fall line to the Alleghenies: at each stage it "did indeed
furnish a new field of opportunity, a gate of escape from the
bondage of the past; and freshness, and confidence, and scorn
of older society, impatience of its restraints and its ideas, and
indifference to its lessons, have accompanied the frontier." [26]
One recalls the spirited satire on frontier conditions, as the above
aspects give birth to violence and disregard for law, in Hugh
Brackenridge's *Modern Chivalry*. Under the satire one feels the
justness of the attack, intensified by our knowledge that Brackenridge grew up "in a democratic Scotch-Irish back-country
settlement." If the frontiersmen during the eighteenth century
did not place their dirty boots on their governors' desks, they
were partially responsible for an inveterate spirit of revolt,

[24] Fiske, *op. cit.*, 124.
[25] F. J. Turner, *The Frontier in American History* (New York, 1920), 30.
[26] *Ibid.*, 38.

shown so brutally in the "massacres" provoked by the "Paxton boys" of Pennsylvania. One is not unprepared to discover resentment against the forms of authority in a territory in which a strong back is more immediately important than a knowledge of debates on predestination. Granting the importance of the frontier in opposing the theocratic Old Way, it must be considered in terms of other and more complex factors.

Reinforcing Edwards's Great Awakening, George Whitefield, especially in the Middle Colonies, challenged the growing complacence of colonial religious thought with his insistence that man "is by nature half-brute and half-devil." It has been suggested that Methodism in effect allied itself with the attitudes of Hobbes and Mandeville in attacking man's nature, and hence by reaction tended to provoke "a primitivism based on the doctrine of natural benevolence." [27]

The "New English Israel" was harried by the Quakers,[28] who preached the priesthood of all believers and the right of private judgment. They denied the total depravity of the natural man and the doctrine of election; they gloried in a loving Father, and scourged the ecclesiastical pomp and ceremony of other religions. They were possessed by a blunt enthusiasm which held the immediate private revelation anterior to scriptural revelation. Faithful to the inner light, the Quakers seemed to neglect Scripture. Although the less extreme Quakers, such as John Woolman, did not blind themselves to the need for personal introspection and self-conquest, Quakerism as a movement tended to place the greater emphasis on morality articulate in terms of fellow-service, and lent momentum to the rise of humanitarianism expressed in prison reform and anti-slavery agitation. Also one may wonder to what extent colonial Quakerism tended to lend sanction to the rising democratic spirit.

In the person of Cotton Mather, until recently considered a

[27] Whitney, *op. cit.*, 83–4.
[28] See R. M. Jones, *The Quakers in the American Colonies* (London, 1921).

bigoted incarnation of the "Puritan spirit . . . become ossified," are discovered forces which, when divorced from Puritan theology, were to become the sharpest wedges splintering the deep-rooted oak of the Old Way. These forces were the authority of reason and science. In *The Christian Philosopher*,[29] basing his attitude on the works of Ray, Derham, Cheyne, and Grew,[30] Mather attempted to shatter the Calvinists' antithesis between science and theology, asserting "that [Natural] Philosophy is no Enemy, but a mighty and wondrous Incentive to Religion."[31] He warned that since even Mahomet with the aid of reason found the Workman in his Work, Christian theologians should fear "lest a Mahometan be called in for thy Condemnation!"[32] Studying nature's sublime order, one must be blind if his thoughts are not carried heavenward to "admire that Wisdom itself!" Although Mather mistrusted Reason, he accepted it as "the voice of God"—an experience which enabled him to discover the workmanship of the Deity in nature. Magnetism, the vegetable kingdom, the stars infer a harmonious order, so wondrous that only a God could have created it. If Reason is no complete substitute for Scripture it offers enough evidence to hiss atheism out of the world: "A Being that must be superior to Matter, even the Creator and Governor of all Matter, is everywhere so conspicuous, that there can be nothing more monstrous than to deny the God that is above."[33] Sir Isaac Newton with his mathematical and experimental proof of the sublime universal order strung on invariable secondary causes, Mather confessed, is "our perpetual Dictator."[34] Conceiving of science as a rebuke to the atheist, and a natural ally to scrip-

---

[29] T. Hornberger's "The Date, the Source, and the Significance of Cotton Mather's Interest in Science," *American Literature*, VI, 413–20 (Jan., 1935), offers evidence to show that Mather's thought in this work is latent in earlier works.

[30] K. Murdock (ed.), *Selections from Cotton Mather* (New York, 1926), xlix–l; see G. L. Kittredge items (Murdock, lxii), and Hornberger, *op. cit.*

[31] Murdock, *op. cit.*, 286.   [32] *Ibid.*, 292.

[33] *Ibid.*, 349.   [34] Riley, *op. cit.*, 196.

tural theology, Mather, like a Newton himself, juxtaposed rationalism and faith in one pyramidal confirmation of the existence, omnipotence, and benevolence of God. Here were variations from Calvinism's common path which, when augmented by English and French liberalism, by the influence of Quakerism and the frontier, were to give rise to democracy, rationalism, and scientific deism. The Church of England through the seventeenth and eighteenth centuries had "pursued a liberal latitudinarian policy which, as a mode of thought, tended to promote deism by emphasizing rational religion and minimizing revelation."[35] It was to be expected that in colonies created by Puritans (or even Quakers), deism would have a less spectacular and extensive success than it appears to have had in the mother country. If militant deism remained an aristocratic cult until the Revolution,[36] scientific rationalism (Newtonianism) long before this, from the time of Mather, became a common ally of orthodoxy. If a "religion of nature" may be defined with Tillotson as "obedience to Natural Law, and the performance of such duties as Natural Light, without any express and supernatural revelation, doth dictate to man," then it was in the colonies, prior to the Revolution, more commonly a buttress to revealed religion than an equivalent to it.

Lockian sensism and Newtonian science were the chief sources of that brand of colonial rationalism which at first complemented orthodoxy, and finally buried it among lost causes. The Marquis de Chastellux was astounded when he found on a center table in a Massachusetts inn an "Abridgment of Newton's Philosophy"; whereupon he "put some questions" to his host "on physics and geometry," with which he "found him well acquainted."[37] Now, even a superficial reading of the eighteenth century discloses countless allusions to Newton, his

---

[35] Quoted in H. M. Morais, *Deism in Eighteenth Century America*, 25.
[36] *Ibid.*, 17. See also G. A. Koch, *Republican Religion*.
[37] *Travels in North America, in the Years 1780, 1781, and 1782* (London, 1787), I, 445.

popularizers, and the implications of his physics and cosmology. As Mr. Brasch suggests, "From the standpoint of the history of science," the extent of the vogue of Newtonianism "is yet very largely unknown history." [38]

In Samuel Johnson's retrospective view, the Yale of 1710 at Saybrook was anything but progressive with its "scholastic cobwebs of a few little English and Dutch systems." [39] The year of Johnson's graduation (1714), however, Mr. Dummer, Yale's agent in London, collected seven hundred volumes, including works of Norris, Barrow, Tillotson, Boyle, Halley, and the second edition (1713) of the *Principia* and a copy of the *Optics*, presented by Newton himself. After the schism of 1715/6 the collection was moved to New Haven, at the time of Johnson's election to a tutorship. It was then, writes Johnson, that the trustees "introduced the study of Mr. Locke and Sir Isaac Newton as fast as they could and in order to this the study of mathematics. The Ptolemaic system was hitherto as much believed as the Scriptures, but they soon cleared up and established the Copernican by the help of Whiston's Lectures, Derham, etc." [40] Johnson studied Euclid, algebra, and conic sections "so as to read Sir Isaac with understanding." He gloomily reviews the "infidelity and apostasy" resulting from the study of the ideas of Locke, Tindal, Bolingbroke, Mandeville, Shaftesbury, and Collins. That Newtonianism and even deism made progress at Yale is the tenor of Johnson's backward glance. About 1716 Samuel Clarke's edition of Rohault was introduced at Yale: Clarke's Rohault [41] was an attack upon this

[38] F. E. Brasch, "Newton's First Critical Disciple in the American Colonies—John Winthrop," in *Sir Isaac Newton, 1727–1927* (Baltimore, 1928), 301.

[39] H. and C. Schneider (eds.), *Samuel Johnson, President of Kings College: His Career and Writings* (New York, 1929), I, 6.

[40] *Ibid.*, I, 8–9. It will be remembered that Thomas Young was struck with science and deism while at Yale: he it was who introduced liberal ideas to that militant prince of deists (with Thomas Paine), Ethan Allen.

[41] *Jacobus Rohaultus physica Latine reddita et annotata ex, Js. Newtonii principiis* (1697).

standard summary of Cartesianism. Ezra Stiles was not certain that Clarke was honest in heaping up notes "not so much to illustrate Rohault as to make him the Vehicle of conveying the peculiarities of the sublimer Newtonian Philosophy." [42] This work was used until 1743 when 'sGravesande's *Natural Philosophy* was wisely substituted. Rector Thomas Clap used Wollaston's *Religion of Nature Delineated* as a favorite text. That there was no dearth of advanced natural science and philosophy, even suggestive of deism, is fairly evident.

Measured by the growth of interest in science in the English universities, Harvard's awareness of new discoveries was not especially backward in the seventeenth century. Since Copernicanism at the close of the sixteenth century had few adherents, [43] it is almost startling to learn that probably by 1659 the Copernican system was openly avowed at Harvard. [44] In 1786 Nathaniel Mather wrote from Dublin: "I perceive the Cartesian philosophy begins to obteyn in New England, and if I conjecture aright the Copernican system too." [45] John Barnard, who was graduated from Harvard in 1710, has written that no algebra was then taught, and wistfully suggests that he had been born too soon, since "now" students "have the great Sir Isaac Newton and Dr. Halley and some other mathematicians for their guides." [46] Although Thomas Robie and Nathan Prince are thought to have known Newton's physics through secondary sources, [47] and, as Harvard tutors, indoctrinated their charges with Newtonianism, it was left to Isaac Greenwood [48] to trans-

[42] *Literary Diary*, I, 556 (1775).

[43] D. Stimson, *The Gradual Acceptance of the Copernican Theory*, 48.

[44] See S. E. Morison, "The Harvard School of Astronomy in the Seventeenth Century," *New England Quarterly*, VII, 3 (March, 1934).

[45] *Ibid.*, 7. In 1672 Harvard received her first telescope. Such men as Winthrop and Thomas Brattle were actively interested in science.

[46] F. Cajori, *The Teaching and History of Mathematics in the United States*, U. S. Bureau of Education, Circular of Information, No. 3, 1890 (Washington, D. C.), 22.

[47] Brasch, *op. cit.*, 308.

[48] *Dictionary of American Biography*, VII, 591-2.

plant from London the popular expositions of Newtonian philosophy. A Harvard graduate in 1721, Greenwood continued his theological studies in London where he attended Desaguliers's lectures on experimental philosophy, based essentially on Newtonianism. From Desaguliers Greenwood learned how

> By Newton's help, 'tis evidently seen
> Attraction governs all the World's machine.[49]

He learned that Scripture is "to teach us Morality, and our Articles of Faith" but not to serve as an instructor in natural philosophy.[50] In fine, Greenwood became devoted to science, and science as it might serve to augment avenues to the religious experience. In London he had come to know Hollis, who in 1727 suggested to Harvard authorities that Greenwood be elected Hollis Professor of Mathematics and Natural and Experimental Philosophy.[51] Greenwood accepted, and until 1737 was at Harvard a propagandist of the new science. In 1727 he advertised in the *Boston News-Letter*[52] that he would give scientific lectures, revolving primarily around "the Discoveries of the incomparable Sir Isaac Newton." From 1727 through 1734 he was a prominent popularizer of Newtonianism in Boston.[53]

It remained for Greenwood's pupil John Winthrop to be the first to teach Newton at Harvard with adequate mechanical and textual materials. Elected in 1738 to the Hollis professorship formerly held by Greenwood, Winthrop adopted 'sGravesande's *Natural Philosophy*, at which time, Cajori observes, "the teach-

---

[49] *The Newtonian System of the World* . . . (Westminster, 1728), 30.
[50] *Ibid.*, 6.
[51] See J. Quincy, *History of Harvard University* (Boston, 1860 [1840]), II, 4–21.
[52] Jan. 12, 1727, Feb. 23, and others. Also see June 13 and July 11 of 1734.
[53] See advertisements in *Boston Gazette*, June 17–24, 1734, quoted in W. G. Bleyer's *Main Currents in the History of American Journalism*, 73–4.

ings of Newton had at last secured a firm footing there." [54]
The year after his election he secured a copy of the *Principia*
(the third edition, 1726, edited by Dr. Henry Pemberton, friend
of Franklin in 1725–1726). According to the astute Ezra Stiles,
Winthrop became a "perfect master of Newton's Principia—
which cannot be said of many Professors of Philosophy in
Europe." [55] That he did not allow Newtonianism to draw him
to deism may be seen in Stiles's gratification that Winthrop
"was a Firm friend to Revelation in opposition to Deism."
Stiles "wish[es] the evangelical Doctors of Grace had made a
greater figure in his Ideal System of divinity," thus inferring that
Winthrop was a rationalist in theology, however orthodox. [56]

A cursory view of the eighteenth-century pulpit discloses
that if the clergy did not become deistic they were not blind
to a natural religion, and often employed its arguments to augment scriptural authority. Aware of the writings of Samuel
Clarke, Wollaston, Whiston, Cudworth, Butler, Hutcheson, [57]
Voltaire, and Locke, Mayhew revolts against total depravity [58]
and the doctrines of election and the Trinity, arraigns himself
against authoritarianism and obscurantism, and though he draws
upon reason for revelation of God's will, he does not seem to
have been latitudinarian in respect to the holy oracles. Although
he often wrote ambiguously concerning the nature of Christ,
he asserted: "That I ever denied, or treated in a bold or ludicrous
manner, the divinity of the Son of God, as revealed in scripture,

[54] *Op. cit.*, 25.

[55] *Literary Diary*, II, 334.

[56] Through the kindness of the Hollis family, Harvard (by 1764) gained
a remarkable collection of scientific instruments, possessed the Boylean
lectures, Transactions of the Royal Society and of the Academy of Science
in Paris, the works of Boyle and Newton, "with a great variety of other
mathematical and philosophical treatises" (Quincy, *op. cit.*, II, 481).
Notable among these items are Chambers's *Cyclopædia*, received in 1743,
and Pemberton's *View of Sir Isaac Newton's Philosophy*, in 1752.

[57] A. Bradford, *Memoir of the Life and Writings of Rev. Jonathan
Mayhew* . . . (Boston, 1838), 18–9, 46.

[58] *Ibid.*, 50.

I absolutely deny." [59] He is antagonistic toward the mystical in Calvinism, convinced that "The love of God is a calm and rational thing, the result of thought and consideration." [60] His biographer thinks that Mayhew was "the first clergyman in New England who expressly and openly opposed the scholastic doctrine of the trinity." [61] Coupling "natural and revealed religion," he does not threaten but he urges that one "ought not to leave the clear light of revelation. . . . It becomes us to adhere to the holy Scriptures as our only rule of faith and practice, discipline and worship." [62] In Mayhew one finds an impotent compromise between Calvinism and the demands of reason, fostered by the Enlightenment. Like Mayhew's, in the main, are the views of Dr. Charles Chauncy, who reconciled the demands of reason and revelation, concluding that "the voice of reason is the voice of God." [63] Jason Haven and Jonas Clarke are typical of the orthodox rationalists who were alive to the implications of science, and to such rationalists as Tillotson and Locke. Haven affirms that "by the light of reason and nature, we are led to believe in, and adore God, not only as the maker, but also as the governor of all things." [64] "Revelation comes in to the assistance of reason, and shews them to us in a clearer light than we could see them without its aid." Clarke observes that "the light of nature teaches, which revelation confirms." [65] Rev. Henry Cumings, illustrating his indebtedness to scientific rationalism, honors "the gracious Parent of the universe, whose

[59] *Ibid.*, 305. Mayhew is on record as saying: "The inspired scriptures are our only rule of faith and conduct" (*ibid.*, 140).

[60] *Ibid.*, 75. On the other hand, he reacts against what deism and orthodox rationalism commonly became: "A religion consisting in nothing but a knowledge of God's attributes, and an external conduct agreeable to his laws, would be a lifeless, insipid thing. It would be neither a source of happiness to ourselves, nor recommend us to the approbation of him, who requires us 'to give him our hearts.'"

[61] *Ibid.*, 464.

[62] *Two Discourses Delivered Oct. 9th, 1760 . . .* (Boston, 1760), 66.

[63] *Election-Sermon*, May 27, 1747 (Boston, 1747), 9.

[64] *A Sermon* [election], May 31, 1769 (Boston, 1769), 5.

[65] *Election-Sermon*, May 30, 1781 (Boston, 1781), 4.

tender mercies are over all his works . . .," [66] a Deity "whose providence governs the world; whose voice all nature obeys; to whose controul all second causes and subordinate agents are subject; and whose sole prerogative it is to dispense blessings or calamities, as to his wisdom seems best." [67] Simeon Howard discovers the "perfections of the Deity, as displayed in the Creation" as well as in the "government and redemption of the world." [68] Both Phillips Payson [69] and Andrew Eliot [70] affirm the identity of "the voice of reason, and the voice of God."

No clergyman of the eighteenth century was more terribly conscious of the polarity of colonial thought than was Ezra Stiles. Abiel Holmes has told the graphic story of Stiles's struggles with deism after reading Pope, Whiston, Boyle, Trenchard and Gordon, Butler, Tindal, Collins, Bolingbroke, and Shaftesbury. [71] If he finally, as a result of his trembling and fearful doubt, reaffirmed zealously his faith in the bibliolatry and relentless dogma of Calvinism, [72] Newtonian rationalism was a means to his recovery, and throughout his life a complement to his Calvinism. [73] Turning from his well-worn Bible, the chief source of his faith, he also kindled his "devotion at the stars." It should be remembered, however, that this tendency among Puritan clergy to call science to the support of theology had been inaugurated by Cotton Mather as early as 1693,[74] and that it was the Puritan Mather whom Franklin acknowledged as having started him on his career and influenced him, by his *Essays to do Good,* throughout life.

[66] *Election-Sermon,* May 28, 1783 (Boston, 1783), 29.
[67] *Ibid.,* 54.
[68] *Election-Sermon,* May 31, 1780 (Boston, 1780), 21.
[69] *Election-Sermon,* May 27, 1778 (Boston, 1778), 7.
[70] *Election-Sermon,* May 29, 1765 (Boston, 1765), 17.
[71] *Life of Ezra Stiles* (Boston, 1798), *passim;* see especially pp. 34–54.
[72] See his *United States Elevated to Glory and Honour. . . ,* May 8, 1783 (Worcester, 1785).
[73] See *Literary Diary* for his inveterate interest in science and the laws of nature; see also I. M. Calder (ed.), *Letters & Papers of Ezra Stiles . . .* (New Haven, 1933).
[74] See Hornberger, *op. cit.,* 419.

Only against this complex and as yet inadequately integrated background of physical conditions and ideas (the dogmas of Puritanism, Quakerism, Methodism, rationalism, scientific deism, economic and political liberalism[75]—against a cosmic, social, and individual attitude, the result of Old-World thought impinging on colonial thought and environment) can one attempt to appraise adequately the mind and achievements of Franklin, whose life was coterminous with the decay of Puritan theocracy and the rise of rationalism, democracy, and science.

II. FRANKLIN'S THEORIES OF EDUCATION

Franklin's penchant for projects manifests itself nowhere more fully than in his schemes of education, both self and formal. One may deduce a pattern of educational principles not undeservedly called Franklin's *theories* of education, theories which he successfully institutionalized, from an examination of his Junto ("the best school of philosophy, morality, and politics that then existed in the province"[76]), his Philadelphia Library Company (his "first project of a public nature"[77]), his *Proposal for*

[75] For full backgrounds, see G. P. Gooch, *English Democratic Ideas in the Seventeenth Century;* W. A. Dunning, *A History of Political Theories from Luther to Montesquieu;* H. L. Osgood, "Political Ideas of the Puritans," *Political Science Quarterly,* VI, 1–29, 201–31; Mellen Chamberlain, *John Adams . . . with Other Essays* (Boston, 1898), especially pp. 19–53, stressing the influence of Puritanism on political liberalism; Alice Baldwin, *The New England Clergy and the American Revolution;* J. W. Thornton, *The Pulpit of the American Revolution* (Boston, 1860), a collection of election sermons edited with an extensive introduction; C. H. Van Tyne, "The Influence of the Clergy . . . in the American Revolution," *American Historical Review,* XIX, 44–64. In stressing the influence on Franklin of European ideas, it is important to remember that, as we shall see, it is probable that some of Franklin's interest in doing good (charity), in science, and in democracy may have been inspired by his exposure during his formative years to American Puritanism.

[76] *The Writings of Benjamin Franklin,* ed. by Albert Henry Smyth (New York, 1905–1907), I, 300; (hereafter referred to as *Writings*). For a scholarly exposition of backgrounds of educational theory in relation to philosophy, especially the cult of progress, see A. O. Hansen's *Liberalism and American Education in the Eighteenth Century,* which includes a valuable bibliography. This work, however, slights Franklin and Jefferson.

[77] *Writings,* I, 312.

Promoting Useful Knowledge among the British Plantations in America, calling for a scientific society of ingenious men or virtuosi, his *Proposals Relating to the Education of Youth in Pensilvania* and *Idea of the English School*, which eventually fathered the University of Pennsylvania, and from his fragmentary notes in his correspondence.

Variously apotheosized, patronized, or damned for his practicality, expediency, and opportunism, dramatized for his allegiance to materiality, Franklin has commonly been viewed (and not only through the popular imagination) as one fostering in the American mind an unimaginative, utilitarian prudence, motivated by the pedestrian virtues of industry, frugality, and thrift. Whatever the educational effect of Franklin's life and writings on American readers, we shall find that his works contain schemes and theories which *transcend* the more mundane habits and utilitarian biases ascribed to him.

Franklin progressively felt "the loss of the learned education" his father had planned for him, as he realized in his hunger for knowledge that he must repair the loss through assiduous reading, accomplished during hours stolen from recreation and sleep.[78] Proudly he confessed that reading was his "only amusement."[79] In 1727 he formed the Junto, or Leather Apron Club, his first educational project. Franklin was never more eclectic than when founding the Junto. To prevent Boston homes from becoming "the porches of hell,"[80] Cotton Mather had created mutual improvement societies through which neighbors would help one another "with a rapturous assiduity."[81] Mather in his *Essays to do Good* proposed:

[78] For an exhaustive survey of the means Franklin pursued to educate himself, and suggestive notes on his ideas of education, see F. N. Thorpe's *Benjamin Franklin and the University of Pennsylvania*, chaps. I–II, 9–203. See also Thomas Woody's *Educational Views of Benjamin Franklin* (New York, 1931), which in addition to relevant selections from Franklin's works contains stimulating observations by the editor.

[79] *Writings*, I, 323.

[80] *Essays to do Good*, with an Introductory Essay by Andrew Thomson (Glasgow, 1825 [1710]), 189.   [81] *Ibid.*, 102.

That a proper number of persons in a neighborhood, whose hearts God hath touched with a zeal to do good, should form themselves into a society, to meet when and where they shall agree, and to consider—"what are the disorders that we may observe rising among us; and what may be done, either by ourselves immediately, or by others through our advice, to suppress those disorders?" [82]

Since Franklin's father was a member of one of Mather's "Associated Families" and since Franklin as a boy read Mather's *Essays* with rapt attention, [83] and since his *Rules for a Club Established for Mutual Improvement* are amazingly congruent with Mather's rules proposed for his neighborly societies, it is not improbable that Franklin in part copied the plans of this older club. One also wonders whether Franklin remembered Defoe's suggestions in *Essays upon Several Projects* (1697) for the formation of "Friendly Societies" in which members covenanted to aid one another. [84] In addition, M. Faÿ has observed that the "ideal which this society [the Junto] adopted was the same that Franklin had discovered in the Masonic lodges of England." [85] Then, too, in London during the period of Desaguliers, Sir Hans Sloane, and Sir Isaac Newton, he would have heard much of the ideals and utility of the Royal Society. Many of the questions discussed by the Junto are suggestive of the calendar of the Royal Society:

Is sound an entity or body?
How may the phenomena of vapors be explained?
What is the reason that the tides rise higher in the Bay of
    Fundy, than the Bay of Delaware?

[82] *Ibid.*, 192–3.
[83] See his letter to Samuel Mather, May 12, 1784 (*Writings*, IX, 208–10).
[84] *The Works of Daniel Defoe*, ed. by Wm. Hazlitt (London, 1843), I.
[85] *Franklin, the Apostle of Modern Times*, 119. Also see his "Learned Societies in Europe and America in the Eighteenth Century," *American Historical Review*, XXXVII, 258 (1932), in which he suggests that the Junto "had Masonic leanings."

How may smoky chimneys be best cured?
Why does the flame of a candle tend upwards in a spire? [86]

The Junto members, like Renaissance gentlemen, were determined to convince themselves that nothing valuable to the
several powers of life should be alien to them. They were urged
to communicate to one another anything significant "in history,
morality, poetry, physic, travels, mechanic arts, or other parts
of knowledge." [87] Surely a humanistic catholicity of interest!
Schemes for getting on materially, suggestions for improving
the laws and protecting the "just liberties of the people," [88]
efforts to aid the strangers in Philadelphia (an embryonic association of commerce), curiosity in the latest remedies used for
the sick and wounded: all were to engage the minds of this as-
siduously curious club. Above all, the members must be "serviceable to *mankind*, to their country, to their friends, or to
themselves." [89] The intensity of the Junto's utilitarian purpose
was matched only by its humanitarian bias. Members must swear
that they "love mankind in general, of what profession or religion soever," [90] and that they believe no man should be per-
secuted "for mere speculative opinions, or his external way of
worship." Also they must profess to "love truth for truth's
sake," to search diligently for it and to communicate it to
others. Tolerance, the empirical method, scientific disinterestedness, and humanitarianism had hardly gained a foothold in
the colonies in 1728. On the other hand, the Junto members
were urged, when throwing a kiss to the world, not to neglect
their individual ethical development. [91] Franklin's humanitarian

---

[86] These and others quoted in Woody, *op. cit.*, 45–6 (reprinted from
Sparks, *The Works of Benjamin Franklin*, II, 9–10).

[87] *Writings*, II, 88.   [88] *Ibid.*, II, 89.

[89] *Ibid.*   [90] *Ibid.*, II, 90.

[91] Questions suggestive of the Junto's interest in moral, political, and
philosophical topics are: "Is self-interest the rudder that steers mankind,
the universal monarch to whom all are tributaries?" which causes one to
suspect that Franklin had challenged his friends with *The Fable of the Bees;*
"Can any one particular form of government suit all mankind?" which

neighborliness is associated with a rigorous ethicism. The members were invited to report "unhappy effects of intemperance," of "imprudence, of passion, or of any other vice or folly," and also "happy effects of temperance, of prudence, of moderation." Franklin reflects sturdily here, and boundlessly elsewhere, the Greek and English emphasis on the Middle Way. If this is prudential, it is an elevated prudence.

The Philadelphia Library Company was born of the Junto and became "the mother of all the North American subscription libraries, now so numerous." [92] The colonists, "having no publick amusements to divert their attention from study, became better acquainted with books, and in a few years were observ'd by strangers to be better instructed and more intelligent than people of the same rank generally are in other countries." [93] It is curious that although many articles have been written describing the Library Company no one seems to include a study of the climate of ideas represented in its volumes.[94] One must be careful not to credit Franklin with solely presiding over the ordering of books. At a meeting in 1732 of the company, Thomas Godfrey, probable inventor of the quadrant and he who learned Latin to read the *Principia*, notified the body that "Mr. Logan had let him know he would willingly give his advice of the choice of the books ... the Committee esteeming

---

may have stirred controversies in the Junto between logical relativists and historic absolutists, the realists and those motivated by a priori abstractions, as, for example, in the Burke-Paine intellectual duel; "Whether it ought to be the aim of philosophy to eradicate the passions?" which may tend to suggest that Franklin would gear philosophy to moral action rather than to arid metaphysics.

[92] *Writings*, I, 312.   [93] *Ibid.*, I, 322.

[94] Since writing this the editors have noted Morais's fragmentary use of the Company's catalogues in *Deism in Eighteenth Century America*. For popular accounts of the general character and function of the Company see L. Stockton, "The Old Philadelphia Library," *Our Continent*, Oct., 1882, 452–9; J. M. Read, Jr., "The Old Philadelphia Library," *Atlantic Monthly*, March, 1868, 299–312; B. Samuel, "The Father of American Libraries," *Century Magazine*, May, 1883, 81–6. The ablest survey is G. M. Abbot's *A Short History of the Library Company of Philadelphia*. He lists, however, only the first books ordered in 1732 through Peter Collinson.

Mr. Logan to be a Gentleman of universal learning, and the best judge of books in these parts, ordered that Mr. Godfrey should wait on him and request him to favour them with a catalogue of suitable books." [95] The first order included: Puffendorf's *Introduction* and *Laws of Nature*, Hayes upon Fluxions, Keill's *Astronomical Lectures*, Sidney on Government, Gordon and Trenchard's *Cato's Letters*, the *Spectator*, *Guardian*, *Tatler*, L'Hospital's *Conic Sections*, Addison's works, Xenophon's *Memorabilia*, Palladio, Evelyn, Abridgement of Philosophical Transactions,'sGravesande's *Natural Philosophy*, Homer's *Odyssey* and *Iliad*, Bayle's *Critical Dictionary*, and Dryden's *Virgil*. As a gift Peter Collinson included Newton's *Principia* in the order. The ancient phalanxes were thoroughly routed! Then there is the MS "List of Books of the Original Philadelphia Library in Franklin's Handwriting" [96] which lends recruits to the modern battalions. Included in this list are: Fontenelle on Oracles, Woodward's *Natural History of Fossils* and *Natural History of the Earth*, Keill's *Examination of Burnet's Theory of the Earth*, *Memoirs of the Royal Academy of Surgery at Paris*, William Petty's *Essays*, Voltaire's *Elements of Sir Isaac Newton's Philosophy*, Halley's *Astronomical Tables*, Hill's *Review of the Works of the Royal Society*, Montesquieu's *Spirit of Laws*, Burlamaqui's *Principles of Natural Law* and *Principles of Politic Law*, Bolingbroke's *Letters on the Study and Use of History*, and Conyer Middleton's *Miscellaneous Works*. From the volumes owned by the Library Company in 1757 it would have been possible for an alert mind to discover all of the implications, philosophic and religious, of the rationale of science. No less could be found here the political speculations which were later to aid the colonists in unyoking themselves from England. The Library was an arsenal capable of supplying

[95] Cited in Abbot, *op. cit.*, 5.
[96] Photostat used as source is in the William Smith Mason Collection in Evanston, Ill.

weapons to rationalistic minds intent on besieging the
fortress of Calvinism. Defenders of natural rights could find
ammunition to wound monarchism; here authors could discover the neoclassic ideals of *curiosa felicitas*, perspicuity,
order, and lucidity reinforced by the emphasis on clarity and
correctness sponsored by the Royal Society and inherent in
Newtonianism as well as Cartesianism. In short, the volumes
contained the ripest fruition of scientific and rationalistic mod-
ernity. One can only conjecture the extent to which this library
would perplex, astonish, and finally convert men to rationalism
and scientific deism, and release them from bondage to throne
and altar.

In 1743 Franklin wrote and distributed among his correspondents *A Proposal for Promoting Useful Knowledge among
the British Plantations in America.* From a letter (Feb. 17,
1735/6) of William Douglass, one-time friend of Franklin's
brother James, to Cadwallader Colden, we learn that some years
before 1736, Colden "proposed the forming a sort of Virtuoso
Society or rather Correspondence." [97] I. W. Riley suggests that
Franklin owes Colden thanks for having stimulated him to form
the American Philosophical Society. [98] There remains no convincing evidence, however, to disprove A. H. Smyth's observation that Franklin's *Proposal* "appears to contain the first suggestions, in any *public form* [editors' italics] for an American
Philosophical Society." P. S. Du Ponceau has noted with compelling evidence that the philosophical society formed in 1744
was the direct descendant of Franklin's Junto. [99] That in part
the Philadelphia Library Company was one of the factors in

---

[97] "The Letters and Papers of Cadwallader Colden, Vol. II, 1730–1742,"
Collections of the New York Historical Society (New York, 1919), II, 146–7.
See also A. M. Keys, *Cadwallader Colden: A Representative Eighteenth-
Century Official* (New York, 1906), 6–7.

[98] *American Philosophy: The Early Schools*, 330.

[99] *An Historical Account of the Origin and Formation of the American
Philosophical Society* (Philadelphia, 1914); J. G. Rosengarten, in "The
American Philosophical Society," tends to agree with Du Ponceau.

the formation of the scientific society may be inferred from Franklin's request that it be founded in Philadelphia, which, "having the advantages of a good growing library," can "be the centre of the Society." [100] The most important factor, however, was obviously the desire to imitate the forms and ideals of the Royal Society of London. Both societies had as their purpose the improvement of "the common stock of knowledge"; neither was to be provincial or national in interests, but was to have in mind the "benefit of mankind in general." A study of Franklin's *Proposal* will suggest the purpose of the Royal Society as interpreted by Thomas Sprat:

Their purpose is, in short, to make faithful Records, of all the Works of Nature, or Art, which can come within their reach: that so the present Age, and posterity, may be able to put a mark on the Errors, which have been strengthned by long prescription: to restore the Truths, that have lain neglected: to push on those, which are already known, to more various uses: and to make the way more passable, to what remains unreveal'd. [101]

The Royal Society, no less than Franklin's *Proposal*, stressed the usefulness of its experimentation. Even as it sought "to overcome the mysteries of all the Works of Nature" [102] through experimentation and induction, the Baconian empirical method, so Franklin urged the cultivation of "all philosophical experiments that let light into the nature of things, tend to increase the power of man over matter, and multiply the conveniences or pleasures of life." [103] Though Franklin may have stopped short of theoretical science,[104] he was not only interested in making

[100] *Writings*, II, 229.
[101] *The History of the Royal Society of London* . . . (2d ed., London, 1702), 61.
[102] *Ibid.*, 64.   [103] *Writings*, II, 230.
[104] In 1750 he wrote: "Nor is it of much importance to us, to know the manner in which nature executes her laws; 'tis enough if we know the laws themselves. 'Tis of real use to know that china left in the air unsupported will fall and break; but *how* it comes to fall, and *why* it breaks,

devices but also in discovering immutable natural laws on which he could base his mechanics for making the world more habitable, less unknown and terrifying. Interpreting natural phenomena in terms of gravity and the laws of electrical attraction and repulsion is to detract from the terror in a universe presided over by a providential Deity, exerting his wrath through portentous comets, "fire-balls flung by an angry God."

Franklin's program is no more miscellaneous, or seemingly pedestrian, than the practices of the Royal Society. As a discoverer of nature's laws and their application to man's use, Franklin, the Newton of electricity, appealed to fact and experiment rather than authority and suggested that education in science may serve, in addition to making the world more comfortable, to make it more habitable and less terrifying. The ideals of scientific research and disinterestedness were dramatized picturesquely by the Tradesman Franklin, who aided the colonist in becoming unafraid.

Although his *Proposals Relating to the Education of Youth in Pensilvania* (1749) furnished the initial suggestion which created the Philadelphia Academy, later the college, and ultimately the University of Pennsylvania, it is easy to overestimate the real significance of Franklin's influence in these schemes unless we remember that political quarrels separated him from those who were nurturing the school in the 1750's. In 1759 Franklin wrote from London to his friend, Professor Kinnersley, concerning the cabal in the Academy against him: "The Trustees have reap'd the full Advantage of my Head, Hands, Heart and Purse, in getting through the first Difficulties of the Design, and when they thought they could do without

are matters of speculation. 'Tis a pleasure indeed to know them, but we can preserve our china without it" (*Writings*, II, 434–5). We remember that even Sir Isaac Newton confessed that "the *cause* of gravity is what I do not pretend to know" (*Works of Richard Bentley*, London, 1838, III, 210). He observed that "Gravity must be caused by an agent acting constantly according to certain laws; but whether this agent be material or immaterial, I have left to the consideration of my readers" (*ibid.*, 212).

me, they laid me aside." [105]   After Franklin failed to secure
Samuel Johnson,[106] Rev. William Smith was made Provost and
Professor of Natural Philosophy of the Academy in 1754. He
quoted Franklin as saying that the Academy had become "a
narrow, bigoted institution, put into the hands of the Proprietary party as an engine of government." [107]

[105] *Pennsylvania Magazine of History and Biography*, XIII, 247–8 (1889).
[106] Franklin was unable to prevail upon Johnson to accept the provost-
ship of the Academy. In 1752 he printed Johnson's *Elementa Philosophica*
and suggested in *Idea of the English School* that it be used in the Academy.
In a letter of 1754 Franklin informs Johnson that the grammatical and
mathematical parts were already being used—the rest would be when the
instructors and pupils were ready for it (E. E. Beardsley, *Life and Correspondence of S. Johnson, D. D.*, 2d ed., New York, 1874, 180–1). In the
Elementa Philosophica Johnson stresses the use of mathematics in man's
study of nature (p. xv).   Through mathematics, an indispensable aid in
"considering that wonderful and amazing Power, that All-comprehending
Wisdom, that inimitable Beauty, that surprizing Harmony, that immutable
Order, which abundantly discover themselves in the Formation and Government of the Universe, we are led to their divine Original, who is the
unexhausted Source, the glorious Fountain of all Perfection . . ." (*ibid.*,
xiii).   The *Elementa* is a rhapsodic manual extolling the discovery of
the Deity in his Work, through the study of the physical laws of the
creation.   Although subordinated to this, there are frequent reactions
against Lockian sensationalism, suggesting an ecstatic mystical union between man and God.   On the whole, the volume is a treatise on the glories
of a natural religion (a religion of course which buttresses rather than
refutes scriptural religion).
[107] Quoted in T. H. Montgomery's *A History of the University of Pennsylvania*, 396.   Smith's educational principles may be partially seen in
his "View of the Philosophy Schools" (1754) printed in H. W. Smith's
Life and Correspondence of the Rev. William Smith (Philadelphia, 1879),
I, 59 f.   Although he conceived Nature as affording only "those fainter
exhibitions of the Deity" (I, 156), he was a sturdy orthodox rationalist,
tending toward, yet not embracing deism.   Emphasizing the principal
writings of Barrow, Maclaurin, Watts, Keill, Locke, Hutcheson, 'sGravesande, Martin, Desaguliers, Rohault (Clarke's edition), Ray, Derham, and
Sir Isaac Newton, Smith suggests the rationalist who buttresses scriptural
revelation with the evidences of Deity through discovery by reason of the
Workman in the Work.   His *Discourses on Public Occasions in America*
(2d ed., London, 1762) are the result "of his office as Head of a seminary
of learning [Philadelphia Academy and College]; in order to advance the
interests of Science, and therewith the interests of true Christianity" (p. vi).
"A General Idea of the College of Mirania" (1762), though written about
1752 while Smith was in New York, suggests the form of his "View": he
observes that "besides his revealed will, God has given intimations of his
will to us, by appealing to our senses in the constitution of our nature,

With Milton, Locke, Fordyce, Walker, Rollin, Turnbull, and "some others" as his sources, Franklin adapted the works of these pioneers in education to provincial uses. (One finds it difficult to discover any original ideas in the *Proposals*.) Like Locke and Milton, he urged that education "supply the succeeding Age with Men qualified to serve the Publick with Honour to themselves, and to their Country." [108] Here he was unlike President Clap, who in 1754 explained that "the Original End and design of Colleges was to instruct and train up persons for the Work of the ministry. . . . The great design of founding this school [Yale] was to educate ministers in our own way." [109] As early as 1722, in *Dogood Paper* No. IV, Franklin caricatured sardonically the narrow theological curriculum of Harvard College.[110] Existing for the citizenry rather than the clergy, offering instruction in English as well as Latin and Greek, in mechanics, physical culture, natural history, gardening, mathematics, and arithmetic rather than in sectarian theology, Franklin's Academy was to be more secular and utilitarian than any other school in the provinces. Indeed, Rev. George Whitefield lamented the want of *"aliquid Christi"* in the curriculum, "to make it as useful as I would desire it might be."

Franklin stressed the need for the acquisition of a clear and concise literary style. He observed: "Reading should also be

and the constitution and harmony of the material universe" (*Discourses*, 44). The same titles and authors are listed as in the "View." A Newtonian rationalist, Smith meditated: "All thy works, with unceasing voice, echo forth thy wondrous praises. The splendid sun, with the unnumbered orbs of heaven, thro' the pathless void, repeat their unwearied circuits, that, to the uttermost bounds of the universe, they may proclaim Thee the source of justest order and unabating harmony" (*ibid.*, 155). Smith arrived at his principles of rationalism apparently without indebtedness to Franklin: there seems to be no evidence that as provost he was merely attempting to fulfill the scientific and rationalistic ideas latent in Franklin's *Proposals*, that he was a tool in Franklin's hands. Indeed, they were anything but friendly to one another. Hence, one feels that the credit for the relatively modern curriculum should be given more abundantly to Smith than to Franklin.

[108] *Writings*, II, 388.
[109] Montgomery, *op. cit.*, 254 note.   [110] *Writings*, II, 9–14.

taught, and pronouncing, properly, distinctly, emphatically; not with an even Tone, which *under-does*, nor a theatrical, which *over-does* Nature." Hence he reflected the virtues of neoclassic perspicuity and correctness. (These plans he more fully expressed in his *Idea of the English School*, published in 1751.) As he grew older he apparently became less tolerant of the teaching of the ancient languages in colonial schools: in *Observations Relative to the Intentions of the Original Founders of the Academy of Philadelphia* (1789), he charged that the Latin school had swallowed the English and that he was hence "surrounded by the Ghosts of my dear departed Friends, beckoning and urging me to use the only Tongue now left us, in demanding that Justice to our Grandchildren, that our Children has [*sic*] been denied." [111] The Latin and Greek languages he considered "in no other light than as the *Chapeau bras* of modern Literature." [112] Like Emerson's, his opposition was to linguistic study rather than to the classical ideas.

Although he emphasized the study of science and mechanics, it is important to observe that he kept his balance. He warned Miss Mary Stevenson in 1760: "There is . . . a prudent Moderation to be used in Studies of this kind. The Knowledge of Nature may be ornamental, and it may be useful; but if, to attain an Eminence in that, we neglect the Knowledge and Practice of essential Duties, we deserve Reprehension." [113] Not without reserve did he champion the Moderns; remembering several provocative scientific observations in Pliny, he wrote to William Brownrigg (Nov. 7, 1773): "It has been of late too much the mode to slight the learning of the ancients." [114] He would not agree with the enthusiastic and trenchant disciple of the

[111] *Writings*, X, 29.
[112] *Ibid.*, X, 31. Compare similar views in Benjamin Rush's "Observations upon the Study of the Latin and Greek Languages," in *Essays, Literary, Moral and Philosophical* (Philadelphia, 1798), and Francis Hopkinson's "An Address to the American Philosophical Society," in *Miscellaneous Essays and Occasional Writings* (Philadelphia, 1792), I.
[113] *Writings*, IV, 22.   [114] *Ibid.*, VI, 153.

moderns, M. Fontenelle, that "We are under an obligation to the ancients for having exhausted almost all the false theories that could be found." [115] Although he would agree that the empirical method of acquiring knowledge is more reasonable than authoritarianism reared on syllogistic foundations, and with Cowley that

Bacon has broke that scar-crow Deity ["Authority"],[116]

he was not blithely confident that science and the knowledge gained from experimentation would create a more rigorously moral race. He wrote to Priestley in 1782: "I should rejoice much, if I could once more recover the Leisure to search with you into the Works of Nature; I mean the *inanimate*, not the *animate* or moral part of them, the more I discover'd of the former, the more I admir'd them; the more I know of the latter, the more I am disgusted with them." [117] He often suggested, "As Men grow more enlightened," but seldom did this clause carry more than an intellectual connotation. Progress in knowledge [118] did not on the whole suggest to Franklin progress in morals or the general progress of mankind.

Essentially classical in morality, extolling a temperance like that of Xenophon, Epictetus, Cicero, Socrates, and Aristotle, Franklin could not cheerily champion the moderns without serious reservations. Considering only progress in knowledge, man may be considered as *pedetentim progredientes*, but, Franklin thought, man seemed to have found it easier to conquer lightning than himself. If science and other contemporaneous knowledge detracted from cosmic terror, it did not solve the problem of the mystery of evil and sin: like Shakespeare, Franklin was perplexed by the inexplicability and ruthlessness of Man's potential and actual malevolence.[119] Thus in stressing

[115] Quoted in J. B. Bury's *The Idea of Progress*, 104. See also Lois Whitney's *Primitivism and the Idea of Progress*, especially chap. V.
[116] Bury, *op. cit.*, 96.   [117] *Writings*, VIII, 451.
[118] For example see *ibid.*, IX, 74, 557.   [119] See *Writings*, VIII, 454.

utility and vocational adaptiveness, Franklin did not forget to stress the need for development of character, man's internal self, and here he did not find the ancients dispensable.[120] If unlike Socrates in his studies of physical nature, he was like the Athenian gadfly in his quest for moral perfection in the teeth of "perpetual temptation," in his strenuous and sober effort to know himself. Too little attention has been paid Franklin's Hellenic sobriety—even as it has had too meagre an influence. Let Molière challenge, "The ancients are the ancients, we are the people of today"; Franklin, although confident that he could learn more of physical nature from Newton than from Aristotle, was not convinced that the wisdom of Epictetus or the Golden Verses of Pythagoras were less salutary than the wit of his own age. A modern in his confidence in the progress of knowledge, Franklin, approaching the problem of morality, wisely saw the ancients and moderns as complementary. Aware of the continuity of the mind and race, he was not willing to dismiss the ancients as fit to be imitated. Yet he failed to discover in the welter of egoistic men any continuous moral progress, although, unlike the determinists, he thought that the individual could improve himself through self-knowledge and self-control. Unlike contemporary exponents of the "original genius" cult who scorned industrious rational study and conformity, Franklin as an educational theorist was the exponent of reason and of conscious intellectual industry and thrift; he would mediate between the study of nature and of man, and, like Aristotle, he would rely not so much upon individualistic self-expression as upon a purposeful *imitation* of those men in the past who had led useful and happy lives.

[120] See R. M. Gummere, "Socrates at the Printing Press. Benjamin Franklin and the Classics," *Classical Weekly*, XXVI, 57–9 (Dec. 5, 1932).

III. FRANKLIN'S LITERARY THEORY AND PRACTICE [121]

Uniting the "wit of Voltaire with the simplicity of Rousseau," Franklin achieved a style "only surpassed by the unimprovable Hobbes of Malmesbury, the paragon of perspicuity." Characterized by simplicity, order, and a trenchant pointedness, his prose style was "a principal means" of his "advancement." [122]

He was "extreamly ambitious . . . to be a tolerable English writer." In the *Autobiography* he recalls that he read books in "polemic divinity," Plutarch's *Lives* (probably Dryden's translation), *Pilgrim's Progress*, Defoe's *Essays upon Several Projects*, Mather's *Essays to do Good*, Xenophon's *Memorabilia*, [123] the *Spectator* papers, and the writings of Shaftesbury and Collins.

Born in Boston, he knew the Bible, [124] characterized by

[121] Several of the following arguments are included in C. E. Jorgenson's "Sidelights on Benjamin Franklin's Principles of Rhetoric," *Revue Anglo-Américaine*, Feb., 1934, 208–22.

[122] Hume wrote to Franklin: "You are the first philosopher, and indeed the first great man of letters for whom we are beholden to her [America]" (*Writings*, IV, 154). Cowper exclaimed that Franklin was "one of the most important [men] in the literary world, that the present age can boast of" (Parton, *op. cit.*, II, 439); for other engaging estimates of Franklin as a man of letters consult C. W. Moulton, *Library of Literary Criticism . . .*, IV, 79–106.

[123] Franklin found in an appendix to Greenwood's *English Grammar* and in the *Memorabilia* specimens of the Socratic method which influenced him to adopt the manner of "the humble inquirer and doubter," to write and harangue with a "modest diffidence." On several occasions he approvingly quotes Pope's rule: "to speak, tho' sure, with seeming Diffidence." Jefferson recognized Franklin's use of this kind of Machiavellian diffidence, noting, "It was one of the rules which, above all others, made Dr. Franklin the most amiable of men in society, never to contradict anybody," and that "if he was urged to announce an opinion, he did it rather by asking questions, as if for information, or by suggesting doubts." In the *Autobiography* Franklin sees the Socratic method as a necessary ally to "doing good," observing that many who mean to be helpful "lessen their power of doing good by a positive, assuming manner, that seldom fails to disgust, tends to create opposition, and to defeat every one of those purposes for which speech was given to us."

[124] Bunyan's dignified simplicity, his "sound and honest Gospel strains," may have been one of Franklin's incentives to write lucidly and compellingly. For Bunyan's literary ideals, see the prefaces to his works,

the apostle of Augustan correctness, Jonathan Swift, as possessing "that simplicity, which is one of the greatest perfections
in any language." If Franklin did not achieve its "sublime
eloquence," he approximated at intervals its directness and
simplicity. In reading Defoe's *Essays* he learned that Queen
Anne's England urged that writers be "as concise as possible"
and avoid all "superfluous crowding in of insignificant words,
more than are needful to express the thing intended." (It is possible that Defoe's efforts "to polish and refine the English
tongue," to avoid "all irregular additions that ignorance and
affectation have introduced," influenced Franklin in favor of
"correctness" and against provincialisms.) Defoe's "explicit,
easy, free, and very plain" rhetoric is Franklin's.

After Franklin's father warned him that his arguments were
not well-ordered and trenchantly expressed, he desperately
sought to acquire a convincing prose style. In 1717 James,
Franklin's elder brother, returned from serving a printer's
apprenticeship in London. James had known and been attracted
to Augustan England, the England of the *Tatler*, *Spectator*, and
Guardian. Familiar is Franklin's narrative of how he patterned
his fledgling style on the pages of the *Spectator* papers, and
learned to satisfy his father—and himself. Like the neoclassicists, Franklin learned to write by imitation, by respectfully
subordinating himself to those he recognized as masters, and
not, like the romanticists, by expressing his own ego in revolt
against convention and conformity to traditional standards. The
group who supplied copy for James's *New England Courant*,
we are told, were trying to write like the *Spectator*. "The very
look of an ordinary first page of the *Courant* is like that of the
Spectator page." [125] In the *Dogood Papers* (1722) and the *Busy-*

especially that to *Grace Abounding*. The best study of Defoe and Swift
as literary theorists is W. Gückel and E. Günther, *D. Defoes und J. Swifts
Belesenheit und literarische Kritik* (Leipzig, 1925).

[125] E. C. Cook, *Literary Influences in Colonial Newspapers, 1704–1750*,
15. This scholarly work shows the great influence in America of neoclassical authors.

Body series (1728) Franklin's writings show a literal indebtedness to the style and even substance of the *Spectator*. [126] If, after the *Busy-Body* essays, Franklin's writings bear little resemblance to the elegance and glow of the *Spectator*, he did learn from it a long-remembered lesson in orderliness. From the *Spectator* he may have learned to temper wit with morality and morality with wit; he may have learned the neoclassic objection to the "unhappy Force of an Imagination, unguided by the Check of Reason and Judgment"; [127] he may have acquired his distrust of foreign phrases when English ones were as good, or better, insisting on the use of native English undefiled. It is interesting but perhaps futile to conjecture to what degree Franklin at this time, on reading *Spectator* No. 160, "On Geniuses" (warning against a servile imitation of ancient authors, a warning which anticipates the cult of original geniuses of later decades), would have been predisposed against ancient literature and languages. If the *Spectator* was partially responsible for his pleasantries at the expense of Greek in *Dogood Paper* No. IV, his attitude toward the ancients is more ostensibly the result of his later preoccupation with the sciences, [128] and of contact with representatives of the deistic time-spirit whose faith in progress led them to underrate the past.

When Franklin went to live in London in 1724–1726, and became familiar with such men of science as Dr. Henry Pemberton and others, he must have become aware of ideals of prose style not a little unlike those practised by the preachers of his Boston. In Boston he had heard (and in the polemical works in his father's library, read) sermons couched in a style satirized in *Hudibras* as a "Babylonish dialect . . . of patched and piebald languages" (ll. 93 ff.). Sensing the disparity between the seven-

---

[126] For a generous catalog of the devices borrowed see *ibid.*, 15 f.
[127] *Spectator*, No. 167.
[128] For a fuller discussion of Franklin's view of the ancients, see section on "Franklin's Theories of Education," p. xxxii above.

teenth-century prose styles and the empirical, logical, and or-
derly method of science, the Royal Society not long after its
inception inaugurated a campaign for a clarity akin to the pattern urged by Hobbes: "The Light of humane minds is Perspicuous Words, *Reason* is the Pace; Encrease of *Science* the *way;*
and the benefit of man-kind the *end.* And on the contrary,
Metaphors, and senseless and ambiguous words, are like *ignes
fatui;* and reasoning upon them, is wandering among innumerable absurdities." [129] Summarizing the intent of the stylistic
reformations instituted by the Royal Society, Thomas Sprat
urged writers "to reject all the amplifications, digressions, and
swellings of style: to return back to the primitive purity, and
shortness, when men deliver'd so many things, almost in an
equal number of words . . . a close, naked, natural way of
speaking; positive expressions; clear senses; a native easiness:
bringing all things as near the Mathematical plainness, as they
can: and preferring the language of Artizans, Countrymen, and
Merchants, before that, of Wits, or Scholars." [130] It is asserted
that the program of the Royal Society "called for stylistic reform as loudly as for reformation in philosophy. Moreover,
this attitude was in the public mind indissolubly associated with
the Society." [131] It is only reasonable to infer that Franklin (as
a member of the Royal Society and as founder of the American
Philosophical Society) was alive to the movement toward "un-

[129] Cited in R. F. Jones, "Science and English Prose Style . . . ," *Publications of the Modern Language Association,* XLV, 982 (Dec., 1930). On
the backgrounds of literary theories underlying the sermons which Franklin
heard, see scholarly studies such as Caroline F. Richardson's *English
Preachers and Preaching, 1640–1670* (New York, 1928), and W. F. Mitchell's *English Pulpit Oratory* (New York, 1932). From 1750 on, however,
the Puritan clergy in America increasingly advocated a simple, clear, and
easy style. See Howard M. Jones, "American Prose Style: 1700–1770,"
Huntington Library Bulletin, No. 6, 115–51 (Nov., 1934).
[130] *History of the Royal Society . . .* (2d ed., London, 1702), 113.
[131] R. F. Jones, *op. cit.,* 989. Tillotson, whom Franklin suggested as a
model worthy of emulation (*Writings,* II, 391), was "another great exponent of the new style" (R. F. Jones, *op. cit.,* 1002).

defiled plainness" which had for half a century been gathering
momentum.[132]

Even as Cartesianism [133] in France is said to have fostered
logic and lucidity of detail, and that which is universally valid
and recognized by all men, and that art which is aloof to the
non-human world, so in England may Newtonianism (which
overthrew Cartesianism) have conditioned writers to develop
a uniform style, purged of tenuous rhetorical devices. An age
characterized by a worship of reason, which was supposed to
be identical in all men, an age deferring to the general
mind of man, would be hostile to the rhetorical caprices of
those expressing their private, idiosyncratic enthusiasms. If
the neoclassic apotheosis of simplicity and freedom from intri-
cacy was the result of a "rationalistic anti-intellectualism," [134]
expressed in terms of hostility to belabored proof of ideas
known to the general will, then it would seem that one of the
factors sturdily conditioning this hostility was Newtonian
science. Admitting that *reason* leads to uniformitarianism, one
may recall that the processes of science are discoverable by
reason, and that such a cosmologist as Newton illustrated
mathematically and empirically a system, grand in its lucidity, and capable of being apprehended by all through
reason. If the deistic fear of "enthusiasm" in religion—
the individual will prevailing against the *consensus gentium*—
parallels, according to Professor Lovejoy, the neoclassic fear of
feeling and the unrestrained play of imagination in art, then
Newtonian science, as it reinforced deism, was no negligible
factor in discrediting enthusiasm, and hence indirectly militating
against originality, emotion, and the unchecked imagination.
Is it not conceivable that the Newtonian [135] cosmology, popu-

[132] L. M. MacLaurin (*Franklin's Vocabulary*, 21) also suggests Franklin's
probable indebtedness to the Royal Society program.

[133] O. Elton, *The Augustan Age*, 8–12.

[134] A. O. Lovejoy, "The Parallel of Deism and Classicism," *Modern
Philology*, XXIX, 281–99 (Feb., 1932).

[135] Franklin's friend Henry Pemberton, in his *View of Sir Isaac Newton's*

larized by a vast discipleship, challenged the scientists and men of letters alike to achieve a corresponding order, clarity, and simplicity in poetry and prose?

After Franklin's return from London, he reinforced his Addison-like style with the rhetorical implications of science and Newtonianism: in his *Preface* (1729) to the *Pennsylvania Gazette* he observed that an editor ought to possess a "great Easiness and Command of Writing and Relating Things clearly and intelligibly, and in few Words." [136] Good writing, in Franklin's opinion, "should proceed regularly from things known to things unknown [surely the method of all inductive reasoning and science] distinctly and clearly without confusion. The words used should be the most expressive that the language affords, provided that they are the most generally understood. Nothing should be expressed in two words that can be as well expressed in one; that is, no synonyms should be used, or very rarely, but the whole should be as short as possible, consistent with clearness; the words should be so placed as to be agreeable to the ear in reading; summarily it should be smooth, clear, and short, for the contrary qualities are displeasing." [137] Like the members of the Royal Society, Franklin would bring the words of written discourse "as near as possible to the spoken." [138] In 1753 he observed: "If my Hypothesis [concerning waterspouts] is not the Truth itself it is [at] least as naked: For I have not with some of our learned Moderns, disguis'd my Nonsense in Greek, cloth'd it in Algebra or adorn'd it with Fluxions. You have it in puris naturalibus." [139] He briefly summarized his rhetorical ideal, in a letter to Hume: "In writings intended for persuasion

Philosophy (London, 1728), had said (pp. 2–3) that the Newtonian thirst for knowledge, especially of the causes of the operations of nature, had become "so general, that all men of letters, I believe, find themselves influenced by it."

[136] *Writings*, II, 157.   [137] *Ibid.*, I, 37.   [138] *Ibid.*, I, ix.
[139] *Ibid.*, III, 121. For his demand that sculpture and music have "beautiful simplicity" of form see *ibid.*, VII, 194; VIII, 578; IV, 210, 377–8, 381; V, 530; VIII, 94. On the basis of confusion of genres, Franklin disliked the opera.

and for general information, one cannot be too clear; and every expression in the least obscure is a fault." [140]

Unlike Jefferson, "no friend to what is called *purism*, but a zealous one" to neology, Franklin had an inveterate antipathy toward the use of colloquialisms, provincialisms, and extravagant innovations. [141] In another letter to Hume, he hoped that "we shall always in America make the best English of this Island [Britain] our standard." [142] If he did not hold the typical eighteenth-century view that "English must be subjected to a process of classical regularizing," [143] neither did he, with his friend Joseph Priestley, espouse the idea of correctness, dependent only on usage. In general, he seems to have had a tendency toward purism; it is not unlikely that as a youth he was influenced by Swift's *Proposal for Correcting, Improving, and Ascertaining the English Tongue*. [144] Striving for correctness, and

[140] *Ibid.*, I, 41. See also X, 33, 51.

[141] Miss MacLaurin's research has disclosed that Franklin's vocabulary (4,062 words, between 1722 and 1751) contained only 19 words which "were discovered to be pure 'Americanisms,' and of these, 6 are the names of herbs or grasses; 1 is derived from the name of an American university, and 1 from the name of an American state" (*op. cit.*, 38–9).

[142] Quoted in Bruce, *op. cit.*, II, 439. Also see his letters to Noah Webster, *Writings*, I, 29; X, 75–6.

[143] S. A. Leonard, *The Doctrine of Correctness in English Usage, 1700–1800*, 14.

[144] See L. Richardson, *A History of Early American Magazines, 1741–1789*, index, for the vogue of Swift. In the library of the *New England Courant*, as early as 1722, there was a copy of *The Tale of a Tub* (T. G. Wright, *Literary Culture in Early New England, 1620–1730*, 187–8). Franklin was probably indebted to the Dean for his prophecies of the death of Titan Leeds (although he could have learned the use of this device from Defoe). In *Idea of the English School* Franklin recommends Swift for use in the sixth class (*Writings*, III, 28). His *Meditation on a Quart Mugg* is undoubtedly derived from Swift's *Meditation upon a Broomstick*, each forced to undergo the indignities of a "dirty wench." In 1757 he made the acquaintance of Dr. John Hawkesworth, who in 1755 had edited Swift's works. It is likely that this friendly union may have helped to produce Franklin's 1773 masterpieces of caustic irony and the disarmingly effective hoaxes. Variously he quotes (acknowledged and otherwise) bits from Swift's poetry and prose. See Herbert Davis's "Swift's View of Poetry," in *Studies in English by Members of University College, Toronto* (1931), collected by M. W. Wallace.

the avoidance of "affected Words or high-flown Phrases" [145] he approximated the *curiosa felicitas* of the neoclassicists. [146]

A solid neoclassicist [147] in style, Franklin accepted the canon of imitation as it was imperfectly understood in the eighteenth century. To the extent, however, that the models were conceived of as approximating the *consensus gentium*, fragments illustrating universal reason, there may be little disparity between neoclassic imitation and Aristotle's use of the term in the sense of imitating a higher ethical reality. His own life, Franklin thought, (with the exception of a few "errata") was "fit to be imitated." [148] A. H. Smyth notes, perhaps extravagantly, "Nothing but the 'Autobiography' of Benvenuto Cellini, or the 'Confessions' of Rousseau, can enter into competition with it." [149] This may suggest a clue to the durable nature of Franklin's life-tale. Cellini, it is true, was tremendously alive to Benvenuto, even as Michel de Montaigne was interested in his own whims, but neither Cellini, nor Montaigne, nor Franklin, could have penned the *Confessions*, the thesis of which is that if Rousseau is not better than other men at least he is different. Cellini, Montaigne, and Franklin, on the other hand, while allowing us to see their fancies and singular biases, tended to emphasize

[145] *Writings*, III, 26.

[146] To suggest that Franklin knew his Horace, see *ibid.*, VI, 150; VIII, 148.

[147] It seems unnecessary to extend a discussion of the didacticism inherent in Franklin's writing. Addison, and the ethical bent of neoclassicism in general, impinging on a mind no small part of which was motivated by its Puritan heritage, help to account for Franklin's ethicism, a lifelong quality. References illustrating his assumed role as *Censor Morum* are: *Writings*, I, 37, 243; II, 4, 50, 101, 110-1, 117, 175. Franklin proposes not only to delight, but also, in the Jonsonian and Meredithian sense, to instruct through a mild catharsis brought about by holding up man's excesses and vagaries for ridicule. He is firm in distinguishing good writing by its "tendency to benefit the reader, by improving his virtue or his knowledge." Consonant with Horace's

"To teach—to please—comprise the poet's views,
    Or else at once to profit and amuse,"

and with Sidney's "to teach delightfully," Franklin's literary purpose included a basic ethical motivation.

[148] *Writings*, I, 226.   [149] *Ibid.*, I, 42-3.

those qualities which they held in common with their age, nation, and even the continuity of mankind. Montaigne, it will be remembered, sought to express *la connaissance de l'homme en général.* With no aspirations to become an original genius, Franklin, both in his prose style and his yearning for perfection, sought the guidance of models, which he conceived as embodying universal reason. Had he been a writer of epics[150] he would with Pope have acquired "from ancient rules a just esteem"— when the rules were, in his mind, "according to nature."

Likewise Franklin is representative of the Enlightenment in his description of the province of the imagination. It is an axiom that "the belief that the imagination ought to be kept in check by reason, pervades the critical literature of the first half of the eighteenth century."[151] Franklin observes that poetasters above all need instruction on how to govern "Fancy [Imagination] with Judgement."[152] He implies that imagination is a power lending an air of unreality to a creation, often like "the Effect of some melancholy Humour."[153] He feared that the unchecked fancy would vitiate his ideals of simplicity and correctness, and a sober and practical argument.

[150] Fully aware "that I am no *Poet born*" (Bruce, *op. cit.*, II, 498), apparently agreeing with his father that poets "were generally beggars" (*Writings* I, 240), Franklin allowed only that writing poetry may improve one's language. Yet *Dogood Paper* No. VII and his estimate of Cowper (characterized by easiness in manner, correctness in language, clarity of expression, perspicuity, and justness of the sentiments) (*ibid.*, VIII, 448–9), and the "Tears of Pleasure" he shed over Thomson, all suggest that he was not wholly blind to poetry. He hoped to see Philadelphia "become the Seat of the *American* Muses" (*ibid.*, II, 245, 110; IV, 181, 184; VI, 437).

[151] A. Bosker, *Literary Criticism in the Age of Johnson*, 34. For important qualifications see the thorough study by Donald F. Bond, "'Distrust' of Imagination in English Neo-Classicism," *Philological Quarterly*, XIV, 54–69 (Jan., 1935). Those interested in considering Franklin with reference to contemporary literary theory will find full materials in J. W. Draper's *Eighteenth-Century English Aesthetics: A Bibliography*, and additions to it by R. S. Crane, *Modern Philology*, XXIX, 25 ff. (1931); W. D. Templeman, *ibid.*, XXX, 309–16; R. D. Havens, *Modern Language Notes*, XLVII, 118–20 (1932).

[152] *Writings*, II, 24.

[153] *Ibid.*, V, 182; also II, 43, and VIII, 128, 163, 604.

Posing as no original genius independent of the wisdom of the ages,[154] confessing that "from a child" he "was fond of reading" and that as a youth "reading was the only amusement" he allowed himself, Franklin was not backward in cataloguing many of the authors who helped to motivate his thought. He seems to have been acquainted with portions of Plato, Aesop, Pliny, Xenophon, Herodotus, Epictetus, Vergil, Horace, Tacitus, Seneca, Sallust, Cicero, Tully, Milton, Jeremy Taylor, Bacon, Dryden, Tillotson, Rabelais,[155] Bunyan, Féne-lon, Chevalier de Ramsay,[156] Pythagoras, Waller, Defoe, Addison and Steele, William Temple, Pope, Swift, Voltaire, Boyle, Algernon Sidney, Trenchard and Gordon,[157] Young, Mandeville, Locke, Shaftesbury, Collins, Bolingbroke, Richardson, Whiston, Watts, Thomson, Burke, Cowper, Darwin, Rowe, Rapin, Herschel, Paley, Lord Kames, Adam Smith, Hume, Robertson, Lavoisier, Buffon, Dupont de Nemours, Whitefield, Pemberton, Blackmore, John Ray, Petty, Turgot, Priestley, Paine, Mirabeau, Quesnay, Raynal, Morellet, and Condorcet, to suggest only the more prominent.[158] Such a catalogue tends to discredit the all too common idea that the untutored tradesman was torpid to the information and wisdom found in books.

If his prose style shows none of the delicate rhythms and haunting imagery of the prose born of the romantic movement, it is nevertheless far from pedestrian. If it seems devoid of imaginative splendor, it is not lacking in force and persuasion.[159] After one has noted Franklin's canon of simplicity

[154] See G. S. Eddy, "Dr. Benjamin Franklin's Library," *Proceedings of the American Antiquarian Society*, N. S. XXXIV, 206–26 (Oct., 1924).
[155] See C. E. Jorgenson, "Benjamin Franklin and Rabelais," *Classical Journal*, XXIX, 538–40 (April, 1934).
[156] *The Travels of Cyrus.*
[157] *Independent Whig* and *Cato's Letters.*
[158] For an interesting summary of Franklin's references to the classics, see R. M. Gummere, *op. cit.*
[159] Add to this, Franklin's use of the Swiftian hoax and complex irony. After writing *Rules by Which a Great Empire May Be Reduced to a Small*

and order, his insistence on correctness, his assumed role
as *Censor Morum*, his acceptance of the doctrine of imitation and the use of imagination guided by reason, one
returns to the question of the degree to which the ideals
of rhetoric fostered by the men of science may have helped to
motivate Franklin's prose style, and to what degree his acceptance of deism augmented by Newtonianism may have furnished
him with a rationale which lent sanction to his demand for a
simple style.

Sir Humphrey Davy found in Franklin's scientific papers a
language lucid and decorous, "almost as worthy of admiration
as the doctrine" [160] they contain. S. G. Fisher buoyantly maintained that Franklin's "is the most effective literary style ever
used by an American." After reading Franklin's paper on stoves
he was "inclined to lay down the principle that the test of literary genius is the ability to be fascinating about stoves." [161]
Whether he writes soberly (albeit tempered by Gallic fancy) of
the mutability of life, as in *The Ephemera*, or of sophisticated
social amenities, as in the letters to Madame Brillon and
Madame Helvétius, or in his memoirs, in which solid fact
follows solid fact, sifted by the years of good fortune,
Franklin's style never loses its compelling charm and vigor.
If he never wrote (or uttered) less than was demanded
by the nature of his subject, neither would he have disgusted
the Clerk of Oxenford who

> Nought o word spak he more than was nede.

One (1773) he explained to a friend: "These odd ways of presenting Mat-
ters to the publick View sometimes occasion them to be more read, talk'd
of, and more attended to" (*Writings*, VI, 137). Parton observes that the
Edict of the King of Prussia "was the nine-days' talk of the kingdom."
Raynal unsuspectingly used Franklin's *Polly Baker*, as an authentic document in his *Histoire* . . . Franklin's *Exporting of Felons to the Colonies*,
The Sale of Hessians, and *A Dialogue between Britain, France, Spain,
Holland, Saxony, and America* illustrate these trenchant devices used to
achieve a political purpose.

[160] *Writings*, I, 49.
[161] *The True Benjamin Franklin*, 158.

He was no formal literary critic such as Boileau, Lessing, or Coleridge, and no acknowledged arbiter of taste, such as Dr. Johnson. Yet Franklin, in voluminous practice, enjoying tremendous
international vogue, proved that his theories bore the acid test
of effectiveness. Indirectly he challenged his readers to honor
principles of rhetoric which could so trenchantly serve the
demands of his catholic pen, and make him one of the most
widely read of all Americans.

IV. FRANKLIN AS PRINTER AND JOURNALIST

Franklin was a printer chiefly because of two proclivities
which were basic in his personality from childhood to old age—
a bent toward practical mechanics ("handiness") and a fondness
for reading (bookishness). Further, he was a journalist and
publisher chiefly because he was a printer.

A thorough printer is both an artisan and an artist; he has
both the manual dexterity of a good workman and the aesthetic
appreciation of the amateur of beauty. Franklin always took
pride in his ability to handle the printer's tools, from the time
when, at the age of twelve, he became "a useful hand" [162] in the
print shop of his brother James, until the very end of his life.
One of the pleasantest anecdotes of the old printer is that which
tells of his visit to the famous Didot printing establishment in
Paris, when he stepped up to a press, and motioning the printer
aside, himself took possession of the machine and printed off
several sheets. Then the American ambassador smiled at the
gaping printers and said, "Do not be astonished, Sirs, it is my
former business." [163]

Even in his boyhood, it was a pleasure to Franklin "to see
good workmen handle their tools," and he tells in his autobiography how much this feeling for tools meant to him throughout
his life. [164] His flair for invention, though founded on this same

---

[162] *Writings*, I, 239.
[163] Smyth's note, *Writings*, VIII, 336.   [164] *Writings*, I, 238.

"handiness," was not always directed toward the production of tools; but in the two fields of "philosophical" experimentation and the printing trade, his dexterity and cleverness in making needful instruments and devices were invaluable.

Partly because of the fact that printers' supplies must be imported from England, and partly because of his natural tool-mindedness, Franklin manufactured more of his own supplies than any other American commercial printer before or since. He cast type, made paper molds, mixed inks, made contributions to press building, did engraving, forwarded experiments in stereotyping, and worked at logotypy. Long after he had retired from the printing business, Franklin continued to influence developments in that field. It is a common saying among printers that one never forgets the smell of printer's ink. Franklin kept touch with his former business through various partnerships, through correspondence with printer friends, through the establishment of a private press in his home at Passy during his ambassadorship to France, and through his personal supervision of the education of his grandson in "the art preservative of arts." "I am too old to follow printing again myself," he wrote to a friend, "but, loving the business, I have brought up my grandson Benjamin to it, and have built and furnished a printing-house for him, which he now manages under my eye." [165]

As to just how adept Franklin was on the distinctively aesthetic side of printing, critics must differ. It has been customary to assume that the output of his shop was far superior to that of the several other printing houses in the colonies. [166] Such broad generalizations are misleading, however; and it is certainly pos-

[165] *Writings*, X, 4 (to Mrs. Catherine Greene, March 2, 1789).
[166] There were eight towns in the colonies which had presses when Franklin went into business for himself: Cambridge, Boston, New York, Philadelphia, Annapolis, New London (Conn.), Woodbridge (N. J.), and Williamsburg. See Isaiah Thomas, *The History of Printing in America* (Worcester, 1810), II, *passim*.

sible to find Parks and even Bradford imprints which compare favorably enough with some of Franklin's. In typography, the phase of printing which affords the widest aesthetic scope, Franklin was by no means a genius. William Parks, of Annapolis and later of Williamsburg, was at least Franklin's peer during the seventeen-thirties and 'forties in the artistic arrangement of type; and William Goddard, who practiced the art a little later in several of the colonies, was his superior. Yet Franklin was an outstanding printer in a region blessed with few good presses. The difference between him and most of the other colonial printers may be stated thus: Franklin maintained a high average of workmanlike (though not inspired) performance, while his contemporaries were inclined to be slovenly, inaccurate, and generally careless.

In the later years of his life Franklin gave no little attention to fine printing, though as a dilettante rather than as a commercial printer. In France he was friendly with François Ambroise Didot, the greatest French printer of his times, and put his grandson Benjamin Franklin Bache to school in Didot's establishment. With Pierre Simon Fournier, who ranked next to Didot among French printers, Franklin corresponded from time to time. In England the American printer maintained touch with prominent practitioners of his craft from the time of his first visit abroad until his death. Samuel Palmer, Franklin's first London employer, was but a mediocre printer; but John Watts, to whose house the young American went after a year at Palmer's, stood much higher in his vocation.[167] Both Watts and Palmer were patrons of William Caslon, from whom Franklin later bought type. But John Baskerville, Caslon's rival, was the founder whom Franklin did most to encourage and to bring to the attention of discriminating printers. The English printer with whom Franklin was upon the terms of

---

[167] "A printer of first-rate eminence," according to Charles Henry Timperley's *A Dictionary of Printers and Printing* (London, 1839), 714 note.

greatest intimacy—and that for many years—was William
Strahan, member of Parliament, King's Printer, and a successful
publisher. Strahan was a man of parts, a great letter writer, and
a friend of David Hume and Samuel Johnson. The latter referred to the Strahan shop as "the greatest printing house in
London." [168] Another correspondent was John Walter, logo-
typer, press builder, and founder of the London *Times*.[169] In all
his letters to his printer friends, Franklin shows not only a lively
interest in improvements and inventions for the trade, but also
an increasing interest in the artistic side of printing and type-
founding.

The "bookish inclination" which Franklin credits in the
Autobiography with being the quality that decided his father to
make a printer of him, appertained to the trade because printers
were commonly publishers and sellers of books and pamphlets,
and often editors and publishers of newspapers. How the young
Franklin satisfied his literary urge in the print shop of his brother
James is a familiar story, and his theories of writing are traced
in another section of this Introduction. The contribution to
literature which he made as a publisher of original books is negligible, but he did his part both as publisher and bookseller to
spread that bookishness to which he felt that he owed much of
his own success. Like all publishers before and since, he was
forced by his customers to issue books of a lower sort than he
could fully approve in order to float editions of more desirable
works: he tells plaintively of his public's preference for "Robin
Hood's Songs" over the Psalms of his beloved Watts. [170] In still

[168] R. A. Austen Leigh, "William Strahan and His Ledgers," in *Transactions of the Bibliographical Society*, N. S. III, 286. For Strahan see also
Spottiswoode & Co.'s *The Story of a Printing House, Being a Short Account
of the Strahans and Spottiswoodes* (London, 1911); and Timperley,
op. cit., 754–6.
[169] See G. S. Eddy, "Correspondence Between Dr. Benjamin Franklin
and John Walter, Regarding the Logographic Process of Printing," *Proceedings of the American Antiquarian Society*, N. S. XXXVIII, 349–69
(Oct., 1928).
[170] *Writings*, II, 175.

another way, Franklin promoted the bookishness of his community: he founded the first of American circulating libraries, and he built up for himself one of the largest private libraries in the country. [171]

Journalism was a common by-product of the printing trade. When Franklin and Meredith took over Keimer's *The Universal Instructor in all Arts and Sciences: and Pennsylvania Gazette* in 1729, there were six other newspapers being published in the colonies—three in Boston and one each in New York, Philadelphia, and Annapolis. The Williamsburg press had a newspaper a few years later, but the other two printing towns in the colonies had to wait some thirty years for journalistic ventures— a newspaper in New London and a magazine in Woodbridge. [172]

The fundamental question to be asked in analyzing a newspaper may be stated thus: What is the editorial conception of the primary function of the press? Franklin had received his early newspaper training on his brother's *New England Courant*, which frankly acknowledged entertainment as its primary function and relegated news to a minor place. Of his contemporaries in 1729, the oldest, the *Boston News-Letter*, held the publication of news to be its sole function; while the *Boston Gazette*, the *New York Gazette*, and the *Maryland Gazette* took much the same attitude. In the main, they were rather dreary reprints of stale European news. Bradford's *American Weekly Mercury*, in Philadelphia, gave somewhat more attention to local news; but with the exception of the Franklin-Breintnal *Busy-Body* papers, contributed in 1728–1729 in order to bring Keimer to his knees, the *Mercury* gave very little attention to the entertainment function. Only the *New England Weekly Journal*, carrying on something of the tradition of the old *Courant*, dealt largely in entertainment as well as in news. This

---

[171] See W. P. and J. P. Cutler, *Life, Journals and Correspondence of Rev. Manasseh Cutler*, I, 269, letter of July 13, 1787; also G. S. Eddy, *op. cit.*
[172] See Thomas, *loc. cit.*

bi-functional policy was the one adopted by Franklin's *Pennsylvania Gazette*, which was always readable and amusing at the same time that it was newsy.

Of the editorial or opinion-forming function of newspapers there was little evidence in Franklin's paper,[173] at least in the field of politics. The obvious reason was the active governmental censorship. It remained for John Peter Zenger to introduce that function into colonial journalism in the *New York Weekly Journal* in 1733: his struggle for the freedom of the press is well known.[174] But the *Pennsylvania Gazette* never became in any degree a political organ while Franklin edited it; and his first political pronouncement was published not in his paper but in a pamphlet, *Plain Truth*, issued just before his retirement from editorial duties.

Two common misconceptions in regard to Franklin's newspaper call for correction: (1) The *Pennsylvania Gazette* was not connected as forerunner or ancestor with the *Saturday Evening Post*. The *Gazette*, a newspaper to the end, closed its file in 1815;[175] the *Post*, a story paper, issued its Volume I, Number 1, in 1821. Throughout much of the latter half of the nineteenth century, the *Post* carried the legend "Founded in 1821" on its front page; and not until after the Curtis Publishing Company bought it in 1897 did it begin to print the words "Founded A.D. 1728 by Benjamin Franklin" on its cover. The sole connection of the *Post* with Franklin lies in the fact that it was first issued

[173] A notable exception was the type of "letter to the editor" which Franklin used as a means of suggesting reforms, such as those affecting the city watch, the fire companies, and the cleaning and lighting of the streets. See J. B. McMaster, *Benjamin Franklin as a Man of Letters*, 82–5.
[174] A correspondent of Franklin's paper commended Zenger's stand (see *Pennsylvania Gazette*, May 11–18, 1738; reprinted in W. G. Bleyer, *Main Currents in the History of American Journalism*, 66–7), but Franklin shrewdly kept his own paper free of factional politics. See Livingston Rutherford, *John Peter Zenger* (New York, 1904).
[175] See Clarence S. Brigham, "American Newspapers to 1820," *Proceedings of the American Antiquarian Society*, N. S. XXXII, 157–9 (April, 1922), for detailed bibliography of the *Gazette*.

from an office at 53 Market Street which Franklin had once occupied.[176] (2) Franklin did not publish a "chain" of newspapers. A "chain" implies some kind of co-operative connection between the various members, but the several papers which Franklin helped to finance had no such relationship. In some he was a six-years partner,[177] keeping his interest until the resident publisher, usually a former employee, was established; to some he made loans or, in the case of relatives, gifts.[178]

One of his journalistic ventures which is not mentioned in the *Autobiography* is the *General Magazine*, of 1741. It missed by three days being the first of American magazines: Andrew Bradford had learned of Franklin's project and, with his *American Magazine*, beat him in the race for priority. But the *American Magazine* was a failure in three monthly numbers, while Franklin's periodical, though more readable, died after its sixth issue.[179] As an initial episode in the history of American magazines, the *General Magazine* has a certain eminence; but Franklin's neglect of it when writing his *Autobiography*, after the events of nearly fifty busy years had apparently crowded it out of his memory, is sufficient commentary on its unimportance.

To the end of his life Franklin was proud of his trade of printing, with its handmaiden journalism. His last will and testament begins: "I, Benjamin Franklin, Printer . . . " Though clearly not the chief interest of his life, it was one to which he was fundamentally and consistently attached.

---

[176] A. H. Smyth, *Philadelphia Magazines and Their Contributors*, 200.

[177] *Writings*, I, 360.

[178] For a list of the printers with whom Franklin had such connections, see M. R. King, "One Link in the First Newspaper Chain, the *South Carolina Gazette*," *Journalism Quarterly*, IX, 257 (Sept., 1932).

[179] For sketches of both magazines, see L. N. Richardson, *A History of Early American Magazines, 1741–1850*, 17–35, and F. L. Mott, *A History of American Magazines, 1741–1850*, 71–7. See also Philip Biddison, "The Magazine Franklin Failed to Remember," *American Literature*, IV, 177 (June, 1932); the writer thinks certain accusations in the Bradford-Franklin controversy over the magazines discreditable to Franklin, so that the latter's lapse of memory saved him "embarrassment."

V. FRANKLIN'S ECONOMIC VIEWS

An eighteenth-century colonial who wrote on paper money, interest, value, and insurance, who discussed a theory of population and the economic aspects of the abolition of slavery, who championed free trade, and who probably lent Adam Smith some information used in his *Wealth of Nations*, who was an empirical agriculturist, who was "half physiocratic before the rise of the physiocratic school"—such a colonial has, indeed, claims to being America's pioneer economist.

Franklin's hatred of negro slavery was conditioned by more than his humanitarian bias. It may be seen that his indictments of black cargoes were the resultant of an interplay of his convictions that economically slavery was enervating and dear and of his abstract sense of religious and ethical justice. One should not minimize, however, his distrust of slavery on other than economic bases. He was acutely influenced by the Quakers of his colony who, like gadflies, were stinging slaveholders to an awareness of their blood traffic, and by the rise of English humanitarianism. In his youth he had published (first edition, 1729; second, 1730), with no little danger to himself and his business, Ralph Sandiford's *A Brief Examination of the Practice of the Times*, an Amos-like vituperative attack on the "unrighteous Gain" of slaveholding. He also published works of Benjamin Lay and John Woolman.[180] Friend of Anthony Benezet, Benjamin Rush, Fothergill, and Granville Sharp, and after 1760 a member of Dr. Bray's Associates, he lent his voice and pen to denouncing slavery on religious and ethical grounds; and in England, after the James Som-

---

[180] See letter to John Wright, Nov. 4, 1789 (*Writings*, X, 60–3). For European backgrounds of Franklin's economic views see Gide and Rist, in Bibliography. On American backgrounds the standard work is E. A. J. Johnson's *American Economic Thought in the Seventeenth Century* (London, 1932), which shows the intimate relation between economic and religious theories.

mersett trial (1772), he "began to agitate for parliamentary action" toward the abolishing of slavery in all parts of the British Empire.[181] Following the Sommersett verdict, Franklin contributed a brief article to the *London Chronicle* (June 18–20, 1772) in which he denounced the "constant butchery of the human species by this pestilential detestable traffic in the bodies and souls of men." [182] Losing his temperamental urbanity when observing "the diabolical Commerce," [183] "the abominable African Trade," he recollects approvingly that a certain French moralist [184] could "not look on a piece of sugar without conceiving it stained with spots of human blood!" [185] Conditioned by Quakerism, by his deism, which suggested that "the most acceptable Service we render him [God] is doing good to his other Children," and by the eighteenth century's growing repugnance toward suffering and pain,[186] Franklin (although he took little part in legislating against slavery in Pennsylvania) became through his writing a model to be imitated, especially in France, by a people more intent on becoming humane than saintly.

His letter to Anthony Benezet (London, July 14, 1773), however, clearly indicates that for economic, as well as humanitarian reasons, he had sought freedom for slaves:

I am glad to hear that such humane Sentiments prevail so much more generally than heretofore; that there is Reason to hope our Colonies may in time get clear of a Practice that

---

[181] Lewis J. Carey, *Franklin's Economic Views* (Garden City, N. Y., 1928), 72.

[182] Cited in Carey, 73. He had used in this article facts lent by Benezet concerning the "detestable commerce" motivated in part by English "laws for promoting the Guinea trade" (*Writings*, V, 431–2).

[183] *Writings*, IX, 627.

[184] In 1779 he professed mortification that the King of France gave "freedom to Slaves, while a king of England is endeavouring to make Slaves of Freemen" (*ibid.*, VII, 402).

[185] *Ibid.*, IX, 404. See also *ibid.*, 6.

[186] Suggestive notes on this point may be found in N. Foerster's article in the *American Review*, IV, 129–46 (Dec., 1934).

disgraces them, and, without producing any equivalent Benefit, is dangerous to their very Existence.[187]

Franklin's view of the economic disabilities of slavery is best expressed in *Observations Concerning the Increase of Mankind, Peopling of Countries, Etc.* (1751). Arguing against British restraint of colonial manufactures, he observed that " 'tis an ill-grounded Opinion that by the Labour of slaves, *America* may possibly vie in Cheapness of Manufactures with *Britain*. The Labour of Slaves can never be so cheap here as the Labour of working Men is in *Britain*." [188] With arithmetic based on empirical scrutiny of existing conditions, resembling the mode of economists following Adam Smith, he charged that slaves are economically unprofitable due to the rate of interest in the colonies, their initial price, their insurance and maintenance, their negligence and malevolence.[189] In addition, "Slaves ... pejorate the Families that use them; the white Children become proud, disgusted with Labour, and being educated in Idleness, are rendered unfit to get a Living by Industry." [190] Slaves are hardly economical investments in terms of colonial character. Looking to the "*English* Sugar *Islands*" where Negroes "have greatly diminish'd the Whites," and deprived the poor of employment, "while a few Families acquire vast Estates," he realized that "population was limited by means of subsistence," [191] which foreshadowed the more pessimistic progressions of Malthus. Having just maintained that "our People must at least be doubled every 20 Years," [192] and intuitively suspecting that the means for subsistence progress more slowly, he exclaimed, "Why increase the Sons of *Africa*, by planting them in *America*, where we have so fair an Opportunity, by excluding all Blacks and Tawneys, of increasing the lovely White and Red?" [193] He saw mere economic extravagance as the short-time effect of

[187] *Writings*, VI, 102. See also VI, 39–40.
[188] *Ibid.*, III, 66.
[189] *Ibid.*, III, 66–7.
[190] *Ibid.*, III, 68.
[191] Carey, *op. cit.*, 69.
[192] *Writings*, III, 65.
[193] *Ibid.*, III, 73.

slavery; he feared that the long-time effect would be to create an aristocracy subsisting at the head of a vast brood of slaves and poor whites.[194]

It was inevitable in a state having no staple crop, such as rice, sugar, tobacco, or cotton, which offered at least economic justification for negro slavery, that abolition of slaves should be urged partially on purely economic grounds, and that Pennsylvania should have been the first colony to legislate in favor of abolition, in 1780. Although one may feel that economic determinism is overly simple and audacious in its doctrinaire interpretations, one can not refuse to see the extent to which economics tended to buttress humane and religious factors in Franklin's mind to make him a persuasive champion of abolition.[195]

A Modest Enquiry into the Nature and Necessity of a Paper Currency [196] has been appraised as "by far the ablest and most original treatise that had been written on the subject up to 1728

[194] That others in the colonies saw slavery as an economically unsound investment (without any reference to its being *malum in se*) may be witnessed in an article in the *Boston News-Letter* (March 3, 1718): "In the previous year there had been eighty burials of Indians and negroes in Boston. The writer argued that the loss of £30 each amounted to £2,400. If white servants had been employed instead, at £15 for the time of each, the 'town had saved £1,200.' A man could procure £12 to £15 to purchase the time of a white servant that could not pay £30 to £50 for a negro or Indian. 'The Whites Strengthens [*sic*] and Peoples the Country, others do not' " (W. B. Weeden, *Economic and Social History of New England, 1620–1789*, Boston, 1891, II, 456). Congruent with Franklin's *Observations* is John Adams's note that "Argument might have some weight in the abolition of slavery in Massachusetts, but the real cause was the multiplication of labouring white people, who would no longer suffer the rich to employ these sable rivals so much to their injury" (*ibid.*, II, 453).

[195] In Franklin's view, slavery was also politically subversive. In 1756 he feared that the slaves, along with servants and loose people in general, would desert to the French (*Writings*, III, 359). Since the danger undoubtedly existed (*ibid.*, VII, 48, 69), Franklin had a right to be sardonic in commenting on Dr. Johnson's advice that slaves be incited "to rise, cut the throats of their purchasers, and resort to the British army, where they should be rewarded with freedom" (*ibid.*, X, 110–1).

[196] Printed in *Maryland Gazette* (Dec. 17, 1728); later as pamphlet (April 3, 1729).

Benjamin Franklin

and was probably the most widely read work on paper currency that appeared in colonial America." [197] That Franklin's interest in paper money was not unique, one may gather from the fact that between 1714 and 1721 "nearly thirty pamphlets appeared" on this subject in Massachusetts alone.[198] One of the 1728 theses at Harvard, answered in the affirmative, was: "Does the issue of paper money contribute to the public good?" [199] "Since there was a scarcity of circulating medium, caused by the constant drain of specie for export," explains Mr. D. R. Dewey, "it is not strange that projects for converting credit into wealth should have sprung up in the colonies." [200] Franklin argued in his *Modest Enquiry* [201] that (1) "A plentiful Currency will occasion Interest to be low," (2) it "will occasion the Trading Produce to bear a good Price," (3) it "will encourage great Numbers of labouring and Handicrafts Men to come and settle in the Country," and (4) it "will occasion a less consumption of European Goods, in proportion to the Number of the People." Thus he saw paper money as a "Morrison's Pill," promising to cure all economic ills.[202] It has been suggested that as a printer Franklin naturally would favor issues of paper money. In view of his later apostasy one should note that in this essay Franklin apparently accepted the current mercantilist notions, best expressed here in his conviction that paper money will secure a favorable balance of trade.

[197] Carey, *op. cit.*, 7. See *Writings* I, 306–7, for Franklin's own account of the effect of this work.
[198] C. J. Bullock, *Essays on the Monetary History of the United States*, 51.
[199] Weeden, *op. cit.*, II, 485.
[200] *Financial History of the United States*, 21. Bullock observes another factor: "Sooner or later all the plantations were deeply involved in the mazes of a fluctuating currency, for the burdens attending the various wars of the eighteenth century were so great as to induce even the most conservative colonies to resort to this easy method of meeting public obligations" (*op. cit.*, 33).
[201] *Writings*, II, 133–5.
[202] See Carey, *op. cit.*, chap. I, for suggestive survey of this pamphlet. Carey points out Franklin's indebtedness to writings of Sir William Petty.

Demands for emissions of paper money were inevitable in a colony in the grip of such a restrictive commercial policy as British mercantilism. It must be observed, however, that Franklin differed from the proper mercantilists to the extent that simple valuable metals were not to be measures of value. Deriving his idea from Sir William Petty, Franklin took labor as the true measure of value,[203]—a position later held by Karl Marx. In his preoccupation with the growth of manufactures and favorable balances of trade, Franklin gave no suggestions that at least by 1767 he was to become an exponent of agrarianism and free trade. One wonders to what extent his warnings against the purchase of "unnecessary Householdstuff, or any superfluous thing," his inveterate emphasis on industry and frugality, were conditioned by his view that such indulgence would essentially cause a preponderance of imports, hence casting against them an unfavorable trade balance. [204]

In 1751 Parliament passed an act regulating in the New England colonies the issue of paper money and preventing them "from adding a legal tender clause thereto"; in 1764 Parliament forbade issue of legal tender money in any of the colonies. As a member of the Pennsylvania assembly, Franklin had successfully sponsored issues of paper money; in London, following the 1764 act, he urged that one of the causes breeding disrespect for Parliament was "the prohibition of making paper money among [us]." [205] Economics blends into politics when we remember that the 1764 restraining legislation was "one of the factors in the subsequent separation, for it caused some of the suffering that

---

[203] Carey (chap. II, "Value and Interest") quotes Franklin: "Riches of a Country are to be valued by the Quantity of Labour its inhabitants are able to purchase, and not by the Quantity of Silver and Gold they possess" (*Writings*, II, 144).

[204] See, for example, *Plan for Saving One Hundred Thousand Pounds*, 1755 (*Writings*, III, 293–5).

[205] *Writings*, IV, 420: *Examination of Benjamin Franklin*. He was obliged to admit that Massachusetts colonists had taken a calmer view of the 1751 act (IV, 428).

inevitably follows in the wake of an unsound monetary policy whose onward course is suddenly checked." [206] In 1766 Franklin was yet an ardent imperialist, who sought politically and economically to keep whole "that fine and noble China Vase, the British Empire." His *Remarks and Facts Concerning American Paper Money* (1767), in answer to Lord Hillsborough's Board of Trade report circulated among British merchants, is an ardent plea for legal tender paper money. He argued that British merchants (since yearly trade balances had regularly been in their favor) had not been deprived of gold and silver, that paper money *had worked* in the Colonies,[207] and that British merchants had lost no more in their colonial dealings than was inevitable in war times. Franklin concluded that since there were no mines in the colonies, paper money was a necessity (arguing here very shrewdly that even English silver "is obliged to the legal Tender for Part of its Value"). Hence, at least for colonies deserving it, the mother country should take off the restraint on legal tender. What Franklin seems not to have known and what the merchants had actually felt (they had their accounts staring at them) was that in the past, especially after 1750, much of the legal tender was in effect nothing but inconvertible fiat money. Mr. Carey quotes from an uncollected item, Franklin's "The Legal Tender of Paper Money in America," in which he threatened that "if the colonies were not allowed to issue legal-tender notes there was no way in which they could retain hard money except by boycotting English goods." [208] Franklin suggested (to S. Cooper, April 22, 1779) that depreciation may not be unmixed evil, since it may be viewed as a tax: "It should

---

[206] G. L. Beer, *British Colonial Policy, 1754-1765*, 188.

[207] Although it is true that Pennsylvania suffered less from paper money because of better security (Carey, *op. cit.*, 23 note), it seems curious that Franklin should have been blind to the evils of inflation and the operations of Gresham's law.

[208] Paper in William Smith Mason Collection; cited in Carey, *op. cit.*, 20. See also *Writings*, V, 189, in which he repeats the threat. British restraint must hence provoke colonial "industry and frugality."

always be remembered, that the original Intention was to sink the Bills by Taxes, which would as effectually extinguish the Debt as an actual Redemption." [209] Not a little Machiavellian for one who was not blind to the sanctity of contracts!

With the Revolution and the attendant depreciation in currency, Franklin tended to warn against over-issues.[210] Like Governor Hutchinson, who said that "the morals of the people depreciate with the currency," Franklin confessed in 1783 "the many Mischiefs, the injustices, the Corruption of Manners, &c., &c., that attended a depreciating Currency." [211] There is no evidence to show that Franklin dissented from the conservative prohibition in the Constitutional Convention of 1787 against issues of legal tender paper.[212]

Deborah Logan (in a letter in 1829) stated that Franklin "once told Dr. Logan that the celebrated Adam Smith, when writing his 'Wealth of Nations,' was in the habit of bringing chapter after chapter as he composed it, to himself, Dr. Price and others of the literati; then patiently hear [sic] their observations, and profit by their discussion and criticism—even sometimes submitting to write whole chapters anew, and even to reverse some of his propositions." [213] James Parton observed that the allusions to the colonies which "constitute the experimental evidence of the essential truth of the book" were supplied by Franklin.[214] But Rae reasonably counters: "It ought of course to be borne in mind that Smith had been in the constant habit of hearing much about the American Colonies and their affairs

[209] *Writings*, VII, 294. Cf. *ibid.*, IX, 231–6.

[210] See *Writings*, VII, 275, 335, 341.

[211] To Josiah Quincy, Sept. 11, 1783 (*Writings*, IX, 93–5).

[212] In 1779 (see *Writings*, VII, 294) Franklin explained that the French knew little of paper currency. Mr. Carey offers convincing evidence to show that Franklin helped to predispose the deputies of the first National Assembly to use assignats (*op. cit.*, 27–33). See *Of the Paper Money of the United States of America* (*Writings*, IX, 231–6).

[213] J. F. Watson, *Annals of Philadelphia* (1844 ed.), I, 533.

[214] Cited by J. Rae in his *Life of Adam Smith* (London, 1895), 265.

during his thirteen years in Glasgow from the intelligent merchants and returned planters of that city."[215]

In general, we may conclude that Franklin and Smith were exponents of free trade in proportion as they were reactionaries against British mercantilism. Each in his reaction tended to elevate the function of agriculture beyond reasonable limits. Unlike the physiocrats and Franklin, however, Adam Smith did not hold that, in terms of wealth-producing, manufacturers were sterile. Even if Franklin saw only agriculture as *productive*, he was not blind to the utility of manufactures, especially after the break with the mother country, when he realized that home industry must be developed to supply the colonial needs formerly satisfied by British exports.[216]

Finally, each was, in varying degrees, an exponent of laissez

[215] *Ibid.*, 266. See Carey's chapter, "Franklin's Influence on Adam Smith," for an exhaustive survey of the *personalia* linking Adam Smith and Franklin. Both were in London in 1773–1776 and were occasional companions, having in 1759 met in Edinburgh at the home of Dr. Robertson. Probably they again met in Glasgow during the same year. Smith could have received copies of Franklin's works through Hume and Lord Kames; among Franklin's works in Smith's library was *Observations Concerning the Increase of Mankind;* when Smith in the *Wealth of Nations* observes that colonial population doubles in every twenty to twenty-five years, it seems reasonable to infer that he was beholden to Franklin for the suggestion. It is within the realm of reasonable inference, says Mr. Carey, that Franklin did, as Parton urges, help to educate Smith in the colonial point of view. T. D. Eliot, in "The Relations Between Adam Smith and Benjamin Franklin before 1776," *Political Science Quarterly*, XXXIX, 67–96 (March, 1924), after calling attention to the lack of extant correspondence between them and the silence of their contemporaries concerning a vital relationship, shows a reasonable hesitancy in observing that little is known about Smith's alleged debt to Franklin. Like Wetzel and Carey, Eliot thinks the debt has been exaggerated. He has been unable to prove Dr. Patten's intuition that in 1759 Franklin went to Smith in Scotland to urge him to write a treatise on colonial policy. In 1765 Turgot met Adam Smith. In the following year he published his *Réflexions sur la formation et la distribution des richesses*, antedating Smith's *Wealth of Nations* by ten years. See J. Delvaille's *Essai sur l'histoire de l'idée de progrès* (Paris, 1910), chap. IV, on Adam Smith; and Carey, *op. cit.*, 152, 158–9, for the relationship between Turgot and Franklin.

[216] Although both Franklin and Smith held to the labor theory of value (Franklin was indebted to Petty for his use of the term), Smith was confirmed in his belief before he knew of Franklin or his works.

faire.[217] Since we shall discover that politically Franklin was less a democrat than is often supposed, we may feel that his belief in free trade led him to embrace reservedly the principle of laissez faire, rather than that free trade, an economic concept, was but a fragment of a larger dogma, namely, that government should be characterized by its passivity, frugality, and maximum negligence. V. L. Parrington quotes[218] from George Whately's *Principles of Trade*, which contained views congenial to Franklin:

When Colbert assembled some wise old merchants of France, and desired their advice and opinion, how he could best serve and promote commerce, their answer, after consultation, was, in three words only, *Laissez-nous faire:* "Let us alone." It is said by a very solid writer of the same nation, that he is well advanced in the science of politics, who knows the full force of that maxim, *Pas trop gouverner:* "Not to govern too much!" *which, perhaps, would be of more use when applied to trade, than in any other public concern.* (Present editors' italics.)

Laissez faire in Franklin's as in Whately's view tended to be synonymous with free trade. Laissez faire was suggested by his insistence on free trade, as he progressively expressed his antipathy for mercantilism, rather than that free trade was simply

---

[217] According to Jacob Viner ("Adam Smith and Laissez Faire," in *Adam Smith, 1776–1926. Lectures to Commemorate the Sesqui-Centennial of the Publication of 'The Wealth of Nations,'* 116–55), "Smith's major claim to fame . . . seems to rest on his elaborate and detailed application to the economic world of the concept of a unified natural order, operating according to natural law, and if left to its own course producing results beneficial to mankind" (p. 118), which suggests, especially in *Theory of Moral Sentiments*, that self-love and social are the same. When Smith came to write the *Wealth of Nations*, he tended, Viner asserts, to distrust the operations of the harmonious natural order—yet Viner admits that many passages tend to corroborate his earlier view expressed in *Theory of Moral Sentiments* and that "There is no possible room for doubt that Smith in general believed that there was, to say the least, a stronger presumption against government activity beyond its fundamental duties of protection against its foreign foes and maintenance of justice" (p. 140). We shall see elsewhere that Franklin seems to have urged a less frugal governmental restraint in activities other than economic.

[218] *The Colonial Mind*, 173. It is generally thought that *Principles of Trade* is "partly" Franklin's "own composition" (Carey, *op. cit.*, 161).

a natural deduction from a more inclusive economic-political dogma.

Writing to the pro-colonial Jonathan Shipley, Bishop of St. Asaph, whose "sweet Retirement" at Twyford he had long enjoyed, Franklin, seeing no hopes of a reconciliation between the colonies and Great Britain, uttered what marked him as the first American disciple of Quesnay's school of economic thought: "Agriculture is the great Source of Wealth and Plenty. By cutting off our Trade you have thrown us *to the Earth*, whence like *Antaeus* we shall rise yearly with fresh Strength and Vigour." [219] Upon learning of the colonists' "Resolutions of Non-Importation" he wrote to "Cousin" Folger that they must promote their own industries, especially those of the "Earth and their Sea, the true Sources of Wealth and Plenty." [220] Learning that the colonists had threatened to boycott English manufacturers by creating their own basic industries, Franklin demurred in a letter to Cadwallader Evans: "Agriculture is truly *productive of new wealth;* manufacturers only change forms, and whatever value they give to the materials they work upon, they in the mean time consume an equal value in provisions, &c. So that riches are not *increased* by manufacturing; the only advantage is, that provisions in the shape of manufactures are more easily carried for sale to foreign markets." [221] *Positions to be Examined, Concerning National Wealth* [222] affords a succinct statement of Franklin's agrarianism. "There seem to be but three ways for a nation to acquire wealth. The first is by *war*, as the Romans did, in plundering their conquered neighbours. This is *robbery*. The second by *commerce*, which is generally *cheating*. The third by *agriculture*,

---

[219] Philadelphia, Sept. 13, 1775: MS letter (unpublished) in W. S. Mason Collection.

[220] London, Sept. 29, 1769: MS letter (unpublished) in W. S. Mason Collection.

[221] London, Feb. 20, 1768 (*Writings*, V, 102).

[222] Dated April 4, 1769 (*ibid.*, V, 200–2).

the only *honest way*, wherein man receives a real increase of the seed thrown into the ground, in a kind of continual miracle, wrought by the hand of God in his favour, as a reward for his innocent life and his virtuous industry." [223] Dupont de Nemours, as early as 1769, had written: "Who does not know that the English have today their Benjamin Franklin, who has adopted the principles and the doctrines of our French economists?" [224] Before attempting to appraise the real indebtedness of Franklin to the physiocrats, it is well to seek to learn how he came in contact with their ideas, and especially why by the year 1767 he was acutely susceptible to their doctrine. In the summer of 1767, in the company of Sir John Pringle, Franklin went to Paris, not an unknown figure to the French savants, who were acquainted with his scientific papers already translated into French by D'Alibard. That he was feted by the Newtons of the physiocrats, François Quesnay and the elder Mirabeau, as "le Savant, le Geomètre, le Physicien, l'homme à qui la nature permet de dévoiler ses secrets," [225] we are assured, when to De Nemours (July 28, 1768) he writes regretfully: "Be so good as to present my sincere respect to that venerable apostle, Dr. Quesnay, and to the illustrious Ami des Hommes (of whose civilities to me at Paris I retain a grateful remembrance). . . . " [226] Having missed Franklin in Paris (1767), De Nemours had sent Franklin "un recueil des principaux traités économiques du Docteur Quesnay" and his own *Physiocratie* (1768), which cast him in the role "of a propagandist of Physiocratic doctrines." [227] Franklin admitted, "I am perfectly charmed with them, and wish I could have stayed in France for some time, to have studied in

[223] *Writings*, V, 202.

[224] Cited by F. W. Garrison in "Franklin and the Physiocrats," *Freeman*, VIII, 154-6 (Oct. 24, 1923).

[225] Dupont de Nemours's opinion of Franklin (*Writings*, V, 153-4).

[226] *Writings*, V, 156. See W. Steell's entertaining "The First Visit to Paris," in *Benjamin Franklin of Paris*, 3-21; also E. E. Hale and E. E. Hale, Jr., *Franklin in France*, I, 7-13.

[227] C. Gide and C. Rist, *A History of Economic Doctrines*, 4 note.

your school, that I might by conversing with its founders have made myself quite a master of that philosophy."[228] That Franklin was not before 1767 unacquainted with the Économistes we learn when he tells Dupont de Nemours that Dr. Templeman had shown him the De Nemours-Templeman correspondence when the latter was Secretary of the London Society for the Encouragement of Arts, Manufactures, and Commerce. A second trip to Paris (in 1769) to confer with Barbeu Dubourg, an avowed physiocrat, concerning his forthcoming translation of Franklin's works, served to acquaint him still further with the doctrines of the new school.

Franklin's agrarianism[229] is congruent with physiocracy[230] in as far as he observed that agriculture alone, of the many industries, produced a surplus of wealth after all of the expenses of production had been paid.[231] Each laborer produced more than

[228] *Writings*, V, 155.

[229] As an *experimental* agriculturist Franklin has been given too little honor. He performed many valuable services in introducing Old-World plants, trees, and fruits to the New, and in encouraging others to carry on practical botanical experiments. Particularly from 1747 to 1757 he experimented in agriculture and was in constant communication with that pioneer scientific husbandman, Jared Eliot. See E. D. Ross's "Benjamin Franklin as an Eighteenth-Century Agriculture Leader," *Journal of Political Economy*, XXXVII, 52–72 (Feb., 1929).

[230] Although no scholarly substitute for the works of Quesnay, Mirabeau, Mercier de la Rivière, Dupont de Nemours, Le Trosne, Abbé Bandeau, Abbé Roubaud, and some pieces of the occasional physiocrat Turgot, the following will enable the student to derive adequately for general purposes the thought of the Économistes: H. Higgs, *The Physiocrats* (1897); Gide and Rist, *op. cit.;* L. H. Haney, *History of Economic Thought* (1911), 133–57; G. Weulersse, *Le mouvement physiocratique en France (de 1756 à 1770)*; A. Smith, *Wealth of Nations*, Bk. IV, chap. IX; J. Bonar, *Philosophy and Political Science* (1893); in addition see critical and interpretative writings of Oncken, Stern, Kines, Hasbach, Schelle, Bauer, Feilbogen, De Lavergne.

[231] An integral idea of the French school was its advocacy of the *impôt unique*—a single tax on land. It is difficult to find evidence to controvert Mr. Carey's assertion that Franklin seems never to have advocated this tax (*op. cit.*, 154). However, in marginalia on a pamphlet by Allan Ramsay, Franklin held: "Taxes must be paid out of the Produce of the Land. There is no other possible Fund" (cited by Carey, 155). Another reference is found in a letter of 1787 to Alexander Small: "Our Legislators are all Land-holders; and they are not yet persuaded, that all taxes are

enough to satisfy his own needs. This surplus the Économistes termed the *produit net*. A worker in manufactures, it was assumed, consumed foodstuffs and other materials in proportion to the value he created in his manufacturing process. Hence there obviously could be no *produit net* accruing from manufactures. Like the physiocrats, Franklin felt that manufactures were *sterile*, to the extent that no new wealth was created. The physiocrats believed, however, that laborers in manufacturing industries *could* create a *produit net* if they stinted themselves in consuming foodstuffs, et cetera, but it was argued that this prudential asceticism was not a characteristic habit. To this extent at least the physiocrats were empirical.

Free trade no less than agrarianism characterized physiocracy. Although Franklin indicated his antagonism toward governmental restraint of trade, internal and among nations, in his antipathy toward British mercantilism, it was not until after he became impregnated with French doctrine that he began to express very fully his advocacy of free trade. After Connecticut imposed a 5% duty on goods imported from neighboring colonies, Franklin wrote to Jared Eliot in 1747 that it was likely that the duty would devolve on the consumer and be "only another mode of Taxing" the purchaser. In addition he recognized that smuggling, virtually a colonial art, would cause the "fair Trader" to "be undersold and ruined." [232] He urged that

---

finally paid by the Land" (*Writings*, IX, 615). It is probable that he felt that a land tax would be dubiously effective in view of the difficulties of collection in sparse settlements.

[232] *Writings*, II, 313 (July 16, 1747). See also *Note Respecting Trade and Manufactures*, London, July 7, 1767 (Sparks, II, 366):

"Suppose a country, X, with three manufactures, as *cloth, silk, iron,* supplying three other countries, A, B, C, but is desirous of increasing the vent, and raising the price of cloth in favor of her own clothiers.

In order to do this, she forbids the importation of foreign cloth from A.

A, in return, forbids silks from X.

Then the silk-workers complain of a decay of trade.

And X, to content them, forbids silks from B.

B, in return, forbids iron ware from X.

the import duty might suggest selfishness, and might also tend
to deter Connecticut commerce.   Here, it must be admitted,
Franklin did not sanction free trade with a priori appeals to the
"natural order," the key in the arch of physiocracy.   He rather
appealed to the instincts and observations of the prudential
tradesman.   His *Plan for Regulating Indian Affairs* (1766), unlike his 1747 letters, *suggested* (if it did not express concretely)
inviolable laws of commerce in the words: "It seems contrary to the Nature of Commerce, for Government to interfere
in the Prices of Commodities. . . .   It therefore seems to me,
that Trade will best find and make its own Rates; and that Government cannot well interfere, unless it would take the whole
Trade into its own hands . . . and manage it by its own Servants
at its own Risque." [233] To Dupont de Nemours he admitted that
British mercantilism had not achieved "that wisdom which sees
the welfare of the parts in the prosperity of the whole." [234]   To
Sir Edward Newenham, representing the County of Dublin, he
expressed admiration for Irish efforts to secure freedom of commerce, "which is the right of all mankind."   "To enjoy all the
advantages of the climate, soil, and situation in which God and
nature have placed us, is as clear a right as that of breathing; and
can never be justly taken from men but as a punishment for
some atrocious crime." [235]   Three years before he met Quesnay
(though after he had read Dupont de Nemours's letters to
Templeman), Franklin sanctioned free trade through appeal to
other than utilitarian prudence: first he admitted that British restraint of colonial commerce, for example with the West Indies,
will tend to prevent colonists from making remittances for

Then the iron-workers complain of decay.
And X forbids the importation of iron from C.
C, in return, forbids cloth from X.
What is got by all these prohibitions?
Answer.—All four find their common stock of the enjoyments and con-
veniences of life diminished."
[233] *Writings*, IV, 469–70.   [234] *Ibid.*, V, 155.
[235] Passy, May 27, 1779 (*Writings*, VII, 332).

British manufactured goods, since "The Cat can yield but her skin." Then with a suggestion of philosophic generalization he hoped that "In time perhaps Mankind may be wise enough to let Trade take its own Course, find its own Channels, and regulate its own Proportions, etc." [236] Restraint of manufactures "deprive[s] us of the Advantage God & Nature seem to have intended us. . . . So selfish is the human Mind! But 'tis well there is One above that rules these Matters with a more equal Hand. He that is pleas'd to feed the Ravens, will undoubtedly take care to prevent a Monopoly of the Carrion." [237] Glorifying the husbandman and suggesting that trade restrictions disturb a natural order, Franklin wrote to David Hartley in 1783 that Great Britain has tended to impede "the mutual communications among men of the gifts of God, and rendering miserable multitudes of merchants and their families, artisans, and cultivators of the earth, the most peaceable and innocent part of the human species." [238]

That Franklin was not without his influence in eighteenth-century economic thought we may gather from Dugald Stewart's opinion that "the expressions *laissez-faire* and *pas trop gouverner* are indebted chiefly for their extensive circulation to the short and luminous comments of Franklin, which had so extraordinary an influence on public opinion in the old and new

---

[236] *Ibid.*, IV, 242–5 (April 30, 1764). As Mr. Carey notes, Franklin in several places, *On the Labouring Poor* and in a letter (IX, 240–8), suggests that private vices—demands for luxuries—make public benefits, hence resembling, if not ultimately derived from, Mandeville's *Fable of the Bees*. Franklin's sanction of free trade is, however, antithetical to Mandeville's 'dog eat dog' basis. (See Kaye's Intro. to *The Fable of the Bees*, xcviii ff.) Franklin in no uncertain terms looks upon trade restrictions definitely as the result of "the abominable selfishness" of men (VII, 332). As long as selfishness is the rule, mercantilism, not economic laissez faire, will be king. It is theoretically probable also that belief in man's innate altruism could furnish emotional if not logical sanction for laissez faire—but this abstraction is in Franklin's case futile, since like Swift he was not blind to man's malevolence!

[237] *Writings*, IV, 245; see also *ibid.*, VIII, 107–8, 261, 19.

[238] *Ibid.*, IX, 41; also 63, 578, 588.

world." [239] Mr. Carey maintains that Franklin, unlike the physiocrats, inveighed against trade regulations because they led to smuggling rather than because to any important degree they violated the "natural order." The physiocrats are tenuous, amorphous, and ambiguous when they seek to define *L'Ordre naturel*. At times Dupont de Nemours seems to identify it with a primitivistic past.[240] Quesnay, on the other hand, says: "Natural right is indeterminate in a state of nature. The right only appears when justice and labour have been established." [241] Again, he asserts: "By entering society and making conventions for their mutual advantage men increase the scope of natural right without incurring any restriction of their liberties, for this is just the state of things that enlightened reason would have chosen." [242] Natural order is a "providential order": "Its laws are irrevocable, pertaining as they do to the essence of matter and the soul of humanity. They are just the expression of the will of God." [243] According to the physiocrats, the laws of the natural order are "unique, eternal, invariable, and universal." [244] Now it is true that nowhere did Franklin assert that his advocacy of laissez faire and agrarianism was neatly dependent on these a priori bases. Even though this is true, there are references (quoted above) which seem to suggest that trade restrictions are violations of the very nature of things. It is not wholly fanciful (bearing in mind Franklin's adoration of a Deity who is the creator and sustainer of immutable, universal physical laws which together present the mind with the concept of a vast, wonderfully harmonized physical machine) to conjecture to what extent this matchless physical harmony tended to challenge him with the possibility of discovering a parallel economic machine operating according to immutable laws capable of proof and human adaptability.

[239] Cited in Carey, *op. cit.*, 160–1.
[240] See Gide and Rist, *op. cit.*, 7 note.
[241] *Ibid.*, 7 note.   [242] *Ibid.*
[243] Mercier de la Rivière, cited in *ibid.*, 8 note.   [244] *Ibid.*, 9–10.

O. H. Taylor has shown that "The evolution of the idea of 'laws' in economics has closely paralleled its evolution in the natural sciences."[245] In searching for these economic constants, "the economic mechanism was regarded as a wise device of the Creator for causing individuals, while pursuing only their own interests, to promote the prosperity of society; and for causing the right adjustment to one another of supplies, demand, prices, and incomes, to take place automatically, in consequence of the free action of all individuals."[246] After giving due weight to the fact that Franklin saw in the doctrine of the physiocrats trenchant arguments to buttress his attacks on British mercantilism, one has cogent evidence for at least raising the question, To what extent may his apprehension of a demonstrable physical harmony have suggested to his speculative mind an economic analogy?[247]

[245] "Economics and the Idea of Natural Law," *Quarterly Journal of Economics*, XLIV, 16 (1929). See also O. H. Taylor's valuable dissertation, "The Idea of a 'Natural Order' in Early Modern Economic Thought," summarized in Harvard University *Summaries of Theses*, 1928, 102–6, and available in manuscript at the Harvard University Library.

[246] Taylor, "Economics and the Idea of Natural Law," *loc. cit.*, 16.

[247] Even this fragmentary view of the more obvious economic principles held by Franklin offers convincing evidence that had he been less incidentally an economist he would have been at least a lesser Adam Smith. Mr. Wetzel, in *Benjamin Franklin as an Economist*, offers a convenient summary of Franklin as an economist, some items suggesting aspects of his views which, had space permitted, we should have included in this study: "1. Money as coin may have a value higher than its bullion value. 2. Natural interest is determined by the rent of so much land as the money loaned will buy. 3. High wages are not inconsistent with a large foreign trade. 4. Population will increase as the means of gaining a living increase. 5. A high standard of living serves to prolong single life, and thus acts as a check upon the increase of population. 6. People are adjusted among the different countries according to the comparative well-being of mankind. 7. The value of an article is determined by the amount of labor necessary to produce the food consumed in making the article. 8. While manufactures are advantageous, only agriculture is truly productive. 9. Manufactures will naturally spring up in a country as the country becomes ripe for them. 10. Free trade with the world will give the greatest return at the least expense. 11. Wherever practicable, State revenue should be raised by direct taxes."

VI. FRANKLIN'S POLITICAL THEORIES

Plague of the Pennsylvania proprietaries, propagandist of the American Revolution, moderator of the Constitutional Convention, Franklin was all through his life a politician and statesman in an age characterized above all by political speculations and changes in the destiny of states. Colonial patriot, "arch rebel of King George III," "idol of the court of Versailles," Franklin was a cyclopedia of political strategy and principles. Only through a genetic survey of Franklin the political theorist can one hope to understand his mind as he changed from imperialist, to revolutionist, to the patriarch of the Constitutional Convention who, like a balance wheel, moderated the extreme party factions.

In the early 1720's, Franklin had breathed a Boston air saturated with discontent between the royal governor and the governed. By 1730 he was printer to the Pennsylvania Assembly and in 1736 was appointed clerk to that body. Yet one learns little of his political biases until 1747, when he published *Plain Truth*. In 1729 he genially asserted that he was "no Party-man," [248] and in 1746 temperately stated,

> Free from the bitter Rage of Party Zeal,
> All those we love who seek the publick Weal.[249]

His *Plain Truth* (November, 1747), directed against the proprietary governor as well as against the Quaker assembly, showed Franklin a party man only if one dedicated to "the publick weal" was a party man. With all respect for the Quaker conscience which checks military activity, Franklin could not, however, condone its virtually prohibiting others from defend-

[248] *Writings*, II, 110.
[249] *Ibid.*, II, 295. In 1736 Franklin wrote: "Faction, if not timely suppressed, may overturn the balance, the palladium of liberty, and crush us under its ruins" (cited in R. G. Gettell, *History of American Political Thought*, 149).

ing the province's border. And the proprietaries had shown
an inveterate unwillingness to arm Pennsylvania—a reluctance
which did not, however, prevent them from collecting taxes and
quitrents. On other questions the governor and his chiefs
had to contend with the opposition of the assembly. Without
opposition, the proprietary government could serenely kennel
itself in its medieval privilege of remaining dumb to an urgent
need: one remembers that eighteenth-century proprietary
colonies were "essentially feudal principalities, upon the gran-
tees of which were bestowed all the inferior regalities and subordinate powers of legislation which formerly belonged to the
counts palatine, while provision was also made for the maintenance of sovereignty in the king [the king paid little attention
to Pennsylvania], and for the realization of the objects of the
grant." [250] While the government remained inert, Pennsylvania
would be a pawn in the steeled hands of the French and their
rum-subsidized Indian mercenaries. Appealing to Scripture
and common sense, Franklin pleaded for "Order, Discipline,
and a few Cannon." [251] Not untruthfully he warned that "we
are like the separate Filaments of Flax before the Thread is
form'd, without Strength, because without Connection, but
UNION would make us strong, and even formidable." [252] Since
war existed, there was no need to consider him a militarist
because he challenged, "The Way to secure Peace is to be prepared for War." [253] In the midst of *Plain Truth* Franklin uttered
what only *before* the time of Locke could be interpreted in
terms of feudal *comitatus:* he entreated his readers to consider,
"if not as Friends, at least as Legislators, that *Protection* is as
truly due from the Government to the People, as *Obedience*
from the People to the Government." [254] Suggestive of the contract theory, this is revolutionary only in a very elementary

[250] W. R. Shepherd, *History of Proprietary Government in Pennsylvania*
(New York, 1896), 5.
[251] *Writings*, II, 351.   [252] *Ibid.*
[253] *Ibid.*, II, 352.   [254] *Ibid.*, II, 347.

way. With the French writhing under the Treaty of Paris, with
appeals to natural rights and the right of revolution, this once
harmless principle took on Gargantuan significance. But Thomas
Penn anticipated wisely enough the ultimate implication of
Franklin's paper; Penn intuitively saw the march of time: "Mr.
Franklin's doctrine that obedience to governors is no more due
them than protection to the people, is not fit to be in the heads
of the unthinking multitude. He is a dangerous man and I
should be glad if he inhabited any other country, as I believe
him of a very uneasy spirit. However, as he is a sort of tribune
of the people, he must be treated with regard." [255] It is difficult
to see how Franklin's passion for order and provincial union, [256]
obviously necessary, could have been considered so illiberally
subversive of the government. By 1747 Franklin had read in
Telemachus that kings exist for the people, not the people for
the kings; he must have read Locke's justification of the "Glorious Revolution" and have become aware of the impetus it gave
to the British authority of consent in its subsequent constitutional history.

After his first political pamphlet, he widened his horizon from
provincial to colonial affairs. Two years before the London
Board of Trade demanded that colonial governors hold a conference with the Iroquois, Franklin seems to have devised plans
for uniting the several colonies. He was aware of the narrow
particularism shown by the provinces; he knew also that since
"Governors are often on ill Terms with their Assemblies," no
concerted military efforts could be achieved without a military

[255] Shepherd, *op. cit.*, 222. In 1764 Penn thought that Franklin was one
"who may lose the government of a post office by grasping at that of a
province" (*ibid.*, 564). In turn one of the proprietors wrote to him:
"Franklin is certainly destined to be our plague" (*ibid.*, 566). Penn professed not to fear "your mighty Goliath." For proof that Franklin's fear
expressed in *Plain Truth* was not idle see *Extracts from Chief Justice
William Allen's Letter Book*, 17, 22-3, 25, 31-2.
[256] *Plain Truth* inspirited the colonists to defend themselves, even if it
failed in its larger purpose; see *Writings*, II, 354, 362.

federation.[257] One remembers that as soon as he could think politically he was an imperialist, a lesser William Pitt, and in his *Increase of Mankind* (1751) could gloat over an envisioned thickly populated America—"What an Accession of Power to the *British* Empire by Sea as well as Land!"[258] When the Board of Trade, after British efforts to bring the colonies together had failed, demanded that something be done, Franklin was appointed one of the commissioners to meet at Albany in 1754. Like Franklin, Governor Glen had admitted that the colonies were "a Rope of Sand . . . loose and inconnected."[259] Franklin's plan, adopted by the commissioners, called for a Governor-General "appointed by the king" and a Grand Council made up of members chosen by the Assembly of each of the colonies, the Governor "to have a negation on all acts of the Grand Council, and carry into execution whatever is agreed on by him and that Council."[260] Surely not a very auspicious beginning for one who later was to favor the legislative over the executive functions of state. The plan included the powers of making Indian treaties of peace and war, of regulating Indian trade and Indian purchases, of stimulating the settling of new lands, of making laws to govern new areas, of raising soldiers, of laying general duties, et cetera.[261] But Franklin did not minimize the lack of cohesion of the colonies. We recollect that "in 1755, at a time

[257] To James Parker, March 20, 1750/51 (*Writings*, III, 40–5). L. C. Wroth, in *An American Bookshelf, 1755* (Philadelphia, 1934), 12 ff., reviews A. Kennedy's *The Importance of Gaining the Friendship of the Indians to the British Interest* (1751), to which was appended a letter, prefiguring the Albany Plan of Union. This letter, Mr. Wroth observes, was by Franklin. C. E. Merriam states that "The storm centre of the democratic movement during the colonial period was the conflict between the governors and the colonial legislatures or assemblies" (*A History of American Political Theories*, 34). Also see E. B. Greene, *The Provincial Governor in the English Colonies of North America*.

[258] *Writings*, III, 71.

[259] Cited in G. L. Beer, *British Colonial Policy, 1754–1765*, 17.

[260] *Writings*, III, 197.

[261] For a suggestive source study see Mrs. L. K. Mathews's "Benjamin Franklin's Plans for a Colonial Union, 1750–1775," *American Political Science Review*, VIII, 393–412 (Aug., 1914).

when their very existence was threatened by the French, Massachusetts and New York engaged in a bitter boundary controversy leading to riot and bloodshed." [262]   The colonies refused to ratify the plan—"their weak Noddles are perfectly distracted," [263] wrote Franklin. He was probably right when he observed in 1789 that had the plan been adopted "the subsequent Separation of the Colonies from the Mother Country might not so soon have happened." [264]   The sending of British regulars to America and the resulting efforts at taxation were not least among the sparks which set off the Revolution.

Franklin's *Three Letters to Governor Shirley* (1754), while expressing no credulous views of the wisdom of the people, maintained in one breath that the colonists were loyal to the Constitution and Crown as ever colonists were and in another that "it is supposed an undoubted right of Englishmen, not to be taxed but by their own consent given through their representatives." [265]   (Shirley had apparently written that the Council in the Albany Plan should be appointed by England, and not by the colonial assemblies.)   Franklin held for the colonists' right to English civil liberty and the right to enjoy the Constitution.   Here again we find a factor later magnified into one of the major causes of the Revolution.

In addition to being lethargic in the defense of the Pennsylvania borders, the proprietor refused "to be taxed except for a trifling Part of his Estate, the Quitrents, located unimprov'd Lands, Money at Interest, etc, etc, being exempted by Instructions to the Governor." [266]   Thereupon Franklin turned from

[262] Cited in Beer, *op. cit.*, 49.
[263] *Writings*, III, 242.
[264] *Ibid.*, III, 226.   As Beer has pointed out (*op. cit.*, 23 note), since the plan was not ratified, it never went before the Crown; hence Franklin's retrospective glance is misleading: "The Crown disapproved it, as having placed too much Weight in the Democratic Part of the Constitution; and every Assembly as having allowed too much to Prerogative.   So it was totally rejected" (*Writings*, III, 227).
[265] *Ibid.*, III, 233.
[266] To Peter Collinson, Nov. 22, 1756 (*Writings*, III, 351).

colonial affairs (which had indeed proved obstinate) to pressing
local matters, when in 1757 he was appointed agent to go to London to demand that the proprietor submit his estates to be taxed.
In the *Report of the Committee of Aggrievances of the Assembly
of Pennsylvania* [267] (Feb. 22, 1757) it was charged that the proprietor had violated the royal charter and the colonists' civil
rights as Englishmen, and had abrogated their natural rights,
rights "inherent in every man, antecedent to all laws." [268]
Later it was but a short step from provincial matters to
colonial rights of revolution. In this *Report* we see Franklin
associated for the first time expressly with the throne-and-altar-
defying concept of natural rights.

Although we have yet to review the evidence which shows
that Franklin at one stage in his political career was an arch-
imperialist, we need to digress to observe an intellectual factor
which, if only fragmentarily expressed in his political thought
during his activities in behalf of Pennsylvania liberties, was to
become a momentous sanction when during the war he became
a diplomat of revolution. From the Stoics, from Cicero, Grotius, Puffendorf, Burlamaqui, and as Rev. Jonathan Mayhew [269]
observes, from Plato and Demosthenes, from Sidney, Milton,
Hoadley, and Locke; in addition, from Gordon and Trenchard
(see *Cato's Letters* and *The Independent Whig*), Blackstone,
Coke—from these and many others, the colonists derived a
pattern of thought known as natural rights, dependent on natural law. [270] There is no better summary of natural rights

[267] As A. H. Smyth says, this was probably *inspired* by Franklin although
not written by him; at any rate "it undoubtedly reflects" his opinions (III,
vi). Isaac Sharpless observes that Franklin "had sympathy with their
[Quakers'] demands for political freedom, but none for their non-military
spirit" (*Political Leaders of Provincial Pennsylvania*, New York, 1919,
178).
[268] *Writings*, III, 372.
[269] A. Bradford, *Memoir of the Life and Writings of Rev. J. Mayhew*
(Boston, 1838), 119.
[270] See for capable studies: B. F. Wright, *American Interpretations of
Natural Law;* C. F. Mullett, *Fundamental Law and the American Revolu-*

than the Declaration of Independence; and of it John Adams remarked: "There is not an idea in it but what has been hackneyed in Congress for two years before." [271] Carl Becker pointedly observes: "Where Jefferson got his ideas is hardly so much a question as where he could have got away from them." [272] A characteristic summary of natural law may be found in Blackstone's *Commentaries:* [273]

This law of nature being coeval with mankind, and dictated by God himself, is of course superior in obligation to any other. It is binding over all the globe, in all countries and at all times: no human laws are of any validity, if contrary to this; and such of them as are valid derive all their force and all their authority, mediately or immediately, from this original. [274]

Discoverable only by reason, natural laws are immutable and universal, apprehensible by all men. As Hamilton wrote,

The origin of all civil government, justly established, must be a voluntary compact between the rulers and the ruled, and must be liable to such limitations as are necessary for the security of the *absolute rights* of the latter; for what original title can any man, or set of men, have to govern others, except their own consent? To usurp dominion over a people in their own despite, or to grasp at a more extensive power than they are willing to intrust, is to violate that law of nature which gives every man a right to his personal liberty, and can therefore confer no obligation to obedience. [275]

tion; D. G. Ritchie, *Natural Rights* (London, 1895), and his "Contributions to the History of the Social Contract Theory," *Political Science Quarterly,* VI, 656–76 (1891); C. Becker, *The Declaration of Independence,* chap. II; C. E. Merriam, *op. cit.,* chap. II; H. J. Laski, *Political Thought in England from Locke to Bentham* (New York, 1920).

[271] Becker, *op. cit.,* 24.   [272] *Ibid.,* 27.
[273] Burke said that nearly as many copies of this work were sold in the colonies as in Great Britain. It will be remembered that Hamilton leaned heavily on Blackstone in *The Farmer Refuted* (1773).
[274] Cited in Wright, *op. cit.,* 11.
[275] *The Farmer Refuted.* For discussion of changes in Hamilton's political theory see F. C. Prescott's Introduction to *Hamilton and Jefferson* (American Writers Series, New York, 1934).

In a pre-social state, real or hypothetical, men possess certain natural rights, the crown of them, according to Locke,[276] being "the mutual preservation of their lives, liberties, and estates, which I call by the general name, property." In entering the social state men through free consent are willing to sacrifice fragments of their natural rights in order to gain civil rights. This process would seem tyrannical were one to forget that the surrender is sanctioned by the principle of consent. Men in sacrificing their rights expect from society (i.e., the governors) civil rights and, in addition, protection of their unsurrendered natural rights. A voluntary compact is achieved between the governor and the governed. If laws are fabricated which contravene these, the governed have retained for themselves the right of forcible resistance. A natural inference from these premises is that sovereignty rests with the people. In the colonies this secular social compact was buttressed by the principle of covenants and natural rights within the churches. Sermons became "textbooks of politics." [277] Miss Baldwin has ably illustrated how before 1763 the clergy in Franklin's native New England

---

[276] Franklin acknowledges his close reading of Locke's *Essay Concerning Human Understanding* (*Writings*, I, 243). In 1749 he urges that Locke be read in the Philadelphia Academy (II, 387) and refers again to the great logician in *Idea of the English School* (III, 28). He is supposed to have defended in spirited debate Locke's treatise on Toleration (I, 179). The catalogues of the Philadelphia Library Company disclose that by 1757 all of Locke's works had been obtained. One may ask how an alert eighteenth-century mind could have escaped the impact of Locke's thought.

It is more difficult to establish satisfactorily a nexus between Rousseau's and Franklin's minds. Mr. George Simpson Eddy has kindly allowed us to consult his "Catalogue of Pamphlets, Once a Part of the Library of Benjamin Franklin, and now owned by the Historical Society of Pennsylvania" in which are included Rousseau's *Préface de la Nouvelle Héloïse* . . . (1761) and *Discours sur l'économie politique* . . . (1760). Even if Rousseau's mistress, Countess d'Houdetot, feted Franklin in 1781, and Franklin was acquainted with Rousseau's physician, Achille-Guillaume le Bègue de Presle, and directly in 1785 mentions Rousseau on child-education (*Writings*, IX, 334), one can not be sure to what extent Rousseau's writings may have aided Franklin in formulating notions similar to the social contract theory (IX, 138).

[277] Cited in A. M. Baldwin, *The New England Clergy and the American Revolution*, 6.

had popularized the "doctrines of natural right, the social contract, and the right of resistance" as well as "the fundamental
principle of American constitutional law, that government,
like its citizens, is bounded by law and when it transcends its
authority it acts illegally." [278]

In an oration commemorating the Boston massacre Dr. Benjamin Church stated the principle of the compact: "A sense of
their wants and weakness in a state of nature, doubtless inclined
them to such reciprocal aids and support, as eventually established society." [279] Defining liberty as "the happiness of living
under laws of our own making by our personal consent or that
of our representatives," [280] he warned that any breach of trust
in the governor "effectually absolves subjects from every bond
of covenant and peace." [281]

Then, too, Newtonian science buttressed the principle of
natural rights. Sir Isaac Newton demonstrated mathematically
that the universe was governed by a fagot of immutable, universal, and harmonious physical laws. These were capable of
being apprehended through reason. Now even as reason discovered the matchless physical harmony, so could reason, men
argued, ferret out unvarying, universal principles of social-
political rights. These principles constituted natural rights,
natural to the extent that all men had the power, if not the capacity, to discover and learn them through use of their native
reason. Newton demonstrated the validity of physical law:
Locke sanctioned the supremacy of reason. Since Franklin

---

[278] *Ibid.*, xii. See also C. H. Van Tyne's able study, "The Influence of
the Clergy, and of Religious and Sectarian Forces, on the American Revolution," *American Historical Review*, XIX, 44–64 (Oct., 1913). He takes
issue with the economic determinists and concludes that of all the causes
of the Revolution religious causes are "among the most important"
(p. 64). The Revolution was in large measure caused by a conflict of
political ideas, and these were disseminated mostly by the clergy.

[279] *An Oration, Delivered March 5, 1773* (Boston, 1773), 6.

[280] *Ibid.*, 10–11.

[281] *Ibid.*, 8. Also see S. Stillman, *Election-Sermon*, May 26, 1779 (Boston,
1779); J. Clarke, *Election-Sermon*, May 30, 1781 (Boston, 1781).

was himself motivated by Newtonian rationalism and was a student of Locke, there is reason to believe that he was vibrantly aware of the extent to which the scientific-rationalistic ideology lent sanction to man's timeless quest for the certitude of "natural rights," antecedent to all laws.

Franklin's mission to London in 1757 as Pennsylvania agent may be understood through an examination of *An Historical Review of the Constitution and Government of Pennsylvania* (London, 1759).[282] If not written by him, at least "the ideas are his." Convinced that the proprietors "seem to have no regard to the Publick Welfare, so the private Point may be gained—'Tis like Firing a House to have Opportunity of stealing a Trencher,"[283] Franklin knew that a brilliant attack had to be made were he to intimidate the proprietary government into assuming its charter responsibilities and granting the colonists what they considered to be inviolable rights. By 1758 his "Patience with the Proprietors is almost tho' not quite spent."[284] A few months later, impatient with unresponsive officials, he wrote to Joseph Galloway: "God knows when we shall see it finish'd, and our Constitution settled firmly on the Foundation of Equity and English Liberty: But I am not discouraged; and only wish my Constituents may have the Patience that I have, and that I find will be absolutely necessary."[285] In 1759 Franklin still found the proprietors "obscure, uncertain and evasive," and was acutely virulent in despising Rev. William Smith, who was in London attacking him and the Quaker Assembly's de-

---

[282] Although Franklin denied having written it (*Writings*, IV, 82), Mr. Ford (*Franklin Bibliography*, 111) asserts that "this work must still be treated as from Franklin's pen." He sent 500 copies to Pennsylvania consigned to his partner, David Hall, for distribution.

[283] To Joseph Galloway, April 11, 1757 (unpublished MS letter in W. S. Mason Collection). For a description of the unpublished Franklin-Galloway correspondence see W. S. Mason's article in *Proceedings of the American Antiquarian Society* for Oct., 1924.

[284] To Joseph Galloway, Feb. 17, 1758 (unpublished MS letter in W. S. Mason Collection).

[285] June 10, 1758 (unpublished MS letter in W. S. Mason Collection).

mands.[286] In the same letter to Galloway he uttered a thought
which he sought to develop during his second trip to London
as Assembly agent in 1764: "For my part, I must own, I am
tired of Proprietary Government, and heartily wish for that
of the Crown."

Turning to *An Historical Review* to learn the political principles sanctioning the Assembly's grievances against its feudal
lords, one finds that the colonists conceived it "our duty to
defend the rights and privileges we enjoy under the royal
charter." [287] Secondly, they reminded the lords that the laws
agreed upon in England (prior to the settling of Pennsylvania)
were "of the nature of an original compact between the proprietary and the freemen, and as such were reciprocally received
and executed." [288] Thirdly, they demanded the right to exercise
the "birthright of every British subject," "to have a property
of [their] own, in [their] estate, person, and reputation; subject
only to laws enacted by [their] own concurrence, either in
person or by [their] representatives." [289] Fourthly, they resisted
the proprietors on basis of their possession of natural rights,
"antecedent to all laws." [290] The editor of the protest charged
that "It is the cause of every man who deserves to be free,
everywhere." [291] It is ironic that this grievance should have
enjoyed the sanction of one who, like Lord Chatham, was an
empire builder, one who proudly wrote, "I am a Briton," and
even during the time he sought to retrieve the Pennsylvania
colonists' lost natural rights, entertained the ideas of a British
imperialist. Franklin little saw that the internal Pennsylvania
struggle was to be contagious, that the provincial revolt was
motivated partially at least by political theories which were to be
given expression *par excellence* when a discontented minority
created the Declaration of Independence. In 1760 Frank-

[286] April 7, 1759 (unpublished MS letter in W. S. Mason Collection).
[287] *The Works of Benjamin Franklin* (Philadelphia, 1809), II, 147.
[288] *Ibid.*, II, 7.   [289] *Ibid.*, II, 1.
[290] *Ibid.*, II, vii.   [291] *Ibid.*, II, xvi.

lin had the satisfaction of witnessing the victory of the Assembly over the Proprietors, although he was not unaware that the right to tax feudal lands was less than that right he had already envisioned—the right to become a royal colony.[292]

But Franklin's pleas for charter, constitutional, and natural rights may be misleading if one considers his position as suggestive of doctrinaire republicanism, of Paine's "Government is the badge of our lost innocence," or of Shelley's

> Kings, priests, and statesmen blast the human flower.

His political activities assert the rights of the governed against the governor; his writings often indirectly suggest the intemperance of the governed, and the need for something more lasting than mere outer freedom. Like Coleridge, who wrote:

> [Man] may not hope from outward forms to win
> The passion and the life, whose fountains are within,

white-locked Father Abraham harangued:

The Taxes are indeed very heavy, and if those laid on by the Government were the only Ones we had to pay, we might more easily discharge them; but we have many others, and much more grievous to some of us. We are taxed twice as much by our *Idleness*, three times as much by our *Pride*, and four times as much by our *Folly;* and from these Taxes the Commissioners cannot ease or deliver us by allowing an Abatement.[293]

---

[292] Apropos of many colonial ferments, not unlike the one we have considered above, Carl Becker writes: "Throughout the eighteenth century, little colonial aristocracies played their part, in imagination clothing their governor in the decaying vesture of Old-World tyrants and themselves assuming the homespun garb, half Roman and half Puritan, of a virtuous republicanism. . . . It was the illusion of sharing in great events rather than any low mercenary motive that made Americans guard with jealous care their legislative independence" (*The Eve of the Revolution*, New Haven, 1918, 60). Also see C. H. Lincoln, *The Revolutionary Movement in Pennsylvania, 1760–1776.*

[293] *Writings*, III, 408–9.

With solid good sense Franklin acknowledged that "happiness in this life rather depends on internals than externals." [294]

His purpose for being in London accomplished, Franklin wrote *The Interest of Great Britain Considered with Regard to Her Colonies, and the Acquisitions of Canada and Guadaloupe* (1760). Since "there is evidence that the pamphlet created much contemporary interest," [295] Franklin undoubtedly had some influence in causing the retention of Canada, a retention which "made the American Revolution inevitable." [296] If the release from French terrorism caused the colonists to become myopic toward advantages lent them as a British colony, it is appropriate in view of Franklin's later advocacy of independence and ironic in view of his then imperialistic principles, that he should have written *The Interest of Great Britain*. Here Franklin, later to be a propagandist of revolution, cast himself in the role of architect of a vast empire. For economic reasons, and for colonial safety, he urged the retention, ridiculing the charge that the colonies were lying in wait to declare their independence from England, if the French were cast out from Canada.

Back in Pennsylvania in 1764 he declared the provincial government "running fast into anarchy and confusion." [297] In his *Cool Thoughts on the Present Situation of Our Public Affairs* (1764) he set up a sturdy antagonism between "Proprietary Interest and Power, and Popular Liberty." Unlike the "lunatic fringe" of liberals who see "Popular Liberty compatible only with a tendency toward anarchy" Franklin urged that the Pennsylvania government lacked "Authority enough to keep the common Peace." [298] The constitutional nature of proprietary government had lost dignity and hence "suffers in the Opinion

---

[294] *Ibid.*, III, 457.
[295] V. W. Crane, "Certain Writings of Benjamin Franklin on the British Empire and the American Colonies," *Papers of the Bibliographical Society*, XXVIII, Pt. I, 6 (1934). Also see W. L. Grant, "Canada vs. Guadaloupe," *American Historical Review*, XVII, 735–43, (Oct., 1911–July, 1912).
[296] Beer, *op. cit.*, 313.
[297] *Writings*, IV, 224.   [298] *Ibid.*, IV, 229.

of the People, and with it the Respect necessary to keep up the Authority of Government." Almost Burkean in his apology for change, he suggested that the popular party demand "rather and only a Change of Governor, that is, instead of self-interested Proprietaries, a gracious King!" His *Narrative of the Late Massacres in Lancaster County* [299] is a bloody tribute to the lack of authority and police power of the current regime. The *Petition to the King* for a royal governor maintained that, torn by "armed Mobs," the government was "weak, unable to support its own Authority, and maintain the common internal Peace of the Province." [300]

While petitioning for a crown colony, he found himself in 1765 faced with a larger than provincial interest—Lord Grenville's Stamp Act forced him into the role of one seeking definition of colonial status. Such was his position in his examination (1766) before the House of Commons relative to the repeal of the Stamp Act. Almost brusquely he told his catechizers that even a moderated stamp act could not be enforced "unless compelled by force of arms." [301] With a preface asserting that colonials before 1763 were proud to be called Old-England men, he summarized: "The authority of parliament was allowed to be valid in all laws, except such as should lay internal taxes. It was never disputed in laying duties to regulate commerce." [302] Parliament, in the colonial view, had no right to lay internal taxes because "we are not represented there." Mr. Merriam observes that in advancing this legal and constitutional issue, the colonists "had in short an antiquated theory as to the position and power of Parliament, and a premature theory of Parliamentary representation." [303]

Franklin referred to the Pennsylvania colonial charter to prove that all that was asked for was the "privileges and liberties of

[299] The massacre led by the "Paxton boys."
[300] *Writings*, IV, 314.   [301] *Writings*, IV, 418.
[302] *Ibid.*, IV, 419. See Beer, *op. cit.*, 294 f.
[303] *A History of American Political Theories*, 46.

Englishmen." When the examiners asked whether the colonists appealing to the Magna Charta and constitutional rights of Englishmen could not with equal force "object to the parliament's right of external taxation," Franklin with cautious ambiguity declared: "They never have hitherto." [304] Franklin's skill in upholding tenuous, almost "metaphysical," constitutional grievances (grievances, however, which were not upheld by constitutional legalists in England) captivated Edmund Burke's imagination: Franklin appeared to him like a schoolmaster catechizing a pack of unruly schoolboys. Conservative in his omission of any appeal to "natural rights," he was radical in his legalistic distinctions between parliamentary rights to levy certain kinds of taxes. His position in 1766 and for several years following was one of seeking legal definitions of the colonial status. Considering the popular excesses in the colonies, Franklin's view was anything but illiberally radical. Trying to counteract "the general Rage against America, artfully work'd up by the Grenville Faction," [305] fearful that the unthinking rabble in the colonies might demonstrate too lustily against duties and the redcoats,[306] Franklin saw, as a result of the constitutional dilemma, the true extent of the fracture:

But after all, I doubt People in Government here will never be satisfied without some Revenue from America, nor America ever satisfy'd with their imposing it; so that Disputes will from this Circumstance besides others, be perpetually arising, till there is a consolidating union of the whole.[307]

His chief demand was for a less ambiguous relation between the mother and her offspring, for a unified, pacific commonwealth

[304] *Writings*, IV, 445–6.
[305] To Joseph Galloway, May 20, 1767 (photostat of unpublished MS letter in W. S. Mason Collection; original in W. L. Clements Library).
[306] To Joseph Galloway, Aug. 20, 1768 (photostat of unpublished MS letter in W. S. Mason Collection; original in W. L. Clements Library).
[307] To Joseph Galloway, April 14, 1767 (photostat of unpublished MS letter in W. S. Mason Collection; original in W. L. Clements Library). Cf. also letter to the same, Jan. 11, 1770, *ibid.*

empire. Until he left for the colonies in 1775, he tire-
lessly sought through conversation, conference, and articles [308]
sent to the British press (in addition he "reprinted everything
from America" that he "thought might help our Common
Cause") to reiterate patiently the colonies' "Charter liberties," [309]
their abhorrence of Parliament-imposed internal taxes, and
the quartering of red-coated battalions. Constantly hoping for
a favorable Ministry (of a Lord Rockingham or a Shelburne), and
bemoaning the physical infirmities of Pitt which rendered him
politically impotent, Franklin felt almost romantically confident
at first of a change that must come. All the while, like Merlin's
gleam, visions of a world-encircling British empire haunted the
Pennsylvania tradesman. A letter to Barbeu Dubourg discloses
at once his belief in an imperial federation [310] and in the sovereignty of the colonial assemblies: "In fact, the British empire
is not a single state; it comprehends many; and, though the
Parliament of Great Britain has arrogated to itself the power of
taxing the colonies, it has no more right to do so, than it has to
tax Hanover. We have the same King, but not the same legislatures." [311] Marginalia by Franklin's hand in an anti-colonial

[308] See, for example, *An Edict by the King of Prussia* (1773)—for its
effect see *Writings*, VI, 146—and *Rules by Which a Great Empire May
Be Reduced to a Small One* (1773). Crane, *op. cit.*, concludes that Franklin
appears as "the chief agent of the American propaganda in England,
especially between 1765 and 1770" (p. 26). For treatment of American
propagandists see P. G. Davidson, "Whig Propagandists of the American
Revolution," *American Historical Review*, XXXIX, 442–53 (April, 1934),
and his *Revolutionary Propagandists in New England, New York and Pennsylvania, 1763–1776* (unpublished dissertation, University of Chicago,
1929); summarized in *Abstracts of Theses*, Humanistic Series VII, 239–42;
F. J. Hinkhouse, *The Preliminaries of the American Revolution as Seen in
the English Press* (New York, 1926).

[309] *Writings*, V, 297.

[310] See R. G. Adams, *Political Ideas of the American Revolution*, 35,
62–3.

[311] Oct. 2, 1770 (*Writings*, V, 280). See also *Causes of the American
Discontents before 1768* (V, 78 f., 160–2). An aspect of his loyalty to the
crown may be seen in his hatred of French desire to separate the colonies
from England (V, 47, 231, 254, 323). The printing of the *Examination*
and other of Franklin's pieces in Europe buttressed the predisposition of

pamphlet written by Dean Tucker indicate how completely he (and here he represented colonial, not private, opinion) had failed to see the growth of parliamentary power: "These Writers against the Colonies all bewilder themselves by supposing the Colonies *within the Realm*, which is not the case, nor ever was." [312]

By 1774 Franklin had discovered the futility of his imperialistic illusions: ministries, fearing the siren colonies, had blocked their ears with wax. The Pennsylvanian knew that "Divine Providence first infatuates the power it designs to ruin." [313] He who had wished for an empire as harmoniously companied as the orbited harmony of celestial bodies lamented while on his way to America in 1775 that "so glorious a Fabric as the present British Empire [was] to be demolished by these Blunderers." [314] Broken was "that fine and noble China Vase, the British Empire." [315] In 1774 he would have gained little cheer from William Livingston's opinion (uttered in 1768): "I take it that clamour is at present our best policy." [316]

His sense of defeat was aggravated by that ugly scene in the Cockpit in 1774 when Wedderburn bespattered the taciturn colonial agent with foul invective. It had been charged that Franklin, the postmaster, had purloined [317] letters of Governor

France to hate Great Britain (V, 231). The best comprehensive treatment of backgrounds is C. H. Van Tyne's *The Causes of the War of Independence.*

[312] *Pennsylvania Magazine of History and Biography*, XXV, 311 (1901). See also *ibid.*, 307–22, and XXVI, 81–90, 255–64 (1902). See *Writings*, VI, 144.

[313] *Writings*, VI, 173.

[314] *Ibid.*, VI, 319. His unpublished letters of 1775 in the Original Correspondence of Benjamin Franklin with the Bishop of St. Asaph (in the W. S. Mason Collection) emphasize his progressive apathy toward a reconciliation. Especially see letters of May 15 and July 7.

[315] *Ibid.*, VI, 460. [316] Cited in Davidson, *op. cit.*, 442.

[317] Hugh Williamson claimed that he actually gave Franklin the letters. Apparently another person went to the office where the letters were archived and posing as an authorized person secured the desired correspondence (D. Hosack, *Biographical Memoir of Hugh Williamson*, New York, 1820, 37 ff.).

Hutchinson and Lieutenant Governor Oliver of Massachusetts and had sent them back to the colonies as proof of the colonists' contention that the royal governors were hostile to their colonial subjects. He whom (as Lord Chatham said) "all Europe held in high Estimation for his Knowledge and Wisdom, and rank'd with our Boyles and Newtons," was decked by Wedderburn "with the choicest flowers of Billingsgate." In the presence of Lord Shelburne, Lord North, the Archbishop of Canterbury, Edmund Burke, Jeremy Bentham, and Priestley, Franklin, "motionless and silent," bore the harangue of the solicitor general for a full three hours.[318] Franklin's eloquent mock humility inspired Horace Walpole to write:

> Sarcastic Sawney, swol'n with spite and prate,
> On silent Franklin poured his venal hate.
> The calm philosopher, without reply,
> Withdrew, and gave his country liberty.

As propagandist for legislative freedom, Franklin, appealing for sanction to legalistic and constitutional liberty more than to natural rights, was no more radical than Edmund Burke. If ever an extreme democrat, Franklin had yet by 1775 to become one. Temperamentally hostile to "drunken electors," the "madness of mobs," he held a patrician attitude toward authority. Earlier, in 1768, he had written from London: "All respect to law and government seems to be lost among the common people, who are moreover continually inflamed by seditious scribblers, to trample on authority and every thing that used to keep them in order." [319] To Georgiana Shipley he sent (*Epitaph* on Squirrel Mungo's death) this Miltonic and unrepublican sentiment:

---

[318] For an interesting account of this episode see Parton, *op. cit.*, I, chap. IX.

[319] *Writings*, V, 134. Franklin and Burke were friendly; see their correspondence. The best exposition of Burke's doctrines is that by John MacCunn, *The Political Philosophy of Edmund Burke* (London, 1913).

Learn hence,
Ye who blindly seek more liberty,
Whether subjects, sons, squirrels or daughters,
That apparent restraint may be real protection
Yielding peace and plenty
With security.[320]

In 1771 he indicted Parliament in a letter to Joseph Galloway: "Its Censures are no more regarded than Popes' Bulls. It is despis'd for its Venality, and abominated for its Injustice." But he hastened to show that he had no illusions that men are natively pure, that only governments are wicked. With almost a Hamiltonian distrust of the public ranks he wrote: "And yet it is not clear that the People deserve a better Parliament, since they are themselves full as corrupt and venal: witness the Sums they accept for their Votes at almost every Election." [321]

Back in the colonies, Franklin remained just long enough to help form a constitution for Pennsylvania,[322] and to aid Jefferson in writing the Declaration of Independence.[323] After the royal governors had dissolved the assemblies and the Continental Congress urged the colonies to form their own constitutions, Franklin assumed leadership in his state and helped to compose a constitution less conservative than those of most

[320] *Ibid.*, V, 439; see also 527.
[321] London, April 20, 1771; unpublished MS letter in W. S. Mason Collection. Compare with Abbé Raynal's opinion that "society is essentially good; government, as is well known, may be, and is but too often evil" (*The Revolution of America*, Dublin, 1781, 45).
[322] M. Eiselen (*Franklin's Political Theories*, Garden City, N. Y., 1928) observes that Franklin as presiding officer had actually little to do with casting the instrument. From his later paper on the Constitution it is possible, however, to see that he accepted most of its major ideas (pp. 57–8). See S. B. Harding, "Party Struggles over the First Pennsylvania Constitution," *Annual Report of the American Historical Association for 1894*, 371–402.
[323] That Franklin "had more to do with the phraseology of the Declaration of Independence than has been recognized up to now" (J. C. Fitzpatrick, *Spirit of the Revolution*, Boston, 1924, 11) has been shown by Becker, *op. cit.*

of the other colonies.[324] Created between July 15 and Sept. 28, 1776, essentially by one who had just worked on and signed the Declaration of Independence, it is not strange that the dominant ideology of this constitution—that of natural rights, the compact theory, and consent of the governed—should be like that of the Declaration. The new constitution has been called the "most democratic constitution yet seen in America." [325] The unicameral legislature, the assembly of representatives, the plan of judicial review of laws every seven years, and other features have been looked upon as demonstrating the dangerous ultra-democratic tendencies of Franklin. The revolutionary Benjamin Rush, who had helped Paine with *Common Sense*, was dismayed because, in his view, Pennsylvania "has substituted mob government for one of the happiest governments in the world. . . . A single legislature is big with tyranny. I had rather live under the government of one man than of seventy-two."[326] One wonders to what extent Franklin was responsible for the unicameral legislature when we know that it "was the natural outcome of Penn's ideas of government as embodied in his various charters." [327] The plural executive, the right of free-

---

[324] See text in S. E. Morison, *Sources and Documents Illustrating the American Revolution, 1764–1788, and the Formation of the Federal Constitution* (Oxford, 1923, 162–76).

[325] C. H. Lincoln, *The Revolutionary Movement in Pennsylvania, 1760–1776*, 277.

[326] Cited in N. G. Goodman, *Benjamin Rush* (Philadelphia, 1934), 62. Another wrote that the unicameral form is good "if men were wise and virtuous as angels" (Lincoln, *op. cit.*, 282; see also 283). The American Philosophical Society, of which Franklin was president, declared against it.

[327] T. F. Moran, *The Rise and Development of the Bicameral System in America* (Johns Hopkins University Studies in Historical and Political Science, 13th ser., V [Baltimore, 1895]), 42. The legislative Council (upper chamber) had been destroyed by the 1701 constitution. See B. A. Konkle, *George Bryan and the Constitution of Pennsylvania* (Philadelphia, 1922), 114. P. L. Ford ("The Adoption of the Pennsylvania Constitution of 1776," *Political Science Quarterly*, X, Sept., 1895, 426–59) observes: "The one-chamber legislature and the annual election were hardly the work of the Convention, for they were merely transfererd from the Penn Charter; having yielded such admirable results in the past, it is not strange that they were grafted into the new instrument" (p. 454).

men to form their militia and elect their own officers, the extension of male suffrage, and other innovations in this constitution were of a radical nature in as far as the populace were given greater liberties and responsibilities than ever before in the colonies. It seems almost incredible that the patrician-minded Franklin, with his Puritan heritage, should have thus almost hurriedly cast himself at the feet of the people. Certain extenuating factors may be mentioned in an attempt not to gloss over but to understand the violent antithesis between Franklin the imperialist and Franklin the revolutionist. To what extent did his antipathy for proprietary governors, as well as the general colonial experience with governors, suggest a joint executive of a council and governor? [328] Since his experience as a Whig propagandist had been to exalt colonial legislatures, to what extent did he see in the unicameral form a plan which would give freest movement to the legislative activity? Prior to 1776 there is little that would suggest that Franklin had any confidence in men, *unchecked.*[329] Yet it is difficult to show that, in the first flush of indignation against England and revolutionary enthusiasm, Franklin did not favor for a time distinctly radical tendencies.

In 1776 he left, as he wrote to Jan Ingenhousz, "to procure those aids from European powers, for enabling us to defend our freedom and independence." [330] He who had "been a Servant to many publicks, thro' a long life" went to Passy, where from

---

[328] Defending (in 1789) the Pennsylvania constitution, Franklin wrote, "Have we not experienced in this Colony, when a Province under the Government of the Proprietors, the Mischiefs of a second Branch existing in the Proprietary Family, countenanced and aided by an Aristocratic Council?" (*Writings*, X, 56.)

[329] In 1775 he submitted to the Second Continental Congress his *Articles of Confederation* (*Writings*, VI, 420–6) which called for a "firm League of Friendship" motivated by a unicameral assembly and a plural executive, a Council of twelve. It was democratic also in its "basing representation upon population instead of financial support" (Eiselen, *op. cit.*, 54).

[330] *Writings*, VII, 48.

the Hôtel de Valentinois of M. Roy de Chaumont he was to direct financial efforts calculated, with Washington's generalship, and the assiduous loyalty of a minority group, to win the Revolution. Welcomed as the apotheosis of "les Insurgens," [331] he was virtually deified; as Turgot expressed it, *Eripuit caelo fulmen sceptrumque tyrannis*. The universality of his vogue in France was primarily due to his deistic naturalism, his wily pleading and activities in behalf of colonial independence, the receptivity of the Gallic mind for any marten-capped child of the New World, and to his scientific thought and experimentation which had fortified Reason in purging the unknown of its terror, helping thus to make the *philosophe* at home in his reasonable world. Three weeks after Franklin arrived in France, one Frenchman said that "it is the mode today for everybody to have an engraving of M. Franklin over the mantelpiece." [332] France overnight became Franklinist when the savant came to dwell at Passy. Even before the victory of Yorktown he became *la mode*. It was to be his success to convert France's unrecognized alliance with the colonies to an open and undisguised alliance, perhaps even to war with England. [333] But even for one who enjoyed, as John Adams wrote, a reputation "more universal than that of Leibnitz or Newton, Frederick or Voltaire," [334] it was to be a difficult task to manipulate a Beaumarchais, a Vergennes, and others, in spite of the well-known and inveterate economic and political grievances which the French held for the English. The virtues he stressed in the *Morals of Chess* he was able to translate into a diplomatic mien,

---

[331] *Ibid.*, VII, 23. No dull sidelight on the quality of Franklin's radicalism during this period is the fact that he brought Thomas Paine to the colonies and was partly responsible for the writing of *Common Sense*. It is alleged that Franklin considered Paine "his adopted political son" (cited in M. D. Conway's *Life of Thomas Paine*, 3d ed., New York, 1893, II, 468). For explication of Paine's political theories see C. E. Merriam, "Political Theories of Thomas Paine," *Political Science Quarterly*, XIV, 389–403.

[332] Hale and Hale, *op. cit.*, I, 70; see also 75.   [333] *Ibid.*, I, 32.

[334] Cited in J. B. Perkins, *France in the American Revolution*, 140.

uniting "perfect silence" with a "generous civility." As a result, his record as minister to France is marked by complete success; but for this "it is by no means certain that American independence would have been achieved until many years later." [335]

Plagued by Frenchmen desiring places in the colonial army, feted by the *philosophes*, sorely vexed by the need for settling countless maritime affairs, embracing and embraced by the venerable Voltaire, corresponding with Hartley concerning exchange of prisoners, shaping alliances and treaties, conducting scientific experiments, investigating Mesmer, intrigued by balloon ascensions, made the darling of several salons, associating in the Lodge of the Nine Sisters with Bailly, Bonneville, Warville, Condorcet, Danton, Desmoulins, D'Auberteuil, Pétion, Saint-Étienne, Sieyès, and others, all men who helped to give shape (or shapelessness) to the French Revolution,[336] Franklin found little time to search for that philosophic repose which he had long coveted. It may be extravagant to say that Franklin was the "Creator of Constitutionalism in Europe," [337] but we know that in 1783 he printed the colonial constitutions for continental distribution.[338] It has been suggested that Franklin was an important formative factor in Condorcet's faith in universal suffrage, a unicameral legislature, and the liberties guaranteed by constitutional law.[339] Then, too, Franklin had signed the Declaration of Independence— a document which the French hailed as the "restoration of

---

[335] *Ibid.*, 127.

[336] See D. J. Hill, "A Missing Chapter of Franco-American History," *American Historical Review*, XXI, 709–19, (July, 1916).

[337] *Ibid.*, 710.

[338] *Writings*, IX, 132. The Duc de la Rochefoucauld translated them into French (IX, 71). Franklin thought they would induce emigration to the colonies. See the scores of requests (on the part of notable Frenchmen) and thanks for copies of the constitutions of the United States listed in *Calendar of the Papers of Benjamin Franklin in the Library of the American Philosophical Society.*

[339] J. S. Schapiro, *Condorcet and the Rise of Liberalism*, 79–81 and *passim.*

humanity's title deeds." [340] The Duc de la Rochefoucauld eulogized the unicameral legislature of Pennsylvania, identifying "this grand idea" and its "maximum of simplicity" as Franklin's creation.[341] Fauchet eulogized him as "one of the foremost builders of our sacred constitution." [342] Along with Helvétius, Mably, Rousseau, and Voltaire, Franklin was considered as one who laid the foundations for the French revolution.[343] Franklin's taciturnity, his "art of listening," his diplomatic reserve, do not suggest a volatile iconoclast doing anything consciously to bring about a republican France. This did not prevent him from becoming a symbol of liberty by his mere presence in the land, stimulating patriots to examine the foundations of the tyrannical authority which they saw or imagined enslaving them. Holding no brief for natural equality, Franklin suggested that "quiet and regular Subordination" is "so necessary to Success." [344] Realist that he was, he became almost obsessed with the innate depravity of men until he was doubtful whether "the Species were really worth producing or preserving." [345] One would not be considered excessively republican who inveighed against the "collected passions, prejudices, and private interests" of collective legislative bodies.[346]

---

[340] *Ibid.*, 222.

[341] Cited in W. T. Franklin's edition, I, 303–4. E. P. Oberholtzer, essentially hostile to Franklin, is obliged to admit that Franklin "seems not to have had more than an advisory part" in making the Constitution of 1776. He adds that if Franklin did not form it, "he was at any rate a loyal defender of its principles," and that he seems to have allowed the French to think that the Constitution was his own (*The Referendum in America*, New York, 1900, 26–42). For Franklin's later defenses of unicameralism, see *Writings*, IX, 645, 674; X, 56–8.

[342] Cited in B. Faÿ, *The Revolutionary Spirit in France and America*, 289. Faÿ shows that in France the "revolutionary leaders" who took lessons from Franklin regarded him as "the prophet and saint of a new religion," as the "high priest of Philosophy." See also E. J. Lowell, *The Eve of the French Revolution* (Boston, 1892), chaps. XVI and XVIII.

[343] B. Faÿ, *The Revolutionary Spirit in France and America*, 302.

[344] *Writings*, VIII, 34.

[345] *Ibid.*, VIII, 452; June 7, 1782 (to Joseph Priestley).

[346] *Ibid.*, IX, 241.

He wrote to Caleb Whitefoord: "It is unlucky ... that the Wise and Good should be as mortal as Common People and that they often die before others are found fit to supply their Places." [347] The great proportion of mankind, weak and selfish, need "the Motives of Religion to restrain them from Vice." [348] No less extreme than J. Q. Adams's retort to Paine's *Rights of Man*, that it is anarchic to trust government "to the custody of a lawless and desperate rabble," was Franklin's distrust of the unthinking majority.[349]

Having helped to free the colonies, Franklin fittingly became, if not one of the fathers of the Constitution, then, due to the serenity with which he helped to moderate the plans of extremists on both sides, at least its godfather. If, as Mr. James M. Beck asserts, the success of the Constitution has been the result of its approximation of the golden mean, between monarchy and anarchy, the section and the nation, the small and the large state, then its success may be attributed not a little to Franklin's genius.[350] After small and large states had waged a fruitless struggle over congressional representation, Franklin spoke:

The diversity of opinion turns on two points. If a proportional representation takes place, the small States contend that their liberties will be in danger. If an equality of votes is to be put in its place, the large States say their money will be in danger. When a broad table is to be made, and the edges <of

[347] *Ibid.*, IX, 330.
[348] *Ibid.*, IX, 521; see also IX, 489.
[349] Although the preponderance of evidence bears out the trustworthiness of this assertion, one can not idly dismiss his *Some Good Whig Principles* or disregard his expressed belief that the people "seldom continue long in the wrong" and if misled they "come right again, and double their former affections" (cited in W. C. Bruce, *Benjamin Franklin, Self-Revealed*, II, 100; also see *Writings*, X, 130). There is a clearly evident polarity in Franklin's mind between ultra-democratic faith and a rigorous observation that if "people" are so constituted, many men are utter rascals. One almost senses a dichotomy between Franklin the politician and Franklin the man and moralist.
[350] See his *The Constitution of the United States* (New York, 1924).

planks do not fit> the artist takes a little from both, and makes a good joint.[351]

The former imperialist could not logically become a state rights advocate. Engrossed essentially in "promoting and securing the common Good," [352] he derided the advantage the greater state would have, asserting that he "was originally of Opinion it would be better if every Member of Congress, or our national Council, were to consider himself rather as a Representative of the whole, than as an Agent for the Interests of a particular State." When Mr. Randolph considered,

To negative all laws, passed by the several States, contravening, in the opinion of the national legislature, the articles of union: (the following words were added to this clause on motion of Mr. Franklin, "or any Treaties subsisting under the authority of the union.") [353]

This is anything but the corollary of a defender of state rights. Franklin was convinced that the permanence of the national view alone could prevent federal anarchy. Addressing himself to the problem of delegated authority Madison observed: "This prerogative of the General Govt. is the great pervading principle that must controul the centrifugal tendency of the States; which, without it, will continually fly out of their proper orbits and destroy the order & harmony of the political system." [354] One is tempted to see here Newton's principle of gravity translated into terms of political nationalism; one wonders whether it is probable that (like Madison's) Franklin's emphasis on the harmony of the whole could have been partly conditioned by the cohesiveness and harmony of universal physical laws incarnate in Newtonian physics, of which he was a master.

[351] *The Records of the Federal Convention*, ed. by Max Farrand, I, 488; see *Writings*, IX, 602–3, 595–9.
[352] *Writings*, IX, 596.
[353] *The Records of the Federal Convention*, I, 47.
[354] *Ibid.*, I, 165.

Franklin was "apprehensive . . .—perhaps too apprehensive, —that the Government of these States may in future times end in a Monarchy." [355] He suggested that moderate rather than kingly salaries paid the chief executive would tend to allay this danger. Between Randolph, who belabored a single executive as the "foetus of monarchy," and Wilson, who harbored it as the "best safeguard against tyranny," stood Franklin, who saw it as subversive of democratic sovereignty but not necessarily fatal. He declared himself emphatically against the motion that the executive have a complete negative.[356] Extolling popular sovereignty, he warned that "In free Governments the rulers are the servants, and the people their superiors & sovereigns." [357] He refused to consider a plan which sought to establish a franchise only for freeholders: "It is of great consequence that we shd. not depress the virtue & public spirit of our common people; of which they displayed a great deal during the war, and which contributed principally to the favorable issue of it." [358] Pinckney had made a motion that rulers should have unencumbered estates:

Doctr Franklin expressed his dislike of every thing that tended to debase the spirit of the common people. If honesty was often the companion of wealth, and if poverty was exposed to peculiar temptation, it was not less true that the possession of property increased the desire of more property— [359] . . . This Constitution will be much read and attended to in Europe, and if it should betray a great partiality to the rich—will not only hurt us in the esteem of the most liberal and enlightened men there, but discourage the common people from removing to this Country.[360]

Pinckney's motion was rejected. Franklin within the Conven-

[355] *Writings*, IX, 593.
[356] *The Records of the Federal Convention*, I, 109.
[357] *Ibid.*, II, 120.   [358] *Ibid.*, II, 204.
[359] Franklin objected to primogeniture and entail.
[360] *Ibid.*, II, 249.

tion did not seem to fear Gerry's threat—"the evils we experience flow from the excess of democracy." [361]

Franklin suggested the adoption of a unicameral legislature, but does not seem to have made any struggle for it. His article of 1789 in defense of the Pennsylvania (unicameral) legislature, however, shows that he clung to the principle as firmly as he had in 1776.[362] He questioned: "The Wisdom of a few Members in one single Legislative Body, may it not frequently stifle bad Motions in their Infancy, and so prevent their being adopted?" In addition the bicameral house is cumbersome and provocative of delay.

Little is known of Franklin's attitude toward the violent controversy attendant upon efforts toward ratification. In his *Ancient Jews and Anti-Federalists* [363] he warned the traducers of the new Constitution against voiding an instrument which in his opinion was as sound as the frailty of human reason would allow it to be. In fact, said he, it "astonishes me, . . . to find this system approaching so near to perfection as it does." [364] He may be said to have been anti-federalistic to the extent that he feared a strong executive, guarded jealously the legislative sphere, worried little about checks and balances, sought to accelerate popular sovereignty; he was federalistic to the extent that he opposed state localism with national sovereignty, was not blind to the depravity of human nature and hence felt the need for a vigorous coercive government. To M. Le Veillard he confessed an almost Hamiltonian distrust of the multitude: The Constitution "has . . . met with great opposition in some States, for we are at present a nation of politicians. And, though there is a general dread of giving too much power to our *governors*, I think we are more in danger from too little obedience in the *governed*." [365] He made the same complaint a year later: "We have been guarding against an evil that old States are most

[361] Gettell, *op. cit.*, 122.   [362] *Writings*, X, 56–8.
[363] *Ibid.*, IX, 698–703.   [364] *Ibid.*, IX, 608.   [365] *Ibid.*, IX, 638.

liable to, *excess of power* in the rulers; but our present danger
seems to be *defect of obedience* in the subjects."[366] It is
difficult to reconcile his inveterate distrust of men with his
activity in behalf of an almost universal franchise, reluctance
to sanction the principle of checks and balances, and belief in
a unicameral legislature; it is difficult to reconcile the Plutarchan
fervor with which he advocated the wisdom of following great
leaders with his fear of a vigorous executive. It is not improbable that those ideas which are generally anti-federalistic in
Franklin's political view are in part the result of his hatred of
proprietary abuses which he witnessed as a provincial statesman
during his middle age.

VII. FRANKLIN AS SCIENTIST AND DEIST

Jan Ingenhousz, the celebrated physician to Maria Theresa
of Austria, wrote a letter to Franklin on May 3, 1780, which
doubtless caused the patriarch of Passy to reflect—not without
sadness of heart—on the diversified fortune which time and
circumstance had devised for him. The physician (no friend to
the American revolution) implored Franklin not to abandon
"entirely the world Nature whose laws made by the supreme
wisdom and is constant and unalterable as its legislature himself [*sic*]." Ingenhousz lamented that Franklin, "a Philosopher
so often and so successfully employed in researches of the most
intricate and the most mysterious operations of Nature,"[367]
should have given his time to politics.

Franklin is now most commonly viewed as a utilitarian
moralist, a successful tradesman and printer, a shrewd propagandist and financier, the diplomat of the Revolution, and if at
all as a scientist, then only as a virtuoso, fashioning devices, such
as open stoves, bifocal spectacles, and lightning rods, for prac-

---

[366] *Writings*, X, 7.
[367] Letter in American Philosophical Society Library; cited by B. M.
Victory, *Benjamin Franklin and Germany*, 128.

tical uses. Probably few general readers are aware that Franklin was a disinterested scientist in the sense that he interrogated nature with an eye to discovering its immutable laws. It is conversely supposed that Franklin himself was unaware of any inclination to pursue natural science to the exclusion of those political achievements which have identified him as one of the wiliest and sagest diplomats of the Enlightenment.

It may be learned, however (not without astonishment), that Franklin almost from the beginning of his participation in politics resented the time given over to such activities, as so much time lost to his speculations and research in natural science. As early as 1752 he wistfully (though realistically) confessed that "business sometimes obliges one to postpone philosophical amusements." [368] A month after this, he wrote to Cadwallader Colden: "I congratulate you on the prospect you have, of passing the remainder of life in philosophical retirement." [369] In the midst of investigating waterspouts, he observed to John Perkins: "How much soever my Inclinations lead me to philosophical Inquiries, I am so engag'd in Business, public and private, that those more pleasing pursuits [of natural science] are frequently interrupted. . . ." [370] He urged Dr. John Fothergill to give himself "repose, delight in viewing the Operations of nature in the vegetable creation." [371] In 1765, upon completing his negotiations in behalf of the Pennsylvania Assembly, he promised Lord Kames that he would "engage in no other" political affairs. [372] To the notable professor of physics of the University of Turin, Giambatista Beccaria, he wrote in 1768 from London (where he had sought to have the Stamp Act rescinded) that he had to "take away entirely" his "attention from philosophical matters, though I have constantly cherished the hope of returning home where I could find leisure to resume

[368] *Writings*, III, 96.
[370] *Ibid.*, III, 107.
[372] *Ibid.*, IV, 377.

[369] *Ibid.*, III, 97.
[371] *Ibid.*, IV, 221.

the studies that I have shamefully put off from time to time." [373]
Again, in 1779, he confessed to Beccaria: "I find myself here
[Passy] immers'd in Affairs, which absorb my Attention, and
prevent my pursuing those Studies in which I always found the
highest Satisfaction; and I am now grown so old, as hardly to
hope for a Return of that Leisure and Tranquillity so necessary
for Philosophical Disquisitions." [374] He longed (in 1782) to
have Congress release him so that he might "spend the Evening
of Life more agreeably in philosophic [devoted to natural
science] Leisure." [375] He who, John Winthrop claimed, "was
good at starting Game for Philosophers," [376] acknowledged that
he had thrown himself on the public, which, "having as it were
eaten my flesh, seemed now resolved to pick my bones." [377]
Reverend Manasseh Cutler visited Franklin a few months before
the patriarch's death. They ardently discussed botany, Franklin
boyish in his eagerness to show the Reverend Mr. Cutler a
massive book, containing "the whole of Linnaeus' Systema
Vegetabilies." "The Doctor seemed extremely fond, through
the course of the visit, of dwelling on Philosophical subjects,
and particularly that of natural History, while the other Gentlemen were swallowed up with politics." [378] In a fictitious (?)
conversation between Joseph II of Austria and Franklin, the
Newton of electricity is reported as explaining that he was early
in life attracted by natural philosophy: "Necessity afterwards
made me a politician. . . . I was Franklin, the *Philosopher* to the
world, long after I had in fact, become Franklin the Poli-

[373] *Ibid.*, V, 165. He repeated this thought to Beccaria in 1773 (*ibid.*, VI,
112). Also see V, 206, 410–1, VII, 49.
[374] *Ibid.*, VII, 418; also see VIII, 211.
[375] *Ibid.*, VIII, 315; also see letter to Priestley, June 7, 1782, VIII, 451;
to Comte de Salmes, July 5, 1785, IX, 361.
[376] *Ibid.*, IX, 652.
[377] *Ibid.*, IX, 621. He wrote this after he was reappointed President of
Pennsylvania in 1787. He confessed, however, that this honor gave him
"no small pleasure."
[378] W. P. and J. P. Cutler, *Life, Journals and Correspondence of Rev.
Manasseh Cutler*, I, 269–70.

tician." [379] After reviewing the evidence, it seems incredulous to doubt that, regardless of his achievements in other fields, Franklin sought his greatest intellectual pleasure in scientific research and speculation, and that his doctrines of scientific deism antedated and conditioned his political, economic, and humanitarian interests.

If Franklin's inventions have been justly praised, his affections for the empirical scientific method and his philosophic interest in Nature's laws have been unjustly ignored. He observed to Ebenezer Kinnersley "that a philosopher cannot be too much on his guard in crediting their ["careless observers'"] relations of things extraordinary, and should never build an hypothesis on any thing but clear facts and experiments, or it will be in danger of soon falling . . . like a house of cards"; [380] and to Abbé Soulavie, "You see I have given a loose to imagination; but I approve much more your method of philosophizing, which proceeds upon actual observation, makes a collection of facts, and concludes no farther than those facts will warrant." [381] In 1782 he wrote to Sir Joseph Banks, president of the Royal Society, that he longed to "sit down in sweet Society with my English philosophic Friends, communicating to each other new Discoveries, and proposing Improvements of old ones; all tending to extend the Power of Man over Matter, avert or diminish the Evils he is subject to, or augment the Number of his Enjoyments." [382] A careful study of his scientific papers discloses that he was not untrained in the method of hypotheses sustained or rejected by patient and laborious experimentation: not fortuitously did he arrive at conclusions in electricity, which were epochal in (1) "His rejection of the two-fluid theory of electricity

[379] *Joseph and Benjamin, A Conversation*, Trans. from a French Manuscript (London, 1787), 72. If this meeting never took place, the reported conversation is anything but "decidedly silly" as Ford opines (*Franklin Bibliography*, #936, 371).

[380] *Writings*, IV, 143.

[381] *Ibid.*, VIII, 601. Also see IX, 53.

[382] *Ibid.*, VIII, 593.

and substitution of the one-fluid theory; (2) his coinage of the appropriate terms *positive* and *negative*, to denote an excess or a deficit of the common electric fluid; (3) his explanation of the Leyden jar, and, notably, his recognition of the paramount rôle played by the glass or dielectric; (4) his experimental demonstration of the identity of lightning and electricity; and (5) his invention of the lightning conductor for the protection of life and property, together with his clear statement of its preventive and protective functions." [383] Not only an inventor, Franklin inductively observed natural phenomena, and drew conclusions until he had created a virtual *Principia* of electricity. His contemporaries were not loath to honor him as a second Newton. Franklin, however, was in all of his researches under a self-confessed yoke which doubtless tended to deny him access to the profoundest reaches of scientific inquiry: from Philadelphia he wrote in 1753 to Cadwallader Colden, eminent mathematician (as well as versatile scientist): "Your skill & Expertness in Mathematical Computations, will afford you an Advantage in these Disquisitions [among them, researches in electricity], that I lament the want of, who am like a Man searching for some thing in a dark Room where I can only grope and guess; while you proceed with a Candle in your Hand." [384]

In an effort to learn the *modus operandi* of Franklin's philosophic thought, let us now review its genetic development, its probable sources, its relation to scientific deism, and the degree to which he achieved that serene repose for which he ever strove. A pioneer American rationalist, not without his claims to being "another Voltaire," Franklin as a youth read those works which were forming or interpreting the thought patterns of the age. Born in an epoch presided over by a Locke and a Newton, an epoch of rationalism and "supernatural" rational-

[383] Brother Potamian and J. J. Walsh, *Makers of Electricity*, 126.
[384] "Letters and Papers of Cadwallader Colden, IV (1748–54)," *Collections of the New York Historical Society* (1920), 372.

ism, alike fed by physico-mathematical speculation, Franklin, barely beyond adolescence, felt the impacts of the age of reason. Scholars before and since M. M. Curtis have explained that "in religion he was a Deist of the type of Lord Herbert of Cherbury." [385] M. Faÿ has sought, without convincing documentary evidence, to interpret Franklin's philosophic mind in terms of Pythagoreanism.[386] We may find that these views are over simple and historically inadequate—even wrong.

Franklin was reared "piously in the Dissenting way" [387] by a "pious and prudent" Calvinistic father who died as he lived, with "entire Dependence on his Redeemer." [388] "Religiously educated as a Presbyterian," [389] young Benjamin was taught that *Major est Scripturae auctoritas quam omnis humani ingenii capacitas.* He was nurtured on the Bible and "books in polemic divinity," and he regularly attended services at the Old South Church. Doubtless without reflection he was led to identify goodness with the church and its worship. He was a part of New England's bibliolatry. Not long before he was apprenticed to his brother James he read Cotton Mather's *Bonifacius—An Essay upon the Good that is to be Devised and Designed by those who desire to Answer the Great End of Life, and to do good while they live,* and Defoe's *Essays upon Several Projects: or Effectual Ways for Advancing the Interests of the Nation.* He confessed in 1784 that *Bonifacius* "gave me such a turn of thinking, as to have an influence on my conduct through life; for I have always set a greater value on the character of a *doer of good* than on any other kind of reputation." [390] Mather, as an exponent of

[385] "An Outline of Philosophy in America," *Western Reserve University Bulletin* (March, 1896). See also I. W. Riley, *American Philosophy: The Early Schools,* 229–65.
[386] *Franklin, the Apostle of Modern Times,* iv.
[387] *Writings,* I, 295.
[388] *Boston News-Letter,* Jan. 17, 1744/5. Also see *1669–1882. An Historical Catalogue of the Old South Church (Third Church), Boston* (Boston, 1883), 304.
[389] *Writings,* I, 324.
[390] *Writings,* IX, 208.

Christian charity, urged that man help his neighbors "with a rapturous assiduity,"[391] that he may discover the "ravishing satisfaction which he might find in relieving the distresses of a poor miserable neighbor."[392] It is ironic that Mather should have apparently aided a young man to divorce himself from the strenuous subtleties of theology. (Franklin was too young to gather that Mather circumspectly warned against a covenant of works, and hence was Pauline in his advocacy of *charity* rather than of humanitarianism.) And from Defoe's *Essays* Franklin received more than a penchant for projects. Like Mather, Defoe observed that "God Almighty has commanded us to relieve and help one another in distress."[393] Defoe seemed to young Franklin to dwell on fellow-service—to promise that the good man need not have understood all of the dogma of Old South meetinghouse.

Apprenticed to James, Franklin admitted that he "now had access to better books."[394] Whatever the extent of James's library in 1718, by 1722 the *New England Courant* collection included Burnet's *History of the Reformation*, *Theory of the Earth*, the *Spectator* papers, *The Guardian*, *Art of Thinking* [Du Port Royal], *The Tale of a Tub*, and the writings of Tillotson.[395] After reading most probably in these, and, as we are told, in Tryon's *Way to Health*, Xenophon's *Memorabilia*, digests of some of Boyle's lectures, Anthony Collins, Locke, and Shaftesbury, Franklin became in his Calvinist religion a "real doubter."[396] He became at the age of sixteen, as a result of reading Boyle's Lectures,[397] a "thorough Deist."[398] We cannot be certain of

---

[391]*Essays to do Good*, with an Introductory Essay by A. Thomson (Glasgow, 1825), 102.   [392]*Ibid.*, 213-4.

[393] *Works of Daniel Defoe*, ed. by Wm. Hazlitt (London, 1843), I, 22.

[394] *Writings*, I, 239.

[395] See *New England Courant*, No. 48, June 25–July 2, 1722.

[396] *Writings*, I, 244.

[397] Consecrated to piety, Robert Boyle at his death left £50 per annum, for a clergyman elected to "preach eight sermons in the year for proving the Christian religion against notorious infidels, *viz.* Atheists, Theists, Pagans, Jews, and Mahometans. . . ." (*Works of Robert Boyle*, London, 1772, I, clxvii.)   [398] *Writings*, I, 295.

the Lectures read by Franklin, but we may observe Bentley's *Folly of Atheism* (1692) and Derham's *Physico-Theology* (1711–1712), which are representative of the series provided for by Boyle. Like Mather's *The Christian Philosopher* (1721) [399] they both employ science and rationalism to reinforce (never as equivalent to or substitute for) scriptural theology. Fed by Newtonian physics, Bentley discovers in gravity "the great basis of all mechanism," the "immediate *fiat* and finger of God, and the executions of the divine law." [400] Gravity, "the powerful cement which holds together this magnificent structure of the world," [401] is the result of the Deity "who *always acts geometrically*." Borrowing from Cockburne, Ray, Bentley, and Fénelon, Derham offers likewise to prove the existence and operations of the Workman from his Work. [402]

It is unlikely that Boyle's Lectures (characterized by orthodox rationalism, augmented by Newtonianism) would alone have precipitated in Franklin a "thorough deism." Not improbably Locke, Shaftesbury, and Anthony Collins (whom Franklin mentions reading) were most militant in overthrowing his inherited bibliolatry. Although he does not say exactly which of Collins's works he read, Collins's rationale is repeated clearly enough in any one of his pieces. Warring against "crackbrain'd Enthusiasts," the "prodigious Ignorance" and "Impositions of Priests," against defective scriptural texts, Collins

---

[399] In his Introduction to *Selections from Cotton Mather* (New York, 1926), xlix-li, K. B. Murdock agrees with I. W. Riley that *The Christian Philosopher* (1721) represents the first stage of the reaction from scriptural Calvinism to the scientific deism of Paine and Franklin. T. Hornberger's "The Date, the Source, and the Significance of Cotton Mather's Interest in Science" (*loc. cit.*) shows that "as early as 1693 Cotton Mather was expressing that delight in the wonder and beauty of design in the external world which Professors Murdock and Riley regard as deistic in tendency," that he "was unconsciously vacillating between two points of view."

[400] *Works of Richard Bentley*, ed. by A. Dyce (London, 1838), III, 74-5.
[401] *Ibid.*, III, 79.
[402] *Physico-Theology* . . . (5th ed., London, 1720), 25-6. God's "exquisite Workmanship" is seen in "every Creature" (p. 27).

defends "our natural Notions" against the authoritarianism of priests. Vilifying the authority of the surplice, he apotheosizes the authority of reason.[403] He intensifies the English tradition of every-man-his-own-priest, and exclaims "How uncertain Tradition is!"[404] From this militant friend of John Locke, Franklin was doubtless impregnated with an *odium theologicum* and an exalted idea of the sanctity of Reason.

Having read *An Essay Concerning Human Understanding*,[405] Franklin may have remembered that Locke there observed, "Nothing that is contrary to, and inconsistent with, the clear and self-evident dictates of reason, has a right to be urged or assented to as a matter of faith, wherein reason hath nothing to do."[406] Like Collins, Locke urged a deistic rationale:

Since then the precepts of Natural Religion are plain, and very intelligible to all mankind, and seldom to come to be controverted; and other revealed truths, which are conveyed to us by books and languages, are liable to the common and natural obscurities and difficulties incident to words; methinks it would become us to be more careful and diligent in observing the former, and less magisterial, positive, and imperious, in imposing our own sense and interpretations of the latter.[407]

[403] See *A Discourse of Free-Thinking* (London, 1713).
[404] *Priestcraft in Perfection* . . . (London, 1710).
[405] *Writings*, I, 243.
[406] A. C. Fraser ed. (Oxford, 1894), II, 425-6.
[407] *Ibid.*, II, 121. For Locke and his place in the age see S. G. Hefel-bower's *The Relation of John Locke to English Deism*. About the time he read Locke, Franklin notes he studied Arnauld and Nicole's *La logique ou l'art de penser*. Mr. G. S. Eddy has informed one of the editors that the Library Company of Philadelphia owns John Ozell's translation of the work (London, 1718), and that this was the copy owned by Franklin. (See Lowndes's *Bibliographer's Manual*, IV, 1930, and *Dictionary of National Biography*, "John Ozell.") In accord with the English deistic and rationalistic tendency, *La logique* admits that Aristotle's authority is not good, that "Men cannot long endure such constraint" (Thomas S. Bayne's trans., 8th ed., Edinburgh and London, n.d., 23). Indebted to Pascal and Descartes, it admits with the latter that geometry and astronomy may help one achieve justness of mind, but it vigorously asserts that this justness of mind is more important than speculative science (p. 1). Anti-sensational, it denies "that all our ideas come through sense" (p. 34),

In addition Franklin may have been influenced by Locke's implied Newtonianism; he would suspect the subtleties of the Old South Church when he read: "For the visible marks of extraordinary wisdom and power appear so plainly in all the works of the creation, that a rational creature, who will but seriously reflect on them, cannot miss the discovery of a Deity." [408] Like Newton, Locke inferred an infinite and benevolent Geometrician from "the magnificent harmony of the universe."

Franklin also read Shaftesbury's *Characteristics*, which Warburton quotes Pope as saying "had done more harm to revealed religion in England than all the works of infidelity put together." [409] Although he may have pondered over Shaftesbury's "virtuoso theory of Benevolence," he was not one to be readily convinced of the innate altruism of man. His Puritan heritage linked with an empirical realism prevented him from becoming prey to Shaftesbury's a priori optimism. He was aware of the potential danger of a complacent trust in natural impulses, which often lead to

The love of sweet security in sin.

To what extent did Franklin's nascent humanitarianism—mildly provoked by the neighborliness of Mather and Defoe—receive

---

affirming that we have within us ideas of things (p. 31). It is uncertain of the value of induction, which "is never a certain means of acquiring perfect knowledge" (p. 265; see also 304, 307, 308, 350). It accords little praise to the sciences and reason, and seems wary of metaphysical speculation, assuring more humbly that "Piety, wisdom, moderation, are without doubt the most estimable qualities in the world" (p. 291). As we shall discover, this work on the whole seems to have had (with the exception of the last very general principle) little formative influence on the young mind which was fast impregnating itself with scientific deism. Were it not for the recurring implications (particularly in the harvest of editions of the *Autobiography*) that *La logique* is as significant for our study as, for example, the works of Locke and Shaftesbury, this note would be pedantic supererogation.

[408] A. C. Fraser, *op. cit.*, I, 99. See also 190, 402–3; II, 65, 68, 352.

[409] Cited in C. A. Moore, "Shaftesbury and the Ethical Poets in England, 1700–1760," *Publications of the Modern Language Association*, XXXI (N. s. XXIV), 276 (June, 1916).

additional sanction from Shaftesbury's doctrine that "compassion is the supreme form of moral beauty, the neglect of it the greatest of all offenses against nature's ordained harmony"? [410] Identifying self-love and social, Shaftesbury saw the divine temper achieved through affection for the public, the "universal good." [411] Born among men who were convinced of the supremacy of scripture, Franklin would at first be astonished (then perhaps liberated) upon reading in the *Characteristics* that "Religion excludes only perfect atheism." [412] From such a piece as Shaftesbury's *An Inquiry Concerning Virtue or Merit* Franklin learned that not all men preserved a union between theology and ethics, scripture and religion. Although Shaftesbury occasionally indicated a reverence for sacred scriptures, the totality of his thought was cast in behalf of natural religion. He was convinced that the "Deity is sufficiently revealed through natural Phenomena." [413] Extolling the apprehension of the Deity through man's uniform reason, Shaftesbury urbanely lampooned enthusiasm, that private revelation which threatened to prevail against the *consensus gentium*.

By 1725 Franklin had divorced theology from morality and morality from conscience, having punctuated his youth with faunish "errata." [414] Although he was as a youth too much at ease in Zion, he did not lose substantial (if then a theoretic) faith in the struggle between the law of the spirit and the law of the members. Nurtured by the Bible, Bunyan, Addison and Steele, Tryon, Socrates, and Xenophon—a blend of Christian and classical traditions—he felt the reasonableness, if not the saintliness, of curbing the resolute sway of his natural self. [415]

[410] *Ibid.*, 271.

[411] J. M. Robertson, ed., *Characteristics* . . . (New York, 1900), I, 27.

[412] *Ibid.*, I, 241–2.   [413] Moore, *op. cit.*, 267.

[414] In *Dogood Paper* No. XIV Franklin suggests (autobiographically?): "In Matters of Religion, he that alters his Opinion on a *religious Account*, must certainly go thro' much Reading, hear many Arguments on both Sides, and undergo many Struggles in his Conscience, before he can come to a full Resolution" (*Writings*, II, 46).

[415] He read Thomas Tryon's *The Way to Health, Long Life and*

After five years with James, a year in Philadelphia where part
of the time he worked with Samuel Keimer,[416] a fanatic

Happiness, probably the second edition (London, 1691), a copy of which
is in the W. S. Mason Collection. Tryon holds that no "greater Happiness" than Attic sobriety is "attainable upon Earth" (p. 1). Divine
Temperance is the "spring head of all Virtues" (p. 33). Inward harmony
"is both the Glory and the Happiness, the Joy and Solace of created
Beings, the celebrated Musick of the Spheres, the Eccho of Heaven, the
Business of Seraphims, and the Imployment of Eternity" (p. 500). From
Xenophon he learned that "self-restraint" is "the very corner-stone of
virtue." The classic core of the *Memorabilia* is the love of the moderate
contending with the love of the incontinent. Franklin has impressed
many as representing an American Socrates. Emerson was certain that
Socrates "had a Franklin-like wisdom" (Centenary Ed., IV, 72). Franklin's
fondness for Socratic centrality, discipline, and knowledge of self is
fragmentarily shown by the aphorisms appropriated in *Poor Richard*.
There are scores of the quality of the following: "He that lives carnally
won't live eternally." "Who has deceived thee so oft as thyself?" "Caesar
did not merit the triumphal car more than he that conquers himself." "If
Passion drives, let Reason hold the Reins." "A man in a Passion rides a
mad Horse." "There are three Things extremely hard, Steel, a Diamond
and to know one's self." Consult T. H. Russell's *The Sayings of Poor
Richard, 1733–1758.*

[416] See S. Bloore, "Samuel Keimer. A Footnote to the Life of Franklin," *Pennsylvania Magazine of History and Biography*, LIV, 255–87 (July,
1930), and "Samuel Keimer," in *Dictionary of American Biography*, X, 288–9.
In 1724 Samuel Keimer (probably with Franklin's aid) reprinted Gordon
and Trenchard's *The Independent Whig*. (See W. J. Campbell's *A Short-
Title Check List of all the Books, Pamphlets, Broadsides, known to have
been printed by Benjamin Franklin*.) Franklin also was acquainted with
their *Cato's Letters*, having helped to set up parts from it while working
on the *New England Courant*. *The Independent Whig* emphasizes humanitarian morality rather than theological dogma, morality which "prompts
us to do good to all Men, and to all Men alike" (London, 1721, xlviii). It
is fearful of metaphysical vagaries (p. 26). Warring against priests and
their "Monkey Tricks at Church" (p. 165)—"One Drop of Priestcraft
is enough to contaminate the Ocean" (p. 168)—it sets up a violent antithesis between reason and authority (p. 212), declaring that "we must
judge from Scripture what is Orthodoxy" *but* "we must judge from
Reason, what is Scripture" (p. 276). Tilting at a Deity "revengeful,
cruel, capricious, impotent, vain, fond of Commendation and Flattery,"
exalting an "All-powerful, All-wise, and All-merciful God" (p. 413),
The Independent Whig, like Franklin's *Articles*, suggests that "it is absurd
to suppose, that we can direct the All-wise Being in the Dispensation of
his Providence; or can flatter or persuade him out of his eternal Decrees"
(p. 436). In *Cato's Letters* (3rd ed., 4 vols., London, 1733), which
were tremendously popular in the American colonies, Franklin could
have read that "The People have no Biass to be Knaves" (I, 178),
that man "cannot enter into the Rationale of God's punishing all Mankind

and bearded Camisard, Franklin, through the duplicity of
Governor Keith, found himself in November, 1724, aboard the
London-Hope, England-bound. It would be unfair to Franklin
were we to think him a primitive colonist to whom England
was an unreal, incalculable land. We remember that James
knew the London of Anne, Addison, Steele, Locke, and Newton. And we have seen that the _New England Courant_ library
was one of which no London gentleman and scholar need have
been ashamed. As a worker on this newspaper Franklin had set
up the names and some indications of the thoughts of such men
as Fénelon, Tillotson, Defoe, Swift, Butler, Bayle, Isaac Watts,
Blount, Burnet, Whiston, Temple, Trenchard and Gordon,
Denham, Garth, Dryden, Milton, Locke, Flamstead, and Newton.[417]

During his two years in London, working successively in the
printing houses of Samuel Palmer and James Watts, he mingled
with many of the leaders of the day. Probably because he had,
while yet in America, read (in the transactions of the Royal
Society) of the virtuosi's interest in asbestos, he wrote to
Sir Hans Sloane, offering to show him purses made of that
novel stuff.[418] And we know that Sir Hans Sloane received

---

for the Sin of their first Parents, which they could not help" (IV, 38),
"That we cannot provoke him, when we intend to adore him; that the
best Way to serve him, is to be serviceable to one another" (IV, 103).
Jesus instituted a natural religion, a worship of One Immutable God, free
from priests, sacrifices, and ceremonies, in which one shows through
"doing Good to men" his adoration for God (IV, 265–6). Here are
observations which could easily have reinforced Franklin's deistic rationale.
For interesting evidence of further deistic and rationalistic works available
to Franklin, see L. C. Wroth's _An American Bookshelf, 1755_.

[417] One of the editors has examined the photostated _New England
Courant_ in the W. S. Mason Collection. For readable accounts of this
newspaper see: W. G. Bleyer, _Main Currents in the History of American
Journalism_, chaps. I–II; C. A. Duniway, _The Development of Freedom of
the Press in Massachusetts_, 97–103; W. C. Ford, "Franklin's New England Courant," _Proceedings of the Massachusetts Historical Society_, LVII,
336–53 (April, 1924); H. F. Kane, "James Franklin Senior, Printer of
Boston and Newport," _American Collector_, III, 17–26 (Oct., 1926).

[418] See _Writings_, II, 52–3.

Franklin in his home at Bloomsbury Square. Before he met other notables he published (what he called later an "erratum") *A Dissertation on Liberty and Necessity, Pleasure and Pain* (1725).[419] Franklin himself said this work was the result of his setting up Wollaston's *The Religion of Nature Delineated*[420] at Palmer's and his not agreeing with the author's "reasonings." Coming to Wollaston's work (with Franklin's *Dissertation* and *Articles of Belief* in mind) we can, however, see much that Franklin agreed with, general principles which do little more than reflect the current patterns of thought. Like Franklin, Wollaston saw Reason as "the great law of our nature."[421] With Locke he denied innate ideas.[422] That part of *The Religion of Nature Delineated* in which he searched with laborious syllogistic reasoning for the Ultimate Cause (which could not produce itself) may have been boring to the less agile mind of the young printer. Wollaston, however, apologized for his syllogistic gymnastics offered in proof of Deity since "much more may those greater motions we see in the world, and the phenomena attending them" afford arguments for such a proof:

I mean the motions of the planets and the heavenly bodies. For *these* must be put into motion, either by one Common mighty Mover, acting upon them immediately, or by causes and laws of His Appointment; or by their respective movers, who, for reasons to which you can by this time be no stranger, must depend upon some *Superior*, that furnished them with the power of doing this.[423]

[419] One of the editors has used the Huth copy now possessed by W. S. Mason. Not included in the Sparks, Bigelow, or Smyth editions of his works, it was printed by Parton as an Appendix to his *Life;* by I. W. Riley, *op. cit.*, and recently edited by L. C. Wroth for The Facsimile Text Society.

[420] Franklin must have been mistaken in his belief that he set up the second edition. The work was privately printed in 1722, reprinted in 1724 and a second time in 1725. Hence Franklin really set up the *third* edition. For an extensive analysis of this work, see C. G. Thompson's dissertation, *The Ethics of William Wollaston* (Boston, 1922).

[421] Wollaston, *op. cit.*, 15.   [422] *Ibid.*, 23.   [423] *Ibid.*, 78–9.

With Newtonian rapture he marveled at "the grandness of this fabric of the world," [424] at "the chorus of planets moving periodically, by uniform laws." Rapt in wonder, he gazed "up to the fixt stars, that radiant numberless host of heaven." Like a Blackmore, Ray, Fontenelle, or Newton, he felt that they were "probably all possest by proper inhabitants." [425] He wondered at the "just and geometrical arrangement of things." [426] These are all sentiments that Franklin expressed in his philosophical juvenilia.[427] But then, Franklin (after reading this sublimated geometry which reduced the parts of creation to an equally sublime simplicity) noted in Wollaston that man must be a free agent,[428] that good and evil are as black and white, distinguishable,[429] that empirically the will is free, the author urging with Johnsonian good sense, "The short way of knowing this certainly is to try." [430] Franklin's *Dissertation* was dedicated to his friend James Ralph and prefaced by a misquotation from Dryden and Lee's *Oedipus*. It purports, as Franklin wrote in 1779, "to prove the doctrine of fate, from the supposed attributes of God . . . that in erecting and governing the world, as he was infinitely wise, he knew what would be best; infinitely good, he must be disposed, and infinitely powerful, he must be able to execute it: consequently all is right." [431] With confidence lent him by his a priori method, he proposed: "I. There is said to be a First Mover, who is called God, Maker of the Universe. II. He is said to be all-wise, all-good, all-powerful." [432] With the nonchalance of an abstractionist, he concluded, "Evil doth not exist." [433] Transcending the sensational necessitarianism [434]

[424] *Ibid.*, 80.   [425] *Ibid.*   [426] *Ibid.*, 83.

[427] It would be interesting to know whether Franklin's much discussed prudential virtues (listed in *Autobiography*) were not in part motivated by Wollaston's pages 173–80.

[428] *Ibid.*, 7.   [429] *Ibid.*, 26.

[430] *Ibid.*, 63 ff.   [431] *Writings*, VII, 412.

[432] *A Dissertation on Liberty and Necessity, Pleasure and Pain* (London, 1725), 4.   [433] *Ibid.*, 5.

[434] For an incisive exposition of the earlier and contemporary controversy regarding freedom of the will, see C. H. Faust and T. H. Johnson's

of Anthony Collins and John Locke, Franklin observed (with an eye on Newton's law of gravitation) that man has liberty, the "Liberty of the same Nature with the Fall of a heavy Body to the Ground; it has Liberty to fall, that is, it meets with nothing to hinder its Fall, but at the same Time it is necessitated to fall, and has no Power or Liberty to remain suspended." [435] As a disciple of Locke's psychology, Franklin reflected his concept of the *tabula rasa* in describing an infant's mind which "is as if it were not." "All our Ideas are first admitted by the Senses and imprinted on the Brain, increasing in Number by Observation and Experience; there they become the Subjects of the Soul's Action."

In the *Dissertation* one can discover the extent to which Franklin had absorbed (if not from Newton's own works, then from his popularizers and intellectual sons such as Pemberton, Franklin's friend) several of the essential tenets of Newtonianism. Here we see his belief in a universe motivated by immutable natural laws comprising a sublimely harmonious system reflecting a Wise Geometrician; a world in which man desires to affect a corresponding inner heaven. Enraptured by the order of the natural laws of Newtonianism, and like a Shaftesbury searching for a demonstrable inner harmony, Franklin (carrying his a priorism to logical absurdity) was unable to reconcile free will with Omniscience, Omnipotence, and Goodness. (In how far was this partly the result of his having been steeped in Calvinism's doctrine of Election?)

The *Dissertation* is as appreciative of Newton's contribution to physics and thought as Thomson's [436] *To the Memory of Sir*

Introduction to *Jonathan Edwards* (American Writers Series, New York, 1935), xliii–lxiv.

[435] *A Dissertation . . .* , 10–1.

[436] In Franklin's liturgy of the '30's (in the *Autobiography*) he quotes from Thomson's *Winter* (lines 217 ff.). While the references to Thomson are few in the complete works, his later influence on Franklin need not be underestimated. See Franklin's letter to W. Strahan (*Writings*, II, 242–3) in which he confesses that "That charming Poet has brought more Tears

Isaac Newton. Not unlike Franklin's framework is Shaftesbury's thought in *An Inquiry Concerning Virtue or Merit.*[437]
Since Franklin acknowledged his reading of Shaftesbury and
since as late as 1730 he borrowed heavily from the *Characteristics*, it seems probable that Shaftesbury lent Franklin in this
case some sanction for his only metaphysical venture.[438]

As one result of his printing *A Dissertation* he made the
acquaintance of Lyons, author of *The Infallibility of Human
Judgement*[439] who introduced him to Mandeville[440] and Dr.

---

of Pleasure into my Eyes than all I ever read before." It is not inconceivable that in Thomson Franklin found additional sanction for his
humanitarian bias. One remembers the wide differences between the
humanitarianism of Thomson and Franklin. Franklin's practical and
masculine humanitarianism keyed to the saving of time and energy was
unlike the sentimental warmheartedness often displayed by Thomson.
Franklin was never moved to tears at beholding the worm's "convulsive
twist in agonizing folds."

[437] Phillips Russell has suggested *Spectator*, No. 183, as Franklin's
probable source in Part II of the *Dissertation*. There, pleasure and pain
are "such constant yoke-fellows." This intuitive assertion can hardly
be conceived as the elaborate metaphysical rationale upon which this
idea rests in Franklin's work.

[438] Robertson, *op. cit.*, 239–40.

[439] London (4th ed.), 1724. A despiser of authoritarianism in religion,
intrigued by the physico-deistic thought of his day, Lyons (with a vituperative force akin to Thomas Paine's) damns those who damn men for
revolting against divine and absolute revelation (p. 25). "Men have
Reason sufficient to find out proper and regular ways for improving and
perfecting their laws." Faith he calls "an unintelligible Chymæra of the
Phantasie" (p. 92). The doctrine of the Trinity "is one of the most nice
Inventions that ever the subtlest Virtuoso constru'd to puzzle the Wit of
Man with" (p. 112). Through faith people make of God "only a confus'd
unintelligible Description of a *Heterogeneous Monster* of their own Making" (p. 117). Deistically he opines that "we shall soon see that the Object
of *True Religion*, and all Rational Mens Speculations, is an Eternal, Un-
changeable, Omnipotent Being, infinitely Good, Just and Wise" (p. 123).
Like Toland he urges, "To pretend to Believe a Thing or the Working of
a Miracle, is a stupid and gaping Astonishment" (p. 195). Although he
enjoyed Franklin's dissertation, he does not in his work hold to Franklin's
necessitarianism: "Nothing interrupts Men, but only as they interrupt
one another" (p. 238). Religion to Lyons is remote from books, but is
found in the "unalterable laws of Nature, which no Authority can destroy,
or Interpolator corrupt" (p. 252).

[440] Although Franklin indicates in his *Autobiography* that he delighted
to listen to Mandeville hold forth at the Horns, there seems to be traceable

Henry Pemberton, who in turn "Promis'd to give me an opportunity, some time or other, of seeing Sir Isaac Newton, *of which I was extreamly desirous;* but this never happened [the italics are the editors']." [441] Dr. Pemberton, physician and mathematician, met Newton in 1722, and during the time Franklin enjoyed his friendship was helping Newton to prepare the third edition of the *Principia.* As a result of his aiding Newton "to discover and understand his writings," [442] Pemberton in 1728 published *A View of Sir Isaac Newton's Philosophy.* It is obvious that Franklin could have discovered few men with a more concentrated and enthusiastic knowledge of Newtonianism than that possessed by Dr. Pemberton. As we have already noted, Franklin undoubtedly derived his appreciation of Newtonian speculation not from grubbing in the *Principia* but from secondary sources. There is no reason to apologize for Franklin on this score when we remember that Voltaire, who popularized Newtonianism in France, exclaimed: "Very few people read Newton because it is necessary to be learned to understand him. But everybody talks about him." Desaguliers, coming to London from Oxford in 1713, observed that "he found all Newtonian philosophy generally receiv'd among persons of all ranks and professions, and even among the ladies by the help of ex-

---

in his writings no direct influence of Mandeville's thought. (One may wonder whether Franklin's use of the name "Horatio" in his 1730 dialogues between Philocles and Horatio could be traced to Mandeville's use of the name in his dialogues between Cleomenes and Horatio.) Mandeville's empirical view of man's essential egoism would have found sympathetic response from Franklin. On the other hand, Mandeville's ethical rigorism (see Kaye's Introd. to *The Fable of the Bees*) differs from the utilitarian cast Franklin sheds over his strenuous ethicism. One may suspect that like a Bunyan, a Swift, a Rabelais, Mandeville would have fortified Franklin against accepting too blithely Shaftesbury's faith in man's innate altruism, even if he did not short-circuit Franklin's growing humanitarianism.

[441] *Writings*, I, 278.

[442] David Brewster, *Life of Sir Isaac Newton* (New York, 1831), 258. For fuller treatment see his *Memoirs of the Life, Writings, and Discoveries of Sir Isaac Newton* (Edinburgh, 1855), II, 378 ff., and *passim.*

periments." [443] Pemberton wrote that the desire after knowledge
of Newtonianism "is by nothing more fully illustrated, than
by the inclination of men to gain an acquaintance with the operations of nature; which disposition to enquire after the causes of
things is so general, that all men of letters, I believe, find themselves influenced by it." [444] Through the sublimated mathematics of the *Principia*, Pemberton observed, "the similitude found
in all parts of the universe makes it undoubted, that the whole
is governed by one supreme being, to whom the original is
owing of the frame of nature, which evidently is the effect of
choice and design." [445] To what extent Franklin later gave evidence of his knowledge of Newtonian speculation we shall
further discover in his *Articles of Belief*.

He returned in the summer of 1726 on the *Berkshire* to Philadelphia with Mr. Denham, a sweetly reasonable Quaker. [446]

[443] Quoted in C. S. Duncan, *op. cit.*, 16. See Desaguliers's *A System
of Experimental Philosophy, Prov'd by Mechanicks* . . . (London, 1719),
and his *The Newtonian System of the World, The Best Model of Government: An Allegorical Poem* (Westminster, 1728). The popularizers of
Newton were legion: see especially Watts, Derham, Ray, Huygens,
Blackmore, Locke, Thomson, Shaftesbury, S. Clarke, Whiston, Keill,
Maclaurin.
[444] *A View of Sir Isaac Newton's Philosophy* (London, 1728), 2–3.
[445] *Ibid.*, 405. Cf. also 13, 18, 181, 406.
[446] Not to be neglected in a summary of the factors influencing Franklin
during his youth is Quakerism. Taught in Boston to suspect the Quakers,
in Philadelphia in the midst of their stronghold he came soon, one may
imagine, to have a sympathetic regard for them. Quakerism, in its
antagonism towards sacraments and ceremonies, in its emphasis on the
priesthood of every man and the right of private judgment, in its strenuous
effort to promote fellow-service, was congenial to the young printer,
reacting against Presbyterianism. Like the radical thought of the age,
Quakerism refused first place to scriptural revelation, which became
secondary to the light within, the dictates of one's heart. Often, we may
suspect, the light within was blended with the concept in deism, that
regardless of the promptings of scripture, each man has within him a
natural sense which enables him to apprehend the truths of nature. The
effort of deism to simplify religion was historically shared by Quakerism.
During the years we have under consideration Franklin was endeavoring
to make a simple worship out of the subtle theology which had been
offered him during his early years. Presbyterianism had frowned upon a
covenant of works; Quakerism attempted to express its covenant with God
in terms of human kindliness, fellowship, and service.

During this journey he wrote his *Journal of a Voyage from London to Philadelphia*, indicating a virtuoso's interest in all novel phenomena of nature. In Philadelphia he worked for Denham, then Keimer, and finally established his own printing house in 1728, a year after founding the Junto,[447] and the year of his *Articles of Belief*. By this time, Franklin, like Hume, wearied of metaphysics. Commonly this creed has been described as illustrating the deism of Lord Herbert of Cherbury. It is true that Franklin admits a God who ought to be worshipped,

[447] It would be interesting to know if M. Faÿ is able to document his statement that the Junto "had Masonic leanings" ("Learned Societies in Europe and America in the Eighteenth Century," *American Historical Review*, XXXVII, 258 [1932]). R. F. Gould (*The History of Freemasonry*, London, 1887, III, 424) conjectures whether where was a lodge in Boston as early as 1720 but can offer no evidence of a real history of Masonry in the colonies until 1730, when colonial Masonry "may be said to have its commencement." Chroniclers of Franklin's Masonic career have found no documentary evidence of his affiliation with Masonry until February, 1731, when he entered St. John's Lodge. See J. F. Sachse, *Benjamin Franklin as a Free Mason;* J. H. Tatsch, *Freemasonry in the Thirteen Colonies* (New York, 1924); *Early Newspaper Accounts of Free Masonry in Pennsylvania, England, Ireland, and Scotland. From 1730 to 1750 by Dr. Benjamin Franklin.* Reprinted from Franklin's *Pennsylvania Gazette* (Philadelphia, 1886); *Masonic Letters of Benjamin Franklin of Philadelphia to H. Price of Boston*, ed. by C. P. MacCalla (Philadelphia, 1888); M. M. Johnson, *The Beginnings of Freemasonry in America* (New York, 1924). See "Prefatory Note" in W. B. Loewy's reprint of Anderson's *Constitutions* (a reprint of Franklin's imprint of 1734) in *Publications of the Masonic Historical Society of New York*, No. 3 (New York, 1905). Arriving in London only seven years after the inauguration of the Grand Lodge, Franklin could hardly have been unaware of the broader speculations of Masonry. In London only a year after Anderson's *Constitutions* were printed (in 1723), he may conceivably have read the volume.

Stressing toleration, the universality of natural religion, morality rather than theology, reason rather than faith, Masonry could easily have augmented these ideas as they were latent or already developed in Franklin's mind. Scholars have yet to work out the extent to which Freemasonry, yokefellow of deism, reinforced free thought and was one of the subversive forces breaking down colonial orthodoxy. B. Faÿ's *Revolution and Freemasonry, 1680–1800* neglects non-political influences of Freemasonry.

Although there is no evidence that Franklin as early as 1728 read such works (popular in the colonies) as De Ramsay's *The Travels of Cyrus* and Rowe's translation of *The Golden Sayings of Pythagoras*, the manner in which oriental lore augmented science and Masonry in fostering deism is an intriguing problem in eighteenth-century colonial letters.

the chief parts of worship being the cultivation of virtue and piety; but there is no suggestion of Lord Herbert's fourth and fifth dogmas, that sin must be atoned for by repentance, and that punishment and rewards follow this life. His reaction against Calvinism may be shown in his failure to include reference to scripture, the experience of faith, and the triune godhead presided over by the redeemer Christ. As a deist he accepted "one supreme, most perfect Being." This Deity is the "Author and Father of the Gods themselves." "Infinite and incomprehensible," He has created many gods, each having "made for himself one glorious Sun, attended with a beautiful and admirable System of Planets." Franklin offered his adoration to that "Wise and Good God, who is the author and owner of our System." It is conventional to suggest that his interest in the plurality of worlds and gods should be traced to Plato's *Timaeus*.[448] In the absence of any conclusive evidence concerning Franklin's study of Plato, and in view of his profound awareness of contemporary scientific and philosophical thought, it seems more reasonable to see the source of this idea in the thought of his own age. Let us remember that with the growth of the heliocentric cosmology there resulted a vast expanse of the unknown, bound to intrigue the speculations of the philosophers of the age. We know that Ray, Fénelon, Blackmore, Huygens, Fontenelle, Shaftesbury, Locke, and Newton all wondered about the plurality of worlds and gods.

In company with the supernatural rationalists and deists, Franklin exalted Reason as the experience through which God is discovered and known. Through Reason he is "capable of observing his Wisdom in the Creation." With Newtonian zeal, upon observing "the glorious Sun, with his attending Worlds," he saw the Deity responsible first for imparting "their prodigious motion," and second for maintaining "the wondrous Laws by

[448] See I. W. Riley, *op. cit.*, 249. Also see C. M. Walsh, "Franklin and Plato," *Open Court*, XX, 129 ff.

which they move." As we have seen above, this argument from the design of creation to a Creator was one of the most influential and popular of the impacts of Newtonian physics. Like Fénelon, Blackmore, and Ray, whom he read and recommended that others read,[449] Franklin exclaimed:

Thy Wisdom, thy Power, and thy Goodness are everywhere clearly seen; in the air and in the water, in the Heaven and on the Earth; Thou providest for the various winged Fowl, and the innumerable Inhabitants of the Water; thou givest Cold and Heat, Rain and Sunshine, in their Season, [et cetera].

In addition to the works mentioned above which aided Franklin in arriving at a natural religion, it is certain that his views and even idiom received stout reinforcement from such a passage as follows from Ray's classic work:

There is no greater, at least no more palpable and convincing argument of the existence of a Deity, than the admirable act and wisdom that discovers itself in the make and constitution, the order and disposition, the ends and uses of all the parts and members of this stately fabric of heaven and earth; for if in the works of art . . . a curious edifice or machine, counsel, design, and direction to an end appearing in the whole frame, and in all the several pieces of it, do necessarily infer the being and operation of some intelligent architect or engineer, why shall not also in the works of nature, that grandeur and magnificence, that excellent contrivance for beauty, order, use &c. which is observable in them, wherein they do as much transcend the effects of human art as infinite power and wisdom exceeds finite, infer the existence and efficacy of an omnipotent and all-wise Creator? [450]

Then he directly referred to the Archbishop of Cambray's *Traité de l'existence et des attributs de Dieu*. Oliver Elton observes

---

[449] See *Writings*, II, 95–6 (1728).
[450] John Ray's *The Wisdom of God Manifested in the Works of the Creation* (London, 1827; first ed. 1691), 31–2.

that this work "with its appeal to popular science, is the chief counterpart in France to the 'physico-theology' current at the time in England." [451] From the skeleton of the smallest animal, "the bones, the tendons, the veins, the arteries, the nerves, the muscles, which compose the body of a single man" [452] to "this vaulted sky" which turns "around so regularly," [453] all show "the infinite skill of its Author." [454] Although Fénelon is applying Cartesian physics, here Descartes reinforced Newtonianism; like Newton, Fénelon argued that cosmic motion is ordered by "immutable laws," so "constant and so salutary." Blackmore's *Creation, a Philosophical Poem* (1712), aiming to demonstrate "the existence of a God from the marks of wisdom, design, contrivance, and the choice of ends and means, which appear in the universe" [455] also furnished additional sanction for Franklin's emphasis on the wondrous laws of the creation and the discovery of the Deity in his Work. Like James Thomson, Blackmore seeks to show how

> The long coherent chain of things we find
> Leads to a Cause Supreme, a wise Creating Mind.[456]

In revolt against the contractile elements in Calvinism, Franklin believed that God "is not offended, when he sees his Children solace themselves in any manner of pleasant exercises and Innocent Delights." [457] In his *Articles of Belief* Franklin retains from his *Dissertation* his a priori concept of the Deity

[451] *The Augustan Age*, 54–5.
[452] *Selections from the Writings of Fénelon*, ed. by Mrs. Follen (Boston, 1861), 51–2.
[453] *Ibid.*, 59.   [454] *Ibid.*, 47.
[455] In Preface to *The Works of the British Poets*, ed. by R. Anderson (London, 1795), 592. Since Franklin frequented Batson's in Cornhill, it is possible that through Dr. Pemberton he might have met Sir R. Blackmore, who was one of its best patrons.
[456] *Ibid.*, 611.
[457] See Ray, *op. cit.*, 143: "I persuade myself, that the beautiful and gracious Author of man's being and faculties, and all things else, delights in the beauty of his creation, and is well pleased with the industry of man, in adorning the earth with beautiful cities and castles. . . ."

as a creator and sustainer of "Wondrous Laws," immutable and beneficent. To the depersonalized First Mover, however, he has added "some of those Passions he has planted in us," and he suggests furthermore that the Deity is mildly providential. A maker of systematic, if inhuman, metaphysics in the *Dissertation*, the author of the *Articles*, in spite of the superficial and embryonic metaphysics, succeeds better in making himself at home in his world. To this embryonic religion (linked with Franklin's obsession with the plurality of worlds and gods—of no real significance save to indicate picturesquely the extent to which he had, with the scientists of his age, extended the limits of the physical universe) Franklin welded a pattern of ethics, prudential but stern.

Mr. Hefelbower's description of the growth of free thought might appropriately be applied to Franklin's *Articles:* "As the supernatural waned in radical Deism, the ethical grew in importance, until religion was but a moral system on a theistic background." [458] Although the metaphysical portions of this work are far too neighborly and casual to be inspiring and provocative of saintliness, the ethical conclusions (would that they were uttered less consciously and complacently!) are worthy of the introspective force of New England's stern mind, of the classic tradition of Socrates and Aristotle, and of England's unbending emphasis on the middle way.[459] One could learn from the *Articles* how to be just, if he did not discover what is meant by the beauty of holiness. In 1728 Franklin, though bewildered by the tenuousness of metaphysics, based his religion on the "everlasting tables of right reason," plumbing the "mighty volumes of visible nature." He was thus our pioneer scientific deist, who discovered his chief sanction in popularized Newtonian physics.

[458] *The Relation of John Locke to English Deism*, 133.
[459] See P. S. Wood, "Native Elements in English Neo-Classicism," *Modern Philology*, XXIV, 201–8 (Nov., 1926).

Following Franklin's formal profession of deism buttressed by
Newtonian science in 1728, one must depend on scattered references to plot the persistence of his philosophic ideology. His
Dialogues between Philocles and Horatio (1730), borrowed [460]
from Shaftesbury's *The Moralists*, suggest that his *moral* speculations were dual and not reconciled; he seems torn between
humanitarian compassion and the self-development of the individual, unable to decide which is the nobler good. One may
observe that this moral bifurcation was inveterate in Franklin's
mind, never resolving itself into a fondness for the idea that
human nature is inexorably the product of institutions and outward social forms. *A Witch Trial at Mount Holly* suggests
that he felt free to handle scriptures with Aristophanic levity.
His intellectual conviction of a matchless physical harmony, as
yet unmatched in the world by a corresponding moral harmony,
is joyously seen in *Preface to Poor Richard, 1735:*

Whatever may be the Musick of the Spheres, how great
soever the Harmony of the Stars, 'tis certain there is no Harmony among the Stargazers; but they are perpetually growling
and snarling at one another like strange Curs. . . . [461]

Even Polly Baker is made to appeal to "nature and nature's
God," [462] discovering in her bastard children the Deity's "divine
skill and admirable workmanship in the formation of their
bodies." In *Proposals Relating to the Education of Youth in
Pensilvania* (1749) Franklin remarked in a note on Natural
Philosophy that "Proper Books may be, Ray's *Wisdom of
God in the Creation*, Derham's *Physico-Theology*, [Pluche's?]
Spectacle de la Nature, &c."[463] *Poor Richard*, in addition to prog-
nostications of weather, survey of roads, Rabelaisian wit, and

[460] See C. E. Jorgenson's "The Source of Benjamin Franklin's Dialogues between Philocles and Horatio (1730)," *American Literature*, VI,
337–9 (Nov., 1934).

[461] *Writings*, II, 203.   [462] *Ibid.*, II, 467.

[463] Facsimile reprint by W. Pepper (Philadelphia, 1931), 27 note.

aphoristic wisdom, was a popular vehicle for the diffusion of a Newtonianism bordering on a mild form of deism.[464]

Since Franklin's interest in science is too commonly discussed as if his research were synonymous with a tinkering and utilitarian inventiveness, it is pertinent to inquire in how far it was at least partially (or even integrally) the result of his philosophic acceptance of Newtonianism. Since his philosophic rationale preceded his activities in science, it will not do to suggest that his interest in science was responsible for his scientific deism. He wrote (August 15, 1745) to Cadwallader Colden, who was receptive to Newtonianism, that he [Franklin] "ought to *study* the sciences" in which hitherto he had merely dabbled.[465] Then follow his electrical experiments. In one of his famous letters on the properties and effects of electricity (sent to Peter Collinson, July 29, 1750) he allowed that the principle of repulsion "affords another occasion of adoring that wisdom which has made all things by weight and measure!"[466] Investigating—like a Newton—nature's *laws*, Franklin at first hand added to his philosophic assurance of the existence of a Deity, observable in the physical order.

In 1739 Franklin met Reverend George Whitefield, whose sermons and journals he printed while the evangelist remained in the colonies.[467] He first angled public opinion through the *Pennsylvania Gazette*, promising to print Whitefield's pieces "if I find sufficient Encouragement."[468] The *Pennsylvania Gazette* piously hoped that Whitefield's heavenly discourses would be ever remembered: "May the Impression on all our Souls remain, to the Honour of God, both in Ministers and People!"[469]

---

[464] See *Almanac* for 1753.   [465] *Writings*, II, 288.
[466] *Ibid.*, II, 429. See also II, 434-5.   [467] See W. J. Campbell, *op. cit.*
[468] No. 570 (Nov. 15, 1739), No. 565 (Oct. 11, 1739), and No. 628 (Dec. 25, 1740), for example, are loaded with tributes to the effective preaching and contagious saintliness of this preacher of the Great Awakening.
[469] No. 618 (Oct. 16, 1740). Franklin's *General Magazine and Historical Chronicle* contains many Whitefield references.

As editor (perhaps even writer of some of those notices) Franklin must have squirmed in praising the activities of one who daily cast all deists in hell! But it should be observed that if Franklin could not accept Methodistic zeal, he loved Whitefield, the man.[470] Even so did Whitefield regard Franklin, the man and printer—though not the scientific deist. Waiting to embark for England in 1740, Whitefield wrote to Franklin from Reedy Island: "Dear Sir, adieu! I do not despair of your seeing the reasonableness of Christianity. Apply to God; be willing to do the Divine Will, and you shall know it." [471] Twelve years later Whitefield wrote to his printer-deist friend: "I find that you grow more and more famous in the learned world. As you have made a pretty considerable progress in the mysteries of electricity, I would now humbly recommend to your diligent unprejudiced pursuit and study the mysteries of the new birth." [472] When troops had been sent to Boston, Franklin wrote a letter to Whitefield (after January 21, 1768) which offers a significant clue for estimating Franklin's philosophy: "I *see* with you that our affairs are not well managed by our rulers here below; I wish I could *believe* with you, that they are well attended to by those above; I rather suspect, from certain circumstances, that though the general government of the universe is well administered, our particular little affairs are perhaps below notice, and left to take the chance of human prudence or imprudence, as either may happen to be uppermost. It is, however, an uncomfortable thought, and I leave it." [473] Whitefield "endorsed his friend's letter with the words, '*Uncomfortable* indeed! and blessed be God, *unscriptural!*' " [474] If in 1786 Frank-

---

[470] *Writings*, II, 316. In general, emotional Methodism was not responsive to science as a basis for rationalistic deism, although to a considerable extent Methodism and deism synchronized in their endeavor to relieve social suffering. See U. Lee's able study, *The Historical Backgrounds of Early Methodist Enthusiasm* (New York, 1931).

[471] Rev. L. Tyerman, *Life of the Reverend George Whitefield* (London, 1876), I, 439.

[472] *Ibid.*, II, 283–4.   [473] *Ibid.*, II, 540–1.   [474] *Ibid.*, II, 541.

lin wrote to an unknown correspondent (perhaps Tom Paine?) [475]
that any arguments "against the Doctrines of a particular
Providence" strike "at the Foundation of all Religion," [476] he also
had written not long before that "the Dispensations of Providence in this World puzzle my weak Reason." [477] Beneath the
taciturn and allegedly complacent, imperturbable Franklin
there is apparent a haunting inquietude. Never dead to his
Calvinist heritage, he sought to establish a providential relationship between the Deity and man's fortunes, not a little chilled
in the presence of the virtually depersonalized Deity of the
Enlightenment. If Calvin's God was wrathful, he was providential; his own Deity, if benevolent and omnipotent, seemed
strangely remote from the ken of man's moral experience.
Science had shown him a Deity existing at the head of a fagot of
immutable laws. If this Creator was picturesquely unlike the
fickle gods of Olympus, he was strangely like them to the
extent that he seemed to exist apart from man's moral nature.
When he wrote to his friend, the Bishop of St. Asaph,
"It seems my Fate constantly to wish for Repose, and never
to obtain it," [478] was he in part longing for the retirement when
he would be able to resolve his doubts as to the workings of
Providence?

M. Marbois, discussing Franklin's religion with John Adams,
quietly noted that "Mr. Franklin adores only great Nature." [479]
Joseph Priestley "lamented that a man of Dr. Franklin's general
good character and great influence should have been an unbeliever in Christianity, and also have done so much as he did to

---

[475] See H. H. Clark's "An Historical Interpretation of Thomas Paine's
Religion," *University of California Chronicle*, XXXV, 56–87 (Jan., 1933),
and "Toward a Reinterpretation of Thomas Paine," *American Literature*,
V, 133–45 (May, 1933).

[476] *Writings*, IX, 520.

[477] *Ibid.*, VIII, 561. See also IX, 506.

[478] Aug. 22, 1784; unpublished letter in W. S. Mason Collection. Also
see *Writings*, VIII, 113; IX, 476, 488, 621.

[479] I. W. Riley, *American Thought from Puritanism to Pragmatism*, 76.

make others unbelievers." [480] This evidence appears untrustworthy in light of his diffident attitude toward church attendance,
even toward scriptures, as it may be discovered in his collected
works. [481] Even if he did not feel the desire to attend formal services, he seemed, like Voltaire, to feel that they were salutary, if
only to furnish the *canaille* with the will to obey authority. In
1751 Franklin's mother, Abiah Franklin, wrote to her son: "I
hope you will look up to God, and thank Him for all His good providences towards you." [482] If he were unable to understand God's
providences, it was certain that he did not seek to disturb
others by calling the concept of a providential deity into question.

In England and France Franklin was revered as the answer
to the Enlightenment's prayer for the ideal philosopher-scien-
tist. Sir John Pringle, [483] one of his warmest friends, in a Royal
Society lecture in honor of Maskelyne, might well have been
describing Franklin's place in eighteenth-century science when
he said: "As much then remains to be explored in the celestial
regions, you [Maskelyne] are encouraged, Sir, by what has been
already attained, to persevere in these hallowed labours, from
which have been derived the greatest improvements in the most
useful arts, and the loudest declarations of the power, the wisdom, and the goodness of the Supreme Architect in the Spacious
and beautiful fabric of the world." [484] To his age Franklin was
"that judicious philosopher," judicious and "enlightened" to
the extent that his experiments showed how men "may per-

[480] Parton, *op. cit.*, I, 546.

[481] He admonished Deborah, his wife, that she "should go oftener to
Church" (*Writings*, IV, 202), and his daughter, Sarah, "Go constantly to
Church, whoever preaches" (*ibid.*, IV, 287).

[482] *Letters to Benjamin Franklin from His Family and Friends, 1751–
1790* (New York, 1859), 10.

[483] Franklin's English friends, Dr. Richard Price, Joseph Priestley, Rev.
David Williams, Dr. John Fothergill, Peter Collinson, Sir Joseph Banks,
Jonathan Shipley, Lord Kames, Sir William Jones, et cetera, though not
all deists, found Newtonian science useful in augmenting their philosophies.

[484] *A Discourse . . .* (London, 1775), 33. For background material on
the history of this concept see L. E. Hicks, *A Critique of Design-Arguments*
(New York, 1883).

ceive not only the direction of Divine Wisdom, but the *goodness* of Providence towards mankind, in having so admirably settled all things in the sublime arrangement of the world, that it should be in the power of men to secure themselves and their habitations against the dire effects of lightning." [485] Turgot's famous epigram on Franklin, the republican-deist, that he snatched sceptres from kings and lightning from the heavens, in part expressed the extent to which the French public conceived of Franklin, the scientist, as detracting from the terror in the cosmos, hence making their reasonable world more habitable.[486] In the popular mind death-dealing lightning had been the visible symbol and proof of Calvin's wrathful and capricious Jehovah. Franklin's dramatic and widely popularized proof that even lightning's secrets were not past finding out, that it acted according to immutable laws and could be made man's captive and menial slave, no doubt had a powerful influence in encouraging the great untheological public to become ultimately more receptive to deism. If Franklin was apotheosized as the apostle of liberty, he was no less sanctified as a "Modern Prometheus." In his own words, he saw science as freeing man "from vain Terrors." [487] To Condorcet, his friend and disciple, Franklin was one who "was enabled to wield a power sufficient to disarm the wrath of Heaven." [488]

He expressed his creed just before his death in the often-quoted letter to Ezra Stiles.[489] Bearing in mind his inveterate scientific deism, we are not surprised that his religion is one created apart from Christian scripture, that Jesus is the conventional, amiable philosopher, respected but not worshipped by

[485] N. Meredith, *Considerations on the Utility of Conductors for Lightning* . . . (London, 1789), 44–5. See especially the characteristic notice in *Monthly Review* . . . , XLII (London, 1770), 199–210, 298–308.

[486] For references see B. Faÿ, *The Revolutionary Spirit in France and America;* E. E. Hale and E. E. Hale, Jr., *Franklin in France;* L. Amiable, *Un loge maçonnique d'avant 1789.* . . .   [487] *Writings,* IX, 436.

[488] W. T. Franklin ed. of Franklin's *Writings* (London, 1818), I, 433.

[489] See similar expression in letter to Mme Brillon, cited in J. M. Stifler, *The Religion of Benjamin Franklin,* 55–6.

the Enlightenment. If he seems convinced in this letter that
God "governs" the universe "by his Providence," we have
seen above that his attitude toward the Deity's relation to man
and his world was anything but sure and free from disturbing
reflection. Convinced that the Deity "ought to be worshipped,"
he next observed "that the most acceptable service we render to
him is doing good to his other children." His a priori concept
of a benevolent Deity whose goodness is expressed in the harmony of the creation, in effect challenged him to attempt to
approximate this kindness in his relations with his fellow men.
Apart from provoking humanitarianism, primarily an ethical
experience guided not by sentimentality but by reason and
practicality, Franklin's natural religion—like deism in general—failed, as scriptural religion does not, to establish a
union between theology, the religious life, and ethical behavior.
It must be seen that Franklin had no confidence in achiev-
ing the good life through mere fellow-service: he continually
urged man to conquer passion through reason, seeming to covet
pagan sobriety more than he did the satisfaction of having aided
man to achieve greater physical ease. If he felt that "to relieve
the misfortunes of our fellow creatures is concurring with the
Deity; it is godlike," [490] he warned against helping those who
had failed to help themselves, implying that the inner growth of
the individual is more significant than his outward charity to
others. Whatever be the ultimate resolution of these antithetic
principles, we see that his humanitarianism was the offspring
of his a priori conceived Deity, augmented by his experiments
in science which led to discovery of nature's laws. His emphasis
on the inward and vertical growth of the individual toward
perfection, on the other hand, may be viewed as the expression
of the introspective force of his Puritan heritage and his knowledge, direct and indirect, of classical literature. As in the polarity
of his thoughts concerning Providence, so here we see that the

[490] *Writings*, III, 135.

modus operandi of his mind is explicable in terms of the interplay of the old and the new, Greek paganism (Socratic self-knowledge) and Christianity and the rationale of the Enlightenment.

Before he became an economist, a statesman, a man of letters, a scientist, he had embraced scientific deism, primarily impelled by Newtonianism. We have observed that it is not improbable that his agrarianism, emphasis on free trade, and tendency toward laissez faire were partially at least the result of his efforts to parallel in economics the harmony of the physical order. Likewise, his views on education were conditioned by his faith in intellectual progress, in the might of Reason, which in turn was in part the result of his scientific deism. Then too, it may well be suggested that his theories of rhetoric were to some degree the result of his rationalistic and scientific habits of mind. We have also seen that his scientific deism was among the motivating factors of his belief in natural rights, which, coupled with his empirical awareness of concrete economic and political abuses issuing from monarchy and imperialistic parliamentarians, made him alive to the sovereignty of the people in their demands for civil and political liberty. This introduction, it is hoped, has made apparent the fact that the growth of Franklin's mind was a complex matter and that it was moulded by a vast multitude of often diverse influences, no one of which alone completely "explains" him. Puritanism, classicism, and neoclassicism were all important influences. Yet perhaps the *modus operandi* of this myriad-minded colonial, this provincial Leonardo, is best explained in reference to the thought pattern of scientific deism. To see the reflection of Newton and his progeny in Franklin's activities, be they economic, political, literary, or philosophical, lends a compelling organic unity to the several sides of his genius, heretofore seen as unrelated. Franklin's mind represents an intellectual coherence—an imperfect counterpart to the physical harmony of the Newtonian order, of which all through his life he was a disciple.

CHRONOLOGICAL TABLE

1706. Benjamin Franklin born in Boston, January 17 (January 6, 1705, O. S.).

1714–16. After a year in Boston Grammar School is sent to learn writing and arithmetic in school kept by George Brownell, from which, after a year, he is taken to assist his father, Josiah, a candlemaker.

1717. James Franklin returns from England, following apprenticeship as printer.

1718. Benjamin is apprenticed to brother James.

1718–23. Period of assiduous reading in Anthony Collins, Shaftesbury, Locke, Addison and Steele, Cotton Mather, Bunyan, Defoe, etc.

1719. Writes and hawks ballads of the "Grub-Street" style, "The Lighthouse Tragedy" and "The Taking of Teach the Pirate."

1721–23. Aids brother in publishing the *New England Courant*. During 1722–23 in charge of paper after James is declared objectionable by the authorities.

1722. His *Dogood Papers* printed anonymously in the *New England Courant*.

1723. Breaks his indentures and leaves for New York; eventually arrives in Philadelphia.

1723–24. Employed by Samuel Keimer, a printer in Philadelphia.

1724. Visits Cotton Mather and Governor Burnet (New York). Meets James Ralph, Grub-Street pamphleteer, historian, and poet in the Thomson tradition. Patronized by Governor Keith. Leaves for London in November on the *London-Hope* to buy type, etc., for printing shop to be set up in his behalf by Keith. Upon arrival he and Ralph take lodgings in Little Britain.

1725–26. Employed in Palmer's and Watts's printing houses.

1725. Publishes *A Dissertation on Liberty and Necessity, Pleasure and Pain*. One result of this is acquaintance with Lyons, author of *The Infallibility of Human Judgement*. Through him Franklin meets Bernard Mandeville and Dr. Henry Pemberton, who is preparing a third edition of Sir Isaac Newton's *Principia*. Is received by Sir Hans Sloane in Bloomsbury Square. Conceives of setting up a swimming school in London.

1726. On July 21, with Mr. Denham, merchant and Quaker, leaves for Philadelphia on the *Berkshire*. Between July 22 and October 11 writes *Journal of a Voyage from London to Philadelphia*. Employed by Denham until latter's death in 1727.

1727. Ill of pleurisy and composes his epitaph. After recovery returns to Keimer's printing house. Forms his Junto club. Employed in Burlington, New Jersey, on a job of printing paper money.

1728. Forms partnership with Hugh Meredith. Writes *Articles of Belief and Acts of Religion*, and *Rules for a Club*— his Junto club "Constitution."

1729. Buys Keimer's *The Universal Instructor in all Arts and Sciences: and Pennsylvania Gazette* (begun December 24, 1728). Changes name to *Pennsylvania Gazette*, first issue, XL, September 25–October 2, 1729. (Published by Franklin until 1748; by Franklin and David Hall from 1748 to 1766, after which Hall, until his death, and others publish it until 1815.) Contributes to *American Weekly Mercury* six papers of *The Busy-Body*, February 4, 1729– March 27, 1729. Writes and prints *A Modest Enquiry into the Nature and Necessity of a Paper Currency*.

1730. Appointed Public Printer by Pennsylvania Assembly (incumbent until 1764). Partnership with Meredith dissolved. Marries Deborah Read (Mrs. Rogers). Prints in *Pennsylvania Gazette* his *Dialogues between Philocles and Horatio*.

1731. First public venture: founds the Philadelphia Library Company, first subscription library in America. Begins partnership with Thomas Whitemarsh, Charleston, S. C. (1732, publishes *South Carolina Gazette*.) Begins Masonic affiliations: enters St. John's Lodge in February. William Franklin born.

1732. Begins *Poor Richard's Almanack* (for 1733). His son Francis Folger Franklin born (dies of smallpox in 1736). Elected junior grand warden of St. John's Lodge.

1733. Begins to study languages, French, Italian, Spanish, and continues Latin.

1734. Elected grand master of Masons of Pennsylvania for 1734–35. Reprints Anderson's *Constitutions*, first Masonic book printed in America.

1735. Writes and prints three pamphlets in defense of Rev. Mr. Hemphill. Prints, in the *Pennsylvania Gazette*, *Protection of Towns from Fire*. Secretary of St. John's Lodge until 1738. Writes introduction for and prints Logan's *Cato's Moral Distiches*, first classic translated and printed in the colonies.

1736. Establishes the Union Fire Company, the first in Philadelphia. Chosen clerk of the Pennsylvania General Assembly.

1737. Appointed postmaster of Philadelphia (incumbent until 1753); also justice of the peace.

1739. Beginning of friendship with the Reverend George Whitefield.

1740. Announces (November 13) *The General Magazine and Historical Chronicle*.

1741. Six issues (January–June) of this magazine (the first planned and the second issued in the colonies). With J. Parker establishes a printing house in New York.

1742. Invents Franklin open stove.

1743. *A Proposal for Promoting Useful Knowledge among the British Plantations in America* (circular letter sent to his friends).

1744. Establishes the American Philosophical Society and becomes its first secretary. Daughter Sarah born. *An Account of the New Invented Pennsylvanian Fire-places.*

Writes preface to and prints Logan's translation of Cicero's *Cato Major*. Reprints Richardson's *Pamela*. Father dies.

1746. *Reflections on Courtship and Marriage*, first of his writings reprinted in Europe. Peter Collinson sends a Leyden vial as gift to Library Company of Philadelphia. Having witnessed Dr. Spence's experiments, Franklin now begins his study of electricity.

1747. *Plain Truth: or, Serious Considerations on the Present State of the City of Philadelphia, and Province of Pennsylvania.*

1748. Withdraws from active service in his printing and bookselling house (Franklin and Hall). *Advice to a Young Tradesman.* Chosen member of the Council of Philadelphia.

1749. Appointed provincial grand master of colonial Masons (through 1750). *Proposals Relating to the Education of Youth in Pensilvania.* Founds academy which later develops into University of Pennsylvania. Reprints Bolingbroke's *On the Spirit of Patriotism.*

1750. Appointed as one of the commissioners to make treaty with the Indians at Carlisle.

1751. *Experiments and Observations on Electricity, made at Philadelphia in America, By Mr. Benjamin Franklin, and Communicated in several Letters to Mr. P. Collinson, of London, F. R. S.* (London.) *Idea of the English School, Sketch'd out for the Consideration of the Trustees of the Philadelphia Academy.* Member of Assembly from Philadelphia (incumbent until 1764). *Observations Concerning the Increase of Mankind, Peopling of Countries, Etc.* Aids Dr. Bond to establish Pennsylvania hospital.

1752. Collinson edition of Franklin's works translated into French. Alleged kite experiment proves identity of lightning and electricity. Invents lightning rod; in September raises one over his own house. Mother dies. Aids in establishing the first fire insurance company in the colonies.

1753. Appointed (jointly with William Hunter) deputy postmaster general of North America Post, a position he held
until 1774. Makes ten-weeks' survey of roads and post
offices in northern colonies. Abbé Nollet attacks Franklin in *Lettres sur l'électricité* (Paris). Beccaria defends
Franklin's electrical theories against Abbé Nollet. Receives M. A. from Harvard and from Yale. Receives Sir
Godfrey Copley medal from the Royal Society.

1754. Proposes Albany Plan of Union. Second edition of
Experiments and Observations on Electricity.

1755. *An Act for the Better Ordering and Regulating such as are
Willing and Desirous to be United for Military Purposes
within the Province of Pennsylvania. A Dialogue Between
X, Y, & Z, concerning the Present State of Affairs in
Pennsylvania.* Aids General Braddock in getting sup-
plies and transportation.

1756. Supervises construction of forts in province of Pennsyl-
vania (a task begun in 1755). Chosen Fellow of the
Royal Society of London. Chosen a member of the
London Society of Arts. *Plan for Settling the Western
Colonies in North America, with Reasons for the Plan.*
M. D'Alibard's edition of Franklin's electrical experi-
ments (French translation). Receives M. A. from Wil-
liam and Mary College.

1757. Appointed colonial agent for Province of Pennsylvania
(arrives in London July 26). *The Way to Wealth* (for
1758). (In 1889 Ford noted: "Seventy editions of it have
been printed in English, fifty-six in French, eleven in
German, and nine in Italian. It has been translated into
Spanish, Danish, Swedish, Welsh, Polish, Gaelic, Rus-
sian, Bohemian, Dutch, Catalan, Chinese, Modern Greek
and Phonetic writing. It has been printed at least four
hundred times, and is today as popular as ever.")

1759. Receives Doctor of Laws degree from University of St.
Andrews. September 5, made burgess and guild-brother
of Edinburgh. *An Historical Review of the Constitution
and Government of Pennsylvania.* (See Ford, pp. 110–111,

where he suggests that this "must still be treated as from Franklin's pen.") *Parable against Persecution*. Meets Adam Smith, Hume, Lord Kames, etc., in home of Dr. Robertson at Edinburgh. Makes many electrical experiments. Chosen honorary member of Philosophical Society of Edinburgh.

1760. Provincial grand master of Pennsylvania Masons. *The Interest of Great Britain Considered with Regard to Her Colonies*. Elected to society of Dr. Bray's Associates. (Corresponding member until 1790.) Successful close of his issue with the proprietaries.

1761. Tour of Holland and Belgium.

1762. Receives degree of Doctor of Civil Law from Oxford. Leaves England in August, arrives in America in October.

1763. Travels through colonies to inspect and regulate post offices.

1764. Appointed agent for Province of Pennsylvania to petition king for change from proprietary to royal government. Leaves for London in November. *Cool Thoughts on the Present Situation of Our Public Affairs. A Narrative of the Late Massacres in Lancaster County. Preface to the Speech of Joseph Galloway, Esq*.

1765. Presents Grenville with resolution of Pennsylvania Assembly against Stamp Act.

1766. Examined in House of Commons relative to repeal of the Stamp Act. *Physical and Meteorological Observations*. With Sir John Pringle visits Germany and Holland (June–August). Chosen foreign member of the Royal Society of Sciences, Göttingen.

1767. With Sir John Pringle visits France (August 28–October 8). Meets French Physiocrats. *Remarks and Facts Concerning American Paper Money*.

1768. Preface to *Letters from a Farmer in Pennsylvania* (J. Dickinson). *A Scheme for a New Alphabet and Reformed Mode of Spelling. Causes of the American Discontents before 1768. Art of Swimming*. Appointed London agent for colony of Georgia.

1769. Visits France (July–August). Appointed New Jersey agent in London. Elected first president of the American Philosophical Society.

1770. Appointed London agent for Massachusetts Assembly.

1771. Begins *Autobiography* (from 1706 to 1731) while visiting the Bishop of St. Asaph at Twyford. Three-months' tour of Ireland and Scotland. Entertained by Hume and Lord Kames. Chosen corresponding member of Learned Society of Sciences, Rotterdam.

1772. Chosen foreign member of Royal Academy of Sciences of Paris.

1773. *Abridgement of the Book of Common Prayer* (with Sir Francis Dashwood). *Rules by Which a Great Empire May Be Reduced to a Small One*. M. Barbeu Dubourg's edition of *Œuvres de M. Franklin*. Sends Hutchinson-Oliver letters to Massachusetts.

1774. Examined by Wedderburn before the Privy Council (January 29) in regard to the Hutchinson-Oliver correspondence. Contributes notes to George Whately's second edition of *Principles of Trade*. Dismissed as deputy postmaster general of North America. Deborah Franklin dies December 19.

1775. First postmaster general under Confederation. Returns to America in May. Member of Philadelphia Committee of Safety. Chosen a delegate to second Continental Congress. *An Account of Negotiations in London for Effecting a Reconciliation between Great Britain and the American Colonies*. Appointed member of Committee of Secret Correspondence.

1776. A commissioner to Canada. Presides over Constitutional Convention of Pennsylvania. Appointed one of committee to frame Declaration of Independence. In September appointed one of three commissioners from Congress to the French court. Leaves Philadelphia October 27; reaches Paris December 21.

1777. Elected member of Loge des Neuf Sœurs. Chosen associate member of Royal Medical Society of Paris.

1778. Assists at initiation of Voltaire in Loge des Neuf Sœurs. Officiates at Masonic funeral service of Voltaire. Signs commercial treaty and alliance for mutual defense with France. *The Ephemera.* Altercation with Arthur Lee.

1779. Minister plenipotentiary to French court. *The Whistle. Morals of Chess.* B. Vaughan edits Franklin's *Political, Miscellaneous, and Philosophical Pieces.*

1780. *Dialogue between Franklin and the Gout.*

1781. Chosen Fellow of American Academy of Arts and Sciences: elected foreign member of Academy of Sciences, Letters, and Arts of Padua, for work in natural philosophy and politics. Appointed one of the peace commissioners to negotiate treaty of peace between England and United States.

1782. Elected Venerable of Loge des Neuf Sœurs.

1783. Signs treaty with Sweden. Prints *Constitutions of the United States.* Elected Honorary Fellow of the Royal Society of Edinburgh. Interest in balloons. Signs the Treaty of Paris with John Jay and John Adams.

1784. With Le Roy, Bailly, Guillotin, Lavoisier, and others, investigates Mesmer's animal magnetism (results in numerous pamphlet reports). *Remarks Concerning the Savages of North America. Advice to Such as Would Remove to America.* Chosen member of Royal Academy of History, Madrid. At Passy resumes work on *Autobiography,* beyond 1731.

1785. *Maritime Observations. On the Causes and Cure of Smoky Chimneys.* Signs treaty of amity and commerce with Prussia. Resigns as minister to French Court, and returns to Philadelphia. President of Council of Pennsylvania (incumbent for three years). Associate member of Academy of Sciences, Literature, and Arts of Lyons. Councillor for Philadelphia until 1788. Member of Philadelphia Society for the Promotion of Agriculture, and Royal Society of Physics, National History and Arts of Orleans, and honorary member of Manchester Literary and Philosophical Society.

1786. Chosen corresponding member of Society of Agriculture of Milan.

1787. President of the Pennsylvania Society for the Abolition of Slavery (incumbent until death). Pennsylvania delegate to Constitutional Convention. Chosen honorary member of Medical Society of London. Aids in establishing the Society for Political Enquiry; elected its first president.

1788. At Philadelphia works on *Autobiography*, from 1731–1757.

1789. *Observations Relative to the Intentions of the Original Founders of the Academy in Philadelphia* and several papers in behalf of abolition of slavery. At Philadelphia resumes *Autobiography*, from 1757 to 1759. Chosen member of Imperial Academy of Sciences of St. Petersburg.

1790. Paper on the slave trade, *To the Editor of the Federal Gazette*, March 23. Dies, April 17, in Philadelphia.

SELECTED BIBLIOGRAPHY

The bibliography for this edition has been revised and brought up to date by C. E. Jorgenson.

I. WORKS

Only the most useful and historically significant editions are here listed. The student interested in other editions of Franklin's works, the publication of his separate pamphlets, his contributions to newspapers and periodicals, and his editorial activities should consult P. L. Ford's *Franklin Bibliography*. Many of these items are conveniently listed in *The Cambridge History of American Literature*, I, p. 442 ff.

The Papers of Benjamin Franklin. Volume I (January 6, 1706 through December 31, 1734). Leonard W. Labaree, Editor, Whitfield J. Bell, Jr., Associate Editor, Helen C. Boatfield and Helene H. Fineman, Assistant Editors. New Haven: 1959.
————. Volume 2 (January 1, 1735 through December 31, 1744). New Haven: 1960.
————. Volume 3 (January 1, 1745 through June 30, 1750). New Haven: 1961. (Projected as a 40 volume edition, published by Yale University Press, this will be definitive. In all aspects, it is a masterwork of editing and encyclopedic, bibliographic references.)
Experiments and Observations on Electricity, made at Philadelphia in America, By Mr. Benjamin Franklin, and Communicated in several Letters to P. Collinson, of London, F. R. S. London: 1751. (For various editions and translations of this and the supplementary letters added to first edition, consult Ford's *Bibliography*.)
Political, Miscellaneous, and Philosophical Pieces; ... Written by Benj. Franklin, LL. D. and F. R. S. ... Now first collected, With Explanatory Plates, Notes, ... [ed. by Benjamin Vaughan]. London: 1779. ("The work is ably performed, many pieces being for the first time printed as Franklin's; and contains valuable notes. But what gives a special value to this collection is that it is the only edition of Franklin's writings [other than his scientific], which was printed during his life time; was done with Franklin's knowledge and consent, and contains an 'errata' made by him for it" [Ford, p.

161]. Review in *Monthly Review*, LXII, pp. 199–210, 298–
308, describes his electrical experiments as constituting a
"principia" of electricity. See also Smyth, VII, pp. 410–13, for
Franklin's own opinion.)

*Mémoires de la vie privée de Benjamin Franklin, écrits par lui-
même, et adressés à son fils; suivis d'un précis historique de sa
vie politique, et de plusieurs pièces, relatives à ce père de la
liberté.* Paris: 1791. (First edition of Franklin's *Autobiography* to the year 1731; translation attributed to Dr. Jacques
Gibelin. "The remainder of his life is a translation from Wil-
mer's *Memoirs* of Franklin, with the most objectionable statements omitted" [Ford, p. 183]. For a succinct history of
Autobiography, editions, printing, translation, and fortunes of
the MS see Bigelow's introduction to *Autobiography*.)

*Memoirs of the Life and Writings of Benjamin Franklin, LL. D.
F. R. S. &c.... Written by himself to a late period, and con-
tinued to the time of his death, by his Grandson; William
Temple Franklin. Now first published from the original MSS.*
3 vols. London: 1818. (The standard collection, according to
A. H. Smyth, until Sparks's edition. Representative review in
Analectic Magazine, XI, pp. 449–84 [June, 1818].)

*The Works of Benjamin Franklin; containing several political
and historical tracts not included in any former edition, and
many letters official and private not hitherto published; with
notes and a life of the author,* by Jared Sparks. 10 vols. Boston: 1836–1840. (Although Sparks took undesirable editorial
liberties with the MSS, rephrasing, emending, and deleting,
this edition still possesses value for its notes and inclusion of
pieces which Smyth does not include, but which *may* have
been written by Franklin. Includes many valuable letters *to*
Franklin. For reviews see *North American Review*, LIX, p.
446, and LXXXIII, p. 402.)

*Autobiography of Benjamin Franklin. Edited from his Manu-
script, with Notes and an Introduction,* by John Bigelow.
Philadelphia: 1868. (To quote Ford: "This is not only the
first appearance of the autobiography from Franklin's own
copy, but also the first publication in English of the four
parts, and the first publication of the very important 'outline'
autobiography. It is therefore the first edition of *the* autobiography" [p. 199].)

*The Life of Benjamin Franklin, written by himself. Now first
edited from original manuscripts and from his printed correspondence and other writings,* by John Bigelow. 3 vols. Philadelphia: 1874. (Bigelow text of *Autobiography* and extracts
from Franklin's other works.)

The Complete Works of Benjamin Franklin including his private as well as his official and scientific correspondence, and numerous letters and documents now for the first time printed with many others not included in any former collection, also the unmutilated and correct version of his autobiography. Comp. and ed. by John Bigelow. 10 vols. New York: 1887–89. (Corrects many of Sparks's errors and adds "some six hundred new pieces." For first time works are chronologically arranged.)

The Writings of Benjamin Franklin, collected and edited with a Life and Introduction, by Albert Henry Smyth. 10 vols. New York: 1905–1907. (The standard edition. It is unfortunate that the editor has omitted pieces which are either too Rabelaisian or too metaphysically radical, such as the *Dissertation* of 1725, or are, in his mind, *probably* not written by Franklin.)

Benjamin Franklin's Memoirs. Parallel Text Edition Comprising the Texts of Franklin's original manuscript, the French translation by Louis Guillaume le Veillard, the French translation published by Buisson, and the version edited by William Temple Franklin, his grandson. Ed., with an introduction and explanatory notes, by Max Farrand, late Director of Research at the Huntington Library. Berkeley and Los Angeles: 1949. (Farrand's scholarship on the *Memoirs* is also found in *The Huntington Library Bulletin,* No. 10, pp. 49–78 [Oct., 1936]. Also published in 1949 in a trade edition which attempts to recreate the fair-copy texts made by B. F. Bache and largely used by W. T. Franklin. For a subtle critique of the Farrand work see Verner W. Crane's article in *Modern Philology,* XLVII, No. 2, pp. 127–34 [Nov., 1949].)

Amacher, Richard E. *Franklin's Wit & Folly. The Bagatelles.* New Brunswick, N.J.: 1953. (Seventeen bagatelles reprinted with scholarly notes on texts and extensive commentary on his friends in various ways alluded to in these spritely moral diversions.)

Butterfield, L. H. "B. Franklin's Epitaph," *New Colophon,* III, pp. 9–30 (1950). (Definitive study of eleven variant MSS.)

A Catalogue of Books Belonging to the Library Company of Philadelphia. A Facsimile of the Edition of 1741, Printed by Benjamin Franklin. With an Introduction by Edwin Wolf 2nd. Philadelphia: 1956. (Useful as an example of Franklin's printing and as an index to the breadth of the library which he founded.)

Cohen, I. Bernard. *Benjamin Franklin's Experiments. A New Edition of Franklin's Experiments and Observations on Elec-*

tricity. Edited, with a Critical and historical Introduction. . . .
Cambridge, Mass.: 1941. (Indispensable. See C. E. Jorgenson's
review in *American Literature*, XIV, pp. 184–87 [May, 1942].
For orientation and bibliography, see also Morris H. Shames,
Great Experiments in Physics. New York: 1960.)

Crane, Verner W. (ed.). *Benjamin Franklin's Letters to the
Press 1758–1775.* Chapel Hill: 1950. (New essays identified
constitute two-thirds of Franklin's writings on politics during
these years. A major contribution.)

*The General Magazine and Historical Chronicle for All The
British Plantations in America.* Published by Benjamin Frank-
lin. Reproduced from the Original Edition, Philadelphia, 1741.
With a Bibliographical Note by Lyon N. Richardson. The
Facsimile Text Society, New York: 1938. (The six issues of
the second colonial magazine, January–June.)

Goodman, Nathan G. (ed.). *A Benjamin Franklin Reader.* New
York: 1945.

———. *Profile of Genius: Poor Richard Pamphlets.* Philadelphia: 1938.

Labaree, Leonard W., and Bell, Whitfield J. Jr. (eds.). *Mr.
Franklin. A Selection From His Personal Letters.* New Haven:
1956. (An attractive piece designed as a "prospectus" of the
monumental Yale Edition of The Papers of Benjamin Franklin.)

McPharlin, Paul (ed.). *Satires and Bagatelles.* Detroit: 1937.

II. COLLECTIONS AND REPRINTS

No attempt has been made to include the learned journal
articles which reprint occasional letters not in Smyth. Letters
which aid in understanding Franklin's mind have been referred
to in the Introduction and Notes.

Chinard, Gilbert. *Les amitiés américaines de Madame d'Houdetot,
d'après sa correspondance inédite avec Benjamin Franklin et
Thomas Jefferson.* Paris: 1924.

Diller, Theodore. *Franklin's Contribution to Medicine.* Brooklyn: 1912. (Able collection of Franklin's letters bearing on
medicine. Franklin is described "as one of the greatest benefactors, friends, and patrons of the medical profession as well
as a most substantial contributor to the science and art of
medicine.")

[Franklin, Benjamin.] *A Dissertation on Liberty and Necessity,
Pleasure and Pain.* Reproduced from the first edition, with a
bibliographical note by Lawrence C. Wroth. The Facsimile

Text Society, New York: 1930. (Although A. H. Smyth omitted this work from his *Writings of Benjamin Franklin*, suggesting that "the work has no value," it is difficult to see how a study of the *modus operandi* of Franklin's mind could be thoroughly made without it. Parton in his *Life and Times of Benjamin Franklin*, and I. W. Riley in his *American Philosophy: The Early Schools* have reprinted it in appendices.)

Franklin, Benjamin. *Poor Richard's Almanack. Being the Almanacks of 1733, 1749, 1756, 1757, 1758, first written under the name of Richard Saunders.* With a foreword by Phillips Russell. Garden City, N. Y.: 1928. ("First facsimile edition of a group of the Almanacks to be published.")

————. *The Prefaces, Proverbs, and Poems of Benjamin Franklin Originally Printed in Poor Richard's Almanacs for 1733–1758.* Collected and ed. by P. L. Ford. Brooklyn: 1890. (Best collection of its kind; in addition contains account of popularity and function of almanacs in colonial period.)

————. *Proposals Relating to the Education of Youth in Pensilvania.* Facsimile reprint, with an introduction by William Pepper. Philadelphia: 1931. (Franklin's notes omitted in Smyth. *Proposals* also reprinted by the William L. Clements Library, Ann Arbor, Michigan: 1927; "though not a facsimile reprint," it does include the notes. Thomas Woody in his *Educational Views of Benjamin Franklin* [New York: 1931] reprints it with the notes.)

————. *The Sayings of Poor Richard, 1733–1758.* Condensed and ed. by T. H. Russell. N.p.: n.d. (Best aphorisms chronologically arranged.)

Goodman, N. G. (ed.). *The Ingenious Dr. Franklin; Selected Scientific Letters of Benjamin Franklin.* Philadelphia: 1931. (Includes several items not published in Smyth edition.)

Letters to Benjamin Franklin, from his Family and Friends, 1751–1790. [Ed. by William Duane.] New York: 1859.

The New-England Courant. A Selection of Certain Issues Containing Writings of Benjamin Franklin Or Published By Him During His Brother's Imprisonment. Reproduced from copies of the originals owned by The Massachusetts Historical Society In Honor of the 250th Anniversary of His Birth. With an Introduction by Perry Miller. (American Academy of Arts and Sciences) Boston: 1956. (Excellent photostats of the paper in which Franklin published his first essays.)

Pepper, William. *The Medical Side of Benjamin Franklin.* Philadelphia: 1911. (Essentially quotations from the A. H. Smyth edition. Franklin is viewed as "an early and great hygienist.")

Roelker, William Greene (ed.). *Benjamin Franklin and Catharine*

Ray Greene: Their Correspondence 1755–1790. Philadelphia: 1949. (A dramatic understatement to say that his letters reveal "a kindly, mellow, domestic side of Franklin, which is little known to the world." Compare Franklin's letters to his dear sister Jane Mecom.)

Stifler, J. M. (ed.). *"My Dear Girl." The Correspondence of Benjamin Franklin with Polly Stevenson, Georgiana and Catherine Shipley.* New York: 1927. (Engaging collection showing Franklin's "capacity for lively and enduring friendship" [p. vii]. Many of the letters *to* Franklin "printed now for the first time." Contains several of Franklin's letters hitherto unpublished.)

Van Doren, Carl (ed.). *Benjamin Franklin's Autobiographical Writings.* New York: 1945. (An excellent array of selections to supplement the *Memoirs.* Included are fifty uncollected pieces and uniformly fine editorial commentary.)

————. *Letters and Papers of Benjamin Franklin and Richard Jackson, 1753–1785.* Philadelphia: 1947. (Important letters, especially between 1762–64, on political and economic issues.)

————. *The Letters of Benjamin Franklin & Jane Mecom.* Published for The American Philosophical Society by Princeton University Press. Princeton: 1950. (Includes 98 letters of Franklin to his sister, "30 of them never before published at all, and several others never published in full or with accurate texts." Fine editorial apparatus.)

III. BIOGRAPHIES

Becker, Carl. "Benjamin Franklin," in *Dictionary of American Biography.* New York: 1931. VI, pp. 585–98. (The most authoritative brief biography.)

Bruce, W. C. *Benjamin Franklin, Self-Revealed.* 2 vols. New York: 1917. (In spite of occasional extravagant statements and a conservative temperament preventing him from discussing Franklin's religion with sympathetic and historical insight, Mr. Bruce has provided a brilliant and perspicuous survey. "Self-revealed" fails to do justice to Bruce's incisive commentary.)

Crane, Verner W. *Benjamin Franklin and a Rising People.* Boston: 1954. (Consider C. E. Jorgenson's review in *American Literature,* XXVII, pp. 426–28 [Nov., 1955].)

Faÿ, Bernard. *Franklin, the Apostle of Modern Times.* Boston: 1929. (A readable critical biography said to be based on "six hundred to nine hundred unpublished letters." Would have been more useful had it been given scholarly documentation. Some new light on Franklin's Masonic activities and his efforts during 1757–62 to effect the growth of a British empire. [Faÿ used the Franklin-Galloway correspondence in the W. S. Mason and W. L. Clements collections.] Believes that Franklin was a "follower of the seventeenth-century English Pythagoreans": since this belief is largely undocumented, one feels it curious that Pythagoreanism should bulk larger than the pattern of thought provoked by Locke and Newton. See very critical reviews by H. M. Jones in *American Literature*, II, pp. 306–12 [Nov., 1930], and W. C. Bruce, *American Historical Review*, XXXV, p. 634 ff. [April, 1930]. The latter concludes that "there is very little, indeed, in the text of the book under review that makes any unquestionably substantial addition to our pre-existing knowledge of Franklin, or is marked by anything that can be termed freshness of interpretation.")

———. *The Two Franklins: Fathers of American Democracy*. Boston: 1933. (Charmingly spirited portrait of patriarchal Franklin of Passy [reworking of materials in *Franklin, the Apostle of Modern Times*]. Faÿ's habit of mingling quotation, paraphrase, and intuition in use of Bache's *Diary* suggests untrustworthy documentation. The second Franklin is, of course, Benjamin Franklin Bache [1769–98, son of Sally Franklin and Richard Bache], editor of the republican *Aurora General Advertiser*. For a judicial, unsympathetic review see A. Guerard's in the *New York Herald Tribune Books*, Oct. 22, 1933. J. A. Krout, in the *American Historical Review*, XXXIX, pp. 741–42 [July, 1934], observes that Faÿ "fails to establish the elder Franklin's paternal relation to the democratic forces of the 'revolutionary' decade after 1790.")

Fisher, S. G. *The True Benjamin Franklin*. Philadelphia: 1899. (Highly prejudiced interpretation with disproportionate attention to Franklin's acknowledged shortcomings.)

Ford, P. L. *The Many-Sided Franklin*. New York: 1899. (A gracefully solid and inclusive standard work.)

Hale, E. E., and Hale, E. E., Jr. *Franklin in France. From Original Documents, Most of Which Are Now Published for the First Time*. 2 vols. Boston: 1877–88. (Convenient collection of letters to Franklin; authors had access to Stevens and American Philosophical Society collections. Franklin letters and documents here given later published in Smyth. Useful chapters on Franklin's friends, his vogue in France, meetings with Voltaire, his activities in science, his interest in balloons, and investigation of Mesmerism. See reviews in *Dial*, VIII, p. 7,

IX, p. 204; *Nation,* XLIV, p. 368; *Athenaeum,* II, p. 77
[1887]; *Atlantic Monthly,* LX, p. 318.)

Keyes, Nelson Beecher. *Benjamin Franklin, An Affectionate
Portrait.* Garden City, New York: 1956.

McMaster, J. B. *Benjamin Franklin as a Man of Letters.* American Men of Letters series. Boston: 1887. (Fullest account of
this aspect of the many-minded Franklin. See also MacLaurin
and Jorgenson items, below.)

More, P. E. *Benjamin Franklin.* Riverside Biographical Series.
Boston: 1900. (Suggestive of a *précis* of Parton's *Life* with
judicial, if not historical, penetration. Stimulating notes, such
as the following: Franklin was "a great pagan, who lapsed
now and then into the pseudo-religious platitudes of the
eighteenth-century deists.")

Morse, John Torrey, Jr. *Benjamin Franklin.* American Statesmen series. Boston: 1889. (Compact account stressing his
political and diplomatic career.)

Parton, James. *Life and Times of Benjamin Franklin.* 2 vols.
New York: 1864. (Although not all works ascribed to Franklin by Parton are by his pen, and although new materials have
been added to the Franklin canon, he remains the most encyclopedic and often the most penetrating of Franklin's biog-
raphers. He deserves credit for printing in an appendix Franklin's *Dissertation on Liberty and Necessity, Pleasure and Pain.*
For reviews see *North American Review* [July, 1864]; *Atlantic
Monthly* [Sept., 1864]; *London Quarterly,* XXIII, p. 483;
Littell's Living Age, LXXXIV, p. 289.)

Russell, Phillips. *Benjamin Franklin, the First Civilized American.* New York: 1926. (The *esprit* and readableness of this
popular work do not offset its lack of precision, historical
scholarship, and taste.)

Scudder, Evarts S. *Benjamin Franklin: A Biography.* London:
1939. (Despite rough errors of fact, a fairly good story of
Franklin as a man of action.)

Smyth, Albert H. "Life of Benjamin Franklin," in Vol. X, pp.
141–510, of *The Writings of Benjamin Franklin.* (Stimulating
survey.)

Swift, Lindsay. *Benjamin Franklin.* Beacon Biographies of
Eminent Americans. Boston: 1910. (Brief series of biographical "impressions" arranged chronologically.)

Van Doren, Carl. *Benjamin Franklin.* New York: 1938. (The
fullest record of Franklin as a man of action but not equally
strong in charting Franklin's rational, deistic mind.)

Weems, Mason L. *The Life of Benjamin Franklin; with many
Choice Anecdotes and Admirable Sayings of this Great Man.*

Baltimore: 1815. (One would think it unfair to smile at a
writer who had the wit to describe Franklin as one who "with
such equal ease, could play the *Newton* or the *Chesterfield*,
and charm alike the lightnings and the ladies." Contains some
imaginative, though intuitive, remarks on Franklin's religion.)

IV. BIOGRAPHICAL AND CRITICAL STUDIES

Abbe, C. "Benjamin Franklin as Meteorologist," *Proceedings of
the American Philosophical Society*, XLV, pp. 117–28 (1906).
("Worthy co-laborer" with Newton, Huygens, Descartes,
Boyle, and Gay-Lussac. He is "the first meteorologist of
America," "pioneer of the rational long-range forecasters.")

Abbot, G. M. *A Short History of the Library Company of
Philadelphia: Compiled from the Minutes, together with some
personal reminiscences.* Philadelphia: 1913.

Adams, Percy G. "Crèvecoeur and Franklin," *Pennsylvania History*, XIV, pp. 2–8 (1947).

Aldridge, Alfred O. "Franklin's 'Shaftesburian' Dialogues Not
Franklin's," *American Literature*, XXI, pp. 152–55 (May,
1949). (The two dialogues between Philocles and Horatio,
The Pennsylvania Gazette, 1730, identified as essays lifted
from a British paper. Many Franklinists erred in accepting
Franklin's statement of authorship in the *Memoirs*! But an
editor seldom "reprints" [plagiarizes!] what he has little belief
in. Thus, though he did not write these pieces, it is reasonable
to assume that he accepted the doctrine they phrased—with
Franklinian perspicuity.)

————. *Franklin and His French Contemporaries.* New York:
1957.

————. "Benjamin Franklin and Philosophical Necessity,"
Modern Language Quarterly, XII, pp. 292–309 (Sept., 1951).

————. "Jacques Barbeu Dubourg, A French Disciple of
Benjamin Franklin," *Proceedings of the American Philosophical Society*, XCV, pp. 331–92 (1951).

————. "Franklin's Deistical Indians." *Proceedings of the
American Philosophical Society*, XCIV, pp. 398–410 (1950).

Amiable, L. *Une loge maçonnique d'avant 1789. La R.˙. L.˙.
Les Neuf Sœurs.* Paris: 1897. (Fullest account of Franklin's
activities in French Freemasonry.)

Analectic Magazine, XI, pp. 449–84 (June, 1818). (Review of
W. T. Franklin's edition of Franklin's works. Complexion of
this eulogy suggested by: "His name is now exalted in Europe
above any others of the eighteenth century.")

Angoff, Charles. *A Literary History of the American People.*

New York: 1931. II, pp. 295–310. (It would be difficult to match the debonair ignorance of this violently hostile essay.)

"A Poem on the Death of Franklin," *Proceedings of the New Jersey Historical Society*, XV, p. 109 (Jan., 1930). (A typical elegy based on theme suggested by Turgot's epigram on Franklin.)

Bache, R. M. "Smoky Torches in Franklin's Honor," *Critic*, XLVIII, pp. 561–66 (June, 1906). (Charming in its caustic though just view that "articles on Franklin have verged on superfluity.")

————. "The So-Called 'Franklin Prayer-Book,' " *Pennsylvania Magazine of History and Biography*, XXI, pp. 225–34 (1897). (See Rev. John Wright's account of the same in *Early Prayer Books of America* [St. Paul: 1896], pp. 386–99.)

Benjamin Franklin and His Circle. A Catalogue of an Exhibition. The Metropolitan Museum of Art, from May 11 through September 13, 1936. New York: 1936. (A dramatic assembly of portraits of Franklin and his associates in France, England, and America along with "pictured views of the scenes of his varied career.")

Biddison, P. "The Magazine Franklin Failed to Remember," *American Literature*, IV, pp. 177–80 (May, 1932). (Survey of the Franklin-Webbe altercation concerning the inauguration of Franklin's *General Magazine, and Historical Chronicle* . . . , 1741.)

Bigelow, John. "Franklin as the Man," *Independent*, LX, pp. 69–72 (Jan. 11, 1906). (Stresses his tolerance, common sense, and "constitutional unwillingness to dogmatize.")

Bleyer, W. G. *Main Currents in the History of American Journalism.* Boston: 1927. (Chapters I–II contain excellent survey of the *New England Courant*, and the *Pennsylvania Gazette* during its formative years. Bibliography, pp. 431–41.)

Bloore, Stephen. "Joseph Breintnall, First Secretary of the Library Company," *Pennsylvania Magazine of History and Biography*, LIX, pp. 42–56 (Jan., 1935). (Valuable notes on Franklin's collaborator in *Busy-Body* series.)

————. "Samuel Keimer. A Foot-note to the Life of Franklin," *Pennsylvania Magazine of History and Biography*, LIV, pp. 255–87 (July, 1930). (Readers of the *Autobiography* will appreciate this excellent study of one who figures prominently in its pages.)

Brett-James, N. G. *The Life of Peter Collinson.* London: [1917]. (Many notes on Franklin-Collinson friendship. Collinson, it is remembered, "started Franklin on his career as a researcher in electricity.")

Buckingham, J. T. *Specimens of Newspaper Literature; with Personal Memoirs, Anecdotes, and Reminiscences.* 2 vols. Boston: 1850. (Vol. I, pp. 49–88, discusses *New England Courant.* Identifies *Dogood Papers* as Franklin's.)

Bullen, H. L. "Benjamin Franklin and What Printing Did for Him," *American Collector,* II, pp. 284–91 (May, 1926).

Butler, Ruth L. *Doctor Franklin, Postmaster General.* Garden City, N. Y.: 1928. (A sturdily documented study illustrating that Franklin "furnished the most highly efficient administration to the postal system during the colonial period.")

Canby, H. S. "Benjamin Franklin," in *Classic Americans.* New York: 1931, pp. 34–45. (Spirited estimate partly vitiated by excessive emphasis on influence of Quakerism; Canby observes that Franklin's mind represents "Quakerism conventionalized, stylized, and Deicized.")

Carey, Lewis J. *Franklin's Economic Views.* Garden City, N. Y.: 1928. (Excellent survey.)

Carlson, C. Lennart. "Samuel Keimer: A Study in the Transit of English Culture to Colonial Pennsylvania," *Pennsylvania Magazine of History and Biography,* LXI, pp. 357–86 (1937).

Cestre, Charles. "Franklin, homme représentatif," *Revue Anglo-Américaine,* pp. 409–23, 505–22 (June, August, 1928).

Cheyney, Edward P. *History of the University of Pennsylvania, 1740–1940.* Philadelphia: 1940.

Chinard, Gilbert. "The Apotheosis of Benjamin Franklin," *Proceedings of The American Philosophical Society,* XCIX, pp. 440–73 (1955).

Choate, J. H. "Benjamin Franklin," in *Abraham Lincoln, and Other Addresses in England.* New York: 1910, pp. 47–94. (Sanely eulogistic biographical survey.)

Christensen, Merton A. "Franklin on the Hemphill Trial: Deism versus Presbyterian Orthodoxy," *William and Mary Quarterly,* X, 3d ser., pp. 422–40 (1953).

Clark, William Bell. *Benjamin Franklin's Privateers, A Naval Epic of the American Revolution.* Baton Rouge: 1956.

Cohen, I. Bernard. *Benjamin Franklin. His Contributions to the American Tradition.* Indianapolis: 1953. (A delightful account in which Cohen makes elaborate comment on the Franklin pieces reprinted.)

———. *Franklin and Newton, An Inquiry into Speculative Newtonian Experimental Science and Franklin's Work in Electricity as an Example Thereof.* Philadelphia: 1956. (An elaborate discussion of Franklin as an "experimental scientist" though "no mathematician." He was "Newtonian" in that he

made an "exact science" of electricity. A major contribution
to an understanding of Franklin's mind as scientist.)

Condorcet, Marquis de. *Éloge de M. Franklin, lu à la séance
publique de l'Académie des Sciences, le 13 Nov., 1790....*
Paris: 1791. (Both a eulogy, and an interpretation of *why*
France, as representative of the Enlightenment, eulogized the
Philadelphia tradesman. By the most sublime of the *phi-
losophes*.)

Cook, E. C. *Literary Influences in Colonial Newspapers, 1704–
1750.* New York: 1912. (Trenchant analysis of Franklin's
indebtedness to Addison and Steele—especially in the *Dogood
Papers*—the character of the *New England Courant,* advertisements of books in *Pennsylvania Gazette,* etc. "Benjamin
Franklin was the only prominent man of the period who
deliberately attempted to spread the knowledge and love of
literature among his countrymen.")

Crane, Verner W. *Benjamin Franklin, Englishman and American.* Baltimore: 1936. (Perceptive portrait of the "fluctua-
tions of Franklin's imperial planning between colonial home-
rule and imperial federation.")

———. "Certain Writings of Benjamin Franklin on the British
Empire and the American Colonies," *Papers of the Bibliographical Society,* XXVIII, Pt. 1, pp. 1–27 (1934). (Newly
identified Franklin papers more than double existing canon.
He becomes "the chief agent of the American propaganda in
England, especially between 1765 and 1770." New canon
promises to "illuminate the development of Franklin's political
ideas." Very significant.)

———. "Three Fables by Benjamin Franklin," *New England
Quarterly,* IX, pp. 499–504 (1936).

Cumston, C. G. "Benjamin Franklin from the Medical View-
point," *New York Medical Journal,* LXXXIX, pp. 3–12 (Jan.
2, 1909). (Useful survey.)

Cutler, W. P., and Cutler, J. P. *Life, Journals and Correspondence of Rev. Manasseh Cutler.* 2 vols. Cincinnati: 1888.
(Portrait of patriarchal Franklin at age of eighty-four.)

Dickinson, A. D. "Benjamin Franklin, Bookman," *Bookman,*
LIII, pp. 197–205 (May, 1921). (Brief account of Franklin
imprints.)

*Discours du Comte de Mirabeau. Dans la séance du 11 Juin, sur
la mort de Benjamin Francklin* [sic] . Imprimé par ordre de
l'Assemblée National. Paris: 1790.

Dorfman, Joseph. *The Economic Mind in American Civilization—1606–1865.* 2 vols. New York: 1946. Vol. I, pp. 178–

95 and *passim*. (Adds to but does not supersede Wetzel and Carey.)

Draper, J. W. "Franklin's Place in the Science of the Last Century," *Harper's Magazine*, LXI, pp. 265–75 (July, 1880). (Franklin's discoveries "were only embellishments of his life." Superficial.)

Duniway, C. A. *The Development of Freedom of the Press in Massachusetts*. Cambridge, Mass.: 1906. (Chapter VI includes account of James Franklin and the *New England Courant*.)

Eddy, G. S. "Dr. Benjamin Franklin's Library," *Proceedings of the American Antiquarian Society*, N. s. XXXIV, pp. 206–26 (Oct., 1924). (This indefatigable scholar has ascertained the titles of 1350 volumes in Franklin's library. This survey article does not list the titles.)

Eiselen, M. R. *Franklin's Political Theories*. Garden City, N. Y.: 1928. (Thoughtful survey.)

———. *The Rise of Pennsylvania Protectionism*. Philadelphia: 1932. (University of Pennsylvania dissertation. Chapter I describes Franklin's holding to laissez faire in a state dominantly protectionist.)

Eliot, T. D. "The Relations Between Adam Smith and Benjamin Franklin before 1776," *Political Science Quarterly*, XXXIX, pp. 67–96 (March, 1924). (Exhaustive documentary data which fails to establish specific and incontrovertible Franklin influence on Smith.)

Ervin, H. "Notes on Franklin's Armonica and the Music Mozart Wrote for It," *Journal of the Franklin Institute*, vol. 262, pp. 329–48 (1956).

"Excerpts from the Papers of Dr. Benjamin Rush," *Pennsylvania Magazine of History and Biography*, XXIX, pp. 15–30 (Jan., 1905). (Includes "Conversations with Franklin," pp. 23–8: Franklin terms Latin and Greek the "quackery of literature"; is alleged to have reprobated the Pennsylvania Constitution of 1776, in that it placed "the Supreme power of the State in the hands of a Single legislature." Other interesting sidelights.)

Farrand, Max (ed.). *The Records of the Federal Convention of 1787*. 3 vols. New Haven: 1911. (Records show Franklin as a sober moderator: when rival factions tended to render the convention impotent, he said, "When a broad table is to be made, and the edges of planks do not fit, the artist takes a little from both, and makes a good joint.")

Fauchet, Claude. *Éloge civique de Benjamin Franklin, prononcé, le 21 Juillet 1790, dans la Rotonde, au nom de la Commune de Paris.* Paris: 1790.

Faÿ, Bernard. "Franklin et Mirabeau collaborateurs," *Revue de Littérature Comparée,* VIII, pp. 5–28 (1928). (Franklin furnished materials for Mirabeau's *Considerations on the Order of Cincinnatus.*)

——. "Learned Societies in Europe and America in the Eighteenth Century," *American Historical Review,* XXXVII, pp. 255–66 (Jan., 1932). (Urges that like all learned societies in the eighteenth century, Franklin's Junto and American Philosophical Society "had Masonic leanings.")

——. "Le credo de Franklin," *Correspondant,* pp. 570–78 (Feb. 25, 1930).

——. "Les débuts de Franklin en France," *Revue de Paris,* pp. 577–605 (Feb. 1, 1931).

——. "Les dernières amours d'un philosophe," *Correspondant,* pp. 381–96 (May 10, 1930).

——. "Le triomphe de Franklin en France," *Revue de Paris,* pp. 872–96 (Feb. 15, 1931).

Ford, P. L. "Franklin as Printer and Publisher," *Century Magazine,* LVII, pp. 803–17 (April, 1899).

Ford, W. C. "Franklin and Chatham," *Independent,* LX, pp. 94–7 (Jan. 11, 1906).

——. "Franklin's New England Courant," *Proceedings of the Massachusetts Historical Society,* LVII, pp. 336–53 (April, 1924).

——. "One of Franklin's Friendships. From Hitherto Unpublished Correspondence between Madame de Brillon and Benjamin Franklin, 1776–1789," *Harper's Magazine,* CXIII, pp. 626–33 (Sept., 1906).

Foster, J. W. "Franklin as a Diplomat," *Independent,* LX, pp. 84–9 (Jan. 11, 1906).

Fox, R. H. *Dr. John Fothergill and His Friends; Chapters in Eighteenth Century Life.* London: 1919. (Franklin and Fothergill, "lovers of nature and keen students of physical science," met in 1757. See also J. C. Lettsom, *Memoirs of John Fothergill,* 4th ed., London: 1786.)

Gallacher, Stuart A. "Franklin's *Way To Wealth:* A Frorileguim of Proverbs and Wise Sayings," *Journal of English and Germanic Philology,* XLVIII, pp. 229–51 (1949).

Garrison, F. W. "Franklin and the Physiocrats," *Freeman,* VIII, pp. 154–6 (Oct. 24, 1923). (Transcended by Carey's chapter in *Franklin's Economic Views,* but has quotation from Dupont de Nemours [1769]: "Who does not know that the English have today their Benjamin Franklin, who has adopted the principles and the doctrines of our French economists?")

Goggio, E. "Benjamin Franklin and Italy," *Romanic Review,* XIX, pp. 302–8 (Oct., 1928). Largely through the efforts of G. Beccaria, "Benjamin Franklin was one of the first Americans to gain eminence and popularity among the people of Italy.")

Goode, G. B. "The Literary Labors of Benjamin Franklin," *Proceedings of the American Philosophical Society,* XXVIII, pp. 177–97 (1890).

Grandgent, C. H. "Benjamin Franklin the Reformer," in *Prunes and Prisms, with Other Odds and Ends.* Cambridge, Mass.: 1928, pp. 86–97. ("The principles advocated in his unfinished exposition [on spelling reform] are those which phoneticians now advocate.")

Gray, Austin K. *Benjamin Franklin's Library. A Short Account of the Library Company of Philadelphia.* New York: 1937.

Greene, S. A. "The Story of a Famous Book," *Atlantic Monthly,* XXVII, pp. 207–12 (Feb., 1871). (A kind of *précis* of Bigelow's Introduction to *Autobiography.*)

Griswold, A. W. "Three Puritans on Prosperity," *New England Quarterly,* VII, pp. 475–93 (Sept., 1934). (Cotton Mather, Timothy Dwight, and Franklin. One wonders by what right Franklin is dubbed the "soul of Puritanism.")

Guedalla, Philip. "Dr. Franklin," in *Fathers of the Revolution.* New York: 1926, pp. 215–34. (Chatty popular review of "the first high-priest of the religion of efficiency.")

Guillois, Antoine. *Le salon de Madame Helvétius.* Paris: 1894.

Gummere, R. M. "Socrates at the Printing Press. Benjamin Franklin and the Classics," *Classical Weekly,* XXVI, pp. 57–59 (Dec. 5, 1932). (Survey of his references to the classics, with occasional estimates of impact on his mind.)

Hale, E. E. "Ben Franklin's Ballads," *New England Magazine,* N. S. XVIII, pp. 505–07 (1898). (Thinks "The Downfall of Piracy," found in Ashton's *Real Sea-Songs,* is "one of the two lost ballads" Franklin mentions in *Autobiography.*)

———. "Franklin as Philosopher and Moralist," *Independent,* LX, pp. 89–93 (Jan. 11, 1906). (Does not go beyond terming Franklin's philosophy common sense.)

Hall, Max. *Benjamin Franklin and Polly Baker: The History of a Literary Deception.* Chapel Hill, N. C.: 1960. (This should satisfy as a definitive bibliographical account.)

Hans, Nicholas, "Franklin, Jefferson, and the English Radicals," *Proceedings of The American Philosophical Society,* XCVIII, pp. 408–26 (Dec., 1954).

Harrison, Frederic. "Benjamin Franklin," in *Memories and Thoughts.* New York: 1906, pp. 119–23. (Keen appraisal.)

Hart, C. H. "Benjamin Franklin in Allegory," *Century Magazine*, XLI (N. S. XIX), pp. 197–204 (Dec., 1890). (The French sanctify Franklin in allegory.)

————. "Who Was the Mother of Franklin's Son? An Inquiry Demonstrating that She Was Deborah Read, Wife of Benjamin Franklin," *Pennsylvania Magazine of History and Biography*, XXXV, pp. 308–14 (July, 1911). (Plausible circumstantial evidence is offered.)

Hays, I. M. *The Chronology of Benjamin Franklin, Founder of the American Philosophical Society*. Philadelphia: 1904.

Hill, D. J. "A Missing Chapter of Franco-American History," *American Historical Review*, XXI, pp. 709–19 (July, 1916). (Political interests of Masonic "Lodge of the Nine Sisters," Paris, of which Franklin was an active member. Franklin described as "creator of constitutionalism in Europe.")

Horner, George F. "Franklin's *Dogood Papers* Re-examined," *Studies in Philology*, XXXVII, pp. 501–23 (1940). (Sharp but inconclusive arguments that "very little is left to be derived from the *Spectator*.")

Houston, E. J. "Franklin as a Man of Science and an Inventor," *Journal of the Franklin Institute*, CLXI, Nos. 4–5, pp. 241–383 (April–May, 1906).

Hulbert, C. *Biographical Sketches of Dr. Benjamin Franklin, General Washington, and Thomas Paine; with an Essay on Atheism and Infidelity*. London: 1820. (Franklin and Washington made almost saintly to contrast with Paine, "a notorious Unbeliever." Quotes one who sees Franklin as "the patriot of the world, the playmate of the lightning, the philosopher of liberty.")

Indian Treaties Printed by Benjamin Franklin 1736–1762. Reproductions in Facsimile, with an Introduction by Carl Van Doren and Historical and Bibliographical Notes by Julian P. Boyd. Philadelphia: 1938. (Dramatic story of a little known series of adventures with his Indian "neighbors.")

Jackson, M. K. *Outlines of the Literary History of Colonial Pennsylvania*. Lancaster, Pa.: 1906. (Especially Chapter III, which surveys Franklin as man of letters.)

Jernegan, M. W. "Benjamin Franklin's 'Electrical Kite' and Lightning Rod," *New England Quarterly*, I, pp. 180–96 (April, 1928). ("The question still remains however whether Franklin flew his kite *before* he heard of the French experiments, and thus discovered the identity of lightning and electricity independently." Summarizes and supersedes: McAdie, A., "The Date of Franklin's Kite Experiment," *Proceedings of the American Antiquarian Society, N. s. XXXIV, pp. 188–205; Rotch, A. L., "Did Benjamin Franklin Fly His Electrical Kite before He Invented the Lightning Rod?" *Proceedings of the American Antiquarian Society,* N. s. XVIII, pp. 115–23.)

Jordan, J. W. "Franklin as a Genealogist," *Pennsylvania Magazine of History and Biography,* XXIII, pp. 1–22 (April, 1899).

Jorgenson, C. E. "A Brand Flung at Colonial Orthodoxy. Samuel Keimer's 'Universal Instructor in All Arts and Sciences,'" *Journalism Quarterly,* XII, pp. 272–77 (Sept., 1935). (Shows deistic tendencies.)

———. "The New Science in the Almanacs of Ames and Franklin," *New England Quarterly,* VIII, pp. 55–61 (Dec., 1935). (Newtonianism and scientific deism diffused through these popular almanacs.)

———. "Sidelights on Benjamin Franklin's Principles of Rhetoric," *Revue Anglo-Américaine,* pp. 208–22 (Feb., 1934). (Franklin's principles in general are consonant with the eighteenth-century neoclassic ideals.)

———. "The Source of Benjamin Franklin's Dialogues between Philocles and Horatio (1730)," *American Literature,* VI, pp. 337–39 (Nov., 1934). (The source is Shaftesbury's "The Moralists," in the *Characteristics.*)

Jusserand, J. J. "Franklin in France," in *Essays Offered to Herbert Putnam. . . .* Ed. by W. W. Bishop and A. Keogh. New Haven: 1929, pp. 226–47. (Delightful summary.)

Kane, Hope F. "James Franklin Senior, Printer of Boston and Newport," *American Collector,* III, pp. 17–26 (Oct., 1926). (A study of his *New England Courant* and his place in the development of freedom of the press.)

Kenny, Robert W. "James Ralph: An Eighteenth-Century Philadelphian in Grub Street," *Pennsylvania Magazine of History and Biography,* LXIV, pp. 218–42 (1940). (For readers of the *Memoirs* who may be curious about Ralph.)

King, A. Hyatt. "The Musical Glasses and Glass Harmonica," *Proceedings of the Royal Musical Association,* 72nd. session, pp. 97–122 (1945–46).

King, M. R. "One Link in the First Newspaper Chain, *The South Carolina Gazette,*" *Journalism Quarterly,* IX, pp. 257–68 (September, 1932). (Franklin's partnership with Thomas Whitemarsh in 1731 is here alleged to have begun the first American newspaper "chain.")

Kite, Elizabeth S. "Benjamin Franklin—Diplomat," *Catholic World,* CXLII, pp. 28–37 (Oct., 1935). (An intelligent and appreciative brief survey of the subject, with a considerable preface showing the extent to which Franklin's worldly success grew out of his religious views.)

Lees, F. "The Parisian Suburb of Passy: Its Architecture in the Days of Franklin," *Architectural Record*, XII, pp. 669–83 (Dec., 1902). (Several good illustrations included.)

Lingelbach, W. E. "B. Franklin, Printer—Some New Source Materials," *American Philosophical Society Library Bulletin*, XCII, No. 2, pp. 89–96 (May, 1948).

Livingston, L. S. *Franklin and His Press at Passy; An Account of the Books, Pamphlets, and Leaflets Printed There, including the Long-Lost Bagatelles*. The Grolier Club, New York: 1914. (For additions to this work begun by L. S. Livingston, see R. G. Adams, "The 'Passy-ports' and Their Press," *American Collector*, IV, pp. 177–80 [Aug., 1927], which includes bibliography useful to study of the Passy imprints.)

MacDonald, William. "The Fame of Franklin," *Atlantic Monthly*, XCVI, pp. 450–62 (Oct., 1905).

Mackay, Constance D'A. *Franklin. A Play.* New York: 1922.

MacLaurin, Lois M. *Franklin's Vocabulary.* Garden City, N. Y.: 1928. (His "conservative ideas about linguistic innovations" are to a notable degree achieved in his practices. For example, of a vocabulary of 4062 words used in his writings between 1722 and 1751, "only 19 were discovered to be pure 'Americanisms.' ")

McMaster, J. B. "Franklin in France," *Atlantic Monthly*, LX, pp. 318–26 (Sept., 1887). (Good survey, based on Hale and Hale, *Franklin in France*.)

Malone, Kemp. "Benjamin Franklin on Spelling Reform," *American Speech*, I, pp. 96–100 (Nov., 1925). (Franklin was the "first American to tackle English phonetics scientifically.")

Mason, W. S. "Franklin and Galloway: Some Unpublished Letters," *Proceedings of the American Antiquarian Society*, N. s. XXXIV, pp. 227–58 (Oct., 1924). (Significant sidelights cast on "the problems of Pennsylvania colonial history from 1757 to 1760." Excellent summary of Franklin's and Galloway's victory over the Proprietors. Mr. Mason's collection includes many valuable letters [Franklin-Galloway] between 1757 and 1772, not published in Smyth.)

Mathews, Mrs. L. K. "Benjamin Franklin's Plans for a Colonial Union, 1750–1775," *American Political Science Review*, VIII, pp. 393–412 (Aug., 1914).

Meet Dr. Franklin. The Franklin Institute, Philadelphia: 1943. (An important symposium which includes essays by: Carl Van Doren, "Meet Doctor Franklin"; Robert A. Millikan,

"Benjamin Franklin as Scientist"; Max Farrand, "Self-Portraiture: The Autobiography"; Conyers Read, "Dr. Franklin as the English Saw Him"; Verner W. Crane, "Franklin's Political Journalism in England"; Robert E. Spiller, "Benjamin Franklin: Student of Life"; George Wharton Pepper, "Molding the Constitution"; Bernhard Knollenberg, "Benjamin Franklin: Philosophical Revolutionist"; Lawrence C. Wroth, "Benjamin Franklin: The Printer at Work"; Carl R. Woodward, "Benjamin Franklin: Adventures in Agriculture"; Julian P. Boyd, "Dr. Franklin: Friend of the Indians"; and a "Concluding Paper" suggesting lines of future scholarship by Carl Van Doren.)

Meister, Charles W. "Franklin as a Proverb Stylist," *American Literature*, XXIV, pp. 157–66 (1952).

Melville, Herman. *Israel Potter*. London: 1923. (Graphic intuitive portrait of Franklin: he lives as a "household Plato," "a practical Magian in linsey-woolsey," a "didactically waggish," prudent courtier who "was everything but a poet.")

Mémoires de l'Abbé Morellet, de l'Académie Française, sur le dix-huitième siècle et sur la Révolution. 2 vols. Paris: 1821. (Especially II, pp. 286–311. Franklin viewed as very emblem of Liberty.)

Miles, Richard D. "The American Image of Benjamin Franklin," *American Quarterly*, IX, pp. 117–43 (Summer, 1957).

Miller, C. William. "Benjamin Franklin's Philadelphia Type," *Studies in Bibliography* (Bibliographical Society, University of Virginia), XI, pp. 179–206 (1958).

———. "Franklin's Type: Its Study Past and Present," *Proceedings of The American Philosophical Society*, XCIX, pp. 418–32 (1955).

Montgomery, T. H. *A History of the University of Pennsylvania from Its Foundation to A. D. 1770.* Philadelphia: 1900.

Monthly Review; or Literary Journal: By Several Hands. London: 1770. XLII, pp. 199–210, 298–308. ("The experiments and observations of Dr. Franklin constitute the *principia* of electricity, and form the basis of a system equally simple and profound.")

More, P. E. "Benjamin Franklin," in *Shelburne Essays*, Fourth Series. New York: 1906, pp. 129–55. (Provocative appraisal: stresses Franklin's "contemporaneity," his tendency to be oblivious to the past—a suggestive, if a moot point.)

Morgan, W. *Memoirs of the Life of Rev. Richard Price.* London: 1815. (Notes on Franklin's relations with Price during early 1760's; meetings at Royal Society and London Coffeehouse.)

Mottay, F. *Benjamin Franklin et la philosophie pratique.* Paris: 1886. (Good model for citizens of a free nation and "le véritable catechisme de l'homme vertueux." Also several just remarks on his style which possesses "les mots épiques d'un Corneille et les élégantes périphrases d'un Racine.")

Moulton, C. W. (ed.). *Library of Literary Criticism of English and American Authors.* Buffalo, N. Y.: 1901. IV, pp. 79–106. (Stimulating assembly of extracts which aids student in discovering the history of Franklin's reputation.)

Mustard, W. P. "Poor Richard's Poetry," *Nation,* LXXXII, pp. 239, 279 (March 22, April 5, 1906). (Indicates Franklin's borrowings from Dryden, Pope, Prior, Gay, Swift, and others.)

Nichols, E. L. "Franklin as a Man of Science," *Independent,* LX, pp. 79–84 (Jan. 11, 1906). (Franklin's mind "turned ever by preference to the utilitarian and away from the theoretical and speculative aspects of things.")

Nolan, J. Bennett. *Benjamin Franklin in Scotland and Ireland 1759 and 1771.* Philadelphia: 1938 (reprinted 1956). (Amazing array of valuable personalia. Excellent notes. See V. W. Crane's review in *New England Quarterly,* XIII, pp. 155–57 [1940].)

———. *General Benjamin Franklin. The Military Career of A Philosopher.* Philadelphia: 1936 (reprinted 1956). (Antiquarian minutiae but important as chief study of Franklin's interlude as a military man.)

"Notice sur Benjamin Franklin," in *Œuvres posthumes de Cabanis.* Paris: 1825, pp. 219–74. (Representative in its rapturous eulogy.)

Oberholtzer, E. P. *The Literary History of Philadelphia.* Philadelphia: 1906. (Chap. II, "The Age of Franklin," written with conservative bias, belabors Franklin who as a statesman "was almost as wrong as Paine and Mirabeau." What Voltaire was to France, Franklin was to his native city and state.)

Oswald, J. C. *Benjamin Franklin in Oil and Bronze.* New York: 1926. ("Probably the features and form of no man who ever lived were delineated so frequently and in such a variety of ways as were those of Benjamin Franklin." Best survey of its kind, including many excellent reproductions.)

———. *Benjamin Franklin, Printer.* Garden City, N. Y.: 1917. (Fullest and ablest account of this phase of Franklin's life.)

Owen, E. D. "Where Did Benjamin Franklin Get the Idea for His Academy?" *Pennsylvania Magazine of History and Biography,* LVIII, pp. 86–94 (Jan., 1934). (Inconclusive evidence attributing it to Dr. Philip Doddridge.)

Pace, Antonio. *Benjamin Franklin and Italy.* Philadelphia: 1958.

(An encyclopedic account of "Franklin's interest in Italy" which "is admittedly a rather minor aspect of his tremendously variegated activity. . . ." Franklin never visited Italy but he corresponded with her scholars and read many Italian books, especially on politics and science. Savants, artists, and statesmen regarded Franklin with veneration.)

Parker, Theodore. "Benjamin Franklin," in *Historic Americans*. Ed. with notes by S. A. Eliot. Boston: 1908 [written in 1858]. (Franklin "thinks, investigates, theorizes, invents, but never does he dream." Although Parker, an idealist and reformer, exalts "the sharp outline of his [Franklin's] exact idea," his humanitarianism, his combining the "rare excellence of Socrates and Bacon" in making things "easy for all to handle and comprehend," he concludes that Franklin is "a saint devoted to the almighty dollar." There are few more readable estimates.)

Parrington, V. L. "Benjamin Franklin," in *The Colonial Mind, 1620–1800*. New York: 1927, pp. 164–78. (Emphasizes Franklin's tendencies toward agrarian democracy; Parrington's indifference to the genetic approach and his chronic economic determinism lead him to slight the primary importance of Franklin's religious and philosophic views in conditioning his other activities.)

Pennington, E. L. "The Work of the Bray Associates in Pennsylvania," *Pennslyvania Magazine of History and Biography*, LVIII, pp. 1–25 (Jan., 1934). (Franklin's humanitarian interest in Negro education. In 1758 he writes from London urging school for instructing young Negroes in Philadelphia.)

Pennsylvania Magazine of History and Biography, XXV, pp. 307–22, 516–26 (1901), XXVI, pp. 81–90, 255–64 (1902). (Reprints one of Dean Tucker's pamphlets with Franklin's annotations. Casts light on Franklin's loyalty to the Crown, while rebellious against Parliament.)

Phillips, William L. "Franklin's Version of the 'Lord's Prayer': A Restoration of the Text," *American Literature*, XXII, pp. 338–41 (Nov., 1950).

Pitt, A. Stuart. "Franklin and the Quaker Movement Against Slavery," *Bulletin of The Friends' Historical Association*, XXXII, pp. 13–31 (1943).

———. "The Sources, Significance, and Date of Franklin's 'An Arabian Tale,' " *Publications of the Modern Language Association of America*, LVII, pp. 155–68 (1942). (Bagatelle interpreted as including the concept of the "Great Chain of Being.")

Potamian, Brother, and Walsh, J. J. *Makers of Electricity*. New

York: 1909. ("Franklin and Some Contemporaries," Chapter II, pp. 68–132, by Brother Potamian, is an excellent survey of Franklin's contributions to the science of electricity.)

Powell, E. P. "A Study of Benjamin Franklin," *Arena,* VIII, pp. 477–91 (Sept., 1893). (Fair survey of Franklin as a diplomatist.)

Priestley, J. *The History and Present State of Electricity, with Original Experiments.* London: 1767. (Many notes observing Franklin's "truly philosophical greatness of mind." Preface contains suggestive generalizations concerning function of the natural philosopher: especially, he who experiments in electricity discerns laws of nature, "that is, of the God of nature himself.")

Rava, Luigi. "La fortuna di Beniamino Franklin in Italia," Prefazione al volume *Beniamino Franklin* di Lawrence Shaw Mayo. Firenze: n. d.

"The Remarkable Benjamin Franklin," *Wisdom,* 23rd Issue, vol. 2, No. 11 (March, 1958).

Repplier, Emma. "Franklin's Trials as a Benefactor," *Lippincott's Magazine,* LXXVII, pp. 63–70 (Jan., 1906). (Concerning those who during the Revolution wrote Franklin for favors and places.)

Riddell, W. R. "Benjamin Franklin and Colonial Money," *Pennsylvania Magazine of History and Biography,* LIV, pp. 52–64 (Jan., 1930).

————. "Benjamin Franklin's Mission to Canada and the Causes of Its Failure," *Pennsylvania Magazine of History and Biography,* XLVIII, pp. 111–58 (April, 1924).

Riley, I. W. *American Philosophy: The Early Schools.* New York: 1907, pp. 229–65. (Conventional view of Franklin's deism; with C. M. Walsh [see below], Riley overemphasizes influence of Plato on Franklin's thought.)

————. *American Thought from Puritanism to Pragmatism and Beyond.* New York: 1915, pp. 68–77. (Graphic glimpses of "most precocious of the American skeptics.")

Rosengarten, J. G. "The American Philosophical Society," reprinted from *Founders' Week Memorial Volume.* Philadelphia: 1908.

Ross, E. D. "Benjamin Franklin as an Eighteenth-Century Agriculture Leader," *Journal of Political Economy,* XXXVII, pp. 52–72 (Feb., 1929). (No "rural sentimentalist," Franklin experimented in agriculture, particularly during 1747–55, as a utilitarian idealist. Quotes one who suggests Franklin was "half physiocratic before the rise of the physiocratic school." Excellent and well-documented survey.)

Ross, John F. "The Character of Poor Richard: Its Source and Alteration," *Publications of the Modern Language Association of America,* LV, pp. 785–94 (1940).

Sachse, J. F. *Benjamin Franklin as a Free Mason.* Philadelphia: 1906. ("To write the history of Franklin as a Freemason is virtually to chronicle the early Masonic history of America." Soundly documented survey. Includes useful chronological table of Franklin's Masonic activities.)

Sainte-Beuve, C. A. *Portraits of the Eighteenth Century.* Tr. by K. P. Wormeley, with a critical introduction by E. Scherer. New York: 1905. I, pp. 311–75. (The two essays on Franklin in *Causeries du lundi* are "here put together," though with no important omissions from either. Brilliant portrait of the "most gracious, smiling, and persuasive utilitarian," one who assigned "no part to human imagination.")

Seipp, Erika. *Benjamin Franklins Religion und Ethik.* Darmstadt: 1932. (Suggestive, though brief, view of Franklin's deism and utilitarianism. Attempts to see his thought in reference to various representative deists. This is not, however, a "source" study.)

Shepherd, W. R. *History of Proprietary Government in Pennsylvania.* New York: 1896. (Franklin emerges as "a sort of tribune to the people," a "mighty Goliath," a "plague" in the eyes of the feudalistic rulers of Pennsylvania, "a huge fief." Author relatively unsympathetic to Franklin.)

Sherman, S. P. "Franklin and the Age of Enlightenment," in *Americans.* New York: 1922, pp. 28–62. (Penetrating survey and estimate.)

Smith, William, D.D. *Eulogium on Benjamin Franklin.* Philadelphia: 1792. (One agrees with P. L. Ford, that this work "forms a somewhat amusing contrast to the savageness of the Doctor's earlier writings against Franklin." Bombastic in its rhetoric and eulogy.)

Smythe, J. H., Jr. (comp.). *The Amazing Benjamin Franklin.* New York: 1929. (Anthology of brief, popular estimates. If individual notes are trivial, the collection illustrates Franklin's many-mindedness, a Renaissance versatility.)

Sonneck, O. G. "Benjamin Franklin's Relation to Music," *Music,* XIX, pp. 1–14 (Nov., 1900).

Steell, Willis. *Benjamin Franklin of Paris, 1776–1785.* New York: 1928. (An undocumented, partly imaginative, popular account.)

Stifler, J. M. *The Religion of Benjamin Franklin.* New York: 1925. (Popular survey. Warm appreciation of Franklin's penchant for projects of a humanitarian sort.)

Stourzh, Gerald. *Benjamin Franklin and American Foreign Policy*. Chicago: 1954. (A provocative study which resolves few of the major ambiguities.)

Stuber, Henry. "Life of Franklin" (a biography meant as a continuation of Franklin's *Autobiography*), in *Columbian Magazine and Universal Asylum*, May, July, September, October, November, 1790, and February, March, May, June, 1791.

Thorpe, F. N. (ed.). *Benjamin Franklin and the University of Pennsylvania*. U. S. Bureau of Education, Circular of Information, No. 2 (1892). Washington: 1893. (See especially Chapters I, II, written by Thorpe, which deal particularly with Franklin's ideas of self and formal education.)

Tilton, Eleanor M. "Lightning Rods and the Earthquake of 1755," *New England Quarterly*, XIII, pp. 85–97 (March, 1940).

Titus, Rev. Anson. "Boston When Ben Franklin Was a Boy," *Proceedings of the Bostonian Society*, pp. 55–72 (1906). (Brief suggestive view of the climate of opinion with regard to inoculation, Newtonianism, and Lockian sensationalism.)

Trent, W. P. "Benjamin Franklin," *McClure's Magazine*, VIII, pp. 273–7 (Jan., 1897). ("The most complete representative of his century that any nation can point to." Franklin "thoroughly represents his age in its practicality, in its devotion to science, in its intellectual curiosity, in its humanitarianism, in its lack of spirituality, in its calm self-content—in short, in its exaltation of prose and reason over poetry and faith." An enthusiastic and wise account.)

Trowbridge, John. "Franklin as a Scientist," *Publications of the Colonial Society of Massachusetts*, XVIII (1917). (Excellent appreciation of Franklin's capacity for inductive reasoning.)

Tuckerman, H. T. "Character of Franklin," *North American Review*, LXXXIII, pp. 402–22 (Oct., 1856). (Praises disinterestedness of Franklin as a scientist, as "one whom Bacon would have hailed as a disciple," although he "is not adapted to beguile us 'along the line of infinite desires.'")

Tudury, M. "Poor Richard," *Bookman*, LXIV, pp. 581–84 (Jan., 1927). (Popular glance at "cynical patriarch of American letters.")

Typothetae Bulletin, XXII, No. 15 (Jan. 11, 1926). (Issue devoted to the printer Franklin.)

Van Doren, Carl. "Benjamin Franklin," in *Literary History of the United States*. Revised edition in one volume. New York: 1953, pp. 101–12. (Useful description of Franklin's breadth of mind and action.)

————. *Jane Mecom: The Favorite Sister of Benjamin Franklin*.

New York: 1950. (Counterpoint to Van Doren's edition of their correspondence.)

Vicq d'Azyr, Félix. *Éloge de Franklin.* N. p.: 1791.

Victory, Beatrice M. *Benjamin Franklin and Germany.* Americana Germanica series, No. 21. Press of the University of Pennsylvania: 1915. (Sources reflecting Franklin's reputation in Germany of particular interest.)

Walsh, C. M. "Franklin and Plato," *Open Court*, XX, pp. 129–33 (March, 1906). (An attempt to interpret his *Articles of Belief*, 1728, in terms of the *Timaeus, Protagoras, Republic*, and *Euthyphro*.)

Webster, Noah. *Dissertations on the English Language: With Notes, Historical and Critical. To which is added, By Way of Appendix, an Essay on a Reformed Mode of Spelling, with Dr. Franklin's Arguments on that Subject.* Boston: 1789. (Notable remarks on Franklin's perspicuous and correct style which is "plain and elegantly neat": he "writes for the child as well as the philosopher.")

Wecter, Dixon. "Poor Richard: The boy who made good," in *The Hero in America, a chronicle of hero-worship.* New York: 1941, Chapter 4.

Wendell, Barrett. *A Literary History of America.* New York: 1900. (Franklin estimate, pp. 92–103.)

Wetzel, W. A. *Benjamin Franklin as an Economist.* Johns Hopkins University Studies in Historical and Political Science, Thirteenth Series, IX, pp. 421–76. Baltimore: 1895. (Useful summary, but superseded by Carey's *Franklin's Economic Views*.)

Wharton, A. H. "The American Philosophical Society," *Atlantic Monthly*, LXI, pp. 611–24 (May, 1888).

Williams, David. "More Light on Franklin's Religious Ideas," *American Historical Review*, XLIII, pp. 803–13 (July, 1938). (Important evidence on Franklin's deistic veneration of the "God of Newton.")

Woodward, Carl R. "Benjamin Franklin: Adventures in Agriculture," *Journal of the Franklin Institute*, CCXXXIV, pp. 207–28 (Sept., 1942).

Wright, Louis B. "Franklin's Legacy to the Gilded Age," *Virginia Quarterly Review*, XX, pp. 268–79 (1946).

Wroth, Lawrence C. "Benjamin Franklin: The Printer at Work," *Journal of the Franklin Institute*, CCXXXIV, pp. 105–32 (Aug., 1942).

Bibliographical suggestions relating to Franklin's American friends and contemporaries will be found following the brief but

scholarly studies in the *Dictionary of American Biography*. Of
these see especially John Adams (also G. Chinard, *Honest John
Adams*, Boston: 1933); Samuel Adams; Ethan Allen; Nathaniel
Ames; Joel Barlow (also V. C. Miller, *Joel Barlow: Revolutionist*,
London, *1791–92*, Hamburg: 1932, and T. A. Zunder, *Early
Days of Joel Barlow*, New Haven: 1934); John Bartram;
William Bartram (also N. Fagin, *William Bartram*, Baltimore:
1933); Hugh H. Brackenridge (also C. Newlin, *Brackenridge*,
Princeton: 1933); Cadwallader Colden; John Dickinson; Philip
Freneau; Francis Hopkinson; T. Jefferson; Cotton Mather; Jona-
than Mayhew; Thomas Paine; David Rittenhouse; Dr. Benjamin
Rush (also N. Goodman, *Rush*, Philadelphia: 1934); Rev.
William Smith; Ezra Stiles; John Trumbull; Noah Webster.

V. THE AGE OF FRANKLIN

Adams, J. T. *Provincial Society, 1690–1763*. (Volume III of
   A History of American Life, ed. by Fox and Schlesinger.)
   New York: 1927. (Contains useful "Critical Essay on
   Authorities" consulted, pp. 324–56, which serves as a guide
   for further study of many phases of the social history of the
   period.)

Adams, R. G. *Political Ideas of the American Revolution*. Durham, N. C.: 1922.

Andrews, C. M. *The Colonial Background of the American
   Revolution*. New Haven: 1924. (Stresses economic factors
   and the need of viewing the subject from the European angle;
   profitably used as companion study to Beer's *British Colonial
   Policy*.)

Baldwin, Alice M. *The New England Clergy and the American
   Revolution*. Durham, N. C.: 1928. (Prior to 1763 the clergy
   popularized "doctrines of natural right, the social contract,
   and the right of resistance" and principles of American
   constitutional law.)

Beard, C. A. *The Economic Origins of Jeffersonian Democracy*.
   New York: 1915. (Suggestive, if *other* factors are not neglected. See C. H. Hull's review in *American Historical Review*, XXII, pp. 401–3.)

Becker, Carl. *The Declaration of Independence; A Study in the
   History of Political Ideas*. New York: 1922. (Excellent
   survey of natural rights, and the extent to which this concept
   was influenced by Newtonianism.)

————. *The Heavenly City of the Eighteenth-Century Philosophers*. New Haven: 1932. (R. S. Crane observes, after calling
   attention to certain obscurities and confusions: "The descrip-

tion of the general temper of the 'philosophers,' the characterization of the principal eighteenth-century historians, much at least of the final chapter on the idea of progress—these can be read with general approval for their content and with a satisfaction in Becker's prose style that is unalloyed by considerations of exegesis or terminology" [*Philological Quarterly*, XIII, pp. 104–6].)

Beer, George L. *British Colonial Policy, 1754–1765.* New York: 1933 [1907].

Bemis, S. F. *The Diplomacy of the American Revolution.* New York: 1935. (Brilliant exposition of French, Spanish, Austrian, and other diplomacy relative to the Revolution. Should be supplemented by Frank Monaghan's *John Jay.*)

Blau, Joseph L. *Men and Movements in American Philosophy.* New York: 1952. (Useful account for the "general reader" who may not be schooled in the language of philosophy.)

Bloch, Léon. *La philosophie de Newton.* Paris: 1908. (A comprehensive, standard exposition.)

Bosker, Aisso. *Literary Criticism in the Age of Johnson.* Groningen: 1930. (Reviewed by N. Foerster in *Philological Quarterly*, XI, pp. 216–17.)

Brasch, F. E. "The Royal Society of London and Its Influence upon Scientific Thought in the American Colonies," *Scientific Monthly*, XXXIII, pp. 336–55, 448–69 (1931). (Useful survey.)

Bridenbaugh, Carl. *Cities in the Wilderness: The First Century of Urban Life in America, 1625–1744.* New York: 1938.

Bridenbaugh, Carl and Jessica. *Rebels and Gentlemen: Philadelphia in the Age of Franklin.* New York: 1942.

Brinton, Crane. *A Decade of Revolutions, 1789–1799.* New York: 1934. (Useful on the pattern of ideas associated with the French Revolution; has a full and up-to-date "Bibliographical Essay," pp. 293–322, with critical commentary.)

Brown, Esther E. *The French Revolution and the American Man of Letters.* Columbia, Mo.: 1951.

Bullock, C. J. *Essays on the Monetary History of the United States.* New York: 1900. (Useful bibliography, pp. 275–88.)

Burnett, E. C. (ed.). *Letters of Members of the Continental Congress.* Washington, D. C.: 1921. (Seven volumes now published include letters to 1784. Contain a mass of new material of first importance, edited with notes, cross references, and introductions.)

Burtt, E. A. *The Metaphysical Foundations of Modern Physical Science; A Historical and Critical Essay.* New York: 1925.

Bury, J. B. *The Idea of Progress.* New York: 1932 (new edition). (Standard English work on the topic. See also Jules Delvaille, *Essai sur l'histoire de l'idée de progrès* [Paris: 1910], a more encyclopedic book.)

Channing, Edward. *A History of the United States*. New York: 1912. (Volumes II–III.)

Clark, Harry Hayden. "Factors to be Investigated in American Literary History from 1787 to 1800," *English Journal*, XXIII, pp. 481–7 (June, 1934). (Suggests the genetic interrelations of classical ideas; neoclassicism; the scientific spirit, rationalism, and deism; primitivism and the idea of progress; physical America and the frontier spirit; agrarianism and laissez faire; Federalism versus Democracy, whether Jeffersonian or French; sentimentalism and humanitarianism; Gothicism; and conflicting currents of aesthetic theory.)

————. "The Influence of Science on American Ideas, from 1775 to 1809," *Transactions of the Wisconsin Academy of Science, Arts, and Letters*, XXXV, pp. 305–49 (1944).

Clark, Harry Hayden (ed.). *Poems of Freneau*. New York: 1929. (F. L. Pattee says of the Introduction, "No one has ever traced out better the ramifications of French Revolution deism in America and the effects of its clash with Puritanism" [*American Literature*, II, pp. 316–17]. Also see Clark's "Thomas Paine's Theories of Rhetoric," *Transactions of the Wisconsin Academy of Sciences, Arts and Letters*, XXVIII, pp. 307–39 [1933], which discusses relationships between deism and literary theory.)

Clark, J. M., J. Viner, and others. *Adam Smith, 1776–1926*. Chicago: 1928. (Brilliant essays on various aspects of Smith's thought and influence. See especially Jacob Viner's "Adam Smith and Laissez-Faire," pp. 116–55, which shows the relations in Smith's mind between economics and religion, between laissez faire and "the harmonious order of nature" posited by the scientific deists.)

Crane, R. S. "Anglican Apologetics and the Idea of Progress, 1699–1745," *Modern Philology*, XXXI, pp. 273–306 (Feb., 1934), pp. 349–82 (May, 1934). (Demonstrates in masterly fashion how the idea of progress grew out of orthodox defenses of revealed religion, current in Franklin's formative years. Modifies the conventional view that the Church was hostile to the idea of progress and that it derived exclusively from the scientific spirit.)

Curti, Merle. *The Growth of American Thought*. New York: 1943.

Davidson, P. G., Jr. "Whig Propagandists of the American

Revolution," *American Historical Review*, XXXIX, pp. 442–53 (April, 1934). (Also see *Revolutionary Propaganda in New England, New York, and Pennsylvania, 1763–1776*. Unpublished dissertation, University of Chicago, 1929.)

"Deism," in *The New Schaff-Herzog Encyclopedia of Religious Knowledge*, III, pp. 391–97 (by Ernst Troeltsch).

De la Fontainerie, F. (tr. and ed.). *French Liberalism and Education in the Eighteenth Century: The Writings of La Chalotais, Turgot, Diderot, and Condorcet on National Education*. New York: 1932. (Convenient source book.)

Dewey, D. R. *Financial History of the United States*. New York: 1924 (9th ed.). (Bristles with bibliographical aids for study of eighteenth century.)

Draper, J. W. *Eighteenth Century English Aesthetics: A Bibliography*. Heidelberg: 1931. (Source materials, pp. 61–128, for aesthetics of literature and drama: includes in appendix, pp. 129–40, ablest secondary works to 1931. An invaluable guide. See additions by R. S. Crane, *Modern Philology*, XXIX, pp. 251 ff. [1931], W. D. Templeman, *ibid.*, XXX, pp. 309–16, R. D. Havens, *Modern Language Notes*, XLVII, pp. 118–20 [1932].)

Drennon, Herbert. "Newtonianism: Its Method, Theology, and Metaphysics," *Englische Studien*, LXVIII, pp. 397–409 (1933–1934). (Other parts of Mr. Drennon's brilliant doctoral dissertation, *James Thomson and Newtonianism* [University of Chicago, 1928], have been published in *Publications of the Modern Language Association*, XLIX, pp. 71–80, March, 1934; in *Studies in Philology*, XXXI, pp. 453–71, July, 1934; and in *Philological Quarterly*, XIV, pp. 70–82, Jan., 1935.)

Ducros, Louis. *French Society in the Eighteenth Century*. Tr. from the French by W. de Geijer; with a Foreword by J. A. Higgs-Walker. London: 1927.

Duncan, C. S. *The New Science and English Literature in the Classical Period*. Menasha, Wis.: 1913. (Scholarly.)

Dunning, W. A. *A History of Political Theories from Luther to Montesquieu*. New York: 1905. Also *A History of Political Theories from Rousseau to Spencer*. New York: 1920. (Standard works.)

Elton, Oliver. *The Augustan Age*. New York: 1899. Also *A Survey of English Literature, 1730–1780*. 2 vols. London: 1928. (Acute on literary trends, though hardly adequate on ideas.)

Evans, Charles. *American Bibliography*. Chicago: 1903–34. (Volumes I–XII, pp. 1639–1799.)

Faÿ, Bernard. *Revolution and Freemasonry, 1680–1800*. Boston: 1935. (Stimulating conjectures vitiated by extravagant and undocumented conclusions.)

————. *The Revolutionary Spirit in France and America*. Tr. by R. Guthrie. New York: 1927. (Especially valuable for notes on the vogue of Franklin in France. Highly important comprehensive survey of French influence in America, and the impetus our revolution gave to French liberalism.)

Fisher, S. G. *The Quaker Colonies. A Chronicle of the Proprietors of the Delaware*. New Haven: 1921. (Useful bibliography, pp. 231–4.)

Fiske, John. *The Beginnings of New England, or the Puritan Theocracy in Its Relations to Civil and Religious Liberty*. Boston: 1896 [1889]. (See also Perry Miller's *Orthodoxy in Massachusetts, 1630–1650. A Genetic Study*. Cambridge, Mass.: 1933.)

Gettell, R. G. *History of American Political Thought*. New York: 1928. (The standard comprehensive treatment of its subject. Has good bibliographies.)

Gide, Charles, and Rist, Charles. *A History of Economic Doctrines from the Time of the Physiocrats to the Present Day*. Authorized translation from the second revised and augmented edition of 1913 under the direction of the late Professor Wm. Smart, by R. Richards. Boston: 1915. (Excellent survey of physiocracy.)

Gierke, Otto. *Natural Law and the Theory of Society, 1500 to 1800*. With a Lecture on The Ideas of Natural Law and Humanity, by Ernst Troeltsch. Tr. with an introduction by E. Barker. 2 vols. Cambridge, England: 1934. (A standard work, with excellent notes, especially valuable on European backgrounds.)

Gohdes, Clarence. "Ethan Allen and his *Magnum Opus*," *Open Court*, XLIII, pp. 128–51 (March, 1929). (Suggests the eighteenth-century battle between revelation and reason, the latter as buttressed by Lockian sensationalism and Newtonian science.)

Green, E. B. *The Provincial Governor in the English Colonies of North America*. Cambridge, Mass.: 1898. (Inveterate divergence between provincial governor and provincial assemblies foreshadowed the American Revolution.)

Halévy, E. *The Growth of Philosophic Radicalism*. Tr. by M. Morris, with a preface by A. D. Lindsay. London: 1928. (A comprehensive, authoritative work.)

Hansen, A. O. *Liberalism and American Education in the Eighteenth Century*. With an introduction by E. H. Reisner.

New York: 1926. (A good bibliography of primary sources and a poor bibliography of secondary sources, pp. 265–96. Although this slights Franklin and deals especially with plans following Franklin's death, it surveys educational ideals with reference to the ideas of the Enlightenment, ideas latent in Franklin's writings.)

Haroutunian, Joseph. *Piety versus Moralism; the Passing of the New England Theology.* New York: 1932. (An important scholarly work arguing reluctantly that Puritanism declined because it was theocentric and inadequate to the social needs of the time. Has an excellent bibliography.)

Hefelbower, S. G. *The Relation of John Locke to English Deism.* Chicago: 1918. (The relation between Locke and the English deists is "not causal, nor do they mark different stages of the same movement"; they are "related as coordinate parts of the larger progressive movement of the age." Stresses Locke's tolerance, rationalism, and natural religion.)

Higgs, Henry. *The Physiocrats. Six Lectures on the French Économistes of the Eighteenth Century.* London: 1897. (Gide and Rist term this a "succinct account" of the physiocratic system.)

Hildeburn, C. R. *Issues of the Pennsylvania Press. A Century of Printing, 1685–1784.* 2 vols. Philadelphia: 1885–1886. (A highly useful guide to what was being read in Pennsylvania year by year.)

Hindle, Brooke. *The Pursuit of Science in Revolutionary America, 1735–1789.* Durham, N. C.: 1956. (Many sidelights on Franklin and his colleagues in the sciences.)

Horton, W. M. *Theism and the Scientific Spirit.* New York: 1933. (Popular accounts of "Copernican world" and "God in the Newtonian world" in Chapters I–II.)

Humphrey, Edward. *Nationalism and Religion in America, 1774–1789.* Boston: 1924.

Jameson, J. F. *The American Revolution Considered as a Social Movement.* Princeton, N. J.: 1926. (Brief and general, but suggestive.)

Jones, H. M. *America and French Culture, 1750–1848.* Chapel Hill, N. C.: 1927. (A monumental, elaborately documented comprehensive work, containing an excellent bibliography.)

Jones, H. M. "American Prose Style: 1700–1770," *Huntington Library Bulletin,* No. 6, pp. 115–51 (Nov., 1934). (Shows that Puritan preachings inculcated the ideal of a simple, lucid, and dignified style.)

Kaye, F. B. (ed.). *The Fable of the Bees: or, Private Vices, Publick Benefits. With a Commentary Critical, Historical,*

and Explanatory. 2 vols. Oxford: 1924. (The introduction is
the most lucid and penetrating commentary on Mandeville in
relation to the pattern of ideas of his age. See L. I. Bredvold's
review in *Journal of English and Germanic Philology,* XXIV,
pp. 586–89, Oct., 1925.)

Koch, G. A. *Republican Religion: The American Revolution
and the Cult of Reason.* New York: 1933. ("A vast body of
facts about a host of obscure figures"—reviewed by H. H.
Clark in *Journal of Philosophy,* XXXI, pp. 135–38. Contains
an elaborate bibliography.)

Kraus, Michael. *The Atlantic Civilization: Eighteenth-Century
Origins.* Ithaca: 1949.

————. "Slavery Reform in the Eighteenth Century: An
Aspect of Transatlantic Intellectual Cooperation," *Pennsylvania Magazine of History and Biography,* LX, pp. 53–66
(1936).

————. *Intercolonial Aspects of American Culture on the Eve
of the Revolution.* New York: 1928. (Scholarly.)

Lecky, W. E. H. *A History of England in the Eighteenth Century.* 7 vols. New York: 1892–93 (new ed.). (A standard
work, containing a finely documented treatment of the political aspects of the American Revolution.)

Leonard, S. A. *The Doctrine of Correctness in English Usage,
1700–1800.* Madison, Wis.: 1929. (Authoritative.)

Lévy-Bruhl, Lucien. *History of Modern Philosophy in France.*
Chicago: 1899.

Lincoln, C. H. *The Revolutionary Movement in Pennsylvania,
1760–1776.* Philadelphia: 1901. (A highly important study
showing that local sectional strife which would have eventually
led to conflict synchronized with the strife between the colony
and England.)

Lovejoy, Arthur O. *The Great Chain of Being: A Study of the
History of an Idea.* Cambridge, Mass.: 1936.

————. "The Parallel of Deism and Classicism," *Modern
Philology,* XXIX, pp. 281–99 (Feb., 1932). ("A systematic
statement of the rationalistic *preconceptions* which, when applied in matters of religion terminated in Deism, when applied
in aesthetics produced Classicism. An illuminating synthesis,
done throughout with characteristic finesse and discrimination"
[*Philological Quarterly,* XII, p. 106, April, 1933].)

McIlwain, C. H. *The American Revolution: A Constitutional
Interpretation.* New York: 1923. (Offers defense of revolution on English constitutional grounds.)

Martin, Kingsley. *French Liberal Thought in the Eighteenth
Century: A Study of Political Ideas from Bayle to Condorcet.*

Boston: 1929. (Stimulating survey of ideology motivating the French Revolution, "a dramatic moment when feudalism, clericalism and divine monarchy collapsed.")

Merriam, C. E. *A History of American Political Theories.* New York: 1924 [1903]. (Authoritative, brief treatment.)

Miller, Perry. *The New England Mind: From Colony to Province.* Cambridge, Mass.: 1953.

Monaghan, Frank. *John Jay, Defender of Liberty.* New York: 1935. (A brilliant biography and a fully documented study of the activities and diplomacy of the Continental Congress. Supplements S. F. Bemis; see above.)

Moore, C. A. "Shaftesbury and the Ethical Poets in England, 1700–1760," *Publications of the Modern Language Association,* XXXI (N. s. XXIV), pp. 264–325 (June, 1916). (Penetrating and brilliant survey of the growth of altruism, to be supplemented by R. S. Crane's studies of earlier sources.)

Morais, Herbert M. *Deism in Eighteenth Century America.* New York: 1934. (If little space is given to the implications of Deism in terms of political, economic, and literary theory, and if the leaders of deistic thought, such as Franklin, Jefferson, and Paine are too lightly dealt with, this work is "substantial, precise, well-documented, modest, cautious, and objective." Has a good bibliography. Reviewed by H. H. Clark, *American Literature,* VI, pp. 467–69, Jan., 1935. See also Morais's "Deism in Revolutionary America, 1763–89," *International Journal of Ethics,* XLII, pp. 434–53, July, 1932.)

————. *The Struggle for American Freedom: The First Two Hundred Years.* New York: 1944.

Morley, John. *Diderot and the Encyclopædists.* 2 vols. London: 1923. (A suggestive survey, parts of which have been superseded by more recent studies.)

Mornet, Daniel. *French Thought in the Eighteenth Century.* Tr. by L. M. Levin. New York: 1929. (Lucid and penetrating survey; suggestive notes on the influence of speculation motivated by science.)

————. *Les origines intellectuelles de la Révolution française (1715–1787).* Paris: 1933. (A brilliant work, concluding that without the extraordinary diffusion of radical ideas in all classes in France, the States-General in 1789 would not have adopted revolutionary measures. See C. Brinton's review, *American Historical Review,* XXXIX, pp. 726–27, 1934.)

Morse, W. N. "Lectures on Electricity in Colonial Times," *New England Quarterly,* VII, pp. 364–74 (June, 1934). (Presents fourteen items on the vogue of electrical experiments, 1747–1765.)

Mott, F. L. *A History of American Magazines, 1741–1850.*
New York: 1930.

Mullett, C. F. *Fundamental Law and the American Revolution,
1760–1776.* New York: 1933. (A highly important scholarly
study, with excellent bibliography of relevant investigations
of recent date. Supplements B. F. Wright.)

Ornstein, Martha. *The Rôle of Scientific Societies in the Seventeenth Century.* New York: 1913. Reprinted, University of
Chicago Press: 1928. (Shows their radical influence. See
suggestive reviews in *American Historical Review,* XXXIV,
pp. 386–27 [1929]; and *Times Literary Supplement* [Lon-
don], p. 679 [Sept. 27, 1928].)

Osgood, H. L. *The American Colonies in the Eighteenth Century.* 4 vols. New York: 1924–25. (Standard work on political aspects.)

Perkins, J. B. *France in the American Revolution.* Boston: 1911.
(Includes able survey of Franklin's efforts in behalf of colonies.)

Richardson, L. N. *A History of Early American Magazines,
1741–1789.* New York: 1931. (An encyclopedic survey indispensable to all students of the period. Enormously documented.)

Robertson, J. M. *A Short History of Free Thought, Ancient
and Modern.* 2 vols. London: 1915. (Third edition, revised
and expanded. An important survey, if somewhat militantly
partisan.)

Roustan, Marius. *The Pioneers of the French Revolution.* Tr.
by F. Whyte, with an Introduction by H. J. Laski. Boston:
1926. (Thesis: "The spirit of the *philosophes* was the spirit of
the Revolution." Highly readable, but inferior to parallel
studies by Martin and Mornet in incisive analysis of patterns
of ideas. Stresses picturesque social aspects.)

Savelle, Max. *The Foundations of American Civilization.* New
York: 1942.

Schapiro, J. S. *Condorcet and the Rise of Liberalism in France.*
New York: 1934. (Condorcet is the "almost perfect expres-
sion of the pioneer liberalism of the period"; he is viewed as
the "last of the encyclopedists and the most universal of all."
A lucid scholarly study, although hardly superseding Alengry's
Condorcet.)

Schlesinger, A. M. "The American Revolution," in *New View-
points in American History.* New York: 1922, pp. 160–83.
(A brief but excellent interpretation, stressing economic
factors, and presenting a useful "Bibliographical Note," pp.
181–83, including references to studies of political and religious

factors. See also studies of the latter by R. G. Adams, Alice Baldwin, Carl Becker, B. F. Wright, C. F. Mullett, C. H. Van Tyne, and Edward Humphrey.)

Schneider, Herbert W. *A History of American Philosophy*. New York: 1946.

——. *The Puritan Mind*. New York: 1930. (An acute scholarly study, with excellent bibliography. The stress on ideas supplements and balances Parrington's tendency to dismiss ideas as by-products of economic factors.)

Smith, T. V. *The American Philosophy of Equality*. Chicago: 1927. (Chapter I includes discussion of "natural rights," with recognition of the influence of European theorists.)

Smyth, A. H. *The Philadelphia Magazines and Their Contributors, 1741–1850*. Philadelphia: 1892. (Brief descriptive account, mostly superseded by the relevant sections in F. L. Mott's and L. N. Richardson's histories.)

Stephen, Leslie. *A History of English Thought in the Eighteenth Century*. 2 vols. London: 1902 (3rd ed.). (As J. L. Laski observes, it is "almost insolent to praise such work." In certain aspects, however, it has been superseded by studies by such men as R. S. Crane, A. O. Lovejoy, H. M. Jones, etc.)

Stimson, Dorothy. *The Gradual Acceptance of the Copernican Theory of the Universe*. Hanover, N. H.: 1917.

Taylor, O. H. "Economics and the Idea of Natural Law," *Quarterly Journal of Economics*, XLIV, pp. 1–39 (Nov., 1929). ("The evolution of the idea of 'law' in economics" paralleling "its evolution in the natural sciences" led to belief in an economic mechanism which "was regarded as a wise device of the Creator for causing individuals, while pursuing only their own interests, to promote the prosperity of society, and for causing the right adjustment to one another of supplies, demands, prices, and incomes, to take place automatically, in consequence of the free action of all individuals." The author suggests that there is evident an incongruous dichotomy between the mechanistic idea of the physiocrats and their assumption that enlightened men "would be able to use government as a scientific tool for carrying out purely rationalistic measures in the common interest." See also outline of his doctoral thesis on this subject, Harvard University *Summaries of Theses* [1928], pp. 102–6. An authoritative study of an important subject.)

Torrey, N. L. *Voltaire and the English Deists*. New Haven: 1930. (Shows Voltaire's great indebtedness to Newtonianism, which he popularized in France, and to earlier deists than Bolingbroke. Authoritative.)

Turberville, A. S. (ed.). *Johnson's England. An Account of the Life and Manners of His Age.* 2 vols. Oxford University Press: 1933. (Although this collaborative work neglects political, religious, economic, and aesthetic ideas, it embodies readable and authoritative surveys of external aspects of social history, viewed from many angles. Contains useful bibliographies. See review by H. H. Clark, *American Review,* II, No. 4 [Feb., 1934].)

Tyler, M. C. *A History of American Literature, 1607–1765.* 2 vols. New York: 1878. Also *The Literary History of the American Revolution.* 2 vols. New York: 1897. (Somewhat grandiloquent but very full survey, including Loyalists. Excellent on literary aspects but partly superseded on ideas. Contains excellent bibliography of primary sources.)

Van Tyne, C. H. *The Causes of the War of Independence.* Boston: 1922. (Brilliant both in interpretation and style, and well balanced in considering economic, political, social, religious, and philosophic factors.)

Veitch, G. S. *The Genesis of Parliamentary Reform.* London: 1913. (Useful for English backgrounds.)

Weld, C. R. *A History of the Royal Society with Memoirs of the Presidents.* 2 vols. London: 1848.

Wendell, Barrett. *Cotton Mather, the Puritan Priest.* Cambridge, Mass.: 1926 [1891]. (A sympathetic study of one of Franklin's masters, based on a deep knowledge of the Puritan spirit.)

Weulersse, Georges. *Le mouvement physiocratique en France (de 1756 à 1770).* 2 vols. Paris: 1910. (The standard treatment.)

White, A. D. *A History of the Warfare of Science with Theology in Christendom.* 2 vols. New York: 1897. (Prominent attention given to colonial eighteenth century.)

Whitney, Lois. *Primitivism and the Idea of Progress in English Popular Literature of the Eighteenth Century.* Baltimore: 1934. (An acute study of the history of an important idea, especially as embodied in novels. Occasionally misleading because Miss Whitney does not always pay necessary attention to the major individuals' change of attitude, to their genetic development. Contains no bibliography. See Bury, above.)

Williams, David. "The Influence of Rousseau on Political Opinion, 1760–1795," *English Historical Review,* XLVIII, pp. 414-30 (1933).

Winsor, Justin (ed.). *Narrative and Critical History of America.* 8 vols. Boston: [1884–] 1889. (Especially valuable for bibliographical notes.)

Wright, B. F. *American Interpretations of Natural Law. A*

Study in the History of Political Thought. Cambridge, Mass.: 1931. (An able outline of main trends, although it neglects evidence both in eighteenth-century sermons and in legal papers of colonial attorneys. Shows strong influence of Grotius, Puffendorf, and Locke on Revolutionary theories. Should be supplemented by C. F. Mullett's parallel book. Reviewed by R. B. Morris, *American Historical Review*, XXXVII, pp. 561–62, [April, 1932].)

Wright, T. G. *Literary Culture in Early New England, 1620–1730*. New Haven: 1920. (Valuable for its check lists of colonial libraries, suggesting books current in Franklin's formative years. The best treatment of its subject although it neglects the literary and aesthetic theories of the period. To be supplemented by books by C. F. Richardson, W. F. Mitchell, and E. C. Cook.)

Further background studies may be found in *The Cambridge History of English Literature*, Cambridge and New York, 1912–14, VIII–XI, and *The Cambridge History of American Literature*, New York, 1917, Vol. I. See also the more up-to-date bibliographies in P. Smith's *A History of Modern Culture*, New York, 1934, II, pp. 647–76; R. S. Crane's *A Collection of English Poems, 1660–1800*, New York, 1932, pp. 1115–42; and especially O. Shepard and P. S. Wood, *English Prose and Poetry, 1660–1800*, Boston, 1934, pp. xxxiii–xxxviii and pp. 937–1067.

VI. BIBLIOGRAPHIES AND CHECK LISTS

Boggess, A. C., and Witmer, E. R. *Calendar of the Papers of Benjamin Franklin in the Library of the University of Pennsylvania*. (Being the Appendix to the *Calendar of the Papers of Benjamin Franklin in the Library of the American Philosophical Society*, edited by I. M. Hays.) Philadelphia: 1908. (This valuable work lists letters to Franklin, letters from Franklin, and miscellaneous letters, with brief notes on the topics discussed in each letter and place of publication in cases where the letters have been published.)

Books Printed by Benjamin Franklin. Born Jan. 17, 1706. New York: 1906. (Lists best known imprints; useful although eclipsed by Campbell.)

Bridgewater, Dorothy W. "Notable Additions to the Franklin Collection," *Yale University Library Gazette*, XX, pp. 21–28 (Oct., 1945).

The Cambridge History of American Literature. New York: 1917. I, pp. 442–52. (Lists of "Collected Works," "Separate

Works," and "Contributions to Periodicals" constitute a convenient abridgment of Ford, but the list, "Biographical and
Critical," limited to two pages, is at best inadequately suggestive.

Campbell, W. J. *The Collection of Franklin Imprints in the
Museum of the Curtis Publishing Company. With a Short-
Title Check List of All the Books, Pamphlets, Broadsides, &c.,
known to have been printed by Benjamin Franklin.* Philadelphia: 1918.

———. *A Short-Title Check List of All the Books, Pamphlets,
Broadsides, &c., known to have been printed by Benjamin
Franklin.* Philadelphia: 1918.

Eddy, George Simpson. "First American, called civilized; some
bibliographical suggestions," *Colophon*, Vol. II, N. s., No. 4,
pp. 602–08 (1937).

Faÿ, B. *Benjamin Franklin bibliographie et étude sur les sources
historiques relatives à sa vie* (Vol. III of *Benjamin Franklin,
bourgeois d'Amérique et citoyen du monde.*) Paris: 1931.
(Faÿ, in *Franklin, the Apostle of Modern Times*, pp. 517–33,
has furnished "only a summary bibliography," which, in spite
of its occasional inaccuracies and infelicities in form, contains
many useful items, American, English, and French; especially
valuable for notes on several manuscript collections. In this
French edition the bibliography is more detailed.)

Ford, P. L. *Franklin Bibliography. A List of Books Written by,
or Relating to Benjamin Franklin.* Brooklyn, N. Y.: 1889.
(The standard, time-honored work, unfortunately not superseded.)

Ford, W. C. *List of the Benjamin Franklin Papers in the Library
of Congress.* Washington, D. C.: 1905.

Hays, I. M. *Calendar of the Papers of Benjamin Franklin in the
Library of the American Philosophical Society.* Vols. II–VI in
*The Record of the Celebration of the Two Hundredth An-
niversary of the Birth of Benjamin Franklin, under the
Auspices of the American Philosophical Society Held at Philadelphia for Promoting Useful Knowledge, April 17 to 20,
1906.* Philadelphia: 1908. (A. H. Smyth purports to have
printed in his ten-volume edition all of Franklin's letters in
this collection. Valuable especially for letters addressed to
Franklin.)

Lingelbach, William E. "Benjamin Franklin's Papers in the
American Philosophical Society," *Proceedings of the American Philosophical Society*, XCIX, pp. 359–80 (1955).

"List of Works in the New York Public Library by or Relating to Benjamin Franklin," *Bulletin of New York Public Library*, X, No. 1. New York: 1906, pp. 29–83.

Mugridge, Donald H. "Scientific Manuscripts of Benjamin Franklin," *Library of Congress Journal of Current Acquisitions*, IV, pp. 12–21 (1947).

Philbrick, Francis S. "Notes on Early Editions and Editors of Franklin," *Proceedings of the American Philosophical Society*, XCVII, pp. 525–64 (1953).

Rosengarten, J. G. "Some New Franklin Papers," *University of Pennsylvania Alumni Register*, pp. 1–7 (July, 1903). (A report to the Board of Trustees saying "there are over five hundred pieces of MS. among the collection of Franklin papers recently added to the Library of the University." These range from 1731 to Franklin's latest correspondence. Only a few of these pieces are described.)

Spiller, Robert E., Willard Thorp, Thomas H. Johnson, Henry Seidel Canby (Eds.). *Literary History of the United States*. New York: 1948. Vol. III, pp. 507–15. (Severely selective but useful. See also "Bibliography Supplement," edited by Richard M. Ludwig. 1959 [second printing 1960], pp. 123–26.)

Stevens, Henry. *Benjamin Franklin's Life and Writings. A Bibliographical Essay on the Stevens Collection of Books and Manuscripts Relating to Doctor Franklin*. London: 1881. (Pp. 21–40 contain a list of "Franklin's Printed Works.")

Swift, Lindsay. "Catalogue of Works Relating to Benjamin Franklin in the Boston Public Library," *Bulletin of the Boston Public Library*, V, pp. 217–31, 276–84, 420–33. Boston: 1883. (Including Dr. S. A. Green's collection, this was the "immediate predecessor" to Ford.)

Consider Lewis Leary's *Articles on American Literature, 1900–1950*. Durham, N. C.: 1954; and the massive references in the notes to the Yale Edition of Franklin papers, 1959 ff.

For current articles the student should consult especially the bibliographies in *Philological Quarterly, American Literature, Publications of the Modern Language Association,* bibliographical bulletins of the Modern Humanities Research Association, and Grace C. Griffin's annual bibliography, *Writings on American History*.

*

Selections from
BENJAMIN FRANKLIN

*

From the AUTOBIOGRAPHY [1]

TWYFORD, at the Bishop of St. Asaph's, 1771.

DEAR SON, I have ever had a Pleasure in obtaining any little Anecdotes of my Ancestors. You may remember the Enquiries I made among the Remains of my Relations when you were with me in England; and the journey I undertook for that purpose. Now imagining it may be equally agreable to you to know the Circumstances of *my* Life, many of which you are yet unacquainted with; and expecting a Weeks uninterrupted Leisure in my present Country Retirement, I sit down to write them for you. To which I have besides some other Inducements. Having emerg'd from the Poverty and Obscurity in which I was born and bred, to a State of Affluence and some Degree of Reputation in the World, and having gone so far thro' Life with a considerable Share of Felicity, the conducing Means I made use of, which, with the Blessing of God, so well succeeded, my Posterity may like to know, as they may find some of them suitable to their own Situations, and therefore fit to be imitated. That Felicity, when I reflected on it, has induc'd me sometimes to say, that were it offer'd to my Choice, I should have no Objection to a Repetition of the same Life from its Beginning, only asking the Advantages Authors have in a second Edition to correct some Faults of the first. So would I if I might, besides corr[ecting] the Faults, change some sinister Accidents and Events of it for others more favourable, but tho' this were deny'd, I should still accept the Offer. However, since such a Repetition is not to be expected, the next Thing most like living one's Life over again, seems to be a *Recollection* of that Life; and to make that Recollection as durable as possible, the putting it down in Writing. Hereby, too, I shall indulge the Inclination so natural in old Men, to be talking of themselves and their own past Actions, and I shall indulge it, without being troublesome to others who thro' respect to Age might think themselves oblig'd

[1] Superior figures through the text refer to notes in pp. 529 ff.

3

to give me a Hearing, since this may be read or not as any one
pleases. And lastly (I may as well confess it, since my Denial of
it will be believ'd by no Body) perhaps I shall a good deal gratify
my own *Vanity*. Indeed I scarce ever heard or saw the introductory Words, *Without vanity I may say*, &c but some vain
thing immediately follow'd. Most People dislike Vanity in
others whatever share they have of it themselves, but I give it
fair Quarter wherever I meet with it, being persuaded that it is
often productive of Good to the Possessor and to others that
are within his Sphere of Action: And therefore in many Cases it
would not be quite absurd if a Man were to thank God for his
Vanity among the other Comforts of Life.—

And now I speak of thanking God, I desire with all Humility
to acknowledge, that I owe the mention'd Happiness of my past
Life to his kind Providence, which led me to the Means I us'd
and gave them Success. My Belief of this, induces me to *hope*,
tho' I must not *presume*, that the same Goodness will still be exercis'd towards me in continuing that Happiness, or in enabling
me to bear a fatal Reverse, which I may experience as others
have done, the Complexion of my future Fortune being known to
him only: in whose Power it is to bless to us even our Afflictions.

The Notes one of my Uncles (who had the same kind of
Curiosity in collecting Family Anecdotes) once put into my
Hands, furnish'd me with several Particulars relating to our Ancestors. From these Notes I learnt that the Family had liv'd in
the same Village, Ecton in Northamptonshire, for 300 Years,
and how much longer he knew not (perhaps from the Time
when the Name *Franklin* that before was the name of an Order
of People, was assum'd by them for a Surname, when others
took surnames all over the kingdom)[,] on a Freehold of about
30 Acres, aided by the Smith's Business, which had continued
in the Family till his Time, the eldest son being always bred to
that Business[.] A Custom which he and my Father both followed as to their eldest Sons.—When I search'd the Register at
Ecton, I found an Account of their Births, Marriages and
Burials, from the Year 1555 only, there being no Register kept
in that Parish at any time preceding.—By that Register I per-

ceiv'd that I was the youngest Son of the youngest Son for 5 Generations back. My Grandfather Thomas, who was born in 1598, lived at Ecton till he grew too old to follow Business longer, when he went to live with his Son John, a Dyer at Banbury in Oxfordshire, with whom my Father serv'd an Apprenticeship. There my Grandfather died and lies buried. We saw his Gravestone in 1758. His eldest Son Thomas liv'd in the House at Ecton, and left it with the Land to his only Child, a Daughter, who, with her Husband, one Fisher of Wellingborough sold it to Mr. Isted, now Lord of the Manor there. My Grandfather had 4 Sons that grew up, viz Thomas, John, Benjamin and Josiah. I will give you what Account I can of them at this distance from my Papers, and if these are not lost in my Absence, you will among them find many more Particulars. Thomas was bred a Smith under his Father, but being ingenious, and encourag'd in Learning (as all his Brothers likewise were) by an Esquire Palmer then the principal Gentleman in that Parish, he qualify'd himself for the Business of Scrivener, became a considerable Man in the County Affairs, was a chief Mover of all publick Spirited Undertakings for the County or Town of Northampton and his own village, of which many instances were told us; and he was at Ecton much taken Notice of and patroniz'd by the then Lord Halifax. He died in 1702, Jan. 6, old Stile, just 4 Years to a Day before I was born. The Account we receiv'd of his Life and Character from some old People at Ecton, I remember struck you as something extraordinary, from its Similarity to what you knew of mine. Had he died on the same Day, you said one might have suppos'd a Transmigration.—John was bred a Dyer, I believe of Woollens. Benjamin, was bred a Silk Dyer, serving an Apprenticeship at London. He was an ingenious Man, I remember him well, for when I was a Boy he came over to my Father in Boston, and lived in the House with us some Years. He lived to a great Age. His Grandson Samuel Franklin now lives in Boston. He left behind him two Quarto Volumes, M.S. of his own Poetry, consisting of little occasional Pieces address'd to his Friends and Relations, of which the following sent to me, is a Specimen. [Although

Franklin wrote in the margin "Here insert it," the poetry is not given.] He had form'd a Shorthand of his own, which he taught me, but, never practising it I have now forgot it. I was nam'd after this Uncle, there being a particular Affection between him and my Father. He was very pious, a great Attender of Sermons of the best Preachers, which he took down in his Shorthand and had with him many Volumes of them. He was also much of a Politician, too much perhaps for his Station. There fell lately into my Hands in London a Collection he had made of all the principal Pamphlets relating to Publick Affairs from 1641 to 1717. Many of the Volumes are wanting, as appears by the Numbering, but there still remains 8 Vols. Folio, and 24 in 4.to and 8.vo.—A Dealer in old Books met with them, and knowing me by my sometimes buying of him, he brought them to me. It seems my Uncle must have left them here when he went to America, which was above 50 years since. There are many of his Notes in the Margins.—

This obscure Family of ours was early in the Reformation, and continu'd Protestants thro' the Reign of Queen Mary, when they were sometimes in Danger of Trouble on Account of their Zeal against Popery. They had got an English Bible, and to conceal and secure it, it was fastened open with Tapes under and within the Frame of a Joint Stool. When my Great Great Grandfather read it [it] to his Family, he turn'd up the Joint Stool upon his Knees, turning over the Leaves then under the Tapes. One of the Children stood at the Door to give Notice if he saw the Apparitor coming, who was an Officer of the Spiritual Court. In that Case the Stool was turn'd down again upon its feet, when the Bible remain'd conceal'd under it as before. This Anecdote I had from my Uncle Benjamin.—The Family continu'd all of the Church of England till about the End of Charles the 2ds Reign, when some of the Ministers that had been outed for Nonconformity, holding Conventicles in Northamptonshire, Benjamin and Josiah adher'd to them, and so continu'd all their Lives. The rest of the Family remain'd with the Episcopal Church.

Josiah, my father, married young, and carried his Wife with

three Children into New England, about 1682. The Conventicles having been forbidden by Law, and frequently disturbed, induced some considerable Men of his Acquaintance to remove to that Country, and he was prevail'd with to accompany them thither, where they expected to enjoy their Mode of Religion with Freedom.—By the same Wife he had 4 Children more born there, and by a second wife ten more, in all 17, of which I remember 13 sitting at one time at his Table, who all grew up to be Men and Women, and married. I was the youngest Son, and the youngest Child but two, and was born in Boston, N. England. My mother, the 2^d wife was Abiah Folger, a daughter of Peter Folger, one of the first Settlers of New England, of whom honourable mention is made by Cotton Mather, in his Church History of that Country, (entitled Magnalia Christi Americana) as *a godly learned Englishman*, if I remember the Words rightly. I have heard that he wrote sundry small occasional Pieces, but only one of them was printed which I saw now many years since. It was written in 1675, in the home-spun Verse of that Time and People, and address'd to those then concern'd in the Government there. It was in favour of Liberty of Conscience, and in behalf of the Baptists, Quakers, and other Sectaries, that had been under Persecution; ascribing the Indian Wars and other Distresses, that had befallen the Country to that Persecution, as so many Judgments of God, to punish so heinous an Offense; and exhorting a Repeal of those uncharitable Laws. The whole appear'd to me as written with a good deal of Decent Plainness and manly Freedom. The six last concluding Lines I remember, tho' I have forgotten the two first of the Stanza, but the Purport of them was that his Censures proceeded from Good will, and therefore he would be known as the Author,

> "Because to be a Libeller, (says he)
>   I hate it with my Heart.
> From* Sherburne Town where now I dwell,
>   My Name I do put here,
>   Without Offense, your real Friend,
>   It is Peter Folgier."

*In MS Franklin notes, "In the Island of Nantucket."

My elder Brothers were all put Apprentices to different
Trades. I was put to the Grammar School at Eight Years of
Age, my Father intending to devote me as the Tithe of his Sons
to the Service of the Church. My early Readiness in learning to
read (which must have been very early, as I do not remember
when I could not read) and the Opinion of all his Friends that I
should certainly make a good Scholar, encourag'd him in this
Purpose of his. My Uncle Benjamin too approv'd of it, and
propos'd to give me all his Shorthand Volumes of Sermons I
suppose as a Stock to set up with, if I would learn his Character.
I continu'd however at the Grammar School not quite one Year,
tho' in that time I had risen gradually from the Middle of the
Class of that Year to be the Head of it, and farther was remov'd
into the next Class above it, in order to go with that into the
third at the End of the Year. But my Father in the mean time,
from a View of the Expence of a College Education which, having so large a Family, he could not well afford, and the mean
Living many so educated were afterwards able to obtain, Reasons that he gave to his Friends in my Hearing, altered his first
Intention, took me from the Grammar School, and sent me to a
School for Writing and Arithmetic kept by a then famous Man,
Mr. Geo. Brownell, very successful in his Profession generally,
and that by mild encouraging Methods. Under him I acquired
fair Writing pretty soon, but I fail'd in the Arithmetic, and
made no Progress in it.—At Ten Years old, I was taken home to
assist my Father in his Business, which was that of a Tallow
Chandler and Sope Boiler. A Business he was not bred to, but
had assumed on his Arrival in New England and on finding his
Dying Trade would not maintain his Family, being in little Request. Accordingly I was employed in cutting Wick for the
Candles, filling the Dipping Mold, and the Molds for cast Candles, attending the Shop, going of Errands, etc.—I dislik'd the
Trade and had a strong Inclination for the Sea; but my Father
declar'd against it; however, living near the Water, I was much
in and about it, learnt early to swim well, and to manage Boats,
and when in a Boat or Canoe with other Boys I was commonly
allow'd to govern, especially in any case of Difficulty; and upon

other Occasions I was generally a Leader among the Boys, and sometimes led them into Scrapes, of wch I will mention one Instance, as it shows an early projecting public Spirit, tho' not then justly conducted. There was a salt Marsh that bounded part of the Mill Pond, on the Edge of which at Highwater, we us'd to stand to fish for Min[n]ows. By much Trampling, we had made it a mere Quagmire. My Proposal was to build a Wharf there fit for us to stand upon, and I show'd my Comrades a large Heap of Stones which were intended for a new House near the Marsh, and which would very well suit our Purpose. Accordingly in the Evening when the Workmen were gone, I assembled a Number of my Playfellows; and working with them diligently like so many Emmets, sometimes two or three to a Stone, we brought them all away and built our little Wharff.—The next Morning the Workmen were surpriz'd at Missing the Stones; which were found in our Wharff; Enquiry was made after the Removers; we were discovered and complain'd of; several of us were corrected by our Fathers; and tho' I pleaded the Usefulness of the Work, mine convinc'd me that nothing was useful which was not honest.

I think you may like to know something of his Person and Character. He had an excellent Constitution of Body, was of middle Stature, but well set and very strong. He was ingenious, could draw prettily, was skill'd a little in Music and had a clear pleasing Voice, so that when he play'd Psalm Tunes on his Violin and sung withal as he sometimes did in an Evening after the Business of the Day was over, it was extreamly agreable to hear. He had a mechanical Genius too, and on occasion was very handy in the Use of other Tradesmen's Tools. But his great Excellence lay in a sound Understanding, and solid Judgment in prudential Matters, both in private and publick Affairs. In the latter indeed he was never employed, the numerous Family he had to educate and the straitness of his Circumstances, keeping him close to his Trade, but I remember well his being frequently visited by leading People, who consulted him for his Opinion in Affairs of the Town or of the Church he belong'd to and show'd a good deal of Respect for his Judgment and advice. He

was also much consulted by private Persons about their affairs
when any Difficulty occurr'd, and frequently chosen an Arbitrator between contending Parties.—At his Table he lik'd to have
as often as he could, some sensible Friend or Neighbour to converse with, and always took care to start some ingenious or useful Topic for Discourse, which might tend to improve the
Minds of his Children. By this means he turn'd our Attention
to what was good, just, and prudent in the Conduct of Life; and
little or no Notice was ever taken of what related to the Victuals
on the Table, whether it was well or ill drest, in or out of season,
of good or bad flavour, preferable or inferior to this or that
other thing of the kind; so that I was bro't up in such a perfect
Inattention to those Matters as to be quite Indifferent what kind
of Food was set before me, and so unobservant of it, that to this
Day, if I am ask'd I can scarce tell a few Hours after Dinner,
what I din'd upon. This has been a Convenience to me in
travelling, where my Companions have been sometimes very
unhappy for want of a suitable Gratification of their more delicate[,] because better instructed[,] tastes and appetites.

My Mother had likewise an excellent Constitution. She
suckled all her 10 Children. I never knew either my Father or
Mother to have any Sickness but that of which they dy'd he at
89, and she at 85 years of age. They lie buried together at Boston, where I some years since placed a Marble Stone over their
Grave with this Inscription:

> JOSIAH FRANKLIN
> And ABIAH his Wife
> Lie here interred.
> They lived lovingly together in Wedlock
> Fifty-five Years.
> Without an Estate or any gainful Employment,
> By constant labour and Industry,
> With God's blessing,
> They maintained a large Family
> Comfortably;
> And brought up thirteen Children,
> And seven Grandchildren
> Reputably.

From this Instance, Reader,
Be encouraged to Diligence in thy Calling,
And Distrust not Providence.
He was a pious and prudent Man,
She a discreet and virtuous Woman.
Their youngest Son,
In filial Regard to their Memory,
Places this Stone.
J. F. born 1655—Died 1744—Ætat 89.
A. F. born 1667—Died 1752——85.

By my rambling Digressions I perceive myself to be grown old. I us'd to write more methodically.—But one does not dress for private Company as for a publick Ball. 'Tis perhaps only Negligence.—

To return. I continu'd thus employ'd in my Father's Business for two Years, that is till I was 12 Years old; and my Brother John, who was bred to that Business having left my Father, married and set up for himself at Rhodeisland, there was all Appearance that I was destin'd to supply his Place and be a Tallow Chandler. But my Dislike to the Trade continuing, my Father was under Apprehensions that if he did not find one for me more agreable, I should break away and get to Sea, as his Son Josiah had done to his great Vexation. He therefore sometimes took me to walk with him, and see Joiners, Bricklayers, Turners, Braziers, etc. at their Work, that he might observe my Inclination, and endeavour to fix it on some Trade or other on Land. It has ever since been a Pleasure to me to see good Workmen handle their Tools; and it has been useful to me, having learnt so much by it, as to be able to do little Jobs myself in my House, when a Workman could not readily be got; and to construct little Machines for my Experiments while the Intention of making the Experiment was fresh and warm in my Mind. My Father at last fix'd upon the Cutler's Trade, and my Uncle Benjamin's Son Samuel who was bred to that Business in London[,] being about that time establish'd in Boston, I was sent to be with him some time on liking. But his Expectations of a Fee with me displeasing my Father, I was taken home again.—

From a Child I was fond of Reading, and all the little Money that came into my Hands was ever laid out in Books. Pleas'd with the Pilgrim's Progress, my first Collection was of John Bunyan's Works, in separate little Volumes. I afterwards sold them to enable me to buy R. Burton's Historical Collections; they were small Chapmen's Books and cheap, 40 or 50 in all.— My Father's little Library consisted chiefly of Books in polemic Divinity, most of which I read, and have since often regretted, that at a time when I had such a Thirst for Knowledge, more proper Books had not fallen in my Way, since it was now re-solv'd I should not be a Clergyman. Plutarch's Lives there was, in which I read abundantly, and I still think that time spent to great ["Great" seems to have been deleted.] Advantage. There was also a Book of Defoe's, called an Essay on Projects, and another of Dr. Mather's, called Essays to do Good which per-haps gave me a Turn of thinking that had an influence on some of the principal future Events of my Life.

This Bookish inclination at length determin'd my Father to make me a Printer, tho' he had already one Son (James) of that Profession. In 1717 my Brother James return'd from England with a Press and Letters to set up his Business in Boston. I lik'd it much better than that of my Father, but still had a Hankering for the Sea.—To prevent the apprehended Effect of such an Inclination, my Father was impatient to have me bound to my Brother. I stood out some time, but at last was persuaded and signed the Indentures, when I was yet but 12 Years old.—I was to serve as an Apprentice till I was 21 Years of Age, only I was to be allow'd Journeyman's Wages during the last Year. In a little time I made great Proficiency in the Business, and became a useful Hand to my Brother. I now had Access to better Books. An Acquaintance with the Apprentices of Booksellers, enabled me sometimes to borrow a small one, which I was careful to re-turn soon and clean. Often I sat up in my Room reading the greatest Part of the Night, when the Book was borrow'd in the Evening and to be return'd early in the Morning[,] lest it should be miss'd or wanted. And after some time an ingenious Trades-man Mr. Matthew Adams who had a pretty Collection of

Books, and who frequented our Printing House, took Notice of me, invited me to his Library, and very kindly lent me such Books as I chose to read. I now took a Fancy to Poetry, and made some little Pieces. My Brother, thinking it might turn to account encourag'd me, and put me on composing two occasional Ballads. One was called The *Lighthouse Tragedy*, and contained an Acc[t] of the drowning of Capt. Worthilake with his Two Daughters; the other was a Sailor Song on the Taking of *Teach* or Blackbeard the Pirate. They were wretched Stuff, in the Grub-street Ballad Stile, and when they were printed he sent me about the Town to sell them. The first sold wonderfully, the Event being recent, having made a great Noise. This flatter'd my Vanity. But my Father discourag'd me, by ridiculing my Performances, and telling me Verse-makers were generally Beggars; so I escap'd being a Poet, most probably a very bad one. But as Prose Writing has been of great Use to me in the Course of my Life, and was a principal Means of my Advancement, I shall tell you how in such a Situation I acquir'd what little Ability I have in that Way.

There was another Bookish Lad in the Town, John Collins by Name, with whom I was intimately acquainted. We sometimes disputed, and very fond we were of Argument, and very desirous of confuting one another. Which disputacious Turn, by the way, is apt to become a very bad Habit, making People often extreamly disagreeable in Company, by the Contradiction that is necessary to bring it into Practice, and thence, besides souring and spoiling the Conversation, is productive of Disgusts and perhaps Enmities where you may have occasion for Friendship. I had caught it by reading my Father's Books of Dispute about Religion. Persons of good Sense, I have since observ'd, seldom fall into it, except Lawyers, University Men, and Men of all Sorts that have been bred at Edinborough. A Question was once some how or other started between Collins and me, of the Propriety of educating the Female Sex in Learning, and their Abilities for Study. He was of Opinion that it was improper, and that they were naturally unequal to it. I took the contrary Side, perhaps a little for Dispute['s] sake. He was naturally more eloquent, had a ready Plenty of Words, and sometimes as I thought bore me down more by his Fluency than by the Strength of his Reasons. As we parted without settling the Point, and were not to see one another again for some time, I sat down to put my Arguments in Writing, which I copied fair and sent to him. He answer'd and I reply'd. Three of [or] four Letters of a Side had pass'd, when my Father happen'd to find my Papers, and read them. Without ent'ring into the Discussion, he took occasion to talk to me about the Manner of my Writing, observ'd that tho' I had the Advantage of my Antagonist in correct Spelling and pointing (which I ow'd to the Printing House) I fell far short in elegance of Expression, in Method and in Perspicuity, of which he convinc'd me by several Instances. I saw the Justice of his Remarks, and thence grew more attentive to the *Manner* in writing, and determin'd to endeavour at Improvement.——

About this time I met with an odd Volume of the Spectator. It was the Third. I had never before seen any of them. I bought it, read it over and over, and was much delighted with it. I thought the Writing excellent, and wish'd if possible to imitate it. With that View, I took some of the Papers, and making short Hints of the Sentiment in each Sentence, laid them by a few Days, and then without looking at the Book, try'd to compleat the Papers again, by expressing each hinted Sentiment at length, and as fully as it had been express'd before, in any suitable Words, that should come to hand.

Then I compar'd my Spectator with the Original, discover'd some of my Faults and corrected them. But I found I wanted a Stock of Words or a Readiness in recollecting and using them, which I thought I should have acquir'd before that time, if I had gone on making Verses, since the continual Occasion for Words of the same Import but of different Length, to suit the Measure, or of different Sound for the Rhyme, would have laid me under a constant Necessity of searching for Variety, and also have tended to fix that Variety in my Mind, and make me Master of it. Therefore I took some of the Tales and turn'd them into Verse: And after a time, when I had pretty well forgotten the Prose, turn'd them back again. I also sometimes jumbled my Collections of Hints into Confusion, and after some Weeks, endeavour'd to reduce them into the best Order, before I began to form the full Sentences, and compleat the Paper. This was to teach me Method in the Arrangement of Thoughts. By comparing my work afterwards with the original, I discover'd many faults and amended them; but I sometimes had the Pleasure of Fancying that in certain Particulars of small Import, I had been lucky enough to improve the Method or the Language and this encourag'd me to think I might possibly in time come to be a tolerable English Writer, of which I was extreamly ambitious.

My Time for these Exercises and for Reading, was at Night, after Work or before it began in the Morning; or on Sundays, when I contrived to be in the Printing House alone, evading as much as I could the common Attendance on publick Worship, which my Father used to exact of me when I was under his Care: And which indeed I still thought a Duty; tho' I could not, as it seemed to me, afford the Time to practise it.

When about 16 Years of Age, I happen'd to meet with a Book, written by one Tryon, recommending a Vegetable Diet. I determined to go into it. My Brother being yet unmarried, did not keep House, but boarded himself and his Apprentices in another Family. My refusing to eat Flesh occasioned an Inconveniency, and I was frequently chid for my singularity. I made myself acquainted with Tryon's Manner of preparing some of his Dishes, such as Boiling Potatoes or Rice, making Hasty Pudding, and a few others, and then propos'd to my Brother, that if he would give me Weekly half the Money he paid for my Board I would board myself. He instantly agreed to it, and I presently found that I could save half what he paid me. This was an additional Fund for buying Books. But I had another Advantage in it. My Brother and the rest going from the Printing House to their Meals, I remain'd there alone, and dispatching presently my light Repast, (which often was no more than a Bisket or a Slice of Bread, a Handful of Raisins or a Tart from the Pastry Cook's, and a Glass of Water) had the rest of the Time till their Return, for Study, in which I made the greater

Progress from that greater Clearness of Head and quicker Apprehension which usually attend Temperance in Eating and Drinking. And now it was that being on some Occasion made asham'd of my Ignorance in Figures, which I had twice failed in Learning when at School, I took Cocker's Book of Arithmetick, and went thro' the whole by myself with great Ease. I also read Seller's and Sturmy's Books of Navigation, and became acquainted with the little Geometry they contain, but never proceeded far in that Science.—And I read about this Time Locke on Human Understanding, and the Art of Thinking by Messrs du Port Royal.

While I was intent on improving my Language, I met with an English Grammar (I think it was Greenwood's) at the End of which there were two little Sketches of the Arts of Rhetoric and Logic, the latter finishing with a Specimen of a Dispute in the Socratic Method. And soon after I procur'd Xenophon's Memorable Things of Socrates, wherein there are many Instances of the same Method. I was charm'd with it, adopted it, dropt my abrupt Contradiction, and positive Argumentation, and put on the humble Enquirer and Doubter. And being then, from reading Shaftsbury and Collins, become a real Doubter in many Points of our religious Doctrine, I found this Method safest for myself and very embarrassing to those against whom I us'd it, therefore I took a Delight in it, practis'd it continually and grew very artful and expert in drawing People even of superior Knowledge into Concessions the Consequences of which they did not foresee, entangling them in Difficulties out of which they could not extricate themselves, and so obtaining Victories that neither myself nor my Cause always deserved.—I continu'd this Method some few years, but gradually left it, retaining only the Habit of expressing myself in Terms of modest Diffidence, never using when I advance any thing that may possibly be disputed, the Words, *Certainly*, *undoubtedly;* or any others that give the Air of Positiveness to an Opinion; but rather say, I conceive, or I apprehend a Thing to be so or so, It appears to me, or I should think it so or so for such and such Reasons, or I imagine it to be so, or it is so if I am not mistaken. This Habit I believe

has been of great Advantage to me, when I have had occasion
to inculcate my Opinions and persuade Men into Measures that
I have been from time to time engag'd in promoting.—And as
the chief Ends of Conversation are to *inform*, or to be *informed*,
to *please* or to *persuade*, I wish wellmeaning sensible Men would
not lessen their Power of doing Good by a Positive assuming
Manner that seldom fails to disgust, tends to create Opposition,
and to defeat every one of those Purposes for which Speech was
given us, to wit, giving or receiving Information, or Pleasure:
For if you would *inform*, a positive dogmatical Manner in advancing your Sentiments, may provoke Contradiction and prevent a candid Attention. If you wish Information and Improvement from the Knowledge of others and yet at the same time
express yourself as firmly fix'd in your present Opinions, modest
sensible Men, who do not love Disputation, will probably leave
you undisturbed in the Possession of your Error; and by such a
Manner you can seldom hope to recommend yourself in *pleasing*
your Hearers, or to persuade those whose Concurrence you
desire.—Pope says, judiciously,

> *Men should be taught as if you taught them not,*
> *And things unknown propos'd as things forgot,—*

farther recommending it to us,

> *To speak tho' sure, with seeming Diffidence.*

And he might have coupled with this Line that which he has
coupled with another, I think less properly,

> *For want of Modesty is want of Sense.*

If you ask why *less properly*, I must repeat the lines;

> "Immodest Words admit of *no* Defence;
> *For* Want of Modesty is Want of Sense."

Now is not *Want of Sense* (where a Man is so unfortunate as to
want it) some Apology for his *Want of Modesty?* and would not
the Lines stand more justly thus?

Immodest Words admit *but this* Defence,
That Want of Modesty is Want of Sense.

This however I should submit to better Judgments.—

My Brother had in 1720 or 21, begun to print a Newspaper.
It was the second that appear'd in America, and was called *The
New England Courant.*² The only one before it, was *the Boston
News Letter.* I remember his being dissuaded by some of his
Friends from the Undertaking, as not likely to succeed, one
Newspaper being in their Judgment enough for America.—
At this time 1771 there are not less than five and twenty.—He
went on however with the Undertaking, and after having
work'd in composing the Types and printing off the Sheets, I
was employ'd to carry the Papers thro' the Streets to the Customers.—He had some ingenious Men among his Friends who
amus'd themselves by writing little Pieces for this Paper, which
gain'd it Credit, and made it more in Demand; and these Gentlemen often visited us.—Hearing their Conversations, and their
Accounts of the Approbation their Papers were receiv'd with, I
was excited to try my Hand among them. But being still a Boy,
and suspecting that my Brother would object to printing any
Thing of mine in his Paper if he knew it to be mine, I contriv'd
to disguise my Hand, and writing an anonymous Paper I put it
in at Night under the Door of the Printing House. It was found
in the Morning and communicated to his Writing Friends when
they call'd in as usual. They read it, commented on it in my
Hearing, and I had the exquisite Pleasure, of finding it met with
their Approbation, and that in their different Guesses at the
Author none were named but Men of some Character among us
for Learning and Ingenuity.—I suppose now that I was rather
lucky in my Judges: And that perhaps they were not really so
very good ones as I then esteem'd them. Encourag'd however
by this, I wrote and convey'd in the same Way to the Press
several more Papers, which were equally approv'd, and I kept
my Secret till my small Fund of Sense for such Performances
was pretty well exhausted, and then I discovered it; when I began to be considered a little more by my Brother's Acquaintance, and in a manner that did not quite please him, as he thought,

probably with reason, that it tended to make me too vain. And perhaps this might be one Occasion of the Differences that we began to have about this Time. Tho' a Brother, he considered himself as my Master, and me as his Apprentice; and accordingly expected the same Services from me as he would from another; while I thought he demean'd me too much in some he requir'd of me, who from a Brother expected more Indulgence. Our Disputes were often brought before our Father, and I fancy I was either generally in the right, or else a better Pleader, because the Judgment was generally in my favour: But my Brother was passionate and had often beaten me, which I took extreamly amiss; and thinking my Apprenticeship very tedious, I was continually wishing for some Opportunity of shortening it, which at length offered in a manner unexpected.*

One of the Pieces in our Newspaper, on some political Point which I have now forgotten, gave Offence to the Assembly. He was taken up, censur'd and imprison'd for a Month by the Speaker's Warrant, I suppose because he would not discover his Author. I too was taken up and examin'd before the Council; but tho' I did not give them any Satisfaction, they contented themselves with admonishing me, and dismiss'd me; considering me perhaps as an Apprentice who was bound to keep his Master's Secrets. During my Brother's Confinement, which I resented a good deal, notwithstanding our private Differences, I had the Management of the Paper, and I made bold to give our Rulers some Rubs in it, which my Brother took very kindly, while others began to consider me in an unfavourable Light, as a young Genius that had a Turn for Libelling and Satyr. My Brother's Discharge was accompany'd with an Order of the House, (a very odd one) *that James Franklin should no longer print the Paper called the New England Courant.* There was a Consultation held in our Printing House among his Friends what he should do in this Case. Some propos'd to evade the Order by changing the Name of the Paper; but my Brother see-

---

*I fancy his harsh and tyrannical Treatment of me, might be a means of impressing me with that Aversion to arbitrary Power that has stuck to me thro' my whole life [*Franklin's note.*]

ing Inconveniences in that, it was finally concluded on as a better Way, to let it be printed for the future under the Name of *Benjamin Franklin*. And to avoid the Censure of the Assembly that might fall on him, as still printing it by his Apprentice, the Contrivance was, that my old Indenture should be return'd to me with a full Discharge on the Back of it, to be shown on Occasion; but to secure to him the Benefit of my Service I was to sign new Indentures for the Remainder of the Term, wch were to be kept private. A very flimsy Scheme it was, but however it was immediately executed, and the Paper went on accordingly under my Name for several Months. At length a fresh Difference arising between my Brother and me, I took upon me to assert my Freedom, presuming that he would not venture to produce the new Indentures. It was not fair in me to take this Advantage, and this I therefore reckon one of the first Errata of my life: But the Unfairness of it weighed little with me, when under the Impressions of Resentment, for the Blows his Passion too often urg'd him to bestow upon me. Tho' he was otherwise not an ill-natur'd Man: Perhaps I was too saucy and provoking.

When he found I would leave him, he took care to prevent my getting Employment in any other Printing-House of the Town, by going round and speaking to every Master, who accordingly refus'd to give me Work. I then thought of going to New York as the nearest Place where there was a Printer: and I was the rather inclin'd to leave Boston, when I reflected that I had already made myself a little obnoxious to the governing Party; and from the arbitrary Proceedings of the Assembly in my Brother's Case it was likely I might if I stay'd soon bring myself into Scrapes; and farther that my indiscrete Disputations about Religion began to make me pointed at with Horror by good People, as an Infidel or Atheist. I determin'd on the Point: but my Father now siding with my Brother, I was sensible that if I attempted to go openly, Means would be used to prevent me. My Friend Collins therefore undertook to manage a little for me. He agreed with the Captain of a New York Sloop for my Passage, under the Notion of my being a young Acquaintance of his that had got a naughty Girl with Child, whose Friends would compel me to marry her, and therefore I could not appear or come away publickly. So I sold some of my Books to raise a little Money, Was taken on board privately, and as we had a fair Wind[,] in three Days I found myself in New York near 300 Miles from home, a Boy of but 17, without the least Recommendation to or Knowledge of any Person in the Place, and with very little Money in my Pocket.

My Inclinations for the Sea, were by this time worne out, or I might now have gratify'd them. But having a Trade, and supposing myself a pretty good Workman, I offer'd my Service to the Printer in the Place, old Mr Wm Bradford, who had been the first Printer in Pensilvania, but remov'd from thence upon the Quarrel of Geo. Keith.—He could give me no Employment, having little to do, and Help enough already: But, says he, my Son at Philadelphia has lately lost his principal Hand, Aquila Rose, by Death. If you go thither I believe he may employ you.—Philadelphia was 100 Miles farther. I set out, however, in a Boat for Amboy, leaving my Chest and Things to follow me round by Sea. In crossing the Bay we met with a Squall that tore our rotten Sails to pieces, prevented our getting into the Kill, and drove us upon Long Island. In our Way a drunken Dutchman, who was a Passenger too, fell overboard; when he was sinking I reach'd thro' the Water to his shock Pate and drew him up so that we got him in again. His ducking sober'd him a little, and he went to sleep, taking first out of his Pocket a Book which he desir'd I would dry for him. It prov'd to be my old favourite Author Bunyan's Pilgrim's Progress in Dutch, finely printed on good Paper with copper Cuts, a Dress better than I had ever seen it wear in its own Language. I have since found that it has been translated into most of the Languages of Europe, and suppose it has been more generally read than any other Book except perhaps the Bible. Honest John was the first that I know of who mix'd Narration and Dialogue, a Method of Writing very engaging to the Reader, who in the most interesting Parts finds himself, as it were brought into the Company, and present at the Discourse. De foe in his Cruso, his Moll Flanders, Religious Courtship, Family Instructor, and other

Pieces, has imitated it with Success. And Richardson has done the same in his Pamela, etc.——

When we drew near the Island we found it was at a Place where there could be no Landing, there being a great Surff on the stony Beach. So we dropt Anchor and swung round towards the Shore. Some People came down to the Water Edge and hallow'd to us, as we did to them. But the Wind was so high and the Surff so loud, that we could not hear so as to understand each other. There were Canoes on the Shore, and we made Signs and hallow'd that they should fetch us, but they either did not understand us, or thought it impracticable. So they went away, and Night coming on, we had no Remedy but to wait till the Wind should abate, and in the mean time the Boatman and I concluded to sleep if we could, and so crouded into the Scuttle with the Dutchman who was still wet, and the Spray beating over the Head of our Boat, leak'd thro' to us, so that we were soon almost as wet as he. In this Manner we lay all Night with very little Rest. But the Wind abating the next Day, we made a Shift to reach Amboy before Night, having been 30 Hours on the Water without Victuals, or any Drink but a Bottle of filthy Rum: The Water we sail'd on being salt.——

In the Evening I found myself very feverish, and went in to Bed. But having read somewhere that cold Water drank plentifully was good for a Fever, I follow'd the Prescription, sweat plentifully most of the Night, my Fever left me, and in the Morning crossing the Ferry, I proceeded on my Journey, on foot, having 50 Miles to Burlington, where I was told I should find Boats that would carry me the rest of the Way to Philadelphia.

It rain'd very hard all the Day, I was thoroughly soak'd, and by Noon a good deal tir'd, so I stopt at a poor Inn, where I staid all Night, beginning now to wish I had never left home. I cut so miserable a Figure too, that I found by the Questions ask'd me I was suspected to be some runaway Servant, and in danger of being taken up on that Suspicion. However I proceeded the next Day, and got in the Evening to an Inn within 8 or 10 Miles of Burlington, kept by one Dr Brown.——

He ent[e]red into Conversation with me while I took some

Refreshment, and finding I had read a little, became very sociable and friendly. Our Acquaintance continu'd as long as he
liv'd. He had been, I imagine, an itinerant Doctor, for there
was no Town in England, or Country in Europe, of which he
could not give a very particular Account. He had some Letters,
and was ingenious, but much of an Unbeliever, and wickedly
undertook, some Years after to travesty the Bible in doggrel
Verse as Cotton had done Virgil. By this means he set many of
the Facts in a very ridiculous Light, and might have hurt weak
minds if his Work had been publish'd:—but it never was.—At
his House I lay that Night, and the next Morning reach'd Burlington.—But had the Mortification to find that the regular
Boats were gone, a little before my coming, and no other expected to go till Tuesday, this being Saturday. Wherefore I returned to an old Woman in the Town of whom I had bought
Gingerbread to eat on the Water, and ask'd her Advice; she invited me to lodge at her House till a Passage by Water should
offer: and being tired with my foot Travelling, I accepted the
Invitation. She understanding I was a Printer, would have had
me stay at that Town and follow my Business, being ignorant of
the Stock necessary to begin with. She was very hospitable,
gave me a Dinner of Ox Cheek with great Goodwill, accepting
only of a Pot of Ale in return. And I thought myself fix'd till
Tuesday should come. However walking in the Evening by
the Side of the River, a Boat came by, which I found was going
towards Philadelphia, with several People in her. They took
me in, and as there was no wind, we row'd all the Way; and
about Midnight not having yet seen the City, some of the Company were confident we must have pass'd it, and would row no
farther, the others knew not where we were, so we put towards
the Shore, got into a Creek, landed near an old Fence[,] with
the Rails of which we made a Fire, the Night being cold, in
October, and there we remain'd till Daylight. Then one of the
Company knew the Place to be Cooper's Creek a little above
Philadelphia, which we saw as soon as we got out of the Creek,
and arriv'd there about 8 or 9 o'Clock, on the Sunday morning,
and landed at the Market street Wharff.—

I have been the more particular in this Description of my Journey, and shall be so of my first Entry into that City, that you may in your Mind compare such unlikely Beginnings with the Figure I have since made there. I was in my Working Dress, my best Cloaths being to come round by Sea. I was dirty from my Journey; my Pockets were stuff'd out with Shirts and Stockings; I knew no Soul, nor where to look for Lodging. I was fatigued with Travelling, Rowing and Want of Rest. I was very hungry, and my whole Stock of Cash consisted of a Dutch Dollar and about a Shilling in Copper. The latter I gave the People of the Boat for my Passage, who at first refus'd it on Acc^t of my Rowing; but I insisted on their taking it, a Man being sometimes more generous when he has but a little Money than when he has plenty, perhaps thro' Fear of being thought to have but little. Then I walk'd up the Street, gazing about, till near the Market House I met a Boy with Bread. I had made many a Meal on Bread, and inquiring where he got it, I went immediately to the Baker's he directed me to in Second Street; and ask'd for Bisket, intending such as we had in Boston, but they it seems were not made in Philadelphia, then I ask'd for a threepenny Loaf, and was told they had none such: so not considering or knowing the Difference of Money and the greater Cheapness nor the Names of his Bread, I bad[e] him give me threepenny worth of any sort. He gave me accordingly three great Puffy Rolls. I was surpriz'd at the Quantity, but took it, and having no room in my Pockets, walk'd off, with a Roll under each Arm, and eating the other. Thus I went up Market Street as far as fourth Street, passing by the Door of Mr. Read, my future Wife's Father, when she standing at the Door saw me, and thought I made as I certainly did a most awkward ridiculous Appearance. Then I turn'd and went down Chestnut Street and part of Walnut Street, eating my Roll all the Way, and coming round found myself again at Market Street Wharff, near the Boat I came in, to which I went for a Draught of the River Water, and being fill'd with one of my Rolls, gave the other two to a Woman and her Child that came down the River in the Boat with us and were waiting to go farther. Thus refresh'd I walk'd again up the Street, which by this time had many clean dress'd People in it who were all walking the same Way; I join'd them, and thereby was led into the great Meeting House of the Quakers near the Market. I sat down among them, and after looking round awhile and hearing nothing said; being very drowsy thro' Labour and want of Rest the preceding Night, I fell fast asleep, and continu'd so till the Meeting broke up, when one was kind enough to rouse me. This was therefore the first House I was in or slept in, in Philadelphia.—

Walking again down towards the River, and looking in the Faces of People, I met a young Quaker Man whose Countenance I lik'd, and accosting him requested he would tell me where a Stranger could get Lodging. We were then near the Sign of the Three Mariners. Here, says he, is one Place that entertains Strangers, but it is not a reputable House; if thee wilt walk with me, I'll show thee a better. He brought me to the Crooked Billet in Water Street. Here I got a Dinner. And while I was eating it, several sly Questions were ask'd me, as it seem'd to be suspected from my youth and Appearance, that I might be some Runaway. After Dinner my Sleepiness return'd: and being shown to a Bed, I lay down without undressing, and slept till Six in the Evening; was call'd to Supper; went to Bed again very early and slept soundly till next Morning. Then I made myself as tidy as I could, and went to Andrew Bradford the Printer's. I found in the Shop the old Man his Father, whom I had seen at New York, and who travelling on horseback had got to Philadelphia before me. He introduc'd me to his Son, who receiv'd me civilly, gave me a Breakfast, but told me he did not at present want a Hand, being lately supply'd with one. But there was another Printer in town lately set up, one Keimer, who perhaps might employ me; if not, I should be welcome to lodge at his House, and he would give me a little Work to do now and then till fuller Business should offer.

The old Gentleman said, he would go with me to the new Printer: And when we found him, Neighbor, says Bradford, I have brought to see you a young Man of your Business, perhaps you may want such a One. He ask'd me a few Questions, put a

Composing Stick in my Hand to see how I work'd, and then said he would employ me soon, tho' he had just then nothing for me to do. And taking old Bradford whom he had never seen before, to be one of the Towns People that had a Good Will for him, enter'd into a Conversation on his present Undertaking and Prospects; while Bradford not discovering that he was the other Printer's Father, on Keimer's saying he expected soon to get the greatest Part of the Business into his own Hands, drew him on by artful Questions and starting little Doubts, to explain all his Views, what Interest he rely'd on, and in what manner he intended to proceed.—I who stood by and heard all, saw immediately that one of them was a crafty old Sophister, and the other a mere Novice. Bradford left me with Keimer, who was greatly surpriz'd when I told him who the old Man was.

Keimer's Printing House I found, consisted of an old shatter'd Press, and one small worn-out Fount of English, which he was then using himself, composing in it an Elegy on Aquila Rose before-mentioned, an ingenious young Man of excellent Character much respected in the Town, Clerk of the Assembly, and a pretty Poet. Keimer made Verses, too, but very indifferently. He could not be said to write them, for his Manner was to compose them in the Types directly out of his Head; so there being no Copy, but one Pair of Cases, and the Elegy likely to require all the Letter[s], no one could help him.—I endeavour'd to put his Press (which he had not yet us'd, and of which he understood nothing) into Order fit to be work'd with; and promising to come and print off his Elegy as soon as he should have got it ready, I return'd to Bradford's who gave me a little Job to do for the present, [and] there I lodged and dieted. A few Days after[,] Keimer sent for me to print off the Elegy. And now he had got another Pair of Cases, and a Pamphlet to reprint, on which he set me to work.—

These two Printers I found poorly Qualified for their Business. Bradford had not been bred to it, and was very illiterate; and Keimer tho' something of a Scholar, was a mere Compositor, knowing nothing of Presswork. He had been one of the French Prophets and could act their enthusiastic Agitations. At this time he did not profess any particular Religion, but something of all on occasion; was very ignorant of the World, and had, as I afterward found, a good deal of the Knave in his Composition. He did not like my Lodging at Bradford's while I work'd with him. He had a House indeed, but without Furniture, so he could not lodge me: But he got me a Lodging at Mr. Read's beforementioned, who was the Owner of his House. And my Chest and Clothes being come by this time, I made rather a more respectable Appearance in the Eyes of Miss Read than I had done when she first happen'd to see me eating my Roll in the Street.——

I began now to have some Acquaintance among the young People of the Town, that were Lovers of Reading with whom I spent my Evenings very pleasantly and gaining Money by my Industry and Frugality, I lived very agreably, forgetting Boston as much as I could, and not desiring that any there should know where I resided, except my Friend Collins who was in my Secret, and kept it when I wrote to him. At length an Incident happened that sent me back again much sooner than I had intended.——

I had a Brother-in-law, Robert Holmes, Master of a Sloop, that traded between Boston and Delaware. He being at New Castle 40 Miles below Philadelphia, heard there of me, and wrote me a Letter, mentioning the Concern of my Friends in Boston at my abrupt Departure, assuring me of their Good will to me, and that every thing would be accommodated to my Mind if I would return, to which he exhorted me very earnestly. I wrote an Answer to his Letter, thank'd him for his Advice, but stated my Reasons for quitting Boston fully, and in such a Light as to convince him I was not so wrong as he had apprehended. Sir William Keith[3] Governor of the Province, was then at New Castle, and Capt. Holmes happening to be in Company with him when my Letter came to hand, spoke to him of me, and show'd him the Letter. The Governor read it, and seem'd surpriz'd when he was told my Age. He said I appear'd a young Man of promising Parts, and therefore should be encouraged: The Printers at Philadelphia were wretched ones, and if I would

set up there, he made no doubt I should succeed; for his Part, he
would procure me the publick Business, and do me every other
Service in his Power. This my Brother-in-Law afterwards told
me in Boston. But I knew as yet nothing of it; when one Day
Keimer and I being at Work together near the Window, we saw
the Governor and another Gentleman (which prov'd to be Col.
French, of New Castle) finely dress'd, come directly across the
Street to our House, and heard them at the Door. Keimer ran
down immediately, thinking it a Visit to him. But the Governor
enquir'd for me, came up, and with a Condescension and Po-
liteness I had been quite unus'd to, made me many Compliments, desired to be acquainted with me, blam'd me kindly for
not having made myself known to him when I first came to the
Place, and would have me away with him to the Tavern where
he was going with Col. French to taste as he said some excellent
Madeira. I was not a little surpriz'd, and Keimer star'd like a
Pig poison'd. I went however with the Governor and Col.
French, to a Tavern [at] the Corner of Third Street, and over the
Madeira he propos'd my Setting up my Business, laid before me
the Probabilities of Success, and both he and Col. French, assur'd me I should have their Interest and Influence in procuring
the Publick Business of both Governments. On my doubting
whether my Father would assist me in it, Sir William said he
would give me a Letter to him, in which he would state the Advantages, and he did not doubt of prevailing with him. So it
was concluded I should return to Boston in the first Vessel with
the Governor's Letter recommending me to my Father. In the
mean time the Intention was to be kept secret, and I went on
working with Keimer as usual, the Governor sending for me
now and then to dine with him, a very great Honour I thought
it, and conversing with me in the most affable, familiar, and
friendly manner imaginable. About the End of April 1724 a
little Vessel offer'd for Boston. I took leave of Keimer as going
to see my Friends. The Governor gave me an ample Letter,
saying many flattering things of me to my Father, and strongly
recommending the Project of my setting up at Philadelphia, as a
Thing that must make my Fortune. We struck on a Shoal in go-

ing down the Bay and sprung a Leak, we had a blustering time
at Sea, and were oblig'd to pump almost continually, at which I
took my Turn. We arriv'd safe however at Boston in about a
Fortnight.—I had been absent Seven Months and my Friends
had heard nothing of me; for my Br. Holmes was not yet return'd; and had not written about me. My unexpected Appearance surpriz'd the Family; all were however very glad to see me
and made me Welcome, except my Brother. I went to see him
at his Printing-House: I was better dress'd than ever while in
his Service, having a genteel new Suit from Head to foot, a
Watch, and my Pockets lin'd with near Five Pounds Sterling in
Silver. He receiv'd me not very frankly, look'd me all over, and
turn'd to his Work again. The JourneyMen were inquisitive
where I had been, what sort of a Country it was, and how I lik'd
it? I prais'd it much, and the happy Life I led in it; expressing
strongly my Intention of returning to it; and one of them asking
what kind of Money we had there, I produc'd a handful of Silver
and spread it before them, which was a kind of Raree Show they
had not been us'd to, Paper being the Money of Boston. Then I
took an Opportunity of letting them see my Watch: and lastly,
(my Brother still grum and sullen) I gave them a Piece of Eight
to drink, and took my Leave.—This Visit of mine offended him
extreamly. For when my Mother some time after spoke to him
of a Reconciliation, and of her Wishes to see us on good Terms
together, and that we might live for the future as Brothers, he
said, I had insulted him in such a Manner before his People that
he could never forget or forgive it. In this however he was
mistaken.—

My Father received the Governor's Letter with some apparent
Surprize; but said little of it to me for some Days; when Capt.
Holmes returning, he show'd it to him, ask'd if he knew Keith,
and what kind of a Man he was: Adding his Opinion that he must
be of small Discretion, to think of setting a Boy up in Business
who wanted yet 3 Years of being at Man's Estate. Holmes said
what he could in favᵣ of the Project; but my Father was clear in
the Impropriety of it; and at last gave a flat Denial to it. Then
he wrote a civil Letter to Sir William thanking him for the

Patronage he had so kindly offered me, but declining to assist me as yet in Setting up, I being in his Opinion too young to be trusted with the Management of a Business so important, and for which the Preparation must be so expensive.——

My Friend and Companion Collins, who was a Clerk at the Post-Office, pleas'd with the Account I gave him of my new Country, determin'd to go thither also: And while I waited for my Fathers Determination, he set out before me by Land to Rhodeisland, leaving his Books which were a pretty Collection of Mathematicks and Natural Philosophy, to come with mine and me to New York where he propos'd to wait for me. My Father, tho' he did not approve Sir William's Proposition was yet pleas'd that I had been able to obtain so advantageous a Character from a Person of such Note where I had resided, and that I had been so industrious and careful as to equip myself so handsomely in so short a time: therefore seeing no Prospect of an Accommodation between my Brother and me, he gave his Consent to my Returning again to Philadelphia, advis'd me to behave respectfully to the People there, endeavour to obtain the general Esteem, and avoid lampooning and libelling to which he thought I had too much Inclination; telling me, that by steady Industry and a prudent Parsimony, I might save enough by the time I was One and Twenty to set me up, and that if I came near the Matter he would help me out with the rest. This was all I could obtain, except some small Gifts as Tokens of his and my Mother's Love, when I embark'd again for New-York, now with their Approbation and their Blessing.——

The Sloop putting in at Newport, Rhodeisland, I visited my Brother John, who had been married and settled there some Years. He received me very affectionately, for he always lov'd me. A Friend of his, one Vernon, having some Money due to him in Pensilvania, about 35 Pounds Currency, desired I would receive it for him, and keep it till I had his Directions what to remit it in. Accordingly he gave me an Order.——This afterwards occasion'd me a good deal of Uneasiness. At Newport we took in a Number of Passengers for New York: Among which were two young Women, Companions, and a grave, sen-

sible Matron-like Quaker-Woman with her Attendants.—I had
shown an obliging readiness to do her some little Services which
impress'd her I suppose with a degree of Good-will towards me.
—Therefore when she saw a daily growing Familiarity between
me and the two Young Women, which they appear'd to encourage, she took me aside and said, Young Man, I am concern'd
for thee, as thou has no Friend with thee, and seems not to know
much of the World, or of the Snares Youth is expos'd to; depend
upon it those are very bad Women, I can see it in all their Actions, and if thee art not upon thy Guard, they will draw thee
into some Danger: they are Strangers to thee, and I advise thee
in a friendly Concern for thy Welfare, to have no Acquaintance
with them. As I seem'd at first not to think so ill of them as she
did, she mention'd some Things she had observ'd and heard
that had escap'd my Notice; but now convinc'd me she was
right. I thank'd her for her kind Advice, and promis'd to follow
it.—When we arriv'd at New York, they told me where they
liv'd, and invited me to come and see them: but I avoided it.
And it was well I did: For the next Day, the Captain miss'd a
Silver Spoon and some other Things that had been taken out of
his Cabbin, and knowing that these were a Couple of Strumpets,
he got a Warrant to search their Lodgings, found the stolen
Goods, and had the Thieves punish'd. So tho' we had escap'd
a sunken Rock which we scrap'd upon in the Passage, I thought
this Escape of rather more Importance to me. At New York I
found my Friend Collins, who had arriv'd there some Time before me. We had been intimate from Children, and had read the
same Books together: But he had the Advantage of more time
for reading, and Studying and a wonderful Genius for Mathematical Learning in which he far outstript me. While I liv'd in
Boston most of my Hours of Leisure for Conversation were
spent with him, and he continu'd a sober as well as an industrious
Lad; was much respected for his Learning by several of the
Clergy and other Gentlemen, and seem'd to promise making a
good Figure in Life: but during my Absence he had acquir'd a
Habit of Sotting with Brandy; and I found by his own Account
and what I heard from others, that he had been drunk every day

since his Arrival at New York, and behav'd very oddly. He had
gam'd too and lost his Money, so that I was oblig'd to discharge
his Lodgings, and defray his Expenses to and at Philadelphia:
Which prov'd extreamly inconvenient to me. The then Governor of N[ew] York, Burnet, Son of Bishop Burnet hearing from
the Captain that a young Man, one of his Passengers, had a great
many Books, desired he would bring me to see him. I waited
upon him accordingly, and should have taken Collins with me
but that he was not sober. The Govr treated me with great
Civility, show'd me his Library, which was a very large one, and
we had a good deal of Conversation about Books and Authors.
This was the second Governor who had done me the Honour to
take Notice of me, which to a poor Boy like me was very pleasing.—We proceeded to Philadelphia. I received on the Way
Vernon's Money, without which we could hardly have finish'd
our Journey. Collins wish'd to be employ'd in some Counting
House; but whether they discover'd his Dramming by his
Breath, or by his Behaviour, tho' he had some Recommendations, he met with no Success in any Application, and continu'd
Lodging and Boarding at the same House with me and at my Expense. Knowing I had that Money of Vernon's he was continually borrowing of me, still promising Repayment as soon as he
should be in Business. At length he had got so much of it, that
I was distress'd to think what I should do, in case of being call'd
on to remit it. His Drinking continu'd, about which we sometimes quarrel'd, for when a little intoxicated he was very frac-
tious. Once in a Boat on the Delaware with some other young
Men, he refused to row in his Turn: I will be row'd home, says he.
We will not row you, says I. You must or stay all Night on the
Water, says he, just as you please. The others said, Let us row;
what signifies it? But my Mind being soured with his other Conduct, I continu'd to refuse. So he swore he would make me row,
or throw me overboard; and coming along stepping on the
Thwarts towards me, when he came up and struck at me I clapt
my Hand under his Crutch, and rising pitch'd him head-fore-
most into the River. I knew he was a good Swimmer, and so
was under little Concern about him; but before he could get

round to lay hold of the Boat, we had with a few Strokes pull'd her out of his Reach. And ever when he drew near the Boat, we ask'd if he would row, striking a few Strokes to slide her away from him.—He was ready to die with Vexation, and obstinately would not promise to row; however seeing him at last beginning to tire, we lifted him in; and brought him home dripping wet in the Evening. We hardly exchang'd a civil Word afterwards; and a West India Captain who had a Commission to procure a Tutor for the Sons of a Gentleman at Barbadoes, happening to meet with him, agreed to carry him thither. He left me then, promising to remit me the first Money he should receive in order to discharge the Debt. But I never heard of him after. The Breaking into this Money of Vernon's was one of the first great Errata of my Life[.] And this Affair show'd that my Father was not much out in his Judgment when he suppos'd me too Young to manage Business of Importance. But Sir William, on reading his Letter, said he was too prudent. There was great Difference in Persons, and Discretion did not always accompany Years, nor was Youth always without it. And since he will not set you up, says he, I will do it myself. Give me an Inventory of the Things necessary to be had from England, and I will send for them. You shall repay me when you are able; I am resolv'd to have a good Printer here, and I am sure you must succeed. This was spoken with such an Appearance of Cordiality, that I had not the least doubt of his meaning what he said. I had hitherto kept the Proposition of my Setting up[,] a Secret in Philadelphia, and I still kept it. Had it been known that I depended on the Governor, probably some Friend that knew him better would have advis'd me not to rely on him, as I afterwards heard it as his known Character to be liberal of Promises which he never meant to keep.—Yet unsolicited as he was by me, how could I think his generous Offers insincere? I believ'd him one of the best Men in the World.—

I presented him an Inventory of a little Print^g House, amounting by my Computation to about 100£ Sterling. He lik'd it, but ask'd me if my being on the Spot in England to chuse the Types and see that every thing was good of the kind, might not be of some Advantage. Then, says he, when there, you may make Acquaintances and establish Correspondencies in the Bookselling and Stationary Way. I agreed that this might be advantageous. Then, says he, get yourself ready to go with Annis; which was the annual Ship, and the only one at that Time usually passing between London and Philadelphia. But it would be some Months before Annis sail'd, so I continu'd working with Keimer, fretting about the Money Collins had got from me; and in daily Apprehensions of being call'd upon by Vernon, which however did not happen for some Years after.—

I believe I have omitted mentioning that in my first Voyage from Boston, being becalm'd off Block Island, our People set about catching Cod and haul'd up a great many. Hitherto I had stuck to my Resolution of not eating animal Food; and on this Occasion, I consider'd with my Master Tryon, the taking every Fish as a kind of unprovoked Murder, since none of them had or ever could do us any Injury that might justify the Slaughter. All this seem'd very reasonable.—But I had formerly been a great Lover of Fish, and when this came hot out of the Frying Pan, it smelt admirably well. I balanc'd some time between Principle and Inclination: till I recollected, that when the Fish were opened, I saw smaller Fish taken out of their Stomachs: Then thought I, if you eat one another, I don't see why we mayn't eat you. So I din'd upon Cod very heartily and continu'd to eat with other People, returning only now and then occasionally to a vegetable Diet. So convenient a thing it is to be a *reasonable Creature*, since it enables one to find or make a Reason for every thing one has a mind to do.

Keimer and I liv'd on a pretty good familiar Footing and agreed tolerably well: for he suspected nothing of my Setting up. He retain'd a great deal of his old Enthusiasms, and lov'd Argumentation. We therefore had many Disputations. I used to work him so with my Socratic Method, and had trepann'd him so often by Questions apparently so distant from any Point we had in hand, and yet by degrees led to the Point, and brought him into Difficulties and Contradictions that at last he grew ridiculously cautious, and would hardly answer me the most common Question, without asking first, *What do you intend to infer from that?* However it gave him so high an Opinion of my Abilities in the Confuting Way, that he seriously propos'd my being his Colleague in a Project he had of setting up a new Sect. He was to preach the Doctrines, and I was to confound all Opponents. When he came to explain with me upon the Doctrines, I found several Conundrums which I objected to, unless I might have my Way a little too, and introduce some of mine. Keimer wore his Beard at full Length, because somewhere in the Mosaic Law it is said, *thou shalt not mar the Corners of thy beard.* He likewise kept the seventh day Sabbath; and these two Points were Essentials with him. I dislik'd both, but agreed to admit them upon Condition of his adopting the Doctrine of using no animal Food. I doubt, says he, my Constitution will not bear that. I assur'd him it would, and that he would be the better for it. He was usually a great Glutton, and I promis'd myself some Diversion in half-starving him. He agreed to try the Practice if I would keep him Company. I did so and we held it for three Months. We had our Victuals dress'd and brought to us regularly by a Woman in the Neighbourhood, who had from me a List of 40 Dishes to be prepar'd for us at different times, in all which there was neither Fish Flesh nor Fowl, and the whim suited me the better at this time from the Cheapness of it, not costing us above 18ᵈ Sterling each, per Week. I have since kept several Lents most strictly, leaving the common Diet for that, and that for the common, abruptly, without the least Inconvenience: So that I think there is little in the Advice of making those Changes by easy Gradations. I went on pleasantly, but Poor Keimer suffer'd grievously, tir'd of the Project, long'd for the Flesh Pots of Egypt, and order'd a roast Pig. He invited me and two Women Friends to dine with him, but it being brought too soon upon the table, he could not resist the Temptation, and ate it all up before we came.—

I had made some Courtship during this time to Miss Read. I had a great Respect and Affection for her, and had some Reason to believe she had the same for me: but as I was about to take a long Voyage, and we were both very young, only a little above

18, it was thought most prudent by her Mother to prevent our going too far at present, as a Marriage if it was to take place would be more convenient after my Return, when I should be as I expected set up in my Business. Perhaps too she thought my Expectations not so well founded as I imagined them to be.—

My chief Acquaintances at this time were, Charles Osborne, Joseph Watson, and James Ralph; all Lovers of Reading. The two first were Clerks to an eminent Scrivener or Conveyancer in the Town, Charles Brogden; the other was Clerk to a Merchant. Watson was a pious sensible young Man, of great Integrity.— The others rather more lax in their Principles of Religion, particularly Ralph, who as well as Collins had been unsettled by me, for which they both made me suffer.—Osborne was sensible, candid, frank, sincere and affectionate to his Friends; but in literary Matters too fond of Criticising. Ralph, was ingenious, genteel in his Manners, and extreamly eloquent; I think I never knew a prettier Talker. Both of them great Admirers of Poetry, and began to try their Hands in little Pieces. Many pleasant Walks we four had together on Sundays into the Woods near Schuylkill, where we read to one another and conferr'd on what we read. Ralph was inclin'd to pursue the Study of Poetry, not doubting but he might become eminent in it and make his Fortune by it, alledging that the best Poets must when they first began to write, make as many Faults as he did.—Osborne dissuaded him, assur'd him he had no Genius for Poetry, and advis'd him to think of nothing beyond the Business he was bred to; that in the mercantile way tho' he had no Stock, he might by his Diligence and Punctuality recommend himself to Employment as a Factor, and in time acquire wherewith to trade on his own Account. I approv'd the amusing one's self with Poetry now and then, so far as to improve one's Language, but no farther. On this it was propos'd that we should each of us at our next Meeting produce a Piece of our own Composing, in order to improve by our mutual Observations, Criticisms and Corrections. As Language and Expression was what we had in View, we excluded all Considerations of Invention, by agreeing that the Task should be a Version of the 18th Psalm, which de-

scribes the Descent of a Deity. When the Time of our Meeting
drew nigh, Ralph call'd on me first, and let me know his Piece
was ready. I told him I had been busy, and having little Inclination had done nothing. He then show'd me his Piece for
my Opinion; and I much approv'd it, as it appear'd to me to have
great Merit. Now, says he, Osborne never will allow the least
Merit in any thing of mine, but makes 1000 Criticisms out of
mere Envy. He is not so jealous of you. I wish therefore you
would take this Piece, and produce it as yours. I will pretend
not to have had time, and so produce nothing: We shall then
see what he will say to it. It was agreed, and I immediately
transcrib'd it that it might appear in my own hand. We met.
Watson's Performance was read: there were some Beauties in it:
but many Defects. Osborne's was read: It was much better.
Ralph did it Justice, remark'd some Faults, but applauded the
Beauties. He himself had nothing to produce. I was backward,
seem'd desirous of being excused, had not had sufficient Time
to correct, etc. but no Excuse could be admitted, produce I must.
It was read and repeated; Watson and Osborne gave up the Contest; and join'd in applauding it immoderately. Ralph only
made some Criticisms and propos'd some Amendments, but I
defended my Text. Osborne was against Ralph, and told him
he was no better a Critic than Poet; so he dropt the Argument.
As they two went home together, Osborne express'd himself
still more strongly in favour of what he thought my Production,
having restrain'd himself before as he said, lest I should think it
Flattery. But who would have imagin'd, says he, that Franklin
had been capable of such a Performance; such Painting, such
Force! such Fire! he has even improv'd the Original! In his common Conversation, he seems to have no Choice of Words; he
hesitates and blunders; and yet, good God, how he writes!—
When we next met, Ralph discover'd the Trick we had plaid
him, and Osborne was a little laught at. This Transaction fix'd
Ralph in his Resolution of becoming a Poet. I did all I could to
dissuade him from it, but he continued scribbling Verses, till
Pope cur'd him. He became however a pretty good Prose
Writer. More of him hereafter. But as I may not have occasion

again to mention the other two, I shall just remark here, that Watson died in my Arms a few Years after, much lamented, being the best of our Set. Osborne went to the West Indies, where he became an eminent Lawyer and made Money, but died young. He and I had made a serious Agreement, that the one who happen'd first to die, should if possible make a friendly Visit to the other, and acquaint him how he found things in that Separate State. But he never fulfill'd his Promise.

The Governor, seeming to like my Company, had me frequently to his House; and his Setting me up was always mention'd as a fix'd thing. I was to take with me Letters recommendatory to a Number of his Friends, besides the Letter of Credit to furnish me with the necessary Money for purchasing the Press and Types, Paper, etc. For these Letters I was appointed to call at different times, when they were to be ready, but a future time was still named.—Thus we went on till the Ship whose Departure too had been several times postponed was on the Point of sailing. Then when I call'd to take my Leave and receive the Letters, his Secretary, Dr. Bard, came out to me and said the Governor was extreamly busy, in writing, but would be down at Newcastle before the Ship, and there the Letters would be delivered to me.

Ralph, tho' married and having one Child, had determined to accompany me in this Voyage. It was thought he intended to establish a Correspondence, and obtain Goods to sell on Commission. But I found afterwards, that thro' some Discontent with his Wife's Relations, he purposed to leave her on their Hands, and never return again.—Having taken leave of my Friends, and interchang'd some Promises with Miss Read, I left Philadelphia in the Ship, which anchor'd at Newcastle. The Governor was there. But when I went to his Lodging, the Secretary came to me from him with the civillest Message in the World, that he could not then see me being engag'd in Business of the utmost Importance, but should send the Letters to me on board, wish'd me heartily a good Voyage and a speedy Return, etc. I return'd on board, a little puzzled, but still not doubting.—

Mr. Andrew Hamilton, a famous Lawyer of Philadelphia, had taken Passage in the same Ship for himself and Son: and with Mr. Denham a Quaker Merchant, and Messrs. Onion and Russel[,] Masters of an Iron Work in Maryland, had engag'd the Great Cabin; so that Ralph and I were forc'd to take up with a Birth in the Steerage: And none on board knowing us, were considered as ordinary Persons.—But Mr. Hamilton and his Son (it was James, since Governor) return'd from New Castle to Philadelphia, the Father being recall'd by a great Fee to plead for a seized Ship.—And just before we sail'd Col. French coming on board, and showing me great Respect, I was more taken Notice of, and with my Friend Ralph invited by the other Gentlemen to come into the Cabin, there being now Room. Accordingly we remov'd thither.

Understanding that Col. French had brought on board the Governor's Dispatches, I ask'd the Captain for those Letters that were to be under my Care. He said all were put into the Bag together; and he could not then come at them; but before we landed in England, I should have an Opportunity of picking them out. So I was satisfy'd for the present, and we proceeded on our Voyage. We had a sociable Company in the Cabin, and lived uncommonly well, having the Addition of all Mr. Hamilton's Stores, who had laid in plentifully. In this Passage Mr. Denham contracted a Friendship for me that continued during his Life. The Voyage was otherwise not a pleasant one, as we had a great deal of bad Weather.

When we came into the Channel, the Captain kept his Word with me, and gave me an Opportunity of examining the Bag for the Governor's Letters. I found none upon which my Name was put, as under my Care; I pick'd out 6 or 7 that by the Hand writing I thought might be the promis'd Letters, especially as one of them was directed to Basket the King's printer, and another to some Stationer. We arriv'd in London the 24th of December, 1724.—I waited upon the Stationer who came first in my Way, delivering the Letter as from Gov. Keith. I don't know such a Person, says he: but opening the Letter, O, this is from Riddlesden; I have lately found him to be a compleat Ras-

cal, and I will have nothing to do with him, nor receive any Letters from him. So putting the Letter into my Hand, he turn'd
on his Heel and left me to serve some Customer. I was sur-
prized to find these were not the Governor's Letters. And after
recollecting and comparing Circumstances, I began to doubt his
Sincerity.—I found my Friend Denham, and opened the whole
Affair to him. He let me into Keith's Character, told me there
was not the least Probability that he had written any Letters for
me, that no one who knew him had the smallest Dependence on
him, and he laught at the Notion of the Governor's giving me a
Letter of Credit, having as he said no Credit to give.—On my
expressing some Concern about what I should do: He advis'd
me to endeavour getting some Employment in the Way of my
Business. Among the Printers here, says he, you will improve
yourself; and when you return to America, you will set up to
greater Advantage.—

We both of us happen'd to know, as well as the Stationer,
that Riddlesden the Attorney, was a very Knave. He had half
ruin'd Miss Read's Father by acquiring his note he bound for
him. By his Letter it appear'd, there was a secret Scheme on foot
to the Prejudice of Hamilton, (suppos'd to be then coming over
with us,) and that Keith was concern'd in it with Riddlesden.
Denham, who was a Friend of Hamilton's, thought he ought to
be acquainted with it. So when he arriv'd in England, which was
soon after, partly from Resentment and Ill-Will to Keith and
Riddlesden, and partly from Good Will to him: I waited
on him, and gave him the Letter. He thank'd me cordially, the
Information being of Importance to him. And from that time
he became my Friend, greatly to my Advantage afterwards on
many Occasions.

But what shall we think of a Governor's playing such pitiful
Tricks, and imposing so grossly on a poor ignorant Boy! It
was a Habit he had acquired. He wish'd to please every body;
and, having little to give, he gave Expectations. He was otherwise an ingenious sensible Man, a pretty good Writer, and a
good Governor for the People, tho' not for his Constituents the
Proprietaries, whose Instructions he sometimes disregarded.—

Several of our best Laws were of his Planning, and pass'd during his Administration.—

Ralph and I were inseparable Companions. We took Lodgings together in Little Britain at 3/6 p[er] Week, as much as we could then afford. He found some Relations, but they were poor and unable to assist him. He now let me know his Intentions of remaining in London, and that he never meant to return to Philad[a]—He had brought no Money with him, the whole he could muster having been expended in paying his Passage. I had 15 Pistoles: So he borrowed occasionally of me, to subsist while he was looking out for Business.—He first endeavoured to get into the Playhouse, believing himself qualify'd for an Actor; but Wilkes to whom he apply'd, advis'd him candidly not to think of that Employment, as it was impossible he should succeed in it.—Then he propos'd to Roberts, a Publisher in Paternoster Row, to write for him a Weekly Paper like the Spectator, on certain Conditions, which Roberts did not approve. Then he endeavour'd to get Employm[t] as a Hackney Writer to copy for the Stationers and Lawyers about the Temple: but could find no Vacancy.—

I immediately got into Work at Palmer's then a famous Printing House in Bartholomew Close; and here I continu'd near a Year. I was pretty diligent; but spent with Ralph a good deal of my Earnings in going to Plays and other Places of Amusement. We had together consum'd all my Pistoles, and now just rubb'd on from hand to mouth. He seem'd quite to forget his Wife and Child, and I by degrees my Engagements wth Miss Read, to whom I never wrote more than one Letter, and that was to let her know I was not likely soon to return. This was another of the great Errata of my Life, which I should wish to correct if I were to live it over again.—In fact, by our Expences, I was constantly kept unable to pay my Passage.

At Palmer's I was employ'd in composing for the second Edition of Woollaston's [sic] Religion of Nature. Some of his Reasonings not appearing to me well-founded, I wrote a little metaphysical Piece, in which I made Remarks on them. It was entitled, *A Dissertation on Liberty and Necessity, Pleasure and pain.* I inscrib'd it to my Friend Ralph.—I printed a small Number. It occasion'd my being more consider'd by Mr. Palmer, as a young Man of some Ingenuity, tho' he seriously Expostulated with me upon the Principles of my Pamphlet which to him appear'd abominable. My printing this Pamphlet was another Erratum.

In our House there lodg'd a young Woman; a Millener, who I think had a Shop in the Cloisters. She had been genteelly bred, was sensible and lively, and of most pleasing Conversation. Ralph read Plays to her in the Evenings, they grew intimate, she took another Lodging, and he follow'd her. They liv'd together some time, but he being still out of Business, and her Income not sufficient to maintain them with her Child, he took a Resolution of going from London, to try for a Country School, which he thought himself well qualify'd to undertake, as he wrote an excellent Hand, and was a Master of Arithmetic and Accounts.—This however he deem'd a Business below him, and confident of future better Fortune when he should be unwilling to have it known that he once was so meanly employ'd, he chang'd his Name, and did me the Honour to assume mine.—For I soon after had a Letter from him, acquainting me, that he was settled in a small Village in Berkshire, I think it was, where he taught reading and writing to 10 or a dozen Boys at 6 pence each p[er] Week, recommending Mrs. T. to my Care, and desiring me to write to him directing for Mr. Franklin Schoolmaster at such a Place. He continu'd to write frequently, sending me large Specimens of an Epic Poem, which he was then composing, and desiring my Remarks and Corrections.—These I gave him from time to time, but endeavour'd rather to discourage his Proceeding. One of Young's Satires was then just publish'd. I copy'd and sent him a great Part of it, which set in a strong Light the Folly of pursuing the Muses with any Hope of Advancement by them. All was in vain. Sheets of the Poem continu'd to come by every Post. In the mean time Mrs. T. having on his Account lost her Friends and Business, was often in Distresses, and us'd to send for me, and borrow what I could spare to help her out of them. I grew fond of her Company, and being at this time under no Religious Restraints, and presuming on my Importance to her, I attempted Familiarities, (another Erratum) which she repuls'd with a proper Resentment, and acquainted him with my Behaviour. This made a Breach between us, and when he return'd again to London, he let me know he thought I had cancell'd all the Obligations he had been under to me.——So I found I was never to expect his Repaying me what I lent to him or advanc'd for him. This was however not then of much Consequence, as he was totally unable: And in the Loss of his Friendship I found myself reliev'd from a Burthen. I now began to think of getting a little Money beforehand; and expecting better Work, I left Palmer's to work at Watts's near Lincoln's Inn Fields, a still greater Printing House. Here I continu'd all the rest of my Stay in London.

While I lodg'd in Little Britain I made an Acquaintance with one Wilcox a Bookseller, whose Shop was at the next Door. He had an immense Collection of second-hand Books. Circulating Libraries were not then in Use; but we agreed that on certain reasonable Terms which I have now forgotten, I might take, read and return any of his Books. This I esteem'd a great Advantage, and I made as much use of it as I could.——

My Pamphlet by some means falling into the Hands of one Lyons, a Surgeon, Author of a Book intitled *The Infallibility of Human Judgment*, it occasioned an Acquaintance between us; he took great Notice of me, call'd on me often, to converse on those Subjects, carried me to the Horns a pale Alehouse in —— Lane, Cheapside, and introduc'd me to Dr. Mandevil[l]e, Author of the Fable of the Bees who had a Club there, of which he was the Soul, being a most facetious entertaining Companion. Lyons too introduced me to Dr. Pemberton, at Batson's Coffee House, who promis'd to give me an Opportunity some time or other of seeing Sir Isaac Newton, of which I was extreamly desirous; but this never happened.

I had brought over a few Curiosities among which the principal was a Purse made of the Asbestos, which purifies by Fire. Sir Hans Sloane heard of it, came to see me, and invited me to his House in Bloomsbury Square; where he show'd me all his

Curiosities, and persuaded me to let him add that to the Number, for which he paid me handsomely.[4]—

At my first Admission into this Printing House, I took to working at Press, imagining I felt a Want of the Bodily Exercise I had been us'd to in America, where Presswork is mix'd with Composing, I drank only Water; the other Workmen, near 50 in Number, were great Guzzlers of Beer. On occasion I carried up and down Stairs a large Form of Types in each hand, when others carried but one in both Hands. They wonder'd to see from this and several Instances that the water-American as they call'd me was *stronger* than themselves who drank *strong* beer. We had an Alehouse Boy who attended always in the House to supply the Workmen. My Companion at the Press, drank every day a Pint before Breakfast, a Pint at Breakfast with his Bread and Cheese; a Pint between Breakfast and Dinner; a Pint at Dinner; a Pint in the Afternoon about Six o'Clock, and another when he had done his Day's-Work. I thought it a detestable Custom.—But it was necessary, he suppos'd, to drink *strong* Beer that he might be *strong* to labour. I endeavour'd to convince him that the Bodily Strength afforded by Beer could only be in proportion to the Grain or Flour of the Barley dissolved in the Water of which it was made; that there was more Flour in a Penny-worth of Bread, and therefore if he would eat that with a Pint of Water, it would give him more Strength than a Quart of Beer.—He drank on however, and had 4 or 5 Shillings to pay out of his Wages every Saturday Night for that muddling Liquor; an Expence I was free from.—And thus these poor Devils keep themselves always under.

Watts after some Weeks desiring to have me in the Composing-Room, I left the Pressmen. A new *Bienvenu* or Sum for Drink; being 5/, was demanded of me by the Compositors. I thought it an Imposition, as I had paid below. The Master thought so too, and forbad[e] my Paying it. I stood out two or three Weeks, was accordingly considered as an Excommunicate, and had so many little Pieces of private Mischief done me, by mixing my Sorts, transposing my Pages, breaking my Matter, etc. etc. and if I were ever so little out of the Room, and all ascrib'd to the Chapel Ghost, which they said ever haunted those not regularly admitted, that notwithstanding the Master's Protection, I found myself oblig'd to comply and pay the Money; convinc'd of the Folly of being on ill Terms with those one is to live with continually. I was now on a fair Footing with them, and soon acquir'd considerable Influence. I propos'd some reasonable Alterations in their Chapel* Laws, and carried them against all Opposition. From my Example a great Part of them, left their muddling Breakfast of Beer and Bread and Cheese, finding they could with me be supply'd from a neighbouring House with a large Porringer of hot Water-gruel, sprinkled with Pepper, crumb'd with Bread, and a Bit of Butter in it, for the Price of a Pint of Beer, viz., three halfpence. This was a more comfortable as well as cheaper Breakfast, and kept their Heads clearer.—Those who continu'd sotting with Beer all day, were often, by not paying, out of Credit at the Alehouse, and us'd to make Interest with me to get Beer, *their Light*, as they phras'd it, *being out*. I watch'd the Pay table on Saturday Night, and collected what I stood engag'd for them, having to pay some times near Thirty Shillings a Week on their Accounts. —This, and my being esteem'd a pretty good Riggite, that is a jocular verbal Satyrist, supported my Consequence in the Society.—My constant Attendance, (I never making a St. Monday), recommended me to the Master; and my uncommon Quickness at Composing, occasion'd my being put upon all Work of Dispatch which was generally better paid. So I went on now very agreeably.—

My Lodging in Little Britain being too remote, I found another in Duke-street opposite to the Romish Chapel. It was two pair of Stairs backwards at an Italian Warehouse. A Widow Lady kept the House; she had a Daughter and a Maid Servant, and a Journey-man who attended the Warehouse, but lodg'd abroad. After sending to enquire my Character at the House where I last lodg'd, she agreed to take me in at the same Rate 3/6 p[er] Week, cheaper as she said from the Protection she ex-

*A Printing House is always called a Chappel [sic], by the Workmen. [*Franklin's note.*]

pected in having a Man lodge in the House. She was a Widow, an elderly Woman, had been bred a Protestant, being a Clergyman's Daughter, but was converted to the Catholic Religion by her Husband, whose Memory she much revered[;] had lived much among People of Distinction, and knew a 1000 Anecdotes of them as far back as the Times of Charles the Second. She was lame in her Knees with the Gout, and therefore seldom stirr'd out of her Room, so sometimes wanted Company; and hers was so highly amusing [Franklin first wrote "agreable"; both it and "amusing" are deleted in the MS.] to me; that I was sure to spend an Evening with her whenever she desired it. Our Supper was only half an Anchovy each, on a very little Strip of Bread and Butter, and half a Pint of Ale between us. But the Entertainment was in her Conversation. My always keeping good Hours, and giving little Trouble in the Family, made her unwilling to part with me; so that when I talk'd of a Lodging I had heard of, nearer my Business, for 2/ a Week, which, intent as I now was on saving Money, made some Difference; she bid me not think of it, for she would abate me two Shillings a Week for the future, so I remain'd with her at 1/6 as long as I staid in London.—

In a Garret of her House there lived a Maiden Lady of 70 in the most retired Manner, of whom my Landlady gave me this Account, that she was a Roman Catholic, had been sent abroad when young and lodg'd in a Nunnery with an Intent of becoming a Nun: but the Country not agreeing with her, she return'd to England, where there being no Nunnery, she had vow'd to lead the Life of a Nun as near as might be done in those Circumstances: Accordingly she had given all her Estate to charitable Uses, reserving only Twelve Pounds a Year to live on, and out of this Sum she still gave a great deal in Charity, living herself on Watergruel only, and using no Fire but to boil it.—She had lived many Years in that Garret, being permitted to remain there gratis by successive Catholic Tenants of the House below, as they deem'd it a Blessing to have her there. A Priest visited her, to confess her every Day. I have ask'd her, says my Landlady, how she, as she liv'd, could possibly find so much Employment for a Confessor? O, says she, it is impossible to avoid *vain Thoughts*. I was permitted once to visit her: She was chearful and polite, and convers'd pleasantly. The Room was clean, but had no other Furniture than a Matras, a Table with a Crucifix and Book, a Stool, which she gave me to sit on, and a Picture over the Chimney of St. *Veronica*, displaying her Handkerchief with the miraculous Figure of Christ's bleeding Face on it, which she explain'd to me with great Seriousness. She look'd pale, but was never sick, and I give it as another Instance on how small an Income Life and Health may be supported.

At Watts's Printinghouse I contracted an Acquaintance with an ingenious young Man, one Wygate, who having wealthy Relations, had been better educated than most Printers, was a tolerable Latinist, spoke French, and lov'd Reading. I taught him and a Friend of his, to swim, at twice going into the River, and they soon became good Swimmers. They introduc'd me to some Gentlemen from the Country who went to Chelsea by Water to see the College and Don Saltero's Curiosities.[5] In our Return, at the Request of the Company, whose Curiosity Wygate had excited, I stript and leapt into the River, and swam from near Chelsea to Blackfryars, performing on the Way many Feats of Activity both upon and under Water, that surpriz'd and pleas'd those to whom they were Novelties.—I had from a Child been ever delighted with this Exercise, had studied and practis'd all Thevenot's Motions and Positions, added some of my own, aiming at the graceful and easy, as well as the Useful. All these I took this Occasion of exhibiting to the Company, and was much flatter'd by their Admiration.—And Wygate, who was desirous of becoming a Master, grew more and more attach'd to me, on that account, as well as from the Similarity of our Studies. He at length propos'd to me travelling all over Europe together, supporting ourselves everywhere by working at our Business. I was once inclin'd to it. But mentioning it to my good Friend Mr. Denham, with whom I often spent an Hour, when I had Leisure. He dissuaded me from it, advising me to think only of returning to Pensilvania, which he was now about to do.

I must record one Trait of this good Man's Character. He
had formerly been in Business at Bristol, but fail'd in Debt to a
Number of People, compounded and went to America. There,
by a close Application to Business as a Merchant, he acquir'd a
plentiful Fortune in a few Years. Returning to England in the
Ship with me, He invited his old Creditors to an Entertainment,
at which he thank'd them for the easy Composition they had
favour'd him with, and when they expected nothing but the
Treat, every Man at the first Remove, found under his Plate an
Order on a Banker for the full Amount of the unpaid Remainder with Interest.

He now told me he was about to return to Philadelphia, and
should carry over a great Quantity of Goods in order to open a
Store there: He propos'd to take me over as his Clerk, to keep
his Books (in which he would instruct me) copy his Letters,
and attend the Store. He added, that as soon as I should be acquainted with mercantile Business he would promote me by
sending me with a Cargo of Flour and Bread etc to the West
Indies, and procure me Commissions from others; which would
be profitable, and if I manag'd well, would establish me handsomely. The Thing pleas'd me, for I was grown tired of London, remember'd with Pleasure the happy Months I had spent in
Pennsylvania, and wish'd again to see it. Therefore I immediately agreed, on the Terms of Fifty Pounds a Year, Pensylvania
Money less indeed than my then present Gettings as a Compositor, but affording a better Prospect.—

I now took leave of Printing; as I thought for ever, and was
daily employ'd in my new Business; going about with Mr. Denham among the Tradesmen, to purchase various Articles, and
seeing them pack'd up, doing Errands, calling upon Workmen
to dispatch, etc. and when all was on board, I had a few Days
Leisure. On one of these Days I was to my Surprise sent for by
a great Man I knew only by Name, a Sir William Wyndham and
I waited upon him. He had heard by some means or other of
my Swimming from Chelsey to Blackfryars, and of my teaching
Wygate and another young Man to swim in a few Hours. He
had two Sons about to set out on their Travels; he wish'd to

have them first taught Swimming; and propos'd to gratify me handsomely if I would teach them.—They were not yet come to Town and my Stay was uncertain, so I could not undertake it. But from this Incident I thought it likely, that if I were to remain in England and open a Swimming School, I might get a good deal of Money. And it struck me so strongly, that had the Overture been sooner made me, probably I should not so soon have returned to America.—After many Years, you and I had something of more Importance to do with one of these Sons of Sir William Wyndham, become Earl of Egremont, which I shall mention in its Place.—[This promise Franklin did not fulfill.]

Thus I spent about 18 Months in London. Most Part of the Time, I work'd hard at my Business, and spent but little upon myself except in seeing Plays, and in Books.—My Friend Ralph had kept me poor. He owed me about 27 Pounds; which I was now never likely to receive; a great Sum out of my small Earnings. I lov'd him notwithstanding, for he had many amiable Qualities.—Tho' I had by no means improv'd my Fortune. But I had pick'd up some very ingenious Acquaintance whose Conversation was of great Advantage to me, and I had read considerably.

We sail'd from Gravesend on the 23^d of July 1726. For the Incidents of the Voyage, I refer you to my Journal, where you will find them all minutely related. Perhaps the most important Part of that Journal is the *Plan* [This Plan is not found in the *Journal* printed in *Writings*, II, 53-86.] to be found in it which I formed at Sea, for regulating my future Conduct in Life. It is the more remarkable, as being formed when I was so young, and yet being pretty faithfully adhered to quite thro' to old Age. —We landed in Philadelphia on the 11th of October, where I found sundry Alterations. Keith was no longer Governor, being superceded by Major Gordon: I met him walking the Streets as a common Citizen. He seem'd a little asham'd at seeing me, but pass'd without saying any thing. I should have been as much asham'd at seeing Miss Read, had not her Fr^{ds}, despairing with Reason of my Return, after the Receipt of my Letter, persuaded her to marry another, one Rogers, a Potter, which was done in my Absence. With him however she was never happy, and soon parted from him, refusing to cohabit with him, or bear his Name[,] it being now said that he had another Wife. He was a worthless Fellow tho' an excellent Workman[,] which was the Temptation to her Friends. He got into Debt, ran away in 1727 or 28. and went to the West Indies, and died there. Keimer had got a better House, a Shop well supply'd with Stationary[,] plenty of new Types, a number of Hands tho' none good, and seem'd to have a great deal of Business.

Mr. Denham took a Store in Water Street, where we open'd our Goods. I attended the Business diligently, studied Accounts, and grew in a little Time expert at selling. We lodg'd and boarded together, he counsell'd me as a Father, having a sincere Regard for me: I respected and lov'd him: and we might have gone on together very happily: But in the Beginning of Feby 172$\frac{6}{7}$ when I had just pass'd my 21st Year, we both were taken ill. My Distemper was a Pleurisy, which very nearly carried me off:—I suffered a good deal, gave up the Point in my own mind, and was rather disappointed when I found my Self recovering; regretting in some degree that I must now some time or other have all that disagreeable Work to do over again.—I forget what his Distemper was. It held him a long time, and at length carried him off. He left me a small Legacy in a nuncupative Will, as a Token of his Kindness for me, and he left me once more to the wide World. For the Store was taken into the Care of his Executors, and my Employment under him ended:—My Brother-in-law Holmes, being now at Philadelphia, advised my Return to my Business. And Keimer tempted me with an Offer of large Wages by the Year to come and take the Management of his Printing-House, that he might better attend his Stationer's Shop.—I had heard a bad Character of him in London, from his Wife and her Friends, and was not fond of having any more to do with him. I try'd for farther Employment as a Merchant's Clerk; but not readily meeting with any, I clos'd again with Keimer.—

I found in *his* House these Hands; Hugh Meredith a Welsh-

Pensilvanian, 30 Years of Age, bred to Country Work: honest, sensible, had a great deal of solid Observation, was something of a Reader, but given to drink: Stephen Potts, a young Country Man of full Age, bred to the Same:—of uncommon natural Parts, and great Wit and Humour, but a little idle. These he had agreed with at extream low Wages, p[er] Week, to be rais'd a Shilling every 3 Months, as they would deserve by improving in their Business, and the Expectation of these high Wages to come on hereafter was what he had drawn them in with. Meredith was to work at Press, Potts at Bookbinding, which he by Agreement, was to teach them, tho' he knew neither one nor t'other. John —— a wild Irishman brought up to no Business, whose Service for 4 Years Keimer had purchas'd from the Captain of a Ship. He too was to be made a Pressman. George Webb, an Oxford Scholar, whose Time for 4 Years he had likewise bought, intending him for a Compositor: of whom more presently. And David Harry, a Country Boy, whom he had taken Apprentice. I soon perceiv'd that the Intention of engaging me at Wages so much higher than he had been us'd to give, was to have these raw cheap Hands form'd thro' me, and as soon as I had instructed them, then, they being all articled to him, he should be able to do without me.—I went on however, very chearfully; put his Printing House in Order, which had been in great Confusion, and brought his Hands by degrees to mind their Business and to do it better.

It was an odd Thing to find an Oxford Scholar in the Situation of a bought Servant. He was not more than 18 Years of Age, and gave me this Account of himself; that he was born in Gloucester, educated at a Grammar School there, had been distinguish'd among the Scholars for some apparent Superiority in performing his Part when they exhibited Plays; belong'd to the Witty Club there, and had written some Pieces in Prose and Verse which were printed in the Gloucester Newspapers.— Thence he was sent to Oxford; where he continu'd about a Year, but not well-satisfy'd, wishing of all things to see London and become a Player. At length receiving his Quarterly Allowance of 15 Guineas, instead of discharging his Debts, he walk'd out of

Town, hid his Gown in a Furz Bush, and footed it to London,
where having no Friend to advise him, he fell into bad Company, soon spent his Guineas, found no means of being introduc'd among the Players, grew necessitous, pawn'd his Cloaths
and wanted Bread. Walking the Street very hungry, and not
knowing what to do with himself, a Crimp's Bill was put into
his Hand, offering immediate Entertainment and Encouragement to such as would bind themselves to serve in America. He
went directly, sign'd the Indentures, was put into the Ship and
came over; never writing a Line to acquaint his Friends what
was become of him. He was lively, witty, good-natur'd, and
a pleasant Companion, but idle, thoughtless and imprudent to
the last Degree.

John the Irishman soon ran away. With the rest I began to
live very agreably; for they all respected me, the more as they
found Keimer incapable of instructing them, and that from me
they learnt something daily. We never work'd on a Saturday,
that being Keimer's Sabbath. So I had two Days for Reading.—
My Acquaintance with ingenious People in the Town, increased. Keimer himself treated me with great Civility, and apparent Regard; and nothing now made me uneasy but my Debt
to Vernon, which I was yet unable to pay being hitherto but a
poor Oeconomist. He however kindly made no Demand of it.

Our Printing-House often wanted Sorts, and there was no
Letter Founder in America. I had seen Types cast at James's in
London, but without much Attention to the Manner: However
I now contriv'd a Mould, made use of the Letters we had, as
Puncheons, struck the Matrices in Lead, and thus supply'd in a
pretty tolerable way all Deficiencies. I also engrav'd several
Things on occasion. I made the Ink, I was Warehouse-man
and every thing, in short quite a Factotum.—

But however serviceable I might be, I found that my Services
became every Day of less Importance, as the other Hands improv'd in the Business. And when Keimer paid my second
Quarter's Wages, he let me know that he felt them too heavy,
and thought I should make an Abatement. He grew by degrees
less civil, put on more of the Master, frequently found Fault,

was captious and seem'd ready for an Out-breaking. I went on nevertheless with a good deal of Patience, thinking that his in- cumber'd Circumstances were partly the Cause. At length a Trifle snapt our Connexion. For a great Noise happening near the Courthouse, I put my Head out of the Window to see what was the Matter. Keimer being in the Street look'd up and saw me, call'd out to me in a loud voice and angry Tone to mind my Business, adding some reproachful Words, that nettled me the more for their Publicity, all the Neighbours who were looking out on the same Occasion being Witnesses how I was treated. He came up immediately into the Printing-House, continu'd the Quarrel, high Words pass'd on both Sides, he gave me the Quarter's Warning we had stipulated, expressing a Wish that he had not been oblig'd to so long a Warning: I told him his Wish was unnecessary for I would leave him that Instant; and so tak- ing my Hat walk'd out of Doors; desiring Meredith whom I saw below to take care of some Things I left, and bring them to my Lodging.—

Meredith came accordingly in the Evening, when we talk'd my Affair over. He had conceiv'd a great Regard for me, and was very unwilling that I should leave the House while he re- main'd in it. He dissuaded me from returning to my native Country which I began to think of. He reminded me that Kei- mer was in debt for all he possess'd, that his Creditors began to be uneasy, that he kept his Shop miserably, sold often without Profit for ready Money, and often trusted without keeping Ac- counts. That he must therefore fail; which would make a Va- cancy I might profit of.—I objected my Want of Money. He then let me know, that his Father had a high Opinion of me, and from some Discourse that had pass'd between them, he was sure would advance Money to set us up, if I would enter into Part- ner Ship with him. My Time, says he, will be out with Keimer in the Spring. By that time we may have our Press and Types in from London: I am sensible I am no Workman. If you like it, Your Skill in the Business shall be set against the Stock I furnish; and we will share the Profits equally.—The Proposal was agre- able, and I consented. His Father was in Town, and approv'd of it, the more as he saw I had great Influence with his Son, had prevail'd on him to abstain long from Dramdrinking, and he hop'd might break him of that wretched Habit entirely, when we came to be so closely connected. I gave an Inventory to the Father, who carry'd it to a Merchant; the Things were sent for; the Secret was to be kept till they should arrive, and in the mean time I was to get work if I could at the other Printing House. But I found no Vacancy there, and so remain'd idle a few Days, when Keimer, on a Prospect of being employ'd to print some Paper-Money, in New Jersey, which would require Cuts and various Types that I only could supply, and apprehending Bradford might engage me and get the Jobb from him, sent me a very civil Message, that old Friends should not part for a few Words the Effect of sudden Passion, and wishing me to return. Meredith persuaded me to comply, as it would give more Opportunity for his Improvement under my daily Instructions.—So I return'd, and we went on more smoothly than for some time before. The New Jersey Jobb was obtained. I contriv'd a Copper-Plate Press for it, the first that had been seen in the Country. I cut several Ornaments and Checks for the Bills. We went together to Burlington, where I executed the Whole to Satisfaction, and he received so large a Sum for the Work, as to be enabled thereby to keep his Head much longer above Water.

At Burlington I made an Acquaintance with many principal People of the Province. Several of them had been appointed by the Assembly a Committee to attend the Press, and take Care that no more Bills were printed than the Law directed. They were therefore by Turns constantly with us, and generally he who attended brought with him a Friend or two for Company. My Mind having been much more improv'd by Reading than Keimer's, I suppose it was for that Reason my Conversation seem'd to be more valu'd. They had me to their Houses, introduc'd me to their Friends and show'd me much Civility, while he, tho' the Master, was a little neglected. In truth he was an odd Fish, ignorant of common Life, fond of rudely opposing receiv'd Opinions, slovenly to extream dirtiness, enthusiastic in some Points of Religion, and a little Knavish withal. We continu'd there near 3 Months, and by that time I could reckon among my acquired Friends, Judge Allen, Samuel Bustill, the Secretary of the Province, Isaac Pearson, Joseph Cooper and several of the Smiths, Members of Assembly, and Isaac Decow the Surveyor General. The latter was a shrewd sagacious old Man, who told me that he began for himself when young by wheeling Clay for the Brickmakers, learnt to write after he was of Age, carry'd the Chain for Surveyors, who taught him Surveying, and he had now by his Industry acquir'd a good Estate; and says he, I foresee, that you will soon work this Man out of his Business and make a Fortune in it at Philadelphia. He had not then the least Intimation of my Intention to set up there or any where. These Friends were afterwards of great use to me, as I occasionally was to some of them. They all continued their Regard for me as long as they lived.—

Before I enter upon my public Appearance in Business it may be well to let you know the then State of my Mind, with regard to my Principles and Morals, that you may see how far those influenc'd the future Events of my Life. My Parent's [*sic*] had early given me religious Impressions, and brought me through my Childhood piously in the Dissenting Way. But I was scarce 15 when, after doubting by turns of several Points as I found them disputed in the different Books I read, I began to doubt of Revelation it self. Some Books against Deism fell into my Hands; they were said to be the Substance of Sermons preached at Boyle's Lectures. It happened that they wrought an Effect on me quite contrary to what was intended by them: For the Arguments of the Deists which were quoted to be refuted, appeared to me much Stronger than the Refutations. In short I soon became a thorough Deist. My Arguments perverted some others, particularly Collins and Ralph: but each of them having afterwards wrong'd me greatly without the least Compunction and recollecting Keith's Conduct towards me, (who was another Freethinker) and my own towards Vernon and Miss Read, which at Times gave me great Trouble, I began to suspect that this Doctrine tho' it might be true, was not very useful.—

My London Pamphlet, which had for its Motto these Lines of
Dryden

> *Whatever is, is right. Tho' purblind Man*
> *Sees but a Part of the Chain, the nearest Link,*
> *His Eyes not carrying to the equal Beam,*
> *That poises all, above.*

And from the Attributes of God, his infinite Wisdom, Goodness and Power concluded that nothing could possibly be
wrong in the World, and that Vice and Virtue were empty Distinctions, no such Things existing: appear'd now not so clever a
Performance as I once thought it; and I doubted whether some
Error had not insinuated itself unperceiv'd, into my Argument,
so as to infect all that follow'd, as is common in metaphysical
Reasonings.—I grew convinc'd that *Truth, Sincerity* and *Integrity* in Dealings between Man and Man, were of the utmost
Importance to the Felicity of Life, and I form'd written Resolutions, (wch still remain in my Journal Book) to practice them
everwhile I lived. Revelation had indeed no weight with me as
such; but I entertain'd an Opinion, that tho' certain Actions
might not be bad *because* they were forbidden by it, or good *because* it commanded them; yet probably those Actions might be
forbidden *because* they were bad for us, or commanded *because*
they were beneficial to us, in their own Natures, all the Circumstances of things considered. And this Persuasion, with the
kind hand of Providence, or some guardian Angel, or accidental
favourable Circumstances and Situations, or all together, preserved me (thro' this dangerous Time of Youth and the hazardous Situations I was sometimes in among Strangers, remote
from the Eye and Advice of my Father) without any *wilful*
gross Immorality or Injustice that might have been expected
from my Want of Religion. I say *wilful*, because the Instances I
have mentioned, had something of *Necessity* in them, from my
Youth, Inexperience, and the Knavery of others. I had therefore a tolerable Character to begin the World with, I valued it
properly, and determin'd to preserve it.—

We had not been long return'd to Philadelphia, before the

New Types arriv'd from London. We settled with Keimer, and left him by his Consent before he heard of it.—We found a House to hire near the Market, and took it. To lessen the Rent, (which was then but 24£ a Year tho' I have since known it let for 70) We took in Tho' Godfrey a Glazier and his Family, who were to pay a considerable Part of it to us, and we to board with them. We had scarce opened our Letters and put our Press in Order, before George House, an Acquaintance of mine, brought a Countryman to us, whom he had met in the Street enquiring for a Printer. All our Cash was now expended in the Variety of Particulars we had been obliged to procure and this Countryman's Five Shillings being our first Fruits, and coming so seasonably, gave me more Pleasure than any Crown I have since earned; and from the Gratitude I felt towards House, has made me often more ready, than perhaps I should otherwise have been to assist young Beginners.

There are Croakers in every Country always boding its Ruin. Such a one then lived in Philadelphia, a Person of Note, an elderly Man, with a wise Look, and very grave Manner of speaking. His Name was Samuel Mickle. This Gentleman, a Stranger to me, stopt one Day at my Door, and asked me if I was the young Man who had lately opened a new Printing House: Being answered in the Affirmative, he said he was sorry for me, because it was an expensive Undertaking and the Expence would be lost; for Philadelphia was a sinking Place, the People already half Bankrupts or near being so; all Appearances to the contrary, such as new Buildings and the Rise of Rents being to his certain Knowledge fallacious; for they were in fact among the Things that would soon ruin us.—And he gave me such a Detail of Misfortunes, now existing or that were soon to exist, that he left me half melancholy. Had I known him before I engaged in this Business, probably I never should have done it.—This Man continued to live in this decaying Place; and to declaim in the same Strain, refusing for many Years to buy a House there, because all was going to Destruction, and at last I had the Pleasure of seeing him give five times as much for one as he might have bought it for, when he first began his Croaking.

I should have mentioned before, that in the Autumn of the preceeding Year I had formed most of my ingenious Acquaintance into a Club of mutual Improvement, which we called the Junto. We met on Friday Evenings. The Rules I drew up required that every Member in his Turn should produce one or more Queries on any Point of Morals, Politics or Natural Philosophy, to be discussed by the Company, and once in three Months produce and read an Essay of his own Writing on any Subject he pleased. Our Debates were to be under the Direction of a President and to be conducted in the sincere Spirit of Enquiry after Truth, without Fondness for Dispute, or Desire of Victory; and to prevent Warmth all Expressions of Positiveness in Opinions or direct Contradiction, were after some time made contraband and prohibited under small pecuniary Penalties.— The first Members were Joseph Breintnal,[6] a Copyer of Deeds for the Scriveners; a good-natur'd friendly middle-ag'd Man, a great Lover of Poetry, reading all he could meet with, and writing some that was tolerable; very ingenious in many little Nicknackeries, and of sensible Conversation. Thomas Godfrey,[7] a self-taught Mathematician, great in his Way, and afterwards Inventor of what is now call'd Hadley's Quadrant. But he knew little out of his way, and was not a pleasing Companion, as like most Great Mathematicians I have met with, he expected universal Precision in every thing said, or was forever denying or distinguishing upon Trifles, to the Disturbance of all Conversation. He soon left us. Nicholas Scull, a Surveyor, afterwards Surveyor-General, who lov'd Books, and sometimes made a few Verses. William Parsons,[8] bred a Shoemaker, but loving Reading, had acquir'd a considerable Share of Mathematics, which he first studied with a View to Astrology that he afterwards laught at. He also became Surveyor General. William Maugridge, a Joiner, a most exquisite Mechanic and a solid sensible Man. Hugh Meredith, Stephen Potts, and George Webb, I have Characteris'd before. Robert Grace, a young Gentleman of some Fortune, generous, lively and witty, a Lover of Punning and of his Friends. And William Coleman, then a Merchant's Clerk, about my Age, who had the coolest clearest Head, the best

Heart, and the exactest Morals, of almost any Man I ever met with. He became afterwards a Merchant of great Note, and one of our Provincial Judges. Our Friendship continued without Interruption to his death upwards of 40 Years. And the club continu'd almost as long[,] and was the best School of Philosophy, and Politics that then existed in the Province; for our Queries which were read the Week preceding their Discussion, put us on reading with Attention upon the several Subjects, that we might speak more to the purpose: and here too we acquired better Habits of Conversation, every thing being studied in our Rules which might prevent our disgusting each other. From hence the long Continuance of the Club, which I shall have frequent Occasion to speak farther of hereafter; But my giving this Account of it here, is to show something of the Interest I had, every one of these exerting themselves in recommending Business to us.——Brientnal particularly procur'd us from the Quakers, the Printing 40 Sheets of their History [William Sewel's], the rest being to be done by Keimer: and upon this we work'd exceeding hard, for the Price was low. It was a Folio, Pro Patria Size, in Pica with Long Primer Notes. I compos'd of it a Sheet a Day, and Meredith work'd it off at Press. It was often 11 at Night and sometimes later, before I had finish'd my Distribution for the next days Work: For the little Jobbs sent in by our other Friends now and then put us back. But so determin'd I was to continue doing a Sheet a Day of the Folio, that one Night when having impos'd my Forms, I thought my Days Work over, one of them by accident was broken and two Pages reduc'd to pie, I immediately distributed and compos'd it over again before I went to bed. And this Industry visible to our Neighbours began to give us Character and Credit; particularly I was told, that mention being made of the new Printing Office at the Merchants every-night Club, the general Opinion was that it must fail, there being already two Printers in the Place, Keimer and Bradford; but Dr. Baird (whom you and I saw many Years after at his native Place, St. Andrews in Scotland) gave a contrary Opinion; for the Industry of that Franklin, says he, is superior to any thing I ever saw of the kind: I see him still at

work when I go home from Club; and he is at Work
again before his Neighbours are out of bed. This struck the
rest, and we soon after had Offers from one of them to Supply us with Stationary. But as yet we did not chuse to engage in
Shop Business.

I mention this Industry the more particularly and the more
freely, tho' it seems to be talking in my own Praise, that those of
my Posterity who shall read it, may know the Use of that Virtue, when they see its Effects in my Favour throughout this
Relation.—

George Webb, who had found a Friend that lent him wherewith to purchase his Time of Keimer, now came to offer himself
as a Journeyman to us. We could not then imploy him, but I
foolishly let him know, as a Secret, that I soon intended to begin
a Newspaper, and might then have Work for him. My Hopes of
Success as I told him were founded on this, that the then only
Newspaper [the *American Weekly Mercury*], printed by Bradford was a paltry thing, wretchedly manag'd, no way entertaining; and yet was profitable to him.—I therefore thought a good
Paper could scarcely fail of good Encouragem^t. I requested
Webb not to mention it, but he told it to Keimer, who immediately, to be beforehand with me, published Proposals for Printing one himself, on which Webb was to be employ'd.—I resented this, and to counteract them, as I could not yet begin our
Paper, I wrote several Pieces of Entertainment for Bradford's
Paper, under the Title of the Busy Body which Brientnal continu'd some Months. By this means the Attention of the Publick was fix'd on that Paper, and Keimers Proposals which we
burlesqu'd and ridicul'd, were disregarded. He began his Paper[9]
however, and after carrying it on three Quarters of a Year, with
at most only 90 Subscribers, he offer'd it to me for a Trifle, and I
having been ready some time to go on with it, took it in hand
directly, and it prov'd in a few years extreamly profitable to me.

I perceive that I am apt to speak in the singular Number,
though our Partnership still continu'd. The Reason may be,
that in fact the whole Management of the Business lay upon me.
Meredith was no Compositor, a poor Pressman, and seldom

sober. My Friends lamented my Connection with him, but I was to make the best of it.

Our first Papers made a quite different Appearance from any before in the Province, a better Type and better printed [In MS is found: "Insert these Remarks, in a Note."]: but some spirited Remarks of my Writing on the Dispute then going on between Govr Burnet and the Massachusetts Assembly, struck the principal People, occasion'd the Paper and the Manager of it to be much talk'd of, and in a few Weeks brought them all to be our Subscribers. Their Example was follow'd by many, and our Number went on growing continually.—This was one of the first good Effects of my having learnt a little to scribble. Another was, that the leading Men, seeing a News Paper now in the hands of one who could also handle a Pen, thought it convenient to oblige and encourage me. Bradford still printed the Votes and Laws and other Publick Business. He had printed an Address of the House to the Governor in a coarse blundering manner; We reprinted it elegantly and correctly, and sent one to every Member. They were sensible of the Difference, it strengthen'd the Hands of our Friends in the House, and they voted us their Printers for the Year ensuing.

Among my Friends in the House I must not forget Mr. Hamilton before mentioned, who was then returned from England and had a Seat in it. He interested himself for me strongly in that Instance, as he did in many others afterwards, continuing his Patronage till his Death.* Mr Vernon about this time put me in mind of the Debt I ow'd him: but did not press me. I wrote him an ingenuous Letter of Acknowledgments, crav'd his Forbearance a little longer which he allow'd me, and as soon as I was able I paid the Principal with Interest and many Thanks.— So that Erratum was in some degree corrected.—

But now another Difficulty came upon me, which I had never the least Reason to expect. Mr. Meredith's Father, who was to have paid for our Printing House according to the Expectations given me, was able to advance only one Hundred Pounds, Currency, which had been paid, and a Hundred more was due to the

* I got his Son once 500 £. [*Franklin's note.*]

Merchant; who grew impatient and su'd us all. We gave Bail,
but saw that if the Money could not be rais'd in time, the Suit
must come to a Judgment and Execution, and our hopeful Prospects must with us be ruined, as the Press and Letters must be
sold for Payment, perhaps at half Price.—In this Distress two
true Friends whose Kindness I have never forgotten nor ever
shall forget while I can remember any thing, came to me separately[,] unknown to each other, and without any Application
from me, offering each of them to advance me all the Money
that should be necessary to enable me to take the whole Business
upon myself if that should be practicable, but they did not like
my continuing the Partnership with Meredith, who as they said
was often seen drunk in the Streets, and playing at low Games in
Alehouses, much to our Discredit. These two Friends were
William Coleman and *Robert Grace.* I told them I could not propose a Separation while any Prospect remain'd of the Merediths
fulfilling their Part of our Agreement. Because I thought myself under great Obligations to them for what they had done
and would do if they could. But if they finally fail'd in their
Performance, and our Partnership must be dissolv'd, I should
then think myself at Liberty to accept the Assistance of my
Friends. Thus the matter rested for some time. When I said to
my Partner, perhaps your Father is dissatisfied at the Part you
have undertaken in this Affair of ours, and is unwilling to advance for you and me what he would for you alone: If that is
the Case, tell me, and I will resign the whole to you and go
about my Business. No[,] says he, my Father has really been
disappointed and is really unable; and I am unwilling to distress
him farther. I see this is a Business I am not fit for. I was bred a
Farmer, and it was a Folly in me to come to Town and put my
Self at 30 Years of Age an Apprentice to learn a new Trade.
Many of our Welsh People are going to settle in North Carolina
where Land is cheap: I am inclin'd to go with them, and following my old Employment. You may find Friends to assist you.
If you will take the Debts of the Company upon you, return to
my Father the hundred Pound he has advanc'd, pay my little
personal Debts, and give me Thirty Pounds and a new Saddle,

I will relinquish the Partnership and leave the whole in your Hands. I agreed to this Proposal. It was drawn up in Writing, sign'd and seal'd immediately. I gave him what he demanded and he went soon after to Carolina; from whence he sent me next Year two long Letters, containing the best Account that had been given of that Country, the Climate, Soil, Husbandry, etc. for in those Matters he was very judicious. I printed them in the Papers, and they gave grate Satisfaction to the Publick.

As soon as he was gone, I recurr'd to my two Friends; and because I would not give an unkind Preference to either, I took half what each had offered and I wanted, of one, and half of the other; paid off the Company Debts, and went on with the Business in my own Name, advertising that the Partnership was dissolved. I think this was in or about the Year 1729 [July 14, 1730].—

About this Time there was a Cry among the People for more Paper-Money, only 15,000£ being extant in the Province and that soon to be sunk. The wealthy Inhabitants oppos'd any Addition, being against all Paper Currency, from an Apprehension that it would depreciate as it had done in New England to the Prejudice of all Creditors.—We had discuss'd this Point in our Junto, where I was on the Side of an Addition, being persuaded that the first small Sum struck in 1723 had done much good, by increasing the Trade[,] Employment, and Number of Inhabitants in the Province, since I now saw all the old Houses inhabited, and many new ones building, where as I remember'd well, that when I first walk'd about the Streets of Philadelphia, eating my Roll, I saw most of the Houses in Walnut Street between Second and Front Streets with Bills on their Doors, to be let; and many likewise in Chesnut Street, and other Streets; which made me then think the Inhabitants of the City were deserting it, one after another.—Our Debates possess'd me so fully of the Subject, that I wrote and printed an anonymous Pamphlet on it, entituled, *The Nature and Necessity of a Paper Currency*. It was well receiv'd by the common People in general; but the Rich Men dislik'd it; for it increas'd and strengthen'd the Clamour for more Money; and they happening to have no Writers

among them that were able to answer it, their Opposition slack-
en'd, and the Point was carried by a Majority in the House. My
Friends there, who conceiv'd I had been of some Service,
thought fit to reward me, by employing me in printing the
Money, a very profitable Jobb, and a great Help to me.—This
was another Advantage gain'd by my being able to write[.] The
Utility of this Currency became by Time and Experience so evident, as never afterwards to be much disputed, so that it grew
soon to 55000,£ and in 1739 to 80,000£ since which it arose
during War to upwards of 350,000£. Trade, Building and Inhabitants all the while increasing. Tho' I now think there are
Limits beyond which the Quantity may be hurtful.—

I soon after obtain'd, thro' my Friend Hamilton, the Printing
of the New Castle Paper Money, another profitable Jobb, as I
then thought it; small Things appearing great to those in small
Circumstances. And these to me were really great Advantages,
as they were great Encouragements. He procured me also the
Printing of the Laws and Votes of that Government which continu'd in my Hands as long as I follow'd the Business.—

I now open'd a little Stationer's Shop. I had in it Blanks of all
Sorts[,] the correctest that ever appear'd among us, being assisted
in that by my Friend Brientnal; I had also Paper, Parchment,
Chapmen's Books, etc. One Whitema[r]sh[,] a Compositor I had
known in London, an excellent Workman now came to me and
work'd with me constantly and diligently, and I took an Apprentice the Son of Aquila Rose. I began now gradually to pay
off the Debt I was under for the Printing-House. In order to
secure my Credit and Character as a Tradesman, I took care not
only to be in *Reality* Industrious and frugal, but to avoid all
Appearances of the Contrary. I drest plainly; I was seen at no
Places of idle Diversion; I never went out a fishing or Shooting;
a Book, indeed, sometimes debauch'd me from my Work; but
that was seldom, snug, and gave no Scandal: and to show that I
was not above my Business, I sometimes brought home the Paper I purchas'd at the Stores, thro' the Streets on a Wheelbar-
row. Thus being esteem'd an industrious thriving young Man,
and paying duly for what I bought, the Merchants who im-

ported Stationary solicited my Custom, others propos'd supplying me with Books, I went on swimmingly.—In the mean time Keimer's Credit and Business declining daily, he was at last forc'd to sell his Printing-house to satisfy his Creditors. He went to Barbadoes, there lived some Years, in very poor Circumstances.

His Apprentice David Harry, whom I had instructed while I work'd with him, set up in his place at Philadelphia, having bought his Materials. I was at first apprehensive of a powerful Rival in Harry, as his Friends were very able, and had a good deal of Interest. I therefore propos'd a Partnership to him; which he, fortunately for me, rejected with Scorn. He was very proud, dress'd like a Gentleman, liv'd expensively, took much Diversion and Pleasure abroad, ran in debt, and neglected his Business, upon which all Business left him; and finding nothing to do, he follow'd Keimer to Barbadoes; taking the Printing-house with him[.] There this Apprentice employ'd his former Master as a Journeyman. They quarrel'd often, Harry went continually behindhand, and at length was forc'd to sell his Types, and return to his Country work in Pensilvania. The Person that bought them, employ'd Keimer to use them, but in a few years he died. There remain'd now no Competitor with me at Philadelphia, but the old one, Bradford, who was rich and easy, did a little Printing now and then by straggling Hands, but was not very anxious about it. However, as he kept the Post Office, it was imagined he had better Opportunities of obtaining News, his Paper was thought a better Distributer of Advertisements than mine, and therefore had many more, which was a profitable thing to him and a Disadvantage to me. For tho' I did indeed receive and send Papers by Post, yet the publick Opinion was otherwise; for what I did send was by Bribing the Riders who took them privately: Bradford being unkind enough to forbid it: which occasion'd some Resentment on my Part; and I thought so meanly of him for it, that when I afterwards came into his Situation, I took care never to imitate it.

I had hitherto continu'd to board with Godfrey who lived in Part of my House with his Wife and Children, and had one

Side of the Shop for his Glazier's Business, tho' he work'd little, being always absorb'd in his Mathematics.—Mrs. Godfrey projected a Match for me with a Relation's Daughter, took Opportunities of bringing us often together, till a serious Courtship on my Part ensu'd, the Girl being in herself very deserving. The old Folks encourag'd me by continual Invitations to Supper, and by leaving us together, till at length it was time to explain. Mrs. Godfrey manag'd our little Treaty. I let her know that I expected as much Money with their Daughter as would pay off my Remaining Debt for the Printinghouse, which I believe was not then above a Hundred Pounds. She brought me Word they had no such Sum to spare. I said they might mortgage their House in the Loan Office.—The Answer to this after some Days was, that they did not approve the Match; that on Enquiry of Bradford they had been inform'd the Printing Business was not a profitable one, the Types would soon be worn out and more wanted, that S. Keimer and D. Harry had fail'd one after the other, and I should probably soon follow them; and therefore I was forbidden the House, and the Daughter shut up.—Whether this was a real Change of Sentiment, or only Artifice, on a Supposition of our being too far engag'd in Affection to retract, and therefore that we should steal a Marriage, which would leave them at Liberty to give or with[h]old what they pleas'd, I know not: But I suspected the latter, resented it, and went no more. Mrs. Godfrey brought me afterwards some more favourable Accounts of their Disposition, and would have drawn me on again: But I declared absolutely my Resolution to have nothing more to do with that Family. This was resented by the Godfreys, we differ'd, and they removed, leaving me the whole House, and I resolved to take no more Inmates. But this Affair having turn'd my Thoughts to Marriage, I look'd round me, and made Overtures of Acquaintance in other Places; but soon found that the Business of a Printer being generally thought a poor one, I was not to expect Money with a Wife unless with such a one, as I should not otherwise think agreable.—In the mean time, that hard-to-be-govern'd Passion of Youth, had hurried me frequently into Intrigues with low Women that fell in

my Way, which were attended with some Expence and great
Inconvenience, besides a continual Risque to my Health by a
Distemper which of all Things I dreaded, tho' by great good
Luck I escaped it.—

A friendly Correspondence as Neighbours and old Acquaintances, had continued between me and Mrs. Read's Family, who
all had a Regard for me from the time of my first Lodging in
their House. I was often invited there and consulted in their
Affairs, wherein I sometimes was of service.—I pity'd poor
Miss Read's unfortunate Situation, who was generally dejected,
seldom chearful, and avoided Company. I consider'd my Giddi-
ness and Inconstancy when in London as in a great degree the
Cause of her Unhappiness; tho' the Mother was good enough to
think the Fault more her own than mine, as she had prevented
our Marrying before I went thither, and persuaded the other
Match in my Absence. Our mutual Affection was revived, but
there were now great Objections to our Union. That Match was
indeed look'd upon as invalid, a preceeding Wife being said to
be livin[g] in England; but this could not easily be prov'd, because of the Distance[.] And tho' there was a Report of his
Death, it was not certain. The[n] tho' it should be true, he had
left many Debts which his Successor might be call'd [on] to pay.
We ventur['d] however, over all these Difficulties, and I [took]
her to Wife Sept. 1. 1730.[10] None of the Inconveniencies
happen[ed] that we had apprehended, she prov'd a good and
faithful Helpmate, assisted me much by attending the Shop, we
throve together, and have ever mutually endeavour'd to make
each other happy. Thus I corrected that great *Erratum* as wel[l]
as I could.

About [th]is Time our Club meeting, not at a Tavern, but in
a little Room of Mr. Grace's set apart for that Purpose; a Proposition was made by me that since our Books were often referr'd
to in our Disquisitions upon the Queries, it might be convenient
to us to have them all together where we met, that upon Occasion they might be consulted; and by thus clubbing our Books
to a common Library, we should, while we lik'd to keep them
together, have each of us the Advantage of using the Books of

all the other Members, which would be nearly as beneficial as if each owned the whole. It was lik'd and agreed to, and we fill'd one End of the Room with such Books as we could best spare. The Number was not so great as we expected; and tho' they had been of great Use, yet some Inconveniencies occurring for want of due Care of them, the Collection after about a Year was separated, and each took his Books home again.

And now I sent on foot my first Project of a public Nature, [th]at for a Subscription Library. [I] drew up the Proposals, got them put into Form by our great Scrivener Brockden, and by the help of my Friends in the Junto, procur'd Fifty Subscribers of 40/ each to begin with and 10/ a Year for 50 Years, the Term our Company was to continue. We afterwards obtain'd a Charter, the Company being increas'd to 100. This was the Mother of all the N American Subscription Libraries now so numerous, is become a great thing itself, and continually increasing.— These Libraries have improv'd the general Conversation of the Americans, made the common Tradesmen and Farmers as intelligent as most Gentlemen from other Countries, and perhaps have contributed in some degree to the Stand so generally made throughout the Colonies in Defence of their Privileges.—[11]

.   .   .   .

This library afforded me the means of improvement by constant study, for which I set apart an hour or two each day, and thus repair'd in some degree the loss of the learned education my father once intended for me. Reading was the only amusement I allow'd myself. I spent no time in taverns, games, or frolicks of any kind; and my industry in my business continu'd as indefatigable as it was necessary. I was indebted for my printing-house; I had a young family coming on to be educated, and I had to contend with for business two printers, who were established in the place before me. My circumstances, however, grew daily easier. My original habits of frugality continuing, and my father having, among his instructions to me when a boy, frequently repeated a proverb of Solomon, "Seest thou a man diligent in his calling, he shall stand before kings, he shall not stand before mean men," I from thence considered industry as a means of obtaining wealth and distinction, which encourag'd me, tho' I did not think that I should ever literally *stand before kings*, which, however, has since happened; for I have stood before *five*, and even had the honour of sitting down with one, the King of Denmark, to dinner.

We have an English proverb that says, "*He that would thrive, must ask his wife.*" It was lucky for me that I had one as much dispos'd to industry and frugality as myself. She assisted me chearfully in my business, folding and stitching pamphlets, tending shop, purchasing old linen rags for the paper-makers, etc., etc. We kept no idle servants, our table was plain and simple, our furniture of the cheapest. For instance, my breakfast was a long time bread and milk (no tea), and I ate it out of a twopenny earthen porringer, with a pewter spoon. But mark how luxury will enter families, and make a progress, in spite of principle: being call'd one morning to breakfast, I found it in a China bowl, with a spoon of silver! They had been bought for me without my knowledge by my wife, and had cost her the enormous sum of three-and-twenty shillings, for which she had no other excuse or apology to make, but that she thought *her* husband deserv'd a silver spoon and China bowl as well as any of his neighbors. This was the first appearance of plate and China in our house, which afterward, in a course of years, as our wealth increas'd, augmented gradually to several hundred pounds in value.

I had been religiously educated as a Presbyterian; and tho' some of the dogmas of that persuasion, such as *the eternal decrees of God, election, reprobation, etc.*, appeared to me unintelligible, others doubtful, and I early absented myself from the public assemblies of the sect, Sunday being my studying day, I never was without some religious principles. I never doubted, for instance, the existence of the Deity; that he made the world, and govern'd it by his Providence; that the most acceptable service of God was the doing good to man; that our souls are immortal; and that all crime will be punished, and virtue rewarded, either here or hereafter. These I esteem'd the essentials of every religion; and, being to be found in all the religions we had in our country, I respected them all, tho' with different degrees of respect, as I found them more or less mix'd with other articles, which, without any tendency to inspire, promote, or confirm morality, serv'd principally to divide us, and make us unfriendly to one another. This respect to all, with an opinion that the worst had some good effects, induc'd me to avoid all discourse that might tend to lessen the good opinion another might have of his own religion; and as our province increas'd in people, and new places of worship were continually wanted, and generally erected by voluntary contribution, my mite for such purpose, whatever might be the sect, was never refused.

Tho' I seldom attended any public worship, I had still an opinion of its propriety, and of its utility when rightly conducted, and I regularly paid my annual subscription for the support of the only Presbyterian minister or meeting we had in Philadelphia. He us'd to visit me sometimes as a friend, and admonish me to attend his administrations, and I was now and then prevail'd on to do so, once for five Sundays successively. Had he been in my opinion a good preacher, perhaps I might have continued, notwithstanding the occasion I had for the Sunday's leisure in my course of study; but his discourses were chiefly either polemic arguments, or explications of the peculiar doctrines of our sect, and were all to me very dry, uninteresting, and unedifying, since not a single moral principle was inculcated or enforc'd, their aim seeming to be rather to make us Presbyterians than good citizens.

At length he took for his text that verse of the fourth chapter of Philippians, "*Finally, brethren, whatsoever things are true, honest, just, pure, lovely, or of good report, if there be any virtue, or any praise, think on these things.*" And I imagin'd, in a sermon on such a text, we could not miss of having some morality. But he confin'd himself to five points only, as meant by the apostle, viz.: 1. Keeping holy the Sabbath day. 2. Being diligent in reading the holy Scriptures. 3. Attending duly the publick worship. 4. Partaking of the Sacrament. 5. Paying a due respect to God's ministers. These might be all good things; but, as they were not the kind of good things that I expected from that text, I despaired of ever meeting with them from any other, was disgusted, and attended his preaching no more. I had some years before compos'd a little Liturgy, or form of prayer, for my own private use (viz., in 1728), entitled *Articles of Belief and Acts of Religion*. I return'd to the use of this, and went no more to the public assemblies. My conduct might be blameable, but I leave it, without attempting further to excuse it; my present purpose being to relate facts, and not to make apologies for them.

It was about this time I conceiv'd the bold and arduous project of arriving at moral perfection. I wish'd to live without committing any fault at any time; I would conquer all that either natural inclination, custom, or company might lead me into. As I knew, or thought I knew, what was right and wrong, I did not see why I might not always do the one and avoid the other. But I soon found I had undertaken a task of more difficulty than I had imagined. While my care was employ'd in guarding against one fault, I was often surprised by another; habit took the advantage of inattention; inclination was sometimes too strong for reason. I concluded, at length, that the mere speculative conviction that it was our interest to be completely virtuous, was not sufficient to prevent our slipping; and that the contrary habits must be broken, and good ones acquired and established, before we can have any dependence on a steady, uniform rectitude of conduct. For this purpose I therefore contrived the following method.

In the various enumerations of the moral virtues I had met with in my reading, I found the catalogue more or less numerous, as different writers included more or fewer ideas under the same name. Temperance, for example, was by some confined to eating and drinking, while by others it was extended to mean the moderating every other pleasure, appetite, inclination, or passion, bodily or mental, even to our avarice and ambition. I propos'd to myself, for the sake of clearness, to use rather more names, with fewer ideas annex'd to each, than a few names with more ideas; and I included under thirteen names of virtues all that at that time occurr'd to me as necessary or desirable, and annexed to each a short precept, which fully express'd the extent I gave to its meaning.

These names of virtues, with their precepts, were:

1. TEMPERANCE

Eat not to dullness; drink not to elevation.

2. SILENCE

Speak not but what may benefit others or yourself; avoid trifling conversation.

3. ORDER

Let all your things have their places; let each part of your business have its time.

4. RESOLUTION

Resolve to perform what you ought; perform without fail what you resolve.

5. FRUGALITY

Make no expense but to do good to others or yourself; *i. e.*, waste nothing.

6. INDUSTRY

Lose no time; be always employ'd in something useful; cut off all unnecessary actions.

7. SINCERITY

Use no hurtful deceit; think innocently and justly, and, if you speak, speak accordingly.

8. JUSTICE

Wrong none by doing injuries, or omitting the benefits that are your duty.

9. MODERATION

Avoid extreams; forbear resenting injuries so much as you think they deserve.

10. CLEANLINESS

Tolerate no uncleanliness in body, cloaths, or habitation.

11. TRANQUILLITY

Be not disturbed at trifles, or at accidents common or unavoidable.

12. CHASTITY

Rarely use venery but for health or offspring, never to dulness, weakness, or the injury of your own or another's peace or reputation.

13. HUMILITY

Imitate Jesus and Socrates.

My intention being to acquire the *habitude* of all these virtues, I judg'd it would be well not to distract my attention by attempting the whole at once, but to fix it on one of them at a time; and, when I should be master of that, then to proceed to another, and so on, till I should have gone thro' the thirteen; and, as the previous acquisition of some might facilitate the acquisition of certain others, I arrang'd them with that view, as they stand above. Temperance first, as it tends to procure that coolness and clearness of head, which is so necessary where constant vigilance was to be kept up, and guard maintained against the unremitting attraction of ancient habits, and the force of perpetual temptations. This being acquir'd and establish'd, Silence would be more easy; and my desire being to gain knowledge at the same time that I improv'd in virtue, and considering that in conversation it was obtain'd rather by the use of the ears than of the tongue, and therefore wishing to break a habit I was getting into of prattling, punning, and joking, which only made me acceptable to trifling company, I gave *Silence* the second place. This and the next, *Order*, I expected would allow me more time for attending to my project and my studies. *Resolution*, once become habitual, would keep me firm in my endeavours to obtain all the subsequent virtues; *Frugality* and Industry freeing me from my remaining debt, and producing affluence and independence, would make more easy the practice of Sincerity and Justice, etc., etc. Conceiving then, that, agreeably to the advice of Pythagoras in his *Golden Verses*, daily examination would be necessary, I contrived the following method for conducting that examination.

I made a little book,[12] in which I allotted a page for each of the virtues. I rul'd each page with red ink, so as to have seven columns, one for each day of the week, marking each column with a letter for the day. I cross'd these columns with thirteen red lines, marking the beginning of each line with the first letter of one of the virtues, on which line, and in its proper column, I might mark, by a little black spot, every fault I found upon examination to have been committed respecting that virtue upon that day.

Form of the Pages

TEMPERANCE.							
EAT NOT TO DULNESS. DRINK NOT TO ELEVATION.							
	S.	M.	T.	W.	T.	F.	S.
T.							
S.	*	*		*		*	
O.	* *	*	*		*	*	*
R.			*			*	
F.		*			*		
I.			*				
S.							
J.							
M.							
C.							
T.							
C.							
H.							

I determined to give a week's strict attention to each of the virtues successively. Thus, in the first week, my great guard was to avoid every the least offence against *Temperance*, leaving the other virtues to their ordinary chance, only marking every evening the faults of the day. Thus, if in the first week I could keep my first line, marked T, clear of spots, I suppos'd the habit of that virtue so much strengthen'd, and its opposite weaken'd, that I might venture extending my attention to include the next, and for the following week keep both lines clear of spots. Proceeding thus to the last, I could go thro' a course compleat in thirteen weeks, and four courses in a year. And like him who, having a garden to weed, does not attempt to eradicate all the bad herbs at once, which would exceed his reach and his strength, but works on one of the beds at a time, and, having accomplish'd the first, proceeds to a second, so I should have, I hoped, the encouraging pleasure of seeing on my pages the progress I made in virtue, by clearing successively my lines of their spots, till in the end, by a number of courses, I should be happy in viewing a clean book, after a thirteen weeks' daily examination.

This my little book had for its motto these lines from Addison's *Cato:*

> Here will I hold. If there's a power above us
> (And that there is, all nature cries aloud
> Thro' all her works), He must delight in virtue;
> And that which he delights in must be happy.

Another from Cicero,

O vitæ Philosophia dux! O virtutum indagatrix expultrixque vitiorum! Unus dies, bene et ex præceptis tuis actus, peccanti immortalitati est anteponendus.

Another from the Proverbs of Solomon, speaking of wisdom or virtue:

Length of days is in her right hand, and in her left hand riches and honour. Her ways are ways of pleasantness, and all her paths are peace.—iii. 16, 17.

And conceiving God to be the fountain of wisdom, I thought it right and necessary to solicit his assistance for obtaining it; to this end I formed the following little prayer, which was prefix'd to my tables of examination, for daily use.

O powerful Goodness! bountiful Father! merciful Guide! Increase in me that wisdom which discovers my truest interest. Strengthen my resolutions to perform what that wisdom dictates. Accept my kind offices to thy other children as the only return in my power for thy continual favours to me.

I used also sometimes a little prayer which I took from Thomson's *Poems*, viz.:

> Father of light and life, thou Good Supreme!
> O teach me what is good; teach me Thyself!
> Save me from folly, vanity, and vice,
> From every low pursuit; and fill my soul
> With knowledge, conscious peace, and virtue pure;
> Sacred, substantial, never-fading bliss!

The precept of *Order* requiring that *every part of my business should have its allotted time*, one page in my little book contain'd the following scheme of employment for the twenty-four hours of a natural day.

THE MORNING. *Question.* What good shall I do this day?	5 6 7	Rise, wash, and address *Powerful Goodness!* Contrive day's business, and take the resolution of the day; prosecute the present study, and breakfast.
	8 9 10 11	Work.
NOON.	12 1	Read, or overlook my accounts, and dine.
	2 3 4 5	Work.
EVENING. *Question.* What good have I done to-day?	6 7 8 9	Put things in their places. Supper. Music or diversion, or conversation. Examination of the day.

$$
\text{NIGHT.} \quad
\left.
\begin{cases}
10 \\
11 \\
12 \\
1 \\
2 \\
3 \\
4
\end{cases}
\right\} \text{Sleep.}
$$

I enter'd upon the execution of this plan for self-examination, and continu'd it with occasional intermissions for some time. I was surpris'd to find myself so much fuller of faults than I had imagined; but I had the satisfaction of seeing them diminish. To avoid the trouble of renewing now and then my little book, which, by scraping out the marks on the paper of old faults to make room for new ones in a new course, became full of holes, I transferr'd my tables and precepts to the ivory leaves of a memorandum book, on which the lines were drawn with red ink, that made a durable stain, and on those lines I mark'd my faults with a black-lead pencil, which marks I could easily wipe out with a wet sponge. After a while I went thro' one course only in a year, and afterward only one in several years, till at length I omitted them entirely, being employ'd in voyages and business abroad, with a multiplicity of affairs that interfered; but I always carried my little book with me.

My scheme of ORDER gave me the most trouble; and I found that, tho' it might be practicable where a man's business was such as to leave him the disposition of his time, that of a journeyman printer, for instance, it was not possible to be exactly observed by a master, who must mix with the world, and often receive people of business at their own hours. *Order*, too, with regard to places for things, papers, etc., I found extreamly difficult to acquire. I had not been early accustomed to it, and, having an exceeding good memory, I was not so sensible of the inconvenience attending want of method. This article, therefore, cost me so much painful attention, and my faults in it vexed me so much, and I made so little progress in amendment, and had such frequent relapses, that I was almost ready to give up the attempt, and content myself with a faulty character in that respect, like the man who, in buying an ax of a smith, my

neighbour, desired to have the whole of its surface as bright as
the edge. The smith consented to grind it bright for him if he
would turn the wheel; he turn'd, while the smith press'd the
broad face of the ax hard and heavily on the stone, which made
the turning of it very fatiguing. The man came every now and
then from the wheel to see how the work went on, and at length
would take his ax as it was, without farther grinding. "No,"
said the smith, "turn on, turn on; we shall have it bright by-and-
by; as yet, it is only speckled." "Yes," says the man, *"but I
think I like a speckled ax best."* And I believe this may have been
the case with many, who, having, for want of some such means
as I employ'd, found the difficulty of obtaining good and breaking bad habits in other points of vice and virtue, have given up
the struggle, and concluded that *"a speckled ax was best"*; for
something, that pretended to be reason, was every now and
then suggesting to me that such extream nicety as I exacted of
myself might be a kind of foppery in morals, which, if it were
known, would make me ridiculous; that a perfect character
might be attended with the inconvenience of being envied and
hated; and that a benevolent man should allow a few faults in
himself, to keep his friends in countenance.

In truth, I found myself incorrigible with respect to Order;
and now I am grown old, and my memory bad, I feel very sensibly the want of it. But, on the whole, tho' I never arrived at the
perfection I had been so ambitious of obtaining, but fell far short
of it, yet I was, by the endeavour, a better and a happier man
than I otherwise should have been if I had not attempted it; as
those who aim at perfect writing by imitating the engraved
copies, tho' they never reach the wish'd-for excellence of those
copies, their hand is mended by the endeavour, and is tolerable
while it continues fair and legible.

It may be well my posterity should be informed that to this
little artifice, with the blessing of God, their ancestor ow'd the
constant felicity of his life, down to his 79th year in which this
is written. What reverses may attend the remainder is in the
hand of Providence; but, if they arrive, the reflection on past
happiness enjoy'd ought to help his bearing them with more

resignation. To Temperance he ascribes his long-continued health, and what is still left to him of a good constitution; to Industry and Frugality, the early easiness of his circumstances and acquisition of his fortune, with all that knowledge that enabled him to be a useful citizen, and obtained for him some degree of reputation among the learned; to Sincerity and Justice, the confidence of his country, and the honorable employs it conferred upon him; and to the joint influence of the whole mass of the virtues, even in the imperfect state he was able to acquire them, all that evenness of temper, and that cheerfulness in conversation, which makes his company still sought for, and agreeable even to his younger acquaintance. I hope, therefore, that some of my descendants may follow the example and reap the benefit.

It will be remark'd that, tho' my scheme was not wholly without religion, there was in it no mark of any of the distinguishing tenets of any particular sect. I had purposely avoided them; for, being fully persuaded of the utility and excellency of my method, and that it might be serviceable to people in all religions, and intending some time or other to publish it, I would not have any thing in it that should prejudice any one, of any sect, against it. I purposed writing a little comment on each virtue, in which I would have shown the advantages of possessing it, and the mischiefs attending its opposite vice; and I should have called my book THE ART OF VIRTUE,* because it would have shown the means and manner of obtaining virtue, which would have distinguished it from the mere exhortation to be good, that does not instruct and indicate the means, but is like the apostle's man of verbal charity, who only, without showing to the naked and hungry how or where they might get clothes or victuals, exhorted them to be fed and clothed.— James ii. 15, 16.

But it so happened that my intention of writing and publishing this comment was never fulfilled. I did, indeed, from time to time, put down short hints of the sentiments, reasonings, etc.,

---

*Nothing so likely to make a man's fortune as virtue. [*Franklin's note.*]

to be made use of in it, some of which I have still by me; but the necessary close attention to private business in the earlier part of my life, and public business since, have occasioned my postponing it; for, it being connected in my mind with *a great and extensive project*, that required the whole man to execute, and which an unforeseen succession of employs prevented my attending to, it has hitherto remain'd unfinish'd.

In this piece it was my design to explain and enforce this doctrine, that vicious actions are not hurtful because they are forbidden, but forbidden because they are hurtful, the nature of man alone considered; that it was, therefore, every one's interest to be virtuous who wish'd to be happy even in this world; and I should, from this circumstance (there being always in the world a number of rich merchants, nobility, states, and princes, who have need of honest instruments for the management of their affairs, and such being so rare), have endeavoured to convince young persons that no qualities were so likely to make a poor man's fortune as those of probity and integrity.

My list of virtues contain'd at first but twelve; but a Quaker friend having kindly informed me that I was generally thought proud; that my pride show'd itself frequently in conversation; that I was not content with being in the right when discussing any point, but was overbearing, and rather insolent, of which he convinc'd me by mentioning several instances; I determined endeavouring to cure myself, if I could, of this vice or folly among the rest, and I added *Humility* to my list, giving an extensive meaning to the word.

I cannot boast of much success in acquiring the *reality* of this virtue, but I had a good deal with regard to the *appearance* of it. I made it a rule to forbear all direct contradiction to the sentiments of others, and all positive assertion of my own. I even forbid myself, agreeably to the old laws of our Junto, the use of every word or expression in the language that imported a fix'd opinion, such as *certainly*, *undoubtedly*, etc., and I adopted, instead of them, *I conceive*, *I apprehend*, or *I imagine* a thing to be so or so; or it *so appears to me at present*. When another asserted something that I thought an error, I deny'd myself the pleasure of contradicting him abruptly, and of showing immediately some absurdity in his proposition; and in answering I began by observing that in certain cases or circumstances his opinion would be right, but in the present case there *appear'd* or *seem'd* to me some difference, etc. I soon found the advantage of this change in my manner; the conversations I engag'd in went on more pleasantly. The modest way in which I propos'd my opinions procur'd them a readier reception and less contradiction; I had less mortification when I was found to be in the wrong, and I more easily prevail'd with others to give up their mistakes and join with me when I happened to be in the right.

And this mode, which I at first put on with some violence to natural inclination, became at length so easy, and so habitual to me, that perhaps for these fifty years past no one has ever heard a dogmatical expression escape me. And to this habit (after my character of integrity) I think it principally owing that I had early so much weight with my fellow-citizens when I proposed new institutions, or alterations in the old, and so much influence in public councils when I became a member; for I was but a bad speaker, never eloquent, subject to much hesitation in my choice of words, hardly correct in language, and yet I generally carried my points.

In reality, there is, perhaps, no one of our natural passions so hard to subdue as *pride*. Disguise it, struggle with it, beat it down, stifle it, mortify it as much as one pleases, it is still alive, and will every now and then peep out and show itself; you will see it, perhaps, often in this history; for, even if I could conceive that I had compleatly overcome it, I should probably be proud of my humility.[13] . . .

Having mentioned *a great and extensive project* which I had conceiv'd, it seems proper that some account should be here given of that project and its object. Its first rise in my mind appears in the following little paper, accidentally preserv'd, viz.:

Observations on my reading history, in Library, May 19th, 1731.

"That the great affairs of the world, the wars, revolutions, etc., are carried on and affected by parties.

"That the view of these parties is their present general interest, or what they take to be such.

"That the different views of these different parties occasion all confusion.

"That while a party is carrying on a general design, each man has his particular private interest in view.

"That as soon as a party has gain'd its general point, each member becomes intent upon his particular interest; which, thwarting others, breaks that party into divisions, and occasions more confusion.

"That few in public affairs act from a meer view of the good of their country, whatever they may pretend; and, tho' their actings bring real good to their country, yet men primarily considered that their own and their country's interest was united, and did not act from a principle of benevolence.

"That fewer still, in public affairs, act with a view to the good of mankind.

"There seems to me at present to be great occasion for raising a United Party for Virtue, by forming the virtuous and good men of all nations into a regular body, to be govern'd by suitable good and wise rules, which good and wise men may probably be more unanimous in their obedience to, than common people are to common laws.

"I at present think that whoever attempts this aright, and is well qualified, can not fail of pleasing God, and of meeting with success.

B. F."

Revolving this project in my mind, as to be undertaken hereafter, when my circumstances should afford me the necessary leisure, I put down from time to time, on pieces of paper, such thoughts as occurr'd to me respecting it. Most of these are lost; but I find one purporting to be the substance of an intended creed, containing, as I thought, the essentials of every known religion, and being free of every thing that might shock the professors of any religion. It is express'd in these words, viz.:

"That there is one God, who made all things.

"That he governs the world by his providence.

"That he ought to be worshiped by adoration, prayer, and thanksgiving.

"But that the most acceptable service of God is doing good to man.

"That the soul is immortal.

"And that God will certainly reward virtue and punish vice, either here or hereafter."

My ideas at that time were, that the sect should be begun and spread at first among young and single men only; that each person to be initiated should not only declare his assent to such creed, but should have exercised himself with the thirteen weeks' examination and practice of the virtues, as in the before-mention'd model; that the existence of such a society should be kept a secret, till it was become considerable, to prevent solicitations for the admission of improper persons, but that the members should each of them search among his acquaintance for ingenuous, well-disposed youths, to whom, with prudent caution, the scheme should be gradually communicated; that the members should engage to afford their advice, assistance, and support to each other in promoting one another's interests, business, and advancement in life; that, for distinction, we should be call'd *The Society of the Free and Easy:* free, as being, by the general practice and habit of the virtues, free from the dominion of vice; and particularly by the practice of industry and frugality, free from debt, which exposes a man to confinement, and a species of slavery to his creditors.

This is as much as I can now recollect of the project, except that I communicated it in part to two young men, who adopted it with some enthusiasm; but my then narrow circumstances, and the necessity I was under of sticking close to my business, occasion'd my postponing the further prosecution of it at that time; and my multifarious occupations, public and private, induc'd me to continue postponing, so that it has been omitted till I have no longer strength or activity left sufficient for such an enterprise; tho' I am still of opinion that it was a practicable scheme, and might have been very useful, by forming a great number of good citizens; and I was not discourag'd by the seeming magnitude of the undertaking, as I have always thought that one man of tolerable abilities may work great changes, and accomplish great affairs among mankind, if he first forms a good plan, and, cutting off all amusements or other employments that would divert his attention, makes the execution of that same plan his sole study and business.

In 1732 I first publish'd my Almanack, under the name of *Richard Saunders;* it was continu'd by me about twenty-five years, commonly call'd *Poor Richard's Almanack.* I endeavour'd to make it both entertaining and useful, and it accordingly came to be in such demand, that I reap'd considerable profit from it, vending annually near ten thousand.[14] And observing that it was generally read, scarce any neighborhood in the province being without it, I consider'd it as a proper vehicle for conveying instruction among the common people, who bought scarcely any other books; I therefore filled all the little spaces that oc-curr'd between the remarkable days in the calendar with pro-verbial sentences, chiefly such as inculcated industry and frugal-ity, as the means of procuring wealth, and thereby securing virtue; it being more difficult for a man in want, to act always honestly, as, to use here one of those proverbs, *it is hard for an empty sack to stand upright.*

These proverbs, which contained the wisdom of many ages and nations, I assembled and form'd into a connected discourse prefix'd to the Almanack of 1757, as the harangue of a wise old man to the people attending an auction. The bringing all these scatter'd counsels thus into a focus enabled them to make greater impression. The piece, being universally approved, was copied in all the newspapers of the Continent; reprinted in Britain on a broad side, to be stuck up in houses; two translations were made of it in French, and great numbers bought by the clergy and gentry, to distribute gratis among their poor parishioners and tenants. In Pennsylvania, as it discouraged useless expense in foreign superfluities, some thought it had its share of influence in producing that growing plenty of money which was observable for several years after its publication.

I considered my newspaper, also, as another means of communicating instruction, and in that view frequently reprinted in it extracts from the Spectator, and other moral writers; and sometimes publish'd little pieces of my own, which had been first compos'd for reading in our Junto. Of these are a Socratic dialogue, tending to prove that, whatever might be his parts and abilities, a vicious man could not properly be called a man of sense; and a discourse on self-denial, showing that virtue was not secure till its practice became a habitude, and was free from the opposition of contrary inclinations. These may be found in the papers about the beginning of 1735.[15]

In the conduct of my newspaper, I carefully excluded all libelling and personal abuse, which is of late years become so disgraceful to our country. Whenever I was solicited to insert any thing of that kind, and the writers pleaded, as they generally did, the liberty of the press, and that a newspaper was like a stage-coach, in which any one who would pay had a right to a place, my answer was, that I would print the piece separately if desired, and the author might have as many copies as he pleased to distribute himself, but that I would not take upon me to spread his detraction; and that, having contracted with my subscribers to furnish them with what might be either useful or entertaining, I could not fill their papers with private altercation, in which they had no concern, without doing them manifest injustice. Now, many of our printers make no scruple of gratifying the malice of individuals by false accusations of the fairest characters among ourselves, augmenting animosity even to the producing of duels; and are, moreover, so indiscreet as to print scurrilous reflections on the government of neighboring states, and even on the conduct of our best national allies, which may be attended with the most pernicious consequences. These things I mention as a caution to young printers, and that they may be encouraged not to pollute their presses and disgrace

their profession by such infamous practices, but refuse steadily,
as they may see by my example that such a course of conduct
will not, on the whole, be injurious to their interests.

.   .   .   .

I had begun in 1733 to study languages; I soon made myself
so much a master of the French as to be able to read the books
with ease. I then undertook the Italian. An acquaintance, who
was also learning it, us'd often to tempt me to play chess with
him. Finding this took up too much of the time I had to spare
for study, I at length refus'd to play any more, unless on this
condition, that the victor in every game should have a right to
impose a task, either in parts of the grammar to be got by heart,
or in translations, etc., which tasks the vanquish'd was to perform upon honour, before our next meeting. As we play'd
pretty equally, we thus beat one another into that language. I
afterwards with a little painstaking, acquir'd as much of the
Spanish as to read their books also.

I have already mention'd that I had only one year's instruction in a Latin school, and that when very young, after which I
neglected that language entirely. But, when I had attained an
acquaintance with the French, Italian, and Spanish, I was surpriz'd to find, on looking over a Latin Testament, that I understood so much more of that language than I had imagined,
which encouraged me to apply myself again to the study of it,
and I met with more success, as those preceding languages had
greatly smooth'd my way.

From these circumstances, I have thought that there is some
inconsistency in our common mode of teaching languages. We
are told that it is proper to begin first with the Latin, and, having
acquir'd that, it will be more easy to attain those modern languages which are deriv'd from it; and yet we do not begin with
the Greek, in order more easily to acquire the Latin. It is true
that, if you can clamber and get to the top of a staircase without using the steps, you will more easily gain them in descending; but certainly, if you begin with the lowest you will with
more ease ascend to the top; and I would therefore offer it to
the consideration of those who superintend the education of our

youth, whether, since many of those who begin with the Latin quit the same after spending some years without having made any great proficiency, and what they have learnt becomes almost useless, so that their time has been lost, it would not have been better to have begun with the French, proceeding to the Italian, etc.; for, tho', after spending the same time, they should quit the study of languages and never arrive at the Latin, they would, however, have acquired another tongue or two, that, being in modern use, might be serviceable to them in common life.

. . . .

Our club, the Junto, was found so useful, and afforded such satisfaction to the members, that several were desirous of introducing their friends, which could not well be done without exceeding what we had settled as a convenient number, viz., twelve. We had from the beginning made it a rule to keep our institution a secret, which was pretty well observ'd; the intention was to avoid applications of improper persons for admittance, some of whom, perhaps, we might find it difficult to refuse. I was one of those who were against any addition to our number, but, instead of it, made in writing a proposal, that every member separately should endeavour to form a subordinate club, with the same rules respecting queries, etc., and without informing them of the connection with the Junto. The advantages proposed were, the improvement of so many more young citizens by the use of our institutions; our better acquaintance with the general sentiments of the inhabitants on any occasion, as the Junto member might propose what queries we should desire, and was to report to the Junto what pass'd in his separate club; the promotion of our particular interests in business by more extensive recommendation, and the increase of our influence in public affairs, and our power of doing good by spreading thro' the several clubs the sentiments of the Junto.

The project was approv'd, and every member undertook to form his club, but they did not all succeed. Five or six only were compleated, which were called by different names, as the Vine, the Union, the Band, etc. They were useful to themselves, and afforded us a good deal of amusement, information, and instruction, besides answering, in some considerable degree, our views of influencing the public opinion on particular occasions, of which I shall give some instances in course of time as they happened.

.   .   .   .

I began now to turn my thoughts a little to public affairs,[16] beginning, however, with small matters. The city watch was one of the first things that I conceiv'd to want regulation. It was managed by the constables of the respective wards in turn; the constable warned a number of housekeepers to attend him for the night. Those who chose never to attend, paid him six shillings a year to be excus'd, which was suppos'd to be for hiring substitutes, but was, in reality, much more than was necessary for that purpose, and made the constableship a place of profit; and the constable, for a little drink, often got such ragamuffins about him as a watch, that respectable housekeepers did not choose to mix with. Walking the rounds, too, was often neglected, and most of the nights spent in tippling. I thereupon wrote a paper to be read in Junto, representing these irregularities, but insisting more particularly on the inequality of this six-shilling tax of the constables, respecting the circumstances of those who paid it, since a poor widow housekeeper, all whose property to be guarded by the watch did not perhaps exceed the value of fifty pounds, paid as much as the wealthiest merchant, who had thousands of pounds' worth of goods in his stores.

On the whole, I proposed as a more effectual watch, the hiring of proper men to serve constantly in that business; and as a more equitable way of supporting the charge, the levying a tax that should be proportion'd to the property. This idea, being approv'd by the Junto, was communicated to the other clubs, but as arising in each of them; and though the plan was not immediately carried into execution, yet, by preparing the minds of people for the change, it paved the way for the law obtained a few years after, when the members of our clubs were grown into more influence.

About this time I wrote a paper (first to be read in Junto, but

it was afterward publish'd) on the different accidents and care-
lessnesses by which houses were set on fire, with cautions
against them, and means proposed of avoiding them. This was
much spoken of as a useful piece, and gave rise to a project,
which soon followed it, of forming a company for the more
ready extinguishing of fires, and mutual assistance in removing
and securing of goods when in danger. Associates in this scheme
were presently found, amounting to thirty. Our articles of
agreement oblig'd every member to keep always in good order,
and fit for use, a certain number of leather buckets, with strong
bags and baskets (for packing and transporting of goods),
which were to be brought to every fire; and we agreed to meet
once a month and spend a social evening together, in discoursing and communicating such ideas as occurred to us upon the
subject of fires, as might be useful in our conduct on such occasions.

The utility of this institution soon appeared, and many more
desiring to be admitted than we thought convenient for one
company, they were advised to form another, which was accordingly done; and this went on, one new company being formed
after another, till they became so numerous as to include most
of the inhabitants who were men of property; and now, at the
time of my writing this, tho' upward of fifty years since its
establishment, that which I first formed, called the Union Fire
Company, still subsists and flourishes, tho' the first members
are all deceas'd but myself and one, who is older by a year than
I am. The small fines that have been paid by members for absence at the monthly meetings have been apply'd to the purchase of fire-engines, ladders, fire-hooks, and other useful imple-
ments for each company, so that I question whether there is a
city in the world better provided with the means of putting a
stop to beginning conflagrations; and, in fact, since these institutions, the city has never lost by fire more than one or two houses
at a time, and the flames have often been extinguished before the
house in which they began has been half consumed.

In 1739 arrived among us from Ireland the Reverend Mr.
Whitefield, who had made himself remarkable there as an itin-

erant preacher. He was at first permitted to preach in some of
our churches; but the clergy, taking a dislike to him, soon refus'd him their pulpits, and he was oblig'd to preach in the fields.
The multitudes of all sects and denominations that attended his
sermons were enormous, and it was matter of speculation to me,
who was one of the number, to observe the extraordinary influence of his oratory on his hearers, and how much they admir'd
and respected him, notwithstanding his common abuse of them,
by assuring them they were naturally *half beasts and half devils*.
It was wonderful to see the change soon made in the manners of
our inhabitants. From being thoughtless or indifferent about
religion, it seem'd as if all the world were growing religious,
so that one could not walk thro' the town in an evening without
hearing psalms sung in different families of every street.

. . . .

I happened soon after to attend one of his sermons, in the
course of which I perceived he intended to finish with a collection, and I silently resolved he should get nothing from me. I
had in my pocket a handful of copper money, three or four silver dollars, and five pistoles in gold. As he proceeded I began
to soften, and concluded to give the coppers. Another stroke of
his oratory made me asham'd of that, and determin'd me to give
the silver; and he finish'd so admirably, that I empty'd my pocket
wholly into the collector's dish, gold and all. At this sermon
there was also one of our club, who, being of my sentiments respecting the building in Georgia and, suspecting a collection
might be intended, had, by precaution, emptied his pockets before he came from home. Towards the conclusion of the discourse, however, he felt a strong desire to give, and apply'd to a
neighbour, who stood near him, to borrow some money for the
purpose. The application was unfortunately [made] to perhaps
the only man in the company who had the firmness not to be
affected by the preacher. His answer was, *At any other time,
Friend Hopkinson, I would lend to thee freely; but not now, for
thee seems to be out of thy right senses."*

. . . .

He [Rev. Whitefield] us'd, indeed, sometimes to pray for my

conversion, but never had the satisfaction of believing that his prayers were heard. Ours was a mere civil friendship, sincere on both sides, and lasted to his death.[17]

The following instance will show something of the terms on which we stood. Upon one of his arrivals from England at Boston, he wrote to me that he should come soon to Philadelphia, but knew not where he could lodge when there, as he understood his old friend and host, Mr. Benezet was removed to Germantown. My answer was, "You know my house; if you can make shift with its scanty accommodations, you will be most heartily welcome." He reply'd, that if I made that kind offer for Christ's sake, I should not miss of a reward. And I returned, *"Don't let me be mistaken; it was not for Christ's sake, but for your sake."* One of our common acquaintance jocosely remark'd, that, knowing it to be the custom of the saints, when they received any favour, to shift the burden of the obligation from off their own shoulders, and place it in heaven, I had contriv'd to fix it on earth.

The last time I saw Mr. Whitefield was in London, when he consulted me about his Orphan House concern, and his purpose of appropriating it to the establishment of a college.

He had a loud and clear voice, and articulated his words and sentences so perfectly, that he might be heard and understood at a great distance, especially as his auditories, however numerous, observ'd the most exact silence. He preach'd one evening from the top of the Court-house steps, which are in the middle of Market-street, and on the west side of Second-street, which crosses it at right angles. Both streets were fill'd with his hearers to a considerable distance. Being among the hindmost in Market-street, I had the curiosity to learn how far he could be heard, by retiring backwards down the street towards the river; and I found his voice distinct till I came near Front-street, when some noise in that street obscur'd it. Imagining then a semicircle, of which my distance should be the radius, and that it were fill'd with auditors, to each of whom I allow'd two square feet, I computed that he might well be heard by more than thirty thousand. This reconcil'd me to the newspaper accounts of his

having preach'd to twenty-five thousand people in the fields,
and to the antient histories of generals haranguing whole armies,
of which I had some times doubted.

.   .   .   .

I had, on the whole, abundant reason to be satisfied with my
being established in Pennsylvania. There were, however, two
things that I regretted, there being no provision for defense,
nor for a compleat education of youth; no militia, nor any college. I therefore, in 1743, drew up a proposal for establishing
an academy; and at that time, thinking the Reverend Mr. Peters,
who was out of employ, a fit person to superintend such an institution, I communicated the project to him; but he, having
more profitable views in the service of the proprietaries, which
succeeded, declin'd the undertaking; and, not knowing another
at that time suitable for such a trust, I let the scheme lie a while
dormant. I succeeded better the next year, 1744, in proposing
and establishing a Philosophical Society. The paper I wrote for
that purpose will be found among my writings, when collected.

.   .   .   .

Peace being concluded, and the association business therefore
at an end, I turn'd my thoughts again to the affair of establishing an academy. The first step I took was to associate in the design a number of active friends, of whom the Junto furnished a
good part; the next was to write and publish a pamphlet, entitled *Proposals Relating to the Education of Youth in Pennsylvania.* This I distributed among the principal inhabitants gratis;
and as soon as I could suppose their minds a little prepared by
the perusal of it, I set on foot a subscription for opening and
supporting an academy; it was to be paid in quotas yearly for
five years; by so dividing it, I judg'd the subscription might be
larger, and I believe it was so, amounting to no less, if I remember right, than five thousand pounds.

In the introduction to these proposals, I stated their publication, not as an act of mine, but of some *publick-spirited gentlemen*, avoiding as much as I could, according to my usual rule,
the presenting myself to the publick as the author of any scheme
for their benefit.

The subscribers, to carry the project into immediate execution, chose out of their number twenty-four trustees, and appointed Mr. Francis, then attorney-general, and myself to draw up constitutions for the government of the academy; which being done and signed, a house was hired, masters engag'd, and the schools opened, I think, in the same year, 1749.

.   .   .   .

In 1746, being at Boston, I met there with a Dr. Spence, who was lately arrived from Scotland, and show'd me some electric experiments. They were imperfectly perform'd, as he was not very expert; but, being on a subject quite new to me, they equally surpris'd and pleased me. Soon after my return to Philadelphia, our library company receiv'd from Mr. P. Collinson, Fellow of the Royal Society of London, a present of a glass tube, with some account of the use of it in making such experiments. I eagerly seized the opportunity of repeating what I had seen at Boston; and, by much practice, acquir'd great readiness in performing those, also, which we had an account of from England, adding a number of new ones. I say much practice, for my house was continually full, for some time, with people who came to see these new wonders.

To divide a little this incumbrance among my friends, I caused a number of similar tubes to be blown at our glass-house, with which they furnish'd themselves, so that we had at length several performers. Among these, the principal was Mr. Kinnersley, an ingenious neighbor, who, being out of business, I encouraged to undertake showing the experiments for money, and drew up for him two lectures, in which the experiments were rang'd in such order, and accompanied with such explanations in such method, as that the foregoing should assist in comprehending the following. He procur'd an elegant apparatus for the purpose, in which all the little machines that I had roughly made for myself were nicely form'd by instrument-makers. His lectures were well attended, and gave great satisfaction; and after some time he went thro' the colonies, exhibiting them in every capital town, and pick'd up some money. In the

West India Islands, indeed, it was with difficulty the experiments could be made, from the general moisture of the air.

Oblig'd as we were to Mr. Collinson for his present of the tube, etc., I thought it right he should be inform'd of our success in using it, and wrote him several letters containing accounts of our experiments. He got them read in the Royal Society, where they were not at first thought worth so much notice as to be printed in their Transactions. One paper, which I wrote for Mr. Kinnersley, on the sameness of lightning with electricity, I sent to Dr. Mitchel, an acquaintance of mine, and one of the members also of that society, who wrote me word that it had been read, but was laughed at by the connoisseurs. The papers, however, being shown to Dr. Fothergill, he thought them of too much value to be stifled, and advis'd the printing of them. Mr. Collinson then gave them to *Cave* for publication in his Gentleman's Magazine; but he chose to print them separately in a pamphlet, and Dr. Fothergill wrote the preface. Cave, it seems, judged rightly for his profit, for by the additions that arrived afterward they swell'd, to a quarto volume, which has had five editions, and cost him nothing for copy-money.

It was, however, some time before those papers were much taken notice of in England. A copy of them happening to fall into the hands of the Count de Buffon, a philosopher deservedly of great reputation in France, and, indeed, all over Europe, he prevailed with M. Dalibard to translate them into French, and they were printed at Paris. The publication offended the Abbé Nollet, preceptor in Natural Philosophy to the royal family, and an able experimenter, who had form'd and publish'd a theory of electricity, which then had the general vogue. He could not at first believe that such a work came from America, and said it must have been fabricated by his enemies at Paris, to decry his system. Afterwards, having been assur'd that there really existed such a person as Franklin at Philadelphia, which he had doubted, he wrote and published a volume of Letters, chiefly address'd to me, defending his theory, and denying the verity of my experiments, and of the positions deduc'd from them.

I once purpos'd answering the abbé, and actually began the

answer; but, on consideration that my writings contain'd a description of experiments which any one might repeat and verify, and if not to be verifi'd, could not be defended; or of observations offer'd as conjectures, and not delivered dogmatically, therefore not laying me under any obligation to defend them; and reflecting that a dispute between two persons, writing in different languages, might be lengthened greatly by mistranslations, and thence misconceptions of one another's meaning, much of one of the abbé's letters being founded on an error in the translation, I concluded to let my papers shift for themselves, believing it was better to spend what time I could spare from public business in making new experiments, than in disputing about those already made. I therefore never answered M. Nollet, and the event gave me no cause to repent my silence; for my friend M. le Roy, of the Royal Academy of Sciences, took up my cause and refuted him; my book was translated into the Italian, German, and Latin languages; and the doctrine it contain'd was by degrees universally adopted by the philosophers of Europe, in preference to that of the abbé; so that he lived to see himself the last of his sect, except Monsieur B——, of Paris, his *élève* and immediate disciple.

What gave my book the more sudden and general celebrity, was the success of one of its proposed experiments, made by Messrs. Dalibard and De Lor at Marly, for drawing lightning from the clouds. This engag'd the public attention every where. M. de Lor, who had an apparatus for experimental philosophy, and lectur'd in that branch of science, undertook to repeat what he called the *Philadelphia Experiments;* and, after they were performed before the king and court, all the curious of Paris flocked to see them. I will not swell this narrative with an account of that capital experiment, nor of the infinite pleasure I receiv'd in the success of a similar one I made soon after with a kite at Philadelphia, as both are to be found in the histories of electricity.

Dr. Wright, an English physician, when at Paris, wrote to a friend, who was of the Royal Society, an account of the high esteem my experiments were in among the learned abroad, and of their wonder that my writings had been so little noticed in England. The Society, on this, resum'd the consideration of the letters that had been read to them; and the celebrated Dr. Watson drew up a summary account of them, and of all I had afterwards sent to England on the subject, which he accompanied with some praise of the writer. This summary was then printed in their Transactions; and some members of the Society in London, particularly the very ingenious Mr. Canton, having verified the experiment of procuring lightning from the clouds by a pointed rod, and acquainting them with the success, they soon made me more than amends for the slight with which they had before treated me. Without my having made any application for that honour, they chose me a member, and voted that I should be excus'd the customary payments, which would have amounted to twenty-five guineas; and ever since have given me their Transactions gratis. They also presented me with the gold medal of Sir Godfrey Copley for the year 1753, the delivery of which was accompanied by a very handsome speech of the president, Lord Macclesfield, wherein I was highly honoured.

.   .   .   .

DOGOOD PAPERS, NO. I

(From Monday March 26. to Monday April 2. 1722.)

To the Author of the New-England Courant.

SIR,

It may not be improper in the first Place to inform your Readers, that I intend once a Fortnight to present them, by the Help of this Paper, with a short Epistle, which I presume will add somewhat to their Entertainment.

And since it is observed, that the Generality of People, now a days, are unwilling either to commend or dispraise what they read, until they are in some measure informed who or what the Author of it is, whether he be *poor* or *rich*, *old* or *young*, a *Scollar* or a *Leather Apron Man*, &c. and give their Opinion of the Performance, according to the Knowledge which they have of the Author's Circumstances, it may not be amiss to begin with a short Account of my past Life and present Condition, that the Reader may not be at a Loss to judge whether or no my Lucubrations are worth his reading.

At the time of my Birth, my Parents were on Ship-board in their Way from *London* to *N. England*. My Entrance into this troublesome World was attended with the Death of my Father, a Misfortune, which tho' I was not then capable of knowing, I shall never be able to forget; for as he, poor Man, stood upon the Deck rejoycing at my Birth, a merciless Wave entred the Ship, and in one Moment carry'd him beyond Reprieve. Thus was the *first* Day which I saw, the *last* that was seen by my Father; and thus was my disconsolate Mother at once made both a *Parent* and a *Widow*.

When we arrived at *Boston* (which was not long after) I was put to Nurse in a Country Place, at a small Distance from the Town, where I went to School, and past my Infancy and Childhood in Vanity and Idleness, until I was bound out Apprentice, that I might no longer be a Charge to my Indigent Mother, who was put to hard Shifts for a Living.

My Master was a Country Minister, a pious good-natur'd young Man, & a Batchelor: He labour'd with all his Might to instil vertuous and godly Principles into my tender Soul, well knowing that it was the most suitable Time to make deep and lasting Impressions on the Mind, while it was yet untainted with Vice, free and unbiass'd. He endeavour'd that I might be instructed in all that Knowledge and Learning which is necessary for our Sex, and deny'd me no Accomplishment that could possibly be attained in a Country Place, such as all Sorts of Needle-Work, Writing, Arithmetick, &c. and observing that I took a more than ordinary Delight in reading ingenious Books, he gave me the free Use of his Library, which tho' it was but small, yet it was well chose, to inform the Understanding rightly and enable the Mind to frame great and noble Ideas.

Before I had liv'd quite two Years with this Reverend Gentleman, my indulgent Mother departed this Life, leaving me as it were by my self, having no Relation on Earth within my Knowledge.

I will not abuse your Patience with a tedious Recital of all the frivolous Accidents of my Life, that happened from this Time until I arrived to Years of Discretion, only inform you that I liv'd a chearful Country Life, spending my leisure Time either in some innocent Diversion with the neighbouring Females, or in some shady Retirement, with the best of Company, *Books*. Thus I past away the Time with a Mixture of Profit and Pleasure, having no Affliction but what was imaginary and created in my own Fancy; as nothing is more common with us Women, than to be grieving for nothing, when we have nothing else to grieve for.

As I would not engross too much of your Paper at once, I will defer the Remainder of my Story until my next Letter; in the mean time desiring your Readers to exercise their Patience, and bear with my Humours now and then, because I shall trouble them but seldom. I am not insensible of the Impossibility of pleasing all, but I would not willingly displease any; and for those who will take Offence where none is intended, they are beneath the Notice of

Your Humble Servant,
SILINC DOGOOD.

As the Favour of Mrs. Dogood's Correspondence is acknowledged by the Publisher of this Paper, lest any of her Letters should miscarry, he desires they may for the future be deliver'd at his Printing-House, or at the Blue Ball in Union-Street, and no Questions shall be ask'd of the Bearer.

DOGOOD PAPERS, NO. IV

(From Monday May 7. to Monday May 14. 1722.)

An sum etiam nunc vel Græcè loqui vel Latinè *docendus?*

CICERO.

To the Author of the New-England Courant.

SIR,

Discoursing the other Day at Dinner with my Reverend Boarder, formerly mention'd, (whom for Distinction sake we will call by the Name of *Clericus*,) concerning the Education of Children, I ask'd his Advice about my young Son *William*, whether or no I had best bestow upon him Academical Learning, or (as our Phrase is) *bring him up at our College:* He perswaded me to do it by all Means, using many weighty Arguments with me, and answering all the Objections that I could form against it; telling me withal, that he did not doubt but that the Lad would take his Learning very well, and not idle away his Time as too many there now-a-days do. These words of *Clericus* gave me a Curiosity to inquire a little more strictly into the present Circumstances of that famous Seminary of Learning; but the Information which he gave me, was neither pleasant, nor such as I expected.

As soon as Dinner was over, I took a solitary Walk into my Orchard, still ruminating on *Clericus's* Discourse with much Consideration, until I came to my usual Place of Retirement under the *Great Apple-Tree;* where having seated my self, and carelessly laid my Head on a verdant Bank, I fell by Degrees into a soft and undisturbed Slumber. My waking Thoughts remained with me in my Sleep, and before I awak'd again, I dreamt the following DREAM.

I fancy'd I was travelling over pleasant and delightful Fields and Meadows, and thro' many small Country Towns and Villages; and as I pass'd along, all Places resounded with the Fame of the Temple of LEARNING: Every Peasant, who had wherewithal, was preparing to send one of his Children at least to this famous Place; and in this Case most of them consulted their own Purses instead of their Childrens Capacities: So that I observed, a great many, yea, the most part of those who were travelling thither, were little better than Dunces and Blockheads. Alas! Alas!

At length I entred upon a spacious Plain, in the Midst of which was erected a large and stately Edifice: It was to this that a great Company of Youths from all Parts of the Country were going; so stepping in among the Crowd, I passed on with them, and presently arrived at the Gate.

The Passage was Kept by two sturdy Porters named *Riches*

and *Poverty*, and the latter obstinately refused to give Entrance
to any who had not first gain'd the Favour of the former; so that
I observed, many who came even to the very Gate, were obliged
to travel back again as ignorant as they came, for want of this
necessary Qualification. However, as a Spectator I gain'd Admittance, and with the rest entred directly into the Temple.

In the Middle of the great Hall stood a stately and magnificent
Throne, which was ascended to by two high and difficult Steps.
On the Top of it sat Learning in awful State; she was
apparelled wholly in Black, and surrounded almost on every
Side with innumerable Volumes in all Languages. She seem'd
very busily employ'd in writing something on half a Sheet of
Paper, and upon Enquiry, I understood she was preparing a
Paper, call'd, *The New-England Courant*. On her Right Hand
sat *English*, with a pleasant smiling Countenance, and handsomely attir'd; and on her left were seated several *Antique Figures* with their Faces vail'd. I was considerably puzzl'd to guess
who they were, until one informed me, (who stood beside me,)
that those Figures on her left Hand were *Latin, Greek, Hebrew,*
&c. and that they were very much reserv'd, and seldom or never
unvail'd their Faces here, and then to few or none, tho' most of
those who have in this Place acquir'd so much Learning as to
distinguish them from *English*, pretended to an intimate Acquaintance with them. I then enquir'd of him, what could be
the Reason why they continued vail'd, in this Place especially:
He pointed to the Foot of the Throne, where I saw *Idleness*,
attended with *Ignorance*, and these (he informed me) were they,
who first vail'd them, and still kept them so.

Now I observed, that the whole Tribe who entred into the
Temple with me, began to climb the Throne; but the Work
proving troublesome and difficult to most of them, they withdrew their Hands from the Plow, and contented themselves to
sit at the Foot, with Madam *Idleness* and her Maid *Ignorance*,
until those who were assisted by Diligence and a docible Temper, had well nigh got up the first Step: But the Time drawing
nigh in which they could no way avoid ascending, they were
fain to crave the Assistance of those who had got up before

them, and who, for the Reward perhaps of a *Pint of Milk*, or a *Piece of Plumb-Cake*, lent the Lubbers a helping Hand, and sat them in the Eye of the World, upon a Level with themselves.

The other Step being in the same Manner ascended, and the usual Ceremonies at an End, every Beetle-Scull seem'd well satisfy'd with his own Portion of Learning, tho' perhaps he was *e'en just* as ignorant as ever. And now the Time of their Departure being come, they march'd out of Doors to make Room for another Company, who waited for Entrance: And I, having seen all that was to be seen, quitted the Hall likewise, and went to make my Observations on those who were just gone out before me.

Some I perceiv'd took to Merchandizing, others to Travelling, some to one Thing, some to another, and some to Nothing; and many of them from henceforth, for want of Patrimony, liv'd as poor as church Mice, being unable to dig, and asham'd to beg, and to live by their Wits it was impossible. But the most Part of the Crowd went along a large beaten Path, which led to a Temple at the further End of the Plain, call'd, *The Temple of Theology*. The Business of those who were employ'd in this Temple being laborious and painful, I wonder'd exceedingly to see so many go towards it; but while I was pondering this Matter in my Mind, I spy'd *Pecunia* behind a Curtain, beckoning to them with her Hand, which Sight immediately satisfy'd me for whose Sake it was, that a great Part of them (I will not say all) travel'd that Road. In this Temple I saw nothing worth mentioning, except the ambitious and fraudulent Contrivances of *Plagius*, who (notwithstanding he had been severely reprehended for such Practices before) was diligently transcribing some eloquent Paragraphs out of *Tillotson's* Works, &c. to embellish his own.

Now I bethought my self in my Sleep, that it was Time to be at Home, and as I fancy'd I was travelling back thither, I reflected in my Mind on the extream Folly of those Parents, who, blind to their Childrens Dulness, and insensible of the Solidity of their Skulls, because they think their Purses can afford it, will needs send them to the Temple of Learning, where, for want of a suitable Genius, they learn little more than how to carry themselves handsomely, and enter a Room genteely, (which might as well be acquir'd at a Dancing-School,) and from whence they return, after Abundance of Trouble and Charge, as great Blockheads as ever, only more proud and self-conceited.

While I was in the midst of these unpleasant Reflections, *Clericus* (who with a Book in his Hand was walking under the Trees) accidentally awak'd me; to him I related my Dream with all its Particulars, and he, without much Study, presently interpreted it, assuring me, *That it was a lively Representation of* HARVARD COLLEGE, *Etcetera.*

> I remain, Sir,
> Your Humble Servant,
> SILENCE DOGOOD.

DOGOOD PAPERS, NO. V

(From Monday May 21. to Monday May 28. 1722.)

Mulier Muliere magis congruet.—TER.

To the Author of the New-England Courant.

SIR,

I shall here present your Readers with a Letter from one, who informs me that I have begun at the wrong End of my Business, and that I ought to begin at Home, and censure the Vices and Follies of my own Sex, before I venture to meddle with your's: Nevertheless, I am resolved to dedicate this Speculation to the Fair Tribe, and endeavour to show, that Mr. *Ephraim* charges Women with being particularly guilty of Pride, Idleness, &c. wrongfully, inasmuch as the Men have not only as great a Share in those Vices as the Women, but are likewise in a great Measure the Cause of that which the Women are guilty of. I think it will be best to produce my Antagonist, before I encounter him.

To Mrs. DOGOOD.

Madam,

My Design in troubling you with this Letter is, to desire you would begin with your own Sex first: Let the first Volley of your Resentments be directed against *Female* Vice; let Female Idleness, Ignorance and Folly, (which are Vices more peculiar to your Sex than to our's,) be the Subject of your Satyrs, but more especially Female Pride, which I think is intollerable. Here is a large Field that wants Cultivation, and which I believe you are able (if willing) to improve with Advantage; and when you have once reformed the Women, you will find it a much easier Task to reform the Men, because Women are the prime Causes of a great many Male Enormities. This is all at present from

Your Friendly Wellwisher,

Ephraim Censorious.

After Thanks to my Correspondent for his Kindness in cutting out Work for me, I must assure him, that I find it a very difficult Matter to reprove Women separate from the Men; for what Vice is there in which the Men have not as great a Share as the Women? and in some have they not a far greater, as in Drunkenness, Swearing, &c.? And if they have, then it follows, that when a Vice is to be reproved, Men, who are most culpable, deserve the most Reprehension, and certainly therefore, ought to have it. But we will wave this point at present, and proceed to a particular Consideration of what my Correspondent calls *Female Vice.*

As for Idleness, if I should *Quære,* Where are the greatest Number of its Votaries to be found, with us or the Men? it might I believe be easily and truly answer'd, *With the latter.* For, notwithstanding the Men are commonly complaining how hard they are forc'd to labour, only to maintain their Wives in Pomp and Idleness, yet if you go among the Women, you will learn, that *they have always more Work upon their Hands than they are able to do,* and that *a Woman's Work is never done,* &c. But however, Suppose we should grant for once, that we are generally more idle than the Men, (without making any Allowance for the *Weakness of the Sex,*) I desire to know whose Fault it is? Are not the Men to blame for their Folly in maintaining us in Idleness? Who is there that can be handsomely supported in Affluence, Ease and Pleasure by another, that will chuse

rather to earn his Bread by the Sweat of his own Brows? And
if a Man will be so fond and so foolish, as to labour hard himself
for a Livelihood, and suffer his Wife in the mean Time to sit in
Ease and Idleness, let him not blame her if she does so, for it
is in a great Measure his own Fault.

And now for the Ignorance and Folly which he reproaches us
with, let us see (if we are Fools and Ignoramus's) whose is the
Fault, the Men's or our's. An ingenious Writer, having this
Subject in Hand, has the following Words, wherein he lays the
Fault wholly on the Men, for not allowing Women the Ad-
vantages of Education.

"I have (says he) often thought of it as one of the most
barbarous Customs in the World, considering us as a civiliz'd
and Christian Country, that we deny the Advantages of Learning to Women. We reproach the Sex every Day with Folly and
Impertinence, while I am confident, had they the Advantages of
Education equal to us, they would be guilty of less than our
selves. One would wonder indeed how it should happen that
Women are conversible at all, since they are only beholding to
natural Parts for all their Knowledge. Their Youth is spent to
teach them to stitch and sow, or make Baubles. They are
taught to read indeed, and perhaps to write their Names, or so;
and that is the Heigth of a Womans Education. And I would
but ask any who slight the Sex for their Understanding, What
is a Man (a Gentleman, I mean) good for that is taught no more?
If Knowledge and Understanding had been useless Additions
to the Sex, God Almighty would never have given them
Capacities, for he made nothing Needless. What has the
Woman done to forfeit the Priviledge of being taught? Does
she plague us with her Pride and Impertinence? Why did we
not let her learn, that she might have had more Wit? Shall we
upraid Women with Folly, when 'tis only the Error of this in-
humane Custom that hindred them being made wiser."

So much for Female Ignorance and Folly; and now let us a
little consider the Pride which my Correspondent thinks is
intolerable. By this Expression of his, one would think he is
some dejected Swain, tyranniz'd over by some cruel haughty

Nymph, who (perhaps he thinks) has no more Reason to be proud than himself. *Alas-a-day!* What shall we say in this Case! Why truly, if Women are proud, it is certainly owing to the Men still; for if they will be such *Simpletons* as to humble themselves at their Feet, and fill their credulous Ears with extravagant Praises of their Wit, Beauty, and other Accomplishments (perhaps where there are none too,) and when Women are by this Means perswaded that they are Something more than humane, what Wonder is it, if they carry themselves haughtily, and live extravagantly. Notwithstanding, I believe there are more Instances of extravagant Pride to be found among Men than among Women, and this Fault is certainly more hainous in the former than in the latter.

Upon the whole, I conclude, that it will be impossible to lash any Vice, of which the Men, are not equally guilty with the Women, and consequently deserve an equal (if not a greater, Share in the Censure. However, I exhort both to amend, where both are culpable, otherwise they may expect to be severely handled by   Sir,

Your Humble Servant,
SILENCE DOGOOD.

N. B. *Mrs.* Dogood *has lately left her Seat in the Country, and come to Boston, where she intends to tarry for the Summer Season, in order to compleat her Observations of the present reigning Vices of the Town.*

DOGOOD PAPERS, NO. VII

(From Monday June 18. to Monday June 25. 1722.)

Give me the Muse, whose generous Force,
Impatient of the Reins,
Pursues an unattempted Course,
Breaks all the Criticks Iron Chains.

WATTS.

To the Author of the New-England Courant.

SIR,

It has been the Complaint of many Ingenious Foreigners,

who have travell'd amongst us, *That good Poetry is not to be expected in* New-England. I am apt to Fancy, the Reason is, not because our Countrymen are altogether void of a Poetical Genius, nor yet because we have not those Advantages of Education which other Countries have, but purely because we do not afford that Praise and Encouragement which is merited, when any thing extraordinary of this Kind is produc'd among us: Upon which Consideration I have determined, when I meet with a Good Piece of *New-England* Poetry, to give it a suitable Encomium, and thereby endeavour to discover to the World some of its Beautys, in order to encourage the Author to go on, and bless the World with more, and more Excellent Productions.

There has lately appear'd among us a most Excellent Piece of Poetry, entituled, *An Elegy upon the much Lamented Death of Mrs.* Mehitebell Kitel, *Wife of Mr.* John Kitel *of* Salem, *Etc.* It may justly be said in its Praise, without Flattery to the Author, that it is the most *Extraordinary* Piece that was ever wrote in *New-England.* The Language is so soft and Easy, the Expression so moving and pathetick, but above all, the Verse and Numbers so Charming and Natural, that it is almost beyond Comparison.

> The Muse *disdains**
> *Those Links and Chains,*
> *Measures and Rules of Vulgar Strains,*
> *And o'er the Laws of Harmony a Sovereign Queen she reigns.*

I find no English Author, Ancient or Modern, whose Elegies may be compar'd with this, in respect to the Elegance of Stile, or Smoothness of Rhime; and for the affecting Part, I will leave your Readers to judge, if ever they read any Lines, that would sooner make them *draw their Breath* and Sigh, if not shed Tears, than these following.

> *Come let us mourn, for we have lost a*
> *Wife, a Daughter, and a Sister,*
> *Who has lately taken Flight, and*
> *greatly we have mist her.*

* Watts. [*Franklin's note.*]

In another place,

Some little Time before she yielded up her Breath,
She said, I ne'er shall hear one Sermon more on Earth.
She kist her Husband some little Time before she expir'd,
Then lean'd her Head the Pillow on, just out of Breath and tir'd.

But the Threefold Appellation in the first Line

—a Wife, a Daughter, and a Sister,

must not pass unobserved. That Line in the celebrated *Watts*,

GUNSTON, *the Just, the Generous, and the Young,*

is nothing Comparable to it. The latter only mentions three Qualifications of *one* Person who was deceased, which therefore could raise Grief and Compassion but for *One*. Whereas the former, (*our most excellent Poet*) gives his Reader a Sort of an Idea of the Death of *Three Persons*, viz.

—a Wife, a Daughter, and a Sister,

which is *Three Times* as great a Loss as the Death of *One*, and consequently must raise *Three Times* as much Grief and Compassion in the Reader.

I should be very much straitened for Room, if I should attempt to discover even half the Excellencies of this Elegy which are obvious to me. Yet I cannot omit one Observation, which is, that the Author has (to his Honour) invented a new Species of Poetry, which wants a Name, and was never before known. His muse scorns to be confin'd to the old Measures and Limits, or to observe the dull Rules of Criticks;

Nor Rapin *gives her Rules to fly, nor* Purcell *Notes to Sing.*
                                                            Watts.

Now 'tis Pity that such an Excellent Piece should not be dignify'd with a particular Name; and seeing it cannot justly be called, either *Epic*, *Sapphic*, *Lyric*, or *Pindaric*, nor any other Name yet invented, I presume it may, (in Honour and Remembrance of the Dead) be called the KITELIC. Thus much in the Praise of *Kitelic Poetry*.

It is certain, that those Elegies which are of our own Growth, (and our Soil seldom produces any other sort of Poetry) are by far the greatest part, wretchedly Dull and Ridiculous. Now since it is imagin'd by many, that our Poets are honest, well-meaning Fellows, who do their best, and that if they had but some Instructions how to govern Fancy with Judgment, they would make indifferent good Elegies; I shall here subjoin a Receipt for that purpose, which was left me as a Legacy, (among other valuable Rarities) by my Reverend Husband. It is as follows,

A Receipt *to make a* New-England Funeral Elegy.

For the Title of your Elegy. *Of these you may have enough ready made to your Hands; but if you should chuse to make it your self, you must be sure not to omit the words Ætatis Suæ, which will Beautify it exceedingly.*

For the Subject of your Elegy. *Take one of your Neighbours who has lately departed this Life; it is no great matter at what Age the Party dy'd, but it will be best if he went away suddenly, being* Kill'd, Drown'd, *or* Frose to Death.

Having chose the Person, take all his Virtues, Excellencies, &c. and if he have not enough, you may borrow some to make up a sufficient Quantity: To these add his last Words, dying Expressions, &c. if they are to be had; mix all these together, and be sure you strain them well. Then season all with a Handful or two of Melancholly Expressions, such as, Dreadful, Deadly, cruel cold Death, unhappy Fate, weeping Eyes, &c. *Have mixed all these Ingredients well, put them into the empty Scull of some* young Harvard; (*but in Case you have ne'er a One at Hand, you may use your own,*) *there let them Ferment for the Space of a Fortnight, and by that Time they will be incorporated into a Body, which take out, and having prepared a sufficient Quantity of double Rhimes, such as* Power, Flower; Quiver, Shiver; Grieve us, Leave us; tell you, excel you; Expeditions, Physicians; Fatigue him, Intrigue him; &c. *you must spread all upon Paper, and if you can procure a Scrap of Latin to put at the End, it will garnish it mightily; then having affixed your Name at the Bottom, with a* Mœstus Composuit, *you will have an Excellent Elegy.*

N. B. *This Receipt will serve when a Female is the Subject of your Elegy, provided you borrow a greater Quantity of Virtues, Excellencies, &c.*

Sir,

Your Servant,

Silence Dogood.

P. S. I shall make no other Answer to *Hypercarpus's* Criticism on my last Letter than this, *Mater me genuit, peperit mox filia matrem.*

DOGOOD PAPERS, NO. XII

(From Monday September 3. to Monday September 10. 1722.)

Quod est in corde sobrii, est in ore ebrii.

To the Author of the New-England Courant.

Sir,

It is no unprofitable tho' unpleasant Pursuit, diligently to inspect and consider the Manners & Conversation of Men, who, insensible of the greatest Enjoyments of humane Life, abandon themselves to Vice from a false Notion of *Pleasure* and *good Fellowship.* A true and natural Representation of any Enormity, is often the best Argument against it and Means of removing it, when the most severe Reprehensions alone, are found ineffectual.

I would in this Letter improve the little Observation I have made on the Vice of *Drunkeness*, the better to reclaim the *good Fellows* who usually pay the Devotions of the Evening to *Bacchus.*

I doubt not but *moderate Drinking* has been improv'd for the Diffusion of Knowledge among the ingenious Part of Mankind, who want the Talent of a ready Utterance, in order to discover the Conceptions of their Minds in an entertaining and intelligible Manner. 'Tis true, drinking does not *improve* our Faculties, but it enables us to use them; and therefore I conclude, that much Study and Experience, and a little Liquor, are of absolute Necessity for some Tempers, in order to make them accomplish'd Orators. *Dic. Ponder* discovers an excellent Judgment when he is inspir'd with a Glass or two of *Claret*, but he passes for a Fool among those of small Observation, who never saw him the better for Drink. And here it will not be improper to observe, That the moderate Use of Liquor, and a well plac'd and well regulated Anger, often produce this same Effect; and some who cannot ordinarily talk but in broken Sentences and false Grammar, do in the Heat of Passion express themselves with as much Eloquence as Warmth. Hence it is that my own Sex are generally the most eloquent, because the most passionate. "It has been said in the Praise of some Men," (says an ingenious Author,) "that they could talk whole Hours together upon any thing; but it must be owned to the Honour of the other Sex, that there are many among them who can talk whole Hours together upon Nothing. I have known a Woman branch out into a long extempore Dissertation on the Edging of a Petticoat, and chide her Servant for breaking a China Cup, in all the Figures of Rhetorick."

But after all it must be consider'd, that no Pleasure can give Satisfaction or prove advantageous to a *reasonable Mind*, which is not attended with the *Restraints of Reason*. Enjoyment is not to be found by Excess in any sensual Gratification; but on the contrary, the immoderate Cravings of the Voluptuary, are always succeeded with Loathing and a palled Apetite. What Pleasure can the Drunkard have in the Reflection, that, while in his Cups, he retain'd only the Shape of a Man, and acted the Part of a Beast; or that from reasonable Discourse a few Minutes before, he descended to Impertinence and Nonsense?

I cannot pretend to account for the different Effects of Liquor on Persons of different Dispositions, who are guilty of Excess in the Use of it. 'Tis strange to see Men of a regular Conversation become rakish and profane when intoxicated with Drink, and yet more surprizing to observe, that some who appear to be the most profligate Wretches when sober, become mighty

religious in their Cups, and will then, and at no other Time address their Maker, but when they are destitute of Reason, and
actually affronting him. Some shrink in the Wetting, and others
swell to such an unusual Bulk in their Imaginations, that they
can in an Instant understand all Arts and Sciences, by the liberal
Education of a little vivyfying *Punch,* or a sufficient Quantity
of other exhilerating Liquor.

And as the Effects of Liquor are various, so are the Characters
given to its Devourers. It argues some Shame in the Drunkards
themselves, in that they have invented numberless Words and
Phrases to cover their Folly, whose proper Significations are
harmless, or have no Signification at all. They are seldom
known to be *drunk,* tho they are very often *boozey, cogey, tipsey,*
fox'd, merry, mellow, fuddl'd, groatable, Confoundedly cut, See
two Moons, are *Among the Philistines, In a very good Humour,*
See the Sun, or, *The Sun has shone upon them;* they *Clip the King's*
English, are *Almost froze, Feavourish, In their Altitudes, Pretty*
well enter'd, &c.[18] In short, every Day produces some new
Word or Phrase which might be added to the Vocabulary of
the *Tiplers:* But I have chose to mention these few, because if
at any Time a Man of Sobriety and Temperance happens to *cut*
himself confoundedly, or is *almoss froze,* or *feavourish,* or accidentally *sees the Sun,* &c. he may escape the Imputation of being
drunk, when his Misfortune comes to be related.

> *I am* SIR,
> *Your Humble Servant,*
> SILENCE DOGOOD.

EDITORIAL PREFACE
TO THE NEW ENGLAND COURANT

(From Monday, February 4, to Monday, February 11, 1723)

The late Publisher of this Paper,[19] finding so many Inconveniences would arise by his carrying the Manuscripts and
publick News to be supervis'd by the Secretary, as to render his
carrying it on unprofitable, has intirely dropt the Undertaking.

The present Publisher having receiv'd the following Piece, desires the Readers to accept of it as a Preface to what they may hereafter meet with in this Paper.

> Non ego mordaci distrinxi Carmine quenquam
> Nulla vonenato Litera onista Joco est.

Long has the Press groaned in bringing forth an hateful, but numerous Brood of Party Pamphlets, malicious Scribbles, and Billinsgate Ribaldry. The Rancour and bitterness it has unhappily infused into Men's minds, and to what a Degree it has sowred and leaven'd the Tempers of Persons formerly esteemed some of the most sweet and affable, is too well known here, to need any further Proof or Representation of the Matter.

No generous and impartial Person then can blame the present Undertaking, which is designed purely for the Diversion and Merriment of the Reader. Pieces of Pleasancy and Mirth have a secret Charm in them to allay the Heats and Tumours of our Spirits, and to make a Man forget his restless Resentments. They have a strange Power to tune the harsh Disorders of the Soul, and reduce us to a serene and placid State of Mind.

The main Design of this Weekly Paper will be to entertain the Town with the most comical and diverting Incidents of Humane Life, which in so large a Place as *Boston* will not fail of a universal Exemplification: Nor shall we be wanting to fill up these Papers with a grateful Interspersion of more serious Morals which may be drawn from the most ludicrous and odd Parts of Life.

As for the Author, that is the next Question. But tho' we profess ourselves ready to oblige the ingenious and courteous Reader with most Sorts of Intelligence, yet here we beg a Reserve. Nor will it be of any Manner of Advantage either to them or to the Writers, that their names should be published; and therefore in this Matter we desire the Favour of you to suffer us to hold our Tongues: Which tho' at this Time of Day it may sound like a very uncommon Request, yet it proceeds from the very Hearts of your Humble Servants.

By this Time the Reader perceives that more than one are engaged in the present Undertaking. Yet is there one Person, an Inhabitant of this Town of *Boston*, whom we honour as a Doctor in the Chair, or a perpetual Dictator.

The Society had design'd to present the Publick with his Effigies, but that the Limner, to whom he was presented for a Draught of his Countenance, descryed (and this he is ready to offer upon Oath) Nineteen Features in his Face, more than ever he beheld in any Humane Visage before; which so raised the Price of his Picture, that our Master himself forbid the Extravagance of coming up to it. And then besides, the Limner objected a Schism in his face, which splits it from his Forehead in a strait Line down to his chin, in such sort, that Mr. Painter protests it is a double Face, and he'll have *Four Pounds* for the Pourtraiture. However, tho' this double Face has spoilt us of a pretty Picture, yet we all rejoiced to see old *Janus* in our Company.

There is no Man in *Boston* better qualified than old *Janus* for a *Couranteer*, or if you please, an *Observator*, being a Man of such remarkable *Opticks*, as to look two ways at once.

As for his Morals, he is a chearly Christian, as the Country Phrase expresses it. A Man of good Temper, courteous Deportment, sound Judgment; a mortal Hater of Nonsense, Foppery, Formality, and endless Ceremony.

As for his club, they aim at no greater Happiness or Honour, than the Publick be made to know, that it is the utmost of their Ambition to attend upon and do all imaginable good Offices to good old *Janus* the Couranteer, who is and always will be the Readers humble Servant.

P. S. Gentle Readers, we design never to let a Paper pass without a Latin Motto if we can possibly pick one up, which carries a Charm in it to the Vulgar, and the learned admire the pleasure of Construing. We should have obliged the World with a Greek scrap or two, but the Printer has no Types, and therefore we intreat the candid Reader not to impute the defect to our Ignorance, for our Doctor can say all the *Greek* Letters by heart.

A DISSERTATION ON LIBERTY
AND NECESSITY,
PLEASURE AND PAIN

To Mr. J. R.

[London, 1725]

Sir,

I have here, according to your Request, given you my *present* Thoughts of the *general State of Things* in the Universe. Such as they are, you have them, and are welcome to 'em; and if they yield you any Pleasure or Satisfaction, I shall think my Trouble sufficiently compensated. I know my Scheme will be liable to many Objections from a less discerning Reader than your self; but it is not design'd for those who can't understand it. I need not give you any Caution to distinguish the hypothetical Parts of the Argument from the conclusive: You will easily perceive what I design for Demonstration, and what for Probability only. The whole I leave entirely to you, and shall value my self more or less on this account, in proportion to your Esteem and Approbation.

. . . .

Sect. I. *Of* Liberty *and* Necessity

I. *There is said to be a* First Mover, *who is called* God, *Maker of the Universe.*

II. *He is said to be all-wise, all-good, all powerful.*

These two Propositions being allow'd and asserted by People of almost every Sect and Opinion; I have here suppos'd them granted, and laid them down as the Foundation of my Argument; What follows then, being a Chain of Consequences truly drawn from them, will stand or fall as they are true or false.

III. *If He is all-good, whatsoever He doth must be good.*

IV. *If He is all-wise, whatsoever He doth must be wise.*

The Truth of these Propositions, with relation to the two first, I think may be justly call'd evident; since, either that infinite Goodness will act what is ill, or infinite Wisdom what is not wise, is too glaring a Contradiction not to be perceiv'd by

any Man of common Sense, and deny'd as soon as understood.
V. *If He is all-powerful, there can be nothing either existing or
acting in the Universe against or without his Consent; and what
He consents to must be good, because He is good; therefore* Evil
doth not exist.

Unde Malum? has been long a Question, and many of the
Learned have perplex'd themselves and Readers to little Purpose
in Answer to it. That there are both Things and Actions to
which we give the Name of *Evil,* is not here deny'd, as *Pain,
Sickness, Want, Theft, Murder,* &c. but that these and the like
are not in reality *Evils, Ills,* or *Defects* in the Order of the
Universe, is demonstrated in the next Section, as well as by
this and the following Proposition. Indeed, to suppose any
Thing to exist or be done, *contrary* to the Will of the Almighty,
is to suppose him not almighty; or that Something (the Cause
of *Evil*) is more mighty than the Almighty; an Inconsistence
that I think no One will defend: And to deny any Thing or
Action, which he consents to the existence of, to be good, is
entirely to destroy his two Attributes of *Wisdom* and *Goodness.*

There is nothing done in the Universe, say the Philosophers,
but what God either does, or permits *to be done.* This, as He is
Almighty, is certainly true: But what need of this Distinction
between *doing* and *permitting?* Why, first they take it for granted
that many Things in the Universe exist in such a Manner as is
not for the best, and that many Actions are done which ought
not to be done, or would be better undone; these Things or
Actions they cannot ascribe to God as His, because they have
already attributed to Him infinite Wisdom and Goodness; Here
then is the Use of the Word *Permit;* He *permits* them to be done,
say they. But we will reason thus: If God permits an Action to
be done, it is because he wants either *Power* or *Inclination* to
hinder it; in saying he wants *Power,* we deny Him to be *almighty;* and if we say He wants *Inclination* or *Will,* it must be,
either because He is not Good, or the Action is not *evil,* (for
all Evil is contrary to the Essence of *Infinite Goodness.*) The
former is inconsistent with his before-given Attribute of Goodness, therefore the latter must be true.

It will be said, perhaps, that *God permits evil Actions to be done, for* wise *Ends and Purposes*. But this Objection destroys itself; for whatever an infinitely good God hath wise Ends in suffering to *be*, must be good, is thereby made good, and cannot be otherwise.

VI. *If a Creature is made by God, it must depend upon God, and receive all its Power from Him; with which Power the Creature can do nothing contrary to the Will of God, because God is Almighty; what is not contrary to His Will, must be agreeable to it; what is agreeable to it, must be good, because He is Good; therefore a Creature can do nothing but what is good.*

This Proposition is much to the same Purpose with the former, but more particular; and its Conclusion is as just and evident. Tho' a Creature may do many Actions which by his Fellow Creatures will be nam'd *Evil*, and which will naturally and necessarily cause or bring upon the Doer, certain *Pains* (which will likewise be call'd *Punishments;*) yet this Proposition proves, that he cannot act what will be in itself really Ill, or displeasing to God. And that the painful Consequences of his evil Actions *(so call'd)* are not, as indeed they ought not to be, *Punishments* or Unhappinesses, will be shewn hereafter.

Nevertheless, the late learned Author of *The Religion of Nature*, (which I send you herewith) has given us a Rule or Scheme, whereby to discover which of our Actions ought to be esteem'd and denominated *good*, and which *evil:* It is in short this, "Every Action which is done according to *Truth*, is good; and every Action contrary to Truth, is evil: To act according to Truth is to use and esteem every Thing as what it is, *&c.* Thus if *A* steals a Horse from *B*, and rides away upon him, he uses him not as what he is in Truth, *viz.* the Property of another, but as his own, which is contrary to Truth, and therefore *evil.*" But, as this Gentleman himself says, (Sect. I. Prop. VI.) "In order to judge rightly what any Thing is, it must be consider'd, not only what it is in one Respect, but also what it may be in any other Respect; and the whole Description of the Thing ought to be taken in: So in this Case it ought to be consider'd, that *A* is naturally a *covetous* Being, feeling an Uneasiness in the want of *B's* Horse, which produces an Inclination for stealing him, stronger than his Fear of Punishment for so doing. This is *Truth* likewise, and *A* acts according to it when he steals the Horse. Besides, if it is prov'd to be a *Truth*, that *A* has not Power over his own Actions, it will be indisputable that he acts according to Truth, and impossible he should do otherwise.

I would not be understood by this to encourage or defend Theft; 'tis only for the sake of the Argument, and will certainly have no *ill Effect*. The Order and Course of Things will not be affected by Reasoning of this Kind; and 'tis as just and necessary, and as much according to Truth, for *B* to dislike and punish the Theft of his Horse, as it is for *A* to steal him.

VII. *If the Creature is thus limited in his Actions, being able to do only such Things as God would have him to do, and not being able to refuse doing what God would have done; then he can have no such Thing as Liberty, Free-will or Power to do or refrain an Action.*

By *Liberty* is sometimes understood the Absence of Opposition; and in this Sense, indeed, all our Actions may be said to be the Effects of our Liberty: But it is a Liberty of the same Nature with the Fall of a heavy Body to the Ground; it has Liberty to fall, that is, it meets with nothing to hinder its Fall, but at the same Time it is necessitated to fall, and has no Power or Liberty to remain suspended.

But let us take the Argument in another View, and suppose ourselves to be, in the common sense of the Word, *Free Agents*. As Man is a Part of this great Machine, the Universe, his regular Acting is requisite to the regular moving of the whole. Among the many Things which lie before him to be done, he may, as he is at Liberty and his Choice influenc'd by nothing, (for so it must be, or he is not at Liberty) chuse any one, and refuse the rest. Now there is every Moment something *best* to be done, which is alone then *good*, and with respect to which, every Thing else is at that Time *evil*. In order to know which is best to be done, and which not, it is requisite that we should have at one View all the intricate Consequences of every Action with respect to the general Order and Scheme of the Universe, both present and future; but they are innumerable and incomprehensible by any Thing but Omniscience. As we cannot know these, we have but as one Chance to ten thousand, to hit on the right Action; we should then be perpetually blundering about in the Dark, and putting the Scheme in Disorder; for every wrong Action of a Part, is a Defect or Blemish in the Order of the Whole. Is it not necessary then, that our Actions should be over-rul'd and govern'd by an all-wise Providence?—How exact and regular is every Thing in the *natural* World! How wisely in every Part contriv'd! We cannot here find the least Defect! Those who have study'd the mere animal and vegetable Creation, demonstrate that nothing can be more harmonious and beautiful! All the heavenly Bodies, the Stars and Planets, are regulated with the utmost Wisdom! And can we suppose less Care to be taken in the Order of the *moral* than in the *natural* System? It is as if an ingenious Artificer, having fram'd a curious Machine or Clock, and put its many intricate Wheels and Powers in such a Dependance on one another, that the whole might move in the most exact Order and Regularity, had nevertheless plac'd in it several other Wheels endu'd with an independent *Self-Motion*, but ignorant of the general Interest of the Clock; and these would every now and then be moving wrong, disordering the true Movement, and making continual Work for the Mender: which might better be prevented, by depriving them of that Power of Self-Motion, and placing them in a Dependance on the regular Part of the Clock.

VIII. *If there is no such Thing as Free-Will in Creatures, there can be neither Merit nor Demerit in Creatures.*

IX. *And therefore every Creature must be equally esteem'd by the Creator.*

These Propositions appear to be the necessary Consequences of the former. And certainly no Reason can be given, why the Creator should prefer in his Esteem one Part of His Works to another, if with equal Wisdom and Goodness he design'd and created them all, since all Ill or Defect, as contrary to his Nature, is excluded by his Power. We will sum up the Argument thus, When the Creator first design'd the Universe, either it was His

Will and Intention that all Things should exist and be in the Manner they are at this Time; or it was his Will they should *be* otherwise, *i.e.* in a different Manner: To say it was His Will Things should be otherwise than they are, is to say Somewhat hath contradicted His Will, and broken His Measures, which is impossible because inconsistent with his Power; therefore we must allow that all Things exist now in a Manner agreeable to His Will, and in consequence of that are all equally Good, and therefore equally esteem'd by Him.

I proceed now to shew, that as all the Works of the Creator are equally esteem'd by Him, so they are, as in Justice they ought to be, equally us'd.

. . . .

Sect. II. *Of* Pleasure *and* Pain.

I. *When a Creature is form'd and endu'd with Life, 'tis suppos'd to receive a Capacity of the Sensation of* Uneasiness *or* Pain.

It is this distinguishes Life and Consciousness from unactive unconscious Matter. To know or be sensible of Suffering or being acted upon is *to live;* and whatsoever is not so, among created Things, is properly and truly *dead.*

All *Pain* and *Uneasiness* proceeds at first from and is caus'd by Somewhat without and distinct from the Mind itself. The Soul must first be acted upon before it can re-act. In the Beginning of Infancy it is as if it were not; it is not conscious of its own Existence, till it has receiv'd the first Sensation of *Pain;* then, and not before, it begins to feel itself, is rous'd, and put into Action; then it discovers its Powers and Faculties, and exerts them to expel the Uneasiness. Thus is the Machine set on work; this is Life. We are first mov'd by *Pain,* and the whole succeeding Course of our Lives is but one continu'd Series of Action with a View to be freed from it. As fast as we have excluded one Uneasiness another appears, otherwise the Motion would cease. If a continual Weight is not apply'd, the Clock will stop. And as soon as the Avenues of Uneasiness to the Soul are choak'd up or cut off, we are dead, we think and act no more.

II. *This Uneasiness, whenever felt, produces* Desire *to be freed from it, great in exact proportion to the Uneasiness.*

Thus is *Uneasiness* the first Spring and Cause of all Action; for till we are uneasy in Rest, we can have no Desire to move, and without Desire of moving there can be no voluntary Motion. The Experience of every Man who has observ'd his own Actions will evince the Truth of this; and I think nothing need be said to prove that the *Desire* will be equal to the *Uneasiness*, for the very Thing implies as much: It is not *Uneasiness* unless we desire to be freed from it, nor a great *Uneasiness* unless the consequent Desire is great.

I might here observe, how necessary a Thing in the Order and Design of the Universe this *Pain* or *Uneasiness* is, and how beautiful in its Place! Let us but suppose it just now banish'd the World entirely, and consider the Consequence of it: All the Animal Creation would immediately stand stock still, exactly in the Posture they were in the Moment Uneasiness departed; not a Limb, not a Finger would henceforth move; we should all be reduc'd to the Condition of Statues, dull and unactive: Here I should continue to sit motionless with the Pen in my Hand thus ———— and neither leave my Seat nor write one Letter more. This may appear odd at first View, but a little Consideration will make it evident; for 'tis impossible to assign any other Cause for the voluntary Motion of an Animal than its *uneasiness* in Rest. What a different Appearance then would the Face of Nature make, without it! How necessary is it! And how unlikely that the Inhabitants of the World ever were, or that the Creator ever design'd they should be, exempt from it!

I would likewise observe here, that the VIIIth Proposition in the preceding Section, viz. *That there is neither Merit nor Demerit,* &c. is here again demonstrated, as infallibly, tho' in another manner: For since *Freedom from Uneasiness* is the End of all our Actions, how is it possible for us to do any Thing disinterested?—How can any Action be meritorious of Praise or Dispraise, Reward or Punishment, when the natural Principle of *Self-Love* is the only and the irresistible Motive to it?

III. *This* Desire *is always fulfill'd or satisfy'd,*

In the *Design* or *End* of it, tho' not in the *Manner:* The first is requisite, the latter not. To exemplify this, let us make a Supposition; A Person is confin'd in a House which appears to be in imminent Danger of Falling, this, as soon as perceiv'd, creates a violent *Uneasiness*, and that instantly produces an equal strong *Desire*, the *End* of which is *freedom from the Uneasiness*, and the *Manner* or Way propos'd to gain this *End*, is *to get out of the House.* Now if he is convinc'd by any Means, that he is mistaken, and the House is not likely to fall, he is immediately freed from his *Uneasiness*, and the *End* of his Desire is attain'd as well as if it had been in the *Manner* desir'd, viz. *leaving the House.*

All our different Desires and Passions proceed from and are reducible to this one Point, *Uneasiness*, tho' the Means we propose to ourselves for expelling of it are infinite. One proposes *Fame*, another *Wealth*, a third *Power*, &c. as the Means to gain this *End;* but tho' these are never attain'd, if the Uneasiness be remov'd by some other Means, the *Desire* is satisfy'd. Now during the Course of Life we are ourselves continually removing successive Uneasinesses as they arise, and the *last* we suffer is remov'd by the *sweet Sleep* of Death.

IV. *The fulfilling or Satisfaction of this* Desire, *produces the Sensation of* Pleasure, *great or small in exact proportion to the* Desire.

Pleasure is that Satisfaction which arises in the Mind upon, and is caus'd by, the accomplishment of our *Desires*, and by no other Means at all; and those Desires being above shewn to be caus'd by our *Pains* or *Uneasinesses*, it follows that *Pleasure* is wholly caus'd by *Pain*, and by no other Thing at all.

V. *Therefore the Sensation of* Pleasure *is equal, or in exact proportion to the Sensation of* Pain.

As the *Desire* of being freed from Uneasiness is equal to the *Uneasiness*, and the *Pleasure* of satisfying that Desire equal to the *Desire*, the *Pleasure* thereby produc'd must necessarily be equal to the *Uneasiness* or *Pain* which produces it: of three Lines, *A*, *B*, and *C*, if *A* is equal to *B*, and *B* to *C*, *C* must be equal to *A*. And as our *Uneasinesses* are always remov'd by some Means or other, it follows that *Pleasure* and *Pain* are in their Nature inseparable: So many Degrees as one Scale of the Ballance descends, so many exactly the other ascends; and one cannot rise or fall without the Fall or Rise of the other: 'Tis impossible to taste of *Pleasure*, without feeling its preceding proportionate *Pain;* or to be sensible of *Pain*, without having its necessary Consequent *Pleasure:* The *highest Pleasure* is only Consciousness of Freedom from the *deepest Pain*, and Pain is not Pain to us unless we ourselves are sensible of it. They go Hand in Hand; they cannot be divided.

You have a View of the whole Argument in a few familiar Examples: The *Pain* of Abstinence from Food, as it is greater or less, produces a greater or less *Desire* of Eating, the Accomplishment of this *Desire* produces a greater or less *Pleasure* proportionate to it. The *Pain* of Confinement causes the *Desire* of Liberty, which accomplish'd, yields a *Pleasure* equal to that *Pain* of Confinement. The *Pain* of Labour and Fatigue causes the *Pleasure* of Rest, equal to that *Pain*. The *Pain* of Absence from Friends, produces the *Pleasure* of Meeting in exact proportion. *&c.*

This is the *fixt Nature* of Pleasure and Pain, and will always be found to be so by those who examine it.

One of the most common Arguments for the future Existence of the Soul, is taken from the generally suppos'd Inequality of Pain and Pleasure in the present; and this, notwithstanding the Difficulty by outward Appearances to make a Judgment of another's Happiness, has been look'd upon as almost unanswerable: but since *Pain* naturally and infallibly produces a *Pleasure* in proportion to it, every individual Creature must, in any State of *Life*, have an equal Quantity of each, so that there is not, on that Account, any Occasion for a future Adjustment.

Thus are all the Works of the Creator *equally* us'd by him; And no Condition of Life or Being is in itself better or preferable to another: The Monarch is not more happy than the Slave, nor the Beggar more miserable than *Crœsus*. Suppose *A*, *B*, and *C*, three distinct Beings; *A* and *B*, animate, capable of *Pleasure* and *Pain*, *C* an inanimate Piece of Matter, insensible of either. *A* receives ten Degrees of *Pain*, which are necessarily succeeded by ten Degrees of *Pleasure:* *B* receives fifteen of *Pain*, and the consequent equal Number of *Pleasure:* *C* all the while lies unconcern'd, and as he has not suffer'd the former, has no right to the latter. What can be more equal and just than this? When the Accounts come to be adjusted, *A* has no Reason to complain that his Portion of *Pleasure* was five Degrees less than that of *B*, for his Portion of *Pain* was five Degrees less likewise: Nor has *B* any Reason to boast that his *Pleasure* was five Degrees greater than that of *A*, for his *Pain* was proportionate: They are then both on the same Foot with *C*, that is, they are neither Gainers nor Losers.

It will possibly be objected here, that even common Experience shews us, there is not in Fact this Equality: "Some we see hearty, brisk and chearful perpetually, while others are constantly burden'd with a heavy Load of Maladies and Misfortunes, remaining for Years perhaps in Poverty, Disgrace, or Pain, and die at last without any Appearance of Recompence." Now tho' 'tis not necessary, when a Proposition is demonstrated to be a general Truth, to shew in what manner it agrees with the particular Circumstances of Persons, and indeed ought not to be requir'd; yet, as this is a common Objection, some Notice may be taken of it: And here let it be observ'd, that we cannot be proper Judges of the good or bad Fortune of Others; we are apt to imagine, that what would give us a great Uneasiness or a great Satisfaction, has the same Effect upon others: we think, for Instance, those unhappy, who must depend upon Charity for a mean Subsistence, who go in Rags, fare hardly, and are despis'd and scorn'd by all; not considering that Custom renders all these Things easy, familiar, and even pleasant. When we see Riches, Grandeur and a chearful Countenance, we easily imagine Happiness accompanies them, when oftentimes 'tis quite otherwise: Nor is a constantly sorrowful Look, attended with continual Complaints, an infallible Indication of Unhappiness. In short, we can judge by nothing but Appearances, and they are very apt to deceive us. Some put on a gay chearful Outside, and appear to the World perfectly at Ease, tho' even then, some inward Sting, some secret Pain imbitters all their Joys, and makes the Ballance even: Others appear continually dejected and full of Sorrow; but even Grief itself is sometimes *pleasant*, and Tears are not always without their Sweetness: Besides, Some take a Satisfaction in being thought unhappy, (as others take a Pride in being thought humble,) these will paint their Misfortunes to others in the strongest Colours, and leave no Means unus'd to make you think them throughly miserable; so great a Pleasure it is to them *to be pitied;* Others retain the Form and outside Shew of Sorrow, long after the Thing itself, with its Cause, is remov'd from the Mind; it is a Habit they have acquir'd and cannot leave. These, with many others that might be given, are Reasons why we cannot make a true Estimate of the *Equality* of the Happiness and Unhappiness of others; and unless we could, Matter of Fact cannot be opposed to this Hypothesis. Indeed, we are sometimes apt to think, that the Uneasinesses we ourselves have had, outweigh our Pleasures; but the Reason is this, the Mind takes no Account of the latter, they flip away un-remark'd, when the former leave more lasting Impressions on the Memory. But suppose we pass the greatest part of Life in Pain and Sorrow, suppose we die by Torments and *think no more*, 'tis no Diminution to the Truth of what is here advanc'd; for the *Pain*, tho' exquisite, is not so to the *last* Moments of Life, the Senses are soon benumm'd, and render'd incapable of transmitting it so sharply to the Soul as at first; She perceives it cannot hold long, and 'tis an *exquisite Pleasure* to behold the immediate Approaches of Rest. This makes an Equivalent tho' Annihilation should follow: For the Quantity of *Pleasure* and *Pain* is not to be measur'd by its Duration, any more than the Quantity of Matter by its Extension; and as one cubic Inch may be made to contain, by Condensation, as much Matter as would fill ten thousand cubic Feet, being more expanded, so one single Moment of *Pleasure* may outweigh and compensate an Age of *Pain*.

It was owing to their Ignorance of the Nature of Pleasure and Pain that the Antient Heathens believ'd the idle Fable of their *Eliẓium*, that State of uninterrupted Ease and Happiness!

The Thing is intirely impossible in Nature! Are not the Pleasures of the Spring made such by the Disagreeableness of the Winter? Is not the Pleasure of fair Weather owing to the Unpleasantness of foul? Certainly. Were it then always Spring, were the Fields always green and flourishing, and the Weather constantly serene and fair, the Pleasure would pall and die upon our Hands; it would cease to be Pleasure to us, when it is not usher'd in by Uneasiness. Could the Philosopher visit, in reality, every Star and Planet with as much Ease and Swiftness as he can now visit their Ideas, and pass from one to another of them in the Imagination; it would be a *Pleasure* I grant; but it would be only in proportion to the *Desire* of accomplishing it, and that would be no greater than the *Uneasiness* suffer'd in the Want of it. The Accomplishment of a long and difficult Journey yields a great *Pleasure;* but if we could take a Trip to the Moon and back again, as frequently and with as much Ease as we can go and come from Market, the Satisfaction would be just the same.

The *Immateriality* of the Soul has been frequently made use of as an Argument for its *Immortality;* but let us consider, that tho' it should be allow'd to be immaterial, and consequently its Parts incapable of Separation or Destruction by any Thing material, yet by Experience we find, that it is not incapable of Cessation of *Thought*, which is its Action. When the Body is but a little indispos'd it has an evident Effect upon the Mind; and a right Disposition of the Organs is requisite to a right Manner of Thinking. In a sound Sleep sometimes, or in a Swoon, we cease to think at all; tho' the Soul is not therefore then annihilated, but *exists* all the while tho' it does not *act;* and may not this probably be the Case after Death? All our Ideas are first admitted by the Senses and imprinted on the Brain, increasing in Number by Observation and Experience; there they become the Subjects of the Soul's Action. The Soul is a mere Power or Faculty of *contemplating* on, and *comparing* those Ideas when it has them; hence springs Reason: But as it can *think* on nothing but Ideas, it must have them before it can *think* at all. Therefore as it may exist before it has receiv'd any Ideas, it may exist before it *thinks*. To remember a Thing, is to have the Idea of it still plainly imprinted on the Brain, which the Soul can turn to and contemplate on Occasion. To forget a Thing, is to have the Idea of it defac'd and destroy'd by some Accident, or the crouding in and imprinting of great variety of other Ideas upon it, so that the Soul cannot find out its Traces and distinguish it. When we have thus lost the Idea of any one Thing, we can *think* no more, or *cease to think*, on that Thing; and as we can lose the Idea of one Thing, so we may of ten, twenty, a hundred, &c. and even of all Things, because they are not in their Nature permanent; and often during Life we see that some Men, (by an Accident or Distemper affecting the Brain,) lose the greatest Part of their Ideas, and remember very little of their past Actions and Circumstances. Now upon *Death*, and the Destruction of the Body, the Ideas contain'd in the Brain, (which are alone the Subjects of the Soul's Action) being then likewise necessarily destroy'd, the Soul, tho' incapable of Destruction itself, must then necessarily *cease to think* or *act*, having nothing left to think or act upon. It is reduc'd to its first unconscious State before it receiv'd any Ideas. And to cease to *think* is but little different from *ceasing to be*.

Nevertheless, 'tis not impossible that this same *Faculty* of contemplating Ideas may be hereafter united to a new Body, and receive a new Set of Ideas; but that will no way concern us who are now living; for the Identity will be lost, it is no longer that same *Self* but a new Being.

I shall here subjoin a short Recapitulation of the Whole, that it may with all its Parts be comprehended at one View.

1. *It is suppos'd that God the Maker and Governour of the Universe, is infinitely wise, good, and powerful.*

2. *In consequence of His infinite Wisdom and Goodness, it is asserted, that whatever He doth must be infinitely wise and good;*

3. *Unless He be interrupted, and His Measures broken by some other Being, which is impossible because He is Almighty.*

4. *In consequence of His infinite Power, it is asserted, that nothing can exist or be done in the Universe which is not agreeable to His Will, and therefore good.*

5. *Evil is hereby excluded, with all Merit and Demerit; and likewise all preference in the Esteem of God, of one Part of the Creation to another.* This is the Summary of the first Part.

Now our common Notions of Justice will tell us, that if all created Things are equally esteem'd by the Creator, they ought to be equally us'd by Him; and that they are therefore equally us'd, we might embrace for Truth upon the Credit, and as the true Consequence of the foregoing Argument. Nevertheless we proceed to confirm it, by shewing *how* they are equally us'd, and that in the following Manner.

1. *A Creature when endu'd with Life or Consciousness, is made capable of Uneasiness or Pain.*

2. *This Pain produces Desire to be freed from it, in exact proportion to itself.*

3. *The Accomplishment of this Desire produces an equal Pleasure.*

4. *Pleasure is consequently equal to Pain.*

From these Propositions it is observ'd,

1. *That every Creature hath as much Pleasure as Pain.*

2. *That Life is not preferable to Insensibility; for Pleasure and Pain destroy one another: That Being which has ten Degrees of Pain subtracted from ten of Pleasure, has nothing remaining, and is upon an equality with that Being which is insensible of both.*

3. *As the first Part proves that all Things must be equally us'd by the Creator because equally esteem'd; so this second Part demonstrates that they are equally esteem'd because equally us'd.*

4. *Since every Action is the Effect of Self-Uneasiness, the Distinction of Virtue and Vice is excluded; and* Prop. VIII. *in* Sect. I. *again demonstrated.*

5. *No State of Life can be happier than the present, because Pleasure and Pain are inseparable.*

Thus both Parts of this Argument agree with and confirm one another, and the Demonstration is reciprocal.

I am sensible that the Doctrine here advanc'd, if it were to be publish'd, would meet with but an indifferent Reception. Mankind naturally and generally love to be flatter'd: Whatever sooths our Pride, and tends to exalt our Species above the rest of the Creation, we are pleas'd with and easily believe, when ungrateful Truths shall be with the utmost Indignation rejected. "What! bring ourselves down to an Equality with the Beasts of the Field! with the *meanest* part of the Creation! 'Tis insufferable!" But, (to use a Piece of *common* Sense) our *Geese* are but *Geese* tho' we may think 'em *Swans;* and Truth will be Truth tho' it sometimes prove mortifying and distasteful.

RULES FOR A CLUB
ESTABLISHED FOR MUTUAL IMPROVEMENT[20]

[1728]

Previous Question, To Be Answered At Every Meeting

Have you read over these queries this morning, in order to consider what you might have to offer the Junto touching any one of them? viz.

1. Have you met with any thing in the author you last read, remarkable, or suitable to be communicated to the Junto? particularly in history, morality, poetry, physic, travels, mechanic arts, or other parts of knowledge.

2. What new story have you lately heard agreeable for telling in conversation?

3. Hath any citizen in your knowledge failed in his business lately, and what have you heard of the cause?

4. Have you lately heard of any citizen's thriving well, and by what means?

5. Have you lately heard how any present rich man, here or elsewhere, got his estate?

6. Do you know of a fellow citizen, who has lately done a worthy action, deserving praise and imitation; or who has lately committed an error, proper for us to be warned against and avoid?

7. What unhappy effects of intemperance have you lately observed or heard; of imprudence, of passion, or of any other vice or folly?

8. What happy effects of temperance, of prudence, of moderation, or of any other virtue?

9. Have you or any of your acquaintance been lately sick or wounded? If so, what remedies were used, and what were their effects?

10. Whom do you know that are shortly going voyages or journeys, if one should have occasion to send by them?

11. Do you think of any thing at present, in which the Junto may be serviceable to *mankind*, to their country, to their friends, or to themselves?

12. Hath any deserving stranger arrived in town since last meeting, that you have heard of? And what have you heard or observed of his character or merits? And whether, think you, it lies in the power of the Junto to oblige him, or encourage him as he deserves?

13. Do you know of any deserving young beginner lately set up, whom it lies in the power of the Junto any way to encourage?

14. Have you lately observed any defect in the laws of your *country*, of which it would be proper to move the legislature for an amendment? Or do you know of any beneficial law that is wanting?

15. Have you lately observed any encroachment on the just liberties of the people?

16. Hath any body attacked your reputation lately? And what can the Junto do towards securing it?

17. Is there any man whose friendship you want, and which the Junto, or any of them, can procure for you?

18. Have you lately heard any member's character attacked, and how have you defended it?

19. Hath any man injured you, from whom it is in the power of the Junto to procure redress?

20. In what manner can the Junto, or any of them, assist you in any of your honourable designs?

21. Have you any weighty affair on hand, in which you think the advice of the Junto may be of service?

22. What benefits have you lately received from any man not present?

23. Is there any difficulty in matters of opinion, of justice,

and injustice, which you would gladly have discussed at this time?

24. Do you see any thing amiss in the present customs or proceedings of the Junto, which might be amended?

Any person to be qualified [as a member of the Junto], to stand up, and lay his hand upon his breast, and be asked these questions, viz.

1. Have you any particular disrespect to any present members? *Answer.* I have not.

2. Do you sincerely declare, that you love mankind in general, of what profession or religion soever? *Answer.* I do.

3. Do you think any person ought to be harmed in his body, name, or goods, for mere speculative opinions, or his external way of worship? *Answer.* No.

4. Do you love truth for truth's sake, and will you endeavour impartially to find and receive it yourself, and communicate it to others? *Answer.* Yes.

ARTICLES OF BELIEF AND ACTS OF RELIGION

IN TWO PARTS [21]

Here will I hold. If there is a Pow'r above us,
(And that there is, all Nature cries aloud,
Thro' all her Works) He must delight in Virtue;
And that which he delights in must be Happy.

　　　　　　　　　　　　　　　　　—CATO.

PART I

Philad^a, Nov. 20: 1728

FIRST PRINCIPLES

I believe there is one supreme, most perfect Being, Author and Father of the Gods themselves. For I believe that Man is not the most perfect Being but one, rather that as there are many Degrees of Beings his Inferiors, so there are many Degrees of Beings superior to him.

Also, when I stretch my Imagination thro' and beyond our System of Planets, beyond the visible fix'd Stars themselves, into that Space that is every Way infinite, and conceive it fill'd with Suns like ours, each with a Chorus of Worlds forever moving round him, then this little Ball on which we move, seems, even in my narrow Imagination, to be almost Nothing, and myself less than nothing, and of no sort of Consequence.

When I think thus, I imagine it great Vanity in me to suppose, that the *Supremely Perfect* does in the least regard such an inconsiderable Nothing as Man. More especially, since it is impossible for me to have any positive clear idea of that which is infinite and incomprehensible, I cannot conceive otherwise than that he *the Infinite Father* expects or requires no Worship or Praise from us, but that he is even infinitely above it.

But, since there is in all Men something like a natural principle, which inclines them to DEVOTION, or the Worship of some unseen Power;

And since Men are endued with Reason superior to all other Animals, that we are in our World acquainted with;

Therefore I think it seems required of me, and my Duty as a Man, to pay Divine Regards to SOMETHING.

I conceive then, that the INFINITE has created many beings or Gods, vastly superior to Man, who can better conceive his Perfections than we, and return him a more rational and glorious Praise.

As, among Men, the Praise of the Ignorant or of Children is not regarded by the ingenious Painter or Architect, who is rather honour'd and pleas'd with the approbation of Wise Men & Artists.

It may be that these created Gods are immortal; or it may be that after many Ages, they are changed, and others Supply their Places.

Howbeit, I conceive that each of these is exceeding wise and good, and very powerful; and that Each has made for himself one glorious Sun, attended with a beautiful and admirable System of Planets.

It is that particular Wise and good God, who is the author

and owner of our System, that I propose for the object of my praise and adoration.

For I conceive that he has in himself some of those Passions he has planted in us, and that, since he has given us Reason whereby we are capable of observing his Wisdom in the Creation, he is not above caring for us, being pleas'd with our Praise, and offended when we slight Him, or neglect his Glory.

I conceive for many Reasons, that he is a *good Being;* and as I should be happy to have so wise, good, and powerful a Being my Friend, let me consider in what manner I shall make myself most acceptable to him.

Next to the Praise resulting from and due to his Wisdom, I believe he is pleas'd and delights in the Happiness of those he has created; and since without Virtue Man can have no Happiness in this World, I firmly believe he delights to see me Virtuous, because he is pleased when he sees Me Happy.

And since he has created many Things, which seem purely design'd for the Delight of Man, I believe he is not offended, when he sees his Children solace themselves in any manner of pleasant exercises and Innocent Delights; and I think no Pleasure innocent, that is to Man hurtful.

I *love* him therefore for his Goodness, and I *adore* him for his Wisdom.

Let me then not fail to praise my God continually, for it is his Due, and it is all I can return for his many Favours and great Goodness to me; and let me resolve to be virtuous, that I may be happy, that I may please Him, who is delighted to see me happy. Amen!

ADORATION

PREL. Being mindful that before I address the Deity, my soul ought to be calm and serene, free from Passion and Perturbation, or otherwise elevated with Rational Joy and Pleasure, I ought to use a Countenance that expresses a filial Respect, mixed wth a kind of Smiling, that Signifies inward Joy, and Satisfaction, and Admiration.

O wise God, my good Father!

Thou beholdest the sincerity of my Heart and of my Devotion; Grant me a Continuance of thy Favour!

1. O Creator, O Father! I believe that thou art Good, and that thou art *pleas'd with the pleasure* of thy children.—Praised be thy name for Ever!

2. By thy Power hast thou made the glorious Sun, with his attending Worlds; from the energy of thy mighty Will, they first received [their prodigious] motion, and by thy Wisdom hast thou prescribed the wondrous Laws, by which they move.—Praised be thy name for Ever!

3. By thy Wisdom hast thou formed all Things. Thou hast created Man, bestowing Life and Reason, and placed him in Dignity superior to thy other earthly Creatures.—Praised be thy name for Ever!

4. Thy Wisdom, thy Power, and thy Goodness are everywhere clearly seen; in the air and in the water, in the Heaven and on the Earth; Thou providest for the various winged Fowl, and the innumerable Inhabitants of the Water; thou givest Cold and Heat, Rain and Sunshine, in their Season, & to the Fruits of the Earth Increase.—Praised be thy name for Ever!

5. Thou abhorrest in thy Creatures Treachery and Deceit, Malice, Revenge, [*Intemperance*,] and every other hurtful Vice; but Thou art a Lover of Justice and Sincerity, of Friendship and Benevolence, and every Virtue. Thou art my Friend, my Father, and my Benefactor.—Praised be thy name, O God, for Ever! Amen!

[After this, it will not be improper to read part of some such Book as Ray's *Wisdom of God in the Creation*, or *Blackmore on the Creation*, or the Archbishop of Cambray's *Demonstration of the Being of a God*, &c., or else spend some Minutes in a serious Silence, contemplating on those Subjects.]

Then sing

MILTON'S HYMN TO THE CREATOR
"These are thy Glorious Works, Parent of Good!
Almighty, Thine this Universal Frame,
Thus wondrous fair! Thyself how wondrous then!

Speak ye who best can tell, Ye Sons of Light,
Angels, for ye behold him, and with Songs
And Choral Symphonies, Day without Night,
Circle his Throne rejoicing you in Heav'n,
On Earth join all ye creatures to extol
Him first, him last, him midst, and without End.
    "Fairest of Stars, last in the Train of Night,
If rather Thou belongst not to the Dawn,
Sure Pledge of Day! thou crown'st the smiling Morn
With thy bright Circlet, Praise him in thy Sphere
While Day arises, that sweet Hour of Prime.
Thou Sun, of this great World, both Eye and Soul,
Acknowledge him thy greater; Sound his Praise
In thy eternal Course; both when thou climb'st,
And when high Noon hast gain'd, and when thou fall'st.
Moon! that now meet'st the orient sun, now fly'st,
With the fixed Stars, fixed in their orb that flies,
And ye five other wandering Fires, that move
In mystic Dance not without Song; resound
His Praise, that out of Darkness called up Light.
Air! and ye Elements! the eldest Birth
Of Nature's womb, that in Quaternion run
Perpetual Circle, multiform, and mix
And nourish all things, let your ceaseless Change
Vary to our great Maker still new Praise.
Ye mists and Exhalations, that now rise
From Hill or steaming lake, dusky or grey,
Till the Sun paint your fleecy skirts with Gold,
In honour to the World's Great Author rise;
Whether to deck with Clouds the uncolor'd sky,
Or wet the thirsty Earth wth falling show'rs,
Rising or falling still advance his Praise.
His Praise, ye Winds! that from 4 quarters blow,
Breathe soft or Loud; and wave your Tops, ye Pines!
With every Plant, in sign of worship wave.
Fountains! and ye that warble, as ye flow
Melodious Murmurs, warbling tune his Praise.
Join voices all ye living souls, ye Birds!
That singing, up to Heaven's high gate ascend,
Bear on your wings, & in your Note his Praise;
Ye that in Waters glide! and ye that walk

The Earth! and stately tread or lowly creep;
Witness *if I be silent*, Ev'n or Morn,
To Hill, or Valley, Fountain, or Fresh Shade,
Made Vocal by my Song, and taught his Praise."

[Here follows the Reading of some Book, or part of a Book, Discoursing on and exciting to Moral Virtue.]

PETITION

Inasmuch as by Reason of our Ignorance We cannot be certain that many Things, which we often hear mentioned in the Petitions of Men to the Deity, would prove real Goods, if they were in our Possession, and as I have reason to hope and believe that the Goodness of my Heavenly Father will not withold from me a suitable share of Temporal Blessings, if by a Virtuous and holy Life I conciliate his Favour and Kindness, Therefore I presume not to ask such things, but rather humbly and with a Sincere Heart, express my earnest desires that he would graciously assist my Continual Endeavours and Resolutions of eschewing Vice and embracing Virtue; which Kind of Supplications will *at least be thus far beneficial, as they remind me* in a solemn manner of my Extensive duty.

That I may be preserved from Atheism & Infidelity, Impiety, and Profaneness, and, in my Addresses to Thee, carefully avoid Irreverence and ostentation, Formality and odious Hypocrisy, —Help me, O Father!

That I may be loyal to my Prince, and faithful to my country, careful for its good, valiant in its defence, and obedient to its Laws, abhorring Treason as much as Tyranny,—Help me, O Father!

That I may to those above me be dutiful, humble, and submissive; avoiding Pride, Disrespect, and Contumacy,—Help me, O Father!

That I may to those below me be gracious, Condescending, and Forgiving, using Clemency, protecting *innocent Distress*, avoiding Cruelty, Harshness, and oppression, Insolence, and unreasonable Severity,—Help me, O Father!

That I may refrain from Censure, Calumny and Detraction; that I may avoid and abhor Deceit and Envy, Fraud, Flattery, and Hatred, Malice, Lying, and Ingratitude,—Help me, O Father!

That I may be sincere in Friendship, faithful in trust, and Impartial in Judgment, watchful against Pride, and against Anger (that momentary Madness),—Help me, O Father!

That I may be just in all my Dealings, temperate in my Pleasures, full of Candour and Ingenuity, Humanity and Benevolence,—Help me, O Father!

That I may be grateful to my Benefactors, and generous to my Friends, exercising Charity and Liberality to the Poor, and Pity to the Miserable,—Help me, O Father!

That I may avoid Avarice and Ambition, Jealousie, and Intemperance, Falsehood, Luxury, and Lasciviousness,—Help me, O Father!

That I may possess Integrity and Evenness of Mind, Resolution in Difficulties, and Fortitude under Affliction; that I may be punctual in performing my promises, Peaceable and prudent in my Behaviour,—Help me, O Father!

That I may have Tenderness for the Weak, and reverent Respect for the Ancient; that I may be Kind to my Neighbours, good-natured to my Companions, and hospitable to Strangers, —Help me, O Father!

That I may be averse to Talebearing, Backbiting, Detraction, Slander, & Craft, and overreaching, abhor Extortion, Perjury, and every Kind of wickedness,—Help me, O Father!

That I may be honest and open-hearted, gentle, merciful, and good, cheerful in spirit, rejoicing in the Good of others,— Help me, O Father!

That I may have a constant Regard to Honour and Probity, that I may possess a perfect innocence and a good Conscience, and at length become truly Virtuous and Magnanimous,—Help me, good God; help me, O Father!*

*At this point the original MS. ends. The subsequent paragraph, including the "Thanks," is found only in William Temple Franklin's transcript, now in the Library of Congress. [*Smyth's note.*]

And, forasmuch as ingratitude is one of the most odious of vices, let me not be unmindful gratefully to acknowledge the favours I receive from Heaven.

THANKS

For peace and liberty, for food and raiment, for corn, and wine, and milk, and every kind of healthful nourishment,— Good God, I thank thee!

For the common benefits of air and light; for useful fire and delicious water,—Good God, I thank thee!

For knowledge, and literature, and every useful art, for my friends and their prosperity, and for the fewness of my enemies, —Good God, I thank thee!

For all thy innumerable benefits; for life, and reason, and the use of speech; for health, and joy, and every pleasant hour,— My good God, I thank thee!

THE BUSY-BODY, NO. 1[22]

Tuesday, February 4th, 1728/9

MR. ANDREW BRADFORD,

I design this to acquaint you, that I, who have long been one of your Courteous Readers, have lately entertain'd some Thoughts of setting up for an Author mySelf; not out of the least Vanity, I assure you, or Desire of showing my Parts, but purely for the Good of my Country.

I have often observ'd with Concern that your Mercury is not always equally entertaining. The Delay of Ships expected in, and want of fresh Advices from Europe, make it frequently very Dull; and I find the Freezing of our River has the same Effect on News as on Trade. With more Concern have I continually observ'd the growing Vices and Follies of my Country-folk; and, tho' Reformation is properly the concern of every Man; that is, Every one ought to mend One; yet 'tis too true in this Case, that what is every Body's Business is nobody's Business; and the Business is done accordingly. I therefore, upon mature Deliberation, think fit to take Nobody's Business wholly into my own Hands; and, out of Zeal for the Publick Good, design to erect mySelf into a Kind of *Censor Morum*; proposing, with your Allowance, to make Use of the *Weekly Mercury* as a Vehicle in which my Remonstrances shall be convey'd to the World.

I am sensible I have in this Particular undertaken a very unthankful Office, and expect little besides my Labour for my Pains. Nay, 'tis probable I may displease a great Number of your Readers, who will not very well like to pay 10 s. a Year for being told of their Faults. But, as most People delight in Censure when they themselves are not the Objects of it, if any are offended at my publickly exposing their private Vices, I promise they shall have the Satisfaction, in a very little Time, of seeing their good Friends and Neighbours in the same Circumstances.

However, let the Fair Sex be assur'd that I shall always treat them and their Affairs with the utmost Decency and Respect. I intend now and then to dedicate a Chapter wholly to their Service; and if my Lectures any Way contribute to the Embellishment of their Minds and brightning of their Understandings, without offending their Modesty, I doubt not of having their Favour and Encouragement.

'Tis certain, that no Country in the World produces naturally finer Spirits than ours; Men of Genius for every kind of Science, and capable of acquiring to Perfection every Qualification that is in Esteem among Mankind. But as few here have the Advantage of good Books, for want of which, good Conversation is still more scarce, it would doubtless have been very acceptable to your Readers, if, instead of an old out-of-date Article from Muscovy or Hungary, you had entertained them with some well-chosen Extract from a good Author. This I shall sometimes do, when I happen to have nothing of my own to say that I think of more Consequence. Sometimes I propose to deliver Lectures of Morality or Philosophy, and (because I am naturally enclin'd to be meddling with Things that don't concern me) perhaps I may sometimes talk Politicks. And if I can by any means furnish out a Weekly Entertainment for the Publick that will give a rational Diversion, and at the same Time be instructive to the Readers, I shall think my Leisure Hours well employ'd: And if you publish this, I hereby invite all ingenious Gentlemen and others (that approve of such an Undertaking) to my Assistance and Correspondence.

'Tis like by this Time, you have a Curiosity to be acquainted with my Name and Character. As I do not aim at publick Praise, I design to remain concealed; and there are such Numbers of our Family and Relations at this Time in the Country, that tho' I've sign'd my Name at full Length, I am not under the least Apprehension of being distinguish'd and discover'd by it. My Character, indeed, I would favour you with, but that I am cautious of praising mySelf, lest I should be told my Trumpeter's dead: And I cannot find in my Heart at present, to say any Thing to my own Disadvantage.

It is very common with Authors, in their first Performances, to talk to their Readers thus; "If this meets with a SUITABLE Reception; Or, If this should meet with DUE Encouragement, I shall hereafter publish, &c." This only manifests the Value they put on their own Writings, since they think to frighten the Publick into their Applause, by threatning, that unless you approve what they have already wrote, they intend never to write again; when perhaps it mayn't be a Pin Matter whether they ever do or no. As I have not observ'd the Criticks to be more favourable on this Account, I shall always avoid saying any Thing of the Kind; and conclude with telling you, that, if you send me a Bottle of Ink and a Quire of Paper by the Bearer, you may depend on hearing further from, Sir, your most humble Servant,

THE BUSY-BODY.

THE BUSY-BODY, NO. 2

Tuesday, February 11, 1728/9

All fools have still an itching to deride,
And fain would be upon the laughing side.
—POPE.

Monsieur de la Rochefoucault tells us somewhere in his Memoirs, that the Prince of Condé delighted much in ridicule, and used frequently to shut himself up for half a day together in his chamber, with a gentleman that was his favorite, purposely to divert himself with examining what was the foible or ridiculous side of every noted person in the court. That gentleman said afterwards in some company, that he thought nothing was more ridiculous in anybody, than this same humour in the Prince; and I am somewhat inclined to be of this opinion. The general tendency there is among us to this embellishment, which I fear has too often grossly imposed upon my loving countrymen instead of wit, and the applause it meets with from a rising generation, fill me with fearful apprehensions for the future reputation of my country. A young man of modesty (which is the most certain indication of large capacities) is hereby discouraged from attempting to make any figure in life; his apprehensions of being out-laughed will force him to continue in a restless obscurity, without having an opportunity of knowing his own merit himself or discovering it to the world, rather than venture to oppose himself in a place where a pun or a sneer shall pass for wit, noise for reason, and the strength of the argument be judged by that of the lungs.

Among these witty gentlemen let us take a view of Ridentius. What a contemptible figure does he make with his train of paltry admirers! This wight shall give himself an hour's diversion with the cock of a man's hat, the heels of his shoes, an unguarded expression in his discourse, or even some personal defect; and the height of his low ambition is to put some one of the company to the blush, who perhaps must pay an equal share of the reckoning with himself. If such a fellow makes laughing the sole end and purpose of his life; if it is necessary to his constitution, or if he has a great desire of growing suddenly fat, let him eat; let him give public notice where any dull stupid rogue may get a quart of four-penny for being laughed at; but it is barbarously unhandsome, when friends meet for the benefit of conversation and a proper relaxation from business, that one should be the butt of the company, and four men made merry at the cost of the fifth.

How different from this character is that of the good-natured, gay Eugenius, who never spoke yet but with a design to divert and please, and who was never yet baulked in his intention. Eugenius takes more delight in applying the wit of his friends, than in being admired himself; and if any one of the company is so unfortunate as to be touched a little too nearly, he will make use of some ingenious artifice to turn the edge of ridicule another way, choosing rather to make himself a public jest, than be at the pain of seeing his friend in confusion.

Among the tribe of laughers, I reckon the petty gentlemen that write satires, and carry them about in their pockets, reading them themselves in all company they happen into; taking an advantage of the ill taste of the town to make themselves famous for a pack of paltry, low nonsense, for which they deserve to be kicked rather than admired, by all who have the least tincture of politeness. These I take to be the most incorrigible of all my readers; nay, I expect they will be squibbing at the Busy-Body himself. However, the only favour he begs of them is this, that if they cannot control their overbearing itch of scribbling, let him be attacked in downright biting lyrics; for there is no satire he dreads half so much as an attempt towards a panegyric.

THE BUSY-BODY, NO. 3

Tuesday, February 18th, 1728/9

Non vultus instantis Tyranni
  Mente quatit solidâ,—neque Auster,
Dux inquieti turbidus Adriæ,
Nec fulminantis magna Jovis manus.
                                —HOR.

It is said that the Persians, in their ancient Constitution, had publick Schools in which Virtue was taught as a Liberal Art or Science; and it is certainly of more Consequence to a Man, that he has learnt to govern his Passions; in spite of Temptation to be just in his Dealings, to be Temperate in his Pleasures, to support himself with Fortitude under his Misfortunes, to behave with Prudence in all Affairs, and in every Circumstance of

Life; I say, it is of much more real Advantage to him to be thus qualified, than to be a Master of all the Arts and Sciences in the World beside.

Virtue alone is sufficient to make a Man Great, Glorious, and Happy. He that is acquainted with Cato, as I am, cannot help thinking as I do now, and will acknowledge he deserves the Name, without being honour'd by it. Cato is a Man whom Fortune has plac'd in the most obscure Part of the Country. His Circumstances are such, as only put him above Necessity, without affording him many Superfluities; Yet who is greater than Cato? I happened but the other Day to be at a House in Town, where, among others, were met Men of the most Note in this Place. Cato had Business with some of them, and knock'd at the Door. The most trifling Actions of a Man, in my Opinion, as well as the smallest Features and Lineaments of the Face, give a nice Observer some Notion of his Mind. Methought he rapp'd in such a peculiar Manner, as seem'd of itself to express there was One, who deserv'd as well as desir'd Admission. He appear'd in the plainest Country Garb; his Great Coat was coarse, and looked old and threadbare; his Linnen was home-spun; his Beard perhaps of Seven Days' Growth; his Shoes thick and heavy; and every Part of his Dress corresponding. Why was this Man receiv'd with such concurring Respect from every Person in the Room, even from those who had never known him or seen him before? It was not an exquisite Form of Person, or Grandeur of Dress, that struck us with Admiration.

I believe long Habits of Virtue have a sensible Effect on the Countenance. There was something in the Air of his Face, that manifested the true Greatness of his Mind, which likewise ap-pear'd in all he said, and in every Part of his Behaviour, obliging us to regard him with a Kind of Veneration. His Aspect is sweetened with Humanity and Benevolence, and at the same Time enboldned with Resolution, equally free from a diffident Bashfulness and an unbecoming Assurance. The Consciousness of his own innate Worth and unshaken Integrity renders him calm and undaunted in the Presence of the most Great and Powerful, and upon the most extraordinary Occasions. His strict Justice and known Impartiality make him the Arbitrator and Decider of all Differences, that arise for many Miles around him, without putting his Neighbours to the Charge, Perplexity, and Uncertainty of Law-Suits. He always speaks the Thing he means, which he is never afraid or asham'd to do, because he knows he always means well, and therefore is never oblig'd to blush, and feel the Confusion of finding himself detected in the Meanness of a Falsehood. He never contrives Ill against his Neighbour, and therefore is never seen with a lowring, suspicious Aspect. A mixture of Innocence and Wisdom makes him ever seriously chearful. His generous Hospitality to Strangers, according to his Ability; his Goodness, his Charity, his Courage in the Cause of the Oppressed, his Fidelity in Friendship, his Humility, his Honesty and Sincerity, his Moderation, and his Loyalty to the Government; his Piety, his Temperance, his Love to Mankind, his Magnanimity, his Publick-Spiritedness, and in fine, his consummate Virtue, make him justly deserve to be esteem'd the Glory of his Country.

> "The Brave do never shun the Light;
>   Just are their Thoughts, and open are their Tempers;
>   Freely without Disguise they love and hate;
>   Still are they found in the fair Face of Day,
>   And Heaven and Men are Judges of their Actions."
>   —ROWE.

Who would not rather chuse, if it were in his Choice, to merit the above Character, than be the richest, the most learned, or the most powerful Man in the Province without it?

Almost every Man has a strong natural Desire of being valu'd and esteem'd by the rest of his Species, but I am concern'd and griev'd to see how few fall into the Right and only infallible Method of becoming so. That laudable Ambition is too commonly misapply'd, and often ill employ'd. Some to make themselves considerable pursue Learning, others grasp at Wealth; some aim at being thought witty; and others are only careful to make the most of an handsome Person; But what is Wit, or Wealth, or Form, or Learning, when compar'd with Virtue?

'Tis true, we love the handsome, we applaud the Learned, and we fear the Rich and Powerful; but we even Worship and adore the Virtuous. Nor is it strange; since Men of Virtue are so rare, so very rare to be found. If we were as industrious to become Good as to make ourselves Great, we should become really Great by being Good, and the Number of valuable Men would be much increased; but it is a Grand Mistake to think of being Great without Goodness; and I pronounce it as certain, that there was never yet a truly Great Man, that was not at the same Time truly Virtuous.

O Cretico! thou sowre Philosopher! Thou cunning States-man! Thou art crafty, but far from being Wise. When wilt thou be esteem'd, regarded, and belov'd like Cato? When wilt thou, among thy Creatures, meet with that unfeign'd respect and warm Good-will, that all Men have for him? Wilt thou never understand, that the cringing, mean, submissive Deport-ment of thy Dependents, is (like the worship paid by Indians to the Devil) rather thro' Fear of the Harm thou may'st do to them, than out of Gratitude for the Favours they have receiv'd of thee? Thou art not wholly void of Virtue; there are many good Things in thee, and many good Actions reported of thee. Be advised by thy Friend. Neglect those musty Authors; let them be cover'd with Dust, and moulder on their proper Shelves; and do thou apply thyself to a Study much more profitable, The knowledge of Mankind and of thySelf.

This is to give Notice, that the Busy-Body strictly forbids all Persons, from this Time forward, of what Age, Sex, Rank, Quality, Degree, or Denomination soever, on any Pretence, to enquire who is the Author of this Paper, on Pain of his Dis-pleasure, (his own near and Dear Relations only excepted).

'Tis to be observ'd, that if any bad Characters happen to be drawn in the Course of these Papers, they mean no particular Person, if they are not particularly apply'd.

Likewise, that the Author is no Party-man, but a general Meddler.

N. B. Cretico lives in a neighbouring Province.

THE BUSY-BODY, NO. 4

Tuesday, February 25, 1728/9.

Ne quid nimis.

In my first Paper I invited the Learned and the Ingenious to join with me in this Undertaking, and I now repeat that Invitation. I would have such Gentlemen take this Opportunity (by trying their Talent in Writing) of diverting themselves and their Friends, and improving the Taste of the Town. And because I would encourage all Wit of our own Growth and Produce, I hereby promise, that whoever shall send me a little Essay on some moral or other Subject, that is fit for publick View in this Manner, (and not basely borrow'd from any other Author,) I shall receive it with Candour, and take care to place it to the best Advantage. It will be hard if we cannot muster up in the whole Country a sufficient Stock of Sense to supply the *Busy-Body* at least for a Twelvemonth.

For my own Part, I have already profess'd, that I have the Good of my Country wholly at Heart in this Design, without the least sinister View; my chief Purpose being to inculcate the noble Principles of Virtue, and depreciate Vice of every kind. But, as I know the Mob hate Instruction, and the Generality would never read beyond the first Line of my Lectures, if they were actually fill'd with nothing but wholesome Precepts and Advice, I must therefore sometimes humor them in their own Way. There are a Set of Great Names in the Province, who are the common Objects of Popular Dislike. If I can now and then overcome my Reluctance, and prevail with myself to satyrize a little one of these Gentlemen, the Expectation of meeting with such a Gratification will induce many to read me through, who would otherwise proceed immediately to the Foreign News. As I am very well assured the greatest Men among us have a sincere Love for their Country, notwithstanding its Ingratitude, and the Insinuations of the Envious and Malicious to the contrary, so I doubt not but they will chearfully tolerate me in the Liberty I design to take for the End above mentioned.

As yet I have but few Correspondents, tho' they begin now to increase. The following Letter, left for me at the Printer's, is one of the first I have receiv'd, which I regard the more for that it comes from one of the Fair Sex, and because I have myself oftentimes suffer'd under the Grievance therein complain'd of.

"TO THE BUSY-BODY

"*Sir*,

"You having set yourself up for a *Censuror Morum*, (as I think you call it), which is said to mean a Reformer of *Manners*, I know no Person more proper to be apply'd to for Redress in all the Grievances we suffer from Want of *Manners*, in some People. You must know I am a single Woman, and keep a Shop in this Town for a Livelyhood. There is a certain Neighbour of mine, who is really agreeable Company enough, and with whom I have had an Intimacy of some Time standing; but of late she makes her visits so excessively often, and stays so very long every Visit, that I am tir'd out of all Patience. I have no Manner of Time at all to myself; and you, who seem to be a wise Man, must needs be sensible that every Person has little Secrets and Privacies, that are not proper to be expos'd even to the nearest Friend. Now I cannot do the least Thing in the World, but she must know all about it; and it is a Wonder I have found an Opportunity to write you this Letter. My Misfortune is, that I respect her very well, and know not how to disoblige her so much as to tell her I should be glad to have less of her Company; for if I should once hint such a Thing, I am afraid she would resent it so as never to darken my Door again.

"But alas, Sir, I have not yet told you half my Affliction. She has two Children, that are just big enough to run about and do pretty Mischief; these are continually along with Mamma, either in my Room or Shop, if I have ever so many Customers or People with me about Business. Sometimes they pull the Goods off my low Shelves down to the Ground, and perhaps where one of them has just been making Water. My Friend takes up the Stuff, and cries, 'Eh! thou little wicked mischievous

Rogue! But, however, it has done no great Damage; 'tis only wet a little;' and so puts it up upon the Shelf again. Sometimes they get to my Cask of Nails behind the Counter, and divert themselves, to my great Vexation, with mixing my Ten-penny, and Eight-penny, and Four-penny, together. I endeavour to conceal my Uneasiness as much as possible, and with a grave Look go to Sorting them out. She cries, 'Don't thee trouble thyself, Neighbour: Let them play a little; I'll put all to rights myself before I go.' But Things are never so put to rights, but that I find a great deal of Work to do after they are gone. Thus, Sir, I have all the Trouble and Pesterment of Children, without the Pleasure of—calling them my own; and they are now so us'd to being here, that they will be content nowhere else. If she would have been so kind as to have moderated her Visits to ten times a Day, and stay'd but half an hour at a Time, I should have been contented, and I believe never have given you this Trouble. But this very Morning they have so tormented me, that I could bear no longer; for, while the Mother was asking me twenty impertinent Questions, the youngest got to my Nails, and with great Delight rattled them by handfuls all over the Floor; and the other, at the same Time, made such a terrible Din upon my Counter with a Hammer, that I grew half distracted. I was just then about to make myself a new Suit of Pinners; but in the Fret and Confusion I cut it quite out of all Manner of Shape, and utterly spoil'd a Piece of the first Muslin.

"Pray, Sir, tell me what I shall do; and talk a little against such unreasonable Visiting in your next Paper; tho' I would not have her affronted with me for a great Deal, for sincerely I love her and her Children, as well, I think, as a Neighbour can, and she buys a great many Things in a Year at my Shop. But I would beg her to consider, that she uses me unmercifully, Tho' I believe it is only for want of Thought. But I have twenty Things more to tell you besides all this: There is a handsome Gentleman, that has a Mind (I don't question) to make love to me, but he can't get the least Opportunity to—O dear! here she comes again; I must conclude, yours, &c.

"PATIENCE."

Indeed, 'tis well enough, as it happens, that she is come to shorten this Complaint, which I think is full long enough already, and probably would otherwise have been as long again. However, I must confess, I cannot help pitying my Correspondent's Case; and, in her Behalf, exhort the Visitor to remember and consider the Words of the Wise Man, "Withdraw thy Foot from the House of thy Neighbour, lest he grow weary of thee, and so hate thee." It is, I believe, a nice thing, and very difficult, to regulate our Visits in such a Manner, as never to give Offence by coming too seldom, or too often, or departing too abruptly, or staying too long. However, in my Opinion, it is safest for most People in a general way, who are unwilling to disoblige, to visit seldom, and tarry but a little while in a Place, notwithstanding pressing invitations, which are many times insincere. And tho' more of your Company should be really desir'd, yet in this Case, too much Reservedness is a Fault more easily excus'd than the Contrary.

Men are subjected to various Inconveniences meerly through lack of a small Share of Courage, which is a Quality very necessary in the common Occurrences of Life, as well as in a Battle. How many Impertinences do we daily suffer with great Uneasiness, because we have not Courage enough to discover our Dislike? And why may not a Man use the Boldness and Freedom of telling his Friends, that their long Visits sometimes incommode him? On this Occasion, it may be entertaining to some of my Readers, if I acquaint them with the *Turkish* Manner of entertaining Visitors, which I have from an Author of unquestionable Veracity; who assures us, that even the Turks are not so ignorant of Civility and the Arts of Endearment, but that they can practise them with as much Exactness as any other Nation, whenever they have a Mind to shew themselves obliging.

"When you visit a Person of Quality," (says he) "and have talk'd over your Business, or the Complements, or whatever Concern brought you thither, he makes a Sign to have Things serv'd in for the Entertainment, which is generally, a little Sweetmeat, a Dish of Sherbet, and another of Coffee; all which are immediately brought in by the Servants, and tender'd to all the Guests in Order, with the greatest Care and Awfulness imaginable. At last comes the finishing Part of your Entertainment, which is, Perfuming the Beards of the Company; a Ceremony which is perform'd in this Manner. They have for the Purpose a small Silver Chaffing-Dish, cover'd with a Lid full of Holes, and fixed upon a handsome Plate. In this they put some fresh Coals, and upon them a piece of *Lignum Aloes*, and shutting it up, the smoak immediately ascends with a grateful Odour thro' the Holes of the Cover. This smoak is held under every one's Chin, and offer'd as it were a Sacrifice to his Beard. The bristly Idol soon receives the Reverence done to it, and so greedily takes in and incorporates the gummy Steam, that it retains the Savour of it, and may serve for a Nosegay a good while after.

"This Ceremony may perhaps seem ridiculous at first hearing, but it passes among the *Turks* for a high Gratification. And I will say this in its Vindication, that its Design is very wise and useful. For it is understood to give a civil Dismission to the Visitants, intimating to them, that the Master of the House has Business to do, or some other Avocation, that permits them to go away as soon as they please, and the sooner after this Ceremony the better. By this Means you may, at any Time, without Offence, deliver yourself from being detain'd from your Affairs by tedious and unseasonable Visits; and from being constrain'd to use that Piece of Hypocrisy, so common in the World, of pressing those to stay longer with you, whom perhaps in your Heart you wish a great Way off for having troubled you so long already."

Thus far my Author. For my own Part, I have taken such a Fancy to this Turkish Custom, that for the future I shall put something like it in Practice. I have provided a Bottle of right French Brandy for the Men, and Citron-Water for the Ladies. After I have treated with a Dram, and presented a Pinch of my best Snuff, I expect all Company will retire, and leave me to pursue my Studies for the Good of the Publick.

ADVERTISEMENT

I give Notice, that I am now actually compiling, and design to publish in a short Time, the true History of the Rise, Growth, and Progress of the renowned Tiff-Club. All Persons who are acquainted with any Facts, Circumstances, Characters, Transactions, &c. which will be requisite to the Perfecting and Embellishment of the said Work, are desired to communicate the same to the Author, and direct their Letters to be left with the Printer hereof.

The Letter, sign'd *"Would-be-Something,"* is come to hand.

PREFACE TO THE PENNSYLVANIA GAZETTE

October 2, 1729

The Pennsylvania Gazette being now to be carry'd on by other Hands, the Reader may expect some Account of the Method we design to proceed in.[23]

Upon a view of Chambers's great Dictionaries, from whence were taken the Materials of the *Universal Instructor in all Arts and Sciences*, which usually made the First Part of this Paper, we find that besides their containing many Things abstruse or insignificant to us, it will probably be fifty Years before the Whole can be gone thro' in this Manner of Publication. There are likewise in those Books continual References from Things under one Letter of the Alphabet to those under another, which relate to the same Subject, and are necessary to explain and compleat it; these taken in their Turn may perhaps be Ten Years distant; and since it is likely that they who desire to acquaint themselves with any particular Art or Science, would gladly have the whole before them in much less time, we believe our Readers will not think such a Method of communicating Knowledge to be a proper One.

However, tho' we do not intend to continue the Publication of those Dictionaries in a regular Alphabetical Method, as has hitherto been done; yet as several Things exhibited from them in the Course of these Papers, have been entertaining to such of the Curious, who never had and cannot have the Advantage of good Libraries; and as there are many Things still behind, which being in this Manner made generally known, may perhaps become of considerable Use, by giving such Hints to the excellent natural Genius's of our Country, as may contribute either to the Improvement of our present Manufactures, or towards the Invention of new Ones; we propose from Time to Time to communicate such particular Parts as appear to be of the most general Consequence.

As to the "Religious Courtship," Part of which has been retal'd to the Publick in these Papers, the Reader may be inform'd, that the whole Book will probably in a little Time be printed and bound up by itself; and those who approve of it, will doubtless be better pleas'd to have it entire, than in this broken interrupted Manner.

There are many who have long desired to see a good News-Paper in Pennsylvania; and we hope those Gentlemen who are able, will contribute towards the making This such. We ask Assistance, because we are fully sensible, that to publish a good News-Paper is not so easy an Undertaking as many People imagine it to be. The Author of a Gazette (in the Opinion of the Learned) ought to be qualified with an extensive Acquaintance with Languages, a great Easiness and Command of Writing and Relating Things clearly and intelligibly, and in few Words; he should be able to speak of War both by Land and Sea; be well acquainted with Geography, with the History of the Time, with the several Interests of Princes and States, the Secrets of Courts, and the Manners and Customs of all Nations. Men thus accomplish'd are very rare in this remote Part of the World; and it would be well if the Writer of these Papers could make up among his Friends what is wanting in himself.

Upon the Whole, we may assure the Publick, that as far as the Encouragement we meet with will enable us, no Care and Pains shall be omitted, that may make the Pennsylvania Gazette as agreeable and useful an Entertainment as the Nature of the Thing will allow.

A DIALOGUE
BETWEEN PHILOCLES AND HORATIO,
MEETING ACCIDENTALLY IN THE FIELDS,
CONCERNING VIRTUE AND PLEASURE

[From the *Pennsylvania Gazette*, June 23, 1730.]²⁴

Philocles. My friend *Horatio!* I am very glad to see you;
prithee, how came such a Man as you alone? and musing too?
What Misfortune in your Pleasures has sent you to Philosophy
for Relief?

Horatio. You guess very right, my dear *Philocles!* We
Pleasure-hunters are never without 'em; and yet, so enchanting
is the Game! we can't quit the Chace. How calm and undisturbed is your Life! How free from present Embarrassments
and future Cares! I know you love me, and look with Compassion upon my Conduct; Shew me then the Path which leads up
to that constant and invariable Good, which I have heard you so
beautifully describe, and which you seem so fully to possess.

Phil. There are few Men in the World I value more than you,
Horatio! for amidst all your Foibles and painful Pursuits of
Pleasure, I have oft observed in you an honest Heart, and a
Mind strongly bent towards Virtue. I wish, from my Soul, I
could assist you in acting steadily the Part of a reasonable Crea-
ture; for, if you would not think it a Paradox, I should tell you
I love you better than you do yourself.

Hor. A Paradox indeed! Better than I do myself! When I
love my dear self so well, that I love every Thing else for my
own sake.

Phil. He only loves himself well, who rightly and judiciously
loves himself.

Hor. What do you mean by that, *Philocles!* You Men of
Reason and Virtue are always dealing in Mysteries, tho' you
laugh at 'em when the Church makes 'em. I think he loves himself very well and very judiciously too, as you call it, who allows
himself to do whatever he pleases.

Phil. What, though it be to the Ruin and Destruction of that very Self which he loves so well! That Man alone loves himself rightly, who procures the greatest possible Good to himself thro' the whole of his Existence; and so pursues Pleasure as not to give for it more than 'tis worth.

Hor. That depends all upon Opinion. Who shall judge what the Pleasure is worth? Supposing a pleasing Form of the fair Kind strikes me so much, that I can enjoy nothing without the Enjoyment of that one Object. Or, that Pleasure in general is so favorite a Mistress, that I will take her as Men do their Wives, for better, for worse; mind no Consequences, nor regarding what's to come. Why should I not do it?

Phil. Suppose, *Horatio*, that a Friend of yours entred into the World about Two-and-Twenty, with a healthful vigorous Body, and a fair plentiful Estate of about Five Hundred Pounds a Year; and yet, before he had reached Thirty, should, by following his Pleasures, and not, as you say, duly regarding Consequences, have run out of his Estate, and disabled his Body to that Degree, that he had neither the Means nor Capacity of Enjoyment left, nor any Thing else to do but wisely shoot himself through the Head to be at rest; what would you say to this unfortunate Man's Conduct? Is it wrong by Opinion or Fancy only? Or is there really a Right and Wrong in the Case? Is not one Opinion of Life and Action juster than another? Or, one Sort of Conduct preferable to another? Or, does that miserable Son of Pleasure appear as reasonable and lovely a Being in your Eyes, as a Man who, by prudently and rightly gratifying his natural Passions, had preserved his Body in full Health, and his Estate entire, and enjoy'd both to a good old Age, and then died with a thankful Heart for the good Things he had received, and with an entire Submission to the Will of Him who first called him into Being? Say, *Horatio!* are these Men equally wise and happy? And is every Thing to be measured by mere Fancy and Opinion, without considering whether that Fancy or Opinion be right?

Hor. Hardly so neither, I think; yet sure the wise and good Author of Nature could never make us to plague us. He could never give us Passions, on purpose to subdue and conquer 'em; nor produce this Self of mine, or any other self, only that it may be denied; for that is denying the Works of the great Creator himself. Self-denial, then, which is what I suppose you mean by Prudence, seems to me not only absurd, but very dishonourable to that Supreme Wisdom and Goodness, which is supposed to make so ridiculous and Contradictious a Creature, that must be always fighting with himself in order to be at rest, and undergo voluntary Hardships in order to be happy: Are we created sick, only to be commanded to be Sound? Are we born under one Law, our Passions, and yet bound to another, that of Reason? Answer me, *Philocles*, for I am warmly concerned for the Honour of Nature, the Mother of us all.

Phil. I find, *Horatio*, my two Characters have affrighted you; so that you decline the Trial of what is Good, by reason: And had rather make a bold Attack upon Providence; the usual Way of you Gentlemen of Fashion, who, when by living in Defiance of the eternal Rules of Reason, you have plunged yourselves into a thousand Difficulties, endeavour to make yourselves easy by throwing the Burden upon Nature. You are, *Horatio*, in a very miserable Condition indeed; for you say you can't be happy if you controul your Passions; and you feel yourself miserable by an unrestrained Gratification of 'em; so that here's Evil, irremediable Evil, either way.

Hor. That is very true, at least it appears so to me: Pray, what have you to say, *Philocles!* in Honour of Nature or Providence; methinks I'm in Pain for her: How do you rescue her? poor Lady!

Phil. This, my dear *Horatio*, I have to say; that what you find Fault with and clamour against, as the most terrible Evil in the World, Self-denial; is really the greatest Good, and the highest Self-gratification: If indeed, you use the Word in the Sense of some weak sour Moralists, and much weaker Divines, you'll have just Reason to laugh at it; but if you take it, as understood by Philosophers and Men of Sense, you will presently see her Charms, and fly to her Embraces, notwithstanding her demure Looks, as absolutely necessary to produce even your own darling sole Good, Pleasure: For, Self-denial is never a Duty, or a reasonable Action, but as 'tis a natural Means of procuring more Pleasure than you can taste without it so that this grave, Saint-like Guide to Happiness, as rough and dreadful as she has been made to appear, is in truth the kindest and most beautiful Mistress in the World.

Hor. Prithee, *Philocles!* do not wrap yourself in Allegory and Metaphor. Why do you teaze me thus? I long to be satisfied, what this Philosophical Self-denial is; the Necessity and Reason of it; I'm impatient, and all on Fire; explain, therefore, in your beautiful, natural easy Way of Reasoning, what I'm to understand by this grave Lady of yours, with so forbidding, downcast Looks, and yet so absolutely necessary to my Pleasures. I stand ready to embrace her; for you know, Pleasure I court under all Shapes and Forms.

Phil. Attend then, and you'll see the Reason of this Philosophical Self-denial. There can be no absolute Perfection in any Creature; because every Creature is derived, and dependent: No created Being can be All-wise, All-good, and All-powerful, because his Powers and Capacities are finite and limited; consequently whatever is created must, in its own Nature, be subject to Error, Irregularity, Excess, and Disorder. All intelligent, rational Agents find in themselves a Power of judging what kind of Beings they are; what Actions are proper to preserve 'em, and what Consequences will generally attend them, what Pleasures they are form'd for, and to what Degree their Natures are capable of receiving them. All we have to do then, *Horatio*, is to consider, when we are surpriz'd with a new Object, and passionately desire to enjoy it, whether the gratifying that Passion be consistent with the gratifying other Passions and Appetites, equal if not more necessary to us. And whether it consists with our Happiness To-morrow, next Week, or next Year; for, as we all wish to live, we are obliged by Reason to take as much Care for our future, as our present Happiness, and not build one upon the Ruins of t'other. But, if thro' the Strength and Power of a present Passion, and thro' want of attending to Consequences, we have err'd and exceeded the Bounds which Nature or Reason have set us; we are then, for our own Sakes, to refrain, or deny ourselves a present momentary Pleasure for a future, constant and durable one: So that this Philosophical Self-denial is only refusing to do an Action which you strongly desire; because 'tis inconsistent with your Health, Fortunes, or Circumstances in the World; or, in other Words, because 'twould cost you more than 'twas worth. You would lose by it, as a Man of Pleasure. Thus you see, *Horatio!* that Self-denial is not only the most reasonable, but the most pleasant Thing in the World.

Hor. We are just coming into Town, so that we can't pursue this Argument any farther at present; you have said a great deal for Nature, Providence, and Reason: Happy are they who can follow such divine Guides.

Phil. *Horatio!* good Night; I wish you wise in your Pleasures.

Hor. I wish, *Philocles!* I could be as wise in my Pleasures as you are pleasantly Wise; your Wisdom is agreeable, your Virtue is amiable, and your Philosophy the highest Luxury. Adieu! thou enchanting Reasoner!

A SECOND DIALOGUE
BETWEEN PHILOCLES AND HORATIO,
CONCERNING VIRTUE AND PLEASURE

[From the *Pennsylvania Gazette*, July 9, 1730.]

Philocles. Dear *Horatio!* where hast thou been these three or four Months? What new Adventures have you fallen upon since I met you in these delightful, all-inspiring Fields, and wondred how such a Pleasure-hunter as you could bear being alone?

Horatio. O *Philocles*, thou best of Friends, because a Friend to Reason and Virtue, I am very glad to see you. Don't you remember, I told you then, that some Misfortunes in my Pleasures had sent me to Philosophy for Relief? But now I do assure you, I can, without a Sigh, leave other Pleasures for those of Philosophy; I can hear the Word *Reason* mentioned, and Virtue praised, without Laughing. Don't I bid fair for Conversion, think you?

Phil. Very fair, *Horatio!* for I remember the Time when Reason, Virtue, and Pleasure, were the same Thing with you: When you counted nothing Good but what pleas'd, nor any thing Reasonable but what you got by; When you made a Jest of a Mind, and the Pleasures of Reflection, and elegantly plac'd your sole Happiness, like the rest of the Animal Creation, in the Gratifications of Sense.

Hor. I did so: But in our last Conversation, when walking upon the Brow of this Hill, and looking down on that broad, rapid River, and yon widely-extended beautifully-varied Plain, you taught me another Doctrine: You shewed me, that Self-denial, which above all Things I abhorred, was really the greatest Good, and the highest Self-gratification, and absolutely necessary to produce even my own darling sole Good, Pleasure.

Phil. True: I told you that Self-denial was never a Duty but when it was a natural Means of procuring more Pleasure than we could taste without it: That as we all strongly desire to live, and to live only to enjoy, we should take as much Care about our future as our present Happiness; and not build one upon the Ruins of 'tother: That we should look to the End, and regard Consequences: and if, thro' want of Attention we had err'd, and exceeded the Bounds which Nature had set us, we were then obliged, for our own Sakes, to refrain or deny ourselves a present momentary Pleasure for a future, constant, and durable Good.

Hor. You have shewn, *Philocles*, that Self-denial, which weak or interested Men have rendred the most forbidding, is really the most delightful and amiable, the most reasonable and pleasant Thing in the World. In a Word, if I understand you aright, Self-denial is, in Truth, Self-recognising, Self-acknowledging, or Self-owning. But now, my Friend! you are to perform another Promise; and shew me the Path which leads up to that constant, durable, and invariable Good, which I have heard you so beautifully describe, and which you seem so fully to possess: Is not this Good of yours a mere Chimera? Can any Thing be constant in a World which is eternally changing! and which appears to exist by an everlasting Revolution of one Thing into another, and where every Thing without us, and every Thing within us, is in perpetual Motion? What is this constant, durable Good, then, of yours? Prithee, satisfy my Soul, for I'm all on Fire, and impatient to enjoy her. Produce this eternal blooming Goddess with never-fading Charms, and see, whether I won't embrace her with as much Eagerness and Rapture as you.

Phil. You seem enthusiastically warm, *Horatio;* I will wait till you are cool enough to attend to the sober, dispassionate Voice of Reason.

Hor. You mistake me, my dear *Philocles!* my Warmth is not so great as to run away with my Reason: it is only just raised enough to open my Faculties, and fit them to receive those eternal Truths, and that durable Good, which you so triumphantly boasted of. Begin, then; I'm prepared.

Phil. I will. I believe, *Horatio!* with all your Skepticism about you, you will allow that Good to be constant which is never absent from you, and that to be durable, which never Ends but with your Being.

Hor. Yes, go on.

Phil. That can never be the Good of a Creature, which when present, the Creature may be miserable, and when absent, is certainly so.

Hor. I think not; but pray explain what you mean; for I am not much used to this abstract Way of Reasoning.

Phil. I mean all the Pleasures of Sense. The Good of Man cannot consist in the mere Pleasures of Sense; because, when any one of those Objects which you love is absent, or can't be come at, you are certainly miserable: and if the Faculty be impair'd, though the Object be present, you can't enjoy it. So that this sensual Good depends upon a thousand Things without and within you, and all out of your Power. Can this then be the Good of Man? Say, *Horatio!* what think you, Is not this a chequer'd, fleeting, fantastical Good? Can that, in any propriety of Speech, be called the Good of Man which even, while he is tasting, he may be miserable; and which when he cannot taste, he is necessarily so? Can that be our Good, which costs us a great deal of Pains to obtain; which cloys in possessing; for which we must wait the Return of Appetite before we can enjoy again? Or, is that our Good, which we can come at without Difficulty; which is heightened by Possession, which never ends in Weariness and Disappointment; and which, the more we enjoy, the better qualified we are to enjoy on?

Hor. The latter, I think; but why do you torment me thus? *Philocles!* shew me this Good immediately.

Phil. I have shewed you what 'tis not; it is not sensual, but 'tis rational and moral Good. It is doing all the Good we can to others, by Acts of Humanity, Friendship, Generosity, and Benevolence: This is that constant and durable Good, which will afford Contentment and Satisfaction always alike, without Variation or Diminution. I speak to your Experience now, *Horatio!* Did you ever find yourself weary of relieving the Miserable? or of raising the Distressed into Life or Happiness? Or rather, don't you find the Pleasure grow upon you by Repetition, and that 'tis greater in the Reflection than in the Act itself? Is there a Pleasure upon Earth to be compared with that which arises from the Sense of making others happy? Can this Pleasure ever be absent, or ever end but with your Being? Does it not always accompany you? Doth not it lie down and rise with you? live as long as you live? give you Consolation in the Article of Death, and remain with you in that gloomy Hour, when all other Things are going to forsake you, or you them?

Hor. How glowingly you paint, *Philocles!* Methinks *Horatio* is amongst the Enthusiasts. I feel the Passion: I am enchantingly convinced; but I don't know why: Overborn by something stronger than Reason. Sure some Divinity speaks within me; but prithee, *Philocles*, give me cooly the Cause, why this rational and moral Good so infinitely excels the meer natural or sensual.

Phil. I think, *Horatio!* that I have clearly shewn you the Difference between merely natural or sensual Good, and rational or moral Good. Natural or sensual Pleasure continues no longer than the Action itself; but this divine or moral Pleasure continues when the Action is over, and swells and grows upon your Hand by Reflection: The one is inconstant, unsatisfying, of short Duration, and attended with numberless Ills; the other is constant, yields full Satisfaction, is durable, and no Evils preceding, accompanying, or following it. But, if you enquire farther into the Cause of this Difference, and would know why the moral Pleasures are greater than the sensual; perhaps the Reason is the same as in all other Creatures, That their Happiness or chief Good consists in acting up to their chief Faculty, or that Faculty which distinguishes them from all Creatures of a different Species. The chief Faculty in a Man is his Reason; and consequently his chief Good; or that which may be justly called his Good, consists not merely in Action, but in reasonable Action. By reasonable Actions, we understand those Actions which are preservative of the human Kind, and naturally tend to produce real and unmixed Happiness; and these Actions, by way of Distinction, we call Actions morally Good.

Hor. You speak very clearly, *Philocles!* but, that no Difficulty may remain upon my Mind, pray tell me what is the real Difference between natural Good and Ill, and moral Good and Ill? for I know several People who use the Terms without Ideas.

Phil. That may be: The Difference lies only in this; that natural Good and Ill is Pleasure and Pain: Moral Good and Ill is Pleasure or Pain produced with Intention and Design; for 'tis the Intention only that makes the Agent morally Good or Bad.

Hor. But may not a Man, with a very good Intention, do an ill Action?

Phil. Yes, but, then he errs in his Judgment, tho' his Design be good. If his Error is inevitable, or such as, all Things considered, he could not help, he is inculpable: But if it arose through want of Diligence in forming his Judgment about the Nature of human Actions, he is immoral and culpable.

Hor. I find, then, that in order to please ourselves rightly, or to do good to others morally, we should take great Care of our Opinions.

Phil. Nothing concerns you more; for, as the Happiness or real Good of Men consists in right Action, and right Action cannot be produced without right Opinion, it behoves us, above all Things in this World, to take Care that our Opinions of Things be according to the Nature of Things. The Foundation of all Virtue and Happiness is Thinking rightly. He who sees an Action is right, that is, naturally tending to Good, and does it because of that Tendency, he only is a moral Man; and he alone is capable of that constant, durable, and invariable Good, which has been the Subject of this Conversation.

Hor. How, my dear philosophical Guide, shall I be able to know, and determine certainly, what is Right and Wrong in Life?

Phil. As easily as you distinguish a Circle from a Square, or Light from Darkness. Look, *Horatio*, into the sacred Book of Nature; read your own Nature, and view the Relation which other Men stand in to you, and you to them; and you'll immediately see what constitutes human Happiness, and consequently what is Right.

Hor. We are just coming into Town, and can say no more at present. You are my good Genius, *Philocles*. You have shewed me what is good. You have redeemed me from the Slavery and Misery of Folly and Vice, and made me a free and happy Being.

Phil. Then I am the happiest Man in the World. Be steady, *Horatio!* Never depart from Reason and Virtue.

Hor. Sooner will I lose my Existence. Good Night, *Philocles.*

Phil. Adieu! dear *Horatio!*

A WITCH TRIAL AT MOUNT HOLLY

[From the *Pennsylvania Gazette*, Oct. 22, 1730.]

"Saturday last, at Mount-Holly, about 8 Miles from this Place [Burlington, N. J.] near 300 People were gathered together to see an Experiment or two tried on some Persons accused of Witchcraft. It seems the Accused had been charged with making their Neighbours' Sheep dance in an uncommon Manner, and with causing Hogs to speak and sing Psalms, etc., to the

great Terror and Amazement of the king's good and peaceable
Subjects in this Province; and the Accusers, being very positive
that if the Accused were weighed in Scales against a Bible, the
Bible would prove too heavy for them; or that, if they were
bound and put into the River they would swim; the said Accused, desirous to make Innocence appear, voluntarily offered
to undergo the said Trials if 2 of the most violent of their Accusers would be tried with them. Accordingly the Time and
Place was agreed on and advertised about the Country; The
Accusers were 1 Man and 1 Woman: and the Accused the same.
The Parties being met and the People got together, a grand
Consultation was held, before they proceeded to Trial; in which
it was agreed to use the Scales first; and a Committee of Men
were appointed to search the Men, and a Committee of Women
to search the Women, to see if they had any Thing of Weight
about them, particularly Pins. After the Scrutiny was over a
huge great Bible belonging to the Justice of the Place was provided, and a Lane through the Populace was made from the
Justice's House to the Scales, which were fixed on a Gallows
erected for that Purpose opposite to the House, that the Justice's
Wife and the rest of the Ladies might see the Trial without coming amongst the Mob, and after the Manner of Moorfields a
large Ring was also made. Then came out of the House a grave,
tall Man carrying the Holy Writ before the supposed Wizard
etc, (as solemnly as the Sword-bearer of London before the
Lord Mayor) the Wizard was first put in the Scale, and over him
was read a Chapter out of the Books of Moses, and then the
Bible was put in the other Scale, (which, being kept down before) was immediately let go; but, to the great Surprize of the
Spectators, Flesh and Bones came down plump, and outweighed
that great good Book by abundance.[25] After the same Manner
the others were served, and their Lumps of Mortality severally
were too heavy for Moses and all the Prophets and Apostles.
This being over, the Accusers and the rest of the Mob, not satisfied with this Experiment, would have the Trial by Water.
Accordingly a most solemn Procession was made to the Mill-
pond, where both Accused and Accusers being stripped (saving

only to the Women their Shifts) were bound Hand and Foot
and severally placed in the Water, lengthways, from the Side
of a Barge or Flat, having for Security only a Rope about the
Middle of each, which was held by some in the Flat. The
accused man being thin and spare with some Difficulty began
to sink at last; but the rest, every one of them, swam very light
upon the Water. A Sailor in the Flat jump'd out upon the
Back of the Man accused thinking to drive him down to the
Bottom; but the Person bound, without any Help, came up
some time before the other. The Woman Accuser being told
that she did not sink, would be duck'd a second Time; when
she swam again as light as before. Upon which she declared,
That she believed the Accused had bewitched her to make her
so light, and that she would be duck'd again a Hundred Times
but she would duck the Devil out of her. The Accused Man,
being surpriz'd at his own Swimming, was not so confident of
his Innocence as before, but said, 'If I am a Witch, it is more
than I know.' The more thinking Part of the Spectators were
of Opinion that any Person so bound and placed in the Water
(unless they were mere Skin and Bones) would swim, till their
Breath was gone, and their Lungs fill'd with Water. But it
being the general Belief of the Populace that the Women's
shifts and the Garters with which they were bound help'd to
support them, it is said they are to be tried again the next warm
Weather, naked."

AN APOLOGY FOR PRINTERS

[From the *Pennsylvania Gazette*, June 10, 1731.]

Being frequently censur'd and condemn'd by different Persons for printing Things which they say ought not to be printed,
I have sometimes thought it might be necessary to make a standing Apology for my self, and publish it once a Year, to be read
upon all Occasions of that Nature. Much Business has hitherto
hindered the execution of this Design; but having very lately
given extraordinary Offence by printing an Advertisement with

a certain N. B. at the End of it, I find an Apology more particularly requisite at this Juncture, tho' it happens when I have not yet Leisure to write such a Thing in the proper Form, and can only in a loose manner throw those Considerations together which should have been the Substance of it.

I request all who are angry with me on the Account of printing things they don't like, calmly to consider these following Particulars.

1. That the Opinions of Men are almost as various as their Faces; an Observation general enough to become a common Proverb, *So many Men so many Minds.*

2. That the Business of Printing has chiefly to do with Mens Opinions; most things that are printed tending to promote some, or oppose others.

3. That hence arises the peculiar Unhappiness of that Business, which other Callings are no way liable to; they who follow Printing being scarce able to do any thing in their way of getting a Living, which shall not probably give Offence to some, and perhaps to many; whereas the Smith, the Shoemaker, the Carpenter, or the Man of any other Trade, may work indifferently for People of all Persuasions, without offending any of them: and the Merchant may buy and sell with Jews, Turks, Hereticks and Infidels of all sorts, and get Money by every one of them, without giving Offence to the most orthodox, of any sort; or suffering the least Censure or Ill will on the Account from any Man whatever.

4. That it is as unreasonable in any one Man or Set of Men to expect to be pleas'd with every thing that is printed, as to think that nobody ought to be pleas'd but themselves.

5. Printers are educated in the Belief, that when Men differ in Opinion, both Sides ought equally to have the Advantage of being heard by the Publick; and that when Truth and Error have fair Play, the former is always an overmatch for the latter: Hence they chearfully serve all contending Writers that pay them well, without regarding on which side they are of the Question in Dispute.

6. Being thus continually employ'd in serving both Parties,

Printers naturally acquire a vast Unconcernedness as to the right or wrong Opinions contain'd in what they print; regarding it only as the Matter of their daily labour: They print things full of Spleen and Animosity, with the utmost Calmness and Indifference, and without the least Ill-will to the Persons reflected on; who nevertheless unjustly think the Printer as much their Enemy as the Author, and join both together in their Resentment.

7. That it is unreasonable to imagine Printers approve of every thing they print, and to censure them on any particular thing accordingly; since in the way of their Business they print such great variety of things opposite and contradictory. It is likewise as unreasonable what some assert, "That Printers ought not to print any Thing but what they approve;" since if all of that Business should make such a Resolution, and abide by it, an End would thereby be put to Free Writing, and the World would afterwards have nothing to read but what happen'd to be the Opinions of Printers.

8. That if all Printers were determin'd not to print any thing till they were sure it would offend no body, there would be very little printed.

9. That if they sometimes print vicious or silly things not worth reading, it may not be because they approve such things themselves, but because the People are so viciously and corruptly educated that good things are not encouraged. I have known a very numerous Impression of Robin Hood's Songs go off in this Province at 2s. per Book, in less than a Twelvemonth; when a small Quantity of David's Psalms (an excellent Version) have lain upon my Hands above twice the Time.

10. That notwithstanding what might be urg'd in behalf of a Man's being allow'd to do in the Way of his Business whatever he is paid for, yet Printers do continually discourage the Printing of great Numbers of bad things, and stifle them in the Birth. I my self have constantly refused to print anything that might countenance Vice, or promote Immorality; tho' by complying in such Cases with the corrupt Taste of the Majority I might have got much Money. I have also always refus'd to print such

things as might do real Injury to any Person, how much soever
I have been solicited, and tempted with Offers of Great Pay;
and how much soever I have by refusing got the Ill-will of those
who would have employ'd me. I have hitherto fallen under the
Resentment of large Bodies of Men, for refusing absolutely to
print any of their Party or Personal Reflections. In this Manner
I have made my self many Enemies, and the constant Fatigue
of denying is almost insupportable. But the Publick being unacquainted with all this, whenever the poor Printer happens
either through Ignorance or much Persuasion, to do any thing
that is generally thought worthy of Blame, he meets with no
more Friendship or Favour on the above Account, than if there
were no Merit in't at all. Thus, as Waller says,

> Poets lose half the Praise they would have got
> Were it but known what they discreetly blot;

Yet are censur'd for every bad Line found in their Works with
the utmost Severity.

I come now to the Particular Case of the N. B. above mention'd, about which there has been more Clamour against me,
than ever before on any other Account.—In the Hurry of other
Business an Advertisement was brought to me to be printed;
it signified that such a Ship lying at such a Wharff, would sail
for Barbadoes in such a Time, and that Freighters and Passengers might agree with the Captain at such a Place; so far is
what's common: But at the Bottom this odd Thing was added,
"N. B. No Sea Hens nor Black Gowns will be admitted on any
Terms." I printed it, and receiv'd my Money; and the Advertisement was stuck up round the Town as usual. I had not so
much Curiosity at that time as to enquire the Meaning of it, nor
did I in the least imagine it would give so much Offence. Several good Men are very angry with me on this Occasion; they
are pleas'd to say I have too much Sense to do such things ig-
norantly; that if they were Printers they would not have done
such a thing on any Consideration; that it could proceed from
nothing but my abundant Malice against Religion and the
Clergy. They therefore declare they will not take any more of

my Papers, nor have any farther Dealings with me; but will hinder me of all the Custom they can. All this is very hard!

I believe it had been better if I had refused to print the said Advertisement. However, 'tis done, and cannot be revok'd. I have only the following few Particulars to offer, some of them in my behalf, by way of Mitigation, and some not much to the Purpose; but I desire none of them may be read when the Reader is not in a very good Humour.

1. That I really did it without the least Malice, and imagin'd the N. B. was plac'd there only to make the Advertisement star'd at, and more generally read.

2. That I never saw the Word Sea-Hens before in my Life; nor have I yet ask'd the meaning of it; and tho' I had certainly known that Black Gowns in that place signified the Clergy of the Church of England, yet I have that confidence in the generous good Temper of such of them as I know, as to be well satisfied such a trifling mention of their Habit gives them no Disturbance.

3. That most of the Clergy in this and the neighbouring Provinces, are my Customers, and some of them my very good Friends; and I must be very malicious indeed, or very stupid, to print this thing for a small Profit, if I had thought it would have given them just Cause of Offence.

4. That if I had much Malice against the Clergy, and withal much Sense; 'tis strange I never write or talk against the Clergy myself. Some have observed that 'tis a fruitful Topic, and the easiest to be witty upon of all others; yet I appeal to the Publick that I am never guilty this way, and to all my Acquaintances as to my Conversation.

5. That if a Man of Sense had Malice enough to desire to injure the Clergy, this is the foolishest Thing he could possibly contrive for that Purpose.

6. That I got Five Shillings by it.

7. That none who are angry with me would have given me so much to let it alone.

8. That if all the People of different Opinions in this Province would engage to give me as much for not printing things

they don't like, as I can get by printing them, I should probably live a very easy Life; and if all Printers were everywhere so dealt by, there would be very little printed.

9. That I am oblig'd to all who take my Paper, and am willing to think they do it out of meer Friendship. I only desire they would think the same when I deal with them. I thank those who leave off, that they have taken it so long. But I beg they would not endeavour to dissuade others, for that will look like Malice.

10. That 'tis impossible any Man should know what he would do if he was a Printer.

11. That notwithstanding the Rashness and Inexperience of Youth, which is most likely to be prevail'd with to do things that ought not to be done; yet I have avoided printing such Things as usually give Offence either to Church or State, more than any Printer that has followed the Business in this Province before.

12. And lastly, That I have printed above a Thousand Advertisements which made not the least mention of *Sea-Hens* or *Black Gowns;* and this being the first Offence, I have the more Reason to expect Forgiveness.

I take leave to conclude with an old Fable, which some of my Readers have heard before, and some have not.

"A certain well-meaning Man and his Son, were travelling towards a Market Town, with an Ass which they had to sell. The Road was bad; and the old Man therefore rid, but the Son went a-foot. The first Passenger they met, asked the Father if he was not ashamed to ride by himself, and suffer the poor Lad to wade along thro' the Mire; this induced him to take up his Son behind him: He had not travelled far, when he met others, who said, they are two unmerciful Lubbers to get both on the Back of that poor Ass, in such a deep Road. Upon this the old Man gets off, and let his Son ride alone. The next they met called the Lad a graceless, rascally young Jackanapes, to ride in that Manner thro' the Dirt, while his aged Father trudged along on Foot; and they said the old Man was a Fool, for suffering it. He then bid his Son come down, and walk with him, and they travell'd on leading the Ass by the Halter; 'till they met another Company, who called them a Couple of senseless Blockheads, for going both on Foot in such a dirty Way, when they had an empty Ass with them, which they might ride upon. The old Man could bear no longer; My Son, said he, it grieves me much that we cannot please all these People. Let me throw the Ass over the next Bridge, and be no further troubled with him."

Had the old Man been seen acting this last Resolution, he would probably have been called a Fool for troubling himself about the different Opinions of all that were pleas'd to find Fault with him: Therefore, tho' I have a Temper almost as complying as his, I intend not to imitate him in this last Particular. I consider the Variety of Humors among Men, and despair of pleasing every Body; yet I shall not therefore leave off Printing. I shall continue my Business. I shall not burn my Press and melt my Letters.

PREFACE TO POOR RICHARD, 1733

COURTEOUS READER,

I might in this place attempt to gain thy Favour, by declaring that I write Almanacks with no other View than that of the publick Good; but in this I should not be sincere; and Men are now adays too wise to be deceiv'd by Pretences how specious soever. The plain Truth of the Matter is, I am excessive poor, and my Wife, good Woman, is, I tell her, excessive proud; she cannot bear, she says, to sit spinning in her Shift of Tow, while I do nothing but gaze at the Stars; and has threatned more than once to burn all my Books and Rattling-Traps (as she calls my Instruments) if I do not make some profitable Use of them for the Good of my Family. The Printer has offer'd me some considerable share of the Profits, and I have thus begun to comply with my Dame's Desire.

Indeed this Motive would have had Force enough to have made me publish an Almanack many Years since, had it not been overpowered by my Regard for my good Friend and Fellow Student Mr. *Titan Leeds*, whose Interest I was extreamly unwilling to hurt: But this Obstacle (I am far from speaking it with Pleasure) is soon to be removed, since inexorable Death, who was never known to respect Merit, has already prepared the mortal Dart, the fatal Sister has already extended her destroying Shears, and that ingenious Man must soon be taken from us. He dies, by my Calculation made at his Request, on Oct. 17. 1733. 3 h. 29 m. P. M. at the very instant of the ♂ of ☉ and ☿: By his own Calculation he will survive till the 26th of the same Month.[26] This small Difference between us we have disputed whenever we have met these 9 Years past; but at length he is inclinable to agree with my Judgment: Which of us is most exact, a little Time will now determine. As therefore these Provinces may not longer expect to see any of his Performances after this Year, I think my self free to take up the Task, and request a share of the publick Encouragement; which I am the more apt to hope for on this Account, that the Buyer of my Almanack may consider himself, not only as purchasing an useful Utensil, but as performing an Act of Charity, to his poor *Friend and Servant*

R. SAUNDERS.

A MEDITATION ON A QUART MUGG [27]

[From the *Pennsylvania Gazette*, July 19, 1733.]

Wretched, miserable, and unhappy Mug! I pity thy luckless Lot, I commiserate thy Misfortunes, thy Griefs fill me with Compassion, and because of thee are Tears made frequently to burst from my Eyes.

How often have I seen him compell'd to hold up his Handle at the Bar, for no other Crime than that of being empty; then snatch'd away by a surly Officer, and plung'd suddenly into a Tub of cold Water: Sad Spectacle, and Emblem of human Penury, oppress'd by arbitrary Power! How often is he hurry'd down into a dismal Vault, sent up fully laden in a cold Sweat, and by a rude Hand thrust into the Fire! How often have I seen it obliged to undergo the Indignities of a dirty Wench; to have

melting Candles dropt on its naked Sides, and sometimes in its
Mouth, to risque being broken into a thousand Pieces, for
Actions which itself was not guilty of! How often is he forced
into the Company of boisterous Sots, who lay all their nonsense,
Noise, profane Swearing, Cursing, and Quarreling, on the
harmless Mug, which speaks not a Word! They overset him,
maim him, and sometimes turn him to Arms offensive or defensive, as they please; when of himself he would not be of
either Party, but would as willingly stand still. Alas! what
Power, or Place, is provided, where this poor Mug, this unpitied
Slave, can have Redress of his Wrongs and Sufferings? Or
where shall he have a Word of Praise bestow'd on him for his
Well doings, and faithful Services? If he prove of a large size,
his Owner curses him, and says he will devour more than he'll
earn: If his Size be small, those whom his Master appoints him
to serve will curse him as much, and perhaps threaten him with
the Inquisition of the Standard. Poor Mug, unfortunate is thy
Condition! Of thy self thou wouldst do no Harm, but much
Harm is done with thee! Thou art accused of many Mischiefs;
thou art said to administer Drunkenness, Poison, and broken
Heads: But none praise thee for the good Things thou yieldest!
Shouldest thou produce double Beer, nappy Ale, stallcop Cyder,
or Cyder mull'd, fine Punch, or cordial Tiff; yet for all these
shouldst thou not be prais'd, but the rich Liquors themselves,
which tho' within thee, will be said to be foreign to thee! And
yet, so unhappy is thy Destiny, thou must bear all their Faults
and Abominations! Hast thou been industriously serving thy
Employers with Tiff or Punch, and instantly they dispatch thee
for Cyder, then must thou be abused for smelling of Rum.
Hast thou been steaming their Noses gratefully, with mull'd
Cyder or butter'd Ale, and then offerest to refresh their Palates
with the best of Beer, they will curse thee for thy Greasiness.
And how, alas! can thy Service be rendered more tolerable to
thee? If thou submittest thyself to a Scouring in the Kitchen,
what must thou undergo from sharp Sand, hot Ashes, and a
coarse Dishclout; besides the Danger of having thy Lips rudely
torn, thy Countenance disfigured, thy Arms dismantled, and

thy whole Frame shatter'd, with violent Concussions in an Iron
Pot or Brass Kettle! And yet, O Mug! if these Dangers thou
escapest, with little Injury, thou must at last untimely fall, be
broken to Pieces, and cast away, never more to be recollected
and form'd into a Quart Mug. Whether by the Fire, or in a
Battle, or choak'd with a Dishclout, or by a Stroke against a
Stone, thy Dissolution happens; 'tis all alike to thy avaritious
Owner; he grieves not for thee, but for the Shilling with which
he purchased thee! If thy Bottom Part should chance to survive,
it may be preserv'd to hold bits of Candles, or Blacking for
Shoes, or Salve for kibed Heels; but all thy other Members will
be for ever buried in some miry Hole; or less carefully disposed
of, so that little Children, who have not yet arrived to Acts of
Cruelty, may gather them up to furnish out their Baby Houses:
Or, being cast upon the Dunghill, they will therewith be
carted into Meadow Grounds; where, being spread abroad and
discovered, they must be thrown to the Heap of Stones, Bones
and Rubbish; or being left until the Mower finds them with his
Scythe, they will with bitter Curses be tossed over the Hedge;
and so serve for unlucky Boys to throw at Birds and Dogs;
until by Length of Time and numerous Casualties, they shall be
press'd into their Mother Earth, and be converted to their
original Principles.

PREFACE TO POOR RICHARD, 1734

Courteous Readers,

   Your kind and charitable Assistance last Year, in purchasing
so large an Impression of my Almanacks, has made my Circumstances much more easy in the World, and requires my grateful
Acknowledgment. My Wife has been enabled to get a Pot of
her own, and is no longer oblig'd to borrow one from a Neighbour; nor have we ever since been without something of our
own to put in it. She has also got a pair of Shoes, two new
Shifts, and a new warm Petticoat; and for my part, I have
bought a second-hand Coat, so good, that I am now not
asham'd to go to Town or be seen there. These Things have

render'd her Temper so much more pacifick than it us'd to be, that I may say, I have slept more, and more quietly within this last Year, than in the three foregoing Years put together. Accept my hearty Thanks therefor, and my sincere Wishes for your Health and Prosperity.

In the Preface to my last Almanack, I foretold the Death of my dear old Friend and Fellow-Student, the learned and ingenious Mr. *Titan Leeds*, which was to be on the 17th of *October*, 1733, 3 h. 29 m. P. M. at the very Instant of the ♂ of ☉ and ☿. By his own Calculation he was to survive till the 26th of the same Month, and expire in the Time of the Eclipse, near 11 o'clock A. M. At which of these Times he died, or whether he be really yet dead, I cannot at this present Writing positively assure my Readers; forasmuch as a Disorder in my own Family demanded my Presence, and would not permit me as I had intended, to be with him in his last Moments, to receive his last Embrace, to close his Eyes, and do the Duty of a Friend in performing the last Offices to the Departed. Therefore it is that I cannot positively affirm whether he be dead or not; for the Stars only show to the Skilful, what will happen in the natural and universal Chain of Causes and Effects; but 'tis well known, that the Events which would otherwise certainly happen at certain Times in the Course of Nature are sometimes set aside or postpon'd for wise and good Reasons by the immediate particular Dispositions of Providence; which particular Dispositions the Stars can by no Means discover or foreshow. There is however (and I cannot speak it without Sorrow) there is the strongest Probability that my dear Friend is *no more;* for there appears in his Name, as I am assured, an Almanack for the Year 1734, in which I am treated in a very gross and unhandsome Manner; in which I am called *a false Predicter, an Ignorant, a conceited Scribler, a Fool, and a Lyar*. Mr. *Leeds* was too well bred to use any Man so indecently and so scurrilously, and moreover his Esteem and Affection for me was extraordinary: So that it is to be feared that Pamphlet may be only a Contrivance of somebody or other, who hopes perhaps to sell two or three Year's Almanacks still, by the sole Force and Virtue of Mr. *Leeds's* Name; but certainly, to put Words into the Mouth of a Gentleman and a Man of Letters, against his Friend, which the meanest and most scandalous of the People might be asham'd to utter even in a drunken Quarrel, is an unpardonable Injury to his Memory, and an Imposition upon the Publick.

Mr. *Leeds* was not only profoundly skilful in the useful Science he profess'd, but he was a Man of *exemplary Sobriety*, a most *sincere Friend*, and an *exact Performer of his Word*. These valuable Qualifications, with many others so much endear'd him to me, that although it should be so, that, contrary to all Probability, contrary to my Prediction and his own, he might possibly be yet alive, yet my Loss of Honour as a Prognosticator, cannot afford me so much Mortification, as his Life, Health and Safety would give me Joy and Satisfaction.

I am, *Courteous and Kind Reader*
                   Your poor Friend and Servant,
Octob. 30. 1733.   R. SAUNDERS.

PREFACE TO POOR RICHARD, 1735

COURTEOUS READER,

This is the third Time of my appearing in print, hitherto very much to my own Satisfaction, and, I have reason to hope, to the Satisfaction of the Publick also; for the Publick is generous, and has been very charitable and good to me. I should be ungrateful then, if I did not take every Opportunity of expressing my Gratitude; for *ingratum si dixeris, omnia dixeris:* I therefore return the Publick my most humble and hearty Thanks.

Whatever may be the Musick of the Spheres, how great soever the Harmony of the Stars, 'tis certain there is no Harmony among the Stargazers; but they are perpetually growling and snarling at one another like strange Curs, or like some Men at their Wives: I had resolved to keep the Peace on my own part, and affront none of them; and I shall persist in that Resolution: But having receiv'd much Abuse from *Titan Leeds* deceas'd (*Titan Leeds* when living would not have us'd me so!) I say, having receiv'd much Abuse from the Ghost of *Titan Leeds*, who pretends to be still living, and to write Almanacks in Spight of me and my Predictions, I cannot help saying, that tho' I take it patiently, I take it very unkindly. And whatever he may pretend, 'tis undoubtedly true that he is really defunct and dead. First because the Stars are seldom disappointed, never but in the Case of wise Men, *sapiens dominabitur astris*, and they foreshow'd his Death at the Time I predicted it. Secondly, 'Twas requisite and necessary he should die punctually at that Time, for the Honour of Astrology, the Art professed both by him and his Father before him. Thirdly, 'Tis plain to every one that reads his last two Almanacks (for 1734 and 35) that they are not written with that *Life* his Performances use to be written with; the Wit is low and flat, the little Hints dull and spiritless, nothing smart in them but *Hudibras's* Verses against Astrology at the Heads of the Months in the last, which no Astrologer but a *dead one* would have inserted, and no Man *living* would or could write such Stuff as the rest. But lastly I convince him in his own Words, that he is dead (*ex ore suo condemnatus est*) for in his Preface to his Almanack for 1734, he says "*Saunders adds another* GROSS FALSHOOD *in his Almanack, viz. that by my own Calculation I shall survive until the 26th of the said Month October* 1733, *which is as untrue as the former.*" Now if it be, as Leeds says, *untrue* and a *gross Falshood* that he surviv'd till the 26th of October 1733, then it is certainly *true* that he died *before* that Time: And if he died before that Time, he is dead now, to all Intents and Purposes, any thing he may say to the contrary notwithstanding. And at what Time before the 26th is it so likely he should die, as at the Time by me predicted, *viz.* the 17th of October aforesaid? But if some People will walk and be troublesome after Death, it may perhaps be born with a little, because it cannot well be avoided unless one would be at the Pains and Expence of laying them in the *Red Sea;* however, they should not presume too much upon the Liberty allow'd them; I know Confinement must needs be mighty irksome to the free Spirit of an Astronomer, and I am too compassionate

to proceed suddenly to Extremities with it; nevertheless, tho'
I resolve with Reluctance, I shall not long defer, if it does not
speedily learn to treat its living Friends with better Manners,

I am, *Courteous Reader, your obliged Friend and Servant*
Octob. 30. 1734   R. SAUNDERS.

HINTS FOR THOSE THAT WOULD BE RICH

[October, 1736—From *Poor Richard*, 1737]

The Use of Money is all the Advantage there is in having
Money.

For £6 a Year you may have the Use of £100 if you are a
Man of known Prudence and Honesty.

He that spends a Groat a day idly, spends idly above £6 a
year, which is the Price of using £100.

He that wastes idly a Groat's worth of his Time per Day,
one Day with another, wastes the Privilege of using £100
each Day.

He that idly loses 5s. worth of time, loses 5s. and might as
prudently throw 5s. in the River.

He that loses 5s. not only loses that Sum, but all the Advantage that might be made by turning it in Dealing, which,
by the time that a young Man becomes old, amounts to a comfortable Bag of Money.

Again, He that sells upon Credit, asks a Price for what he
sells equivalent to the Principal and Interest of his Money for
the Time he is like to be kept out of it: therefore He that buys
upon Credit, pays Interest for what he buys. And he that pays
ready Money, might let that Money out to Use; so that He that
possesses any Thing he has bought, pays Interest for the Use
of it.

Consider then when you are tempted to buy any unnecessary
Householdstuff, or any superfluous thing, whether you will be
willing to pay *Interest, and Interest upon Interest* for it as long
as you live; and more if it grows worse by using.

Yet, in buying goods, 'tis best to pay Ready Money, because, He that sells upon Credit, expects to lose 5 *per Cent* by bad Debts; therefore he charges, on all he sells upon Credit, an Advance that shall make up for that Deficiency.

Those who pay for what they buy upon Credit, pay their Share of this Advance.

He that pays ready Money, escapes or may escape that Charge.

A Penny sav'd is Twopence clear,
A Pin a Day is a Groat a Year.

TO JOSIAH FRANKLIN [28]

Philadelphia, April 13, 1738.

HONOURED FATHER,

I have your favours of the 21st of March, in which you both seem concerned lest I have imbibed some erroneous opinions. Doubtless I have my share; and when the natural weakness and imperfection of human understanding is considered, the unavoidable influence of education, custom, books, and company upon our ways of thinking, I imagine a man must have a good deal of vanity who believes, and a good deal of boldness who affirms, that all the doctrines he holds are true, and all he rejects are false. And perhaps the same may be justly said of every sect, church, and society of men, when they assume to themselves that infallibility, which they deny to the Pope and councils.

I think opinions should be judged of by their influences and effects; and, if a man holds none that tend to make him less virtuous or more vicious, it may be concluded he holds none that are dangerous; which I hope is the case with me.

I am sorry you should have any uneasiness on my account; and if it were a thing possible for one to alter his opinions in order to please another, I know none whom I ought more willingly to oblige in that respect than yourselves. But, since it is no more in a man's power to *think* than to *look* like another, methinks all that should be expected from me is to keep my mind open to conviction, to hear patiently and examine attentively, whatever is offered me for that end; and, if after all I continue in the same errors, I believe your usual charity will induce you to rather pity and excuse, than blame me. In the mean time your care and concern for me is what I am very thankful for.

My mother grieves, that one of her sons is an Arian, another an Arminian. What an Arminian or an Arian is, I cannot say that I very well know. The truth is, I make such distinctions very little my study. I think vital religion has always suffered, when orthodoxy is more regarded than virtue; and the Scriptures assure me, that at the last day we shall not be examined what we *thought*, but what we *did;* and our recommendation will not be, that we said, *Lord! Lord!* but that we did good to our fellow creatures. See Matt. xxv.

As to the freemasons, I know no way of giving my mother a better account of them than she seems to have at present, since it is not allowed that women should be admitted into that secret society. She has, I must confess, on that account some reason to be displeased with it; but for any thing else, I must entreat her to suspend her judgment till she is better informed, unless she will believe me, when I assure her that they are in general a very harmless sort of people, and have no principles or practices that are inconsistent with religion and good manners.

We have had great rains here lately, which, with the thawing of snow on the mountains back of our country, have made vast floods in our rivers, and, by carrying away bridges, boats, &c., made travelling almost impracticable for a week past; so that our post has entirely missed making one trip.

I hear nothing of Dr. Crook, nor can I learn any such person has ever been here.

I hope my sister Jenny's child is by this time recovered. I am your dutiful son.

                                                    B. FRANKLIN.

PREFACE TO POOR RICHARD, 1739

KIND READER,

Encouraged by thy former Generosity, I once more present thee with an Almanack, which is the 7th of my Publication. While thou art putting Pence in my Pocket, and furnishing my Cottage with necessaries, *Poor Dick* is not unmindful to do something for thy Benefit. The Stars are watch'd as narrowly as old *Bess* watch'd her Daughter, that thou mayst be acquainted with their Motions, and told a Tale of their Influences and Effects, which may do thee more good than a Dream of last Year's Snow.

Ignorant Men wonder how we Astrologers foretell the Weather so exactly, unless we deal with the old black Devil. Alas! 'tis as easy as ****** For Instance; The Stargazer peeps at the Heavens thro' a long Glass: He sees perhaps TAURUS, or the great Bull, in a mighty Chafe, stamping on the Floor of his House, swinging his Tail about, stretching out his Neck, and opening wide his Mouth. 'Tis natural from these Appearances to judge that this furious Bull is puffing, blowing and roaring. Distance being consider'd and Time allow'd for all this to come down, there you have Wind and Thunder. He spies perhaps VIRGO (or the Virgin;) she turns her Head round as it were to see if any body observ'd her; then crouching down gently, with her Hands on her Knees, she looks wistfully for a while right forward. He judges rightly what she's about: And having calculated the Distance and allow'd Time for its Falling, finds that next Spring we shall have a fine *April* shower. What can be more natural and easy than this? I might instance the like in many other particulars; but this may be sufficient to prevent our being taken for Conjurors. O the wonderful Knowledge to be found in the Stars! Even the smallest Things are written there, if you had but Skill to read: When my Brother J-m-n erected a Scheme to know which was best for his sick Horse, to sup a new-laid Egg, or a little Broth, he found that the Stars plainly gave their Verdict for Broth, and the

Horse having sup'd his Broth;—Now, what do you think became of that Horse? You shall know in my next.

Besides the usual Things expected in an Almanack, I hope the profess'd Teachers of Mankind will excuse my scattering here and there some instructive Hints in Matters of Morality and Religion. And be not thou disturbed, O grave and sober Reader, if among the many serious Sentences in my Book, thou findest me trifling now and then, and talking idly. In all the Dishes I have hitherto cook'd for thee, there is solid Meat enough for thy Money. There are Scraps from the Table of Wisdom, that will if well digested, yield strong Nourishment to thy Mind. But squeamish Stomachs cannot eat without Pickles; which, 'tis true are good for nothing else, but they provoke an Appetite. The Vain Youth that reads my Almanack for the sake of an idle Joke, will perhaps meet with a serious Reflection, that he may ever after be the better for.

Some People observing the great Yearly Demand for my Almanack, imagine I must by this Time have become rich, and consequently ought to call myself *Poor Dick* no longer. But, the Case is this,

When I first begun to publish, the Printer made a fair Agreement with me for my Copies, by Virtue of which he runs away with the greatest Part of the Profit.—However, much good may't do him; I do not grudge it him; he is a Man I have a great Regard for, and I wish his Profit ten times greater than it is. For I am, dear Reader, his, as well as thy

Affectionate Friend
R. Saunders.

A PROPOSAL

FOR PROMOTING USEFUL KNOWLEDGE AMONG THE BRITISH PLANTATIONS IN AMERICA

Philadelphia, May 14, 1743.

The English are possessed of a long tract of continent, from Nova Scotia to Georgia, extending north and south through different climates, having different soils, producing different plants, mines, and minerals, and capable of different improvements, manufactures, &c.

The first drudgery of settling new colonies, which confines the attention of people to mere necessaries, is now pretty well over; and there are many in every province in circumstances that set them at ease, and afford leisure to cultivate the finer arts and improve the common stock of knowledge. To such of these who are men of speculation, many hints must from time to time arise, many observations occur, which if well examined, pursued, and improved, might produce discoveries to the advantage of some or all of the British plantations, or to the benefit of mankind in general.

But as from the extent of the country such persons are widely separated, and seldom can see and converse or be acquainted with each other, so that many useful particulars remain uncommunicated, die with the discoverers, and are lost to mankind; it is, to remedy this inconvenience for the future, proposed,

That one society be formed of *virtuosi* or ingenious men, residing in the several colonies, to be called *The American Philosophical Society*, who are to maintain a constant correspondence.

That Philadelphia, being the city nearest the centre of the continent colonies, communicating with all of them northward and southward by post, and with all the islands by sea, and having the advantage of a good growing library, be the centre of the Society.

That at Philadelphia there be always at least seven members, viz. a physician, a botanist, a mathematician, a chemist, a mechanician, a geographer, and a general natural philosopher, besides a president, treasurer, and secretary.

That these members meet once a month, or oftener, at their own expense, to communicate to each other their observations and experiments, to receive, read, and consider such letters, communications, or queries as shall be sent from distant members; to direct the dispersing of copies of such communications as are valuable, to other distant members, in order to procure their sentiments thereupon.

That the subjects of the correspondence be: all new-discovered plants, herbs, trees, roots, their virtues, uses, &c.; methods of propagating them, and making such as are useful, but particular to some plantations, more general; improvements of vegetable juices, as ciders, wines, &c.; new methods of curing or preventing diseases; all new-discovered fossils in different countries, as mines, minerals, and quarries; new and useful improvements in any branch of mathematics; new discoveries in chemistry, such as improvements in distillation, brewing, and assaying of ores; new mechanical inventions for saving labour, as mills and carriages, and for raising and conveying of water, draining of meadows, &c.; all new arts, trades, and manufactures, that may be proposed or thought of; surveys, maps, and charts of particular parts of the sea-coasts or inland countries; course and junction of rivers and great roads, situation of lakes and mountains, nature of the soil and productions; new methods of improving the breed of useful animals; introducing other sorts from foreign countries; new improvements in planting, gardening, and clearing land; and all philosophical experiments that let light into the nature of things, tend to increase the power of man over matter, and multiply the conveniences or pleasures of life.

That a correspondence, already begun by some intended members, shall be kept up by this Society with the ROYAL SOCIETY of London, and with the DUBLIN SOCIETY.

That every member shall have abstracts sent him quarterly, of every thing valuable communicated to the Society's Secretary at Philadelphia; free of all charge except the yearly payment hereafter mentioned.

That, by permission of the postmaster-general, such communications pass between the Secretary of the Society and the members, postage-free.

That, for defraying the expense of such experiments as the Society shall judge proper to cause to be made, and other contingent charges for the common good, every member send a piece of eight per annum to the treasurer, at Philadelphia, to form a common stock, to be disbursed by order of the President with the consent of the majority of the members that can conveniently be consulted thereupon, to such persons and places where and by whom the experiments are to be made, and otherwise as there shall be occasion; of which disbursements an exact account shall be kept, and communicated yearly to every member.

That, at the first meetings of the members at Philadelphia, such rules be formed for regulating their meetings and transactions for the general benefit, as shall be convenient and necessary; to be afterwards changed and improved as there shall be occasion, wherein due regard is to be had to the advice of distant members.

That, at the end of every year, collections be made and printed, of such experiments, discoveries, and improvements, as may be thought of public advantage; and that every member have a copy sent him.

That the business and duty of the Secretary be to receive all letters intended for the Society, and lay them before the President and members at their meetings; to abstract, correct, and methodize such papers as require it, and as he shall be directed to do by the President, after they have been considered, debated, and digested in the Society; to enter copies thereof in the Society's books, and make out copies for distant members; to answer their letters by direction of the President, and keep records of all material transactions of the Society.

Benjamin Franklin, the writer of this Proposal, offers himself to serve the Society as their secretary, till they shall be provided with one more capable.

SHAVERS AND TRIMMERS

[From the *Pennsylvania Gazette*, June 23, 1743.]

Alexander Miller, Peruke-maker, in *Second-street*, *Philadelphia*, takes Opportunity to acquaint his Customers, that he intends to leave off the Shaving Business after the 22d of *August* next.

To Mr. Franklin

Sir,

It is a common Observation among the People of *Great Britain* and *Ireland*, that the Barbers are reverenced by the lower Classes of the Inhabitants of those Kingdoms, and in the more remote Parts of those Dominions, as the sole Oracles of Wisdom and Politicks. This at first View seems to be owing to the odd Bent of Mind and peculiar Humour of the People of those Nations: But if we carry this Observation into other Parts, we shall find the same Passion equally prevalent throughout the whole civilized World; and discover in every little Market-Town and Village the 'Squire, the Exciseman, and even the Parson himself, listening with as much Attention to a Barber's News, as they would to the profound Revelations of a Chancellor of the Exchequer, or principal Secretary of State.

Antiquity likewise will furnish us with many Confirmations of the Truth of what I have here asserted. Among the old *Romans* the Barbers were understood to be exactly of the same Complection I have hear described. I shall not trouble your Readers with a Multitude of Examples taken from Antiquity. I shall only quote one Passage in *Horace*, which may serve to illustrate the Whole, and is as follows.

> Strenuus et fortis, causisq; Philippus agendis
> Clarus, ab officiis octavam circiter horam
> Dum redit: atq; foro nimium distare carinas
> Jam grandis natu queritur, conspexit, ut aiunt,
> Adrasum quendam vacuâ tonsoris in umbrâ.
> Cultello proprios purgantem leniter ungues.
>   Hor. Epist. Lib. 1. 7.

By which we may understand, that the *Tonsoris Umbra*, *or* Barber's Shop, was the common Rendezvous of every idle Fellow, who had no more to do than to pair his Nails, talk Politicks, and see, and to be seen.

But to return to the Point in Question. If we would know why the Barbers are so eminent for their Skill in Politicks, it will be necessary to lay aside the Appellation of Barber, and confine ourselves to that of Shaver and Trimmer, which will naturally lead us to consider the near Relation which subsists between Shaving, Trimming and Politicks, from whence we shall discover that Shaving and Trimming is not the Province of the Mechanic alone, but that there are their several Shavers and Trimmers at Court, the Bar, in Church and State.

And first, Shaving or Trimming, in a strict mechanical Sense of the Word, signifies a cutting, sheering, lopping off, and fleecing us of those Excrescencies of Hair, Nails, Flesh, &c., which burthen and disguise our natural Endowments. And is not the same practised over the whole World, by Men of every Rank and Station? Does not the corrupt Minister lop off our Privileges and fleece us of our Money? Do not the Gentlemen of the long Robe find means to cut off those Excrescencies of the Nation, Highwaymen, Thieves and Robbers? And to look into the Church, who has been more notorious for shaving and fleecing, than that Apostle of Apostles, that Preacher of Preachers, the Rev. Mr. G. W.?[29] But I forbear making farther mention of this spiritual Shaver and Trimmer, lest I should affect the Minds of my Readers as deeply as his Preaching has affected their Pockets.

The second Species of Shavers and Trimmers are those who, according to the *English* Phrase, *make the best of a bad Market:* Such as cover (what is called by an eminent Preacher) *their poor Dust* in tinsel Cloaths and gaudy Plumes of Feathers. A Star, and Garter, for Instance, adds Grace, Dignity and Lustre to a gross corpulent Body; and a competent Share of religious Horror thrown into the Countenance, with proper Distortions of the Face, and the Addition of a lank Head of Hair, or a long Wig and Band, commands a most profound Respect to Insolence and Ignorance. The Pageantry of the Church of *Rome* is too well known for me to instance: It will not however be amiss to observe, that his Holiness the Pope, when he has a Mind to fleece his Flock of a good round Sum, sets off the Matter with Briefs, Pardons, Indulgencies, &c. &c. &c.

The Third and last Kind of Shavers and Trimmers are those who (in Scripture Language) are carried away with every Wind of Doctrine. The Vicars of Bray, and those who ex-

change their Principles with the Times, may justly be referred
to this Class. But the most odious Shavers and Trimmers of
this Kind, are a certain set of Females, called (by the polite
World) JILTS. I cannot give my Readers a more perfect Idea
of these than by quoting the following Lines of the Poet:

> Fatally fair they are, and in their Smiles
> The Graces, little Loves, and young Desires inhabit:
> But they are false luxurious in their Appetites,
> And all the Heav'n they hope for, is Variety.
> One Lover to another still succeeds,
> Another and another after that,
> And the last Fool is welcome as the former;
> 'Till having lov'd his Hour out, he gives his Place,
> And mingles with the Herd that went before him.
> > *Rowe's Fair Penitent.*

Lastly, I cannot but congratulate my Neighbours on the
little Favour which is shown to Shavers and Trimmers by the
People of this Province. The Business is at so low an Ebb,
that the worthy Gentleman whose Advertisement I have chosen
for the Motto of my Paper, acquaints us he will leave it off
after the 22d of *August* next. I am of Opinion that all possible
Encouragement ought to be given to Examples of this Kind,
since it is owing to this that so perfect an Understanding is
cultivated among ourselves, and the Chain of Friendship is
brightened and perpetuated with our good Allies, the *Indians*.
The Antipathy which these sage Naturalists bear to Shaving
and Trimming, is well known.

I am, Yours, &c.

TO THE PUBLICK

* * * Causis Philippus agendis
Clarus, * * *
S. P. D.

[From the *Pennsylvania Gazette*, June 30, 1743.]

My Paper on Shavers and Trimmers, in the last *Gazette*, being
generally condemn'd, I at first imputed it to the Want of Taste

and Relish for Pieces of that Force and Beauty, which none but University-bred Gentlemen can *produce:* But upon Advice of Friends, whose Judgment I could depend on, I examined *myself* and to my Shame must confess, that I found myself to be an uncircumcised Jew, whose Excrescencies of Hair, Nails, Flesh, &c. did burthen and disguise my Natural Endowments; but having my Hair and Nails since lopp'd off and shorn, and my fleshly Excrescencies circumcised, I now appear in my wonted Lustre, and expect a speedy Admission among the *Levites*, which I have already the Honour of among the Poets and Natural Philosophers. I have one Thing more to add, which is, That I had no real Animosity against the Person whose Advertisement I made the Motto of my Paper; but (as may appear to all who have been Big with Pieces of this Kind) what I had long on my Mind, I at last unburden'd myself of. O! these JILTS still run in my Mind.

N.B. The Publick perhaps may suppose this Confession forced upon me; but if they *repair* to the P— Pe in Secondstreet, they may see Me, or the Original hereof under my own Hand, and be convinced that this is genuine.

PREFACE TO LOGAN'S TRANSLATION OF "CATO MAJOR"[30]

The Printer to the Reader

This Version of Cicero's Tract *de Senectute*, was made Ten Years since, by the Honourable and Learned Mr. Logan, of this City; undertaken partly for his own Amusement, (being then in his 60th Year, which is said to be nearly the Age of the Author when he wrote it) but principally for the Entertainment of a Neighbour then in his grand Climacteric; and the Notes were drawn up solely on that Neighbour's Account, who was not so well acquainted as himself with the Roman History and Language: Some other Friends, however, (among whom I had the Honour to be ranked) obtained Copies of it in MS. And, as I believed it to be in itself equal at least, if not far preferable to any other Translation of the same Piece extant in our Language, besides the Advantage it has of so many valuable Notes, which at the same time they clear up the Text, are highly instructive and entertaining; I resolved to give it an Impression, being confident that the Publick would not unfavourably receive it.

A certain Freed-man of *Cicero's* is reported to have said of a medicinal Well, discovered in his Time, wonderful for the Virtue of its Waters in restoring Sight to the Aged, That it was a Gift of the bountiful Gods to Men, to the end that all might now have the Pleasure of reading his Master's Works. As that Well, if still in being, is at too great a Distance for our Use, I have, *Gentle Reader*, as thou seest, printed this Piece of *Cicero's* in a large and fair Character, that those who begin to think on the Subject of Old Age, (which seldom happens till their Sight is somewhat impair'd by its Approaches) may not, in Reading, by the *Pain* small Letters give the Eyes, feel the *Pleasure* of the Mind in the least allayed.

I shall add to these few Lines my hearty Wish, that this first Translation of a *Classic* in this *Western World*, may be followed with many others, performed with equal Judgment and Success; and be a happy Omen, that *Philadelphia* shall become the Seat of the *American* Muses.

Philadelphia, Febr. 29. 1743/4.

TO JOHN FRANKLIN, AT BOSTON [31]

Philadelphia [March 10], 1745.

—Our people are extremely impatient to hear of your success at Cape Breton. My shop is filled with thirty inquirers at the coming in of every post. Some wonder the place is not yet taken. I tell them I shall be glad to hear that news three months hence. Fortified towns are hard nuts to crack; and your teeth have not been accustomed to it. Taking strong places is a particular trade, which you have taken up without serving an apprenticeship to it. Armies and veterans need skilful engineers to direct them in their attack. Have you any? But some seem to think forts are as easy taken as snuff. Father Moody's prayers look tolerably modest. You have a fast and prayer day for that purpose; in which I compute five hundred thousand petitions were offered up to the same effect in New England, which added to the petitions of every family morning and evening, multiplied by the number of days since January 25th, make forty-five millions of prayers; which, set against the prayers of a few priests in the garrison, to the Virgin Mary, give a vast balance in your favour.

If you do not succeed, I fear I shall have but an indifferent opinion of Presbyterian prayers in such cases, as long as I live. Indeed, in attacking strong towns I should have more dependence on *works*, than on *faith;* for, like the kingdom of heaven, they are to be taken by force and violence; and in a French garrison I suppose there are devils of that kind, that they are not to be cast out by prayers and fasting, unless it be by their own fasting for want of provisions. I believe there is Scripture in what I have wrote, but I cannot adorn the margin with quotations, having a bad memory, and no Concordance at hand; besides no more time than to subscribe myself, &c.

B. Franklin.

PREFACE TO POOR RICHARD, 1746

Who is *Poor Richard?* People oft enquire,
Where lives? What is he? never yet the nigher.
Somewhat to ease your Curiositee,
Take these slight Sketches of my Dame and me.
    Thanks to kind Readers and a careful Wife,
With plenty bless'd, I lead an easy Life;
My business Writing; less to drain the Mead,
Or crown the barren Hill with useful Shade;
In the smooth Glebe to see the Plowshare worn,
And fill the Granary with needful Corn.
Press nectareous Cyder from my loaded Trees,
Print the sweet Butter, turn the Drying Cheese.
Some Books we read, tho' few there are that hit

The happy Point where Wisdom joins with Wit;
That set fair Virtue naked to our View,
And teach us what is *decent*, what is *true*.
The Friend sincere, and honest Man, with Joy
Treating or treated oft our Time employ.
Our Table next, Meals temperate; and our Door
Op'ning spontaneous to the bashful Poor.
Free from the bitter Rage of Party Zeal,
All those we love who seek the publick Weal.
    Nor blindly follow Superstitious Love,
Which cheats deluded Mankind o'er and o'er,
Not over righteous, quite beyond the Rule,
Conscience perplext by every canting Tool.
Nor yet when Folly hides the dubious Line,
When Good and Bad the blended Colours join:
Rush indiscreetly down the dangerous Steep,
And plunge uncertain in the darksome Deep.
Cautious, if right; if wrong resolv'd to part
The Inmate Snake that folds about the Heart.
Observe the *Mean*, the *Motive*, and the *End*,
Mending ourselves, or striving still to mend.
Our Souls sincere, our Purpose fair and free,
Without Vain Glory or Hypocrisy:
Thankful if well; if ill, we kiss the Rod;
Resign with Hope, and put our Trust in God.

THE SPEECH OF POLLY BAKER [32]

[Printed in the *Gentleman's Magazine*, April, 1747.]

The Speech of Miss Polly Baker before a Court of Judicature, at Connecticut near Boston in New England; where she was prosecuted the fifth time, for having a Bastard Child: Which influenced the Court to dispense with her Punishment, and which induced one of her Judges to marry her the next Day— by whom she had fifteen Children.

"May it please the honourable bench to indulge me in a few

words: I am a poor, unhappy woman, who have no money to fee lawyers to plead for me, being hard put to it to get a living. I shall not trouble your honours with long speeches; for I have not the presumption to expect that you may, by any means, be prevailed on to deviate in your Sentence from the law, in my favour. All I humbly hope is, that your honours would charitably move the governor's goodness on my behalf, that my fine may be remitted. This is the fifth time, gentlemen, that I have been dragg'd before your court on the same account; twice I have paid heavy fines, and twice have been brought to publick punishment, for want of money to pay those fines. This may have been agreeable to the laws, and I don't dispute it; but since laws are sometimes unreasonable in themselves, and therefore repealed; and others bear too hard on the subject in particular circumstances, and therefore there is left a power somewhere to dispense with the execution of them; I take the liberty to say, that I think this law, by which I am punished, both unreasonable in itself, and particularly severe with regard to me, who have always lived an inoffensive life in the neighbourhood where I was born, and defy my enemies (if I have any) to say I ever wrong'd any man, woman, or child. Abstracted from the law, I cannot conceive (may it please your honours) what the nature of my offense is. I have brought five fine children into the world, at the risque of my life; I have maintain'd them well by my own industry, without burthening the township, and would have done it better, if it had not been for the heavy charges and fines I have paid. Can it be a crime (in the nature of things, I mean) to add to the king's subjects, in a new country, that really wants people? I own it, I should think it rather a praiseworthy than a punishable action. I have debauched no other woman's husband, nor enticed any other youth; these things I never was charg'd with; nor has any one the least cause of complaint against me, unless, perhaps, the ministers of justice, because I have had children without being married, by which they have missed a wedding fee. But can this be a fault of mine? I appeal to your honours. You are pleased to allow I don't want sense; but I must be stupified to the last degree, not to prefer the honourable state of wedlock to the condition I have lived in. I always was, and still am willing to enter into it; and doubt not my behaving well in it, having all the industry, frugality, fertility, and skill in economy appertaining to a good wife's character. I defy any one to say I ever refused an offer of that sort: on the contrary, I readily consented to the only proposal of marriage that ever was made me, which was when I was a virgin, but too easily confiding in the person's sincerity that made it, I unhappily lost my honour by trusting to his; for he got me with child, and then forsook me.

"That very person, you all know, he is now become a magistrate of this country; and I had hopes he would have appeared this day on the bench, and have endeavoured to moderate the Court in my favour; then I should have scorn'd to have mentioned it; but I must now complain of it, as unjust and unequal, that my betrayer and undoer, the first cause of all my faults and miscarriages (if they must be deemed such), should be advanced to honour and power in this government that punishes my misfortunes with stripes and infamy. I should be told, 'tis like, that were there no act of Assembly in the case, the precepts of religion are violated by my transgressions. If mine is a religious offense, leave it to religious punishments. You have already excluded me from the comforts of your church communion. Is not that sufficient? You believe I have offended heaven, and must suffer eternal fire: Will not that be sufficient? What need is there then of your additional fines and whipping? I own I do not think as you do, for, if I thought what you call a sin was really such, I could not presumptuously commit it. But, how can it be believed that heaven is angry at my having children, when to the little done by me towards it, God has been pleased to add his divine skill and admirable workmanship in the formation of their bodies, and crowned the whole by furnishing them with rational and immortal souls?

"Forgive me, gentlemen, if I talk a little extravagantly on these matters; I am no divine, but if you, gentlemen, must be making laws, do not turn natural and useful actions into crimes by your prohibitions. But take into your wise consideration the great and growing number of batchelors in the country, many of whom, from the mean fear of the expences of a family, have never sincerely and honourably courted a woman in their lives; and by their manner of living leave unproduced (which is little better than murder) hundreds of their posterity to the thousandth generation. Is not this a greater offense against the publick good than mine? Compel them, then, by law, either to marriage, or to pay double the fine of fornication every year. What must poor young women do, whom customs and nature forbid to solicit the men, and who cannot force themselves upon husbands, when the laws take no care to provide them any, and yet severely punish them if they do their duty without them; the duty of the first and great command of nature and nature's God, *encrease and multiply;* a duty, from the steady performance of which nothing has been able to deter me, but for its sake I have hazarded the loss of the publick esteem, and have frequently endured publick disgrace and punishment; and therefore ought, in my humble opinion, instead of a whipping, to have a statue erected to my memory."

PREFACE TO POOR RICHARD, 1747

Courteous Reader,

This is the 15th Time I have entertain'd thee with my annual Productions; I hope to thy Profit as well as mine. For besides the astronomical Calculations, and other Things usually contain'd in Almanacks, which have their daily Use indeed while the Year continues, but then become of no Value, I have constantly interspers'd *moral* Sentences, *prudent* Maxims, and *wise* Sayings, many of them containing *much good Sense* in *very few* Words, and therefore apt to leave *strong* and *lasting* Impressions on the Memory of young Persons, whereby they may receive Benefit as long as they live, when both Almanack and Almanack-maker have been long thrown by and forgotten. If I now and then insert a Joke or two, that seem to have little in them, my Apology *is* that such may have their Use, since perhaps for their Sake light airy Minds peruse the rest, and so are struck by somewhat of more Weight and Moment. The Verses on the Heads of the Months are also generally design'd to have the same Tendency. I need not tell thee that not many of them are of my own Making. If thou hast any Judgment in Poetry, thou wilt easily discern the Workman from the Bungler. I know as well as thee, that I am no *Poet born;* and it is a Trade I never learnt, nor indeed could learn. *If I make Verses, 'tis in Spight—of Nature and my Stars, I write.* Why then should I give my Readers *bad Lines* of my own, when *good Ones* of other People's are so plenty? 'Tis methinks a poor Excuse for the bad Entertainment of Guests, that the Food we set before them, tho' coarse and ordinary, *is of one's own Raising, off one's own Plantation,* &c. when there is Plenty of what is ten times better, to be had in the Market.—On the contrary, I assure ye, my Friends, that I have procur'd the best I could for ye, and *much Good may't do ye.* . . .

I am thy poor Friend, to serve thee,

R. SAUNDERS.

TO PETER COLLINSON

Philad^a, Augt 14, 1747.

SIR

I have lately written two long Letters to you on the Subject of Electricity, one by the Governor's Vessel, the other per Mesnard. On some further Experiments since I have observ'd a Phenomenon or two, that I cannot at present account for on the Principle laid down in those Letters, and am therefore become a little diffident of my Hypothesis, and asham'd that I have express'd myself in so positive a manner. In going on with these Experiments how many pretty Systems do we build which we soon find ourselves oblig'd to destroy! If there is no other Use discover'd of Electricity this however is something considerable, that it may *help to make a vain man humble.*

I must now request that you would not Expose those Letters; or if you communicate them to any Friends you would at least conceal my Name. I have not Time to add but that I am, Sir,

Your obliged and most hum^e Servt

B. FRANKLIN.

PREFACE TO POOR RICHARD IMPROVED, 1748

KIND READER

The favourable Reception my annual Labours have met with from the Publick these 15 Years past, has engaged me in Gratitude to endeavour some Improvements of my Almanack. And since my Friend *Taylor* is no more, whose *Ephemerides* so long and so agreeably serv'd and entertain'd these Provinces, I have taken the Liberty to imitate his well-known Method, and give two Pages for each Month; which affords me Room for several valuable Additions, as will best appear on Inspection and Comparison with former Almanacks. Yet I have not so far follow'd his Method, as not to continue my own when I thought it preferable; and thus my Book is increas'd to a Size beyond his, and contains much more Matter.

> Hail Night serene! thro' Thee where'er we turn
> Our wond'ring Eyes, Heav'n's Lamps profusely burn;
> And Stars unnumber'd all the Sky adorn.
> But lo!—what's that I see appear?
> It seems far off a pointed flame;
> From Earthwards too the shining Meteor came:
> How swift it climbs th' etherial Space!
> And now it traverses each Sphere,
> And seems some knowing Mind, familiar to the Place,
> Dame, hand my Glass, the longest, strait prepare;
> 'Tis He—'tis TAYLOR's Soul, that travels there.
> O stay! thou happy Spirit, stay,
> And lead me on thro' all th' unbeaten Wilds of Day;
> Where Planets in pure Streams of Ether driven,
> Swim thro' the blue Expanse of Heav'n.
> There let me, thy Companion, stray
> From Orb to Orb, and now behold

Unnumber'd Suns, all Seas of molten Gold,
And trace each Comet's wandring Way.—

Souse down into Prose again, my Muse; for Poetry's no more
thy Element, than Air is that of the Flying-Fish; whose Flights,
like thine, are therefore always short and heavy.—

ADVICE TO A YOUNG TRADESMAN
[1748]

TO MY FRIEND, A. B.:

As you have desired it of me, I write the following hints,
which have been of service to me, and may, if observed, be so
to you.

Remember, that *time* is money. He that can earn ten shillings
a day by his labour, and goes abroad, or sits idle, one half of
that day, though he spends but sixpence during his diversion or
idleness, ought not to reckon *that* the only expense; he has
really spent, or rather thrown away, five shillings besides.

Remember, that *credit* is money. If a man lets his money
lie in my hands after it is due, he gives me the interest, or so
much as I can make of it during that time. This amounts to a
considerable sum where a man has good and large credit, and
makes good use of it.

Remember, that money is of the prolific, generating nature.
Money can beget money, and its offspring can beget more, and
so on. Five shillings turned is six, turned again it is seven and
three-pence, and so on till it becomes an hundred pounds. The
more there is of it, the more it produces every turning, so that
the profits rise quicker and quicker. He that kills a breeding
sow, destroys all her offspring to the thousandth generation.
He that murders a crown, destroys all that it might have produced, even scores of pounds.

Remember, that six pounds a year is but a groat a day. For
this little sum (which may be daily wasted either in time or
expense unperceived) a man of credit may, on his own security,
have the constant possession and use of an hundred pounds.

So much in stock, briskly turned by an industrious man, produces great advantage.

Remember this saying, *The good paymaster is lord of another man's purse.* He that is known to pay punctually and exactly to the time he promises, may at any time, and on any occasion, raise all the money his friends can spare. This is sometimes of great use. After industry and frugality, nothing contributes more to the raising of a young man in the world than punctuality and justice in all his dealings; therefore never keep borrowed money an hour beyond the time you promised, lest a disappointment shut up your friend's purse for ever.

The most trifling actions that affect a man's credit are to be regarded. The sound of your hammer at five in the morning, or nine at night, heard by a creditor, makes him easy six months longer; but, if he sees you at a billiard-table, or hears your voice at a tavern, when you should be at work, he sends for his money the next day; demands it, before he can receive it, in a lump.

It shows, besides, that you are mindful of what you owe; it makes you appear a careful as well as an honest man, and that still increases your credit.

Beware of thinking all your own that you possess, and of living accordingly. It is a mistake that many people who have credit fall into. To prevent this, keep an exact account for some time, both of your expenses and your income. If you take the pains at first to mention particulars, it will have this good effect: you will discover how wonderfully small, trifling expenses mount up to large sums, and will discern what might have been, and may for the future be saved, without occasioning any great inconvenience.

In short, the way to wealth, if you desire it, is as plain as the way to market. It depends chiefly on two words, *industry* and *frugality;* that is, waste neither *time* nor *money*, but make the best use of both. Without industry and frugality nothing will do, and with them every thing. He that gets all he can honestly, and saves all he gets (necessary expenses excepted), will certainly become *rich*, if that Being who governs the world, to whom all should look for a blessing on their honest endeavours, doth not, in his wise providence, otherwise determine.

AN OLD TRADESMAN.

TO GEORGE WHITEFIELD

Philadelphia, July 6, 1749.

DEAR SIR

Since your being in England, I have received two of your favours and a box of books to be disposed of. It gives me great pleasure to hear of your welfare and that you purpose soon to return to America.

We have no news here worth writing to you. The affair of the building remains in *statu quo*, there having been no new application to the Assembly about it, or anything done in consequence of the former.

I have received no money on your account from Mr. Thanklin, or from Boston. Mrs. Read and your other friends here, in general, are well, and will rejoice to see you again.

I am glad to hear that you have frequent opportunities of preaching among the great. If you can gain them to a good and exemplary life, wonderful changes will follow in the manners of the lower ranks; for *ad exemplum regis*, etc. On this principle, Confucius, the famous Eastern reformer, proceeded. When he saw his country sunk in vice, and wickedness of all kinds triumphant, he applied himself first to the grandees; and having, by his doctrine, won *them* to the cause of virtue, the commons followed in multitudes. The mode has a wonderful influence on mankind; and there are numbers who, perhaps, fear less the being in hell, than out of the fashion. Our most western reformations began with the ignorant mob; and when numbers of them were gained, interest and party views drew in the wise and great. Where both methods can be used, reformations are likely to be more speedy. O that some method could be found to make them lasting! He who discovers that will, in my opinion, deserve more, ten thousand times, than the inventor of the longitude.

My wife and family join in the most cordial salutations to you and good Mrs. Whitefield.

I am, dear Sir, your very affectionate friend, and most obliged humble Servant

BENJAMIN FRANKLIN.

PROPOSALS RELATING TO THE EDUCATION OF YOUTH IN PENSILVANIA

PHILADELPHIA: PRINTED IN THE YEAR, MDCCXLIX [33]

Advertisement to the Reader.

It has long been regretted as a Misfortune to the Youth of this Province, that we have no ACADEMY, in which they might receive the Accomplishments of a regular Education. The following Paper of Hints towards forming a Plan for that Purpose, is so far approv'd by some publick-spirited Gentlemen, to whom it has been privately communicated, that they have directed a Number of Copies to be made by the Press, and properly distributed, in order to obtain the Sentiments and Advice of Men of Learning, Understanding, and Experience in these Matters; and have determined to use their Interest and best Endeavours, to have the Scheme, when compleated, carried gradually into Execution; in which they have Reason to believe they shall have the hearty Concurrence and Assistance of many who are Wellwishers to their Country. Those who incline to favour the Design with their Advice, either as to the Parts of Learning to be taught, the Order of Study, the Method of Teaching, the Œconomy of the School, or any other Matter of Importance to the Success of the Undertaking, are desired to communicate their Sentiments as soon as may be, by Letter directed to B. FRANKLIN, *Printer*, in PHILADELPHIA."

PROPOSALS

The good Education of Youth has been esteemed by wise Men in all Ages, as the surest Foundation of the Happiness both of private Families and of Commonwealths. Almost all

Governments have therefore made it a principal Object of their Attention, to establish and endow with proper Revenues, such Seminaries of Learning, as might supply the succeeding Age with Men qualified to serve the Publick with Honour to themselves, and to their Country.

Many of the first Settlers of these Provinces were Men who had received a good Education in *Europe*, and to their Wisdom and good Management we owe much of our present Prosperity. But their Hands were full, and they could not do all Things. The present Race are not thought to be generally of equal Ability: For though the *American* Youth are allow'd not to want Capacity; yet the best Capacities require Cultivation, it being truly with them, as with the best Ground, which unless well tilled and sowed with profitable Seed, produces only ranker Weeds.

That we may obtain the Advantages arising from an Increase of Knowledge, and prevent as much as may be the mischievous Consequences that would attend a general Ignorance among us, the following *Hints* are offered towards forming a Plan for the Education of the Youth of *Pennsylvania*, viz.

It is propos'd,

That some Persons of Leisure and publick Spirit apply for a CHARTER, by which they may be incorporated, with Power to erect an ACADEMY for the Education of Youth, to govern the same, provide Masters, make Rules, receive Donations, purchase Lands, etc., and to add to their Number, from Time to Time such other Persons as they shall judge suitable.

That the Members of the Corporation make it their Pleasure, and in some Degree their Business, to visit the Academy often, encourage and countenance the Youth, countenance and assist the Masters, and by all Means in their Power advance the Usefulness and Reputation of the Design; that they look on the Students as in some Sort their Children, treat them with Familiarity and Affection, and, when they have behav'd well, and gone through their Studies, and are to enter the World, zealously unite, and make all the Interest that can be made to establish them, whether in Business, Offices, Marriages, or any other Thing for their Advantage, preferably to all other Persons whatsoever even of equal Merit.

And if Men may, and frequently do, catch such a Taste for cultivating Flowers, for Planting, Grafting, Inoculating, and the like, as to despise all other Amusements for their Sake, why may not we expect they should acquire a Relish for that *more useful* Culture of young Minds. *Thompson* says,

> " 'Tis Joy to see the human Blossoms blow,
> When infant Reason grows apace, and calls
> For the kind Hand of an assiduous Care.
> Delightful Task! to rear the tender Thought,
> To teach the young Idea how to shoot;
> To pour the fresh Instruction o'er the Mind,
> To breathe th' enliv'ning Spirit, and to fix
> The generous Purpose in the glowing Breast."

That a House be provided for the ACADEMY, if not in the Town, not many Miles from it; the Situation high and dry, and if it may be, not far from a River, having a Garden, Orchard, Meadow, and a Field or two.

That the House be furnished with a Library (if in the Country, if in the Town, the Town Libraries may serve) with Maps of all Countries, Globes, some mathematical Instruments, an Apparatus for Experiments in Natural Philosophy, and for Mechanics; Prints, of all Kinds, Prospects, Buildings, Machines, &c.

That the Rector be a Man of good Understanding, good Morals, diligent and patient, learn'd in the Languages and Sciences, and a correct pure Speaker and Writer of the *English* Tongue; to have such Tutors under him as shall be necessary.

That the boarding Scholars diet together, plainly, temperately, and frugally.

That, to keep them in Health, and to strengthen and render active their Bodies, they be frequently exercis'd in Running, Leaping, Wrestling, and Swimming, &c.

That they have peculiar Habits to distinguish them from other Youth, if the Academy be in or near the Town; for this,

among other Reasons, that their Behaviour may be the better
observed.

As to their Studies, it would be well if they could be
taught *every Thing* that is useful, and *every Thing* that is ornamental: But Art is long, and their Time is short. It is therefore propos'd that they learn those Things that are likely to be
most useful and *most ornamental*. Regard being had to the
several Professions for which they are intended.

All should be taught to write a *fair Hand*, and swift, as that
is useful to All. And with it may be learnt something of
Drawing, by Imitation of Prints, and some of the first Principles of Perspective.

Arithmetick, Accounts, and some of the first Principles of
Geometry and *Astronomy*.

The *English* Language might be taught by Grammar; in
which some of our best Writers, as *Tillotson, Addison, Pope,
Algernoon Sidney, Cato's Letters,* &c., should be Classicks: the
Stiles principally to be cultivated, being the *clear* and the
concise. Reading should also be taught, and pronouncing,
properly, distinctly, emphatically; not with an even Tone,
which *under-does*, nor a theatrical, which *over-does* Nature.

To form their Stile they should be put on Writing Letters
to each other, making Abstracts of what they read; or writing
the same Things in their own Words; telling or writing Stories
lately read, in their own Expressions. All to be revis'd and
corrected by the Tutor, who should give his Reasons, and
explain the Force and Import of Words, &c.

To form their Pronunciation, they may be put on making
Declamations, repeating Speeches, delivering Orations, &c.;
The Tutor assisting at the Rehearsals, teaching, advising,
correcting their Accent, &c.

But if History be made a constant Part of their Reading,
such as the Translations of the *Greek* and *Roman* Historians,
and the modern Histories of ancient *Greece* and *Rome*, &c. may
not almost all Kinds of useful Knowledge be that Way introduc'd to Advantage, and with Pleasure to the Student? As
Geography, by reading with Maps, and being required

to point out the Places *where* the greatest Actions were done, to give their old and new Names, with the Bounds, Situation, Extent of the Countries concern'd, &c.

CHRONOLOGY, by the Help of *Helvicus* or some other Writer of the Kind, who will enable them to tell *when* those Events happened; what Princes were Cotemporaries, what States or famous Men flourish'd about that Time, &c. The several principal Epochas to be first well fix'd in their Memories.

ANTIENT CUSTOMS, religious and civil, being frequently mentioned in History, will give Occasion for explaining them; in which the Prints of Medals, Basso-Relievos, and antient Monuments will greatly assist.

MORALITY, by descanting and making continual Observations on the Causes of the Rise or Fall of any Man's Character, Fortune, Power &c. mention'd in History; the Advantages of Temperance, Order, Frugality, Industry, Perseverance &c. &c. Indeed the general natural Tendency of Reading good History must be, to fix in the Minds of Youth deep Impressions of the Beauty and Usefulness of Virtue of all Kinds, Publick Spirit, Fortitude, &c.

History will show the wonderful Effects of ORATORY, in governing, turning and leading great Bodies of Mankind, Armies, Cities, Nations. When the Minds of Youth are struck with Admiration at this, then is the Time to give them the Principles of that Art, which they will study with Taste and Application. Then they may be made acquainted with the best Models among the antients, their Beauties being particularly pointed out to them. Modern Political Oratory being chiefly performed by the Pen and Press, its Advantages over the Antient in some Respects are to be shown; as that its Effects are more extensive, more lasting, &c.

History will also afford frequent Opportunities of showing the Necessity of a *Publick Religion*, from its Usefulness to the Publick; the Advantage of a Religious Character among private Persons; the Mischiefs of Superstition, &c. and the Excellency of the CHRISTIAN RELIGION above all others antient or modern.

History will also give Occasion to expatiate on the Advantage of Civil Orders and Constitutions; how Men and their Properties are protected by joining in Societies and establishing Government; their Industry encouraged and rewarded, Arts invented, and Life made more comfortable: The Advantages of *Liberty*, Mischiefs of *Licentiousness*, Benefits arising from good Laws and a due Execution of Justice, &c. Thus may the first Principles of sound *Politicks* be fix'd in the Minds of Youth.

On *Historical* Occasions, Questions of Right and Wrong, Justice and Injustice, will naturally arise, and may be put to Youth, which they may debate in Conversation and in Writing. When they ardently desire Victory, for the Sake of the Praise attending it, they will begin to feel the Want, and be sensible of the Use of *Logic*, or the Art of Reasoning to *discover* Truth, and of Arguing to *defend* it, and *convince* Adversaries. This would be the Time to acquaint them with the Principles of that Art. Grotius, Puffendorff, and some other Writers of the same Kind, may be used on these Occasions to decide their Disputes. Publick Disputes warm the Imagination, whet the Industry, and strengthen the natural Abilities.

When Youth are told, that the Great Men whose Lives and Actions they read in History, spoke two of the best Languages that ever were, the most expressive, copious, beautiful; and that the finest Writings, the most correct Compositions, the most perfect Productions of human Wit and Wisdom, are in those Languages, which have endured Ages, and will endure while there are Men; that no Translation can do them Justice, or give the Pleasure found in Reading the Originals; that those Languages contain all Science; that one of them is become almost universal, being the Language of Learned Men in all Countries; that to understand them is a distinguishing Ornament, &c. they may be thereby made desirous of learning those Languages, and their Industry sharpen'd in the Acquisition of them. All intended for Divinity, should be taught the *Latin* and *Greek;* for Physick, the *Latin*, *Greek*, and *French;* for Law, the *Latin* and *French;* Merchants, the *French*, *German*, and

Spanish: And though all should not be compell'd to learn *Latin, Greek,* or the modern foreign Languages; yet none that have an ardent Desire to learn them should be refused; their *English,* Arithmetick and other Studies absolutely necessary, being at the same Time not neglected.

If the new *Universal History* were also read, it would give a *connected* Idea of human Affairs, so far as it goes, which should be follow'd by the best modern Histories, particularly of our Mother Country; then of these Colonies; which should be accompanied with Observations on their Rise, Encrease, Use to *Great Britain,* Encouragements, Discouragements, etc. the Means to make them flourish, secure their Liberties, &c.

With the History of Men, Times, and Nations, should be read at proper Hours or Days, some of the best *Histories of Nature,* which would not only be delightful to Youth, and furnish them with Matter for their Letters, &c. as well as other History; but afterwards of great Use to them, whether they are Merchants, Handicrafts, or Divines; enabling the first the better to understand many Commodities, Drugs, &c; the second to improve his Trade or Handicraft by new Mixtures, Materials, &c., and the last to adorn his Discourses by beautiful Comparisons, and strengthen them by new Proofs of Divine Providence. The Conversation of all will be improved by it, as Occasions frequently occur of making Natural Observations, which are instructive, agreeable, and entertaining in almost all Companies. *Natural History* will also afford Opportunities of introducing many Observations, relating to the Preservation of Health, which may be afterwards of great Use. *Arbuthnot* on Air and *Aliment, Sanctorius* on Perspiration, *Lemery* on Foods, and some others, may now be read, and a very little Explanation will make them sufficiently intelligible to Youth.

While they are reading Natural History, might not a little *Gardening, Planting, Grafting, Inoculating,* etc., be taught and practised; and now and then Excursions made to the neighbouring Plantations of the best Farmers, their Methods observ'd and reason'd upon for the Information of Youth? The

Improvement of Agriculture being useful to all, and Skill in
it no Disparagement to any.

The History of *Commerce*, of the Invention of Arts, Rise of
Manufactures, Progress of Trade, Change of its Seats, with the
Reasons, Causes, &c., may also be made entertaining to Youth,
and will be useful to all. And this, with the Accounts in other
History of the prodigious Force and Effect of Engines and
Machines used in War, will naturally introduce a Desire to be
instructed in *Mechanicks*, and to be inform'd of the Principles
of that Art by which weak Men perform such Wonders,
Labour is sav'd, Manufactures expedited, &c. This will be the
Time to show them Prints of antient and modern Machines, to
explain them, to let them be copied, and to give Lectures in
Mechanical Philosophy.

With the whole should be constantly inculcated and cultivated, that *Benignity of Mind*, which shows itself in *searching
for* and *seizing* every Opportunity *to serve* and *to oblige;* and is
the Foundation of what is called GOOD BREEDING; highly useful to the Possessor, and most agreeable to all.

The Idea of what is *true Merit* should also be often presented to Youth, explain'd and impress'd on their Minds, as
consisting in an *Inclination* join'd with an *Ability* to serve Mankind, one's Country, Friends and Family; which *Ability* is
(with the Blessing of God) to be acquir'd or greatly encreas'd
by *true Learning;* and should indeed be the great *Aim* and
End of all Learning.

IDEA OF THE ENGLISH SCHOOL

Sketch'd out for the Consideration of the Trustees of
the Philadelphia Academy [1751][34]

It is expected that every Scholar to be admitted into this
School, be at least able to pronounce and divide the Syllables
in Reading, and to write a legible Hand. None to be receiv'd
that are under   Years of Age.

FIRST OR LOWEST CLASS

Let the first Class learn the *English Grammar* Rules, and at the same time let particular Care be taken to improve them in *Orthography*. Perhaps the latter is best done by *Pairing* the Scholars, two of those nearest equal in their Spelling to be put together; let these strive for Victory, each propounding Ten Words every Day to the other to be spelt. He that spells truly most of the other's Words, is Victor for that Day; he that is Victor most Days in a Month, to obtain a Prize, a pretty neat Book of some Kind useful in their future Studies. This Method fixes the Attention of Children extreamly to the Orthography of Words, and makes them good Spellers very early. 'Tis a Shame for a Man to be so ignorant of this little Art, in his own Language, as to be perpetually confounding Words of like Sound and different Significations; the Consciousness of which Defect, makes some Men, otherwise of good Learning and Understanding, averse to Writing even a common Letter.

Let the Pieces read by the Scholars in this Class be short, such as *Croxall's* Fables,[35] and little Stories. In giving the Lesson, let it be read to them; let the Meaning of the difficult Words in it be explained to them, and let them con it over by themselves before they are called to read to the Master, or Usher; who is to take particular Care that they do not read too fast, and that they duly observe the Stops and Pauses. A Vocabulary of the most usual difficult Words might be formed for their Use, with Explanations; and they might daily get a few of those Words and Explanations by Heart, which would a little exercise their Memories; or at least they might write a Number of them in a small Book for the Purpose, which would help to fix the Meaning of those Words in their Minds, and at the same Time furnish every one with a little Dictionary for his future Use.

THE SECOND CLASS

to be taught Reading with Attention, and with proper Modulations of the Voice, according to the Sentiments and Subject. Some short Pieces, not exceeding the Length of a *Spectator*, to be given this Class as Lessons (and some of the easier *Spectators* would be very suitable for the Purpose.) These Lessons might be given over Night as Tasks, the Scholars to study them against the Morning. Let it then be required of them to give an Account, first of the Parts of Speech, and Construction of one or two Sentences; this will oblige them to recur frequently to their Grammar, and fix its principal Rules in their Memory. Next of the *Intention* of the Writer, or the *Scope* of the Piece; the Meaning of each Sentence, and of every uncommon Word. This would early acquaint them with the Meaning and Force of Words, and give them that most necessary Habit, of Reading with Attention.

The Master then to read the Piece with the proper Modulations of Voice, due Emphasis, and suitable Action, where Action is required; and put the Youth on imitating his Manner.

Where the Author has us'd an Expression not the best, let it be pointed out; and let his Beauties be particularly remarked to the Youth.

Let the Lessons for Reading be varied, that the Youth may be made acquainted with good Stiles of all Kinds in Prose and Verse, and the proper Manner of reading each Kind. Sometimes a well-told Story, a Piece of a Sermon, a General's Speech to his Soldiers, a Speech in a Tragedy, some Part of a Comedy, an Ode, a Satyr, a Letter, Blank Verse, Hudibrastick, Heroic, &c. But let such Lessons for Reading be chosen, as contain some useful Instruction, whereby the Understandings or Morals of the Youth, may at the same Time be improv'd.

It is requir'd that they should first study and understand the Lessons, before they are put upon reading them properly, to which End each Boy should have an *English* Dictionary, to help him over Difficulties. When our Boys read *English* to us, we are apt to imagine *they* understand what *they* read, because *we* do, and because 'tis their Mother Tongue. But they often read as Parrots speak, knowing little or nothing of the Meaning. And it is impossible a Reader should give the due Modulation to his Voice, and pronounce properly, unless his Understanding goes before his Tongue, and makes him Master of the Sentiment. Accustoming Boys to read aloud what they do not first understand, is the Cause of those even set Tones so common among Readers, which when they have once got a Habit of using, they find so difficult to correct: By which Means, among Fifty Readers, we scarcely find a good One. For want of good Reading, Pieces publish'd with a View to influence the Minds of Men for their own or the publick Benefit, lose Half their Force. Were there but one good Reader in a Neighbourhood, a publick Orator might be heard throughout a Nation with the same Advantages, and have the same Effect on his Audience, as if they stood within the Reach of his Voice.

THE THIRD CLASS

to be taught Speaking properly and gracefully, which is near of Kin to good Reading, and naturally follows it in the Studies of Youth. Let the Scholars of this Class begin with learning the Elements of Rhetoric from some short System, so as to be able to give an Account of the most usual Tropes and Figures. Let all their bad Habits of Speaking, all Offences against good Grammar, all corrupt or foreign Accents, and all improper Phrases, be pointed out to them. Short Speeches from the *Roman*, or other History, or from our *Parliamentary Debates*, might be got by heart, and deliver'd with the proper Action, &c. Speeches and Scenes in our best Tragedies and Comedies (avoiding every Thing that could injure the Morals of Youth) might likewise be got by Rote, and the Boys exercis'd in delivering or acting them; great Care being taken to form their Manner after the truest Models.

For their farther Improvement, and a little to vary their Studies, let them now begin to read *History*, after having got by Heart a short Table of the principal Epochas in Chronology. They may begin with *Rollin's Antient and Roman Histories*, and proceed at proper Hours as they go thro' the subsequent Classes, with the best Histories of our own Nation and Colonies. Let Emulation be excited among the Boys by giving, Weekly, little Prizes, or other small Encouragements to those who are able to give the best Account of what they have read, as to Times,

Places, Names of Persons, &c. This will make them read with Attention, and imprint the History well in their Memories. In remarking on the History, the Master will have fine Opportunities of instilling Instruction of various Kinds, and improving the Morals as well as the Understandings of Youth.

The Natural and Mechanic History contain'd in the *Spectacle de la Nature*, might also be begun in this Class, and continued thro' the subsequent Classes by other Books of the same Kind: For next to the Knowledge of *Duty*, this Kind of Knowledge is certainly the most useful, as well as the most entertaining. The Merchant may thereby be enabled better to understand many Commodities in Trade; the Handicraftsman to improve his Business by new Instruments, Mixtures and Materials; and frequently Hints are given of new Manufactures, or new Methods of improving Land, that may be set on foot greatly to the Advantage of a Country.

THE FOURTH CLASS

to be taught Composition. Writing one's own Language well, is the next necessary Accomplishment after good Speaking. 'Tis the Writing-Master's Business to take Care that the Boys make fair Characters, and place them straight and even in the Lines: But to *form their Stile*, and even to take Care that the Stops and Capitals are properly disposed, is the Part of the *English* Master. The Boys should be put on Writing Letters to each other on any common Occurrences, and on various Subjects, imaginary Business, &c., containing little Stories, Accounts of their late Reading, what Parts of Authors please them, and why; Letters of Congratulation, of Compliment, of Request, of Thanks, of Recommendation, of Admonition, of Consolation, of Expostulation, Excuse, &c. In these they should be taught to express themselves clearly, concisely, and naturally, without affected Words or high-flown Phrases. All their Letters to pass through the Master's Hand, who is to point out the Faults, advise the Corrections, and commend what he finds right. Some of the best Letters published in our own Language, as *Sir William Temple's*, those of *Pope*, and his Friends, and some others, might be set before the Youth as Models, their Beauties pointed out and explained by the Master, the Letters themselves transcrib'd by the Scholar.

Dr. Johnson's *Ethices Elementa*,[36] or First Principles of Morality, may now be read by the Scholars, and explain'd by the Master, to lay a solid Foundation of Virtue and Piety in their Minds. And as this Class continues the Reading of History, let them now at proper Hours receive some farther Instruction in Chronology, and in that Part of Geography (from the Mathematical Master), which is necessary to understand the Maps and Globes. They should also be acquainted with the modern Names of the Places they find mention'd in antient Writers. The Exercises of good Reading, and proper Speaking, still continued at suitable Times.

FIFTH CLASS

To improve the Youth in *Composition*, they may now, besides continuing to write Letters, begin to write little Essays in Prose, and sometimes in Verse, not to make them Poets, but for this Reason, that nothing acquaints a Lad so speedily with Variety of Expression, as the Necessity of finding such Words and Phrases as will suit with the Measure, Sound, and Rhime of Verse, and at the same time well express the Sentiment. These Essays should all pass under the Master's Eye, who will point out their Faults, and put the Writer on correcting them. Where the Judgment is not ripe enough for forming new Essays, let the Sentiments of a *Spectator* be given, and requir'd to be cloath'd in a Scholar's own Words; or the Circumstances of some good Story, the Scholar to find Expression. Let them be put sometimes on abridging a Paragraph of a diffuse Author, sometimes on dilating or amplifying what is wrote more closely. And now let Dr. Johnson's *Noetica*, or First Principles of Human Knowledge, containing a Logic, or Art of Reasoning, &c. be read by the Youth, and the Difficulties that may occur to them be explained by the Master. The Reading of History, and the Exercises of good Reading and just Speaking, still continued.

SIXTH CLASS

In this Class, besides continuing the Studies of the preceding, in History, Rhetoric, Logic, Moral and Natural Philosophy, the best *English* Authors may be read and explain'd; as *Tillotson*, *Milton*, *Locke*, *Addison*, *Pope*, *Swift*, the higher Papers in the *Spectator* and *Guardian*, the best Translations of *Homer*, *Virgil*, and *Horace*, of *Telemachus*, *Travels of Cyrus*, &c.[37]

Once a Year let there be publick Exercises in the Hall, the Trustees and Citizens present. Then let fine gilt Books be given as Prizes to such Boys as distinguish themselves and excel the others in any Branch of Learning, making three Degrees of Comparison; giving the best Prize to him that performs best; a less valuable One to him that comes up next to the best; and another to the third. Commendations, Encouragement and Advice to the rest; keeping up their Hopes, that by Industry they may excel another Time. The Names of those that obtain the Prizes to be yearly printed in a List.

The Hours of each Day are to be divided and dispos'd in such a Manner, as that some Classes may be with the Writing-Master, improving their Hands, others with the Mathematical Master, learning Arithmetick, Accompts, Geography, Use of the Globes, Drawing, Mechanicks, &c.; while the rest are in the *English* School, under the *English* Master's Care.

Thus instructed, Youth will come out of this School fitted for learning any Business, Calling or Profession, except such wherein Languages are required; and tho' unacquainted with any antient or foreign Tongue, they will be Masters of their own, which is of more immediate and general Use; and withal will have attain'd many other valuable Accomplishments; the Time usually spent in acquiring those Languages, often without Success, being here employ'd in laying such a Foundation of Knowledge and Ability, as, properly improv'd, may qualify them to pass thro' and execute the several Offices of civil Life, with Advantage and Reputation to themselves and Country.

B. F.

TO C[ADWALLADER] C[OLDEN] ESQ. AT NEW YORK

Communicated to Mr. Collinson

[Philadelphia] 1751.

SIR,

I inclose you answers, such as my present hurry of business will permit me to make, to the principal queries contained in yours of the 28th instant, and beg leave to refer you to the latter piece in the printed collection of my papers, for farther explanation of the difference between what are called *electrics per se*, and *non-electrics*. When you have had time to read and consider these papers, I will endeavour to make any new experiments you shall propose, that you think may afford farther light or satisfaction to either of us; and shall be much obliged to you for such remarks, objections, &c., as may occur to you.

I forget whether I wrote you that I have melted brass pins and steel needles, inverted the poles of the magnetic needle, given a magnetism and polarity to needles that had none, and fired dry gunpowder by the electric spark. I have five bottles that contain 8 or 9 gallons each, two of which charg'd, are sufficient for those purposes: but I can charge and discharge them altogether. There are no bounds (but what expence and labour give) to the force man may raise and use in the electrical way: for bottle may be added to bottle *in infinitum*, and all united and discharged together as one, the force and effect proportioned to their number and size. The greatest known effects of common lightning may, I think, without much difficulty, be exceeded in this way, which a few years since could not have been believed, and even now may seem to many a little extravagant to suppose. So we are got beyond the skill of *Rabelais's* devils of two years old, who, he humorously says, had only learnt to thunder and lighten a little round the head of a cabbage.[38]

I am, with sincere respect,

Your most obliged humble servant,

B. FRANKLIN.

EXPORTING OF FELONS TO THE COLONIES

[From the *Pennsylvania Gazette*, May 9, 1751.]

To the Printers of the Gazette

By a Passage in one of your late Papers, I understand that
the Government at home will not suffer our mistaken Assemblies to make any Law for preventing or discouraging the Importation of Convicts from Great Britain, for this kind Reason,
'*That such Laws are against the Publick Utility, as they tend
to prevent the* IMPROVEMENT *and* WELL PEOPLING *of the Colonies.*'

Such a tender *parental* Concern in our *Mother Country* for
the *Welfare* of her *Children*, calls aloud for the highest *Returns*
of Gratitude and Duty. This every one must be sensible of:
But 'tis said, that in our present Circumstances it is absolutely
impossible for us to make *such* as are adequate to the Favour.
I own it; but nevertheless let us do our Endeavour. 'Tis something to show a grateful Disposition.

In some of the uninhabited Parts of these Provinces, there
are Numbers of these venomous Reptiles we call RATTLE-
SNAKES; Felons-convict from the Beginning of the World:
These, whenever we meet with them, we put to Death, by
Virtue of an old Law, *Thou shalt bruise his Head.* But as this is
a sanguinary Law, and may seem too cruel; and as however
mischievous those Creatures are with us, they may possibly
change their Natures, if they were to change the Climate; I
would humbly propose, that this general Sentence of *Death* be
changed for *Transportation.*

In the Spring of the Year, when they first creep out of their
Holes, they are feeble, heavy, slow, and easily taken; and if a
small Bounty were allow'd *per* Head, some Thousands might
be collected annually, and *transported* to *Britain.* There I would
propose to have them carefully distributed in *St. James's Park,*
in the *Spring-Gardens* and other Places of Pleasure about *London;* in the Gardens of all the Nobility and Gentry throughout

the Nation; but particularly in the Gardens of the *Prime Ministers*, the *Lords of Trade* and *Members of Parliament;* for to them
we are *most particularly* obliged.

There is no human Scheme so perfect, but some Inconveniencies may be objected to it: Yet when the Conveniencies
far exceed, the Scheme is judg'd rational, and fit to be executed.
Thus Inconveniencies have been objected to that *good* and *wise*
Act of Parliament, by virtue of which all the *Newgates* and
Dungeons in *Britain* are emptied into the Colonies. It has been
said, that these Thieves and Villains introduc'd among us, spoil
the Morals of Youth in the Neighbourhoods that entertain
them, and perpetrate many horrid Crimes: But let not *private
Interests* obstruct *publick* Utility. Our *Mother* knows what is
best for us. What is a little *Housebreaking, Shoplifting,* or *Highway Robbing;* what is a *Son* now and then *corrupted* and *hang'd,*
a Daughter *debauch'd* and *pox'd,* a Wife *stabb'd,* a Husband's
Throat cut, or a Child's *Brains beat out* with an Axe, compar'd
with this 'IMPROVEMENT and WELL PEOPLING of the Colonies!'

Thus it may perhaps be objected to my Scheme, that the
Rattle-Snake is a mischievous Creature, and that his changing
his Nature with the Clime is a mere Supposition, not yet confirm'd by sufficient Facts. What then? Is not Example more
prevalent than Precept? And may not the honest rough British
Gentry, by a Familiarity with these Reptiles, learn to *creep,* and
to *insinuate,* and to *slaver,* and to *wriggle* into Place (and perhaps
to *poison* such as stand in their Way) Qualities of no small
Advantage to Courtiers! In comparison of which 'IMPROVE-
MENT and PUBLICK UTILITY,' what is a *Child* now and then kill'd
by their venomous Bite, . . . or even a favourite *Lap Dog?*

I would only add, that this exporting of Felons to the Colonies, may be consider'd as a *Trade,* as well as in the Light of a
Favour, Now all Commerce implies Returns: Justice requires
them: There can be no Trade without them. And *Rattle-Snakes*
seem the most *suitable Returns* for the *Human Serpents* sent us
by our *Mother* Country. In this, however, as in every other
Branch of Trade, she will have the Advantage of us. She will
reap *equal* Benefits without equal Risque of the Inconveniencies

and Dangers. For the *Rattle-Snake* gives Warning before he attempts his Mischief; which the Convict does not. I am

Yours, &c.

AMERICANUS.

OBSERVATIONS

CONCERNING THE INCREASE OF MANKIND, PEOPLING OF COUNTRIES, ETC.

Written in Pensilvania, 1751 [39]

1. Tables of the Proportion of Marriages to Births, of Deaths to Births, of Marriages to the Numbers of Inhabitants, &c., form'd on Observaions [*sic*] made upon the Bills of Mortality, Christnings, &c., of populous Cities, will not suit Countries; nor will Tables form'd on Observations made on full-settled old Countries, as *Europe*, suit new Countries, as *America*.

2. For People increase in Proportion to the Number of Marriages, and that is greater in Proportion to the Ease and Convenience of supporting a Family. When families can be easily supported, more Persons marry, and earlier in Life.

3. In Cities, where all Trades, Occupations, and Offices are full, many delay marrying till they can see how to bear the Charges of a Family; which Charges are greater in Cities, as Luxury is more common: many live single during Life, and continue Servants to Families, Journeymen to Trades; &c. hence Cities do not by natural Generation supply themselves with Inhabitants; the Deaths are more than the Births.

4. In Countries full settled, the Case must be nearly the same; all Lands being occupied and improved to the Heighth; those who cannot get Land, must Labour for others that have it; when Labourers are plenty, their Wages will be low; by low Wages a family is supported with Difficulty; this Difficulty deters many from Marriage, who therefore long continue Servants and single. Only as the Cities take Supplies of People from the Country, and thereby make a little more Room in the Country; Marriage is a little more encourag'd there, and the Births exceed the Deaths.

5. *Europe* is generally full settled with Husbandmen, Manufacturers, &c., and therefore cannot now much increase in People: *America* is chiefly occupied by Indians, who subsist mostly by Hunting. But as the Hunter, of all Men, requires the greatest Quantity of Land from whence to draw his Subsistence, (the Husbandman subsisting on much less, the Gardner on still less, and the Manufacturer requiring least of all), the *Europeans* found *America* as fully settled as it well could be by Hunters; yet these, having large Tracks, were easily prevail'd on to part with Portions of Territory to the new Comers, who did not much interfere with the Natives in Hunting, and furnish'd them with many Things they wanted.

6. Land being thus plenty in *America*, and so cheap as that a labouring man, that understands Husbandry, can in a short Time save Money enough to purchase a Piece of new Land sufficient for a Plantation, whereon he may subsist a Family, such are not afraid to marry; for, if they even look far enough forward to consider how their Children, when grown up, are to be provided for, they see that more Land is to be had at rates equally easy, all Circumstances considered.

7. Hence Marriages in *America* are more general, and more generally early, than in *Europe*. And if it is reckoned there, that there is but one Marriage per Annum among 100 persons, perhaps we may here reckon two; and if in *Europe* they have but 4 Births to a Marriage (many of their Marriages being late), we may here reckon 8, of which if one half grow up, and our Marriages are made, reckoning one with another at 20 Years of Age, our People must at least be doubled every 20 Years.

8. But notwithstanding this Increase, so vast is the Territory of *North America*, that it will require many Ages to settle it fully; and, till it is fully settled, Labour will never be cheap here, where no Man continues long a Labourer for others, but gets a Plantation of his own, no Man continues long a Journeyman to a Trade, but goes among those new Settlers, and sets up for himself, &c. Hence Labour is no cheaper now in *Pennsylvania*, than it was 30 Years ago, tho' so many Thousand labouring People have been imported.

9. The Danger therefore of these Colonies interfering with their Mother Country in Trades that depend on Labour, Manufactures, &c., is too remote to require the attention of *Great-Britain*.

10. But in Proportion to the Increase of the Colonies, a vast Demand is growing for British Manufactures, a glorious Market wholly in the Power of *Britain*, in which Foreigners cannot interfere, which will increase in a short Time even beyond her Power of supplying, tho' her whole Trade should be to her Colonies: Therefore *Britain* should not too much restrain Manufactures in her Colonies. A wise and good Mother will not do it. To distress, is to weaken, and weakening the Children weakens the whole Family.

11. Besides if the Manufactures of *Britain* (by reason of the *American* Demands) should rise too high in Price, Foreigners who can sell cheaper will drive her Merchants out of Foreign Markets; Foreign Manufactures will thereby be encouraged and increased, and consequently foreign Nations, perhaps her Rivals in Power, grow more populous and more powerful; while her own Colonies, kept too low, are unable to assist her, or add to her Strength.

12. 'Tis an ill-grounded Opinion that by the Labour of slaves, *America* may possibly vie in Cheapness of Manufactures with *Britain*. The Labour of Slaves can never be so cheap here as the Labour of working Men is in *Britain*. Any one may compute it. Interest of Money is in the Colonies from 6 to 10 per Cent. Slaves one with another cost 30£ Sterling per Head. Reckon then the Interest of the first Purchase of a Slave, the Insurance or Risque on his Life, his Cloathing and Diet, Expences in his Sickness and Loss of Time, Loss by his Neglect of Business (Neglect is natural to the Man who is not to be benefited by his own Care or Diligence), Expence of a Driver to keep him at Work, and his Pilfering from Time to Time, almost every Slave being *by Nature* a Thief, and compare the whole Amount with the Wages of a Manufacturer of Iron or Wood in *England*, you will see that Labour is much cheaper there than it ever can be by Negroes here. Why then will

Americans purchase Slaves? Because Slaves may be kept as long as a *Man* pleases, or has Occasion for their Labour; while hired Men are continually leaving their masters (often in the midst of his Business,) and setting up for themselves.—Sec. 8.

13. As the Increase of People depends on the Encouragement of Marriages, the following Things must diminish a Nation, viz. 1. *The being conquered;* for the Conquerors will engross as many Offices, and exact as much Tribute or Profit on the Labour of the conquered, as will maintain them in their new Establishment, and this diminishing the Subsistence of the Natives, discourages their Marriages, and so gradually diminishes them, while the foreigners increase. 2. *Loss of Territory.* Thus, the *Britons* being driven into *Wales*, and crowded together in a barren Country insufficient to support such great Numbers, diminished 'till the People bore a Proportion to the Produce, while the *Saxons* increas'd on their abandoned lands; till the Island became full of *English.* And, were the *English* now driven into *Wales* by some foreign Nation, there would in a few Years, be no more Englishmen in *Britain*, than there are now people in *Wales*. 3. *Loss of Trade.* Manufactures exported, draw Subsistence from Foreign Countries for Numbers; who are thereby enabled to marry and raise Families. If the Nation be deprived of any Branch of Trade, and no new Employment is found for the People occupy'd in that Branch, it will also be soon deprived of so many People. 4. *Loss of Food.* Suppose a Nation has a Fishery, which not only employs great Numbers, but makes the Food and Subsistence of the People cheaper. If another Nation becomes Master of the Seas, and prevents the Fishery, the People will diminish in Proportion as the Loss of Employ and Dearness of Provision, makes it more difficult to subsist a Family. 5. *Bad Government and insecure Property.* People not only leave such a Country, and settling Abroad incorporate with other Nations, lose their native Language, and become Foreigners, but, the Industry of those that remain being discourag'd, the Quantity of Subsistence in the Country is lessen'd, and the Support of a Family becomes more difficult. So heavy Taxes tend to diminish a People. 6. *The Introduction of Slaves.*

The Negroes brought into the *English* Sugar *Islands* have greatly diminish'd the Whites there; the Poor are by this Means deprived of Employment, while a few Families acquire vast Estates; which they spend on Foreign Luxuries, and educating their Children in the Habit of those Luxuries; the same Income is needed for the Support of one that might have maintain'd 100. The Whites who have Slaves, not labouring, are enfeebled, and therefore not so generally prolific; the Slaves being work'd too hard, and ill fed, their Constitutions are broken, and the Deaths among them are more than the Births; so that a continual Supply is needed from *Africa*. The Northern Colonies, having few Slaves, increase in Whites. Slaves also pejorate[40] the Families that use them; the white Children become proud, disgusted with Labour, and being educated in Idleness, are rendered unfit to get a Living by Industry.

14. Hence the Prince that acquires new Territory, if he finds it vacant, or removes the Natives to give his own People Room; the Legislator that makes effectual Laws for promoting of Trade, increasing Employment, improving Land by more or better Tillage, providing more Food by Fisheries; securing Property, &c. and the Man that invents new Trades, Arts, or Manufactures, or new Improvements in Husbandry, may be properly called *Fathers* of their Nation, as they are the Cause of the Generation of Multitudes, by the Encouragement they afford to Marriage.

15. As to Privileges granted to the married, (such as the *Jus trium Liberorum* among the *Romans*,) they may hasten the filling of a Country that has been thinned by War or Pestilence, or that has otherwise vacant Territory; but cannot increase a People beyond the Means provided for their Subsistence.

16. Foreign Luxuries and needless Manufactures, imported and used in a Nation, do, by the same Reasoning, increase the People of the Nation that furnishes them, and diminish the People of the Nation that uses them. Laws, therefore, that prevent such Importations, and on the contrary promote the Exportation of Manufactures to be consumed in Foreign Countries, may be called (with Respect to the People that make them)

generative Laws, as, by increasing Subsistence they encourage Marriage. Such Laws likewise strengthen a Country, doubly, by increasing its own People and diminishing its Neighbours.

17. Some *European* Nations prudently refuse to consume the Manufactures of *East-India:* — They should likewise forbid them to their Colonies; for the Gain to the Merchant is not to be compar'd with the Loss, by this Means, of People to the Nation.

18. Home Luxury in the Great increases the Nation's Manufacturers employ'd by it, who are many, and only tends to diminish the Families that indulge in it, who are few. The greater the common fashionable Expence of any Rank of People, the more cautious they are of Marriage. Therefore Luxury should never be suffer'd to become common.

19. The great Increase of Offspring in particular Families is not always owing to greater Fecundity of Nature, but sometimes to Examples of Industry in the Heads, and industrious Education; by which the Children are enabled to provide better for themselves, and their marrying early is encouraged from the Prospect of good Subsistence.

20. If there be a Sect, therefore, in our Nation, that regard Frugality and Industry as religious Duties, and educate their Children therein, more than others commonly do; such Sect must consequently increase more by natural Generation, than any other sect in *Britain*.

21. The Importation of Foreigners into a Country, that has as many Inhabitants as the present Employments and Provisions for Subsistence will bear, will be in the End no Increase of People; unless the New Comers have more Industry and Frugality than the Natives, and then they will provide more Subsistence, and increase in the Country; but they will gradually eat the Natives out. Nor is it necessary to bring in Foreigners to fill up any occasional Vacancy in a Country; for such Vacancy (if the Laws are good, sec. 14, 16,) will soon be filled by natural Generation. Who can now find the Vacancy made in *Sweden*, *France*, or other Warlike Nations, by the Plague of Heroism, 40 years ago; in *France*, by the Expulsion of the

Protestants; in *England*, by the Settlement of her Colonies; or in *Guinea*, by 100 Years Exportation of Slaves, that has blacken'd half *America?* The thinness of Inhabitants in *Spain* is owing to National Pride and Idleness, and other Causes, rather than to the Expulsion of the Moors, or to the making of new Settlements.

22. There is, in short, no Bound to the prolific Nature of Plants or Animals, but what is made by their crowding and interfering with each other's means of Subsistence. Was the Face of the Earth vacant of other Plants, it might be gradually sowed and overspread with one Kind only; as, for Instance, with Fennel; and were it empty of other Inhabitants, it might in a few Ages be replenish'd from one Nation only; as, for Instance, with *Englishmen.* Thus there are suppos'd to be now upwards of One Million *English* Souls in *North-America*, (tho' 'tis thought scarce 80,000 have been brought over Sea,) and yet perhaps there is not one the fewer in *Britain*, but rather many more, on Account of the Employment the Colonies afford to Manufacturers at Home. This Million doubling, suppose but once in 25 Years, will, in another Century, be more than the People of *England*, and the greatest Number of *Englishmen* will be on this Side the Water. What an Accession of Power to the *British* Empire by Sea as well as Land! What Increase of Trade and Navigation! What Numbers of Ships and Seamen! We have been here but little more than 100 years, and yet the Force of our Privateers in the late War, united, was greater, both in Men and Guns, than that of the whole *British* Navy in Queen *Elizabeth's* Time. How important an Affair then to *Britain* is the present Treaty for settling the Bounds between her Colonies and the *French*, and how careful should she be to secure Room enough, since on the Room depends so much the Increase of her People.

23. In fine, a Nation well regulated is like a Polypus; take away a Limb, its Place is soon supply'd; cut it in two, and each deficient Part shall speedily grow out of the Part remaining. Thus if you have Room and Subsistence enough, as you may by dividing, make ten Polypes out of one, you may of one

make ten Nations, equally populous and powerful; or rather increase a Nation ten fold in Numbers and Strength.[41]

And since Detachments of *English* from *Britain*, sent to *America*, will have their Places at Home so soon supply'd and increase so largely here; why should the *Palatine Boors* be suffered to swarm into our Settlements and, by herding together, establish their Language and Manners, to the Exclusion of ours? Why should *Pennsylvania*, founded by the *English*, become a Colony of *Aliens*, who will shortly be so numerous as to Germanize us instead of our Anglifying them, and will never adopt our Language or Customs any more than they can acquire our Complexion?

24. Which leads me to add one Remark, that the Number of purely white People in the World is proportionably very small. All *Africa* is black or tawny; *Asia* chiefly tawny; *America* (exclusive of the new Comers) wholly so. And in *Europe*, the *Spaniards*, *Italians*, *French*, *Russians*, and *Swedes*, are generally of what we call a swarthy Complexion; as are the *Germans* also, the *Saxons* only excepted, who, with the *English*, make the principal Body of White People on the Face of the Earth. I could wish their Numbers were increased. And while we are, as I may call it, *Scouring* our Planet, by *clearing America* of Woods, and so making this Side of our Globe reflect a brighter Light to the Eyes of Inhabitants in *Mars* or *Venus*, why should we, in the Sight of Superior Beings, darken its People? Why increase the Sons of *Africa*, by planting them in *America*, where we have so fair an Opportunity, by excluding all Blacks and Tawneys, of increasing the lovely White and Red? But perhaps I am partial to the Complexion of my Country, for such Kind of Partiality is natural to Mankind.

TO PETER COLLINSON [42]
Electrical Kite
[Philadelphia] Oct. 19, 1752.

Sir,

As frequent mention is made in public papers from *Europe* of the success of the *Philadelphia* experiment for drawing the electric fire from clouds by means of pointed rods of iron erected on high buildings, &c., it may be agreeable to the curious to be informed, that the same experiment has succeeded in *Philadelphia*, though made in a different and more easy manner, which is as follows:

Make a small cross of two light strips of cedar, the arms so long as to reach to the four corners of a large thin silk handkerchief when extended; tie the corners of the handkerchief to the extremities of the cross, so you have the body of a kite; which being properly accommodated with a tail, loop, and string, will rise in the air, like those made of paper; but this being of silk, is fitter to bear the wet and wind of a thunder-gust without tearing. To the top of the upright stick of the cross is to be fixed a very sharp-pointed wire, rising a foot or more above the wood. To the end of the twine, next the hand, is to be tied a silk ribbon, and where the silk and twine join, a key may be fastened. This kite is to be raised when a thunder-gust appears to be coming on, and the person who holds the string must stand within a door or window, or under some cover, so that the silk ribbon may not be wet; and care must be taken that the twine does not touch the frame of the door or window. As soon as any of the thunder-clouds come over the kite, the pointed wire will draw the electric fire from them, and the kite, with all the twine, will be electrified, and the loose filaments of the twine will stand out every way, and be attracted by an approaching finger. And when the rain has wet the kite and twine, so that it can conduct the electric fire freely, you will find it stream out plentifully from the key on the approach of your knuckle. At this key the phial may be charged; and from electric fire thus obtained, spirits may be kindled, and all the other electric experiments be performed, which are usually done by the help of a rubbed glass globe or tube, and thereby the sameness of the electric matter with that of lightning completely demonstrated.

B. Franklin.

[Note.—The *Almanack* for 1753 which follows is an exact facsimile of the copy in the W. S. Mason Collection, here reproduced through the kindness of Mr. Mason. See note 43.]

Poor RICHARD improved:

BEING AN

ALMANACK

AND

EPHEMERIS

OF THE

MOTIONS of the SUN and MOON;

THE TRUE

PLACES and ASPECTS of the PLANETS;

THE

RISING and *SETTING* of the *SUN;*

AND THE

Rifing, Setting *and* Southing *of the* Moon,

FOR THE

YEAR of our LORD 1753:

Being the Firft after LEAP-YEAR.

Containing alfo,
The Lunations, Conjunctions, Eclipfes, Judgment of the Weather, Rifing and Setting of the Planets, Length of Days and Nights, Fairs, Courts, Roads, &c. Together with ufeful Tables, chronological Obfervations, and entertaining Remarks.

Fitted to the Latitude of Forty Degrees, and a Meridian of near five Hours Weft from *London;* but may, without fenfible Error, ferve all the NORTHERN COLONIES.

By *RICHARD SAUNDERS,* Philom.

PHILADELPHIA:

Printed and Sold by B. FRANKLIN, and D. HALL.

The Anatomy of Man's Body as govern'd by the
Twelve Constellations.

♈   The Head and Face.

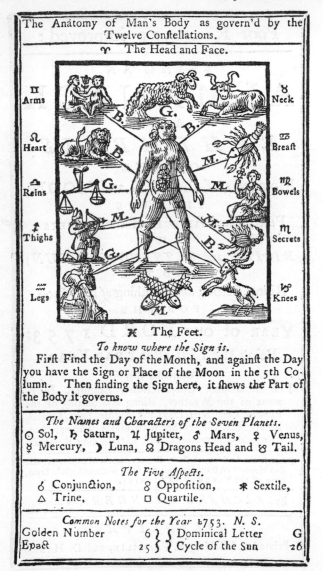

♓   The Feet.

To know where the Sign is.

First Find the Day of the Month, and against the Day
you have the Sign or Place of the Moon in the 5th Column. Then finding the Sign here, it shews the Part of
the Body it governs.

The Names and Characters of the Seven Planets.
☉ Sol, ♄ Saturn, ♃ Jupiter, ♂ Mars, ♀ Venus,
☿ Mercury, ☽ Luna, ☊ Dragons Head and ☋ Tail.

The Five Aspects.
☌ Conjunction,   ☍ Opposition,   ⚹ Sextile,
△ Trine,   □ Quartile.

Common Notes for the Year 1753. N. S.

Golden Number	6	Dominical Letter	G
Epact	25	Cycle of the Sun	26

Courteous Reader,

THIS is the twentieth Time of my addressing thee in this Manner, and I have reason to flatter myself my Labours have not been unacceptable to the Publick. I am particularly pleas'd to understand that my *Predictions of the Weather* give such general Satisfaction; and indeed, such Care is taken in the Calculations, on which those Predictions are founded, that I could almost venture to say, there's not a single One of them, promising *Snow*, *Rain*, *Hail*, *Heat*, *Frost*, *Fogs*, *Wind*, or *Thunder*, but what comes to pass *punctually* and *precisely* on the very *Day*, in some Place or other on this little *diminutive* Globe of ours; (and when you consider the vast Distance of the Stars from whence we take our Aim, you must allow it no small Degree of Exactness to hit any Part of it) I say on this Globe; for tho' in other Matters I confine the Usefulness of my *Ephemeris* to the *Northern Colonies*, yet in that important Matter of the Weather, which is of such *general* Concern, I would have it more extensively useful, and therefore take in both Hemispheres, and all Latitudes from *Hudson's Bay* to *Cape Horn*.

You will find this Almanack in my former Method, only conformable to the *New-Stile* established by the Act of Parliament, which I gave you in my last at length; the new Act since made for Amendment of that first Act, not affecting us in the least, being intended only to regulate some Corporation Matters in *England*, be fore unprovided for. I have only added a Column in the second Page of each Month, containing the Days of the *Old Stile* opposite to their corresponding Days in the *New*, which may, in many Cases, be of Use; and so conclude (believing you will excuse a short Preface, when it is to make Room for something better)

Thy Friend and Servant,

R. SAUNDERS.

HYMN *to the* CREATOR, *from* Psalm CIV.

AWAKE, my Soul! with Joy thy God adore;
  Declare his Greatness; celebrate his Pow'r;
Who, cloath'd with Honour, and with Glory crown'd,
Shines forth, and cheers his Universe around.
Who with a radiant Veil of heavenly Light
Himself conceals from all created Sight.
Who rais'd the spacious Firmament on high,
And spread the azure Curtain of the Sky.
Whose awful Throne Heav'n's starry Arch sustains,
Whose Presence not Heav'n's vast Expanse restrains.
Whose Ways unsearchable no Eye can find,
The Clouds his Chariot, and his Wings the Wind
Whom Hosts of mighty Angels own their Lord,
And flaming Seraphim fulfil his Word.
Whose Pow'r of old the solid Earth did found,
Self-pois'd, self-center'd, and with Strength girt round;
                                                      From

From her appointed Sphere forbid to fly,
Or rush unbalanc'd thro' the trackless Sky.
To reas'ning Man the sov'reign Rule assign'd,
His Delegate o'er each inferior Kind :
Too soon to fall from that distinguish'd Place,
His Honours stain'd with Guilt and foul Disgrace.

He saw the Pride of Earth's aspiring Lord,
And in his Fury gave the dreadful Word :
Straight o'er her peopled Plains his Floods were pour'd,
And o'er her Mountains the proud Billows roar'd.
Athwart the Face of Earth the Deluge sweeps,
And whelms the impious Nations in the Deeps:
Again God spake——and at his pow'rful Call
The raging Floods assuage, the Waters fall,
The Tempests hear his Voice, and straight obey,
And at his Thunder's Roar they haste away :
From off the lofty Mountains they subside,
And gently thro' the winding Vallies glide,
Till in the spacious Caverns of the Deep
They sink together, and in Silence sleep.
There he hath stretch'd abroad their liquid Plains,
And there Omnipotence their Rage restrains,
That Earth no more her Ruins may deplore,
And guilty Mortals dread their Wrath no more.

He bids the living Fountains burst the Ground,
And bounteous spread their Silver Streams around :
Down from the Hills they draw their shining Train,
Diffusing Health and Beauty o'er the Plain.
There the fair Flocks allay the Summer's Rage,
And panting Savages their Flame assuage.
On their sweet winding Banks th' aerial Race
In artless Numbers warble forth his Praise,
Or chant the harmless Raptures of their Loves,
And cheer the Plains, and wake the vocal Groves.
Forth from his Treasures in the Skies he pours
His precious Blessings in refreshing Show'rs.
Each dying Plant with Joy new Life receives,
And thankful Nature smiles, and Earth revives.
The fruitful Fields with Verdure he bespreads,
The Table of the Race that haunts the Meads,
And bids each Forest, and each flow'ry Plain
Send forth their native Physic for the Swain.

Thus

Thus doth the various Bounty of the Earth
Support each Species crowding into Birth.
In purple Streams she bids her Vintage flow,
And Olives on her Hills luxuriant grow,
One with its generous Juice to cheer the Heart,
And one illustrious Beauty to impart ;
And Bread of all Heav'n's precious Gifts the chief
From desolating Want the sure Relief.
Which with new Life the feeble Limbs inspires,
And all the Man with Health and Courage fires.
The Cloud-topt Hills with waving Woods are crown'd,
Which wide extend their sacred Shades around,
There *Lebanon*'s proud Cedars nod their Heads ;
There *Bashan*'s lofty Oaks extend their Shades :
The pointed Firs rise tow'ring to the Clouds,
And Life and warbling Numbers fill the Woods.
  Nor gentle Shades alone, nor verdant Plains,
Nor fair enamell'd Meads, nor flow'ry Lawns,
But e'en rude Rocks and dreary Desarts yield
Retreats for the wild Wand'rers of the Field.
Thy Pow'r with Life and Sense all Nature fills,
Each Element with varied Being swells,
Race after Race arising view the Light,
Then silent pass away, and sink in Night.
The Gift of Life thus boundlesly bestow'd,
Proclaims th' exhaustless Hand, the Hand of God.
  Nor less thy Glory in th' etherial Spheres,
Nor less thy ruling Providence appears.
There from on high the gentle Moon by Night
In solemn Silence sheds her Silver Light,
And thence the glorious Sun pours forth his Beams,
Thence copious spreads around his quick'ning Streams.
Each various Orb enjoys the golden Day,
And Worlds of Life hang on his chearful Ray.
Thus Light and Darkness their fix'd Course maintain,
And still the kind Vicissitudes remain :
For when pale Night her sable Curtain spreads,
And wraps all Nature in her awful Shades,
Soft Slumbers gently seal each mortal Eye,
Stretch'd at their Ease the weary Lab'rers lie.
The restless Soul 'midst Life's vain Tumults tost,
Forgets her Woes, and ev'ry Care is lost.

                                        Then

JANUARY. *I Month.*

Then from their Dens the rav'nous Monſters creep,
Whilſt in their Folds the harmleſs Beſtial ſleep.
The ſurious Lion roams in queſt of Prey,
To gorge his Hunger till the Dawn of Day;
His hideous Roar with Terror ſhakes the Wood,
As from his Maker's Hand he aſks his Food.
Again the Sun his Morning Beams diſplays,
And fires the eaſtern Mountain with his Rays.

Before

		Remark. days, &c.	⊙ ri.	⊙ ſet	☽ pl.	Aſpects, &c.
1	2	CIRCUMCISION.	7 24	4 36	♐ 11	☽ with ♂
2	3	*Clouds and*	7 24	4 36	23	☽ with ♄
3	4	*cold, with*	7 23	4 37	♑ 5	♃ riſe 4 23
4	5	*ſnow;*	7 23	4 37	17	*Tis againſt*
5	6	Days inc. 4 m.	7 23	4 37	29	☽ with ☿ *ſome*
6	7	EPIPHANY.	7 22	4 38	♒ 10	♂ riſe 4 44
7	G	1 p. Epiph.	7 22	4 38	22	☽ w. ♀ *Mens*
8	2	*wind and*	7 21	4 39	♓ 4	*Principle to pay*
9	3	*falling*	7 21	4 39	16	*Intereſt, and*
10	4	Days inc. 10 m	7 20	4 40	28	*ſeems againſt*
11	5	*weather,*	7 19	4 41	♈ 10	♃ ſ. 11 6 *others*
12	6	*then*	7 18	4 42	23	♄ riſe 5 42
13	7	*very cold,*	7 17	4 43	♉ 6	Sirius ſo. 10 52
14	G	2 p. Epiph.	7 16	4 44	19	✱ ♄ ♀ *Intereſt*
15	2	Day incr. 18 m.	7 16	4 44	♊ 2	7 ✱'s ſo. 7 42
16	3	*wintry*	7 15	4 45	16	♃ ſo. 10 39
17	4	*weather;*	7 14	4 46	♋ 0	♂ riſe 4 36
18	5	*but grows more*	7 13	4 47	15	☽ with ♃ to
19	6	Day 9 36 long.	7 12	4 48	♌ 1	⊙ in ♒ *pay*
20	7	*moderate,*	7 12	4 48	17	△ ♃ ♀ *the*
21	G	3 p. Epiph.	7 11	4 49	♍ 3	*Principal.*
22	2	*followed by*	7 10	4 50	18	♀ ſets 8 2
23	3	*clouds, wind*	7 9	4 51	♎ 2	*Philoſophy as*
24	4	*and*	7 8	4 52	15	*well as Foppery*
25	5	Conv. St. PAUL.	7 7	4 53	28	✱ ♂ ☿ *often*
26	6	Day incr. 38 m.	7 6	4 54	♏ 11	*changes Faſhion.*
27	7	*cold, with*	7 5	4 55	24	♄ riſe 4 48
28	G	4 p. Epiph.	7 4	4 56	♐ 7	7 ✱s ſou. 6 47
29	2	*ſnow or*	7 3	4 57	19	Sirius ſou. 9 44
30	3	K. Char. behead.	7 2	4 58	♑ 1	☽ with ♄ & ♂
31	4	*rain.*	7 1	4 59	13	☽ with ☿

JANUARY hath XXXI Days.

D. H.		Planets Places.						
New ☽ 4 8 mor.	D.	☉	♄	♃	♂	♀	☿	☽sL.
First Q. 12 at noon.		♑	♐	♋	♐	♒	♑	
Full ● 19 10 mor.	1	12	29	11	7	15	26	N. 2
Last Q. 26 4 mor.	6	17	30	10	11	21	24	5
☊ { 12 ♏ 12 Deg.	12	23	♑0	9	15	29	19	2
22 11	17	28	1	8	19	♓5	14	S. 4
31 10	22	♒3	1	8	22	11	13	4
	27	8	2	7	26	17	15	N. 1

D.	☽ rise	☽ sou.	T.	Old Stile
1	4 39	M 4 1	12	
2	5 33	10 30	1	
3	Moon	11 19	2	
4	sets.	12 6	3	24
5	A.	A. 53	3	25
6	7 0	1 36	3	26
7	8 0	2 18	5	27
8	8 54	3 0	6	28
9	9 50	3 43	6	29
10	10 47	4 27	7	30
11	11 46	5 19	8	31
12	12 50	5 55	8	
13	M. 50	6 44	9	
14	1 51	7 34	10	3
15	2 52	8 28	11	4
16	3 56	9 23	12	5
17	4 57	10 22	1	6
18	Moon	11 21	2	7
19	rises	12 25	3	8
20	A.	Morn.	3	9
21	7 56	1 30	4	10
22	9 11	2 26	5	11
23	10 18	3 16	6	12
24	11 19	4 5	7	13
25	12 22	4 54	7	14
26	M 22	5 43	8	15
27	1 17	6 34	9	16
28	2 21	7 26	10	17
29	3 16	8 14	11	18
30	4 3	9 3	12	19
31	4 44	9 51	12	20

THE Greatness of that Power, which has been exerted in the Creation, though every Object in Nature shews it, will best appear by considering a little the GREAT Works, properly so called, of Nature; the Sun, and Planets, and the fixed Stars. The Sun and Moon, the most conspicuous to us of all the celestial Bodies, are the only ones mentioned in the sacred Text: But the Invention of that noblest of Instruments the Telescope, and the Sagacity of the Astronomers of later Ages, whose Observations have improved and corrected those of the foregoing, afford us a very different Idea of the Solar System, from what the single Consideration of those two most conspicuous Bodies gives us. As this may probably fall into the Hands of some, who have not Leisure or Opportunities of reading Books of Astronomy, the following brief View of our System, and of the Immensity of the Creation, according to the Theory of the Moderns, may not be unacceptable.

It is proper, in the first Place, just to mention, That the real Magnitudes, Distances, Orbits, and other Affections of the Bodies of our System are determined by what Astronomers call their Parallaxes, and by their Elongations from the Sun, and their apparent Magnitudes, and other analogical Methods, which would take up by far too much Time to explain here; by which it is possible to determine
mine

FEBRUARY. *II Month.*

Before him fly the Horrors of the Night;
He looks upon the World—and all is Light.
Then the lone Wand'rers of the dreary Waste
Affrighted to their Holds return in Haste,
To Man give up the World, his native Reign,
Who then resumes his Pow'r, and rules the Plain.
  How various are thy Works, Creator wise!
How to the Sight Beauties on Beauties rise!

Where

		Remark. days, &c.	☉ ris	☉ set	☽ pl.	Aspects, &c.
1	5	Days 10 h. long.	7 0	5 0	♑ 25	♃ sou. 9 28
2	6	Purification *V. M.*	6 59	5 1	♒ 7	♂ rise 4 20
3	7	*Clouds*	6 58	5 2	19	*Setting too good*
4	G	5 p. Epiph.	6 56	5 4	♓ 1	*an Example*
5	2	*and wind,*	6 55	5 5	13	☿ rise 5 34
6	3	*with*	6 54	5 6	25	☌ ☽ ♀ ☌ ♄ ♂
7	4	*falling*	6 53	5 7	♈ 7	♀ sets 8 2 *is a*
8	5	Days incr. 1 6	6 52	5 8	20	*Kind of Slander*
9	6	*weather,*	6 51	5 9	♉ 3	*seldom forgiven;*
10	7	*then fair*	6 50	5 10	16	*'tis* Scandalum
11	G	6 p. Epiph.	6 48	5 12	29	Magnatum.
12	2	*and cold;*	6 47	5 13	♊ 13	□ ♃ ♀ *A great*
13	3	*changeable*	6 46	5 14	27	♄ rise 3 49
14	4	Valentine.	6 45	5 15	♋ 12	☽ w. ♃ *Talker*
15	5	Days inc. 1 22	6 43	5 17	27	□ ♂ ♀ *may be*
16	6	*and like for*	6 42	5 18	♌ 12	7 *s sets 1 0
17	7	*rain, or snow,*	6 41	5 19	27	♃ sou. 8 21
18	G	Septuagesima.	6 40	5 20	♍ 12	☉ in ♓ *no Fool,*
19	2	*then follows*	6 38	5 22	26	Sirius sou. 8 21
20	3	Day 10 46 long.	6 37	5 23	♎ 10	♂ rise 4 5
21	4	*clear and cold*	6 36	5 24	24	♀ sets 9 0
22	5	*weather; but*	6 35	5 25	♏ 8	✶ ☉ ♄ *but he*
23	6	*soon changes to*	6 33	5 27	21	*is one that*
24	7	St. Matthias.	6 32	5 28	♐ 3	△ ☉ ♃ *relies*
25	G	Sexagesima.	6 31	5 29	15	*on him.*
26	2	*snow*	6 30	5 30	27	♄ rises 3 0
27	3	*or cold rain.*	6 28	5 32	♑ 9	☽ with ♄
28	4	Day inc. 1 56 m.	6 27	5 33	21	☽ with ♂

FEBRUARY hath XXVIII Days.

	D.	H.	
New ☽	3	3	mor.
First Q.	10	12	aft.
Full ●	17	3	aft.
Last Q.	24	7	aft.
☊ 12 ♍		9	Deg.
☊ 22		8	
☊ 28		7	

Planets Places.

D.	☉	♄	♃	♂	♀	☿	☽'s L.
	♒	♑	♋	♑	♓	♑	
1	13	2	7	0	23	19	N. 5
6	18	3	7	3	29	24	4
12	24	3	6	7	♈ 6	♒ 0	S. 3
17	29	4	6	11	12	7	5
22	♓ 4	4	6	14	17	14	0
27	19	4	6	18	23	22	N. 4

D.	☽ rise		☽ sou.		T.	
1	5	29	10	39	1	21
2	Moon		11	24	2	22
3	sets		A.	9	3	23
4	A.		12	52	3	24
5	7	45	1	35	4	25
6	8	39	2	18	5	26
7	9	39	3	1	6	27
8	10	41	3	50	6	28
9	11	44	4	38	7	29
10	12	47	5	29	8	30
11	M.	47	6	19	9	31
12	1	43	7	18	10	Feb.
13	2	46	8	17	11	
14	3	41	9	16	12	3
15	4	34	10	15	1	4
16	Moon		11	14	2	5
17	rises		12	10	3	6
18	A.		Morn		3	7
19	7	53	1	6	4	8
20	9	2	1	57	4	9
21	10	9	2	48	5	10
22	11	19	3	40	6	11
23	12	17	4	32	7	12
24	M.	17	5	20	8	13
25	1	8	6	8	9	14
26	2	0	6	58	9	15
27	2	48	7	47	10	16
28	3	27	8	34	11	17

mine their Magnitudes and Diſtances, when thoſe Diſtances are not too great to yield a Parallax. Aſtronomers, for Example, know certainly the Diſtance of the Moon from the Earth, *viz.* 240 thouſand Miles, becauſe the Moon yields a very ſenſible Parallax; and they know, that the Sun's Diſtance from the Earth is very probably, at leaſt, ten thouſand Times the Diameter or Thickneſs of the Earth, which is about eight thouſand Miles, and brings the whole Diſtance to about eighty Millions of Miles. It is, I ſay, hardly to be doubted, that the Diſtance from the Sun to the Earth is, at leaſt, eighty Millions of Miles; but it is not certainly known, whether it is not a great deal more. In the Year 1761, the Diſtance of all the Planets from the Sun will be determined to a great Degree of Exactneſs by Obſervations on a Tranſit of the Planet *Venus* over the Face of the Sun, which is to happen the 6th of *May*, O. S. in that Year. But, according to the preſent Theory, the Sun, to appear of the Magnitude he does to our Eyes at the Diſtance of eighty Millions of Miles, muſt be a Body a great many hundred thouſand Times larger than the Earth, ſo that if his Centre were placed where that of the Earth is, his outward Surface would extend one hundred and forty thouſand Miles higher than the Orbit of the Moon, his Diameter or Thickneſs being ſeven hundred and ſixty thouſand Miles, whereas that of the Earth is but about eight thouſand. This amazing World

of

MARCH. *III Month.*

Where Goodneſs worthy of a God beſtows
His Gifts on all, and without Bounds o'erflows ;
Where Wiſdom bright appears, and Pow'r divine,
And where Infinitude itſelf doth ſhine ;
Where Excellence inviſible's expreſt,
And in his glorious Works the God appears confeſt.
  With Life thy Hand hath ſtock'd this earthly Plain,
Nor leſs the ſpacious Empire of the Main.

There

		Remark. days, &c.	☉ riſ.	☉ ſet	☽ pl.	Aſpects, &c.
1	5	St. DAVID.	6 26	5 34	♒ 3	✱ ♀ ☿ *When*
2	6	*Cool and*	6 24	5 36	15	7 *s ſet 12 0
3	7	*windy,*	6 23	5 37	27	☽ w. ☿ *Reaſon*
4	G	Shrove Sunday.	6 22	5 38	♓ 9	♃ ſou. 7 25
5	2	*then ſnow.*	6 20	5 40	21	♀ ſets 9 28
6	3	Shrove-Tueſday.	6 19	5 41	♈ 4	*preaches, if you*
7	4	Aſh-Wedneſday.	6 18	5 42	17	✱ ♄ ☿ *won't*
8	5	Days 11 28 long.	6 16	5 44	♉ 0	☽ w. ♀ *hear her*
9	6	*follow'd by ſharp*	6 15	5 45	13	♂ ri. 3 50 *ſhe'll*
10	7	*nipping weather ;*	6 14	5 46	26	△ ♄ ♀ *box your*
11	G	1ſt in Lent.	6 12	5 48	♊ 9	Sirius ſo. 7 6.
12	2	Day inc. 2 28 m.	6 11	5 49	23	☍ ♄ ♃ *Ears.*
13	3	*now fine and*	6 10	5 50	♋ 7	☽ with ♃
14	4	Ember Week,	6 8	5 52	21	♄ riſe 2 4.
15	5	*pleaſant for*	6 7	5 53	♌ 6	♃ ſet 2 9
16	6	*the ſeaſon ;*	6 6	5 54	21	Sirius ſet 11 51
17	7	St. PATRICK.	6 4	5 56	♍ 6	♂ riſe 3 43
18	G	2d in Lent.	6 3	5 57	21	7*s ſet 11 4
19	2	*then*	6 2	5 58	♎ 5	☌ ☉ ☿ Equal
20	3	Days 12 long.	6 0	6 0	19	☉ in ♈ Day and
21	4	*clouds*	5 59	6 1	♏ 3	□ ♄ ☿ Night.
22	5	*and*	5 58	6 2	17	✱ ♂ ☿ *It is not*
23	6	*high winds*	5 56	6 4	♐ 0	□ ♃ ☿ *Leiſure*
24	7	Days inc. 3 h.	5 55	6 5	12	♀ ſets 9 57
25	G	Annunciation.	5 54	6 6	24	□ ☉ ♄ *that is*
26	2	*with rain and*	5 52	6 8	♑ 6	☽ with ♄ *not*
27	3	*cold, but*	5 51	6 9	18	□ ☉ ♃ *uſed.*
28	4	*grows*	5 50	6 10	♒ 0	♄ riſe 1 17
29	5	*more*	5 48	6 12	12	☽ with ♂
30	6	*moderate.*	5 47	6 13	24	Sirius ſet 11 0
31	7	Day 12 30 long.	5 45	6 15	♓ 6	♃ ſets 1 15

MARCH hath XXXI Days.

	D. H.			
New ☽	4 11 aft.			
First Q.	12 10 mor.			
Full ●	19 1 mor.			
Last Q.	26 at noon.			

		m	7 Deg.
☿	12	♏	7 Deg.
	22		6
	31		6

Planets Places.

D.	☉	♄	♃	♂	♀	☿	☽'s L.
	♓	♑	♋	♑	♈	♓	
4	14	5	6	22	29	0	N. 4
9	19	5	6	26	♉ 4	9	S. 1
12	22	5	6	28	7	15	4
17	27	5	6	♒ 2	12	25	4
22	♈ 2	5	7	6	17	♈ 6	N. 1
27	7	6	7	19	23	16	5

D.	☽ rise	☽ sou.	T.	
1	4 49	M 2 1	12 18	of Fire turns once round in about twenty-five Days. This is known by a Number of dusky Spots, which appear upon the Sun's Face, so as to be seen sometimes with the naked Eye, when he shines through a thin Cloud or Mist; but are always observable with the Help of a Telescope, with a dark Glass for the Security of the Eye. These Spots could not be visible at the Distance of the Sun, if they were not as large as the whole Earth; but such of them as appear of a considerable Breadth, as they often do, must be still vastly larger. They never continue long to make the same Appearance; but are always rising and vanishing again. They are probably Exhalations floating in the Sun's Atmosphere at some Distance from his Body, or Masses of Cynder fallen from that Atmosphere upon his Surface.
2	4 44	10 6	1 19	
3	Moon	10 50	1 20	
4	sets	11 34	2 21	
5	A.	A. 17	3 22	
6	7 35	1 4	4 23	
7	8 35	1 51	4 24	
8	9 40	2 41	5 25	
9	10 39	3 30	6 26	
10	11 44	4 22	7 27	
11	12 43	5 15	8 28	
12	M. 43	6 13	9 29	
13	1 36	7 10	10 10	
14	2 27	8 7	11 1	
15	3 19	9 4	1 2	
16	4 2	10 1	1 3	
17	4 42	10 58	1 4	
18	Moon	11 54	2 5	This glorious Luminary, the Centre of our System, has six opaque Globes, commonly called the Planets, going round him at different Distances, and in different Periods, but all from West to East, as follows.
19	rises	12 44	3 6	
20	A.	M. 44	3 7	
21	9 3	1 37	4 8	
22	10 32	2 30	5 9	
23	11 15	3 24	6 10	1. *Mercury*, a Body considerably inferior in Size to the Earth, performs his Course in about three Months, which is his Year, at the Distance of thirty Millions of Miles from the Sun. The Heat of the Sun in *Mercury* (if there be no Provision made for mitigating it) must be such, as, if it were the same on the Earth, would keep all the Waters upon it constantly boiling: And the Brightness of the Sun's
24	12 44	4 12	7 11	
25	M. 45	5 0	8 12	
26	0 43	5 49	8 13	
27	1 29	6 38	9 14	
28	2 12	7 24	10 15	
29	2 47	8 10	11 16	
30	3 21	8 54	11 17	
31	3 50	9 38	12 18	

APRIL. *IV Month.*

There the tall Ships the rolling Billows sweep,
And bound triumphant o'er th' unfathom'd Deep.
There great Leviathan in regal Pride,
The scaly Nations crouding by his Side,
Far in the dark Recesses of the Main
O'er Nature's Wastes extends his boundless Reign.
Round the dark Bottoms of the Mountains roves,
The hoary Deep swells dreadful as he moves.

Now

		Remark. days, &c.	⊙ ris	⊙ set	☽ pl	Aspects, &c.
1	G	4th in Lent.	5 44	6 16	♓ 18	♂ rise 3 22
2	2	*Rain, and*	5 43	6 17	♈ 0	*The Good-will*
3	3	*mild*	5 42	6 18	13	*of the Governed*
4	4	*weather,*	5 40	6 20	26	☽ w. ☿ *will be*
5	5	Days inc. 3 32 m.	5 39	6 21	♉ 9	✶ ⊙ ♂ *starv'd,*
6	6	*grows windy*	5 38	6 22	22	♀ sets 10 26 *if*
7	7	*and cool, then*	5 37	6 23	♊ 6	☽ w. ☿ *not fed*
8	G	5th in Lent.	5 35	6 25	20	7 ✶s sets 9 50 *by*
9	2	*warm and*	5 34	6 26	♋ 4	☽ with ♃ *the*
10	3	*springing,*	5 33	6 27	18	*good Deeds of*
11	4	Days 12 56 long.	5 32	6 28	♌ 2	*the Governors.*
12	5	*follow'd*	5 30	6 30	16	♄ rise 12 21
13	6	*by clouds*	5 29	6 31	♍ 1	7 ✶s sets 9 30
14	7	*and rain,*	5 28	6 32	15	☽ set 12 26
15	G	Palm Sunday.	5 26	6 34	29	Sirius set 10 2
16	2	*then fair and*	5 25	6 35	♎ 13	♂ rise 2 55
17	3	*pleasant again ;*	5 24	6 36	27	☿ sets 10 37
18	4	Days 13 16 long.	5 23	6 37	♏ 10	*Paintings and*
19	5	Maund. Thursday	5 22	6 38	23	⊙ in ♉ *Fight-*
20	6	Good Friday.	5 20	6 40	♐ 6	*ings are best*
21	7	*now rain*	5 19	6 41	19	7 ✶s set 9 0
22	G	Easter-day.	5 18	6 42	♑ 2	☽ with ♄
23	2	St. George.	5 17	6 43	14	Sirius sets 9 33
24	3	*and cool,*	5 16	6 44	26	*seen at a*
25	4	St. Mark.	5 15	6 45	♒ 8	△ ⊙ ♄
26	5	Pr. Will. b. 1721	5 13	6 47	20	*distance.*
27	6	*then clouds*	5 12	6 48	♓ 2	☽ with ♂
28	7	Day 13 38 long.	5 11	6 49	14	♄ rise 11 20
29	G	1 past Easter.	5 10	6 50	26	✶ ⊙ ♃
30	2	*and wind.*	5 8	6 52	♈ 9	♃ sets 11 37

APRIL hath xxx Days.

	D.	H.
New ☽	3	2 aft.
First Q.	10	5 aft.
Full ●	17	2 aft.
Last Q.	25	8 mor.
☊ 12 ♏		6 Deg.
22		6
30		6

Planets Places.

D.	☉	♄	♃	♂	♀	☿	☽'s L.
	♈	♑	♋	♒	♉	♈	
1	12	6	7	13	28	26	N. 4
6	17	6	8	16	♊ 3	♉ 4	S. 1
12	23	6	8	21	8	12	5
17	28	6	9	24	12	17	1
22	♉ 3	6	9	28	15	19	N. 4
27	8	6	10	♓ 1	18	19	4

D	☽ rise	☽ sou.	T.	
1	4 19	10 21	1	21
2	Moon	11 4	2	22
3	sets.	11 53	2	23
4	A.	A. 41	3	24
5	8 38	1 32	4	25
6	9 41	2 22	5	26
7	10 48	3 19	6	27
8	11 51	4 16	7	28
9	12 40	5 14	8	29
10	M. 40	6 11	9	30
11	1 25	7 6	10	31
12	2 6	8 0	11	Apr.
13	2 46	8 53	11	
14	3 25	9 46	12	3
15	4 0	10 38	1	4
16	Moon	11 29	2	5
17	rises	12 21	3	6
18	A.	M. 21	3	7
19	8 52	1 12	4	8
20	9 56	2 6	5	9
21	10 53	3 0	6	10
22	11 39	3 49	6	11
23	12 17	4 37	7	12
24	M. 17	5 28	8	13
25	0 49	6 20	9	14
26	1 23	7 0	10	15
27	1 58	7 40	10	16
28	2 30	8 23	11	17
29	3 1	9 6	12	18
30	3 28	9 55	12	19

Sun's Light must be such as would be quite intolerable to Eyes like ours. But it does not follow, that *Mercury* is therefore uninhabitable; since it can be no Difficulty for the Divine Power and Wisdom to accommodate the Inhabitants to the Place they are to inhabit; as the Cold we see Frogs and Fishes bear very well, would soon deprive any of our Species of Life. To an Eye such as ours, the Sun, seen from this Planet, would appear seven times as large as he does to us. He is always so near the Sun, that we have no Opportunity of discovering whether he turns round upon his own Axis, or not, and consequently cannot determine what Length the Days and Nights in *Mercury* are. He is seen sometimes with Telescopes horned like the Moon, and sometimes like a Half moon, but never fully illuminated, because that Side of the Planet, on which the Sun shines, is never turned full towards us, except when he is so near the Sun, as to be lost in the Brightness of his Beams. His enlightned Side is always towards the Sun, which shews, that he only shines with the borrowed Light of the Sun. That this Planet revolves round the Sun in an Orbit nearer to him, than that of the Earth, is plain, because he is never seen opposite to the Sun, but always in the West, when he is seen at Sun-setting, and in the East, when he is seen at Sun-rising; and that, never beyond the Distance of twenty-eight degrees from the Sun (a Degree is about

C twice

MAY. *V Month.*

Now views the awful Throne of antient Night,
Then mounts exulting to the Realms of Light;
Now launches to the Deep, now ſtems the Shore,
An Ocean ſcarce contains the wild Uproar.
Whate'er of Life repleniſhes the Flood,
Or walks the Earth, or warbles thro' the Wood,
In Nature's various Wants to thee complains,
The Hand, which gave the Life, the Life ſuſtains.

To

		Remark. days, &c.	☉ riſ	☉ ſet	☽ pl.	Aſpects, &c.
1	3	PHILIP & JACOB.	5 7	6 53	♈ 22	♂ riſe 2 30
2	4	*Rain and*	5 6	6 54	♉ 5	♀ ſet 10 28
3	5	Day inc. 4 40	5 5	6 55	18	☽ w ☿ ⚹ ♄ ♂
4	6	*guſts*	5 3	6 57	♊ 2	*If you would*
5	7	*in ſome*	5 2	6 58	16	☽ with ♀ *reap*
6	G	2 paſt Eaſter.	5 1	6 59	♋ 0	☌ ☉ ☿ *Praiſe*
7	2	*places, with*	5 0	7 0	14	☽ with ♃ *you*
8	3	*thunder,*	4 59	7 1	28	7*s ſet 7 56
9	4	Day 14 4 long.	4 58	7 2	♌ 13	*muſt ſow the*
10	5	*then fine*	4 57	7 3	27	Sirius ſet 8 27
11	6	*growing*	4 56	7 4	♍ 11	⚹ ♂ ☿ *Seeds,*
12	7	*weather,*	4 56	7 4	25	♄ riſe 10 28
13	G	3 paſt Eaſter.	4 55	7 5	♎ 9	⚹ ♃ ☿ *Gentle*
14	2	*pleaſant,*	4 54	7 6	23	♃ ſet 10 49
15	3	*with*	4 53	7 7	♏ 6	♂ riſe 2 3
16	4	Day inc. 5 6	4 52	7 8	19	*Words and*
17	5	*wind and*	4 51	7 9	♐ 2	♀ ſet 9 46
18	6	*flying*	4 50	7 10	15	*uſeful Deeds.*
19	7	*clouds,*	4 49	7 11	28	Ignorance *leads*
20	G	4 paſt Eaſter.	4 48	7 12	♑ 10	☉ in ♊ ☌ ☽ ♄
21	2	*follow'd*	4 47	7 13	22	*Men into a.*
22	3	Days 14 28 long.	4 46	7 14	♒ 4	*Party, and*
23	4	*by heat,*	4 45	7 15	16	Shame *keeps*
24	5	*then*	4 44	7 16	28	*them from get-*
25	6	*rain and*	4 44	7 16	♓ 10	*ting out again.*
26	7	*thunder,*	4 43	7 17	22	☽ with ♂
27	G	Rogation Sunday	4 42	7 18	♈ 4	♄ riſe 9 26
28	2	Day inc. 5 26	4 42	7 18	17	♃ ſet 10 6
29	3	K. Cha. reſto.	4 41	7 19	♉ 0	♂ riſe 1 32
30	4	*pleaſant.*	4 41	7 19	13	☽ with ☿ *Haſte*
31	5	Aſcenſion Day.	4 40	7 20	27	*makes Waſte.*

May hath xxxi Days.

	D. H.						
New ☽	3 2 mor.						
First Q.	9 10 aft.						
Full ●	17 2 mor.						
Last Q.	24 12 aft.						

Planets Places.

D.	☉	♄	♃	♂	♀	☿	☽s L.
	♉	♑	♋	♓	♊	♉	
2	12	6	10	5	21	17	N. 0
7	17	6	11	9	23	14	S. 5
12	22	6	11	13	25	12	3
17	27	5	12	17	27	11	N. 2
22	♊ 2	5	14	20	26	11	1
27	6	5	15	24	25	14	3

	☽			
{	12	♏	6	Deg.
☾	22		6	
{	31		5	

D.	☽rise	☽ sou.	T.	
1	4 ☉	10 44	1	20
2	Moon	11 31	2	21
3	sets	A. 21	3	22
4	A	1 17	4	23
5	9 43	2 14	5	24
6	10 40	3 12	6	25
7	11 29	4 10	7	26
8	12 3	5 6	8	27
9	M. 3	6 2	9	28
10	0 48	6 54	10	29
11	1 23	7 45	10	30
12	2 2	8 37	11	31
13	2 36	9 29	12	May
14	3 12	10 20	1	3
15	3 45	11 8	2	4
16	Moon	11 56	2	5
17	rises	13 48	3	6
18	A.	M. 48	3	7
19	9 31	1 42	4	8
20	10 14	2 30	5	9
21	10 51	3 19	6	10
22	11 29	4 6	7	11
23	12 0	4 53	7	12
24	Morn	5 36	8	13
25	0 27	6 19	9	14
26	0 56	7 2	10	15
27	1 27	7 45	10	16
28	1 58	8 32	11	17
29	2 30	9 20	12	18
30	3 8	10 13	1	19
31	Moon	11 6	2	20

twice the apparent Breadth of the Moon.) The same Considerations prove, that the next Planet, viz.

2. *Venus* revolves round the Sun in an Orbit including that of *Mercury* within it : For she is always seen in the Neighbourhood of the Sun, and never appears in the West when the Sun is in the East, nor contrariwise ; nor ever removes above forty-eight Degrees from him. When she is on one Side of her Orbit, she is our Morning- and on the other, our Evening Star. This Planet turns round upon its own Axis in twenty-three Hours, as the Earth does in twenty-four. *Venus* performs her annual Revolution round the Sun in two hundred twenty-four Days, at the Distance of about fifty-nine Millions of Miles from the Sun. She is nearly of the Size of the Earth. She appears through a Telescope exactly as the Moon does to the naked Eye, partly enlightened, and partly dark, and with the same Inequalities on her Face as on that of the Moon. Some Astronomers fancy they have seen a Satellite or Moon near *Venus*, like that belonging to the Earth : But it is not yet certain whether they have deceived themselves or not.

3. The Earth, which we inhabit, possesses the next Place in the Solar System, and, at the Distance of about eighty Millions of Miles, as above, performs her yearly Revolution round the Sun in about three hundred sixty-five Days, and at the same time, as a Bowl upon a

Bowling-

JUNE *VI Month.*

To each th' appointed Sustenance bestows,
To each the noxious and the healthful shows.
Thou spread'st thy Bounty—meagre Famine flies:
Thou hid'st thy Face—their vital Vigour dies.
Thy pow'ful Word again restores their Breath;
Renew'd Creation triumphs over Death.
Th' Almighty o'er his Works casts down his Eye,
And views their various Excellence with Joy;
His

		Remark. days, &c.	☉ ris	☉ set	☽ pl.	Aspects, &c.
1	6	*Clouds and*	4 40	7 20	♊ 11	♀ set 8 17
2	7	*like for*	4 39	7 21	25	☽ with ♀ *Many*
3	G	6 past Easter.	4 39	7 21	♋ 9	☽ with ♃ *have*
4	2	*rain, with*	4 39	7 21	24	*quarrel'd about*
5	3	Day 14 44 long.	4 38	7 22	♌ 9	*Religion, that*
6	4	*wind and*	4 38	7 22	23	☿ rise 3 28
7	5	*thunder;*	4 38	7 22	♍ 7	*never practis'd*
8	6	Days inc 5 36	4 37	7 23	21	☌ ☉ ♀ *it.*
9	7	*flying*	4 37	7 23	♎ 5	Sudden Power
10	G	Whitsunday.	4 37	7 23	19	□ ♄ ♂ *is apt to*
11	2	St. BARNABAS.	4 36	7 24	♏ 2	*be insolent,* Sud
12	6	*clouds, warm*	4 36	7 24	15	♄ ri. 8 13 den
13	4	Ember Week.	4 36	7 24	28	♃ set 9 8
14	5	Days 14 50	4 35	7 25	♐ 11	♂ rise 12 52
15	6	*and inclin'd*	4 35	7 25	24	Liberty *saucy;*
16	7	*to rain,*	4 35	7 25	♑ 6	☌ ☽ ♄ ✱ ♂ ☿
17	G	Trinity Sunday	4 35	7 25	18	*that behaves best*
18	2	Days inc. 5 40	4 35	7 25	♒ 0	☌ ♀ ☿ *which*
19	3	*with wind*	4 35	7 25	12	*has grown gra-*
20	4	*and*	4 35	7 25	24	✱ ♂ ♀ *dually.*
21	5	Corp Christ.	4 35	7 25	♓ 6	☉ in ♋
22	6	K. Geo. Acces.	4 35	7 25	18	*He that best un*
23	7	*thunder,*	4 35	7 25	♈ 0	*derstands the*
24	G	St. JOHN Baptist.	4 35	7 25	12	☌ ☽ ♂ ☍ ☉ ♄
25	2	*then*	4 35	7 25	25	*World, least*
26	3	*cooler,*	4 35	7 25	♉ 8	♃ set 8 32 *likes*
27	4	*but soon*	4 35	7 25	21	♄ rise 7 8 *it.*
28	5	Days 14 50	4 35	7 25	♊ 5	☌ ☽ ♀ ☍ ♄ ☿
29	6	*grows hot again.*	4 36	7 24	19	♂ rise 12 14
30	7	St. PETER.	4 36	7 24	♋ 4	☽ with ☿

King GEORGE's 27th Year begins the 22d Day

JUNE hath xxx Days.

	D.	H.
New ☽	1	at noon.
First Q.	8	6 mor.
Full ●	15	at noon.
Last Q.	23	4 aft.
New ☽	30	9 aft.
☊	12 ♏	5 Deg.
	22	4
	30	3

Planets Places.

D.	☉	♄	♃	♂	♀	☿	☽'s L.
	♊	♑	♋	♓	♊	♉	
1	11	5	16	27	23	18	S. 3
6	16	4	18	♈ 1	20	23	5
12	22	4	19	5	15	♊ 1	N. 1
17	26	4	20	9	13	10	5
22	♋ 1	3	21	13	11	20	4
27	6	3	22	16	10	♋ 1	S. 1

D.	☽ set.	☽ sou.	T.		
					Bowling-green not only proceeds forward, but
1	sets	A. 3	3	21	likewise turns round upon its own Axis, To
2	A.	1 0	4	22	does the Earth turn once round upon its Axis
3	9 15	1 58	4	23	as it goes along, every twenty-four Hours. It
4	10 7	2 56	5	24	is astonishing, and even frightful to think, that
5	10 49	3 52	6	25	this vast and cumbrous Globe of Earth and
6	11 25	4 47	7	26	Sea, which is almost twenty-five thousand
7	12 0	5 38	8	27	Miles in Circumference, has received such an
8	Morn	6 28	9	28	Impulse from the Almighty Arm, as has car-
9	0 34	7 20	10	29	ried it constantly for above these five thousand
10	1 8	8 11	11	30	Years, that we know of, round the Sun at
11	1 42	8 58	11	31	the Rate of at least fifty thousand Miles every
12	2 16	9 46	12	June	Hour, which it must absolutely do, to go round
13	2 57	10 38	1		the Sun in a Year at the Distance of eighty
14	Moon	11 29	2	3	Millions of Miles from him. So that, if an
15	rises	12 23	3	4	Angel were to come from some other World,
16	A.	M. 23	3	5	and to place himself near the Earth's Way,
17	8 51	1 9	4	6	he would see it pass by him with a Swiftness,
18	9 26	1 55	4	7	to which that of a Cannon Ball is but as one
19	10 0	2 40	5	8	to one hundred, and would be left behind by
20	10 27	3 24	6	9	it no less than the above Number of Miles in
21	10 53	4 8	7	10	the Space of one Hour. There is no more
22	11 23	4 50	7	11	Reason to doubt, that the Earth goes in this
23	11 51	5 32	8	12	Manner round the Sun, than there would be
24	12 22	6 18	9	13	for a Passenger in a Ship on smooth Water,
25	M 22	7 4	10	14	who saw the Objects upon Land continually
26	0 55	7 53	10	15	passing by, to doubt whether the Vessel he
27	1 32	8 42	11	16	was in, or the Shore, was in Motion. We see
28	2 14	9 39	12	17	the Sun continually changes his Place with re-
29	Moon	10 36	1	18	spect to the fixed Stars, and must own it to be
30	sets	11 37	2	19	highly improbable that this Change of Place

is owing to any Change in the whole Heavens, which,

JULY. *VII Month.*

His Works with Rev'rence own his pow'rful Hand,
And humble Nature waits his dread Command,
He looks upon the Earth—her Pillars ſhake,
And from her Centre her Foundations quake.
The Hills he touches—Clouds of Smoke ariſe,
And ſulph'rous Streams mount heavy to the Skies.
Whilſt Life informs this Frame, that Life ſhall be
(O Firſt and Greateſt !) ſacred all to Thee.

Thy

		Remark. days, &c.	☉ riſ	☉ ſet	☽ pl.	Aſpects, &c.
1	G	2 paſt Trin.	4 36	7 24	♋ 19	☽ with ♃
2	2	Days dec. 2 m.	4 36	7 24	♌ 4	☌ ☉ ☿ Anger
3	3	*Clouds*	4 37	7 23	19	*is never without*
4	4	*and*	4 37	7 23	♍ 4	*a Reaſon, but*
5	5	*wind,*	4 37	7 23	18	*ſeldom with a*
6	6	*then hot,*	4 38	7 22	♎ 2	*good One.*
7	7	Days dec. 6 m.	4 38	7 22	16	♀ riſe 2 27
8	G	3 paſt Trin.	4 39	7 21	29	*He that is of*
9	2	*follow'd by*	4 39	7 21	♏ 12	□ ♃ ♂ ☌ ♃ ☿
10	3	*rain and*	4 40	7 20	25	*Opinion Money*
11	4	*thunder-*	4 40	7 20	♐ 8	*will do every*
12	5	*guſts*	4 41	7 19	20	♄ ſou. 10 42
13	6	*in many*	4 41	7 19	♑ 2	☽ w. ♄ *Thing,*
14	7	Days dec. 14 m.	4 42	7 18	14	♂ riſe 11 38
15	G	4 paſt Trin.	4 43	7 17	26	*may well be*
16	2	*places, then*	4 43	7 17	♒ 8	*ſuſpected of*
17	3	*more*	4 44	7 16	20	♀ riſe 2 3
18	4	*ſettled and*	4 45	7 15	♓ 2	☌ ☉ ♃ *doing*
19	5	Days dec 20 m.	4 45	7 15	14	⚹ ♀ ☿ *every*
20	6	*ſome what*	4 46	7 14	26	7 *s riſe 12 6
21	7	*cooler ; but*	4 47	7 13	♈ 8	△ ♄ ♂ *Thing*
22	G	5 paſt Trin.	4 48	7 12	21	☉ in ♌ *for*
23	2	*grows hot*	4 49	7 11	♉ 4	☽ w. ♂ *Money.*
24	3	Dog Days begin	4 50	7 10	17	*An ill Wound,*
25	4	St. JAMES.	4 50	7 10	♊ 0	*but not an ill*
26	5	*again, and*	4 51	7 9	14	☽ w. ♀ *Name,*
27	6	Day 14 16 long.	4 52	7 8	28	□ ☉ ♂ *may be*
28	7	*thunder fol-*	4 53	7 7	♋ 13	♄ ſou. 9 30
29	G	6 paſt Trin.	4 54	7 6	28	☽ w. ♃ *healed.*
30	2	*lows with*	4 55	7 5	♌ 13	♂ riſe 10 58
31	3	*rain.*	4 56	7 4	28	☽ with ☿

JULY hath XXXI Days.

	D. H.						
First Q.	7 at noon.						
Full ●	15 6 mor.						
Last Q.	23 6 mor.						
New ☽	30 1 mor.						

Planets Places.

D.	☉	♄	♃	♂	♀	☿	☽'s L.
	♋	♑	♋	♈	♊	♋	
2	11	3	23	20	10	11	S. 5
7	16	2	24	23	11	21	1
12	20	2	25	26	12	♌ 1	N. 4
17	25	2	26	29	14	11	5
22	♌ 0	1	27	♉ 2	17	20	1
27	5	1	29	5	20	28	S. 4

☍ { 12 ♏ 2 Deg. / 22 1 / 31 0 }

D.	☽ sets	☽ fou.	T.		
1	A.	A. 38	3	20	which, considering the Distance of the starry
2	8 38	1 34	4	21	Heavens, would require a Motion infinitely
3	9 19	2 32	5	22	more rapid than that above ascribed to the
4	9 57	3 27	6	23	Earth. As for the common Objection against
5	10 30	4 19	7	24	the Earth's Motion, that we are not sensible
6	11 5	5 9	8	25	of it, and that a Stone thrown up from the
7	11 37	5 59	8	26	Earth ought not to fall down upon the same
8	12 13	6 48	9	27	Place again ; it is answered at once by the a-
9	M. 13	7 37	10	28	bove Comparison of a Ship, from which (as
10	0 53	8 29	11	29	has been often found by Experiment) a Ball
11	1 33	9 19	12	30	fired directly up in the Air, does not fall be-
12	2 24	10 12	1		hind the Ship, let her Motion be ever so swift,
13	3 15	10 59	1		but, partaking of the Ship's Motion, is car-
14	Moon	11 45	2		ried forward in the Air, and falls down again
15	rise	12 34	3		upon the Deck. And as to the Objections
16	A.	M. 34	3	4	taken from some Scripture Expressions, which
17	8 21	1 12	4	5	seem to contradict the Theory of the Earth's
18	8 50	1 55	4	6	Motion, it is plain, from innumerable Instan-
19	9 20	2 38	5	7	ces, that Revelation was not given to Man-
20	9 49	3 22	6	8	kind to make them Philosophers or deep Rea-
21	10 18	4 6	7	9	soners, but to improve them in Virtue and
22	10 50	4 54	7	10	Piety ; and that it was therefore proper it
23	11 26	5 42	8	11	should be expressed in a Manner accommoda-
24	12 7	6 30	9	12	ted to common Capacities and popular Opi-
25	M. 7	7 23	10	13	nions in all Points merely speculative, and
26	0 50	8 20	11	14	which were not to have any direct Influence
27	1 45	9 18	12	15	upon the Hearts and Lives of Men. The
28	2 47	10 18	1	16	Truth of the Matter is, that the Demon-
29	4 0	11 18	2	17	strations given by the incomparable Sir *Isaac*
30	Moon	A. 16	3	18	*Newton*, have established the Doctrine of the
31	sets	1 15	4	19	Motion of the Earth and other Planets, and
				20	the Comets round the Sun, and of the se-

condary

AUGUST. *VIII Month.*

Thy Praise my Morning Song, my daily Theme,
My Ev'ning Subject, and my Midnight Dream;
When Grief oppresses, and when Pain assails;
When all the Man, and all the Stoic fails;
When fierce Tentation's stormy Billows roll;
When Guilt and Horror overwhelm my Soul;
With outward Ills contending Passions join'd,
To shake frail Virtue, and unhinge the Mind;
When

		Remark. days, &c.	☉ ris	☉ set	☽ pl.	Aspects, &c.
1	4	Lammas Day.	4 57	7 3	♍ 13	♀ rise 1 40
2	5	*More tempe-*	4 58	7 2	27	*When out of Fa-*
3	6	Days dec. 46 m.	4 58	7 2	♎ 11	*vour, none know*
4	7	*rate, then*	4 59	7 1	25	*thee; when in,*
5	G	7 past Trin.	5 0	7 0	♏ 9	*thou dost not*
6	2	*clouds, with*	5 1	6 59	22	△ ♂ ☿ *know*
7	3	*rain*	5 2	6 58	♐ 5	7 *s rise 10 55
8	4	Day 13 54 long.	5 3	6 57	17	*thyself.*
9	5	*and*	5 4	6 56	29	☽ with ♄
10	6	St. Lawrence.	5 5	6 55	♑ 11	*A lean Award*
11	7	*thunder;*	5 6	6 54	23	☿ sets 7 54
12	G	8 past Trin.	5 8	6 52	♒ 5	♄ sou. 8 30
13	2	*sultry weather,*	5 9	6 51	17	♃ rises 3 32
14	3	*clouds, and*	5 10	6 50	29	♂ rise 10 25
15	4	Assum. V. MARY.	5 11	6 49	♓ 11	7 *s rise 10 25
16	5	*rain;*	5 13	6 47	23	*is better than a*
17	6	Days dec. 1 18	5 14	6 46	♈ 5	♀ rise 1 37
18	7	*then more*	5 15	6 45	17	*fat Judgment.*
19	G	9 past Trin.	5 16	6 44	29	God, Parents,
20	2	Day 13 26 long.	5 17	6 43	♉ 12	*and* Instructors,
21	3	*temperate,*	5 18	6 42	25	☽ with ♂ *can*
22	4	*clear*	5 20	6 40	♊ 8	☉ in ♍ △ ☉ ♄
23	5	*and fair;*	5 21	6 39	22	*never be*
24	6	St. BARTHOL.	5 22	6 38	♋ 6	7 *s rise 9 52
25	7	*flying*	5 24	6 36	21	☽ with ♀ *re-*
26	G	10 past Trin.	5 25	6 35	♌ 6	☽ w. ♃ *quited.*
27	2	Days dec. 1 42	5 26	6 34	21	♄ sou. 7 36
28	3	*clouds and*	5 27	6 33	♍ 6	♃ rise 2 54
29	4	*perhaps*	5 28	6 32	21	☽ with ☿
30	5	Day 13 h. long	5 30	6 30	♎ 6	△ ♂ ☿
31	6	*rain.*	5 31	6 29	21	♂ rise 9 54

August hath XXXI Days.

	D. H.
First Q.	5	8 aft.
Full ●	13	9 aft.
Last Q.	21	9 aft.
New ☽	28	10 mor.

☌	12 ♎ 29 Deg.
	22	29
	31	28

Planets Places.

D.	☉	♄	♃	♂	♀	☿	D s L.
	♌	♑	♌	♉	♊	♍	
1	9	1	0	8	24	5	S. 4
6	14	1	1	11	28	11	N. 2
12	20	0	2	15 ♋ 4	14	17	5
17	25	0	3	17	9	22	2
22	♍ 0	0	4	20	14	24	S. 3
27	4	0	5	23	19	25	5

D.	☽ set	☽ fou	T.	Secondary Planets or Satellites round their Pri-
1	8 A.25	2 A. 9	5	21	maries, in such a Manner, as leaves no Room
2	9	3	3	1	6	22	for any, but such as do not understand them,
3	9	37	3	53	6	23	to hesitate about it. The Sun's apparent Ri-
4	10	12	4	44	7	24	sing and Setting is therefore owing to the
5	10	56	5	36	8	25	Earth's turning round upon its own Axis; and
6	11	37	6	28	9	26	his apparent Change of Place among the fixed
7	12	22	7	18	10	27	Stars, to our real Change of Situation round
8	M. 22	8	18	11	28	the Sun. The different Seasons of the Year,
9	1	12	8	57	11	29	with all their delightful Varieties, are owing
10	2	2	9	45	12	30	to the most simple Contrivance that can be
11	2	52	10	33	1	31	imagined, viz. The Inclination of the Earth's
12	Moon	11	18	2	Au.	Axis to the Plane of the Ecliptic. Any Per-
13	rises	12	3	2	son who has not an Opportunity of seeing an
14	A.	M.	3	3	Orrery, may easily represent this by an Apple
15	7	25	0	36	3	4	or any other round Body with a Wire thrust
16	7	43	1	20	5	through the Middle of it, and carried round
17	8	22	2	4	5	6	a Table having a Candle placed on the Mid-
18	8	51	2	49	5	7	dle; if the lower End of the Wire be made
19	9	25	3	33	6	8	to touch the Table all the Way round, and to
20	10	3	4	23	7	9	lean a little, the upper End still pointing to-
21	10	47	5	13	8	10	wards the same Side of the Room, by turning
22	11	42	6	10	9	11	the Skewer round, as it is carried along, it
23	12	37	7	6	12	12	will be easy to understand how the Earth's
24	M. 37	8	6	11	13	Turning once round upon her own Axis, makes
25	1	39	9	6	12	14	a Day and a Night; and by carrying the Ap-
26	2	51	10	4	1	15	ple round the Table, it will be easy to shew
27	4	5	11	1	2	16	how the Sun (represented by the Candle) must
28	Moon	11	58	2	17	seem to change Place with regard to the fixed
29	sets.	A. 55	3	18	Stars; and by observing how differently the
30	7 A.46	1	50	4	19	Light of the Candle enlightens the different
31	8	23	2	45	5	20	Parts of the Apple as the Wire points to-

D

ward

SEPTEMBER. IX *Month.*

When Nature sinks ; when Death's dark Shades arise,
And this World's Glories vanish from these Eyes ;
Then may the Thought of Thee be ever near,
To calm the Tumult, and compose the Fear.
In all my Woes thy Favour my Defence ;
Safe in thy Mercy, not my Innocence,
And through what future Scenes thy Hand may guide
My wond'ring Soul, and thro' what States untry'd,
                                              What

		Remark. days, &c.	☉ ris	☉ set	☽ pl.	Aspects, &c.
1	7	Dog Days end	5 32	6 28	♏ 5	* ♀ ☿ He that
2	G	11 past Trin.	5 33	6 27	18	* ♂ ♀ builds
3	2	Clouds	5 34	6 26	♐ 1	♀ rises 1 51
4	3	and	5 35	6 25	14	before he counts
5	4	Days dec. 2 2	5 36	6 24	27	☽ with ♄ the
6	5	like for	5 38	6 22	♑ 9	Cost, acts fool-
7	6	rain ; then	5 39	6 21	21	7 *s rise 9 0
8	7	Nativ. V. MARY.	5 40	6 20	♒ 3	ishly ; and he
9	G	12 past Trin	5 41	6 19	15	that counts be-
10	2	wind,	5 43	6 17	27	fore he builds,
11	3	Days 12 32 long.	5 44	6 16	♓ 8	finds he did not
12	4	Days dec. 2 22	5 46	6 14	20	♄ set 11 16
13	5	fair and	5 47	6 13	♈ 2	7*s rise 8 40
14	6	Holy Rood.	5 49	6 11	14	♃ ri. 2 11 count
15	7	pleasant,	5 50	6 10	26	☌ ♃ ♀ wisely.
16	G	13 past Trin.	5 51	6 9	♉ 9	♂ rise 9 11
17	2	Days 12 16 long.	5 53	6 7	22	♀ rise 2 14
18	3	for some	5 54	6 6	♊ 5	☽ with ♂
19	4	Ember Week.	5 56	6 4	18	Patience in
20	5	days ;	5 57	6 3	♋ 2	Market, is
21	6	St. MATTHEW.	5 58	6 2	16	worth Pounds
22	7	then clouds	6 0	6 0	♌ 0	☉ in ♎ □ ☉ ♄
23	G	14 past Trin.	6 1	5 59	14	☽ w. ♃ & ♀ in a
24	2	with wind	6 3	5 57	29	△ ☉ ♂ Year.
25	3	and	6 4	5 56	♍ 14	☽ w. ☿ Danger
26	4	rain	6 5	5 55	29	7*s rise 7 52 is
27	5	Days decr. 3 h.	6 7	5 53	♎ 14	♄ set 10 21
28	6	towards the end.	6 8	5 52	28	♃ rise 1 30
29	7	St. MICHAEL.	6 9	5 51	♏ 12	♂ r. 8 32 Sauce
30	G	15 past Trin.	6 11	5 49	26	for Prayers.

SEPTEMBER hath xxx Days.

	D.	H.
First Q.	4	8 mor.
Full ●	12	at noon.
Last Q.	20	4 mor.
New ☽	26	9 aft.

☊	12	♎ 28	Deg.
	22	28	
	30	28	

Planets Places.

D.	☉	♄	♃	♂	♀	☿	☽'s L.
	♍	♑	♌	♉	♋	♍	
1	9	0	6	25	24	24	N. 1
6	14	0	7	27	29	20	5
12	20	0	9	29	♌ 6	14	3
17	25	0	9	♊ 0	11	12	S. 2
22	♎ 0	0	10	2	17	13	5
27	5	0	11	2	23	17	1

D.	☽ set	☽ sou.	T.	
1	9 1	3 36	6	21
2	9 41	4 27	7	22
3	10 23	5 17	8	23
4	11 16	6 6	9	24
5	12 10	7 1	10	25
6	M. 10	7 56	10	26
7	0 54	8 41	11	27
8	1 50	9 26	12	28
9	2 48	10 11	1	29
10	3 48	10 57	1	30
11	4 37	11 37	2	31
12	Moon	12 22	3	Sept.
13	rises.	M. 22	3	
14	7 A. 7	0 57	4	3
15	7 39	1 43	4	4
16	8 14	2 30	5	5
17	8 57	3 22	6	6
18	9 43	4 14	7	7
19	10 37	5 8	8	8
20	11 39	6 2	9	9
21	12 41	6 59	9	10
22	M. 41	7 55	18	11
23	1 44	8 52	11	12
24	2 53	9 48	12	13
25	Moon	10 43	1	14
26	sets	11 37	2	15
27	A.	A. 31	3	16
28	7 e	1 25	4	17
29	7 39	2 19	5	18
30	8 23	3 13	6	19

ward it, or from it, the Cause of the Difference of the Seasons, of the Length of the Days and Nights, of the Sun's shining more directly or more obliquely upon different Parts of the Earth, and of the Heat of Summer, and Cold of Winter, may be made plain to any Capacity. That the Earth is of a round, or nearly round Figure, is plain from the Shadow it casts upon the Face of the Moon in a partial Eclipse of the Moon, which is always round, and never of any other Figure. It is also manifest from what is always observed at Sea, *viz.* That a Ship, as it approaches, first shews its Masts and Sails, and by Degrees its lower Parts, till it becomes all visible; and, as it goes off, its Hulk is first lost, and then its Sails and upper Parts, till it be quite hid by the Convexity or Roundness of the Surface of the Ocean.

As the Earth is carried round the Sun once in a Year, so is the Moon carried round the Earth once in about twenty-seven Days, accompanying her in her whole Revolution, at the above-mentioned Distance of two hundred and forty thousand Miles, and keeping always the same Face towards the Earth. That the Moon goes round the Earth, as her Centre, is evident to the Eye. For, when she is between the Sun and the Earth, she is invisible to us, her dark Side being turned toward us. When she goes a little Way forward in her Revolution, so as to come from between

us

OCTOBER. *X Month.*

What distant Seats soe'er I may explore,
When frail Mortality shall be no more;
If aught of meek or contrite in thy Sight
Shall fit me for the Realms of Bliss and Light,
Be this the Bliss of all my future Days,
To view thy Glories, and to sing thy Praise.
When the dread Hour, ordain'd of old, shall come,
Which brings on stubborn Guilt its righteous Doom,
When

		Remark. days, &c.	☉ ris	☉ set	☽ pl.	Aspects, &c.
1	2	*Moderate*	6 12	5 48	♐ 10	*If you have*
2	3	*and plea-*	6 13	5 47	23	♀ rise 3 45
3	4	Day 11 32 long.	6 14	5 46	♑ 5	☽ with ♄ *no*
4	5	*sant, but*	6 15	5 45	17	*Honey in your*
5	6	*soon turns*	6 16	5 44	29	7 *s rise 7 20
6	7	Days dec. 3 26	6 18	5 42	♒ 11	⚹ ☉ ♃ □ ♂ ♀
7	G	16 past Trin.	6 19	5 41	23	□ ♄ ☿ *Pot,*
8	2	*to rain,*	6 20	5 40	♓ 5	△ ♂ ☿ *have*
9	3	*with high*	6 21	5 39	17	*some in your*
10	4	*wind, and*	6 22	5 38	29	*Mouth.*
11	5	*cool,*	6 23	5 37	♈ 11	*A Pair of*
12	6	Days dec. 3 40	6 25	5 35	23	♄ sets 9 33
13	7	*then more*	6 26	5 34	♉ 6	⚹ ♃ ☿ *good*
14	G	17 past Trin.	6 27	5 33	19	7 *s rise 6 46
15	2	*settled*	6 29	5 31	♊ 2	☽ with ♂ *Ears*
16	3	Day 11 h. long.	6 30	5 30	15	♃ rises 12 42
17	4	*and fair,*	6 31	5 29	29	Sirius ri. 12 0
18	5	St. Luke.	6 32	5 28	♋ 13	♂ rises 7 20
19	6	*warm,*	6 34	5 26	27	♀ rises 3 23
20	7	Days dec. 4 h.	6 35	5 25	♌ 11	☽ with ♃ *will*
21	G	18 past Trin.	6 37	5 23	25	*drain dry an*
22	2	K. Geo. II. cro.	6 38	5 22	♍ 9	☌ ☉ ☿ *hun-*
23	3	*and flying*	6 39	5 21	24	☉ in ♏ ☌ ☽ ♀
24	4	*clouds,*	6 40	5 20	♎ 9	⚹ ♄ ☿ *dred*
25	5	Crispin.	6 41	5 19	23	⚹ ☉ ♄ *Tongues.*
26	6	*then*	6 43	5 17	♏ 7	☽ with ☿
27	7	Days 10 32 long.	6 44	5 16	21	♄ set 8 40
28	G	Simon and Jude.	6 45	5 15	♐ 4	Sirius ri. 11 20
29	2	*cold rain,*	6 46	5 14	17	△ ♂ ♀
30	3	*and wind.*	6 48	5 12	♑ 0	☌ ☽ ♄ □ ♄ ♀
31	4		6 49	5 11	13	♃ rise 11 55

OCTOBER hath xxxi Days.

	D.	H.	
Firſt Q.	3	11	aft.
Full ●	12	4	mor.
Laſt Q.	19	10	mor.
New ☽	26	5	mor.
☋ 12	♎	28	Deg.
22		28	
31		28	

Planets Places.

D.	☉	♄	♃	♂	♀	☿	☽'s L.
	♎	♑	♌	♊	♌	♍	
2	9	1	12	3	28	24	N. 4
7	14	1	13	3	♍4	♎2	5
12	19	1	14	4	10	11	0
17	24	1	14	3	16	20	S. 4
22	29	2	15	2	22	29	4
27	♏4	2	15	1	28	♏7	N. 2

D.	☽ ſets		☽ ſou.		T.	
1	9	18	4 A.	10	7	20
2	10	9	5	7	8	21
3	11	2	5	56	8	22
4	11	58	6	44	9	23
5	12	54	7	31	10	24
6	M.	54	8	17	11	25
7	1	46	9	1	12	26
8	2	42	9	45	12	27
9	3	42	10	30	1	28
10	4	36	11	14	2	29
11	Moon		11	57	2	30
12	riſes		12	41	3	Oct.
18	6 A.	24	M.	41	3	
14	7	5	1	25	4	3
15	7	48	2	19	5	4
16	8	37	3	13	6	5
17	9	38	4	11	7	6
18	10	46	5	9	8	7
19	11	55	6	5	9	8
20	Morn.		7	0	10	9
21	1	0	7	50	10	10
22	2	4	8	40	11	11
23	3	14	9	36	12	12
24	4	27	10	31	1	13
25	Moon		11	24	2	14
26	ſets		A.	17	3	15
27	A.		1	10	4	16
28	7	9	2	3	5	17
29	8	0	2	56	5	18
30	8	56	3	48	6	19
31	9	42	4	39	7	20

us and the Sun, we ſee a ſmall Part of her Body enlightned, and ſo on ſtill more and more, till ſhe comes to be in Oppoſition to the Sun, and then we ſee all that Side of her which the Sun ſhines upon, when we ſay ſhe is full; though the Sun does not, in Reality, enlighten any more of her Body at Full than at new Moon; only her enlightened Side is turned towards us in the one Caſe, and from us in the other. This whole Matter may be made very plain to any Capacity in the ſame Manner as is above directed with regard to the Earth's Revolution round the Sun, by carrying a ſmaller Apple or Ball to repreſent the Moon round the firſt, which repreſents the Earth, and obſerving how the Light of the Candle ſhining upon the little Ball muſt appear to a Fly or other Inſect placed upon the large one. Whenever the Moon happens to come exactly between the Earth and the Sun, ſhe ſtops the Light of the Sun, and then we ſay, the Sun is eclipſed; and according as the Moon happens to cover a Part or the Whole of the Sun's Face, we call the Eclipſe partial or total. Sometimes a total Eclipſe of the Sun happens when the Moon is at her greateſt Diſtance from the Earth (for ſhe does not go round the Earth in an exact Circle, as neither do any of the reſt of the primary or ſecondary Planets round their Centers) and then, as all Objects appear ſmaller according to their Diſtance, ſhe does not cover the whole Face of the Sun, but a part

E of

NOVEMBER. *XI Month.*

When Storms of Fire on Sinners ſhall be pour'd,
And all th' Obdurate in thy Wrath devour'd;
May I then hope to find a lowly Place
To ſtand the meaneſt of th' etherial Race;
Swift at thy Word to wing the liquid Sky,
And on thy humbleſt Meſſages to fly:
Howe'er thy bliſsful Sight may raiſe my Soul,
While vaſt Eternity's long Ages roll,

Perfection

		Remark. days, &c.	☉ riſ	☉ ſet	☽ pl.	Aſpects, &c.
1	5	All Saints.	6 50	5 10	♑ 25	♂ riſe 6 13
2	6	Days dec. 4 32	6 51	5 9	♒ 7	*Serving God is*
3	7	*Clouds*	6 52	5 8	19	*Doing Good to*
4	G	20 paſt Trin.	6 53	5 7	♓ 1	*Man, but Pray-*
5	2	Powder Plot.	6 54	5 6	13	*ing is thought*
6	3	Day 10 10 long.	6 55	5 5	25	♀ riſe 4 2 *an*
7	4	*and threa-*	6 56	5 4	♈ 7	*eaſier Service,*
8	5	*tens cold*	6 58	5 2	19	□ ☉ ♃ *and*
9	6	*rain or ſnow,*	6 59	5 1	♉ 2	*therefore more*
10	7	K. Geo. II. b. 1683	7 0	5 0	15	Sirius ri. 10 27
11	G	21 paſt Trin.	7 1	4 59	28	☽ with ♂ *gene-*
12	2	*then*	7 3	4 57	♊ 11	✱ ♃ ♀ *rally*
13	3	*pleaſant*	7 4	4 56	25	♄ ſets 7 35 *cho-*
14	4	Days dec. 5 h.	7 5	4 55	♋ 9	♃ ri. 11 4 *ſen.*
15	5	*and ſuita-*	7 6	4 54	23	7*s ſou. 12 4
16	6	*to the*	7 7	4 53	♌ 7	☍ ☉ ♂ *Nothing*
17	7	*ſeaſon,*	7 8	4 52	21	☽ w ♃ *humbler*
18	G	22 paſt Trin.	7 9	4 51	♍ 5	♂ ſou. 11 51
19	2	*but follow'd*	7 10	4 50	19	Sirius riſes 9 51
20	3	Day 9 38 long.	7 11	4 49	♎ 3	♀ riſe 4 29
21	4	*by cold*	7 12	4 48	17	☉ in ♐ *than*
22	5	*cloudy,*	7 12	4 48	♏ 1	☌ ☽ ♀ △ ♃ ☿
23	6	Days dec. 5 16	7 13	4 47	15	Ambition, *when*
24	7	*weather,*	7 14	4 46	29	*it is about to*
25	G	23 paſt Trin.	7 15	4 45	♐ 12	7*s ſou. 11 26
26	2	*with ſnow*	7 16	4 44	25	☌ ☽ ☿ ✱ ♄ ♀
27	3	*or rain*	7 16	4 44	♑ 8	☽ with ♄
28	4	Days dec. 5 24	7 17	4 43	21	♄ ſets 6 37
29	5	*and wind.*	7 18	4 42	♒ 3	♃ riſes 9 57
30	6	St. ANDREW.	7 18	4 42	15	*climb.*

NOVEMBER hath xxx Days.

	D.	H.
First Q.	2	6 aft.
Full ●	10	8 aft.
Last Q.	17	7 aft.
New ☽	24	8 aft.

☊		
12	♎ 27	Deg
22	27	
30	26	

Planets Places.

D.	☉	♄	♃	♂	♀	☿	☽'s L
	♏	♑	♌	♉	♎	♏	
1	9	2	16	0	4	15	N. 5
6	14	3	16	28	10	23	3
12	20	3	17	26	17	♐ 2	S. 3
17	25	4	17	24	23	10	5
22	♐ 1	4	17	22	0	17	0
27	6	5	17	21	♏ 6	24	N. 5

D.	☽ sets	☽ sou.	T.	
1	10 45	5 29	8	21
2	11 44	6 15	9	22
3	12 40	7 0	10	23
4	M. 40	7 44	10	24
5	1 35	8 27	11	25
6	2 30	9 10	12	26
7	3 21	9 53	12	27
8	4 23	10 39	1	28
9	Moon	11 25	2	29
10	rises	12 14	3	30
11	A.	M. 14	3	31
12	6 37	1 6	4	Nov.
13	7 32	2 4	5	
14	8 33	3 1	6	3
15	9 39	3 56	6	4
16	10 48	4 51	7	5
17	11 58	5 43	8	6
18	Morn.	6 35	9	7
19	1 4	7 26	10	8
20	2 6	8 16	11	9
21	3 15	9 8	12	10
22	4 25	10 0	1	11
23	Moon	10 55	1	12
24	sets	11 50	2	13
25	A	A. 42	3	14
26	6 34	1 34	4	15
27	7 31	2 27	5	16
28	8 23	3 19	6	17
29	9 25	4 4	7	18
30	10 20	4 49	7	19

of his Body is ſeen round the Moon like a ſhining Ring. But, if the Moon happens to come between the Earth and Sun, when ſhe is at her leaſt Diſtance from the Earth, ſhe appears then ſo large as to cover the whole Face of the Sun, and makes, for ſome Minutes, a Darkneſs equal to that of Twilight. When the Earth comes exactly between the Sun and the Moon, ſhe darkens a Part or the Whole of the Moon's Face, and makes an Eclipſe of the Moon. The Earth being a Body about thirty or forty Times larger than the Moon, caſts a Shadow large enough to eclipſe the Moon, if her Diameter were three Times greater than it is, whereas the Shadow of the Moon can never eclipſe the whole Face of the Earth together. If the Moon revolved round the Earth in the ſame Plane as the Earth goes round the Sun, there would be conſtantly an Eclipſe of the Sun every New, and of the Moon every full Moon. But to prevent this Inconvenience, the Author of Nature has ordered Matters ſo, that the Courſe of the Moon round the Earth is ſometimes above and ſometimes below that of the Earth round the Sun, ſo that their Shadows generally miſs one another. Theſe Motions are ſo exactly regulated, that Aſtronomers can foretel Eclipſes to Minutes at an hundred Years Diſtance, than which there is not a more remarkable Inſtance either of human Sagacity, or of the Truth of that Expreſſion of

Scrip

DECEMBER. *XII Month.*

Perfection on Perfection tow'ring high,
Glory on Glory rais'd, and Joy on Joy,
Each Pow'r improving in the bright'ning Mind,
To humble Virtues, lofty Knowledge join'd ;
Be this my highest Aim, howe'er I soar,
Before thy Footstool prostrate to adore,
My brightest Crown before thy Feet to lay,
My Pride to serve, my Glory to obey.

E N D.

		Remark. days, &c.	☉ris	☉ſet	☽ pl.	Aspects, &c.
1	7	Day 9 24 long.	7 19	4 41	♒ 27	*The diſcontented*
2	G	Advent Sunday.	7 19	4 41	♓ 9	♂ ſou. 10 32
3	2	*Cold and*	7 20	4 40	21	*Man finds no*
4	3	Days dec. 5 30.	7 20	4 40	♈ 3	*eaſy Chair.*
5	4	*raw, then*	7 21	4 39	15	Sirius riſe 8 41
6	5	Days 9 18 long.	7 22	4 38	27	☌ ♄ ☿ □ ♃ ♀
7	6	*more plea-*	7 22	4 38	♉ 10	♀ riſes 5 0
8	7	Concep. V. M.	7 23	4 37	23	☌ ☽ ♂ △ ☉ ♃
9	G	2d in Advent.	7 23	4 37	♊ 7	7 *s ſou. 10 28
10	2	*ſant,*	7 24	4 36	21	*Virtue and a*
11	3	Days 9 12 long.	7 24	4 36	♋ 5	*Trade, are*
12	4	*froſt and*	7 24	4 36	19	♃ riſe 9 1
13	5	St. Lucy.	7 24	4 36	♌ 3	Sirius riſe 8 7
14	6	Days decr. 5 40	7 25	4 35	17	☽ with ♃ *a*
15	7	*flying clouds,*	7 25	4 35	♍ 2	□ ♃ ♂ *Child's*
16	G	3d in Advent.	7 25	4 35	16	7 *s ſou. 9 56
17	2	*then more*	7 25	4 35	♎ 0	♂ ſou. 9 14
18	3	*moderate*	7 25	4 35	14	♀ riſes 5 23
19	4	Ember Week.	7 25	4 35	28	*beſt Portion.*
20	5	*and clear,*	7 25	4 35	♏ 12	*Gifts much*
21	6	St. Thomas.	7 25	4 35	25	☉ in ♑ Shor. D
22	7	Days 9 10 long.	7 25	4 35	♐ 8	☌ ☽ ♀ ☌ ♄ ☿
23	G	4th in Advent.	7 25	4 35	21	Sirius riſes 7 23
24	2	*but windy,*	7 25	4 35	♑ 4	☽ with ♄ & ☿
25	3	CHRIST born.	7 25	4 35	17	☌ ☉ ☿ *expect-*
26	4	St. Stephen.	7 25	4 35	29	*ed, are paid,*
27	5	St. John.	7 25	4 35	♒ 11	♃ riſe 7 51
28	6	Innocents.	7 25	4 35	23	7 *s ſou. 9 0
29	7	Days 9 10 long.	7 25	4 35	♓ 5	☌ ☉ ♄ *not*
30	G	*cold and cloudy.*	7 24	4 36	17	△ ♃ ♀ *given.*
31	2	Silveſter.	7 24	4 36	29	Sirius riſe 6 48

DECEMBER hath XXXI Days.

	D.	H.
First Q.	2	4 aft
Full ●	10	8 mor.
Last Q.	17	5 mor.
New ☽	24	10 mor.
☊	12 ♎	25 Deg
	22	24
	31	23

Planets Places.

D.	☉	♄	♃	♂	♀	☿	☽'s L.
	♐	♑	♌	♉	♏		
2	11	5	17	20	12	1	N. 4
7	16	6	17	19	18	7	S. 1
12	21	6	17	18	25	11	5
17	26	7	17	17	♐ 1	12	2
22	♑ 1	8	16	18	7	8	N. 3
27	6	8	16	18	13	1	5

D.	☽ sets	☽ sou.	T.	
1	11 20	5 30	8	20
2	12 14	6 10	9	21
3	M. 14	6 54	9	22
4	1 7	7 38	10	23
5	2 6	8 21	11	24
6	3 0	9 4	12	25
7	4 0	9 54	12	26
8	5 0	10 43	1	27
9	Moon	11 40	2	28
10	rises	12 36	3	29
11	A.	M. 36	3	30
12	7 17	1 36	4	Dec.
13	8 20	2 30	5	
14	9 30	3 24	6	3
15	10 50	4 18	7	4
16	11 53	5 11	8	5
17	12 55	6 2	9	6
18	M. 55	6 53	9	7
19	1 59	7 44	10	8
20	3 8	8 36	11	9
21	4 12	9 28	12	10
22	5 10	10 20	1	11
23	Moon	11 12	2	12
24	sets	A. 4	3	13
25	A.	12 53	3	14
26	6 59	1 42	4	15
27	7 58	2 27	5	16
28	8 53	3 11	6	17
29	9 52	3 55	6	18
30	10 49	4 39	7	19
31	11 45	5 21	8	20

Scripture, "That the Works of God are all "made in Number, Weight and Meaſure." It is certain, by Obſervations made with good Teleſcopes, that, though the Face of the Moon is covered with innumerable Inequalities like the Mountains upon the Earth, there is no great Collection of Waters upon it, like our Oceans; nor is there any Reaſon, from her Appearance through thoſe Inſtruments, to ſuppoſe ſhe has any ſuch Appendage belonging to her as our Atmoſphere of Air. If the Moon is inhabited (as ſhe may for any Thing we know) thoſe who live on one Side or Hemiſphere never can ſee our World, and thoſe who live on the other can never loſe Sight of it, except when the Earth comes between them and the Sun, as ſhe keeps always one Side turned towards us. Thoſe who live about the middle Parts of the Hemiſphere that looks towards the Earth, muſt ſee it always directly over their Heads with much the ſame Appearances as the Moon makes to us, ſometimes horned, ſometimes half, and ſometimes wholly illuminated, but of a vaſtly greater Bulk than the Moon appears to us. It ſeems highly probable, that the Attraction of the Moon acting more ſtrongly upon the Fluid than the ſolid Parts of our Terraqueous Globe is the Cauſe of our Tides, as they anſwer ſo exactly to her Motions and Diſtances from us, and other Circumſtances. To enter upon that Theory, however, would be beſide my preſent Purpoſe. [*Remainder in our next.*]

ECLIPSES, 1753.

THIS Year there will be four Eclipſes, two of the *Sun*, and two of the *Moon*.

The Firſt Eclipſe will be of the *Moon*, on *Tueſday*, the 17th Day of *April*, about Two a Clock in the Afternoon, and therefore it cannot be ſeen here; but in *London* the Moon will riſe five Digits eclipſed.

The Second will be of the *Sun*, on *Thurſday*, the 3d of *May*, about Two a Clock in the Morning, therefore inviſible.

The Third Eclipſe will be of the *Moon*, on *Friday*, the 12th Day of *October*, in the Morning, when, if the Air be clear, the Moon will be ſeen eclipſed almoſt ſix Digits; it begins at 26 min. after Two, and ends at 56 min. paſt Four, ſo that the whole Duration is two Hours and thirty Minutes.

The TYPE.

North.

East.

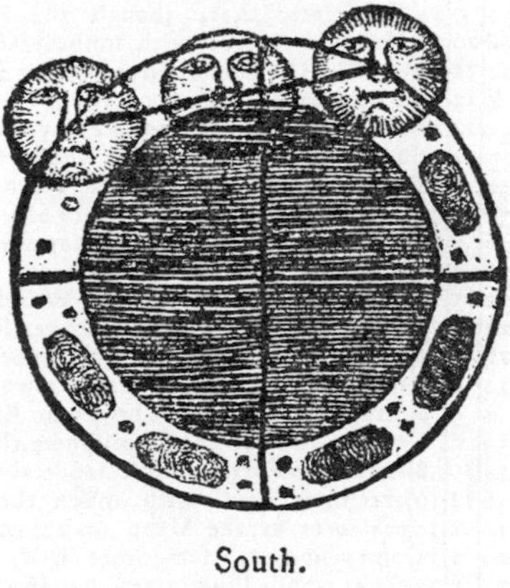

West.

South.

The Fourth is a *Solar* Eclipſe on *Friday*, the 26th of *October*, about Five a Clock in the Morning, inviſible here.

On *Sunday*, the 6th Day of *May*, in the Morning, the Planet *Mercury* may be ſeen to make a black Spot in in the *Sun's* Body, according to the following Calculation.

	D.	h.	m.	
Middle Time of the true ☌ 1753, *May*	5	15	43	P. M
Equation of Time, add			4	
Apparent Time of the true ☌		5	15	47
Mean Anomaly of the *Sun*,	10	6	21	
Mean Anomaly of *Mercury*,	10	19	47	

Diff. of the ☉ from the ☊ Log. 5,004518
    ☿ from the ☉   4,656557
    ☿ from the ☊   4,745839

Geocentrick Longitude ☉ and ☿	♉ 15°	53'	0"	
Geocentrick Latitude,		3	19	
Anomaly of Commutation,	6	0	0	
Inclination, or Heliocentrick Lat. of ☿ S.A.		4	3	
Elongation to six Hours before the true ☌		23	24	
Difference of Latitude in six Hours,		4	18	
Angle of the visible Way,	10	25		
Nearest Approach of their Centers,		3	15	
Motion from the Middle to the true ☌			35	
Latitude of ☿ at the Middle,		3	4	
Motion of Half the visible Way,		15	24	
Motion of Half Duration,		15	9	
Diff. of Lat. between the Mid. Begin. & End,		2	47	
Geocentrick Latitude at the Beginning, S. A.		0	17	
Geocentrick Latitude at the End, S. A.		5	51	
Time from the true ☌ to the Middle,		9	4	
Time of Half Duration,	3	53		
The Arch of the ☉'s Perimeter at the Begin.	1	2		
The Arch of the ☉'s Perimeter at the End,	21	48		
Apparent Semidiameter of the *Sun*,		15	45	
Apparent Semidiameter of ☿		0	6	
Mercury enters the Sun's Disk, *May* 5,	11	44	P. M.	
Middle or nearest Approach of the Centers,	15	37		
True Conjunction,	15	46		
Mercury emerges out of the Disk,	19	31		
Total Duration of this Eclipse,	7	47		

   The astronomical Time when *Mercury* goes off the Sun's Disk, being reduced to common Time, is *May* the 6th, at 31 min. after Seven in the Morning. The *Sun* rises at 1 min. past Five, and if you get up betimes, and put on your Spectacles, you will see *Mercury* rise
in

in the *Sun*, and will appear like a small black Patch in a Lady's Face.

The TYPE of this Eclipse at Sun-rising.

North.

SUN,

Ecliptick,

East.   West.

Orb of Mercury.

South.

Dr. *Halley* puts this Conjunction an Hour forwarder than by this Calculation.

THIS is to give Notice to all Persons that shall have Occasion of transporting themselves, Goods, Wares, or Merchandize from Philadelphia to New-York, or from the latter to the former, That by JOSEPH BORDEN, junior, there is a Stage-boat, well fitted and kept for that Purpose, Nicholas George, Master, and, if Wind and Weather permit, will attend at the Crooked Billet Wharff, in Philadelphia, every Monday and Tuesday in every Week, and proceed up to Borden-Town (not Burlington) on Wednesday, and on Thursday Morning a Stage-waggon, with a choice good Awning, kept by Joseph Richards, will be ready to receive them, and proceed directly to John Cluck's, opposite the City of Perth-Amboy, who keeps a House of good Entertainment; and on Friday a Stage-boat, with a large commodious Cabbin, kept by Daniel Obryant, will be ready to receive them, and proceed directly to New-York, and give her Attendance at the Whitehall Slip, near the Half Moon Battery. If People be ready at the Stage Days and Places, 'tis believed they may pass quicker by Twenty-four Hours than any other Way as our Land Carriage is ten Miles shorter than by Way of Burlington, and our Waggon does not fail to go thro' in a Day. We expect to give better Satisfaction this Year than last, by reason we are more acquainted with the Nature of the Business, and have more convenient Boats, Waggons and Stages, and will endeavour to use People in the best Manner we are capable of; and hope all good People will give it the Encouragement it deserves, and us, as the Promoters of such a publick Good. JOSEPH BORDEN, junior, JOSEPH RICHARDS, and DANIEL OBRYANT.

N. B. Joseph Borden's Shallop, Charles Vandyke, Master, will also be at Philadelphia every Friday and Saturday in every Week; enquire for him at the Queen's Head; he proceeds to Borden-Town (not Burlington) on Sunday, and the Stage-waggon also proceeds to Amboy every Monday in every Week.

Mayor's Courts for the City

ARE held quarterly at *Annapolis*, viz The laſt tueſday in *January*, *April*, *July* and *October*.

How to ſecure Houſes, &c. from LIGHTNING.

IT has pleaſed God in his Goodneſs to Mankind, at length to
diſcover to them the Means of ſecuring their Habitations and
other Buildings from Miſchief by Thunder and Lightning. The
Method is this: Provide a ſmall Iron Rod (it may be made of
the Rod-iron uſed by the Nailers) but of ſuch a Length, that one
End being three or four Feet in the moiſt Ground, the other may
be ſix or eight Feet above the higheſt Part of the Building. To
the upper End of the Rod faſten about a Foot of Braſs Wire, the
Size of a common Knitting-needle, ſharpened to a fine Point; the
Rod may be ſecured to the Houſe by a few ſmall Staples. If the
Houſe or Barn be long, there may be a Rod and Point at each End,
and a middling Wire along the Ridge from one to the other. A
Houſe thus furniſhed will not be damaged by Lightning, it being attracted by the Points, and paſſing thro the Metal into the Ground
without hurting any Thing. Veſſels alſo, having a ſharp pointed Rod
fix'd on the Top of their Maſts, with a Wire from the Foot of the
Rod reaching down, round one of the Shrouds, to the Water, will
not be hurt by Lightning.

QUAKERS General Meetings are kept,

AT Philadelphia, the 3d Sunday in March. At Che-
ſter-River, the 2d Sunday in April. At Duck-
Creek, the 3d Sunday in April. At Salem, the 4th
Sunday in April. At Weſt River on Whitſunday. At
Little Egg-Harbour, the 3d Sunday in May. At Fluſh-
ing, the laſt Sunday in May, and laſt in Nov. At Se-
tacket, the 1ſt Sunday in June. At New-town, (Long-
Iſland) the laſt Sunday in June. At Newport, the 2d
Friday in June. At Weſtbury, the laſt Sunday in Au-
guſt, and laſt in February. At Philadelphia, the 3d Sun-
day in September. At Nottingham, the laſt Monday in
September. At Cecil, the 1ſt Saturday in October.
At Choptank the 2d Saturday in October. At Little-
Creek, the 3d Sunday in October At Shrewſbury the
4th Sunday in October. At Matinicok the laſt Sunday
in October.

FAIRS are kept,

At Noxonton April 29, and October 21. Cohanſie May 5, and
October 27. Wilmington May 9, and November 4. Salem May
12, and October 31. Newcaſtle May 14, and Nov. 14. Cheſter May
16, and Oct. 16. Briſtol May 19, and Nov. 9. Burlington May 21,
and Nov. 12. Philadelphia May 27, and November 27. Lancaſter
June 12, and Nov. 12. Marcus-Hook Oct. 10. Annapolis May 12,
and Oct. 10. Charleſtown May 3, and Oct. 29.

Supreme Courts *in* Pennsylvania, *are held,*

AT *Philadelphia*, the tenth Day of *April*, and the twenty-fourth Day of *September*.

Courts of Quarter Sessions, are held,

AT *Philadelphia*, the 1st Monday in *March, June, September* and *December*. At *Newtown*, for *Bucks* County, on the 11th Day following (inclusive) in every of the Months aforesaid. At *Chester*, the last Tuesday in *May, August, November* and *February*. At *Lancaster*, the 1st Tuesday in each. At York, the last Tuesday in April, July, October and January. At *Cumberland*, the Tuesdays preceding York Courts. At *Reading*, for *Berks* County, the Tuesd. next after *Lancaster* Co. At *Easton*, for *Northampton* County, the Tuesd. next aft. *Bucks* Co.

Courts of Common Pleas, are held,

AT *Philadelphia*, the 1st Wednesday after the Quarter-Sessions in *March, June, Sept.* and *Decem.* At *Newtown*, the 9th Day following (inclusive) in every of the Months aforesaid. At *Chester*, the last Tuesday in *May, August, Novem* and *Febr.* At *Lancaster*, the 1st Tuesd. in the Months aforesaid. At *Sussex*, the 1st, at *Kent*, the 2d, and at *Newcastle*, the 3d Tuesday in the same Months.

Mayor's Courts in Philadelphia, *are held,*

THE first Tuesday in *January, April, July*, and the last Tuesday in *October*.

Supreme Courts in New-Jersey, *are held,*

AT *Amboy*, the 3d tuesday in *March*, and the 2d tuesday in *August*. At *Burlington*, the 2d tuesday in *May*, and the 1st tuesday in *November*.

Courts for Trial of Causes brought to issue in the Supreme Court, are held,

FOR *Salem* and *Cape May* Counties the 3d, for *Gloucester* the 4th tuesday in *April*. For *Hunterdon*, the 1st tuesday in *May*. For *Somerset* the 2d, For *Bergen* the 4th tuesday in *October* For *Essex*, the next tuesd. following. For *Monmouth*, the next tuesday after that.

General Sessions and County Courts, are held,

IN *Bergen* County, the 1st tuesday in *January* and *October*, and the 2d tuesday in *June*. In *Essex* the 2d tuesday in *January* and *May*, the 3d tuesday in *June*, and 4th in *September*. In *Middlesex* the 3d tuesdays in *January, April* and *July*, and the 2d tuesday in *October*. In *Somerset*, the first tuesdays in *January*,

April and *October*, and the 2d tuesdays in *June*. In *Monmouth*, the 4th tuesdays in *January*, *April* and *July*, and 3d in *October*. In *Hunterdon*, the first tuesdays in *February* and *August*, the 3d in *May*, and 4th in *October*. In *Burlington*, the 1st tuesdays in *May* and *November*, and the 2d in *February* and *August*. In *Gloucester*, the 2d tuesday in *June*, 3d in *September*, and 4th in *December* and *March*. In *Salem*, the 1st tuesday in *June*, 3d in *February* and *August*, and 4th in *November*. In *Cape-May*, the 1st tuesday in *February* and *August*, the 3d in *May*, and the 4th tuesday in *October*. For the Borough-town of *Trenton*, the 1st tuesday in *March*, 1st in *June*, 1st in *September*, and the 1st in *December*.

Supreme Courts in New-York, *are held*,

AT *New-York*, the 3d tuesday in *April*, last in *July*, and 3d in *October* and *January*. At *Richmond*, the 2d tuesday in *April*. At *Orange*, 1st tuesday in *June*. At *Dutchess*, the 2d tuesday in *June*. At *Ulster*, the thursday following. At *Albany*, the 4th tuesday in *June*. At *Queen's* County the 1st, at *Suffolk* the 2d, at *King's* County the 3d, and at *West Chester* the 4th tuesday in *September*.

Courts of Sessions and Common Pleas,

AT *New-York*, the 1st tuesday in *May*, *August*, *November* and *February*. At *Albany* the 1st tuesday in *June* and *October*, and 3d tuesday in *January* At *West Chester*, the 4th tuesday in *May* and *October*. In *Ulster*, the 1st tuesdays in *May*, and 3d in *Sept.* In *Richmond*, the 3d tuesday in *March*, and 4th in *September*. In *King's*, the 3d tuesday in *April* and *October*. In *Queen's*, the 3d tuesday in *May* and *September*. In *Suffolk*, the last tuesday in *March*, and first in *October*. In *Orange*, the last tuesday in *April* and *October*. In *Dutchess* County, the 3d tuesday in *May* and *October*.

Provincial Courts in Maryland,

TWO in a Year held at *Annapolis*, viz. The 2d tuesday in *April* and *September*.

County Courts. At *Talbot*, *Baltimore*, *Worcester*, and *St. Mary's*, the 1st tuesday in *March*, *June*, *August* and *November*. At *Dorchester*, *Cæcil*, *Ann-Arundel*, and *Charles* Counties, the 2d tuesday in the same Months ; at *Kent*, *Calvert*, *Frederick*, and *Somerset*, the 3d tuesday in the same Months ; at *Queen Anne's* and *Prince George's* the 4th tuesday in the same Months.

ROADS Northeastward.

FRom *Philadelphia* to *Bristol* 20, to *Trenton* 10, to
Prince-Town 12, to *Kingston* 3, to *Brunswick* 12,
to *Amboy* 12, to the *Narrows* 18, to *Flat-Bush* 5, to
New-York 5, to *Kingsbridge* 18, to *East-Chester* 6, to
Newrochell 4, to *Rye* 4, to *Horseneck* 7, to *Stanford* 7,
to *Norwalk* 10, to *Fairfield* 12, to *Stratford* 8, to *Mil-
ford* 4, to *Newhaven* 10, to *Branford* 10, to *Gilford* 12,
to *Killingsworth* 10, to *Seabrook* 10, to *New-London* 18,
to *Stonington* 15, to *Pemberton* 10, to *Darby* 3, to *French-
town* 24, to *Providence* 20, to *Woodcock's* 15, to *Billend's*
10, to *White's* 7, to *Dedham* 6, to *Boston* 10, to *Lyn* 9, to
Salem 8, to *Ipswich* 14, to *Newberry* 11, to *Hampton* 9, to
Portsmouth 13, to *York* 9, to *Wells* 14, to *Kennebunk* 6, to
Biddeford 14, to *Scarborough* 7, to *Falmouth* 13, to *Yar-
mouth* 10, to *Brunswick* 15, to *Richmond* 16, to *Taconick
Falls* 33, *to Norridgewock* 31.   In all 600 Miles.

ROADS Southwestward.

FRom *Philadelphia* to *Darby* 7, to *Chester* 9, to *Bran-
dewyne* 14, to *Newcastle* 6, to *Elk River* 17, to *N.
East* 7, to *Sasquehanna* 9, to *Gunpowder Ferry* 25, to *Pe-
tapsco Ferry* 20, to *Annapolis* 30, to *Queen Ann's Ferry*
13, to *Upper Marlborough* 9, to *Port Tobacco* 30, to *Hoe's
Ferry* 10, to *Southern's Ferry* 30, to *Arnold's Ferry* 36, to
Clayborn's Ferry 22, to *Freneaux* 12, to *Williamsburg* 16,
to *Hog-Island* 7, to *Isle of Wight Court-House* 18, to
Nansemond Court-House 20, to *Bennet's Creek-Bridge* 30,
to *Edenton* 30, over the *Sound* to *Bell's Ferry* 8, to
Bath-Town, on *Pamlico-River* 45, to *Grave's Ferry*, on
Neu's River 32, to *Whittock River* 20, to *New-River
Ferry* 30, to *Newtown*, on *Cape-Fear River*, 45, to
Lockwood's Folly 15, to *Shallot River* 8, to the *Eastern*
End of *Long-Bay* 22, to the *Western* End of *Long-Bay*
25, to *George-Town, Wynyaw*, 30, to *Santee Ferry* 12,
to *Jonah Collins's* 18, to *Hobcaw Ferry*, against *Charles
Town*, 30   In all 767 Miles

BIbles, Common-Prayers, Testaments, Spelling-books,
Psalters, Primmers, Copy-books for Children, and
all Sorts of Stationary, to be sold by DAVID HALL, at
the *New-Printing-Office*, in *Market-street, Philadelphia*.

TO JOSEPH HUEY

Philadelphia, June 6, 1753.

Sir,

I received your kind Letter of the 2d inst., and am glad to hear that you increase in Strength; I hope you will continue mending, 'till you recover your former Health and firmness. Let me know whether you still use the Cold Bath, and what Effect it has.

As to the Kindness you mention, I wish it could have been of more Service to you. But if it had, the only Thanks I should desire is, that you would always be equally ready to serve any other Person that may need your Assistance, and so let good Offices go round, for Mankind are all of a Family.

For my own Part, when I am employed in serving others, I do not look upon myself as conferring Favours, but as paying Debts. In my Travels, and since my Settlement, I have received much Kindness from Men, to whom I shall never have any Opportunity of making the least direct Return. And number-less Mercies from God, who is infinitely above being benefited by our Services. Those Kindnesses from Men, I can therefore only Return on their Fellow Men; and I can only shew my Grati-tude for these mercies from God, by a readiness to help his other Children and my Brethren. For I do not think that Thanks and Compliments, tho' repeated weekly, can discharge our real Obligations to each other, and much less those to our Creator. You will see in this my Notion of good Works, that I am far from expecting [(as you suppose) that I shall ever][44] to merit Heaven by them. By Heaven we understand a State of Happiness, infinite in Degree, and eternal in Duration: I can do nothing to deserve such rewards: He that for giving a Draught of Water to a thirsty Person, should expect to be paid with a good Plantation, would be modest in his Demands, compar'd with those who think they deserve Heaven for the little good they do on Earth. Even the mix'd imperfect Pleas-ures we enjoy in this World, are rather from God's Goodness than our Merit; how much more such Happiness of Heaven.

For my own part I have not the Vanity to think I deserve it, the Folly to expect it, nor the Ambition to desire it; but content myself in submitting to the Will and Disposal of that God who made me, who has hitherto preserv'd and bless'd me, and in whose Fatherly Goodness I may well confide, that he will never make me miserable, and that even the Afflictions I may at any time suffer shall tend to my Benefit.

The Faith you mention has doubtless its use in the World. I do not desire to see it diminished, nor would I endeavour to lessen it in any Man. But I wish it were more productive of good Works, than I have generally seen it: I mean real good Works, Works of Kindness, Charity, Mercy, and Publick Spirit; not Holiday-keeping, Sermon-Reading or Hearing; performing Church Ceremonies, or making long Prayers, filled with Flatteries and Compliments, despis'd even by wise Men, and much less capable of pleasing the Deity. The worship of God is a Duty; the hearing and reading of Sermons may be useful; but, if Men rest in Hearing and Praying, as too many do, it is as if a Tree should Value itself on being water'd and putting forth Leaves, tho' it never produc'd any Fruit.

Your great Master tho't much less of these outward Appearances and Professions than many of his modern Disciples. He prefer'd the *Doers* of the Word, to the meer *Hearers*; the Son that seemingly refus'd to obey his Father, and yet perform'd his Commands, to him that profess'd his Readiness, but neglected the Work; the heretical but charitable Samaritan, to the uncharitable tho' orthodox Priest and sanctified Levite; & those who gave Food to the hungry, Drink to the Thirsty, Raiment to the Naked, Entertainment to the Stranger, and Relief to the Sick, tho' they never heard of his Name, he declares shall in the last Day be accepted, when those who cry Lord! Lord! who value themselves on their Faith, tho' great enough to perform Miracles, but have neglected good Works, shall be rejected. He profess'd, that he came not to call the Righteous but Sinners to repentance; which imply'd his modest Opinion, that there were some in his Time so good, that they need not hear even him for Improvement; but now-a-days we have scarce a little

Parson, that does not think it the Duty of every Man within his Reach to sit under his petty Ministrations; and that whoever omits them [offends God. I wish to such more humility, and to you health and happiness, being your friend and servant,]

B. FRANKLIN.

THREE LETTERS TO GOVERNOR SHIRLEY [45]

LETTER I

Concerning the Voice of the People in Choosing the Rulers by Whom Taxes are Imposed

Tuesday Morning [December 17, 1754].

SIR,

I return you the loose sheets of the plan, with thanks to your Excellency for communicating them.

I apprehend, that excluding the *people* of the colonies from all share in the choice of the grand council will give extreme dissatisfaction, as well as the taxing them by act of Parliament, where they have no representative. It is very possible, that this general government might be as well and faithfully administered without the people, as with them; but where heavy burthens have been laid on them, it has been found useful to make it, as much as possible, their own act; for they bear better when they have, or think they have some share in the direction; and when any public measures are generally grievous, or even distasteful to the people, the wheels of government move more heavily.

LETTER II

On the Imposition of Direct Taxes upon the Colonies without Their Consent

Wednesday Morning [December 18, 1754].

SIR,

I mentioned it yesterday to your Excellency as my opinion, that excluding the *people* of the colonies from all share in the choice of the grand council, would probably give extreme dissatisfaction, as well as the taxing them by act of Parliament, where they have no representative. In matters of general concern to the people, and especially where burthens are to be laid upon them, it is of use to consider, as well what they will be apt to think and say, as what they ought to think; I shall therefore, as your Excellency requires it of me, briefly mention what of either kind occurs to me on this occasion.

First they will say, and perhaps with justice, that the body of the people in the colonies are as loyal, and as firmly attached to the present constitution, and reigning family, as any subjects in the king's dominions.

That there is no reason to doubt the readiness and willingness of the representatives they may choose, to grant from time to time such supplies for the defence of the country, as shall be judged necessary, so far as their abilities will allow.

That the people in the colonies, who are to feel the immediate mischiefs of invasion and conquest by an enemy in the loss of their estates, lives and liberties, are likely to be better judges of the quantity of forces necessary to be raised and maintained, forts to be built and supported, and of their own abilities to bear the expence, than the parliament of England at so great a distance.

That governors often come to the colonies merely to make fortunes, with which they intend to return to Britain; are not always men of the best abilities or integrity; have many of them no estates here, nor any natural connexions with us, that should make them heartily concerned for our welfare; and might possibly be fond of raising and keeping up more forces than necessary, from the profits accruing to themselves, and to make provision for their friends and dependants.

That the counsellors in most of the colonies being appointed by the crown, on the recommendation of governors, are often of small estates, frequently dependant on the governors for offices, and therefore too much under influence.

That there is therefore great reason to be jealous of a power in such governors and councils, to raise such sums as they shall judge necessary, by draft on the lords of the treasury, to be afterwards laid on the colonies by act of parliament, and paid by the people here; since they might abuse it by projecting useless expeditions, harassing the people, and taking them from their labour to execute such projects, merely to create offices and employments, and gratify their dependants, and divide profits.

That the parliament of England is at a great distance, subject to be misinformed and misled by such Governors and Councils, whose united interests might probably secure them against the effect of any complaint from hence.

That it is supposed an undoubted right of Englishmen, not to be taxed but by their own consent given through their representatives.

That the colonies have no representatives in parliament.

That to propose taxing them by parliament, and refuse them the liberty of choosing a representative council, to meet in the colonies, and consider and judge of the necessity of any general tax, and the quantum, shews suspicion of their loyalty to the crown, or of their regard for their country, or of their common sense and understanding, which they have not deserved.

That compelling the colonies to pay money without their consent, would be rather like raising contributions in an enemy's country, than taxing of Englishmen for their own public benefit.

That it would be treating them as a conquered people, and not as true British subjects.

That a tax laid by the representatives of the colonies might easily be lessened as the occasions should lessen, but being once laid by parliament under the influence of the representations made by Governors, would probably be kept up and continued for the benefit of Governors, to the grievous burthen and discouragement of the colonies, and prevention of their growth and increase.

That a power in Governors to march the inhabitants from one end of the British and French colonies to the other, being a country of at least 1500 square miles, without the approbation or the consent of their representatives first obtained, such expeditions might be grievous and ruinous to the people, and would put them on footing with the subjects of France in Canada, that now groan under such oppression from their Governor, who for two years past has harrassed them with long and destructive marches to Ohio.

That if the colonies in a body may be well governed by governors and councils appointed by the crown, without representatives, particular colonies may as well or better be so governed; a tax may be laid upon them all by act of parliament for support of government, and their assemblies may be dismissed as an useless part of the constitution.

That the powers proposed by the Albany Plan of Union, to be vested in a grand council representative of the people, even with regard to military matters, are not so great as those the colonies of Rhode Island and Connecticut are entrusted with by their charters, and have never abused; for by this plan, the president-general is appointed by the crown, and controls all by his negative; but in those governments, the people choose the Governor, and yet allow him no negative.

That the British colonies bordering on the French are properly frontiers of the British empire; and the frontiers of an empire are properly defended at the joint expence of the body of the people in such empire: It would now be thought hard by act of parliament to oblige the Cinque Ports or seacoasts of Britain to maintain the whole navy, because they are more immediately defended by it, not allowing them at the same time a vote in choosing members of the parliament; and if the frontiers in America bear the expence of their own defence, it seems hard to allow them no share in voting the money, judging of the necessity and sum, or advising the measures.

That besides the taxes necessary for the defence of the frontiers, the colonies pay yearly great sums to the mother-country unnoticed: For taxes paid in Britain by the land-holder or artificer, must enter into and increase the price of the produce of land and of manufactures made of it; and great part of this is paid by consumers in the colonies, who thereby pay a considerable part of the British taxes.

We are restrained in our trade with foreign nations, and

where we could be supplied with any manufacture cheaper from them, but must buy the same dearer from Britain; the difference of price is a clear tax to Britain.

We are obliged to carry a great part of our produce directly to Britain; and where the duties laid upon it lessen its price to the planter, or it sells for less than it would in foreign markets; the difference is a tax paid to Britain.

Some manufactures we could make, but are forbidden, and must take them of British merchants; the whole price is a tax paid to Britain.

By our greatly increasing the demand and consumption of British manufactures, their price is considerably raised of late years; the advantage is clear profit to Britain, and enables its people better to pay great taxes; and much of it being paid by us, is clear tax to Britain.

In short, as we are not suffered to regulate our trade, and restrain the importation and consumption of British superfluities (as Britain can the consumption of foreign superfluities) our whole wealth centers finally amongst the merchants and inhabitants of Britain, and if we make them richer, and enable them better to pay their taxes, it is nearly the same as being taxed ourselves, and equally beneficial to the crown.

These kind of secondary taxes, however, we do not complain of, though we have no share in the laying, or disposing of them; but to pay immediate heavy taxes, in the laying, appropriation, and disposition of which we have no part, and which perhaps we may know to be as unnecessary, as grievous, must seem hard measure to Englishmen, who cannot conceive, that by hazarding their lives and fortunes, in subduing and settling new countries, extending the dominion, and increasing the commerce of the mother nation, they have forfeited the native rights of Britons, which they think ought rather to be given to them, as due to such merit, if they had been before in a state of slavery.

These, and such kind of things as these, I apprehend, will be thought and said by the people, if the proposed alteration of the Albany plan should take place. Then the administration of the board of governors and councils so appointed, not having any representative body of the people to approve and unite in its measures, and conciliate the minds of the people to them, will probably become suspected and odious; dangerous animosities and feuds will arise between the governors and governed; and every thing go into confusion.

Perhaps I am too apprehensive in this matter; but having freely given my opinion and reasons, your Excellency can judge better than I whether there be any weight in them, and the shortness of the time allowed me, will, I hope, in some degree excuse the imperfections of this scrawl.

With the greatest respect, and fidelity, I have the honour to be,

Your Excellency's most obedient, and most humble servant.

B. FRANKLIN.

LETTER III

On the Subject of Uniting the Colonies More Intimately with Great Britain, by Allowing Them Representatives in Parliament

Boston, Dec. 22, 1754.

SIR,

Since the conversation your Excellency was pleased to honour me with, on the subject of *uniting the colonies* more intimately with Great Britain, by allowing them *representatives in parliament*, I have something further considered that matter, and am of opinion, that such a union would be very acceptable to the colonies, provided they had a reasonable number of representatives allowed them; and that all the old acts of Parliament restraining the trade or cramping the manufactures of the colonies be at the same time repealed, and the British subjects *on this side the water* put, in those respects, on the same footing with those in Great Britain, till the new Parliament, representing the whole, shall think it for the interest of the whole to reënact some or all of them. It is not that I imagine so many representatives will be allowed the colonies, as to have any great weight by their numbers; but I think there might be sufficient to occasion those laws to be better and more impartially considered, and perhaps to overcome the interest of a petty corporation, or of any particular set of artificers or traders in England, who heretofore seem, in some instances, to have been more regarded than all the colonies, or than was consistent with the general interest, or best national good. I think too, that the government of the colonies by a parliament, in which they are fairly represented, would be vastly more agreeable to the people, than the method lately attempted to be introduced by royal instructions, as well as more agreeable to the nature of an English constitution, and to English liberty; and that such laws as now seem to bear hard on the colonies, would (when judged by such a Parliament for the best interest of the whole) be more cheerfully submitted to, and more easily executed.

I should hope too, that by such a union, the people of Great Britain, and the people of the colonies, would learn to consider themselves, as not belonging to a different community with different interests, but to one community with one interest; which I imagine would contribute to strengthen the whole, and greatly lessen the danger of future separations.

It is, I suppose, agreed to be the general interest of any state, that its people be numerous and rich; men enough to fight in its defence, and enough to pay sufficient taxes to defray the charge; for these circumstances tend to the security of the state, and its protection from foreign power: But it seems not of so much importance, whether the fighting be done by John or Thomas, or the tax paid by William or Charles. The iron manufacture employs and enriches British subjects, but is it of any importance to the state, whether the manufacturers live at Birmingham, or Sheffield, or both, since they are still within its bounds, and their wealth and persons still at its command? Could the Goodwin Sands be laid dry by banks, and land equal to a large country thereby gained to England, and presently filled with English inhabitants, would it be right to deprive such inhabitants of the common privileges enjoyed by other Englishmen, the right of vending their produce in the same ports, or of making their own shoes, because a merchant or a shoemaker, living on the old land, might fancy it more for his advantage to trade or make shoes for them? Would this be right, even if the land were gained at the expence of the state? And would it not seem less right, if the charge and labour of gaining the additional territory to Britain had been borne by the settlers themselves? And would not the hardship appear yet greater, if the people of the new country should be allowed no representatives in the parliament enacting such impositions?

Now I look on the colonies as so many counties gained to Great Britain, and more advantageous to it than if they had been gained out of the seas around its coasts, and joined to its land: For being in different climates, they afford greater variety of produce, and being separated by the ocean, they increase much more its shipping and seamen; and since they are all included in the British empire, which has only extended itself by their means; and the strength and wealth of the parts are the strength and wealth of the whole; what imports it to the general state, whether a merchant, a smith, or a hatter, grow rich in Old or New England? And if, through increase of people, two smiths are wanted for one employed before, why may not the *new* smith be allowed to live and thrive in the *new* country, as well as the *old* one in the *old?* In fine, why should the countenance of a state be *partially* afforded to its people, unless it be most in favour of those who have most merit? And if there be any difference, those who have most contributed to enlarge Britain's empire and commerce, increase her strength, her wealth, and the numbers of her people, at the risk of their own lives and private fortunes in new and strange countries, methinks ought rather to expect some preference. With the greatest respect and esteem, I have the honour to be

Your Excellency's most obedient and most humble servant,

B. FRANKLIN.

TO MISS CATHERINE RAY [46] [AT BLOCK ISLAND]

Philadelphia, March 4, 1755.

DEAR KATY:—

Your kind letter of January 20th is but just come to hand, and I take this first opportunity of acknowledging the favour. It gives me great pleasure to hear, that you got home safe and well that day. I thought too much was hazarded, when I saw you put off to sea in that very little skiff, tossed by every wave. But the call was strong and just, a sick parent. I stood on the shore, and looked after you, till I could no longer distinguish you, even with my glass; then returned to your sister's, praying for your safe passage. Towards evening all agreed that you must certainly be arrived before that time, the weather having been so favourable; which made me more easy and cheerful, for I had been truly concerned for you.

I left New England slowly, and with great reluctance.[47] Short day's journeys, and loitering visits on the road, for three or four weeks, manifested my unwillingness to quit a country, in which I drew my first breath, spent my earliest and most pleasant days, and had now received so many fresh marks of the people's goodness and benevolence, in the kind and affectionate treatment I had everywhere met with. I almost forgot I had a *home*, till I was more than half way towards it; till I had, one by one, parted with all my New England friends, and was got into the western borders of Connecticut, among mere strangers. Then, like an old man, who, having buried all he loved in this world, begins to think of heaven, I began to think of and wish for home; and, as I drew nearer, I found the attraction stronger and stronger. My diligence and speed increased with my impatience. I drove on violently, and made such long stretches, that a very few days brought me to my own house, and to the arms of my good old wife and children, where I remain, thanks to God, at present well and happy.

Persons subject to the *hyp* complain of the northeast wind, as increasing their malady. But since you promised to send me kisses in that wind, and I find you as good as your word, it is to me the gayest wind that blows, and gives me the best spirits. I write this during a northeast storm of snow, the greatest we have had this winter. Your favours come mixed with the snowy fleeces, which are pure as your virgin innocence, white as your lovely bosom, and—as cold. But let it warm towards some worthy young man, and may Heaven bless you both with every kind of happiness.

I desired Miss Anna Ward[48] to send you over a little book I left with her, for your amusement in that lonely island. My respects to your good father, and mother, and sister. Let me often hear of your welfare, since it is not likely I shall ever again have the pleasure of seeing you. Accept mine, and my wife's sincere thanks for the many civilities I receive from you and your relations; and do me the justice to believe me, dear girl, your affectionate, faithful friend, and humble servant,

B. FRANKLIN.

P. S. My respectful compliments to your good brother Ward, and sister; and to the agreeable family of the Wards at Newport, when you see them.   Adieu.

TO PETER COLLINSON

Philadelphia, Aug. 25, 1755.

DEAR SIR,—

As you have my former papers on Whirlwinds, &c., I now send you an account of one which I had lately an opportunity of seeing and examining myself.

Being in *Maryland*, riding with Colonel *Tasker*, and some other gentlemen to his country-seat, where I and my son were entertained by that amiable and worthy man with great hospitality and kindness, we saw in the vale below us, a small whirlwind beginning in the road, and shewing itself by the dust it raised and contained. It appeared in the form of a sugar-loaf, spinning on its point, moving up the hill towards us, and enlarging as it came forward. When it passed by us, its smaller part near the ground, appeared no bigger than a common barrel, but widening upwards, it seemed, at 40 or 50 feet high, to be 20 or 30 feet in diameter. The rest of the company stood looking after it, but my curiosity being stronger, I followed it, riding close by its side, and observed its licking up, in its progress, all the dust that was under its smaller part. As it is a common opinion that a shot, fired through a water-spout, will break it, I tried to break this little whirlwind, by striking my whip frequently through it, but without any effect. Soon after, it quitted the road and took into the woods, growing every moment larger and stronger, raising, instead of dust, the old dry leaves with which the ground was thick covered, and making a great noise with them and the branches of the trees, bending some tall trees round in a circle swiftly and very surprizingly, though the progressive motion of the whirl was not so swift but that a man on foot might have kept pace with it; but the circular motion was amazingly rapid. By the leaves it was now filled with, I could plainly perceive that the current of air they were driven by, moved upwards in a spiral line; and when I saw the trunks and bodies of large trees invelop'd in the passing whirl, which continued intire after it had left them I no longer wondered that my whip had no effect on it in its smaller state. I accompanied it about three quarters of a mile, till some limbs of dead trees, broken off by the whirl, flying about and falling near me, made me more apprehensive of danger; and then I stopped, looking at the top of it as it went on, which was visible, by means of the leaves contained in it, for a very great height above the trees. Many of the leaves, as they got loose from the upper and widest part, were scattered in the wind; but so great was their height in the air, that they appeared no bigger than flies. My son, who was by this time come up with me, followed the whirlwind till it left the woods, and crossed an old tobacco-field, where, finding neither dust nor leaves to take up, it gradually became invisible below as it went away over that field. The course of the general wind then blowing was along with us as we travelled, and the progressive motion of the whirlwind was in a direction nearly opposite, though it did not keep a strait line, nor was its progressive motion uniform, it making little sallies on either hand as it went, proceeding sometimes faster and sometimes slower, and seeming sometimes for a few seconds almost stationary, then starting forward pretty fast again. When we rejoined the company, they were admiring the vast height of the leaves now brought by the common wind, over our heads. These leaves accompanied us as we travelled, some falling now and then round about us, and some not reaching the ground till we had gone near three miles from the place where we first saw the whirlwind begin. Upon my asking Colonel *Tasker* if such whirlwinds were common in *Maryland*, he answered pleasantly, "No, not at all common; but we got this on purpose to treat Mr. Franklin." And a very high treat it was, to

Dear Sir,

Your affectionate friend and humble servant,

B. F[RANKLIN].

TO MISS CATHERINE RAY

Philadelphia, Sept. 11, 1755.

Begone, business, for an hour, at least, and let me chat a little with my Katy.

I have now before me, my dear girl, three of your favours, viz. of March the 3d, March the 30th, and May the 1st. The first I received just before I set out on a long journey, and the others while I was on that journey, which held me near six weeks. Since my return, I have been in such a perpetual hurry of public affairs of various kinds, as renders it impracticable for me to keep up my private correspondences, even those that afforded me the greatest pleasure.

You ask in your last, how I do, and what I am doing, and whether everybody loves me yet, and why I make them do so.

In regard to the first, I can say, thanks to God, that I do not remember I was ever better. I still relish all the pleasures of life, that a temperate man can in reason desire, and through favour I have them all in my power. This happy situation shall continue as long as God pleases, who knows what is best for his creatures, and I hope will enable me to bear with patience and dutiful submission any change he may think fit to make that is less agreeable. As to the second question, I must confess but don't you be jealous), that many more people love me now, than ever did before; for since I saw you I have been enabled to do some general services to the country, and to the army, for which both have thanked and praised me, and say they love me. They say so, as you used to do; and if I were to ask any favours of them, they would, perhaps, as readily refuse me; so that I find little real advantage in being beloved, but it pleases my humour.

Now it is near four months since I have been favoured with a single line from you; but I will not be angry with you, because it is my fault. I ran in debt to you three or four letters; and as I did not pay, you would not trust me any more, and you had some reason. But, believe me, I am honest; and, tho' I should never make equal returns, you shall see I will keep fair accounts. Equal returns I can never make, tho' I should write to you by every post; for the pleasure I receive from one of yours is more than you can have from two of mine. The small news, the domestic occurrences among our friends, the natural pictures you draw of persons, the sensible observations and reflections you make, and the easy, chatty manner in which you express every thing, all contribute to heighten the pleasure; and the more as they remind me of those hours and miles, that we talked away so agreeably, even in a winter journey, a wrong road, and a soaking shower.

I long to hear whether you have continued ever since in that monastery [Block Island]; or have broke into the world again, doing pretty mischief; how the lady Wards do, and how many of them are married, or about it; what is become of Mr. B— and Mr. L—, and what the state of your heart is at this instant? But that, perhaps, I ought not to know; and, therefore, I will not conjure, as you sometimes say I do. If I could conjure, it should be to know what was that *oddest question about me that ever was thought of*, which you tell me a lady had just sent to ask you.

I commend your prudent resolutions, in the article of granting favours to lovers. But, if I were courting you, I could not hardly approve such conduct. I should even be malicious enough to say you were too *knowing*, and tell you the old story of the Girl and the Miller. I enclose you the songs you write for, and with them your Spanish letter with a translation. I honour that honest Spaniard for loving you. It showed the goodness of his taste and judgement. But you must forget him, and bless some worthy young Englishman.

You have spun a long thread, five thousand and twenty-two

yards. It will reach almost from Rhode Island hither. I wish I had hold of one end of it, to pull you to me. But you would break it rather than come. The cords of love and friendship are longer and stronger, and in times past have drawn me farther; even back from England to Philadelphia. I guess that some of the same kind will one day draw you out of that Island.

I was extremely pleased with the turf you sent me. The Irish people, who have seen it, say it is the right sort; but I cannot learn that we have any thing like it here. The cheeses, particularly one of them, were excellent. All our friends have tasted it, and all agree that it exceeds any English cheese they ever tasted. Mrs. Franklin was very proud, that a young lady should have so much regard for her old husband, as to send him such a present. We talk of you every time it comes to table. She is sure you are a sensible girl, and a notable housewife, and talks of bequeathing me to you as a legacy; but I ought to wish you a better, and hope she will live these hundred years; for we are grown old together, and if she has any faults, I am so used to 'em that I don't perceive 'em; as the song says,

> "Some faults we have all, and so has my Joan,
>   But then they're exceedingly small;
> And, now I am used, they are like my own,
>   I scarcely can see 'em at all,
>   My dear friends,
>   I scarcely can see 'em at all."

Indeed, I begin to think she has none, as I think of you. And since she is willing I should love you, as much as you are willing to be loved by me, let us join in wishing the old lady a long life and a happy.

With her respectful compliments to you, to your good mother and sisters, present mine, though unknown; and believe me to be, dear girl, your affectionate friend and humble servant,

                                                    B. FRANKLIN.

P. S. Sally[49] says, "Papa, my love to Miss Katy."—If it was not quite unreasonable, I should desire you to write to me every post, whether you hear from me or not. As to your spelling, don't let those laughing girls put you out of conceit with it. It is the best in the world, for every letter of it stands for something.

TO MISS CATHERINE RAY

Philadelphia, Oct. 16, 1755.

DEAR KATY

Your Favour of the 28th of June came to hand but the 28th of September, just 3 Months after it was written. I had, two Weeks before, wrote you a long Chat, and sent it to the Care of your Brother Ward. I hear you are now in Boston, gay and lovely as usual. Let me give you some fatherly Advice. Kill no more Pigeons than you can eat—Be a good Girl and dont forget your Catechism.—Go constantly to Meeting—or church —till you get a good Husband,—then stay at home, & nurse the Children, and live like a Christian—Spend your spare Hours, in sober Whisk, Prayers, or learning to cypher—You must practise *addition* to your Husband's Estate, by Industry and Frugality; *subtraction* of all unnecessary Expenses; *Multiplication* (I would gladly have taught you that myself, but you thought it was time enough, & wou'dn't learn) he will soon make you a Mistress of it. As to *Division*, I say with Brother Paul, *Let there be no Division among ye.* But as your good Sister Hubbard (my love to her) is well acquainted with *The Rule of Two*, I hope you will become an expert in the *Rule of Three;* that when I have again the pleasure of seeing you, I may find you like my Grape Vine, surrounded with Clusters, plump, juicy, blushing, pretty little rogues, like their Mama. Adieu. The Bell rings, and I must go among the Grave ones, and talk Politicks.

Your affectionate Friend

B. FRANKLIN.

P. S. The Plums came safe, and were so sweet from the Cause you mentioned, that I could scarce taste the Sugar.

TO MRS. JANE MECOM

Philadelphia, February 12, 1756.

DEAR SISTER,

I condole with you on the loss of our dear brother.[50] As our number grows less, let us love one another proportionably more.

I am just returned from my military expedition, and now my time is taken up in the Assembly. Providence seems to require various duties of me. I know not what will be next; but I find, the more I seek for leisure and retirement from business, the more I am engaged in it. Benny, I understand, inclines to leave Antigua. He may be in the right. I have no objections. My love to brother and to your children. I am, dearest sister, your affectionate brother,

B. FRANKLIN.

TO MISS E. HUBBARD [51]

Philadelphia, February 23, 1756.

—I condole with you. We have lost a most dear and valuable relation. But it is the will of God and nature, that these mortal bodies be laid aside, when the soul is to enter into real life. This is rather an embryo state, a preparation for living. A man is not completely born until he be dead. Why then should we grieve, that a new child is born among the immortals, a new member added to their happy society?

We are spirits. That bodies should be lent us, while they can afford us pleasure, assist us in acquiring knowledge, or in doing good to our fellow creatures, is a kind and benevolent act of God. When they become unfit for these purposes, and afford us pain instead of pleasure, instead of an aid become an incumbrance, and answer none of the intentions for which they were given, it is equally kind and benevolent, that a way is provided by which we may get rid of them. Death is that way. We ourselves, in some cases, prudently choose a partial death. A mangled painful limb, which cannot be restored, we willingly cut off. He who plucks out a tooth, parts with it freely, since the pain goes with it; and he, who quits the whole body, parts at once with all pains and possibilities of pains and diseases which it was liable to, or capable of making him suffer.

Our friend and we were invited abroad on a party of pleasure, which is to last for ever. His chair was ready first, and he is gone before us. We could not all conveniently start together; and why should you and I be grieved at this, since we are soon to follow, and know where to find him?

Adieu.   B. FRANKLIN.

TO REV. GEORGE WHITEFIELD

New York, July 2, 1756.

DEAR SIR:

I received your Favour of the 24th of February with great Pleasure, as it inform'd me of your Welfare, and express'd your continu'd Regard for me. I thank you for the Pamphlet you enclos'd to me. As we had just observ'd a Provincial Fast on the same Occasion, I thought it very seasonable to be publish'd in Pennsylvania, and accordingly reprinted it immediately.

You mention your frequent wish that you were a Chaplain to an American Army. I sometimes wish that you and I were jointly employ'd by the Crown, to settle a Colony on the Ohio. I imagine we could do it effectually, and without putting the Nation to much expence. But I fear we shall never be called upon for such a Service. What a glorious Thing it would be, to settle in that fine Country a large strong Body of Religious and Industrious People! What a Security to the other Colonies; and Advantage to Britain, by Increasing her People, Territory, Strength and Commerce. Might it not greatly facilitate the Introduction of pure Religion among the Heathen, if we could, by such a Colony, show them a better Sample of Christians than they commonly see in our Indian Traders, the most vicious and abandoned Wretches of our Nation? ... Life, like a dramatic Piece, should not only be conducted with Regularity, but methinks it should finish handsomely. Being now in the last Act,

I begin to cast about for something fit to end with. Or if mine be more properly compar'd to an Epigram, as some of its few Lines are but barely tolerable, I am very desirous of concluding with a bright Point. In such an Enterprise I could spend the Remainder of Life with Pleasure; and I firmly believe God would bless us with Success, if we undertook it with a sincere Regard to his Honour, the Service of our gracious King, and (which is the same thing) the Publick Good.

I thank you cordially for your generous Benefaction to the German School. They go on pretty well, and will do better, when Mr. Smith,[52] who has at present the principal Care of them, shall learn to mind Party-writing and Party Politicks less, and his proper Business more; which I hope time will bring about.

I thank you for your good Wishes and Prayers, and am, with the greatest Esteem and Affection, Dear Sir

Your most obedient humble Servant

My best Respects to⎱
  Mrs. Whitefield ⎰
                                          B. FRANKLIN.

THE WAY TO WEALTH

Preface to *Poor Richard Improved*: 1758.[53]

COURTEOUS READER,

I have heard that nothing gives an Author so great Pleasure, as to find his Works respectfully quoted by other learned Authors. This Pleasure I have seldom enjoyed; for tho' I have been, if I may say it without Vanity, an *eminent Author* of Almanacks annually now a full Quarter of a Century, my Brother Authors in the same Way, for what Reason I know not, have ever been very sparing in their Applauses; and no other Author has taken the least Notice of me, so that did not my Writings produce me some solid *Pudding*, the great Deficiency of *Praise* would have quite discouraged me.

I concluded at length, that the People were the best Judges of my Merit; for they buy my Works; and besides, in my Rambles, where I am not personally known, I have frequently heard one or other of my Adages repeated, with, *as Poor Richard says*, at the End on't; this gave me some Satisfaction, as it showed not only that my Instructions were regarded, but discovered likewise some Respect for my Authority; and I own, that to encourage the Practice of remembering and repeating those wise Sentences, I have sometimes *quoted myself* with great Gravity.

Judge then how much I must have been gratified by an Incident I am going to relate to you. I stopt my Horse lately where a great Number of People were collected at a Vendue of Merchant Goods. The Hour of Sale not being come, they were conversing on the Badness of the Times, and one of the Company call'd to a plain clean old Man, with white Locks, *Pray, Father* Abraham, *what think you of the Times? Won't these heavy Taxes quite ruin the Country? How shall we ever be able to pay them? What would you advise us to?*——Father *Abraham* stood up, and reply'd, If you'd have my Advice, I'll give it you in short, for a *Word to the Wise is enough*, and *many Words won't fill a Bushel*, as *Poor Richard says*. They join'd in desiring him to speak his Mind, and gathering round him, he proceeded as follows;

"Friends, says he, and Neighbours, the Taxes are indeed very heavy, and if those laid on by the Government were the only Ones we had to pay, we might more easily discharge them; but we have many others, and much more grievous to some of us. We are taxed twice as much by our *Idleness*, three times as much by our *Pride*, and four times as much by our *Folly*, and from these Taxes the Commissioners cannot ease or deliver us by allowing an Abatement. However let us hearken to good Advice, and something may be done for us; *God helps them that help themselves*, as *Poor Richard* says, in his Almanack of 1733.

It would be thought a hard Government that should tax its People one tenth Part of their *Time*, to be employed in its Service. But *Idleness* taxes many of us much more, if we reckon all that is spent in absolute *Sloth*, or doing of nothing, with that which is spent in idle Employments or Amusements, that amount to nothing. *Sloth*, by bringing on Diseases, absolutely shortens Life. *Sloth, like Rust, consumes faster than Labour wears, while the used Key is always bright*, as *Poor Richard* says. But *dost thou love Life, then do not squander Time, for that's the Stuff Life is made of*, as *Poor Richard* says.—How much more than is necessary do we spend in Sleep! forgetting that *The sleeping Fox catches no Poultry*, and that *there will be sleeping enough in the Grave*, as *Poor Richard* says. If Time be of all Things the most precious, *wasting Time* must be, as *Poor Richard* says, *the greatest Prodigality*, since, as he elsewhere tells us, *Lost Time is never found again;* and what we call *Time-enough, always proves little enough:* Let us then up and be doing, and doing to the Purpose; so by Diligence shall we do more with less Perplexity. *Sloth makes all Things difficult, but Industry all easy*, as *Poor Richard* says; and *He that riseth late, must trot all Day, and shall scarce overtake his Business at Night.* While *Laziness travels so slowly, that Poverty soon overtakes him*, as we read in *Poor Richard*, who adds, *Drive thy Business, let not that drive thee;* and *Early to Bed, and early to rise, makes a Man healthy, wealthy and wise.*

So what signifies *wishing* and *hoping* for better Times. We may make these Times better if we bestir ourselves. *Industry need not wish*, as *Poor Richard* says, and *He that lives upon Hope will die fasting. There are no Gains, without Pains;* then *Help Hands, for I have no Lands*, or if I have, they are smartly taxed. And, as *Poor Richard* likewise observes, *He that hath a Trade hath an Estate*, and *He that hath a Calling, hath an Office of Profit and Honour;* but then the *Trade* must be worked at, and the *Calling* well followed, or neither the *Estate*, nor the *Office*, will enable us to pay our Taxes.—If we are industrious we shall never starve; for, as *Poor Richard* says, *At the working Man's House* Hunger *looks in, but dares not enter.* Nor will the Bailiff or the Constable enter, for *Industry pays Debts, while Despair encreaseth them*, says *Poor Richard.*—What though you have found no Treasure, nor has any rich Relation left you a Legacy, *Diligence is the Mother of Good luck*, as *Poor Richard* says, *and God gives all Things to Industry.* Then *plough deep, while Sluggards sleep, and you shall have Corn to sell and to keep*, says *Poor Dick.* Work while it is called To-day, for you know not how much you may be hindered To-morrow, which makes *Poor*

Richard say, *One To-day is worth two To-morrows;* and farther, *Have you somewhat to do To-morrow, do it To-day.* If you were a Servant, would you not be ashamed that a good Master should catch you idle? Are you then your own Master, *be ashamed to catch yourself idle,* as *Poor Dick* says. When there is so much to be done for yourself, your Family, your Country, and your gracious King, be up by Peep of Day; *Let not the Sun look down and say, Inglorious here he lies.* Handle your Tools without Mittens; remember that *the Cat in Gloves catches no Mice,* as *Poor Richard* says. 'Tis true there is much to be done, and perhaps you are weak handed, but stick to it steadily, and you will see great Effects, for *constant Dropping wears away Stones,* and by *Diligence and Patience the Mouse ate in two the Cable;* and *little Strokes fell great Oaks,* as *Poor Richard* says in his Almanack, the Year I cannot just now remember.

Methinks I hear some of you say, *Must a Man afford himself no Leisure?*—I will tell thee, my Friend, what *Poor Richard* says, *Employ thy Time well if thou meanest to gain Leisure;* and *since thou art not sure of a Minute, throw not away an Hour.* Leisure, is Time for doing something useful; this Leisure the diligent Man will obtain, but the lazy Man never; so that, as *Poor Richard* says, a *Life of Leisure and a Life of Laziness are two Things.* Do you imagine that Sloth will afford you more Comfort than Labour? No, for as *Poor Richard* says, *Trouble springs from Idleness, and grievous Toil from needless Ease. Many without Labour, would live by their* WITS *only, but they break for want of Stock.* Whereas Industry gives Comfort, and Plenty, and Respect: *Fly Pleasures, and they'll follow you. The diligent Spinner has a large Shift;* and *now I have a Sheep and a Cow, every Body bids me Good morrow;* all which is well said by *Poor Richard.*

But with our Industry, we must likewise be *steady, settled* and *careful,* and oversee our own Affairs *with our own Eyes,* and not trust too much to others; for, as *Poor Richard* says,

> *I never saw an oft removed Tree,*
> *Nor yet an oft removed Family,*
> *That throve so well as those that settled be.*

And again, *Three Removes is as bad as a Fire;* and again, *Keep thy Shop, and thy Shop will keep thee;* and again, *If you would have your Business done, go; If not, send.* And again,

> *He that by the Plough would thrive,*
> *Himself must either hold or drive.*

And again, *The Eye of a Master will do more Work than both his Hands;* and again, *Want of Care does us more Damage than Want of Knowledge;* and again, *Not to oversee Workmen, is to leave them your Purse open.* Trusting too much to others Care is the Ruin of many; for, as the *Almanack* says, *In the Affairs of this World, Men are saved, not by Faith, but by the Want of it;* but a Man's own Care is profitable; for, saith *Poor Dick, Learning is to the Studious,* and *Riches to the Careful,* as well as *Power to the Bold,* and *Heaven to the Virtuous.* And farther, *If you would have a faithful Servant, and one that you like, serve yourself.* And again, he adviseth to Circumspection and Care, even in the smallest Matters, because sometimes *a little Neglect may breed great Mischief;* adding, *For want of a Nail the Shoe was lost; for want of a Shoe the Horse was lost; and for want of a Horse the Rider was lost,* being overtaken and slain by the Enemy, all for want of Care about a Horse shoe Nail.

So much for Industry, my Friends, and Attention to one's own Business; but to these we must add *Frugality,* if we would make our *Industry* more certainly successful. A Man may, if he knows not how to save as he gets, *keep his Nose all his Life to the Grindstone,* and die not worth a *Groat* at last. *A fat Kitchen makes a lean Will,* as *Poor Richard* says; and,

> *Many Estates are spent in the Getting,*
> *Since Women for Tea forsook Spinning and Knitting,*
> *And Men for Punch forsook Hewing and Splitting.*

If you would be wealthy, says he, in another Almanack, *think of Saving as well as of Getting: The* Indies *have not made* Spain *rich, because her* Outgoes *are greater than her* Incomes. Away then with your expensive Follies, and you will not have so much Cause to complain of hard Times, heavy Taxes, and chargeable Families; for, as *Poor Dick* says,

> *Women and Wine, Game and Deceit,*
> *Make the Wealth small, and the Wants great.*

And farther, *What maintains one Vice, would bring up two Children.* You may think perhaps, That a *little* Tea, or a *little* Punch now and then, Diet a *little* more costly, Clothes a *little* finer, and a *little* Entertainment now and then, can be no *great* Matter; but remember what *Poor Richard* says, *Many a* Little *makes a* Mickle; and farther, *Beware of* little *Expences; a small Leak will sink a great Ship;* and again, *Who Dainties love, shall Beggars prove;* and moreover, *Fools make Feasts, and wise Men eat them.*

Here you are all got together at this Vendue of *Fineries* and *Knicknacks.* You call them *Goods,* but if you do not take Care, they will prove *Evils* to some of you. You expect they will be sold *cheap,* and perhaps they may for less than they cost; but if you have no Occasion for them, they must be *dear* to you. Remember what *Poor Richard* says, *Buy what thou hast no Need of, and ere long thou shalt sell thy Necessaries.* And again, *At a great Pennyworth pause a while:* He means, that perhaps the Cheapness is *apparent* only, and not *real;* or the Bargain, by straitning thee in thy Business, may do thee more Harm than Good. For in another Place he says, *Many have been ruined by buying good Pennyworths.* Again, *Poor Richard* says, *'Tis foolish to lay out Money in a Purchase of Repentance;* and yet this Folly is practised every Day at Vendues, for want of minding the Almanack. *Wise Men,* as *Poor Dick* says, *learn by others Harms, Fools scarcely by their own;* but *Felix quem faciunt aliena Pericula cautum.* Many a one, for the Sake of Finery on the Back, have gone with a hungry Belly, and half starved their Families; *Silks and Sattins, Scarlet and Velvets,* as *Poor Richard* says, *put out the Kitchen Fire.* These are not the *Necessaries* of Life; they can scarcely be called the *Conveniencies,* and yet only because they look pretty, how many *want* to *have* them. The *artificial* Wants of Mankind thus become more numerous than the *natural;* and, as *Poor Dick* says, *For one* poor *Person, there are an hundred* indigent. By these, and other Extravagancies, the Genteel are reduced to Poverty, and forced to borrow of those whom they formerly despised, but who through *Industry* and

Frugality have maintained their Standing; in which Case it appears plainly, that a *Ploughman on his Legs is higher than a Gentleman on his Knees*, as *Poor Richard* says. Perhaps they have had a small Estate left them which they knew not the Getting of; they think *'tis Day, and will never be Night;* that a little to be spent out of *so much*, is not worth minding; (*a Child and a Fool*, as *Poor Richard* says, *imagine* Twenty Shillings *and Twenty Years can never be spent*) but, *always taking out of*, the *Meal-tub, and never putting in, soon comes to the Bottom;* then, as *Poor Dick* says, *When the Well's dry, they know the Worth of Water.* But this they might have known before, if they had taken his Advice; *If you would know the Value of Money, go and try to borrow some;* for, *he that goes a borrowing goes a sorrowing;* and indeed so does he that lends to such People, when he goes *to get it in again.*—*Poor Dick* farther advises, and says,

> *Fond* Pride of Dress *is sure a very Curse;*
> *E'er* Fancy *you consult, consult your Purse.*

And again, *Pride is as loud a Beggar as Want, and a great deal more saucy.* When you have bought one fine Thing you must buy ten more, that your Appearance may be all of a Piece; but *Poor Dick* says, *'Tis easier to* suppress *the first Desire, than to* satisfy *all that follow it.* And 'tis as truly Folly for the Poor to ape the Rich, as for the Frog to swell, in order to equal the Ox.

> *Great Estates may venture more,*
> *But little Boats should keep near Shore.*

'Tis however a Folly soon punished; for *Pride that dines on Vanity sups on Contempt*, as *Poor Richard* says. And in another Place, *Pride breakfasted with Plenty, dined with Poverty, and supped with Infamy.* And after all, of what Use is this *Pride of Appearance*, for which so much is risked, so much is suffered? It cannot promote Health, or ease Pain; it makes no Increase of Merit in the Person, it creates Envy, it hastens Misfortune.

> *What is a Butterfly? At best*
> *He's but a Caterpillar drest.*
> *The gaudy Fop's his Picture just,*

as *Poor Richard* says.

But what Madness must it be to *run in Debt* for these Superfluities! We are offered, by the Terms of this Vendue, *Six Months Credit;* and that perhaps has induced some of us to attend it, because we cannot spare the ready Money, and hope now to be fine without it. But, ah, think what you do when you run in Debt; *You give to another, Power over your Liberty.* If you cannot pay at the Time, you will be ashamed to see your Creditor; you will be in Fear when you speak to him; you will make poor pitiful sneaking Excuses, and by Degrees come to lose your Veracity, and sink into base downright lying; for, as *Poor Richard* says, *The second Vice is Lying, the first is running in Debt.* And again, to the same Purpose, *Lying rides upon Debt's Back.* Whereas a freeborn *Englishman* ought not to be ashamed or afraid to see or speak to any Man living. But Poverty often deprives a Man of all Spirit and Virtue: *'Tis hard for an empty Bag to stand upright,* as *Poor Richard* truly says. What would you think of that Prince, or that Government, who should issue an Edict forbidding you to dress like a Gentleman or a Gentlewoman, on Pain of Imprisonment or Servitude? Would you not say, that you are free, have a Right to dress as you please, and that such an Edict would be a Breach of your Privileges, and such a Government tyrannical? And yet you are about to put yourself under that Tyranny when you run in Debt for such Dress! Your Creditor has Authority at his Pleasure to deprive you of your Liberty, by confining you in Goal [*sic*] for Life, or to sell you for a Servant, if you should not be able to pay him! When you have got your Bargain, you may, perhaps, think little of Payment; but *Creditors, Poor Richard* tells us, *have better Memories than Debtors;* and in another Place says, *Creditors are a superstitious Sect, great Observers of set Days and Times.* The Day comes round before you are aware, and the Demand is made before you are prepared to satisfy it. Or if you bear your Debt in Mind, the Term which at first seemed so long, will, as it lessens, appear extreamly short. *Time* will seem to have added Wings to his Heels as well as Shoulders. *Those have a short Lent,* saith *Poor Richard, who owe Money to be paid at Easter.* Then since, as he says, *The Borrower is a*

Slave to the Lender, and the Debtor to the Creditor, disdain the Chain, preserve your Freedom; and maintain your Independency: Be *industrious* and *free; be frugal* and *free.* At present, perhaps, you may think yourself in thriving Circumstances, and that you can bear a little Extravangance [*sic*] without Injury; but,

> *For Age and Want, save while you may;*
> *No Morning Sun lasts a whole Day,*

as *Poor Richard* says—Gain may be temporary and uncertain, but ever while you live, Expence is constant and certain; and *'tis easier to build two Chimnies than to keep one in Fuel*, as *Poor Richard* says. So *rather go to Bed supperless than rise in Debt.*

> *Get what you can, and what you get hold;*
> *'Tis the Stone that will turn all your Lead into Gold,*

as *Poor Richard* says. And when you have got the Philosopher's Stone, sure you will no longer complain of bad Times, or the Difficulty of paying Taxes.

This Doctrine, my Friends, is *Reason* and *Wisdom;* but after all, do not depend too much upon your own *Industry*, and *Frugality*, and *Prudence*, though excellent Things, for they may all be blasted without the Blessing of Heaven; and therefore ask that Blessing humbly, and be not uncharitable to those that at present seem to want it, but comfort and help them. Remember *Job* suffered, and was afterwards prosperous.

And now to conclude, *Experience keeps a dear School, but Fools will learn in no other, and scarce in that;* for it is true, *we may give Advice, but we cannot give Conduct*, as *Poor Richard* says: However, remember this, *They that won't be counselled, can't be helped,* as *Poor Richard* says: And farther, That *if you will not hear Reason, she'll surely rap your Knuckles.*

Thus the old Gentleman ended his Harangue. The People heard it, and approved the Doctrine and immediately practised the contrary, just as if it had been a common Sermon; for the Vendue opened, and they began to buy extravagantly, notwithstanding all his Cautions, and their own Fear of Taxes.—I found the good Man had thoroughly studied my Almanacks, and digested all I had dropt on those Topicks during the Course of Five-and-twenty Years. The frequent Mention he made of me must have tired any one else, but my Vanity was wonderfully delighted with it, though I was conscious that not a tenth Part of the Wisdom was my own which he ascribed to me, but rather the *Gleanings* I had made of the Sense of all Ages and Nations. However, I resolved to be the better for the Echo of it; and though I had at first determined to buy Stuff for a new Coat, I went away resolved to wear my old One a little longer. *Reader*, if thou wilt do the same, thy Profit will be as great as mine.

> *I am, as ever,*
> *Thine to serve thee,*
>
> *July 7, 1757.*   RICHARD SAUNDERS.

TO HUGH ROBERTS

London, September 16, 1758.

DEAR FRIEND,

Your kind letter of June 1st gave me great pleasure. I thank you for the concern you express about my health, which at present seems tolerably confirmed by my late journey into different parts of the kingdom, that have been highly entertaining as well as useful to me. Your visits to my little family in my absence are very obliging, and I hope you will be so good as to continue them. Your remark on the thistle and the Scotch motto made us very merry, as well as your string of puns. You will allow me to claim a little merit or demerit in the last, as having had some hand in making you a punster; but the wit of the first is keen, and all your own.

Two of the former members of the Junto you tell me are departed this life, Potts and Parsons.[54] Odd characters both of them. Parsons a wise man, that often acted foolishly; Potts a wit, that seldom acted wisely. If *enough* were the means to make a man happy, one had always the *means* of happiness, without ever enjoying the *thing;* the other had always the *thing*, without ever possessing the *means*. Parsons, even in his prosperity, always fretting; Potts, in the midst of his poverty, ever laughing. It seems, then, that happiness in this life rather depends on internals than externals; and that, besides the natural effects of wisdom and virtue, vice and folly, there is such a thing as a happy or an unhappy constitution. They were both our friends, and loved us. So, peace to their shades. They had their virtues as well as their foibles; they were both honest men, and that alone, as the world goes, is one of the greatest of characters. They were old acquaintances, in whose company I formerly enjoyed a great deal of pleasure, and I cannot think of losing them, without concern and regret.

I shall, as you suppose, look on every opportunity you give me of doing you service, as a favour, because it will afford me pleasure. I know how to make you ample returns for such favours, by giving you the pleasure of building me a house. You may do it without losing any of your own time; it will only take some part of that you now spend in other folks' business. It is only jumping out of their waters into mine.

I am grieved for our friend Syng's loss. You and I, who esteem him, and have valuable sons ourselves, can sympathize with him sincerely. I hope yours is perfectly recovered, for your sake as well as for his own. I wish he may be, in every respect, as good and as useful as his father. I need not wish him more; and can only add, that I am, with great esteem, dear friend, yours affectionately,

B. FRANKLIN.

P. S. I rejoice to hear of the prosperity of the Hospital, and send the wafers. I do not quite like your absenting yourself from that good old club, the Junto. Your more frequent presence might be a means of keeping them from being all engaged in measures not the best for public welfare. I exhort you, therefore, to return to your duty; and, as the Indians say, to confirm my words, I send you a Birmingham tile. I thought the neatness of the figures would please you.

TO MRS. JANE MECOM

London, September 16, 1758.

Dear Sister,

I received your favour of June 17. I wonder you have had no letter from me since my being in England. I have wrote you at least two, and I think a third before this, and what was next to waiting on you in person, sent you my picture. In June last I sent Benny a trunk of books, and wrote to him; I hope they are come to hand, and that he meets with encouragement in his business. I congratulate you on the conquest of Cape Breton, and hope as your people took it by praying, the first time, you will now pray that it may never be given up again, which you then forgot. Billy is well, but in the country. I left him at Tunbridge Wells, where we spent a fortnight, and he is now gone with some company to see Portsmouth. We have been together over a great part of England this summer, and among other places, visited the town our father was born in, and found some relations in that part of the country still living.

Our cousin Jane Franklin, daughter of our uncle John, died about a year ago. We saw her husband, Robert Page, who gave us some old letters to his wife, from uncle Benjamin. In one of them, dated Boston, July 4, 1723, he writes that your uncle Josiah has a daughter Jane, about twelve years old, a good-humoured child. So keep up to your character, and don't be angry when you have no letters. In a little book he sent her, called "None but Christ," he wrote an acrostick on her name, which for namesake's sake, as well as the good advice it contains, I transcribe and send you, viz.

> "Illuminated from on high,
>   And shining brightly in your sphere,
> Ne'er faint, but keep a steady eye,
>   Expecting endless pleasures there.
>
> "Flee vice as you'd a serpent flee;
>   Raise *faith* and *hope* three stories higher,
> And let Christ's endless love to thee
>   Ne'er cease to make thy love aspire.

Kindness of heart by words express,
Let your obedience be sincere,
In prayer and praise your God address,
Nor cease, till he can cease to hear."

After professing truly that I had a great esteem and veneration for the pious author, permit me a little to play the com-
mentator and critic on these lines. The meaning of *three stories
higher* seems somewhat obscure. You are to understand, then,
that *faith, hope,* and *charity* have been called the three steps of
Jacob's ladder, reaching from earth to heaven; our author calls
them *stories*, likening religion to a building, and these are the
three stories of the Christian edifice. Thus improvement in
religion is called *building up* and *edification. Faith* is then the
ground floor, *hope* is up one pair of stairs. My dear beloved
Jenny, don't delight so much to dwell in those lower rooms,
but get as fast as you can into the garret, for in truth the best
room in the house is *charity.* For my part, I wish the house
was turned upside down; 'tis so difficult (when one is fat) to go
up stairs; and not only so, but I imagine *hope* and *faith* may be
more firmly built upon *charity*, than *charity* upon *faith* and
hope. However that may be, I think it the better reading to
say—

"Raise faith and hope one story higher."

Correct it boldly, and I'll support the alteration; for, when you
are up two stories already, if you raise your building three
stories higher you will make five in all, which is two more than
there should be, you expose your upper rooms more to the
winds and storms; and, besides, I am afraid the foundation will
hardly bear them, unless indeed you build with such light stuff
as straw and stubble, and that, you know, won't stand fire.
Again, where the author says,

"Kindness of heart by words express,"

strike out *words*, and put in *deeds.* The world is too full of
compliments already. They are the rank growth of every soil,
and choak the good plants of benevolence, and beneficence;

nor do I pretend to be the first in this comparison of words and actions to plants; you may remember an ancient poet, whose works we have all studied and copied at school long ago.

> "A man of words and not of deeds
> Is like a garden full of weeds."

'Tis a pity that good works, among some sorts of people, are so little valued, and good words admired in their stead: I mean seemingly pious discourses, instead of humane benevolent actions. Those they almost put out of countenance, by calling morality *rotten morality*, righteousness *ragged righteousness*, and even filthy rags—and when you mention virtue, pucker up their noses as if they smelt a stink; at the same time that they eagerly snuff up an empty canting harangue, as if it was a posey of the choicest flowers: So they have inverted the good old verse, and say now

> "A man of deeds and not of words
> Is like a garden full of ———"

I have forgot the rhyme, but remember 'tis something the very reverse of perfume. So much by way of commentary.

My wife will let you see my letter, containing an account of our travels, which I would have you read to sister Dowse, and give my love to her. I have no thoughts of returning till next year, and then may possibly have the pleasure of seeing you and yours; taking Boston in my way home. My love to brother and all your children, concludes at this time from, dear Jenny, your affectionate brother,

B. FRANKLIN.

TO LORD KAMES[55]

London, May 3, 1760.

MY DEAR LORD,

I have endeavoured to comply with your request in writing something on the present situation of our affairs in America, in order to give more correct notions of the British interest with regard to the colonies, than those I found many sensible men

possessed of. Inclosed you have the production, such as it is.
I wish it may in any degree be of service to the public. I shall
at least hope this from it, for my own part, that you will consider it as a letter from me to you, and take its length as some
excuse for being so long a-coming.[56]

I am now reading with great pleasure and improvement your
excellent work, *The Principles of Equity*. It will be of the greatest advantage to the Judges in our colonies, not only in those
which have Courts of Chancery, but also in those which, having
no such courts, are obliged to mix equity with the common law.
It will be of more service to the colony Judges, as few of them
have been bred to the law. I have sent a book to a particular
friend, one of the Judges of the Supreme Court in Pennsylvania.

I will shortly send you a copy of the Chapter you are pleased
to mention in so obliging a manner; and shall be extremely
obliged in receiving a copy of the collection of *Maxims for the
Conduct of Life*, which you are preparing for the use of your
children. I purpose likewise a little work for the benefit of
youth, to be called *The Art of Virtue*.[57] From the title I think
you will hardly conjecture what the nature of such a book
may be. I must therefore explain it a little. Many people lead
bad lives that would gladly lead good ones, but know not *how*
to make the change. They have frequently *resolved* and *endeavoured* it; but in vain, because their endeavours have not
been properly conducted. To expect people to be good, to be
just, to be temperate, &c., without *shewing* them *how* they should
become so, seems like the ineffectual charity mentioned by the
Apostle, which consisted in saying to the hungry, the cold, and
the naked, "Be ye fed, be ye warmed, be ye clothed," without
shewing them how they should get food, fire, or clothing.

Most people have naturally *some* virtues, but none have
naturally *all* the virtues. To *acquire* those that are wanting, and
secure what we acquire, as well as those we have naturally, is
the subject of *an art*. It is as properly an art as painting, navigation, or architecture. If a man would become a painter,
navigator, or architect, it is not enough that he is *advised* to be

one, that he is *convinced* by the arguments of his adviser, that it would be for his advantage to be one, and that he resolves to be one, but he must also be taught the principles of the art, be shewn all the methods of working, and how to acquire the habits of using properly all the instruments; and thus regularly and gradually he arrives, by practice, at some perfection in the art. If he does not proceed thus, he is apt to meet with difficulties that discourage him, and make him drop the pursuit.

My *Art of Virtue* has also its instruments, and teaches the manner of using them. Christians are directed to have faith in Christ, as the effectual means of obtaining the change they desire. It may, when sufficiently strong, be effectual with many: for a full opinion, that a Teacher is infinitely wise, good, and powerful, and that he will certainly reward and punish the obedient and disobedient, must give great weight to his precepts, and make them much more attended to by his disciples. But many have this faith in so weak a degree, that it does not produce the effect. Our *Art of Virtue* may, therefore, be of great service to those whose faith is unhappily not so strong, and may come in aid of its weakness. Such as are naturally well disposed, and have been so carefully educated, as that good habits have been early established, and bad ones prevented, have less need of this art; but all may be more or less benefited by it. It is, in short, to be adapted for universal use. I imagine what I have now been writing will seem to savour of great presumption: I must therefore speedily finish my little piece, and communicate the manuscript to you, that you may judge whether it is possible to make good such pretensions. I shall at the same time hope for the benefit of your corrections.
I am, &c.   B. FRANKLIN.

TO MISS MARY STEVENSON [58]

Craven Street, June 11, 1760.

DEAR POLLY:

'Tis a very sensible Question you ask, how the Air can affect the Barometer, when its Opening appears covered with Wood?

If indeed it was so closely covered as to admit of no Communication of the outward Air to the Surface of the Mercury, the Change of Weight in the Air could not possibly affect it. But the least Crevice is sufficient for the Purpose; a Pinhole will do the Business. And if you could look behind the Frame to which your Barometer is fixed, you would certainly find some small Opening.

There are indeed some Barometers in which the Body of Mercury at the lower End is contain'd in a close Leather Bag, and so the Air cannot come into immediate Contact with the Mercury; yet the same Effect is produc'd. For, the Leather being flexible, when the Bag is press'd by any additional Weight of Air, it contracts, and the Mercury is forced up into the Tube; when the Air becomes lighter, and its Pressure less, the Weight of the Mercury prevails, and it descends again into the Bag.

Your Observation on what you have lately read concerning Insects is very just and solid. Superficial Minds are apt to despise those who make that Part of the Creation their Study, as mere Triflers; but certainly the World has been much oblig'd to them. Under the Care and Management of Man, the Labours of the little Silkworm afford Employment and Subsistence to Thousands of Families, and become an immense Article of Commerce. The Bee, too, yields us its delicious Honey, and its Wax useful to a Multitude of Purposes. Another Insect, it is said, produces the Cochineal, from whence we have our rich Scarlet Dye. The Usefulness of the Cantharides, or Spanish Flies, in Medicine, is known to all, and Thousands owe their Lives to that Knowledge. By human Industry and Observation, other Properties of other Insects may possibly be hereafter discovered, and of equal Utility. A thorough Acquaintance with the Nature of these little Creatures may also enable Mankind to prevent the Increase of such as are noxious, or secure us against the Mischiefs they occasion. These Things doubtless your Books make mention of: I can only add a particular late Instance which I had from a Swedish Gentleman of good Credit. In the green Timber, intended for Ship-building at the King's Yards in that Country, a kind of Worms were found, which every year became more numerous and more pernicious, so that the Ships were greatly damag'd before they came into Use. The King sent Linnæus, the great Naturalist, from Stockholm, to enquire into the Affair, and see if the Mischief was capable of any Remedy. He found, on Examination, that the Worm was produced from a small Egg, deposited in the little Roughnesses on the Surface of the Wood, by a particular kind of Fly or Beetle; from whence the Worm, as soon as it was hatched, began to eat into the Substance of the Wood, and after some time came out again a Fly of the Parent kind, and so the Species increased. The season in which this Fly laid its Eggs, Linnæus knew to be about a Fortnight (I think) in the Month of May, and at no other time of the Year. He therefore advis'd, that, some Days before that Season, all the green Timber should be thrown into the Water, and kept under Water till the Season was over. Which being done by the King's Order, the Flies missing their usual Nest, could not increase; and the Species was either destroy'd or went elsewhere; and the Wood was effectually preserved; for, after the first Year, it became too dry and hard for their purpose.

There is, however, a prudent Moderation to be used in Studies of this kind. The Knowledge of Nature may be ornamental, and it may be useful; but if, to attain an Eminence in that, we neglect the Knowledge and Practice of essential Duties, we deserve Reprehension. For there is no Rank in Natural Knowledge of equal Dignity and Importance with that of being a good Parent, a good Child, a good Husband or Wife, a good Neighbour or Friend, a good Subject or Citizen, that is, in short, a good Christian. Nicholas Gimcrack, therefore, who neglected the Care of his Family, to pursue Butterflies, was a just Object of Ridicule, and we must give him up as fair Game to the satyrist.

Adieu, my dear Friend, and believe me ever

Yours affectionately,

B. FRANKLIN.

TO MRS. DEBORAH FRANKLIN

London, June 27, 1760.

MY DEAR CHILD,

I wrote a Line to you by the Pacquet, to let you know we were well, and I promis'd to write you fully by Capt. Budden, and answer all your Letters, which I accordingly now sit down to do. I am concern'd that so much Trouble should be given you by idle Reports concerning me. Be satisfied, my dear, that while I have my Senses, and God vouchsafes me his Protection, I shall do nothing unworthy the Character of an honest Man, and one that loves his Family.

I have not yet seen Mr. Beatty, nor do I know where to write to him. He forwarded your Letter to me from Ireland. The Paragraph of your Letter inserted in the Papers, related to the Negro School. I gave it to the Gentlemen concern'd, as it was a Testimony in favour of their pious Design. But I did not expect they would have printed it with your Name. They have since chosen [me] one of the Society, and I am at present Chairman for the current year. I enclose you an Account of their Proceedings.[59]

I did not receive the *Prospect of Quebec*, which you mention that you sent me. Peter continues with me, and behaves as well as I can expect, in a Country where there are many Occasions of spoiling Servants, if they are ever so good. He has as few Faults as most of them, and I see with only one Eye, and hear only with one Ear; so we rub on pretty comfortably. King, that you enquire after, is not with us. He ran away from our House, near two Years ago, while we were absent in the Country; But was soon found in Suffolk, where he had been taken in the Service of a Lady, that was very fond of the Merit of making him a Christian, and contributing to his Education and Improvement. As he was of little Use, and often in Mischief, Billy consented to her keeping him while we stay in England. So the Lady sent him to School, has him taught to read and write, to play on the Violin and French Horn, with some other Accomplishments more useful in a Servant. Whether she will finally be willing to part with him, or persuade Billy to sell him to her, I know not. In the mean time he is no Expence to us. The dried Venison was very acceptable, and I thank you for it. We have had it constantly shav'd to eat with our Bread and Butter for Breakfast, and this Week saw the last of it. The Bacon still holds out, for we are choice of it. Some Rashers of it, yesterday relish'd a Dish of Green Pease. Mrs. Stevenson thinks there was never any in England so good. The smok'd Beef was also excellent.

The Accounts you give me of the Marriages of our friends are very agreeable. I love to hear of every thing that tends to increase the Number of good People. You cannot conceive how shamefully the Mode here is a single Life. One can scarce be in the Company of a Dozen Men of Circumstance and Fortune, but what it is odds that you find on enquiry eleven of them are single. The great Complaint is the excessive Expensiveness of English Wives.

I am extreamly concern'd with you at the Misfortune of our Friend Mr. Griffith. How could it possibly happen? 'Twas a terrible Fire that of Boston. I shall contribute here towards the Relief of the Sufferers. Our Relations have escap'd I believe generally; but some of my particular Friends must have suffer'd greatly.

I think you will not complain this Year, as you did the last, of being so long without a Letter. I have wrote to you very frequently; and shall not be so much out of the Way of writing this Summer as I was the last. I hope our friend Bartram is safely return'd to his Family. Remember me to him in the kindest Manner.

Poor David Edwards died this Day Week, of a Consumption. I had a Letter from a Friend of his, acquainting me that he had been long ill, and incapable of doing his Business, and was at Board in the Country. I fear'd he might be in Straits, as he never was prudent enough to lay up any thing. So I wrote to him immediately, that, if he had occasion, he might draw on me for Five Guineas. But he died before my Letter got to hand. I hear the Woman, at whose House he long lodg'd and boarded, has buried him and taken all he left, which could not be much, and there are some small Debts unpaid. He maintained a good Character at Bury, where he lived some years, and was well respected, to my Knowledge, by some Persons of Note there. I wrote to you before, that we saw him at Bury, when we went thro' Suffolk into Norfolk, the Year before last. I hope his good Father, my old Friend, continues well.

Give my Duty to Mother, and Love to my dear Sally. Remember me affectionately to all Enquiring Friends, and believe me ever, my dearest Debby, your loving Husband,

B. FRANKLIN.

TO JARED INGERSOLL[60]

Philadelphia, December 11, 1762.

DEAR SIR:—

I thank you for your kind congratulations. It gives me pleasure to hear from an old friend; it will give me much more pleasure to see him. I hope, therefore, nothing will prevent the journey you propose for next summer and the favour you intend me of a visit. I believe I must make a journey early in the spring to Virginia, but purpose being back again before the hot weather. You will be kind enough to let me know beforehand what time you expect to be here, that I may not be out of the way, for that would mortify me exceedingly.

I should be glad to know what it is that distinguishes Connecticut religion from common religion. Communicate, if you please, some of these particulars that you think will amuse me as a virtuoso. When I travelled in Flanders, I thought of your excessively strict observation of Sunday; and that a man could hardly travel on that day among you upon his lawful occasions without hazard of punishment; while, where I was, every one travelled, if he pleased, or diverted himself in any other way; and in the afternoon both high and low went to the play or the opera, where there was plenty of singing, fiddling and dancing. I looked around for God's judgments, but saw no signs of them. The cities were well built and full of inhabitants, the markets filled with plenty, the people well favoured and well clothed, the fields well tilled, the cattle fat and strong, the fences, houses, and windows all in repair, and no Old Tenor anywhere in the country; which would almost make one suspect that the Deity is not so angry at that offence as a New England Justice.

I left our friend Mr. Jackson [61] well, and I had the great pleasure of finding my little family well when I came home, and my friends as cordial and more numerous than ever. May every prosperity attend you and yours. I am, dear friend, yours affectionately,   B. FRANKLIN.

TO MISS MARY STEVENSON

Philad[a], March 25, 1763.

MY DEAR POLLEY,

Your pleasing Favour of Nov. 11 is now before me. It found me as you suppos'd it would, happy with my American Friends and Family about me; and it made me more happy in showing me that I am not yet forgotten by the dear Friends I left in England. And indeed, why should I fear they will ever forget me, when I feel so strongly that I shall ever remember them!

I sympathise with you sincerely in your Grief at the Separation from your old Friend, Miss Pitt. The Reflection that she is going to be more happy, when she leaves you, might comfort you, if the Case was likely to be so circumstanc'd; but when the Country and Company she has been educated in, and those she is removing to, are compared, one cannot possibly expect it. I sympathize no less with you in your Joys. But it is not merely on your Account, that I rejoice at the Recovery of your dear Dolly's Health. I love that dear good Girl myself, and I love her other Friends. I am, therefore, made happy by what must contribute so much to the Happiness of them all. Remember me to her, and to every one of that worthy and amiable Family, most affectionately.

Remember me in the same manner to your and my good Doctor and Mrs. Hawkesworth.[62] You have lately, you tell me, had the Pleasure of spending three Days with them at

Mr. Stanley's. It was a sweet Society! I too, once partook of that same Pleasure, and can therefore feel what you must have felt. Remember me also to Mr. and Mrs. Stanley,[63] and to Miss Arlond.

Of all the enviable Things England has, I envy it most its People. Why should that petty Island, which compar'd to America, is but like a stepping-Stone in a Brook, scarce enough of it above Water to keep one's Shoes dry; why, I say, should that little Island enjoy in almost every Neighbourhood, more sensible, virtuous, and elegant Minds, than we can collect in ranging 100 Leagues of our vast forests? But 'tis said the Arts delight to travel Westward. You have effectually defended us in this glorious War, and in time you will improve us. After the first Cares for the Necessaries of Life are over, we shall come to think of the Embellishments. Already some of our young Geniuses begin to lisp Attempts at Painting, Poetry, and Music. We have a young Painter now studying at Rome.[64] Some specimens of our Poetry I send you, which if Dr. Hawkesworth's fine Taste cannot approve, his good Heart will at least excuse. The Manuscript Piece is by a young Friend of mine, and was occasion'd by the Loss of one of his Friends, who lately made a Voyage to Antigua to settle some Affairs, previous to an intended Marriage with an amiable young Lady here, but unfortunately died there. I send it to you, because the Author is a great Admirer of Mr. Stanley's musical Compositions, and has adapted this Piece to an Air in the 6th *Concerto* of that Gentleman, the sweetly solemn Movement of which he is quite in Raptures with. He has attempted to compose a *Recitativo* for it, but not being able to satisfy himself in the Bass, wishes I could get it supply'd. If Mr. Stanley would condescend to do that for him, thro' your Intercession, he would esteem it as one of the highest Honours, and it would make him excessively happy. You will say that a *Recitativo* can be but a poor Specimen of our Music. 'Tis the best and all I have at present, but you may see better hereafter.

I hope Mr. Ralph's[65] Affairs are mended since you wrote. I know he had some Expectations, when I came away, from a

Hand that would help him. He has Merit, and one would think ought not to be so unfortunate.

I do not wonder at the behaviour you mention of Dr. Smith towards me, for I have long since known him thoroughly. I made that Man my Enemy by doing him too much Kindness. 'Tis the honestest Way of acquiring an Enemy. And, since 'tis convenient to have at least one Enemy, who by his Readiness to revile one on all Occasions, may make one careful of one's Conduct, I shall keep him an Enemy for that purpose; and shall observe your good Mother's Advice, never again to receive him as a Friend. She once admir'd the benevolent Spirit breath'd in his Sermons. She will now see the Justness of the Lines your Laureat Whitehead addresses to his Poets, and which I now address to her.

> "Full many a peevish, envious, slanderous Elf
> Is, in his Works, Benevolence itself.
> For all Mankind, unknown, his Bosom heaves;
> He only injures those, with whom he lives.
> Read then the Man;—does *Truth* his Actions guide,
> Exempt from *Petulance*, exempt from *Pride?*
> To social Duties does his Heart attend,
> As Son, as Father, Husband, Brother, *Friend?*
> *Do those, who know him, love him?* If they do,
> You've *my* Permission: you may love him too."

Nothing can please me more than to see your philosophical Improvements when you have Leisure to communicate them to me. I still owe you a long Letter on that Subject, which I shall pay. I am vex'd with Mr. James, that he has been so dilatory in Mr. Maddison's *Armonica.* I was unlucky in both the Workmen, that I permitted to undertake making those Instruments. The first was fanciful, and never could work to the purpose, because he was ever conceiving some new Improvement, that answer'd no End. The other I doubt is absolutely idle. I have recommended a Number to him from hence, but must stop my hand.

Adieu, my dear Polly, and believe me as ever, with the sincerest Esteem and Regard, your truly affectionate Friend and humble Servant,

B. FRANKLIN.

P. S. My love to Mrs. Tickell and Mrs. Rooke, and to Pitty, when you write to her. Mrs. Franklin and Sally desire to be affectionately remember'd to you. I find the printed Poetry I intended to enclose will be too bulky to send per the Packet. I shall send it by a Ship, that goes shortly from hence.

TO JOHN FOTHERGILL, M.D.[66]

March 14, 1764.

DEAR DOCTOR,—

I received your favour of the 10th of December. It was a great deal for one to write whose time was so little his own. By the way, when do you intend to live?—*i.e.*, to enjoy life. When will you retire to your villa, give yourself repose, delight in viewing the operations of nature in the vegetable creation, assist her in her works, get your ingenious friends at times about you, make them happy with your conversation, and enjoy theirs: or, if alone, amuse yourself with your books and elegant collections?

To be hurried about perpetually from one sick chamber to another is not living. Do you please yourself with the fancy that you are doing good? You are mistaken. Half the lives you save are not worth saving, as being useless, and almost all the other half ought not to be saved, as being mischievous. Does your conscience never hint to you the impiety of being in constant warfare against the plans of Providence? Disease was intended as the punishment of intemperence, sloth, and other vices, and the example of that punishment was intended to promote and strengthen the opposite virtues. But here you step in officiously with your Art, disappoint those wise intentions of nature, and make men safe in their excesses, whereby you seem to me to be of just the same service to society as some favourite first minister who out of the great benevolence of his heart should procure pardons of all criminals that applied to him; only think of the consequences.

You tell me the Quakers are charged on your side of the water with being, by their aggressions, the cause of the war. Would you believe it that they are charged here, not with offending the Indians and thereby provoking the war, but with gaining their friendship by presents, supplying them privately with arms and ammunition, and engaging them to fall upon and murder the poor white people on the frontiers? Would you think it possible that thousands even here should be made to believe this, and many hundreds of them be raised in arms, not only to kill some converted Indians, supposed to be under the Quakers' protection, but to punish the Quakers who were supposed to give that protection? Would you think these people audacious enough to avow such designs in a public declaration sent to the Governor? Would you imagine that innocent Quakers, men of fortune and character, should think it necessary to fly for safety out of Philadelphia into the Jersies, fearing the violence of such armed mobs, and confiding little in the power or inclination of the government to protect them? And would you imagine that strong suspicions now prevail that those mobs, after committing so barbarous murders hitherto unpunished, are privately tampered with to be made instruments of government to awe the Assembly into proprietary measures? And yet all this has happened within a few weeks past.

More wonders. You know that I don't love the proprietary and that he does not love me. Our totally different tempers forbid it. You might therefore expect that the late new appointments of one of his family would find me ready for opposition. And yet when his nephew arrived, our Governor, I considered government as government, and paid him all respect, gave him on all occasions my best advice, promoted in the Assembly a ready compliance with every thing he proposed or recommended, and when those daring rioters, encouraged by general approbation of the populace, treated his proclamation with contempt, I drew my pen in the cause; wrote a pamphlet (that I have sent you) to render the rioters unpopular; promoted an association to support the authority of the Government and defend the Governor by taking arms, signed it first myself and was followed by several hundreds, who took arms accordingly. The Governor offered me the command of them, but I chose to carry a musket and strengthen his authority by setting an example of obedience to his order. And would you think it, this proprietary Governor did me the honour, in an alarm, to run to my house at midnight, with his counsellors at his heels, for advice, and made it his head-quarters for some time. And within four and twenty hours, your old friend was a common soldier, a counsellor, a kind of dictator, an ambassador to the country mob, and on his returning home, nobody again. All this has happened in a few weeks.

More wonders! The Assembly received a Governor of the Proprietary family with open arms, addressed him with sincere expressions of kindness and respect, opened their purses to them, and presented him with six hundred pounds; made a Riot Act and prepared a Militia Bill immediately, at his instance, granted supplies, and did everything that he requested, and promised themselves great happiness under his administration. But suddenly his dropping all inquiries after the murderers, and his answering the disputes of the rioters privately and refusing the presence of the Assembly who were equally concerned in the matters contained in their remonstrance, brings him under suspicion; his insulting the Assembly without the least provocation by charging them with disloyalty and with making an infringement on the King's prerogatives, only because they had presumed to name in a bill offered for his assent a trifling officer (somewhat like one of your toll-gatherers at a turnpike) without consulting him, and his refusing several of their bills or proposing amendments needless disgusting.

These things bring him and his government into sudden contempt. All regard for him in the Assembly is lost. All hopes of happiness under a Proprietary Government are at an end. It has now scarce authority enough to keep the common peace, and was another to come, I question, though a dozen men were sufficient, whether one could find so many in Philadelphia willing to rescue him or his Attorney General, I won't say from hanging, but from any common insult. All this too happened in a few weeks.

In fine, everything seems in this country, once the land of peace and order, to be running fast into anarchy and confusion. But we hope there is virtue enough in your great nation to support a good Prince in the execution of a good government and the exercise of his just prerogatives against all the attempts of unreasonable faction. I have been already too long. Adieu, my dear friend, and believe me ever, yours affectionately,

B. FRANKLIN.

TO SARAH FRANKLIN

Reedy Island, 7 at night, November 8, 1764.

MY DEAR SALLY,

We got down here at sunset, having taken in more live stock at Newcastle, with some other things we wanted. Our good friends, Mr. Galloway, Mr. Wharton, and Mr. James, came with me in the ship from Chester to Newcastle and went ashore there. It was kind to favour me with their good company as far as they could. The affectionate leave taken of me by so many friends at Chester was very endearing. God bless them and all Pennsylvania.

My dear child, the natural prudence and goodness of heart God has blest you with make it less necessary for me to be particular in giving you advice. I shall therefore only say, that the more attentively dutiful and tender you are towards your good mamma, the more you will recommend yourself to me. But why should I mention *me*, when you have so much higher a promise in the commandments, that such conduct will recommend you to the favour of God. You know I have many enemies, all indeed on the public account, (for I cannot recollect that I have in a private capacity given just cause of offence to any one whatever,) yet they are enemies, and very bitter ones; and you must expect their enmity will extend in some degree to you, so that your slightest indiscretions will be magnified into crimes, in order the more sensibly to wound and afflict me. It is therefore the more necessary for you to be extremely circumspect in all your behaviour, that no advantage may be given to their malevolence.

Go constantly to church, whoever preaches. The act of devotion in the Common Prayer Book is your principal business there, and if properly attended to, will do more towards amending the heart than sermons generally can do. For they were composed by men of much greater piety and wisdom, than our common composers of sermons can pretend to be; and therefore I wish you would never miss the prayer days; yet I do not mean you should despise sermons, even of the preachers you dislike, for the discourse is often much better than the man, as sweet and clear waters come through very dirty earth. I am the more particular on this head, as you seemed to express a little before I came away some inclination to leave our church, which I would not have you do.

For the rest, I would only recommend to you in my absence, to acquire those useful accomplishments, arithmetic and bookkeeping. This you might do with ease, if you would resolve not to see company on the hours you set apart for those studies.

We expect to be at sea to-morrow, if this wind holds; after which I shall have no opportunity of writing to you, till I arrive (if it please God I do arrive) in England. I pray that his blessing may attend you, which is worth more than a thousand of mine, though they are never wanting. Give my love to your brother and sister, [67] as I cannot write to them, and remember me affectionately to the young ladies your friends, and to our good neighbours. I am, my dear child, your affectionate father,

B. FRANKLIN.

From A NARRATIVE OF THE LATE MASSACRES

IN LANCASTER COUNTY, OF A NUMBER OF INDIANS, FRIENDS OF THIS PROVINCE, BY PERSONS UNKNOWN. WITH SOME OBSERVATIONS ON THE SAME. [68]

[1764]

... On *Wednesday*, the 14th of *December*, 1763, Fifty-seven Men, from some of our Frontier Townships, who had projected the Destruction of this little Commonwealth, came, all well mounted, and armed with Firelocks, Hangers and Hatchets, having travelled through the Country in the Night, to *Conestogoe* Manor. There they surrounded the small Village of *Indian* Huts, and just at Break of Day broke into them all at once. Only three Men, two Women, and a young Boy, were found at home, the rest being out among the neighbouring White People, some to sell the Baskets, Brooms and Bowls they manufactured, and others on other Occasions. These poor defenceless Creatures were immediately fired upon, stabbed, and hatcheted to Death! The good *Shehaes*, among the rest, cut to Pieces in his Bed. All of them were scalped and otherwise horribly mangled. Then their Huts were set on Fire, and most of them burnt down. When the Troop, pleased with their own Conduct and Bravery, but enraged that any of the poor *Indians* had escaped the Massacre, rode off, and in small Parties, by different Roads, went home.

The universal Concern of the neighbouring White People on hearing of this Event, and the Lamentations of the younger *Indians*, when they returned and saw the Desolation, and the butchered half-burnt Bodies of their murdered Parents and other Relations, cannot well be expressed.

. . . .

Notwithstanding this Proclamation [by the Governor], those cruel men again assembled themselves, and hearing that the remaining fourteen *Indians* were in the Workhouse at *Lancaster*, they suddenly appeared in that Town, on the 27th of *December*. Fifty of them, armed as before, dismounting, went directly to the Workhouse, and by Violence broke open the Door, and entered with the utmost Fury in their Countenances. When the poor Wretches saw they had *no Protection* nigh, nor could possibly escape, and being without the least Weapon for Defence, they divided into their little Families, the Children clinging to the Parents; they fell on their Knees, protested their Innocence, declared their Love to the *English*, and that, in their whole Lives, they had never done them Injury; and in this Posture they all received the Hatchet! Men, Women and little

Children were every one inhumanly murdered!—in cold Blood!

The barbarous Men who committed the atrocious Fact, in defiance of Government, of all Laws human and divine, and to the eternal Disgrace of their Country and Colour, then mounted their Horses, huzza'd in Triumph, as if they had gained a Victory, and rode off—*unmolested!*

The Bodies of the Murdered were then brought out and exposed in the Street, till a Hole could be made in the Earth to receive and cover them.

But the Wickedness cannot be covered, the Guilt will lie on the whole Land, till Justice is done on the Murderers. THE BLOOD OF THE INNOCENT WILL CRY TO HEAVEN FOR VENGEANCE.

.   .   .   .

If an *Indian* injures me, does it follow that I may revenge that Injury on all *Indians?* It is well known, that *Indians* are of different Tribes, Nations and Languages, as well as the White People. In *Europe* if the *French*, who are White People, should injure the *Dutch*, are they to revenge it on the *English*, because they too are White People? The only Crime of these poor Wretches seems to have been, that they had a reddish-brown Skin, and black Hair; and some People of that Sort, it seems, had murdered some of our Relations. If it be right to kill Men for such a Reason, then, should any Man, with a freckled Face and red Hair, kill a Wife or Child of mine, it would be right for me to revenge it, by killing all the freckled red-haired Men, Women and Children, I could afterwards anywhere meet with.

But it seems these People think they have a better Justification; nothing less than the *Word of God.* With the Scriptures in their Hands and Mouths, they can set at nought that express Command, *Thou shalt do no Murder;* and justify their Wickedness by the Command given *Joshua* to destroy the Heathen. Horrid Perversion of Scripture and of Religion! To father the worst of Crimes on the God of Peace and Love! Even the *Jews*, to whom that particular Commission was directed, spared the *Gibeonites*, on Account of their Faith once given. The Faith of this Government has been frequently given to those *Indians;* but that did not avail them with People who despise Government.

We pretend to be *Christians*, and, from the superior Light we enjoy, ought to exceed *Heathens*, *Turks*, *Saracens*, *Moors*, *Negroes* and *Indians*, in the Knowledge and Practice of what is right. I will endeavour to show, by a few Examples from Books and History, the Sense those People have had of such Actions.

Homer wrote his Poem, called the *Odyssey*, some Hundred Years before the Birth of Christ. He frequently speaks of what he calls not only *the Duties*, but *the Sacred Rites of Hospitality*, (exercised towards Strangers, while in our House or Territory) as including, besides all the common Circumstances of Entertainment, full Safety and Protection of Person, from all Danger of Life, from all Injuries, and even Insults. The Rites of Hospitality were called *sacred*, because the Stranger, the Poor, and the Weak, when they applied for Protection and Relief, were, from the Religion of those Times, supposed to be sent by the Deity to try the Goodness of Men, and that he would avenge the Injuries they might receive, where they ought to have been protected. These Sentiments therefore influenced the Manners of all Ranks of People, even the meanest; for we find that when *Ulysses* came, as a poor Stranger, to the Hut of Eumæus, the Swineherd, and his great Dogs ran out to tear the ragged Man, *Eumæus* drave them away with Stones; and

> "'Unhappy Stranger!' (thus the faithful Swain
> Began, with Accent gracious and humane,)
> 'What Sorrow had been mine, if at *my* Gate
> Thy rev'rend Age had met a shameful Fate!
> But enter this my homely Roof, and see
> Our Woods not void of Hospitality.'
> He said, and seconding the kind Request,
> With friendly Step precedes the unknown Guest,
> A shaggy Goat's soft Hide beneath him spread,
> And with fresh Rushes heap'd an ample Bed.
> Joy touch'd the Hero's tender Soul, to find
> So just Reception from a Heart so kind:

And ['][Oh, ye Gods! with all your Blessings grace'
(He thus broke forth) 'this Friend of human Race![']
     The Swain reply'd. [']It never was our guise
To slight the Poor, or aught humane despise.
For Jove unfolds the hospitable Door,
'Tis Jove that sends the Stranger and the Poor.[']" [69]

These Heathen People thought, that after a Breach of the
Rites of Hospitality, a Curse from Heaven would attend them
in every thing they did, and even their honest Industry in their
Callings would fail of Success. Thus when *Ulysses* tells *Eumæus*,
who doubted the Truth of what he related, "If I deceive you
in this, I should deserve Death, and I consent that you should
put me to Death;" *Eumæus* rejects the Proposal, as what would
be attended with both Infamy and Misfortune, saying ironically,

"Doubtless, O Guest! great Laud and Praise were mine,
If, after social Rites and Gifts bestow'd,
I stain'd my Hospitable Hearth with Blood.
How would the Gods my righteous Toils succeed,
And bless the Hand that made a Stranger bleed?
No more."—

Even an open Enemy, in the Heat of Battle, throwing down
his Arms, submitting to his Foe, and asking Life and Protection,
was supposed to acquire an immediate Right to that Protection.
Thus one describes his being saved, when his Party was defeated;

"We turn'd to Flight; the gath'ring Vengeance spread
On all Parts round, and Heaps on Heaps lie dead.
The radiant Helmet from my Brows unlac'd,
And lo, on Earth my Shield and Javelin cast,
I meet the Monarch with a Suppliant's Face,
Approach his Chariot, and his Knees embrace.
He heard, he sav'd, he plac'd me at his Side;
My State he pity'd, and my Tears he dry'd;
Restrain'd the Rage the vengeful Foe express'd,
And turn'd the deadly Weapons from my Breast.
Pious to guard the Hospitable Rite,
And fearing Jove, whom Mercy's Works delight."

The Suitors of *Penelope* are by the same ancient Poet described as a sett of lawless Men, who were *regardless of the sacred Rites of Hospitality*. And therefore when the Queen was informed they were slain, and that by *Ulysses*, she, not believing that *Ulysses* was returned, says,

> "Ah no! some God the Suitors Deaths decreed,
> Some God descends, and by his Hand they bleed:
> Blind, to contemn the Stranger's righteous Cause,
> And violate all hospitable Laws!
> . . . The Powers they defy'd;
> But Heav'n is just, and by a God they dy'd."

. . . .

Now I am about to mention something of *Indians*, I beg that I may not be understood as framing Apologies for *all Indians*. I am far from desiring to lessen the laudable Spirit of Resentment in my Countrymen against those now at War with us, so far as it is justified by their Perfidy and Inhumanity. I would only observe, that the *Six Nations*, as a Body, have kept Faith with the *English* ever since we knew them, now near an Hundred Years; and that the governing Part of those People have had Notions of Honour, whatever may be the Case with the Rum-debauched, Trader-corrupted Vagabonds and Thieves on the *Sasquehannah* and *Ohio*, at present in Arms against us.

. . . .

Unhappy People! to have lived in such Times, and by such Neighbours! We have seen, that they would have been safer among the ancient *Heathens*, with whom the Rites of Hospitality were *sacred*. They would have been considered as *Guests* of the Publick, and the Religion of the Country would have operated in their Favour. But our Frontier People call themselves *Christians!* They would have been safer, if they had submitted to the *Turks;* for ever since *Mahomet's* Reproof to *Khaled*, even the cruel *Turks* never kill Prisoners in cold Blood. These were not even Prisoners. But what is the Example of *Turks* to Scripture *Christians?* They would have been safer, though they had been taken in actual War against the *Saracens*, if they had once drank Water with them. These were not taken in War against us, and have drank with us, and we with them, for Fourscore Years. But shall we compare *Saracens* to *Christians?*

They would have been safer among the *Moors* in *Spain*, though they had been Murderers of Sons; if Faith had once been pledged to them, and a Promise of Protection given. But these have had the Faith of the *English* given to them many Times by the Government, and, in Reliance on that Faith, they lived among us, and gave us the Opportunity of murdering them. However, what was honourable in *Moors*, may not be a Rule to us; for we are *Christians!* They would have been safer it seems among *Popish Spaniards*, even if Enemies, and delivered into their Hands by a Tempest. These were not Enemies; they were born among us, and yet we have killed them all. But shall we imitate *idolatrous Papists*, we that are *enlightened Protestants?* They would have even been safer among the *Negroes* of *Africa*, where at least one manly Soul would have been found, with Sense, Spirit and Humanity enough, to stand in their Defence. But shall *Whitemen* and *Christians* act like a *Pagan Negroe?* In short it appears, that they would have been safe in any Part of the known World, except in the Neighbourhood of the CHRISTIAN WHITE SAVAGES of *Peckstang* and *Donesgall!*

O, ye unhappy Perpetrators of this horrid Wickedness! reflect a Moment on the Mischief ye have done, the Disgrace ye have brought on your Country, on your Religion, and your Bible, on your Families and Children! Think on the Destruction of your captivated Country-folks (now among the wild *Indians*) which probably may follow, in Resentment of your Barbarity! Think on the Wrath of the United *Five Nations*, hitherto our Friends, but now provoked by your murdering one of their Tribes, in Danger of becoming our bitter Enemies. Think of the mild and good Government you have so audaciously insulted; the Laws of your King, your Country, and your God, that you have broken; the infamous Death that hangs over your Heads; for Justice, though slow, will come at last. All good People everywhere detest your Actions. You have imbrued your Hands in innocent Blood; how will you make them clean? The dying Shrieks and Groans of the Murdered, will often sound in your Ears: Their Spectres will sometimes attend you, and affright even your innocent Children! Fly where you will, your Consciences will go with you. Talking in your Sleep shall betray you, in the Delirium of a Fever you yourselves shall make your own Wickedness known.

. . . .

Let us rouze ourselves, for Shame, and redeem the Honour of our Province from the Contempt of its Neighbours; let all good Men join heartily and unanimously in Support of the Laws, and in strengthening the Hands of Government; that JUSTICE may be done, the Wicked punished, and the Innocent protected; otherwise we can, as a People, expect no Blessing from Heaven; there will be no Security for our Persons or Properties; Anarchy and Confusion will prevail over all; and Violence without Judgment, dispose of every Thing.

. . . .

TO THE EDITOR OF A NEWSPAPER

Monday, May 20, [1765].

SIR,

In your Paper of Wednesday last, an ingenious Correspondent that calls himself THE SPECTATOR, and dates from *Pimlico*, under the Guise of Good Will to the News-writers, whom he calls an "useful Body of Men in this great City," has, in my Opinion, artfully attempted to turn them & their Works into Ridicule, wherein if he could succeed, great Injury might be done to the Public as well as to those good People.

Supposing, Sir, that the "*We hears*" they give us of this & t'other intended Voyage or Tour of this & t'other great Personage, were mere Inventions, yet they at least offer us an innocent Amusement while we read, and useful Matter of Conversation when we are dispos'd to converse.

Englishmen, Sir, are too apt to be silent when they have nothing to say; too apt to be sullen when they are silent; and, when they are sullen, to hang themselves. But, by these *We hears*, we are supplied with abundant funds of Discourse, we discuss the Motives for such Voyages, the Probability of their being undertaken, and the Practicability of their Execution. Here we display our Judgment in Politics, our Knowledge of the Interests of Princes, and our Skill in Geography, and (if we have it) show our Dexterity moreover in Argumentation. In the mean time, the tedious Hour is kill'd, we go home pleas'd with the Applauses we have receiv'd from others, or at least with those we secretly give to ourselves: We sleep soundly, & live on, to the Comfort of our Families. But, Sir, I beg leave to say, that all the Articles of News that seem improbable are not mere Inventions. Some of them, I can assure you on the Faith of a Traveller, are serious Truths. And here, quitting Mr. Spectator of Pimlico, give me leave to instance the various numberless Accounts the Newswriters have given us, with so much honest Zeal for the welfare of *Poor Old England*, of the establishing Manufactures in the Colonies to the Prejudice of those of this Kingdom. It is objected by superficial Readers, who yet pretend to some Knowledge of those Countries, that such Establishments are not only improbable, but impossible, for that their Sheep have but little Wooll, not in the whole sufficient for a Pair of Stockings a Year to each Inhabitant; and that, from the Universal Dearness of Labour among them, the Working of Iron and other Materials, except in some few coarse Instances, is impracticable to any Advantage.

Dear Sir, do not let us suffer ourselves to be amus'd with such groundless Objections. The very Tails of the American Sheep are so laden with Wooll, that each has a little Car or Waggon on four little Wheels, to support & keep it from trailing on the Ground.[70] Would they caulk their Ships, would they fill their Beds, would they even litter their Horses with Wooll, if it were not both plenty and cheap? And what signifies Dearness of Labour, when an English Shilling passes for five and Twenty? Their engaging 300 Silk Throwsters here in one Week, for New York, was treated as a Fable, because, forsooth, they have "no Silk there to throw." Those, who made this Objection, perhaps did not know, that at the same time the Agents from the King of Spain were at Quebec to contract for 1000 Pieces of Cannon to be made there for the Fortification of Mexico, and at N York engaging the annual Supply of woven Floor-Carpets for their West India Houses, other Agents from the Emperor of China were at Boston treating about an Exchange of raw Silk for Wooll, to be carried in Chinese Junks through the Straits of Magellan.

And yet all this is as certainly true, as the Account said to be from Quebec, in all the Papers of last Week, that the Inhabitants of Canada are making Preparations for a Cod and Whale Fishery this "Summer in the upper Lakes." Ignorant People may object that the upper Lakes are fresh, and that Cod and Whale are Salt Water Fish: But let them know, Sir, that Cod, like other Fish when attack'd by their Enemies, fly into any Water where they can be safest; that Whales, when they have a mind to eat Cod, pursue them wherever they fly; and that the grand Leap of the Whale in that Chase up the Fall of Niagara is esteemed, by all who have seen it, as one of the finest Spectacles in Nature. Really, Sir, the World is grown too incredulous. It is like the Pendulum ever swinging from one Extream to another. Formerly every thing printed was believed, because it was in print. Now Things seem to be disbelieved for just the very same Reason. Wise Men wonder at the present Growth of Infidelity. They should have consider'd, when they taught People to doubt the Authority of Newspapers and the Truth of Predictions in Almanacks, that the next Step might be a Disbelief in the well vouch'd Accts of Ghosts Witches, and Doubts even of the Truths of the Creed!

Thus much I thought it necessary to say in favour of an honest Set of Writers, whose comfortable Living depends on collecting & supplying the Printers with News at the small Price of Sixpence an Article, and who always show their Regard to Truth, by contradicting in a subsequent Article such as are wrong,—for another Sixpence,—to the great Satisfaction & Improvement of us Coffee-house Students in History & Politics, and the infinite Advantage of all future Livies, Rapins, Robertsons, Humes, and McAulays, who may be sincerely inclin'd to furnish the World with that *rara Avis*, a true History. I am, Sir, your humble Servant,   A TRAVELLER.

TO LORD KAMES

Craven Street, London, June 2, 1765.

My Dear Lord,

... In my passage to America I read your excellent work, the *Elements of Criticism*, in which I found great entertainment: much to admire and nothing to reprove. I only wished you had examined more fully the subject of Music, and demonstrated, that the pleasure which artists feel in hearing much of that composed in the modern taste, is not the natural pleasure arising from melody or harmony of sounds, but of the same kind with the pleasure we feel on seeing the surprising feats of tumblers and rope-dancers, who execute difficult things. For my part I take this to be really the case, and suppose it is the reason why those, who being unpractised in music, and therefore unacquainted with those difficulties have little or no pleasure in hearing this music. Many pieces of it are mere compositions of tricks. I have sometimes, at a concert, attended by a common audience, placed myself so as to see all their faces, and observed no signs of pleasure in them during the performance of a great part that was admired by the performers themselves; while a plain old *Scottish tune*, which they disdained, and could scarcely be prevailed on to play, gave manifest and general delight.

Give me leave on this occasion to extend a little the sense of your position, that "Melody and Harmony are separately agreeable, and in union delightful," and to give it as my opinion, that the reason why the Scotch tunes have lived so long, and will probably live for ever (if they escape being stifled in modern affected ornament), is merely this, that they are really compositions of melody and harmony united, or rather that their melody is harmony. I mean the simple tunes sung by a single voice. As this will appear paradoxical, I must explain my meaning. In common acceptation, indeed, only an agreeable *succession* of sounds is called *Melody*, and only the *co-existence* of agreeing sounds, *Harmony*. But, since the memory is capable of retaining for some moments a perfect idea of the pitch of a past sound, so as to compare with it the pitch of a succeeding sound, and judge truly of their agreement or disagreement, there may and does arise from thence a sense of harmony between the present and past sounds, equally pleasing with that between two present sounds.

Now the construction of the old Scotch tunes is this, that almost every succeeding *emphatical* note is a third, a fifth, an octave, or in short some note that is in concord with the preceding note. Thirds are chiefly used, which are very pleasing concords. I use the word *emphatical* to distinguish those notes which have a stress laid on them in singing the tune, from the lighter connecting notes, that serve merely, like grammar articles, to tack the others together.

That we have a most perfect idea of a sound just past, I might appeal to all acquainted with music, who know how easy it is to repeat a sound in the same pitch with one just heard. In tuning an instrument, a good ear can as easily determine that two strings are in unison by sounding them separately, as by sounding them together; their disagreement is also as easily, I believe I may say more easily and better distinguished, when sounded separately; for when sounded together, though you know by the beating that one is higher than the other, you cannot tell which it is. [I have ascribed to memory the ability of comparing the pitch of a present tone with that of one past. But, if there should be, as possibly there may be, something in the ear, similar to what we find in the eye, that ability would not be entirely owing to memory. Possibly the vibrations given to the auditory nerves by a particular sound may actually continue some time after the cause of those vibrations is past, and the agreement or disagreement of a subsequent sound become by comparison with them more discernible. For the impression made on the visual nerves by a luminous object will continue for twenty or thirty seconds. Sitting in a room, look earnestly at the middle of a window a little while when the day is bright, and then shut your eyes; the figure of the window will still remain in the eye, and so distinct that you may count the panes.

A remarkable circumstance attending this experiment, is, that the impression of forms is better retained than that of colors;

for after the eyes are shut, when you first discern the image of
the window, the panes appear dark, and the cross bars of the
sashes, with the window frames and walls, appear white or
bright; but, if you still add to the darkness in the eyes by cover-
ing them with your hand, the reverse instantly takes place, the
panes appear luminous and the cross bars dark. And by removing the hand they are again reversed. This I know not how to
account for. Nor for the following; that, after looking long
through green spectacles, the white paper of a book will on first
taking them off appear to have a blush of red; and, after long
looking through red glasses, a greenish cast; this seems to intimate a relation between green and red not yet explained.]

Farther, when we consider by whom these ancient tunes
were composed, and how they were first performed, we shall
see that such harmonical succession of sounds was natural and
even necessary in their construction. They were composed by
the minstrels of those days to be played on the harp accompanied by the voice. The harp was strung with wire, [which
gives a sound of long continuance,] and had no contrivance, like
that in the modern harpsichord, by which the sound of the preceding could be stoppt, the moment a succeeding note began.
To avoid *actual* discord, it was therefore necessary that the succeeding emphatic note should be a chord with the preceding, as
their sounds must exist at the same time. Hence arose that
beauty in those tunes that has so long pleased, and will please
for ever, though men scarce know why. That they were originally composed for the harp, and of the most simple kind, I
mean a harp without any half notes but those in the natural
scale, and with no more than two octaves of strings, from
C to C, I conjecture from another circumstance, which is, that
not one of those tunes, really ancient, has a single artificial half
note in it, and that in tunes where it was most convenient for
the voice to use the middle notes of the harp, and place the
key in F, there the B, which if used should be a B flat, is
always omitted by passing over it with a third. The connoisseurs in modern music will say, I have no taste; but I cannot
help adding, that I believe our ancestors, in hearing a good song,

distinctly articulated, sung to one of those tunes, and accompanied by the harp, felt more real pleasure than is communicated by the generality of modern operas, exclusive of that arising from the scenery and dancing. Most tunes of late composition, not having this natural harmony united with their melody, have recourse to the artificial harmony of a bass, and other accompanying parts. This support, in my opinion, the old tunes do not need, and are rather confused than aided by it. Whoever has heard James Oswald play them on his violoncello, will be less inclined to dispute this with me. I have more than once seen tears of pleasure in the eyes of his auditors; and yet, I think, even *his* playing those tunes would please more, if he gave them less modern ornament. My son, when we parted, desired me to present his Affectionate respects to you, Lady Kames, and your amiable children: be so good with those, to accept mine, and believe me, with sincerest esteem, my dear Lord, &c.

B. FRANKLIN.

P.S. I do promise myself the pleasure of seeing you and my other friends in Scotland, before I return to America.

LETTER
CONCERNING THE GRATITUDE OF AMERICA[71]

AND THE PROBABILITY AND EFFECTS OF A UNION WITH GREAT
BRITAIN; AND CONCERNING THE REPEAL OR SUSPENSION
OF THE STAMP ACT

[London,] January 6, 1766.

SIR,

I have attentively perused the paper you sent me, and am of opinion, that the measure it proposes, of an union with the colonies, is a wise one; but I doubt it will hardly be thought so here, till it is too late to attempt it. The time has been, when the colonies would have esteemed it a great advantage, as well as honour to be permitted to send members to Parliament; and would have asked for that privilege, if they could have had the least hopes of obtaining it. The time is now come when they are indifferent about it, and will probably not ask it, though they might accept it if offered them; and the time will come, when they will certainly refuse it. But if such an union were now established (which methinks it highly imports this country to establish) it would probably subsist as long as Britain shall continue a nation. This people, however, is too proud, and too much despises the Americans, to bear the thought of admitting them to such an equitable participation in the government of the whole.

Then the next best thing seems to be, leaving them in the quiet enjoyment of their respective constitutions; and when money is wanted for any public service, in which they ought to bear a part, calling upon them by requisitorial letters from the crown (according to the long-established custom) to grant such aids as their loyalty shall dictate, and their abilities permit. The very sensible and benevolent author of that paper seems not to have known, that such a constitutional custom subsists, and has always hitherto been practised in America; or he would not have expressed himself in this manner; "It is evident, beyond a doubt, to the intelligent and impartial, that after the very extraordinary efforts, which were effectually made by Great Britain in the late war to save the colonists from destruction, and attended of necessity with an enormous load of debts in consequence, that the same colonists, now firmly secured from foreign enemies, should be somehow induced to contribute some proportion towards the exigencies of state in future." This looks as if he conceived the war had been carried on at the sole expense of Great Britain, and the colonies only reaped the benefit, without hitherto sharing the burden, and were therefore now indebted to Britain on that account. And this is the same kind of argument that is used by those, who would fix on the colonies the heavy charge of unreasonableness and ingratitude, which I think your friend did not intend.

Please to acquaint him, then, that the fact is not so; that, every year during the war, requisitions were made by the crown on the colonies for raising money and men; that accordingly they made more extraordinary efforts, in proportion to their abilities, than Britain did; that they raised, paid, and clothed, for five or six years, near twenty-five thousand men, besides providing for other services, as building forts, equipping guardships, paying transports, &c. And that this was more than their fair proportion is not merely an opinion of mine, but was the judgment of government here, in full knowledge of all the facts; for the then ministry, to make the burthen more equal, recommended the case to Parliament, and obtained a reimbursement to the Americans of about two hundred thousand pounds sterling every year; which amounted only to about two fifths of their expense; and great part of the rest lies still a load of debt upon them; heavy taxes on all their estates, real and personal, being laid by acts of their assemblies to discharge it, and yet will not discharge it in many years.

While, then, these burdens continue; while Britain restrains the colonies in every branch of commerce and manufactures that she thinks interferes with her own; while she drains the colonies, by her trade with them, of all the cash they can procure by every art and industry in any part of the world, and thus keeps them always in her debt; (for they can make no law to discourage the importation of your to *them* ruinous superfluities, as *you* do the superfluities of France; since such a law would immediately be reported against by your Board of Trade, and repealed by the crown;) I say, while these circumstances continue, and while there subsists the established method of royal requisitions for raising money on them by their own assemblies on every proper occasion; can it be necessary or prudent to distress and vex them by taxes laid here, in a Parliament wherein they have no representative, and in a manner which they look upon to be unconstitutional and subversive of their most valuable rights? And are they to be thought unreasonable and ungrateful if they oppose such taxes?

Wherewith, they say, shall we show our loyalty to our gracious King, if our money is to be given by others, without asking our consent? And, if the Parliament has a right thus to take from us a penny in the pound, where is the line drawn that bounds that right, and what shall hinder their calling, whenever they please, for the other nineteen shillings and eleven pence? Have we then any thing that we can call our own? It is more than probable, that bringing representatives from the colonies to sit and act here as members of Parliament, thus uniting and consolidating your dominions, would in a little time remove these objections and difficulties, and make the future government of the colonies easy; but, till some such thing is done, I apprehend no taxes, laid there by Parliament here, will ever be collected, but such as must be stained with blood; and I am sure the profit of such taxes will never answer the expense of collecting them, and that the respect and affection of the Americans to this country will in the struggle be totally lost, perhaps never to be recovered; and therewith all the commercial and political advantages, that might have attended the continuance of this respect and this affection.

In my own private judgment, I think an immediate repeal of the Stamp Act would be the best measure for this country; but a suspension of it for three years, the best for that. The repeal would fill them with joy and gratitude, reëstablish their respect and veneration for Parliament, restore at once their ancient and natural love for this country, and their regard for every thing that comes from it; hence the trade would be renewed in all its branches; they would again indulge in all the expensive superfluities you supply them with, and their own new-assumed home industry would languish. But the suspension, though it might continue their fears and anxieties, would at the same time keep up their resolutions of industry and frugality; which in two or three years would grow into habits, to their lasting advantage. However, as the repeal will probably not be now agreed to, from what I think a mistaken opinion, that the honour and dignity of government is better supported by persisting in a wrong measure once entered into, than by rectifying an error as soon as it is discovered; we must allow the next best thing for the advantage of both countries, is the suspension; for, as to executing the act by force, it is madness, and will be ruin to the whole.

The rest of your friend's reasonings and propositions appear to me truly just and judicious. I will therefore only add, that I am as desirous of his acquaintance and intimacy, as he was of my opinion.

I am, with much esteem,

Your obliged friend,

B. FRANKLIN.

TO LORD KAMES

London, April 11, 1767.

MY DEAR LORD,—

I received your obliging favour of January the 19th. You have kindly relieved me from the pain I had long been under. You are goodness itself. I ought to have answered yours of December 25. 1765. I never received a letter that contained sentiments more suitable to my own. It found me under much agitation of mind on the very important subject it treated. It fortified me greatly in the judgment I was inclined to form (though contrary to the general vogue) on the then delicate and critical situation of affairs between Great Britain and her Colonies, and on that weighty point, their *Union*. You guessed aright in supposing that I would not be a *mute in that play*. I was extremely busy, attending Members of both Houses, informing, explaining, consulting, disputing, in a continual hurry from morning to night, till the affair was happily ended. During the course of it, being called before the House of Commons, I spoke my mind pretty freely. Inclosed I send you the imperfect account that was taken of that examination. "You will there see how entirely we agree, except in a point of fact, of which you could not but be misinformed; the papers at that time being full of mistaken assertions, that the colonies had been the cause of the war, and had ungratefully refused to bear any part of the expence of it.

I send it you now, because I apprehend some late incidents are likely to revive the contest between the two countries. I fear it will be a mischievous one. It becomes a matter of great importance that clear ideas should be formed on solid principles, both in Britain and America, of the true political relation between them, and the mutual duties belonging to that relation. Till this is done, they will be often jarring. I know none whose knowledge, sagacity and impartiality qualify him so thoroughly for such a service, as yours do you. I wish therefore you would consider it. You may thereby be the happy instrument of great good to the nation, and of preventing much mischief and bloodshed. I am fully persuaded with you, that a *Consolidating Union*, by a fair and equal representation of all the parts of this empire in Parliament, is the only firm basis on which its political grandeur and prosperity can be founded. Ireland once wished it, but now rejects it. The time has been, when the colonies might have been pleased with it: they are now *indifferent* about it; and if it is much longer delayed, they too will *refuse* it. But the pride of this people cannot bear the thought of it, and therefore it will be delayed. Every man in England seems to consider himself as a piece of a sovereign over America; seems to jostle himself into the throne with the King, and talks of *our subjects in the Colonies*. The Parliament cannot well and wisely make laws suited to the Colonies, without being properly and truly informed of their circumstances, abilities, temper, &c. This it cannot be, without representatives from thence: and yet it is fond of this power, and averse to the only means of acquiring the necessary knowledge for exercising it; which is desiring to be *omnipotent*, without being *omniscient*.

I have mentioned that the contest is likely to be revived. It is on this occasion. In the same session with the stamp act, an act was passed to regulate the quartering of soldiers in America; when the bill was first brought in, it contained a clause, empowering the officers to quarter their soldiers in private houses: this we warmly opposed, and got it omitted. The bill passed, however, with a clause, that empty houses, barns, &c., should be hired for them, and that the respective provinces where they were should pay the expence and furnish firing, bedding, drink, and some other articles to the soldiers *gratis*. There is no way for any province to do this, but by the Assembly's making a law to raise the money. The Pennsylvanian Assembly has made such a law: the New York Assembly has refused to do it: and now all the talk here is of sending a force to compel them.

The reasons given by the Assembly to the Governor, for the refusal, are, that they understand the act to mean the furnishing such things to soldiers, only while on their march through the country, and not to great bodies of soldiers, to be fixt as at present, in the province; the burthen in the latter case being greater than the inhabitants can bear: That it would put it in the power of the Captain-General to oppress the province at pleasure, &c. But there is supposed to be another reason at bottom, which they intimate, though they do not plainly express it; to wit, that it is of the nature of an *internal tax* laid on them by Parliament, which has no right so to do. Their refusal is here called *Rebellion*, and punishment is thought of.

Now waving that point of right, and supposing the Legislatures in America subordinate to the Legislature of Great Britain, one might conceive, I think, a power in the superior Legislature to forbid the inferior Legislatures making particular laws; but to enjoin it to make a particular law contrary to its own judgment, seems improper; an Assembly or Parliament not being an *executive* officer of Government, whose duty it is, in law-making, to obey orders, but a *deliberative* body, who are to consider what comes before them, its propriety, practicability, or possibility, and to determine accordingly: The very nature of a Parliament seems to be destroyed, by supposing it may be bound, and compelled by a law of a superior Parliament, to make a law contrary to its own judgment.

Indeed, the act of Parliament in question has not, as in other acts, when a duty is enjoined, directed a penalty on neglect or refusal, and a mode of recovering that penalty. It seems, therefore, to the people in America as a mere requisition, which they are at liberty to comply with or not, as it may suit or not suit the different circumstances of different provinces. Pennsylvania has therefore voluntarily complied. New York, as I said before, has refused. The Ministry that made the act, and all their adherents, call for vengeance. The present Ministry are perplext, and the measures they will finally take on the occasion, are yet unknown. But sure I am, that, if *Force* is used, great mischief will ensue; the affections of the people of America to this country will be alienated; your commerce will be diminished; and a total separation of interests be the final consequence.

It is a common, but mistaken notion here, that the Colonies were planted at the expence of Parliament, and that therefore the Parliament has a right to tax them, &c. The truth is, they were planted at the expence of private adventurers, who went over there to settle, with leave of the King, given by charter. On receiving this leave, and those charters, the adventurers voluntarily engaged to remain the King's subjects, though in a foreign country; a country which had not been conquered by either King or Parliament, but was possessed by a free people.

When our planters arrived, they purchased the lands of the natives, without putting King or Parliament to any expence. Parliament had no hand in their settlement, was never so much as consulted about their constitution, and took no kind of notice of them, till many years after they were established. I except only the two modern Colonies, or rather attempts to make Colonies, (for they succeed but poorly, and as yet hardly deserve the name of Colonies), I mean Georgia and Nova Scotia, which have hitherto been little better than Parliamentary jobs. Thus all the colonies acknowledge the King as their sovereign; his Governors there represent his person: Laws are made by their Assemblies or little Parliaments, with the Governor's assent, subject still to the King's pleasure to confirm or annul them: Suits arising in the Colonies, and differences between Colony and Colony, are determined by the King in Council. In this view, they seem so many separate little states, subject to the same Prince. The *sovereignty of the* King is therefore easily understood. But nothing is more common here than to talk of the *sovereignty* of PARLIAMENT, and the *sovereignty of* THIS NATION over the Colonies; a kind of sovereignty, the idea of which is not so clear, nor does it clearly appear on what foundation it is established. On the other hand, it seems necessary for the common good of the empire, that a power be lodged somewhere, to regulate its general commerce: this can be placed nowhere so properly as in the Parliament of Great Britain; and therefore, though that power has in some instances been executed with great partiality to Britain, and prejudice to the Colonies, they have nevertheless always submitted to it. Custom-houses are established in all of them, by virtue of laws made here, and the duties constantly paid, except by a few smugglers, such as are here and in all countries; but internal taxes laid on them by Parliament, are still and ever will be objected to, for the reasons that you will see in the mentioned Examination.

Upon the whole, I have lived so great a part of my life in Britain, and have formed so many friendships in it, that I love it, and sincerely wish it prosperity; and therefore wish to see that Union, on which alone I think it can be secured and established. As to America, the advantages of such a union to her are not so apparent. She may suffer at present under the arbitrary power of this country; she may suffer for a while in a separation from it; but these are temporary evils that she will outgrow. Scotland and Ireland are differently circumstanced. Confined by the sea, they can scarcely increase in numbers, wealth and strength, so as to overbalance England. But America, an immense territory, favoured by Nature with all advantages of climate, soil, great navigable rivers, and lakes, &c. must become a great country, populous and mighty; and will, in a less time than is generally conceived, be able to shake off any shackles that may be imposed on her, and perhaps place them on the imposers. In the mean time, every act of oppression will sour their tempers, lessen greatly, if not annihilate the profits of your commerce with them, and hasten their final revolt; for the seeds of liberty are universally found there, and nothing can eradicate them. And yet, there remains among that people, so much respect, veneration and affection for Britain, that, if cultivated prudently, with kind usage, and tenderness for their privileges, they might be easily governed still for ages, without force, or any considerable expence. But I do not see here a suf-

ficient quantity of the wisdom, that is necessary to produce such
a conduct, and I lament the want of it.

I borrowed at Millar's the new edition of your *Principles of
Equity*, and have read with great pleasure the preliminary discourse on the Principles of Morality. I have never before met
with any thing so satisfactory on the subject. While reading it,
I made a few remarks as I went along. They are not of much
importance, but I send you the paper.

I know the lady you mention; having, when in England before, met her once or twice at Lord Bath's. I remember I then
entertained the same opinion of her that you express. On the
strength of your kind recommendation, I purpose soon to wait
on her.

This is unexpectedly grown a long letter. The visit to Scotland, and the *Art of Virtue*, we will talk of hereafter. It is now
time to say, that I am, with increasing esteem and affection, my
dear friend, yours ever,[72]

B. FRANKLIN.

TO MISS MARY STEVENSON

Paris, Sept. 14, 1767.

DEAR POLLY,

I am always pleas'd with a Letter from you, and I flatter myself you may be sometimes pleas'd in receiving one from me,
tho' it should be of little Importance, such as this, which is to
consist of a few occasional Remarks made here, and in my
Journey hither.

Soon after I left you in that agreable Society at Bromley, I
took the Resolution of making a Trip with Sir John Pringle[73]
into France. We set out the 28th past. All the way to Dover
we were furnished with PostChaises, hung so as to lean forward, the Top coming down over one's Eyes, like a Hood, as if
to prevent one's seeing the Country; which being one of my
great Pleasures, I was engag'd in perpetual Disputes with the
Innkeepers, Hostlers, and Postilions, about getting the Straps
taken up a Hole or two before, and let down as much behind,

they insisting that the Chaise leaning forward was an Ease to the Horses, and that the contrary would kill them. I suppose the chaise leaning forward looks to them like a Willingness to go forward, and that its hanging back shows a Reluctance. They added other Reasons, that were no Reasons at all, and made me, as upon a 100 other Occasions, almost wish that Mankind had never been endow'd with a reasoning Faculty, since they know so little how to make use of it, and so often mislead themselves by it, and that they had been furnish'd with a good sensible Instinct instead of it.

At Dover, the next Morning, we embark'd for Calais with a Number of Passengers, who had never been before at sea. They would previously make a hearty Breakfast, because, if the Wind should fail, we might not get over till Supper time. Doubtless they thought that when they had paid for their Breakfast, they had a Right to it, and that, when they had swallowed it they were sure of it. But they had scarce been out half an Hour, before the Sea laid Claim to it, and they were oblig'd to deliver it up. So it seems there are Uncertainties, even beyond those between the Cup and the Lip. If ever you go to Sea, take my Advice, and live sparingly a Day or two beforehand. The Sickness, if any, will be lighter and sooner over. We got to Calais that Evening.

Various Impositions we suffer'd from Boatmen, Porters, &c. on both Sides the Water. I know not which are most rapacious, the English or French, but the latter have, with their Knavery, the most Politeness.

The Roads we found equally good with ours in England, in some Places pav'd with smooth Stone, like our new Streets, for many Miles together, and Rows of Trees on each Side, and yet there are no Turnpikes. But then the poor Peasants complain'd to us grievously, that they were oblig'd to work upon the Roads full two Months in the Year, without being paid for their Labour. Whether this is Truth, or whether, like Englishmen, they grumble Cause or no Cause, I have not yet been able fully to inform myself.

The Women we saw at Calais, on the Road, at Bouloigne,

and in the Inns and Villages, were generally of dark Complexions; but arriving at Abbeville we found a sudden Change, a Multitude of both Women and Men in that Place appearing remarkably fair. Whether this is owing to a small Colony of Spinners, Wool-combers, and Weavers, brought hither from Holland with the Woollen Manufacture about 60 Years ago; or to their being less expos'd to the Sun, than in other Places, their Business keeping them much within Doors, I know not. Perhaps as in some other Cases, different Causes may club in producing the Effect, but the Effect itself is certain. Never was I in a Place of greater Industry, Wheels and Looms going in every House.

As soon as we left Abbeville, the Swarthiness return'd. I speak generally, for here are some fair Women at Paris, who I think are not whiten'd by Art. As to Rouge, they don't pretend to imitate Nature in laying it on. There is no gradual Diminution of the Colour, from the full Bloom in the Middle of the Cheek to the faint Tint near the Sides, nor does it show itself differently in different Faces. I have not had the Honour of being at any Lady's Toylette to see how it is laid on, but I fancy I can tell you how it is or may be done. Cut a Hole of 3 Inches Diameter in a Piece of Paper; place it on the Side of your Face in such a Manner as that the Top of the Hole may be just under your Eye; then with a Brush dipt in the Colour, paint Face and Paper together; so when the Paper is taken off there will remain a round Patch of Red exactly the Form of the Hole. This is the Mode, from the Actresses on the Stage upwards thro' all Ranks of Ladies to the Princesses of the Blood, but it stops there, the Queen not using it, having in the Serenity, Complacence, and Benignity that shine so eminently in, or rather through her Countenance, sufficient Beauty, tho' now an old Woman, to do extreamly well without it.

You see I speak of the Queen as if I had seen her, and so I have; for you must know I have been at Court. We went to Versailles last Sunday, and had the Honour of being presented to the King; he spoke to both of us very graciously and chearfully, is a handsome Man, has a very lively Look, and appears younger than he is. In the Evening we were at the *Grand Couvert*, where the Family sup in Publick. The Form of their Sitting at the Table was this: The table was as you see half a Hollow Square, the Service Gold. When either made a Sign for Drink, the Word was given by one of the Waiters; *A boire pour*

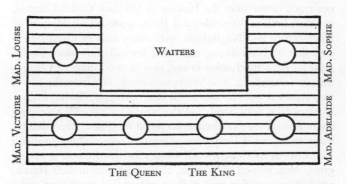

le Roy, or, *A boire pour la Reine.* Then two persons within the Square approach'd, one with Wine[,] the other with Water in *Caraffes;* each drank a little Glass of what he brought, and then put both the *Caraffes* with a Glass on a Salver, and presented it. Their Distance from each other was such, as that other Chairs might have been plac'd between any two of them. An Officer of the Court brought us up thro' the Crowd of Spectators, and plac'd Sir John so as to stand between the King and Madame Adelaide, and me between the Queen and Madame Victoire. The King talk'd a good deal to Sir John, asking many Questions about our Royal Family; and did me too the Honour of taking some Notice of me; that's saying enough, for I would not have you think me so much pleas'd with this King and Queen, as to have a Whit less regard than I us'd to have for ours. No Frenchman shall go beyond me in thinking my own King and Queen the very best in the World, and the most amiable.

Versailles has had infinite Sums laid out in building it and supplying it with Water. Some say the Expences exceeded 80 Millions Sterling. The Range of Building is immense; the Gar-

den-Front most magnificent, all of hewn Stone; the Number of
Statues, Figures, Urns, &c., in Marble and Bronze of exquisite
Workmanship, is beyond Conception. But the Waterworks are
out of Repair, and so is great Part of the Front next the Town,
looking with its shabby half-Brick Walls, and broken Windows,
not much better than the Houses in Durham Yard. There is,
in short, both at Versailles and Paris, a prodigious Mixture of
Magnificence and Negligence, with every kind of Elegance except that of Cleanliness, and what we call *Tidyness*. Tho' I
must do Paris the Justice to say, that in two Points of Cleanliness they exceed us. The Water they drink, tho' from the River,
they render as pure as that of the best Spring, by filtring it thro'
Cisterns fill'd with Sand; and the Streets by constant Sweeping
are fit to walk in, tho' there is no pav'd footPath. Accordingly,
many well-dress'd People are constantly seen walking in them.
The Crowds of Coaches and Chairs for this Reason is not so
great. Men, as well as Women, carry Umbrellas in their Hands,
which they extend in case of Rain or two [*sic*] much sun; and a
Man with an Umbrella not taking up more than 3 foot square,
or 9 square feet of the Street, when, if in a Coach, he would
take up 240 square feet, you can easily conceive that tho' the
Streets here are narrower they may be much less encumber'd.
They are extreamly well pav'd, and the Stones, being generally
Cubes, when worn on one Side, may be turn'd and become
new.

The Civilities we everywhere receive give us the strongest
Impressions of the French Politeness. It seems to be a Point
settled here universally, that Strangers are to be treated with
Respect; and one has just the same Deference shewn one here
by being a Stranger, as in England by being a Lady. The Cus-
tomhouse Officers at Port St. Denis, as we enter'd Paris, were
about to seize 2 doz of excellent Bordeaux Wine given us at
Boulogne, and which we brought with us; but, as soon as they
found we were Strangers, it was immediately remitted on that
Account. At the Church of Notre Dame, where we went to see
a magnificent Illumination, with Figures, &c., for the deceas'd
Dauphiness, we found an immense Crowd, who were kept out

by Guards; but, the Officer being told that we were Strangers from England, he immediately admitted us, accompanied and show'd us every thing. Why don't we practise this Urbanity to Frenchmen? Why should they be allowed to outdo us in any thing?

Here is an Exhibition of Paintings like ours in London, to which Multitudes flock daily. I am not Connoisseur enough to judge which has most Merit. Every Night, Sundays not excepted here are Plays or Operas; and tho' the Weather has been hot, and the Houses full, one is not incommoded by the Heat so much as with us in Winter. They must have some Way of changing the Air, that we are not acquainted with. I shall enquire into it.

Travelling is one Way of lengthening Life, at least in Appearance. It is but about a Fortnight since we left London, but the Variety of Scenes we have gone through makes it seem equal to Six Months living in one Place. Perhaps I have suffered a greater Change, too, in my own Person, than I could have done in Six Years at home. I had not been here Six Days, before my Taylor and Perruquier had transform'd me into a Frenchman. Only think what a Figure I make in a little Bag-Wig and naked Ears! They told me I was become 20 Years younger, and look'd very galante;

So being in Paris where the Mode is to be sacredly follow'd I was once very near making Love to my Friend's Wife.

This Letter shall cost you a Shilling, and you may consider it cheap, when you reflect, that it has cost me at least 50 Guineas to get into the Situation, that enables me to write it. Besides, I might, if I had staied at home, have won perhaps two Shillings of you at Cribbidge. By the Way, now I mention Cards, let me tell you that Quadrille is quite out of Fashion here, and English Whisk all the Mode at Paris and the Court.

And pray look upon it as no small Matter, that surrounded as I am by the Glories of this World, and Amusements of all Sorts, I remember you and Dolly and all the dear good Folks at Bromley. 'Tis true, I can't help it, but must and ever shall remember you all with Pleasure.

Need I add, that I am particularly, my dear good Friend, yours most affectionately,

B. FRANKLIN.

ON THE LABOURING POOR

[From the *Gentleman's Magazine*, April, 1768.]

SIR,

I have met with much invective in the papers, for these two years past, against the hard-heartedness of the rich, and much complaint of the great oppressions suffered in this country by the labouring poor. Will you admit a word or two on the other side of the question? I do not propose to be an advocate for oppression or oppressors. But when I see that the poor are, by such writings, exasperated against the rich, and excited to insurrections, by which much mischief is done, and some forfeit their lives, I could wish the true state of things were better understood, the poor not made by these busy writers more uneasy and unhappy than their situation subjects them to be, and the nation not brought into disrepute among foreigners, by public groundless accusations of ourselves, as if the rich in England had no compassion for the poor, and Englishmen wanted common humanity.

In justice, then to this country, give me leave to remark, that the condition of the poor here is, by far, the best in Europe, for that, except in England and her American colonies, there is not in any country of the known world, not even in Scotland or Ireland, a provision by law to enforce a support of the poor. Everywhere else necessity reduces to beggary. This law was not made by the poor. The legislators were men of fortune. By that act they voluntarily subjected their own estates, and the estates of all others, to the payment of a tax for the maintenance of the poor, incumbering those estates with a kind of rent-charge for that purpose, whereby the poor are vested with an inheritance, as it were, in all the estates of the rich. I wish they were benefited by this generous provision in any degree equal to the good intention, with which it was made, and is continued:

But I fear the giving mankind a dependance on any thing for support, in age or sickness, besides industry and frugality during youth and health, tends to flatter our natural indolence, to encourage idleness and prodigality, and thereby to promote and increase poverty, the very evil it was intended to cure; thus multiplying beggars instead of diminishing them.

Besides this tax, which the rich in England have subjected themselves to, in behalf of the poor, amounting in some places to five or six shillings in the pound, of the annual income, they have, by donations and subscriptions, erected numerous schools in various parts of the kingdom, for educating gratis the children of the poor in reading and writing, and in many of those schools the children are also fed and cloathed. They have erected hospitals at an immense expence for the reception and cure of the sick, the lame, the wounded, and the insane poor, for lying-in women, and deserted children. They are also continually contributing towards making up losses occasioned by fire, by storms, or by floods, and to relieve the poor in severe seasons of frost, in times of scarcity, &c., in which benevolent and charitable contributions no nation exceeds us. Surely, there is some gratitude due for so many instances of goodness.

Add to this all the laws made to discourage foreign manufactures, by laying heavy duties on them, or totally prohibiting them, whereby the rich are obliged to pay much higher prices for what they wear and consume, than if the trade was open: These are so many laws for the support of our labouring poor, made by the rich, and continued at their expence; all the difference of price, between our own and foreign commodities, being so much given by our rich to our poor; who would indeed be enabled by it to get by degrees above poverty, if they did not, as too generally they do, consider every encrease of wages, only as something that enables them to drink more and work less; so that their distress in sickness, age, or times of scarcity, continues to be the same as if such laws had never been made in their favour.

Much malignant censure have some writers bestowed upon the rich for their luxury and expensive living, while the poor are starving, &c.; not considering that what the rich expend, the labouring poor receive in payment for their labour. It may seem a paradox if I should assert, that our labouring poor do in every year receive *the whole revenue of the nation;* I mean not only the public revenue, but also the revenue or clear income of all private estates, or a sum equivalent to the whole.

In support of this position I reason thus. The rich do not work for one another. Their habitations, furniture, cloathing, carriages, food, ornaments, and every thing in short, that they or their families use and consume, is the work or produce of the labouring poor, who are, and must be continually, paid for their labour in producing the same. In these payments the revenues of private estates are expended, for most people live up to their incomes. In cloathing or provision for troops, in arms, ammunition, ships, tents, carriages, &c. &c., (every particular the produce of labour,) much of the public revenue is expended. The pay of officers, civil and military, and of the private soldiers and sailors, requires the rest; and they spend that also in paying for what is produced by the labouring poor.

I allow that some estates may increase by the owners spending less than their income; but then I conceive that other estates do at the same time diminish by the owners spending more than their income, so that when the enriched want to buy more land, they easily find lands in the hands of the impoverished, whose necessities oblige them to sell; and thus this difference is equalled. I allow also, that part of the expence of the rich is in foreign produce or manufactures, for producing which the labouring poor of other nations must be paid; but then I say, we must first pay our own labouring poor for an equal quantity of our manufactures or produce, to exchange for those foreign productions, or we must pay for them in money, which money, not being the natural produce of our country, must first be purchased from abroad, by sending out its value in the produce or manufactures of this country, for which manufactures our labouring poor are to be paid. And indeed, if we did not export more than we import, we could have no money at all. I allow farther, that there are middle men, who make a profit, and even get estates, by purchasing the labour of the poor, and selling it at advanced prices to the rich; but then they cannot enjoy that profit, or the income of estates, but by spending them in employing and paying our labouring poor, in some shape or other, for the products of industry. Even beggars, pensioners, hospitals, and all that are supported by charity, spend their incomes in the same manner. So that finally, as I said at first, *our labouring poor receive annually the whole of the clear revenues of the nation*, and from us they can have no more.

If it be said that their wages are too low, and that they ought to be better paid for their labour, I heartily wish any means could be fallen upon to do it, consistent with their interest and happiness; but, as the cheapness of other things is owing to the plenty of those things, so the cheapness of labour is in most cases owing to the multitude of labourers, and to their underworking one another in order to obtain employment. How is this to be remedied? A law might be made to raise their wages; but, if our manufactures are too dear, they will not vend abroad, and all that part of employment will fail, unless by fighting and conquering we compel other nations to buy our goods, whether they will or no, which some have been mad enough at times to propose.

Among ourselves, unless we give our working people less employment, how can we, for what they do, pay them higher than we do? Out of what fund is the additional price of labour to be paid, when all our present incomes are, as it were, mortgaged to them? Should they get higher wages, would that make them less poor, if, in consequence, they worked fewer days of the week proportionably? I have said, a law might be made to raise their wages; but I doubt much whether it could be executed to any purpose, unless another law, now indeed almost obsolete, could at the same time be revived and enforced; a law, I mean, that many have often heard and repeated, but few have ever duly considered. Six *days shalt thou labour*. This is as positive a part of the commandment, as that which says, *The* seventh *day thou shalt rest*. But we remember well to observe the indulgent part, and never think of the other. *Saint*

Monday is generally as duly kept by our working people as *Sunday;* the only difference is, that, instead of employing their time cheaply at church, they are wasting it expensively at the alehouse.   I am, Sir, &c.

MEDIUS.

TO DUPONT DE NEMOURS[74]

London, July 28, 1768.

I received your obliging letter of the 10th May, with the most acceptable present of your *Physiocratie*, which I have read with great pleasure, and received from it a great deal of instruction. There is such a freedom from local and national prejudices and partialities, so much benevolence to mankind in general, so much goodness mixt with the wisdom, in the principles of your new philosophy, that I am perfectly charmed with them, and wish I could have stayed in France for some time, to have studied in your school, that I might by conversing with its founders have made myself quite a master of that philosophy. ... I had, before I went into your country, seen some letters of yours to Dr. Templeman, that gave me a high opinion of the doctrines you are engaged in cultivating and of your personal talents and abilities, which made me greatly desirous of seeing you. Since I had not that good fortune, the next best thing is the advantage you are so good to offer me of your correspondence, which I shall ever highly value, and endeavour to cultivate with all the diligence I am capable of.

I am sorry to find that that wisdom which sees the welfare of the parts in the prosperity of the whole, seems yet not to be known in this country. ... We are so far from conceiving that what is best for mankind, or even for Europe in general, may be best for us, that we are even studying to establish and extend a separate interest of Britain, to the prejudice of even Ireland and our colonies. ... It is from your philosophy only that the maxims of a contrary and more happy conduct are to be drawn, which I therefore sincerely wish may grow and increase till it becomes the governing philosophy of the human species, as it must be that of superior beings in better worlds. I will take the liberty of sending you a little fragment that has some tincture of it, which, on that account, I hope may be acceptable.

Be so good as to present my sincere respect to that venerable apostle, Dr. Quesnay, and to the illustrious Ami des Hommes (of whose civilities to me at Paris I retain a grateful remembrance), and believe me to be, with real and very great esteem Sir,

Your obliged and most obedient humble servant

B. FRANKLIN.

TO JOHN ALLEYNE[75]

Craven Street, [August 9, 1768].

DEAR SIR

You made an Apology to me for not acquaint^g me sooner with your Marriage. I ought now to make an Apology to you for delaying so long the Answer to your Letter. It was mislaid or hid among my Papers and much Business put it out of my Mind, or prevented my looking for it and writing when I thought of it. So this Account between us if you please may stand balanced. I assure you it gave me great Pleasure to hear you were married, and into a Family of Reputation. This I learnt from the Public Papers. The Character you give me of your Bride (as it includes every Qualification that in the married State conduces to mutual Happiness) is an Addition to that Pleasure. Had you consulted me, as a Friend, on the Occasion, Youth on both sides I should not have thought any Objection. Indeed, from the matches that have fallen under my Observation, I am rather inclin'd to think, that early ones stand the best Chance for Happiness. The Tempers and habits of young People are not yet become so stiff and uncomplying, as when more advanced in Life; they form more easily to each other, and hence many Occasions of Disgust are removed. And if Youth has less of that Prudence, that is necessary to conduct a Family, yet the Parents and elder Friends of young married Persons are generally at hand to afford their Advice, which amply supplies that Defect; and, by early Marriage, Youth is sooner form'd to regular and useful Life; and possibly some of those Accidents, Habits or Connections, that might have injured either the Constitution, or the Reputation, or both, are thereby happily prevented.

Particular Circumstances of particular Persons may possibly sometimes make it prudent to delay entering into that State; but in general, when Nature has render'd our Bodies fit for it, the Presumption is in Nature's Favour, that she has not judg'd amiss in making us desire it. Late Marriages are often attended, too, with this further Inconvenience, that there is not the same Chance the parents shall live to see their offspring educated. "*Late Children,*" says the Spanish Proverb, "*are early Orphans.*" A melancholy Reflection to those, whose Case it may be! With us in America, Marriages are generally in the Morning of Life; our Children are therefore educated and settled in the World by Noon; and thus, our Business being done, we have an Afternoon and Evening of chearful Leisure to ourselves; such as your Friend at present enjoys. By these early Marriages we are blest with more Children; and from the Mode among us, founded in Nature, of every Mother suckling and nursing her own Child, more of them are raised. Thence the swift Progress of Population among us, unparallel'd in Europe.

In fine, I am glad you are married, and congratulate you most cordially upon it. You are now more in the way of becoming a useful Citizen; and you have escap'd the unnatural State of Celibacy for Life, the Fate of many here, who never intended it, but who, having too long postpon'd the Change of their Condition, find at length, that 'tis too late to think of it, and so live all their Lives in a Situation that greatly lessens a Man's Value. An odd Volume of a Set of Books you know is not worth its proportion of the Set, and what think you of the Usefulness of an odd Half of a Pair of Scissors? It cannot well cut any thing. It may possibly serve to scrape a Trencher.

Pray make my Compliments and best Wishes acceptable to your Spouse. I am old and heavy and grow a little indolent, or I should ere this have presented them in Person. I shall make but small Use of the old Man's Privilege, that of giving Advice to younger Friends. Treat your Wife always with Respect; it will procure Respect to you, not from her only but from all that observe it. Never use a slighting Expression to her, even in jest, for Slights in Jest, after frequent bandyings, are apt to end in angry earnest. Be studious in your Profession, and you will be learned. Be industrious and frugal, and you will be rich. Be sober and temperate, and you will be healthy. Be in general virtuous, and you will be happy. At least, you will, by such Conduct, stand the best Chance for such Consequences. I pray God to bless you both; being ever your affectionate Friend.

B. FRANKLIN.

TO THE PRINTER OF THE LONDON CHRONICLE[76]

August 18, 1768.

QUERIES, *recommended to the Consideration of those Gentlemen who are for vigorous measures with the Americans.*

1. Have the Colonists *refused* to answer any reasonable requisitions made to their *Assemblies* by the mother country?

2. If they have *not refused* to grant reasonable aids in the way, which they think consistent with *liberty*, why must they be stripped of their property without their own *consent*, and in a way, which they think *inconsistent* with liberty?

3. What is it for a people to be *enslaved* and *tributary*, if this be not, viz. to be *forced* to give up their property at the arbitrary pleasure of persons, to whose authority they have not *submitted* themselves, nor *chosen* for the purpose of imposing taxes upon them? Wherein consisted the impropriety of King Charles's demanding ship money by his sole authority, but in its being an exercise of power by the King, which the people had not *given* the King? Have the people of America, as the people of Britain, by sending representatives, *consented* to a power in the British parliament to tax them?

4. Has not the British parliament, by repealing the stamp act,

acknowledged that they judged it *improper?* Is there any difference between the stamp act, and the act obliging the Americans to pay *whatever we please,* for articles which they *cannot do without,* as glass and paper? Is there any difference as to justice between our treatment of the colonists, and the tyranny of the Carthaginians over their conquered Sardinians, when they obliged them to take all their corn from them, and at whatever price they pleased to set upon it?

5. If that be true, what is commonly said, viz. That the mother country gains *two millions* a year by the colonies, would it not have been wiser to have gone on quietly in the *happy way* we were in, till our gains by those rising and flourishing countries should amount to *three, four* or *five* millions a year, than by these new fashioned vigorous measures to kill the goose which lays the golden eggs? Would it not have been better policy, instead of *taxing* our colonists, to have done whatever we could to *enrich* them; and encourage them to take off our articles of *luxury,* on which we may put our own price, and thus draw them into paying us a *voluntary* tax; than deluge them in blood, thin their countries, impoverish and distress them, interrupt their commerce, force them on bankruptcy, by which our merchants must be ruined, or tempt them to emigrations, or alliances with our enemies?

6. The late war could not have been *carried on* without America, nor without Scotland? Have we treated America and Scotland in such a manner as is likely in future wars to encourage their zeal for the common cause? Or is England alone to be the Drawcansir of the world, and to bully not only their enemies, but her *friends?*

7. Are not the subjects of Britain concerned to check a ministry, who, by this rage of heaping taxes on taxes, are only drawing into their own hands more and more wealth and power, while they are hurting the *commercial* interest of the empire in general, at the same time that, amidst profound *peace,* the national debt and burden on the public continue undiminished?

N. M. C. N. P. C. H.

POSITIONS TO BE EXAMINED, CONCERNING
NATIONAL WEALTH

Dated April 4, 1769.

1. All food or subsistence for mankind arises from the earth or waters.

2. Necessaries of life, that are not food, and all other conveniences, have their values estimated by the proportion of food consumed while we are employed in procuring them.

3. A small people, with a large territory, may subsist on the productions of nature, with no other labour than that of gathering the vegetables and catching the animals.

4. A large people, with a small territory, finds these insufficient, and, to subsist, must labour the earth, to make it produce greater quantities of vegetable food, suitable for the nourishment of men, and of the animals they intend to eat.

5. From this labour arises a *great increase* of vegetable and animal food, and of materials for clothing, as flax, wool, silk, &c. The superfluity of these is wealth. With this wealth we pay for the labour employed in building our houses, cities, &c., which are therefore only subsistence thus metamorphosed.

6. *Manufactures* are only *another shape* into which so much provisions and subsistence are turned, as were equal in value to the manufactures produced. This appears from hence, that the manufacturer does not, in fact, obtain from the employer, for his labour, *more* than a mere subsistence, including raiment, fuel, and shelter; all which derive their value from the provisions consumed in procuring them.

7. The produce of the earth, thus converted into manufactures, may be more easily carried to distant markets than before such conversion.

8. *Fair commerce* is, where equal values are exchanged for equal, the expense of transport included. Thus, if it costs A in England as much labour and charge to raise a bushel of wheat, as it costs B in France to produce four gallons of wine, then are four gallons of wine the fair exchange for a bushel of wheat,

A and B meeting at half distance with their commodities to make the exchange. The advantage of this fair commerce is, that each party increases the number of his enjoyments, having, instead of wheat alone, or wine alone, the use of both wheat and wine.

9. Where the labour and expense of producing both commodities are known to both parties, bargains will generally be fair and equal. Where they are known to one party only, bargains will often be unequal, knowledge taking its advantage of ignorance.

10. Thus, he that carries one thousand bushels of wheat abroad to sell, may not probably obtain so great a profit thereon, as if he had first turned the wheat into manufactures, by subsisting therewith the workmen while producing those manufactures; since there are many expediting and facilitating methods of working, not generally known; and strangers to the manufactures, though they know pretty well the expense of raising wheat, are unacquainted with those short methods of working, and, thence being apt to suppose more labour employed in the manufactures than there really is, are more easily imposed on in their value, and induced to allow more for them than they are honestly worth.

11. Thus the advantage of having manufactures in a country does not consist, as is commonly supposed, in their highly advancing the value of rough materials, of which they are formed; since, though six pennyworth of flax may be worth twenty shillings, when worked into lace, yet the very cause of its being worth twenty shillings is, that, besides the flax, it has cost nineteen shillings and sixpence in subsistence to the manufacturer. But the advantage of manufactures is, that under their shape provisions may be more easily carried to a foreign market; and, by their means, our traders may more easily cheat strangers. Few, where it is not made, are judges of the value of lace. The importer may demand forty, and perhaps get thirty, shillings for that which cost him but twenty.

12. Finally, there seem to be but three ways for a nation to acquire wealth. The first is by *war*, as the Romans did, in

plundering their conquered neighbours. This is *robbery*. The second by *commerce*, which is generally *cheating*. The third by *agriculture*, the only *honest way*, wherein man receives a real increase of the seed thrown into the ground, in a kind of continual miracle, wrought by the hand of God in his favour, as a reward for his innocent life and his virtuous industry.

TO MISS MARY STEVENSON

Saturday Evening, Septr 2, 1769.

Just come home from a Venison Feast, where I have drank more than a Philosopher ought, I find my dear Polly's chearful, chatty Letter that exhilirates me more than all the Wine.

Your good Mother says there is no Occasion for any Intercession of mine in your behalf. She is sensible that she is more in fault than her Daughter. She received an affectionate, tender Letter from you, and she has not answered it, tho' she intended to do it; but her Head, not her Heart, has been bad, and unfitted her for Writing. She owns, that she is not so good a Subject as you are, and that she is more unwilling to pay Tribute to Cesar, and has less Objection to Smuggling; but 'tis not, she says, mere Selfishness or Avarice; 'tis rather an honest Resentment at the Waste of those Taxes in Pensions, Salaries, Perquisites, Contracts, and other Emoluments for the Benefit of People she does not love, and who do not deserve such Advantages, because— I suppose—because they are not of her Party.

Present my Respects to your good Landlord and his Family. I honour them for their conscientious Aversion to illicit Trading. There are those in the World, who would not wrong a Neighbour, but make no Scruple of cheating the King. The Reverse, however, does not hold; for whoever scruples cheating the King, will certainly not wrong his Neighbour.

You ought not to wish yourself an Enthusiast. They have, indeed, their imaginary Satisfactions and Pleasures, but these are often ballanc'd by imaginary Pains and Mortifications. You can continue to be a good Girl, and thereby lay a solid Foundation for expected future Happiness, without the Enthusiasm that may perhaps be necessary to some others. As those Beings, who have a good sensible Instinct, have no need of Reason, so those, who have Reason to regulate their Actions, have no Occasion for Enthusiasm. However, there are certain Circumstances in Life, sometimes, wherein 'tis perhaps best not to hearken to Reason. For instance; possibly, if the Truth were known, I have Reason to be jealous of this same insinuating, handsome young Physician;[77] but, as it flatters more my Vanity, and therefore gives me more Pleasure, to suppose you were in Spirits on acc^t of my safe Return, I shall turn a deaf Ear to Reason in this Case, as I have done with Success in twenty others. But I am sure you will always give me Reason enough to continue ever your affectionate Friend,

B. FRANKLIN.

P. S. Our Love to Mrs. Tickell. We all long for your Return. Your Dolly was well last Tuesday; the Girls were there on a Visit to her; I mean at Bromley. Adieu. No time now to give you any acc^t of my French Journey.

TO JOSEPH PRIESTLEY

London, Sept. 19: 1772.

DEAR SIR,

In the Affair of so much Importance to you, wherein you ask my Advice, I cannot for want of sufficient Premises, advise you *what* to determine, but if you please I will tell you *how*. When those difficult Cases occur, they are difficult, chiefly because while we have them under Consideration, all the Reasons *pro* and *con* are not present to the Mind at the same time; but sometimes one Set present themselves, and at other times another, the first being out of Sight. Hence the various Purposes or Inclinations that alternately prevail, and the Uncertainty that perplexes us.

To get over this, my Way is, to divide half a Sheet of Paper by a Line into two Columns; writing over the one *Pro*, and over the other *Con.* Then during three or four Days Consideration, I put down under the different Heads short Hints of the different Motives, that at different Times occur to me, *for* or *against* the Measure. When I have thus got them all together in one View, I endeavour to estimate their respective Weights; and where I find two, one on each side, that seem equal, I strike them both out. If I find a Reason *pro* equal to some two Reasons *con*, I strike out the three. If I judge some two Reasons *con*, equal to some three Reasons *pro*, I strike out the five; and thus proceeding I find at length where the Ballance lies; and if after a Day or two of farther Consideration, nothing new that is of Importance occurs on either side, I come to a Determination accordingly. And, tho' the Weight of Reasons cannot be taken with the Precision of Algebraic Quantities, yet, when each is thus considered, separately and comparatively, and the whole lies before me, I think I can judge better, and am less liable to make a rash Step; and in fact I have found great Advantage from this kind of Equation, in what may be called *Moral* or *Prudential Algebra.*

Wishing sincerely that you may determine for the best, I am ever, my dear Friend, yours most affectionately,

B. FRANKLIN.

TO MISS GEORGIANA SHIPLEY[78]

London, September 26, 1772.

DEAR MISS,

I lament with you most sincerely the unfortunate end of poor MUNGO. Few squirrels were better accomplished; for he had had a good education, had travelled far, and seen much of the world. As he had the honour of being, for his virtues, your favourite, he should not go, like common skuggs, without an elegy or an epitaph. Let us give him one in the monumental style and measure, which, being neither prose nor verse, is perhaps the properest for grief; since to use common language would look as if we were not affected, and to make rhymes would seem trifling in sorrow.

EPITAPH.

Alas! poor MUNGO!
Happy wert thou, hadst thou known
Thy own felicity.
Remote from the fierce bald eagle,
Tyrant of thy native woods,
Thou hadst nought to fear from his piercing talons,
Nor from the murdering gun
Of the thoughtless sportsman.
Safe in thy wired castle,
GRIMALKIN never could annoy thee.
Daily wert thou fed with the choicest viands,
By the fair hand of an indulgent mistress;
But, discontented,
Thou wouldst have more freedom.

Too soon, alas! didst thou obtain it;
And wandering,
Thou art fallen by the fangs of wanton, cruel RANGER!

Learn hence,
Ye who blindly seek more liberty,
Whether subjects, sons, squirrels or daughters,
That apparent restraint may be real protection;
Yielding peace and plenty
With security.

You see, my dear Miss, how much more decent and proper this broken style is, than if we were to say, by way of epitaph,

Here SKUGG
Lies snug,
As a bug
In a rug.

and yet, perhaps, there are people in the world of so little feeling as to think that this would be a good-enough epitaph for poor Mungo.

If you wish it, I shall procure another to succeed him; but perhaps you will now choose some other amusement.

Remember me affectionately to all the good family, and believe me ever,

Your affectionate friend,

B. FRANKLIN.

TO PETER FRANKLIN

[No date.]⁷⁹

DEAR BROTHER,

I like your ballad, and think it well adapted for your purpose of discountenancing expensive foppery, and encouraging industry and frugality. If you can get it generally sung in your country, it may probably have a good deal of the effect you hope and expect from it. But as you aimed at making it general, I wonder you chose so uncommon a measure in poetry, that none of the tunes in common use will suit it. Had you fitted it to an old one, well known, it must have spread much faster than I doubt it will do from the best new tune we can get compos'd for it. I think too, that if you had given it to some country girl in the heart of the *Massachusetts,* who has never heard any other than psalm tunes, or *Chevy Chace,* the *Children in the Wood,* the *Spanish Lady,* and such old simple ditties, but has naturally a good ear, she might more probably have made a pleasing popular tune for you, than any of our masters here, and more proper for your purpose, which would best be answered, if every word could as it is sung be understood by all that hear it, and if the emphasis you intend for particular words could be given by the singer as well as by the reader; much of the force and impression of the song depending on those circumstances. I will however get it as well done for you as I can.

Do not imagine that I mean to depreciate the skill of our composers of music here; they are admirable at pleasing *practised* ears, and know how to delight *one another;* but, in composing for songs, the reigning taste seems to be quite out of nature, or rather the reverse of nature, and yet like a torrent, hurries them all away with it; one or two perhaps only excepted.

You, in the spirit of some ancient legislators, would influence the manners of your country by the united powers of poetry and music. By what I can learn of *their* songs, the music was simple, conformed itself to the usual pronunciation of words, as to measure, cadence or emphasis, &c., never disguised and confounded the language by making a long syllable short, or a short one long, when sung; their singing was only a more pleasing, because a melodious manner of speaking; it was capable of all the graces of prose oratory, while it added the pleasure of harmony. A modern song, on the contrary, neglects all the proprieties and beauties of common speech, and in their place introduces its *defects* and *absurdities* as so many graces. I am afraid you will hardly take my word for this, and therefore I must endeavour to support it by proof. Here is the first song I lay my hand on. It happens to be a composition of one of our greatest masters, the ever-famous *Handel*. It is not one of his juvenile performances, before his taste could be improved and formed: It appeared when his reputation was at the highest, is greatly admired by all his admirers, and is really excellent in its kind. It is called, "*The additional* Favourite *Song in* Judas Maccabeus." Now I reckon among the defects and improprieties of common speech, the following, viz.

1. *Wrong placing the accent or emphasis*, by laying it on words of no importance, or on wrong syllables.

2. *Drawling;* or extending the sound of words or syllables beyond their natural length.

3. *Stuttering;* or making many syllables of one.

4. *Unintelligibleness;* the result of the three foregoing united.

5. *Tautology;* and

6. *Screaming*, without cause.

For the *wrong placing of the accent, or emphasis*, see it on the word *their* instead of being on the word *vain*.

with *their* . . vain   my - ste - rious   art.

And on the word *from*, and the wrong syllable *like*.

God - *like* wis - dom *from* . . . a - bove.

For the *drawling*, see the last syllable of the word *wounded*.
And in the syllable *wis*, and the word *from*, and syllable *bove*.

Nor can heal the wound-*ed* heart.

God-*like* *wis* - dom *from* a - bove.

For the *stuttering*, see the words *ne'er relieve*, in

Ma - gic charms can *ne'er* . . re - *lieve* you.

Here are four syllables made of one, and eight of three; but this
is moderate. I have seen in another song, that I cannot now find,
seventeen syllables made of three, and sixteen of one. The latter
I remember was the word *charms;* viz. *cha, a, a, a, a, a, a, a, a,
a, a, a, a, a, a, arms.* Stammering with a witness!

For the *unintelligibleness;* give this whole song to any taught
singer, and let her sing it to any company that have never heard
it; you shall find they will not understand three words in ten.
It is therefore that at the oratorios and operas one sees with
books in their hands all those who desire to understand what
they hear sung by even our best performers.

For the *Tautology;* you have, *with their vain mysterious art,*
twice repeated; *magic charms can ne'er relieve you,* three times.

Nor can heal the wounded heart, three times. *Godlike wisdom from above*, twice; and, *this alone can ne'er deceive you*, two or three times. But this is reasonable when compared with *the Monster Polypheme, the Monster Polypheme*, a hundred times over and over, in his admired *Acis and Galatea*.

As to the *screaming;* perhaps I cannot find a fair instance in this song; but whoever has frequented our operas will remember many. And yet here methinks the words *no* and *e'er*, when sung to these notes, have a little of the air of *screaming*, and would actually be screamed by some singers.

No   ma - gic   charms   can *e'er*   re - lieve you.

I send you inclosed the song with its music at length. Read the words without the repetitions. Observe how few they are, and what a shower of notes attend them: You will then perhaps be inclined to think with me, that though the words might be the principal part of an ancient song, they are of small importance in a modern one; they are in short only a *pretence for singing*.

I am, as ever,
Your affectionate brother,
B. FRANKLIN.

P. S. I might have mentioned *inarticulation* among the defects in common speech that are assumed as beauties in modern singing. But as that seems more the fault of the singer than of the composer, I omitted it in what related merely to the composition. The fine singer, in the present mode, stifles all the hard consonants, and polishes away all the rougher parts of words that serve to distinguish them one from another; so that you hear nothing but an admirable pipe, and understand no more of the song, than you would from its tune played on any other instrument. If ever it was the ambition of musicians to make instruments that should imitate the human voice, that ambition seems now reversed, the voice aiming to be like an instrument. Thus wigs were first made to imitate a good natural head of hair; but when they became fashionable, though in unnatural forms, we have seen natural hair dressed to look like wigs.

ON THE PRICE OF CORN, AND MANAGEMENT OF THE POOR[80]

TO THE PUBLIC

I am one of that class of people, that feeds you all, and at present is abused by you all; in short I am a *farmer*.

By your newspapers we are told, that God had sent a very short harvest to some other countries of Europe. I thought this might be in favour of Old England; and that now we should get a good price for our grain, which would bring millions among us, and make us flow in money; that to be sure is scarce enough.

But the wisdom of government forbade the exportation.

"Well," says I, "then we must be content with the market price at home."

"No;" say my lords the mob, "you sha'nt have that. Bring your corn to market if you dare; we'll sell it for you for less money, or take it for nothing."

Being thus attacked by both ends *of the constitution*, the head and tail *of government*, what am I to do?

Must I keep my corn in the barn, to feed and increase the breed of rats? Be it so; they cannot be less thankful than those I have been used to feed.

Are we farmers the only people to be grudged the profits of our honest labour? And why? One of the late scribblers against us gives a bill of fare of the provisions at my daughter's wedding, and proclaims to all the world, that we had the insolence to eat beef and pudding! Has he not read the precept in the good Book, *Thou shalt not muzzle the mouth of the ox that treadeth out the corn;* or does he think us less worthy of good living than our oxen?

"O, but the manufacturers! the manufacturers! they are to be favoured, and they must have bread at a cheap rate!"

Hark ye, Mr. Oaf; the farmers live spendidly, you say. And pray, would you have them hoard the money they get? Their fine clothes and furniture, do they make them themselves, or for one another, and so keep the money among them? Or do they employ these your darling manufacturers, and so scatter it again all over the nation?

The wool would produce me a better price, if it were suffered to go to foreign markets; but that, Messieurs the Public, your laws will not permit. It must be kept all at home, that our *dear* manufacturers may have it the cheaper. And then, having yourselves thus lessened our encouragement for raising sheep, you curse us for the scarcity of mutton!

I have heard my grandfather say, that the farmers submitted to the prohibition on the exportation of wool, being made to expect and believe, that, when the manufacturer bought his wool cheaper, they should also have their cloth cheaper. But the deuce a bit. It has been growing dearer and dearer from that day to this. How so? Why, truly, the cloth is exported; and that keeps up the price.

Now, if it be a good principle, that the exportation of a commodity is to be restrained, that so our people at home may have it the cheaper, stick to that principle, and go thorough-stitch with it. Prohibit the exportation of your cloth, your leather, and shoes, your iron ware, and your manufactures of all sorts, to make them all cheaper at home. And cheap enough they will be, I will warrant you; till people leave off making them.

Some folks seem to think they ought never to be easy till England becomes another Lubberland, where it is fancied that streets are paved with penny-rolls, the houses tiled with pancakes, and chickens, ready roasted, cry, "Come eat me."

I say, when you are sure you have got a good principle, stick to it, and carry it through. I hear it is said, that though it was *necessary and right* for the ministry to advise a prohibition of the exportation of corn, yet it was *contrary to law;* and also, that though it was *contrary to law* for the mob to obstruct wagons, yet it was *necessary and right*. Just the same thing to a tittle. Now they tell me, an act of indemnity ought to pass in favour of the ministry, to secure them from the consequences of having acted illegally. If so, pass another in favour of the mob. Others say, some of the mob ought to be hanged, by way of example. If so,—but I say no more than I have said before, *when you are sure that you have a good principle, go through with it.*

You say, poor labourers cannot afford to buy bread at a high price, unless they had higher wages. Possibly. But how shall we farmers be able to afford our labourers higher wages, if you will not allow us to get, when we might have it, a higher price for our corn?

By all that I can learn, we should at least have had a guinea a quarter more, if the exportation had been allowed. And this money England would have got from foreigners.

But, it seems, we farmers must take so much less, that the poor may have it so much cheaper.

This operates, then, as a tax for the maintenance of the poor. A very good thing you will say. But I ask, Why a partial tax? why laid on us farmers only? If it be a good thing, pray, Messieurs the Public, take your share of it, by indemnifying us a little out of your public treasury. In doing a good thing, there is both honour and pleasure; you are welcome to your share of both.

For my own part, I am not so well satisfied of the goodness of this thing. I am for doing good to the poor, but I differ in opinion about the means. I think the best way of doing good to the poor, is, not making them easy *in* poverty, but leading or driving them *out* of it. In my youth, I travelled much, and I observed in different countries, that the more public provisions were made for the poor, the less they provided for themselves, and of course became poorer. And, on the contrary, the less was done for them, the more they did for themselves, and became richer. There is no country in the world where so many provisions are established for them; so many hospitals to receive them when they are sick or lame, founded and maintained by voluntary charities; so many almshouses for the aged of both sexes, together with a solemn general law made by the rich to subject their estates to a heavy tax for the support of the poor. Under all these obligations, are our poor modest, humble, and thankful? And do they use their best endeavours to maintain themselves, and lighten our shoulders of this burthen? On the contrary, I affirm, that there is no country in the world in which the poor are more idle, dissolute, drunken, and insolent. The day you passed that act, you took away from before their eyes the greatest of all inducements to industry, frugality, and sobriety, by giving them a dependence on somewhat else than a careful accumulation during youth and health, for support in age or sickness.

In short, you offered a premium for the encouragement of idleness, and you should not now wonder, that it has had its effect in the increase of poverty. Repeal that law, and you will soon see a change in their manners. *Saint Monday* and *Saint Tuesday* will soon cease to be holidays. SIX *days shalt thou labour*, though one of the old commandments long treated as out of date, will again be looked upon as a respectable precept; industry will increase, and with it plenty among the lower people; their circumstances will mend, and more will be done for their happiness by inuring them to provide for themselves, than could be done by dividing all your estates among them.

Excuse me, Messieurs the Public, if, upon this *interesting* subject, I put you to the trouble of reading a little of *my* nonsense. I am sure I have lately read a great deal of *yours*, and therefore from you (at least from those of you who are writers) I deserve a little indulgence.

I am yours, &c.

ARATOR.

AN EDICT BY THE KING OF PRUSSIA [81]

[From the *Gentleman's Magazine*, October, 1773.]

Dantzic, Sept. 5, [1773].

We have long wondered here at the supineness of the English nation, under the Prussian impositions upon its trade entering our port. We did not, till lately, know the claims, ancient and modern, that hang over that nation; and therefore could not suspect that it might submit to those impositions from a sense of duty or from principles of equity. The following Edict, just made publick, may, if serious, throw some light upon this matter.

"FREDERIC, by the grace of God, King of Prussia, &c. &c. &c., to all present and to come, (*à tous présens et à venir*,) Health. The peace now enjoyed throughout our dominions, having afforded us leisure to apply ourselves to the regulation of commerce, the improvement of our finances, and at the same time the easing our domestic subjects in their taxes: For these causes, and other good considerations us thereunto moving, we hereby make known, that, after having deliberated these affairs in our council, present our dear brothers, and other great officers of the state, members of the same, we, of our certain knowledge, full power, and authority royal, have made and issued this present Edict, viz.

"Whereas it is well known to all the world, that the first German settlements made in the Island of Britain, were by colonies of people, subject to our renowned ducal ancestors, and drawn from their dominions, under the conduct of Hengist, Horsa, Hella, Uff, Cerdicus, Ida, and others; and that the said colonies have flourished under the protection of our august house for ages past; have never been emancipated therefrom; and yet have hitherto yielded little profit to the same: And whereas we ourself have in the last war fought for and defended the said colonies, against the power of France, and thereby enabled them to make conquests from the said power in America, for which we have not yet received adequate compensation: And whereas it is just and expedient that a revenue should be raised from the said colonies in Britain, towards our indemnification; and that those who are descendants of our ancient subjects, and thence still owe us due obedience, should contribute to the replenishing of our royal coffers as they must have done, had their ancestors remained in the territories now to us appertaining: We do therefore hereby ordain and command, that, from and after the

date of these presents, there shall be levied and paid to our officers of the *customs*, on all goods, wares, and merchandizes, and
on all grain and other produce of the earth, exported from the
said Island of Britain, and on all goods of whatever kind imported into the same, a duty of four and a half per cent *ad valo-
rem*, for the use of us and our successors. And that the said
duty may more effectually be collected, we do hereby ordain,
that all ships or vessels bound from Great Britain to any other
part of the world, or from any other part of the world to Great
Britain, shall in their respective voyages touch at our port of
Koningsberg, there to be unladen, searched, and charged with
the said duties.

"And whereas there hath been from time to time discovered
in the said island of Great Britain, by our colonists there, many
mines or beds of iron-stone; and sundry subjects, of our ancient
dominion, skilful in converting the said stone into metal, have in
time past transported themselves thither, carrying with them and
communicating that art; and the inhabitants of the said island,
presuming that they had a natural right to make the best use they
could of the natural productions of their country for their own
benefit, have not only built furnaces for smelting the said stone
into iron, but have erected plating-forges, slitting-mills, and
steel-furnaces, for the more convenient manufacturing of the
same; thereby endangering a diminution of the said manufacture
in our ancient dominion;—we do therefore hereby farther ordain, that, from and after the date hereof, no mill or other engine
for slitting or rolling of iron, or any plating-forge to work with
a tilt-hammer, or any furnace for making steel, shall be erected
or continued in the said island of Great Britain: And the Lord
Lieutenant of every county in the said island is hereby commanded, on information of any such erection within his county,
to order and by force to cause the same to be abated and destroyed; as he shall answer the neglect thereof to us at his peril.
But we are nevertheless graciously pleased to permit the inhabitants of the said island to transport their iron into Prussia, there
to be manufactured, and to them returned; they paying our
Prussian subjects for the workmanship, with all the costs of

commission, freight, and risk, coming and returning; any thing herein contained to the contrary notwithstanding.

"We do not, however, think fit to extend this our indulgence to the article of wool; but, meaning to encourage, not only the manufacturing of woollen cloth, but also the raising of wool, in our ancient dominions, and to prevent both, as much as may be, in our said island, we do hereby absolutely forbid the transportation of wool from thence, even to the mother country, Prussia; and that those islanders may be farther and more effectually restrained in making any advantage of their own wool in the way of manufacture, we command that none shall be carried out of one county into another; nor shall any worsted, bay, or woollen yarn, cloth, says, bays, kerseys, serges, frizes, druggets, cloth-serges, shalloons, or any other drapery stuffs, or woollen manufactures whatsoever, made up or mixed with wool in any of the said counties, be carried into any other county, or be water-borne even across the smallest river or creek, on penalty of forfeiture of the same, together with the boats, carriages, horses, &c., that shall be employed in removing them. Nevertheless, our loving subjects there are hereby permitted (if they think proper) to use all their wool as manure for the improvement of their lands.

"And whereas the art and mystery of making hats hath arrived at great perfection in Prussia, and the making of hats by our remoter subjects ought to be as much as possible restrained: And forasmuch as the islanders before mentioned, being in possession of wool, beaver and other furs, have presumptuously conceived they had a right to make some advantage thereof, by manufacturing the same into hats, to the prejudice of our domestic manufacture: We do therefore hereby strictly command and ordain, that no hats or felts whatsoever, dyed or undyed, finished or unfinished, shall be loaded or put into or upon any vessel, cart, carriage, or horse, to be transported or conveyed out of one county in the said island into another county, or to any other place whatsoever, by any person or persons whatsoever; on pain of forfeiting the same, with a penalty of five hundred pounds sterling for every offence. Nor shall any hat-maker, in any of the said counties, employ more than two apprentices, on penalty of five pounds sterling per month; we intending hereby, that such hatmakers, being so restrained, both in the production and sale of their commodity, may find no advantage in continuing their business. But, lest the said islanders should suffer inconveniency by the want of hats, we are farther graciously pleased to permit them to send their beaver furs to Prussia; and we also permit hats made thereof to be exported from Prussia to Britain; the people thus favoured to pay all costs and charges of manufacturing, interest, commission to our merchants, insurance and freight going and returning, as in the case of iron.

"And, lastly, being willing farther to favour our said colonies in Britain, we do hereby also ordain and command, that all the *thieves*, highway and street robbers, house-breakers, forgerers, murderers, s—d—tes, and villains of every denomination, who have forfeited their lives to the law in Prussia; but whom we, in our great clemency, do not think fit here to hang, shall be emptied out of our gaols into the said island of Great Britain, for the better peopling of that country.

"We flatter ourselves, that these our royal regulations and commands will be thought just and reasonable by our much-favoured colonists in England; the said regulations being copied from their statutes of 10 and 11 William III. c. 10, 5 Geo. II. c. 22, 23, Geo. II. c. 29, 4 Geo. I. c. 11, and from other equitable laws made by their parliaments; or from instructions given by their Princes; or from resolutions of both Houses, entered into for the good government of their *own colonies in Ireland and America*.

"And all persons in the said island are hereby cautioned not to oppose in any wise the execution of this our Edict, or any part thereof, such opposition being high treason; of which all who are suspected shall be transported in fetters from Britain to Prussia, there to be tried and executed according to the Prussian law.

"Such is our pleasure.

"Given at Potsdam, this twenty-fifth day of the month of

August, one thousand seven hundred and seventy-three, and in the thirty-third year of our reign.

"By the King, in his Council.

"RECHTMAESSIG, *Sec.*"

Some take this Edict to be merely one of the King's *Jeux d'Esprit:* others suppose it serious, and that he means a quarrel with England; but all here think the assertion it concludes with, "that these regulations are copied from acts of the English parliament respecting their colonies," a very injurious one; it being impossible to believe, that a people distinguished for their love of liberty, a nation so wise, so liberal in its sentiments, so just and equitable towards its neighbours, should, from mean and injudicious views of petty immediate profit, treat its own children in a manner so arbitrary and tyrannical!

RULES BY WHICH A GREAT EMPIRE MAY BE REDUCED TO A SMALL ONE

Presented to a late Minister, when he entered upon his Administration

[From the *Gentleman's Magazine*, Sept., 1773.]

An ancient Sage boasted, that, tho' he could not fiddle, he knew how to make a *great city* of a *little one*. The science that I, a modern simpleton, am about to communicate, is the very reverse.

I address myself to all ministers who have the management of extensive dominions, which from their very greatness are become troublesome to govern, because the multiplicity of their affairs leaves no time for *fiddling*.

I. In the first place, gentlemen, you are to consider, that a great empire, like a great cake, is most easily diminished at the edges. Turn your attention, therefore, first to your *remotest* provinces; that, as you get rid of them, the next may follow in order.

II. That the possibility of this separation may always exist, take special care the provinces are never incorporated with the mother country; that they do not enjoy the same common rights, the same privileges in commerce; and that they are governed by *severer* laws, all of *your enacting*, without allowing them any share in the choice of the legislators. By carefully making and preserving such distinctions, you will (to keep to my simile of the cake) act like a wise ginger-bread-baker, who, to facilitate a division, cuts his dough half through in those places where, when baked, he would have it *broken to pieces*.

III. Those remote provinces have perhaps been acquired, purchased, or conquered, at the *sole expence* of the settlers, or their ancestors, without the aid of the mother country. If this should happen to increase her *strength*, by their growing numbers, ready to join in her wars; her *commerce*, by their growing demand for her manufactures; or her *naval power*, by greater employment for her ships and seamen, they may probably suppose some merit in this, and that it entitles them to some favour; you are therefore to *forget it all, or resent it*, as if they had done you injury. If they happen to be zealous whigs, friends of liberty, nurtured in revolution principles, *remember all that* to their prejudice, and resolve to punish it; for such principles, after a revolution is thoroughly established, are of *no more use; they* are even *odious* and *abominable*.

IV. However peaceably your colonies have submitted to your government, shewn their affection to your interests, and patiently borne their grievances; you are to *suppose* them always inclined to revolt, and treat them accordingly. Quarter troops among them, who by their insolence may *provoke* the rising of mobs, and by their bullets and bayonets *suppress* them. By this means, like the husband who uses his wife ill *from suspicion*, you may in time convert your *suspicions* into *realities*.

V. Remote provinces must have *Governors* and *Judges*, to represent the Royal Person, and execute everywhere the delegated parts of his office and authority. You ministers know, that much of the strength of government depends on the *opinion* of the people; and much of that opinion on the *choice of rulers* placed immediately over them. If you send them wise and good men for governors, who study the interest of the colonists, and advance their prosperity, they will think their King wise and good, and that he wishes the welfare of his subjects. If you send them learned and upright men for Judges, they will think him a lover of justice. This may attach your provinces more to his government. You are therefore to be careful whom you recommend for those offices. If you can find prodigals, who have ruined their fortunes, broken gamesters or stockjobbers, these may do well as *governors;* for they will probably be rapacious, and provoke the people by their extortions. Wrangling proctors and pettifogging lawyers, too, are not amiss; for they will be for ever disputing and quarrelling with their little parliaments. If withal they should be ignorant, wrong-headed, and insolent, so much the better. Attorneys' clerks and Newgate solicitors will do for *Chief Justices*, especially if they hold their places *during your pleasure;* and all will contribute to impress those ideas of your government, that are proper for a people *you would wish to renounce it*.

VI. To confirm these impressions, and strike them deeper, whenever the injured come to the capital with complaints of maladministration, oppression, or injustice, punish such suitors with long delay, enormous expence, and a final judgment in favour of the oppressor. This will have an admirable effect every way. The trouble of future complaints will be prevented, and Governors and Judges will be encouraged to farther acts of oppression and injustice; and thence the people may become more disaffected, and at length desperate.

VII. When such Governors have crammed their coffers, and made themselves so odious to the people that they can no longer remain among them, with safety to their persons, *recall and reward* them with pensions. You may make them *baronets* too, if that respectable order should not think fit to resent it. All will contribute to encourage new governors in the same practice, and make the supreme government, *detestable*.

VIII. If, when you are engaged in war, your colonies should vie in liberal aids of men and money against the common enemy, upon your simple requisition, and give far beyond their abilities, reflect that a penny taken from them by your power is more honourable to you, than a pound presented by their benevolence; despise therefore their voluntary grants, and resolve to harass them with novel taxes. They will probably complain to your parliaments, that they are taxed by a body in which they have no representative, and that this is contrary to common right. They will petition for redress. Let the Parliaments flout their claims, reject their petitions, refuse even to suffer the reading of them, and treat the petitioners with the utmost contempt. Nothing can have a better effect in producing the alienation proposed; for though many can forgive injuries, *none ever forgave contempt.*

IX. In laying these taxes, never regard the heavy burthens those remote people already undergo, in defending their own frontiers, supporting their own provincial governments, making new roads, building bridges, churches, and other public edifices, which in old countries have been done to your hands by your ancestors, but which occasion constant calls and demands on the purses of a new people. Forget the *restraints* you lay on their trade for *your own* benefit, and the advantage a *monopoly* of this trade gives your exacting merchants. Think nothing of the wealth those merchants and your manufacturers acquire by the colony commerce; their encreased ability thereby to pay taxes at home; their accumulating, in the price of their commodities, most of those taxes, and so levying them from their consuming customers; all this, and the employment and support of thousands of your poor by the colonists, you are *intirely to forget.* But remember to make your arbitrary tax more grievous to your provinces, by public declarations importing that your power of taxing them has *no limits;* so that when you take from them without their consent one shilling in the pound, you have a clear right to the other nineteen. This will probably weaken every idea of *security in their property*, and convince them, that under such a government they *have nothing they can call their own;* which can scarce fail of producing the *happiest consequences!*

X. Possibly, indeed, some of them might still comfort themselves, and say, "Though we have no property, we have yet *something* left that is valuable; we have constitutional *liberty*, both of person and of conscience. This King, these Lords, and these Commons, who it seems are too remote from us to know us, and feel for us, cannot take from us our *Habeas Corpus* right, or our right of trial *by a jury of our neighbours;* they cannot deprive us of the exercise of our religion, alter our ecclesiastical constitution, and compel us to be Papists, if they please, or Mahometans." To annihilate this comfort, begin by laws to perplex their commerce with infinite regulations, impossible to be remembered and observed; ordain seizures of their property for every failure; take away the trial of such property by Jury, and give it to arbitrary Judges of your own appointing, and of the lowest characters in the country, whose salaries and emoluments are to arise out of the duties or condemnations, and whose appointments are *during pleasure*. Then let there be a formal declaration of both Houses, that opposition to your edicts is *treason*, and that any person suspected of treason in the provinces may, according to some obsolete law, be seized and sent to the metropolis of the empire for trial; and pass an act, that those there charged with certain other offences, shall be sent away in chains from their friends and country to be tried in the same manner for felony. Then erect a new Court of Inquisition among them, accompanied by an armed force, with instructions to transport all such suspected persons; to be ruined by the expence, if they bring over evidences to prove their innocence, or be found guilty and hanged, if they cannot afford it. And, lest the people should think you cannot possibly go any farther, pass another solemn declaratory act, "that King, Lords, Commons had, hath, and of right ought to have, full power and authority to make statutes of sufficient force and validity to bind the unrepresented provinces IN ALL CASES WHATSOEVER." This will include *spiritual* with temporal, and, taken together, must operate wonderfully to your purpose; by convincing them, that they are at present under a power something like that spoken of in the scriptures, which can not only *kill their bodies*, but *damn their souls* to all eternity, by compelling them, if it pleases, *to worship the Devil*.

XI. To make your taxes more odious, and more likely to procure resistance, send from the capital a board of officers to superintend the collection, composed of the most *indiscreet*, *ill-bred*, and *insolent* you can find. Let these have large salaries out of the extorted revenue, and live in open, grating luxury upon the sweat and blood of the industrious; whom they are to worry continually with groundless and expensive prosecutions before the abovementioned arbitrary revenue Judges; *all at the cost of the party prosecuted*, tho' acquitted, because *the King is to pay no costs*. Let these men, *by your order*, be exempted from all the common taxes and burthens of the province, though they and their property are protected by its laws. If any revenue officers are *suspected* of the least tenderness for the people, discard them. If others are justly complained of, protect and reward them. If any of the under officers behave so as to provoke the people to drub them, promote those to better offices: this will encourage others to procure for themselves such profitable drubbings, by multiplying and enlarging such provocations, and *all will work towards the end you aim at*.

XII. Another way to make your tax odious, is to misapply the produce of it. If it was originally appropriated for the *defence* of the provinces, the better support of government, and the administration of justice, where it may be *necessary*, then apply none of it to that *defence*, but bestow it where it is *not necessary*, in augmented salaries or pensions to every governor, who has distinguished himself by his enmity to the people, and by calumniating them to their sovereign. This will make them pay it more unwillingly, and be more apt to quarrel with those that collect it and those that imposed it, who will quarrel again with them, and all shall contribute to your *main purpose*, of making them *weary of your government*.

XIII. If the people of any province have been accustomed to support their own Governors and Judges to satisfaction, you are to apprehend that such Governors and Judges may be thereby influenced to treat the people kindly, and to do them justice. This is another reason for applying part of that revenue in larger salaries to such Governors and Judges, given, as their commissions are, *during your pleasure* only; forbidding them to take any salaries from their provinces; that thus the people may no longer hope any kindness from their Governors, or (in Crown cases) any justice from their Judges. And, as the money thus misapplied in one province is extorted from all, probably *all will resent the misapplication.*

XIV. If the parliaments of your provinces should dare to claim rights, or complain of your administration, order them to be harrassed with *repeated dissolutions.* If the same men are continually returned by new elections, adjourn their meetings to some country village, where they cannot be accommodated, and there keep them *during pleasure;* for this, you know, is your PREROGATIVE; and an excellent one it is, as you may manage it to promote discontents among the people, diminish their respect, and *increase their disaffection.*

XV. Convert the brave, honest officers of your *navy* into pimping tide-waiters and colony officers of the *customs.* Let those, who in time of war fought gallantly in defence of the commerce of their countrymen, in peace be taught to prey upon it. Let them learn to be corrupted by great and real smugglers; but (to shew their diligence) scour with armed boats every bay, harbour, river, creek, cove, or nook throughout the coast of your colonies; stop and detain every coaster, every wood-boat, every fisherman, tumble their cargoes and even their ballast inside out and upside down; and, if a penn'orth of pins is found unentered, let the whole be seized and confiscated. Thus shall the trade of your colonists suffer more from their friends in time of peace, than it did from their enemies in war. Then let these boats crews land upon every farm in their way, rob the orchards, steal the pigs and the poultry, and insult the inhabitants. If the injured and exasperated farmers, unable to procure other justice, should attack the aggressors, drub them, and burn their boats; you are to call this *high treason and rebellion,* order fleets and armies into their country, and threaten to carry all the offenders three thousand miles to be hanged, drawn, and quartered. *O! this will work admirably!*

XVI. If you are told of discontents in your colonies, never

believe that they are general, or that you have given occasion for them; therefore do not think of applying any remedy, or of changing any offensive measure. Redress no grievance, lest they should be encouraged to demand the redress of some other grievance. Grant no request that is just and reasonable, lest they should make another that is unreasonable. Take all your informations of the state of the colonies from your Governors and officers in enmity with them. Encourage and reward these *leasing-makers;* secrete their lying accusations, lest they should be confuted; but act upon them as the clearest evidence; and believe nothing you hear from the friends of the people: suppose all *their* complaints to be invented and promoted by a few factious demagogues, whom if you could catch and hang, all would be quiet. Catch and hang a few of them accordingly; and the *blood of the Martyrs* shall *work miracles* in favour of your purpose.

XVII. If you see *rival nations* rejoicing at the prospect of your disunion with your provinces, and endeavouring to promote it; if they translate, publish, and applaud all the complaints of your discontented colonists, at the same time privately stimulating you to severer measures, let not that *alarm* or offend you. Why should it, since you all mean *the same thing?*

XVIII. If any colony should at their own charge erect a fortress to secure their port against the fleets of a foreign enemy, get your Governor to betray that fortress into your hands. Never think of paying what it cost the country, for that would look, at least, like some regard for justice; but turn it into a citadel to awe the inhabitants and curb their commerce. If they should have lodged in such fortress the very arms they bought and used to aid you in your conquests, seize them all; it will provoke like *ingratitude* added to *robbery*. One admirable effect of these operations will be, to discourage every other colony from erecting such defences, and so your enemies may more easily invade them; to the great disgrace of your government, and of course *the furtherance of your project*.

XIX. Send armies into their country under pretence of protecting the inhabitants; but, instead of garrisoning the forts on their frontiers with those troops, to prevent incursions, demolish those forts, and order the troops into the heart of the country, that the savages may be encouraged to attack the frontiers, and that the troops may be protected by the inhabitants. This will seem to proceed from your ill will or your ignorance, and contribute farther to produce and strengthen an opinion among them, *that you are no longer fit to govern them.*

XX. Lastly, invest the General of your army in the provinces, with great and unconstitutional powers, and free him from the controul of even your own Civil Governors. Let him have troops enow under his command, with all the fortresses in his possession; and who knows but (like some provincial Generals in the Roman empire, and encouraged by the universal discontent you have produced) he may take it into his head to set up for himself? If he should, and you have carefully practised these few *excellent rules* of mine, take my word for it, all the provinces will immediately join him; and you will that day (if you have not done it sooner) get rid of the trouble of governing them, and all the *plagues* attending their *commerce* and connection from henceforth and for ever.

Q. E. D.

TO WILLIAM FRANKLIN

London, October 6, 1773.

DEAR SON,

I wrote to you the 1st of last month, since which I have received yours of July 29, from New York. I know not what letters of mine Governor H[utchinson] could mean, as advising the people to insist on their independency. But whatever they were, I suppose he has sent copies of them hither, having heard some whisperings about them. I shall however, be able at any time to justify every thing I have written; the purport being uniformly this, that they should carefully avoid all tumults and every violent measure, and content themselves with verbally keeping up their claims, and holding forth their rights whenever occasion requires; secure, that, from the growing importance of

America, those claims will ere long be attended to and acknowledged.

From a long and thorough consideration of the subject, I am indeed of opinion, that the parliament has no right to make any law whatever, binding on the colonies; that the king, and not the king, lords, and commons collectively, is their sovereign; and that the king, with their respective parliaments, is their only legislator. I know your sentiments differ from mine on these subjects. You are a thorough government man, which I do not wonder at, nor do I aim at converting you. I only wish you to act uprightly and steadily, avoiding that duplicity, which in Hutchinson, adds contempt to indignation. If you can promote the prosperity of your people, and leave them happier than you found them, whatever your political principles are, your memory will be honoured.

I have written two pieces here lately for the *Public Advertiser*, on American affairs, designed to expose the conduct of this country towards the colonies in a short, comprehensive, and striking view, and stated, therefore, in out-of-the-way forms, as most likely to take the general attention. The first was called "*Rules by which a Great Empire may be reduced to a small one;*" the second, "*An Edict of the King of Prussia.*" I sent you one of the first, but could not get enough of the second to spare you one, though my clerk went the next morning to the printer's, and wherever they were sold. They were all gone but two. In my own mind I preferred the first, as a composition for the quantity and variety of the matter contained, and a kind of spirited ending of each paragraph. But I find that others here generally prefer the second.

I am not suspected as the author, except by one or two friends; and have heard the latter spoken of in the highest terms, as the keenest and severest piece that has appeared here for a long time. Lord Mansfield, I hear, said of it, that it *was very* ABLE *and very* ARTFUL *indeed;* and would do mischief by giving here a bad impression of the measures of government; and in the colonies, by encouraging them in their contumacy. It is reprinted in the *Chronicle*, where you will see it, but stripped of all the capitaling and italicing, that intimate the allusions and mark the emphasis of written discourses, to bring them as near as possible to those spoken: printing such a piece all in one even small character, seems to me like repeating one of Whitefield's sermons in the monotony of a schoolboy.

What made it the more noticed here was, that people in reading it were, as the phrase is, *taken in*, till they had got half through it, and imagined it a real edict, to which mistake I suppose the King of Prussia's *character* must have contributed. I was down at Lord Le Despencer's when the post brought that day's papers. Mr. Whitehead was there, too, (Paul Whitehead, the author of "Manners,") who runs early through all the papers, and tells the company what he finds remarkable. He had them in another room, and we were chatting in the breakfast parlour, when he came running in to us, out of breath, with the paper in his hand. Here! says he, here's news for ye! *Here's the King of Prussia, claiming a right to this kingdom!* All stared, and I as much as anybody; and he went on to read it. When he had read two or three paragraphs, a gentleman present said, *Damn his impudence, I dare say, we shall hear by next post that he is upon his march with one hundred thousand men to back this.* Whitehead, who is very shrewd, soon after began to smoke it, and looking in my face said, *I'll be hanged if this is not some of your American jokes upon us.* The reading went on, and ended with abundance of laughing, and a general verdict that it was a fair hit: and the piece was cut out of the paper and preserved in my Lord's collection.

I do not wonder that Hutchinson should be dejected. It must be an uncomfortable thing to live among people who he is conscious universally detest him. Yet I fancy he will not have leave to come home, both because they know not well what to do with him, and because they do not very well like his conduct. I am ever your affectionate father,

B. FRANKLIN.

PREFACE TO "AN ABRIDGMENT
OF THE BOOK OF COMMON PRAYER"[82]
[1773]

The editor of the following abridgment of the Liturgy of
the Church of England thinks it but decent and respectful to
all, more particularly to the reverend body of clergy, who adorn
the Protestant religion by their good works, preaching, and
example, that he should humbly offer some reason for such an
undertaking. He addresses himself to the serious and discerning. He professes himself to be a Protestant of the Church of
England, and holds in the highest veneration the doctrines of
Jesus Christ. He is a sincere lover of social worship, deeply
sensible of its usefulness to society; and he aims at doing some
service to religion, by proposing such abbreviations and omissions in the forms of our Liturgy (retaining everything he thinks
essential) as might, if adopted, procure a more general attendance. For, besides the differing sentiments of many pious and
well-disposed persons in some speculative points, who in general have a good opinion of our Church, it has often been observed and complained of, that the Morning and Evening Service, as practised in England and elsewhere, are so long, and filled
with so many repetitions, that the continued attention suitable
to so serious a duty becomes impracticable, the mind wanders,
and the fervency of devotion is slackened. Also the propriety
of saying the same prayer more than once in the same service
is doubted, as the service is thereby lengthened without apparent necessity; our Lord having given us a short prayer as an
example, and censured the heathen for thinking to be heard
because of much speaking.

Moreover, many pious and devout persons, whose age or infirmities will not suffer them to remain for hours in a cold
church, especially in the winter season, are obliged to forego the
comfort and edification they would receive by their attendance
at divine service. These, by shortening the time, would be relieved, and the younger sort, who have had some principles of

religion instilled into them, and who have been educated in a belief of the necessity of adoring their Maker, would probably more frequently, as well as cheerfully, attend divine service, if they were not detained so long at any one time. Also many well disposed tradesmen, shopkeepers, artificers, and others, whose habitations are not remote from churches, could, and would, more frequently at least, find [time to attend divine service on other than Sundays, if the prayers were reduced to a much narrower compass.

Formerly there were three services performed at different times of the day, which three services are now usually joined in one. This may suit the convenience of the person who officiates, but it is too often inconvenient and tiresome to the congregation. If this abridgment, therefore, should ever meet with acceptance, the well-disposed clergy who are laudably desirous to encourage the *frequency* of divine service, may promote so great and good a purpose by repeating it three times on a Sunday, without so much fatigue to themselves as at present. Suppose, at nine o'clock, at eleven, and at one in the evening; and by preaching no more sermons than usual of a moderate length; and thereby accommodate a greater number of people with convenient hours.

These were general reasons for wishing and proposing an abridgment. In attempting it we do not presume to dictate even to a single Christian. We are sensible there is a proper authority in the rulers of the Church for ordering such matters; and whenever the time shall come when it may be thought not unreasonable to revise our Liturgy, there is no doubt but every suitable improvement will be made, under the care and direction of so much learning, wisdom, and piety, in one body of men collected. Such a work as this must then be much better executed. In the meantime this humble performance may serve to show the practicability of shortening the service near one half, without the omission of what is essentially necessary; and we hope, moreover, that the book may be occasionally of some use to families, or private assemblies of Christians.

To give now some account of particulars. We have presumed upon this plan of abridgment to omit the First Lesson, which is taken from the Old Testament, and retain only the Second from the New Testament, which, we apprehend, is more suitable to teach the so-much-to-be-revered doctrine of Christ, and of more immediate importance to Christians;] although the Old Testament is allowed by all to be an accurate and concise history, and, as such, may more properly be read at home.

[We do not conceive it necessary for Christians to make use of more than one creed. Therefore, in this abridgment are omitted the Nicene Creed and that of St. Athanasius. Of the Apostle's Creed we have retained the parts that are most intelligible and most essential. And as the *Father*, *Son*, and *Holy Ghost* are there confessedly and avowedly a part of the belief, it does not appear necessary, after so solemn a confession, to repeat again, in the Litany, the *Son* and *Holy Ghost*, as that part of the service is otherwise very prolix.

The Psalms being a collection of odes written by different persons, it hath happened that many of them are on the same subjects and repeat the same sentiments—such as those that complain of enemies and persecutors, call upon God for protection, express a confidence therein, and thank him for it when afforded. A very great part of the book consists of repetitions of this kind, which may therefore well bear abridgment. Other parts are merely historical, repeating the mention of facts more fully narrated in the preceding books, and which, relating to the ancestors of the Jews, were more interesting to them than to us. Other parts are *local*, and allude to places of which we have no knowledge, and therefore do not affect us. Others are *personal*, relating to the particular circumstances of David or Solomon, as kings, and can therefore seldom be rehearsed with any propriety by private Christians. Others imprecate, in the most bitter terms, the vengeance of God on our adversaries, contrary to the spirit of Christianity, which commands us to love our enemies, and to pray for those that hate us and despitefully use us. For these reasons it is to be wished that the same liberty were by the governors of our Church allowed to the minister with regard to the *reading Psalms*, as is taken by the clerk with regard to those that are to be sung, in directing the parts that he may judge most suitable to be read at the time, from the present circumstances of the congregation, or the tenor of his sermon, by saying, "Let us *read*" such and such parts of the Psalms named. Until this is done our abridgment, it is hoped, will be found to contain what may be most generally proper to be joined in by an assembly of Christian people. The Psalms are still apportioned to the days of the month, as heretofore, though the several parts for each day are generally a full third shorter.

We humbly suppose the same service contained in this abridgment might properly serve for all the saints' days, fasts, and feasts, reading only the Epistle and Gospel appropriated to each day of the month.

The Communion is greatly abridged, on account of its great length; nevertheless, it is hoped and believed that all those parts are retained which are material and necessary.

Infant Baptism in Churches being performed during divine service, would greatly add to the length of that service, if it were not abridged. We have ventured, therefore, to leave out the less material parts.

The Catechism, as a compendium of systematic theology, which learned divines have written folio volumes to explain, and which, therefore, it may be presumed, they thought scarce intelligible without such expositions, is, perhaps, taken altogether, not so well adapted to the capacities of children as might be wished. Only those plain answers, therefore, which express our duty towards God, and our duty towards our neighbor, are retained here. The rest is recommended to their reading and serious consideration, when more years shall have ripened their understanding.]

The Confirmation is here shortened.

The Commination, and all cursing of mankind, is, we think, best omitted in this abridgment.

The form of solemnization of Matrimony is often abbreviated by the officiating minister at his discretion. We have selected what appears to us the material parts, and which we humbly hope, will be deemed sufficient.

The long prayers in the service for the Visitation of the Sick seem not so proper, when the afflicted person is very weak and in distress.

The Order for the Burial of the Dead is very solemn and moving; nevertheless, to preserve the health and lives of the living, it appeared to us that this service ought particularly to be shortened. For numbers standing in the open air with their hats off, often in tempestuous weather, during the celebration, its great length is not only inconvenient, but may be dangerous to the attendants. We hope, therefore, that our abridgment of it will be approved by the rational and prudent.

The Thanksgiving of women after childbirth being, when read, part of the service of the day, we have also, in some measure, abridged that.

Having thus stated very briefly our motives and reasons, and our manner of proceeding in the prosecution of this work, we hope to be believed, when we declare the rectitude of our intentions. We mean not to lessen or prevent the practice of religion, but to honour and promote it. We acknowledge the excellency of our present Liturgy, and, though we have shortened it, we have not presumed to alter a word in the remaining text; not even to substitute *who* for *which* in the Lord's Prayer, and elsewhere, although it would be more correct. We respect the characters of bishops and other dignitaries of our Church, and, with regard to the inferior clergy we wish that they were more equally provided for, than by that odious and vexatious as well as unjust method of gathering tithes in kind, which creates animosities and litigations, to the interruption of the good harmony and respect which might otherwise subsist between the rectors and their parishioners.

And thus, conscious of upright meaning, we submit this abridgment to the serious consideration of the prudent and dispassionate, and not to enthusiasts and bigots; being convinced in our own breasts, that this shortened method, or one of the same kind better executed, would further religion, increase unanimity, and occasion a more frequent attendance on the worship of God.

A PARABLE AGAINST PERSECUTION[83]

1. And it came to pass after these things, that Abraham sat in the door of his tent, about the going down of the sun.

2. And behold a man, bent with age, coming from the way of the wilderness, leaning on a staff.

3. And Abraham arose and met him, and said unto him, Turn in, I pray thee, and wash thy feet, and tarry all night, and thou shalt arise early in the morning, and go on thy way.

4. But the man said, Nay, for I will abide under this tree.

5. And Abraham pressed him greatly; so he turned, and they went into the tent; and Abraham baked unleavened bread, and they did eat.

6. And when Abraham saw that the man blessed not God, he said unto him, Wherefore dost thou not worship the most high God, Creator of heaven and earth?

7. And the man answered and said, I do not worship thy God, neither do I call upon his name; for I have made to myself a god, which abideth always in mine house, and provideth me with all things.

8. And Abraham's zeal was kindled against the man, and he arose and fell upon him, and drove him forth with blows into the wilderness.

9. And God called unto Abraham, saying, Abraham, where is the stranger?

10. And Abraham answered and said, Lord, he would not worship thee, neither would he call upon thy name; therefore have I driven him out from before my face into the wilderness.

11. And God said, Have I borne with him these hundred and ninety and eight years, and nourished him, and cloathed him, notwithstanding his rebellion against me; and couldst not thou, who art thyself a sinner, bear with him one night?

12. And Abraham said, Let not the anger of the Lord wax hot against his servant; lo, I have sinned; lo, I have sinned; forgive me, I pray thee.

13. And Abraham arose, and went forth into the wilderness, and sought diligently for the man, and found him, and returned

with him to the tent; and when he had entreated him kindly, he sent him away on the morrow with gifts.

14. And God spake again unto Abraham, saying, For this thy sin shall thy seed be afflicted four hundred years in a strange land;

15. But for thy repentance will I deliver them; and they shall come forth with power, and with gladness of heart, and with much substance.

A PARABLE ON BROTHERLY LOVE [84]

1. In those days there was no worker of iron in all the land. And the merchants of Midian passed by with their camels, bearing spices, and myrrh, and balm, and wares of iron.

2. And Reuben bought an axe of the Ishmaelite merchants, which he prized highly, for there was none in his father's house.

3. And Simeon said unto Reuben his brother, "Lend me, I pray thee, thine axe." But he refused, and would not.

4. And Levi also said unto him, "My brother, lend me, I pray thee, thine axe;" and he refused him also.

5. Then came Judah unto Reuben, and entreated him, saying, "Lo, thou lovest me, and I have always loved thee; do not refuse me the use of thine axe."

6. But Reuben turned from him, and refused him likewise.

7. Now it came to pass, that Reuben hewed timber on the bank of the river, and his axe fell therein, and he could by no means find it.

8. But Simeon, Levi, and Judah had sent a messenger after the Ishmaelites with money, and had bought for themselves each an axe.

9. Then came Reuben unto Simeon, and said, "Lo, I have lost mine axe, and my work is unfinished; lend me thine, I pray thee."

10. And Simeon answered him, saying, "Thou wouldest not lend me thine axe, therefore will I not lend thee mine."

11. Then went he unto Levi, and said unto him, "My brother, thou knowest my loss and my necessity; lend me, I pray thee, thine axe."

12. And Levi reproached him, saying, "Thou wouldest not lend me thine axe when I desired it, but I will be better than thou, and will lend thee mine."

13. And Reuben was grieved at the rebuke of Levi and being ashamed, turned from him, and took not the axe, but sought his brother Judah.

14. And as he drew near, Judah beheld his countenance as it were covered with grief and shame; and he prevented him, saying, "My brother, I know thy loss; but why should it trouble thee? Lo, have I not an axe that will serve both thee and me? Take it, I pray thee, and use it as thine own."

15. And Reuben fell on his neck, and kissed him, with tears, saying, "Thy kindness is great, but thy goodness in forgiving me is greater. Thou are indeed my brother, and whilst I live, will I surely love thee."

16. And Judah said, "Let us also love our other brethren; behold, are we not all of one blood?"

17. And Joseph saw these things, and reported them to his father Jacob.

18. And Jacob said, "Reuben did wrong, but he repented. Simeon also did wrong; and Levi was not altogether blameless.

19. "But the heart of Judah is princely. Judah hath the soul of a king. His father's children shall bow down before him, and he shall rule over his brethren."

TO WILLIAM STRAHAN [85]

Philadª July 5, 1775.

MR. STRAHAN,

You are a Member of Parliament, and one of that Majority which has doomed my Country to Destruction.—You have begun to burn our Towns, and murder our People.—Look upon your Hands! They are stained with the Blood of your Relations!—You and I were long Friends:—You are now my Enemy,—and I am

Yours,

B. FRANKLIN.

TO JOSEPH PRIESTLEY

Philadelphia, July 7, 1775.

DEAR FRIEND,

The Congress met at a time when all minds were so exasperated by the perfidy of General Gage, and his attack on the country people, that propositions of attempting an accommodation were not much relished; and it has been with difficulty that we have carried another humble petition to the crown, to give Britain one more chance, one opportunity more, of recovering the friendship of the colonies; which, however, I think she has not sense enough to embrace, and so I conclude she has lost them for ever.

She has begun to burn our seaport towns; secure, I suppose, that we shall never be able to return the outrage in kind. She may doubtless destroy them all; but, if she wishes to recover our commerce, are these the probable means? She must certainly be distracted; for no tradesman out of Bedlam ever thought of encreasing the number of his customers, by knocking them on the head; or of enabling them to pay their debts, by burning their houses. If she wishes to have us subjects, and that we should submit to her as our compound sovereign, she is now giving us such miserable specimens of her government, that we shall ever detest and avoid it, as a complication of robbery, murder, famine, fire, and pestilence.

You will have heard, before this reaches you, of the treacherous conduct [of General Gage] to the remaining people in Boston, in detaining their *goods*, after stipulating to let them go out with their *effects*, on pretence that merchants' goods were not effects; the defeat of a great body of his troops by the country people at Lexington; some other small advantages gained in skirmishes with their troops; and the action at Bunker's Hill, in which they were twice repulsed, and the third time gained a dear victory. Enough has happened, one would think, to convince your ministers, that the Americans will fight, and that this is a harder nut to crack than they imagined.

We have not yet applied to any foreign power for assistance, nor offered our commerce for their friendship. Perhaps we never may; yet it is natural to think of it, if we are pressed. We have now an army on our establishment, which still holds yours besieged. My time was never more fully employed. In the morning at six, I am at the Committee of Safety, appointed by the Assembly to put the province in a state of defence; which committee holds till near nine, when I am at the Congress, and that sits till after four in the afternoon. Both these bodies proceed with the greatest unanimity, and their meetings are well attended. It will scarce be credited in Britain, that men can be as diligent with us from zeal for the public good, as with you for thousands per annum. Such is the difference between uncorrupted new states, and corrupted old ones.

Great frugality and great industry are now become fashionable here. Gentlemen, who used to entertain with two or three courses, pride themselves now in treating with simple beef and pudding. By these means, and the stoppage of our consumptive trade with Britain, we shall be better able to pay our voluntary taxes for the support of our troops. Our savings in the article of trade amount to near five millions sterling per annum.

I shall communicate your letter to Mr. Winthrop; but the camp is at Cambridge, and he has as little leisure for philosophy as myself. Believe me ever with sincere esteem, my dear friend, yours most affectionately,

B. FRANKLIN.

TO A FRIEND IN ENGLAND[86]

Philadelphia, Oct. 3, 1775.

DEAR SIR,

I wish as ardently as you can do for peace, and should rejoice exceedingly in coöperating with you to that end. But every ship from Britain brings some intelligence of new measures that tend more and more to exasperate; and it seems to me, that until you have found by dear experience the reducing us by force impracticable, you will think of nothing fair and reasonable.

We have as yet resolved only on defensive measures. If you

would recall your forces and stay at home, we should meditate
nothing to injure you. A little time so given for cooling on
both sides would have excellent effects. But you will goad and
provoke us. You despise us too much; and you are insensible
of the Italian adage, that there is no *little enemy*. I am persuaded
that the body of the British people are our friends; but they are
changeable, and by your lying Gazettes may soon be made our
enemies. Our respect for them will proportionably diminish,
and I see clearly we are on the high road to mutual Enmity [,]
hatred and detestation. A separation of course will be inevitable.
'Tis a million of pities so fair a plan as we have hitherto been
engaged in, for increasing strength and empire with *public felicity*,
should be destroyed by the mangling hands of a few blundering
ministers. It will not be destroyed; God will protect and prosper
it, you will only exclude yourselves from any share in it. We
hear, that more ships and troops are coming out. We know,
that you may do us a great deal of mischief, and are determined
to bear it patiently as long as we can. But, if you flatter yourselves with beating us into submission, you know neither the
people nor the country. The Congress are still sitting, and will
wait the result of their *last* petition. Yours, &c.

B. FRANKLIN.

TO LORD HOWE

Philadelphia, July 30th,[87] 1776.

MY LORD,

I receiv'd safe the Letters your Lordship so kindly forwarded
to me, and beg you to accept my thanks.

The official dispatches, to which you refer me, contain nothing
more than what we had seen in the Act of Parliament, viz. Offers
of Pardon upon Submission, which I was sorry to find, as it
must give your Lordship Pain to be sent upon so fruitless a
Business.

Directing Pardons to be offered to the Colonies, who are the
very Parties injured, expresses indeed that Opinion of our Ignorance, Baseness, and Insensibility, which your uninform'd and
proud Nation has long been pleased to entertain of us; but it

can have no other effect than that of increasing our Resentments. It is impossible we should think of Submission to a Government, that has with the most wanton Barbarity and Cruelty burnt our defenceless Towns in the midst of Winter, excited the Savages to massacre our Peacefull Farmers, and our Slaves to murder their Masters, and is even now bringing foreign Mercenaries to deluge our Settlements with Blood. These atrocious Injuries have extinguished every remaining Spark of Affection for that Parent Country we once held so dear; but, were it possible for *us* to forget and forgive them, it is not possible for *you* (I mean the British Nation) to forgive the People you have so heavily injured. You can never confide again in those as Fellow Subjects, and permit them to enjoy equal Freedom, to whom you know you have given such just Cause of lasting Enmity. And this must impel you, were we again under your Government, to endeavour the breaking our Spirit by the severest Tyranny, and obstructing, by every Means in your Power, our growing Strength and Prosperity.

But your Lordship mentions "the King's paternal solicitude for promoting the Establishment of lasting *Peace* and Union with the Colonies." If by Peace is here meant a Peace to be entered into between Britain and America, as distinct States now at War, and his Majesty has given your Lordship Powers to treat with us of such a Peace, I may venture to say, though without Authority, that I think a Treaty for that purpose not yet quite impracticable, before we enter into foreign Alliances. But I am persuaded you have no such Powers. Your nation, though, by punishing those American Governors, who have fomented the Discord, rebuilding our burnt Towns, and repairing as far as possible the mischiefs done us, might yet recover a great Share of our Regard, and the greatest Part of our growing Commerce, with all the Advantage of that additional Strength to be derived from a Friendship with us; but I know too well her abounding Pride and deficient Wisdom, to believe she will ever take such salutary Measures. Her Fondness for Conquest, as a warlike Nation, her lust of Dominion, as an ambitious one, and her wish for a gainful Monopoly, as a commercial One, (none of them legitimate Causes of War,) will all join to hide from her Eyes every view of her true Interests, and continually goad her on in those ruinous distant Expeditions, so destructive both of Lives and Treasure, that must prove as pernicious to her in the End, as the Crusades formerly were to most of the Nations in Europe.

I have not the Vanity, my Lord, to think of intimidating by thus predicting the Effects of this War; for I know it will in England have the Fate of all my former Predictions, not to be believed till the Event shall verify it.

Long did I endeavour, with unfeigned and unwearied Zeal, to preserve from breaking that fine and noble China Vase, the British Empire; for I knew, that, being once broken, the separate Parts could not retain even their Shares of the Strength and Value that existed in the Whole, and that a perfect Reunion of those Parts could scarce ever be hoped for. Your Lordship may possibly remember the tears of Joy that wet my Cheek, when, at your good Sister's in London, you once gave me Expectations that a Reconciliation might soon take Place. I had the Misfortune to find those Expectations disappointed, and to be treated as the Cause of the Mischief I was laboring to prevent. My Consolation under that groundless and malevolent Treatment was, that I retained the Friendship of many wise and good Men in that country, and, among the rest, some Share in the Regard of Lord Howe.

The well-founded Esteem, and, permit me to say, Affection, which I shall always have for your Lordship, makes it Painful to me to see you engaged in conducting a War, the great Ground of which, as expressed in your Letter, is "the necessity of preventing the American trade from passing into foreign Channels." To me it seems, that neither the Obtaining or Retaining of any trade, how valuable soever, is an Object for which men may justly spill each other's Blood; that the true and sure Means of extending and securing Commerce is the goodness and Cheapness of Commodities; and that the profit of no trade can ever be equal to the Expence of compelling it, and of holding it, by Fleets and Armies.

I consider this War against us, therefore, as both unjust and unwise; and I am persuaded, that cool, dispassionate Posterity will condemn to Infamy those who advised it; and that even Success will not save from some Degree of Dishonor those, who voluntarily engaged to Conduct it. I know your great motive in coming hither was the hope of being Instrumental in a Reconciliation; and I believe, when you find *that* to be impossible on any Terms given you to propose, you will relinquish so odious a Command, and return to a more honourable private Station.

With the greatest and most sincere Respect, I have the Honour to be, my Lord, your Lordship's most obedient humble Servant,

B. FRANKLIN.

THE SALE OF THE HESSIANS [88]

FROM THE COUNT DE SCHAUMBERGH TO THE BARON HOHENDORF, COMMANDING THE HESSIAN TROOPS IN AMERICA

Rome, February 18, 1777.

MONSIEUR LE BARON:—

On my return from Naples, I received at Rome your letter of the 27th December of last year. I have learned with unspeakable pleasure the courage our troops exhibited at Trenton, and you cannot imagine my joy on being told that of the 1,950 Hessians engaged in the fight, but 345 escaped. There were just 1,605 men killed, and I cannot sufficiently commend your prudence in sending an exact list of the dead to my minister in London. This precaution was the more necessary, as the report sent to the English ministry does not give but 1,455 dead. This would make 483,450 florins instead of 643,500 which I am entitled to demand under our convention. You will comprehend the prejudice which such an error would work in my finances, and I do not doubt you will take the necessary pains to prove that Lord North's list is false and yours correct.

The court of London objects that there were a hundred wounded who ought not to be included in the list, nor paid for as dead; but I trust you will not overlook my instructions to you on quitting Cassel, and that you will not have tried by human succor to recall the life of the unfortunates whose days could not be lengthened but by the loss of a leg or an arm. That would be making them a pernicious present, and I am sure they would rather die than live in a condition no longer fit for my service. I do not mean by this that you should assassinate them; we should be humane, my dear Baron, but you may insinuate to the surgeons with entire propriety that a crippled man is a reproach to their profession, and that there is no wiser course than to let every one of them die when he ceases to be fit to fight.

I am about to send to you some new recruits. Don't economize them. Remember glory before all things. Glory is true wealth. There is nothing degrades the soldier like the love of money. He must care only for honour and reputation, but this reputation must be acquired in the midst of dangers. A battle gained without costing the conqueror any blood is an inglorious success, while the conquered cover themselves with glory by perishing with their arms in their hands. Do you remember that of the 300 Lacedæmonians who defended the defile of Thermopylæ, not one returned? How happy should I be could I say the same of my brave Hessians!

It is true that their king, Leonidas, perished with them: but things have changed, and it is no longer the custom for princes of the empire to go and fight in America for a cause with which they have no concern. And besides, to whom should they pay the thirty guineas per man if I did not stay in Europe to receive them? Then, it is necessary also that I be ready to send recruits to replace the men you lose. For this purpose I must return to Hesse. It is true, grown men are becoming scarce there, but I will send you boys. Besides, the scarcer the commodity the higher the price. I am assured that the women and little girls have begun to till our lands, and they get on not badly. You did right to send back to Europe that Dr. Crumerus who was so successful in curing dysentery. Don't bother with a man who is subject to looseness of the bowels. That disease makes bad soldiers. One coward will do more mischief in an engagement than ten brave men will do good. Better that they burst in their barracks than fly in a battle, and tarnish the glory of our arms. Besides, you know that they pay me as killed for all who die from disease, and I don't get a farthing for runaways. My trip to Italy, which has cost me enormously, makes it desirable that there should be a great mortality among them. You will therefore promise promotion to all who expose themselves; you will exhort them to seek glory in the midst of dangers; you will say to Major Maundorff that I am not at all content with his saving the 345 men who escaped the massacre of Trenton. Through the whole campaign he has not had ten men killed in consequence of his orders. Finally, let it be your principal object to prolong the war and avoid a decisive engagement on either side, for I have made arrangements for a grand Italian opera, and I do not wish to be obliged to give it up. Meantime I pray God, my dear Baron de Hohendorf, to have you in his holy and gracious keeping.

MODEL OF A LETTER OF RECOMMENDATION [89]

Paris, April 2, 1777.

Sir:—

The bearer of this, who is going to America, presses me to give him a Letter of Recommendation, tho' I know nothing of him, not even his Name. This may seem extraordinary, but I assure you it is not uncommon here. Sometimes, indeed one unknown Person brings another equally unknown, to recommend him; and sometimes they recommend one another! As to this Gentleman, I must refer you to himself for his Character and Merits, with which he is certainly better acquainted than I can possibly be. I recommend him however to those Civilities, which every Stranger, of whom one knows no Harm, has a Right to; and I request you will do him all the good Offices, and show him all the Favour that, on further Acquaintance, you shall find him to deserve. I have the Honour to be, etc.

[B. F.]

TO ————

Passy, Oct. 4, 1777.

SIR,

I am much obliged by your communication of the letter from England. I am of your opinion, that it is not proper for publication here. Our friend's expressions concerning Mr. Wilson, will be thought too angry to be made use of by one philosopher when speaking of another, and on a philosophical question. He seems as much heated about this *one point*, as the Jansenists and Molinists were about the *five*. As to my writing any thing on the subject, which you seem to desire, I think it not necessary, especially as I have nothing to add to what I have already said upon it in a paper read to the committee, who ordered the conductors at Purfleet; which paper is printed in the last French edition of my writings.

I have never entered into any controversy in defence of my philosophical opinions; I leave them to take their chance in the world. If they are *right*, truth and experience will support them; if *wrong*, they ought to be refuted and rejected. Disputes are apt to sour one's temper, and disturb one's quiet. I have no private interest in the reception of my inventions by the world, having never made, nor proposed to make, the least profit by any of them. The King's changing his *pointed* conductors for *blunt* ones is, therefore, a matter of small importance to me. If I had a wish about it, it would be that he had rejected them altogether as ineffectual. For it is only since he thought himself and family safe from the thunder of Heaven, that he dared to use his own thunder in destroying his innocent subjects.[90] I am, Sir, yours, &c.

B. FRANKLIN.

TO DAVID HARTLEY [91]

Passy, Oct. 14, 1777.

DEAR SIR,

I received duly your letter of May 2, 1777, including a copy of one you had sent me the year before, which never came to hand, and which it seems has been the case with some I wrote to you from America. Filled tho' our letters have always been with sentiments of good will to both countries, and earnest desires of preventing their ruin and promoting their mutual felicity, I have been apprehensive, that, if it were known that a correspondence subsisted between us, it might be attended with inconvenience to you. I have therefore been backward in writing, not caring to trust the post, and not well knowing whom else to trust with my letters. But being now assured of a safe conveyance, I venture to write to you, especially as I think the subject such an one as you may receive a letter upon without censure.

Happy should I have been, if the honest warnings I gave, of the fatal separation of interests, as well as of affections, that must attend the measures commenced while I was in England, had been attended to, and the horrid mischief of this abominable war been thereby prevented. I should still be happy in any successful endeavours for restoring peace, consistent with the liberties, the safety, and honour of America. As to our submitting to the government of Great Britain, it is vain to think of it. She has given us, by her numberless barbarities in the prosecution of the war, and in the treatment of prisoners, by her malice in bribing slaves to murder their masters, and savages to massacre the families of farmers, with her baseness in rewarding the unfaithfulness of servants, and debauching the virtue of honest seamen, intrusted with our property, so deep an impression of her depravity, that we never again can trust her in the management of our affairs and interests. It is now impossible to persuade our people, as I long endeavoured, that the war was merely ministerial, and that the nation bore still a good will to us. The infinite number of addresses printed in your gazettes, all approving this conduct of your government towards us, and encouraging our destruction by every possible means, the great majority in Parliament constantly manifesting the same sentiments, and the popular public rejoicings on occasion of any news of the slaughter of an innocent and virtuous people, fighting only in defence of their just rights; these, together with the recommendations of the same measures by even your celebrated moralists and divines, in their writings and sermons, that are cited approved and applauded in your great national assemblies; all join in convincing us, that you are no longer the magnanimous and enlightened nation, we once esteemed you, and that you are unfit and unworthy to govern us, as not being able to govern your own passions.

But, as I have said, I should be nevertheless happy in seeing peace restored. For tho', if my friends and the friends of liberty and virtue, who still remain in England, could be drawn out of it, a continuance of this war to the ruin of the rest would give me less concern, I cannot, as that removal is impossible, but wish for peace for their sakes, as well as for the sake of humanity, and preventing further carnage.

This wish of mine, ineffective as it may be, induces me to mention to you, that, between nations long exasperated against each other in war, some act of generosity and kindness towards prisoners on one side has softened resentment, and abated animosity on the other, so as to bring on an accommodation. You in England, if you wish for peace, have at present the opportunity of trying this means, with regard to the prisoners now in your goals [*sic*]. They complain of very severe treatment. They are far from their friends and families, and winter is coming on, in which they must suffer extremely, if continued in their present situation; fed scantily on bad provisions, without warm lodging, clothes, or fire, and not suffered to invite or receive visits from their friends, or even from the humane and charitable of their enemies.

I can assure you, from my own certain knowledge, that your people, prisoners in America, have been treated with great kindness; they have been served with the same rations of wholesome provisions with our own troops, comfortable lodgings have been provided for them, and they have been allowed large bounds of villages in a healthy air, to walk and amuse themselves with on their parole. Where you have thought fit to employ contractors to supply your people, these contractors have been protected and aided in their operations. Some considerable act of kindness towards our people would take off the reproach of inhumanity in that respect from the nation, and leave it where it ought with more certainty to lay, on the conductors of your war in America. This I hint to you, out of some remaining good will to a nation I once sincerely loved. But, as things are, and in my present temper of mind, not being over fond of receiving obligations, I shall content myself with proposing, that your government would allow us to send or employ a commissary to take some care of those unfortunate people. Perhaps on your representations this might speedily be obtained in England, though it was refused most inhumanly at New York.

If you could have leisure to visit the goals [*sic*] in which they are confined, and should be desirous of knowing the truth relative to the treatment they receive, I wish you would take the trouble of distributing among the most necessitous according to their wants, two or three hundred pounds, for which your drafts on me here shall be punctually honour'd. You could then be able to speak with some certainty to the point in Parliament, and this might be attended with good effect.

If you cannot obtain for us permission to send a commissary, possibly you may find a trusty, humane, discreet person at Plymouth, and another at Portsmouth, who would undertake to communicate what relief we may be able to afford those unhappy, brave men, martyrs to the cause of liberty. [Your King will not reward you for taking this trouble, but God will.] I shall not mention the good will of America; you have what is better, the applause of your own good conscience. Our captains have set at liberty above 200 of your people, made prisoners by our armed vessels and brought into France, besides a great number dismissed at sea on your coasts, to whom vessels were given to carry them in: But you have not returned us a man in exchange. If we had sold your people to the Moors at Sallee, as you have many of ours to the African and East India Companies, could you have complained?

In revising what I have written, I found too much warmth in it, and was about to strike out some parts. Yet I let them go, as they will afford you this one reflection; "If a man naturally cool, and render'd still cooler by old age, is so warmed by our treatment of his country, how much must those people in general be exasperated against us? And why are we making inveterate enemies by our barbarity, not only of the present inhabitants of a great country, but of their infinitely more numerous posterity; who will in future ages detest the name of *Englishman*, as much as the children in Holland now do those of *Alva* and *Spaniard*." This will certainly happen, unless your conduct is speedily changed, and the national resentment falls where it ought to [fall] heavily, on your ministry, [or perhaps rather on the King, whose will they only execute].

With the greatest esteem and affection, and best wishes for your prosperity, I have the honour to be, dear Sir, &c.

B. FRANKLIN.

A DIALOGUE BETWEEN BRITAIN, FRANCE, SPAIN, HOLLAND, SAXONY AND AMERICA[92]

Britain. Sister of Spain, I have a Favour to ask of you. My Subjects in America are disobedient, and I am about to chastize them; I beg you will not furnish them with any Arms or Ammunition.

Spain. Have you forgotten, then, that when my Subjects in the Low Countries rebelled against me, you not only furnish'd them with military Stores, but join'd them with an Army and a Fleet? I wonder how you can have the Impudence to ask such a Favour of me, or the Folly to expect it!

Britain. You, my dear Sister of France, will surely not refuse me this Favour.

France. Did you not assist my Rebel Hugenots with a Fleet and an Army at Rochelle? And have you not lately aided privately and sneakingly my Rebel Subjects in Corsica? And do you not at this Instant keep their Chief, pension'd, and ready to head a fresh Revolt there, whenever you can find or make an Opportunity? Dear Sister, you must be a little silly!

Britain. Honest Holland! You see it is remembered that I was once your Friend; you will therefore be mine on this Occasion. I know, indeed, you are accustom'd to smuggle with these Rebels of mine. I will wink at that; sell 'em as much Tea as you please, to enervate the Rascals, since they will not take it of me; but for God's sake don't supply them with any Arms!

Holland. 'T is true you assisted me against Philip, my Tyrant of Spain, but have I not assisted you against one of your Tyrants;* and enabled you to expell him? Surely that Accompt, as we Merchants say, is *ballanced*, and I am nothing in your Debt. I have indeed some Complaints against *you*, for endeavouring to starve me by your *Navigation Acts;* but, being peaceably dispos'd, I do not quarrel with you for that. I shall only go on quietly with my own Business. Trade is my Profession: 't is all I have to subsist on. And, let me tell you, I shall make no scruple (on the prospect of a good Market for that Commodity) even to send my ships to Hell and supply the Devil with Brimstone. For you must know, I can insure in London against the Burning of my Sails.

America to Britain. Why, you old bloodthirsty Bully! You who have been everywhere vaunting your own Prowess, and defaming the Americans as poltroons! You who have boasted of being able to march over all their Bellies with a single Regiment! You who by Fraud have possessed yourself of their strongest Fortress, and all the arms they had stored up in it! You who have a disciplin'd Army in their Country, intrench'd to the Teeth, and provided with every thing! Do *you* run about begging all Europe not to supply those poor People with a little Powder and Shot? Do you mean, then, to fall upon them naked and unarm'd, and butcher them in cold Blood? Is this your Courage? Is this your Magnanimity?

Britain. Oh! you wicked—Whig—Presbyterian—Serpent! Have you the Impudence to appear before me after all your Disobedience? Surrender immediately all your Liberties and Properties into my Hands, or I will cut you to Pieces. Was it for this that I planted your country at so great an Expence? That I protected you in your Infancy, and defended you against all your Enemies?

*James 2d. [*Franklin's note.*]

America. I shall not surrender my Liberty and Property, but with my Life. It is not true, that my Country was planted at your expence. Your own Records refute that Falshood to your Face. Nor did you ever afford me a Man or a Shilling to defend me against the Indians, the only Enemies I had upon my own Account. But, when you have quarrell'd with all Europe, and drawn me with you into all your Broils, then you value yourself upon protecting me from the Enemies you have made for me. I have no natural Cause of Difference with Spain, France, or Holland, and yet by turns I have join'd with you in Wars against them all. You would not suffer me to make or keep a separate Peace with any of them, tho' I might easily have done it to great Advantage. Does your protecting me in those Wars give you a Right to fleece me? If so, as I fought for you, as well as you for me, it gives me a proportionable Right to fleece you. What think you of an American Law to make a Monopoly of you and your Commerce, as you have done by your Laws of me and mine? Content yourself with that Monopoly if you are Wise, and learn Justice if you would be respected!

Britain. You impudent b——h! Am not I your Mother Country? Is that not a sufficient Title to your Respect and Obedience?

Saxony. Mother country! Hah, hah, he! What Respect have *you* the front to claim as a Mother Country? You know that *I* am *your* Mother Country, and yet you pay me none. Nay, it is but the other day, that you hired Ruffians* to rob me on the Highway,† and burn my House!‡ For shame! Hide your Face and hold your Tongue. If you continue this Conduct, you will make yourself the Contempt of Europe!

Britain. O Lord! Where are my friends?

France, Spain, Holland, and Saxony, all together. Friends! Believe us, you have none, nor ever will have any, 'till you mend your Manners. How can we, who are your Neighbours, have

---

* Prussians.

† They enter'd and rais'd Contributions in Saxony.

‡ And they burnt the fine Suburbs of Dresden, the Capital of Saxony. [*Franklin's notes.*]

any regard for you, or expect any Equity from you, should your Power increase, when we see how basely and unjustly you have us'd both your *own Mother and your own Children?*

TO CHARLES DE WEISSENSTEIN[93]

Passy, July 1, 1778.

SIR,

I received your letter, dated at Brussels the 16th past. My vanity might possibly be flattered by your expressions of compliment to my understanding, if your *proposals* did not more clearly manifest a mean opinion of it.

You conjure me, in the name of the omniscient and just God, before whom I must appear, and by my hopes of future fame, to consider if some expedient cannot be found to put a stop to the desolation of America, and prevent the miseries of a general war. As I am conscious of having taken every step in my power to prevent the breach, and no one to widen it, I can appear cheerfully before that God, fearing nothing from his justice in this particular, though I have much occasion for his mercy in many others. As to my future fame, I am content to rest it on my past and present conduct, without seeking an addition to it in the crooked, dark paths, you propose to me, where I should most certainly lose it. This your solemn address would therefore have been more properly made to your sovereign and his venal Parliament. He and they, who wickedly began, and madly continue, a war for the desolation of America, are alone accountable for the consequences.

You endeavour to impress me with a bad opinion of French faith; but the instances of their friendly endeavours to serve a race of weak princes, who, by their own imprudence, defeated every attempt to promote their interest, weigh but little with me, when I consider the steady friendship of France to the Thirteen United States of Switzerland, which has now continued inviolate two hundred years. You tell me, that she will certainly cheat us, and that she despises us already. I do not believe that she will cheat us, and I am not certain that she despises us; but

I see clearly that you are endeavouring to cheat us by your conciliatory bills; that you actually despised our understandings, when you flattered yourselves those artifices would succeed; and that not only France, but all Europe, yourselves included, most certainly and for ever would despise us, if we were weak enough to accept your insidious propositions.

Our expectations of the future grandeur of America are not so magnificent, and therefore not so vain or visionary, as you represent them to be. The body of our people are not merchants, but humble husbandmen, who delight in the cultivation of their lands, which, from their fertility and the variety of our climates, are capable of furnishing all the necessaries and conveniences of life without external commerce; and we have too much land to have the least temptation to extend our territory by conquest from peaceable neighbours, as well as too much justice to think of it. Our militia, you find by experience, are sufficient to defend our lands from invasion; and the commerce with us will be defended by all the nations who find an advantage in it. We, therefore, have not the occasion you imagine, of fleets or standing armies, but may leave those expensive machines to be maintained for the pomp of princes, and the wealth of ancient states. We propose, if possible, to live in peace with all mankind; and after you have been convinced, to your cost, that there is nothing to be got by attacking us, we have reason to hope, that no other power will judge it prudent to quarrel with us, lest they divert us from our own quiet industry, and turn us into corsairs preying upon theirs. The weight therefore of an independent empire, which you seem certain of our inability to bear, will not be so great as you imagine. The expense of our civil government we have always borne, and can easily bear, because it is small. A virtuous and laborious people may be cheaply governed. Determining, as we do, to have no offices of profit, nor any sinecures or useless appointments, so common in ancient or corrupted states, we can govern ourselves a year, for the sum you pay in a single department, or for what one jobbing contractor, by the favour of a minister, can cheat you out of in a single article.

You think we flatter ourselves, and are deceived into an opinion that England *must* acknowledge our independency. We, on the other hand, think you flatter yourselves in imagining such an acknowledgment a vast boon, which we strongly desire, and which you may gain some great advantage by granting or withholding. We have never asked it of you; we only tell you, that you can have no treaty with us but as an independent state; and you may please yourselves and your children with the rattle of your right to govern us, as long as you have done with that of your King's being King of France, without giving us the least concern, if you do not attempt to exercise it. That this pretended right is indisputable, as you say, we utterly deny. Your Parliament never had a right to govern us, and your King has forfeited it by his bloody tyranny. But I thank you for letting me know a little of your mind, that, even if the Parliament should acknowledge our independency, the act would not be binding to posterity, and that your nation would resume and prosecute the claim as soon as they found it convenient from the influence of your passions, and your present malice against us. We suspected before, that you would not be actually bound by your conciliatory acts, longer than till they had served their purpose of inducing us to disband our forces; but we were not certain, that you were knaves by principle, and that we ought not to have the least confidence in your offers, promises, or treaties, though confirmed by Parliament.

I now indeed recollect my being informed, long since, when in England, that a certain very great personage, then young, studied much a certain book, called *Arcana Imperii*.[94] I had the curiosity to procure the book and read it. There are sensible and good things in it, but some bad ones; for, if I remember rightly, a particular king is applauded for his politically exciting a rebellion among his subjects, at a time when they had not strength to support it, that he might, in subduing them, take away their privileges, which were troublesome to him; and a question is formally stated and discussed, *Whether a prince, who, to appease a revolt, makes promises of indemnity to the revolters, is obliged to fulfil those promises*. Honest and good men would say, Ay; but this politician says, as you say, No. And he gives this pretty reason, that, though it was right to make the promises, because otherwise the revolt would not be suppressed, yet it would be wrong to keep them, because revolters ought to be punished to deter from future revolts.

If these are the principles of your nation, no confidence can be placed in you; it is in vain to treat with you; and the wars can only end in being reduced to an utter inability of continuing them.

One main drift of your letter seems to be, to impress me with an idea of your own impartiality, by just censures of your ministers and measures, and to draw from me propositions of peace, or approbations of those you have enclosed to me which you intimate may by your means be conveyed to the King directly, without the intervention of those ministers. You would have me give them to, or drop them for, a stranger, whom I may find next Monday in the church of Notre Dame, to be known by a rose in his hat. You yourself, Sir, are quite unknown to me; you have not trusted me with your true name. Our taking the least step towards a treaty with England through you, might, if you are an enemy, be made use of to ruin us with our new and good friends. I may be indiscreet enough in many things; but certainly, if I were disposed to make propositions (which I cannot do, having none committed to me to make), I should never think of delivering them to the Lord knows who, to be carried to the Lord knows where, to serve no one knows what purposes. Being at this time one of the most remarkable figures in Paris, even my appearance in the church of Notre Dame, where I cannot have any conceivable business, and especially being seen to leave or drop any letter to any person there, would be a matter of some speculation, and might, from the suspicions it must naturally give, have very mischievous consequences to our credit here.

The very proposing of a correspondence so to be managed, in a manner not necessary where fair dealing is intended, gives just reason to suppose you intend the contrary. Besides, as your court has sent Commissioners to treat with the Congress, with all the powers that could be given them by the crown under the act of Parliament, what good purpose can be served by privately obtaining propositions from us? Before those Commissioners went, we might have treated in virtue of our general powers, (with the knowledge, advice, and approbation of our friends), upon any propositions made to us. But, under the present circumstances, for us to make propositions, while a treaty is supposed to be actually on foot with the Congress, would be extremely improper, highly presumptuous with regard to our constituents, and answer no good end whatever.

I write this letter to you, notwithstanding; (which I think I can convey in a less mysterious manner, and guess it may come to your hands;) I write it because I would let you know our sense of your procedure, which appears as insidious as that of your conciliatory bills. Your true way to obtain peace, if your ministers desire it, is, to propose openly to the Congress fair and equal terms, and you may possibly come sooner to such a resolution, when you find, that personal flatteries, general cajolings, and panegyrics on our *virtue* and *wisdom* are not likely to have the effect you seem to expect; the persuading us to act basely and foolishly, in betraying our country and posterity into the hands of our most bitter enemies, giving up or selling our arms and warlike stores, dismissing our ships of war and troops, and putting those enemies in possession of our forts and ports.

This proposition of delivering ourselves, bound and gagged, ready for hanging, without even a right to complain, and without a friend to be found afterwards among all mankind, you would have us embrace upon the faith of an act of Parliament! Good God! an act of your Parliament! This demonstrates that you do not yet know us, and that you fancy we do not know you; but it is not merely this flimsy faith, that we are to act upon; you offer us *hope*, the hope of PLACES, PENSIONS, and PEERAGES. These, judging from yourselves, you think are motives irresistible. This offer to corrupt us, Sir, is with me your credential, and convinces me that you are not a private volunteer in your application. It bears the stamp of British court character. It is even the signature of your King. But think for a moment in what light it must be viewed in America. By PLACES, you mean places among us, for you take care by a special article to secure your own to yourselves. We must then pay the salaries in order to enrich ourselves with these places. But you will give us PENSIONS, probably to be paid too out of your expected American revenue, and which none of us can accept without deserving, and perhaps obtaining, a SUS-*pension*. PEERAGES! alas! Sir, our long observation of the vast servile majority of your peers, voting constantly for every measure proposed by a minister, however weak or wicked, leaves us small respect for that title. We consider it as a sort of *tar-and-feather* honour, or a mixture of foulness and folly, which every man among us, who should accept it from your King, would be obliged to renounce, or exchange for that conferred by the mobs of their own country, or wear it with everlasting infamy. I am, Sir, your humble Servant,

                                                              B. FRANKLIN.

THE EPHEMERA[95]

An Emblem of Human Life

[1778]

You may remember, my dear friend, that when we lately spent that happy day in the delightful garden and sweet society of the Moulin Joly, I stopt a little in one of our walks, and staid some time behind the company. We had been shown numberless skeletons of a kind of little fly, called an ephemera, whose successive generations, we were told, were bred and expired within the day. I happened to see a living company of them on a leaf, who appeared to be engaged in conversation. You know I understand all the inferior animal tongues: my too great application to the study of them is the best excuse I can give for the little progress I have made in your charming language. I listened through curiosity to the discourse of these little creatures; but as they, in their national vivacity, spoke three or four together,

I could make but little of their conversation. I found, however, by some broken expressions that I heard now and then, they were disputing warmly on the merit of two foreign musicians, one a *cousin,* the other a *moscheto;* in which dispute they spent their time, seemingly as regardless of the shortness of life as if they had been sure of living a month. Happy people! thought I, you live certainly under a wise, just, and mild government, since you have no public grievances to complain of, nor any subject of contention but the perfections and imperfections of foreign music. I turned my head from them to an old grey-headed one, who was single on another leaf, and talking to himself. Being amused with his soliloquy, I put it down in writing, in hopes it will likewise amuse her to whom I am so much indebted for the most pleasing of all amusements, her delicious company and heavenly harmony.

"It was," said he, "the opinion of learned philosophers of our race, who lived and flourished long before my time, that this vast world, the Moulin Joly, could not itself subsist more than eighteen hours; and I think there was some foundation for that opinion, since, by the apparent motion of the great luminary that gives life to all nature, and which in my time has evidently declined considerably towards the ocean at the end of our earth, it must then finish its course, be extinguished in the waters that surround us, and leave the world in cold and darkness, necessarily producing universal death and destruction. I have lived seven of those hours, a great age, being no less than four hundred and twenty minutes of time. How very few of us continue so long! I have seen generations born, flourish, and expire. My present friends are the children and grandchildren of the friends of my youth, who are now, alas, no more! And I must soon follow them; for, by the course of nature, though still in health, I cannot expect to live above seven or eight minutes longer. What now avails all my toil and labor, in amassing honey-dew on this leaf, which I cannot live to enjoy! What the political struggles I have been engaged in, for the good of my compatriot inhabitants of this bush, or my philosophical studies for the benefit of our race in general! for, in politics, what can laws do without morals? Our present race of ephemeræ will in a course of minutes become corrupt, like those of other and older bushes, and consequently as wretched. And in philosophy how small our progress! Alas! art is long, and life is short! My friends would comfort me with the idea of a name, they say, I shall leave behind me; and they tell me I have lived long enough to nature and to glory. But what will fame be to an ephemera who no longer exists? And what will become of all history in the eighteenth hour, when the world itself, even the whole Moulin Joly, shall come to its end, and be buried in universal ruin?"

To me, after all my eager pursuits, no solid pleasures now remain, but the reflection of a long life spent in meaning well, the sensible conversation of a few good lady ephemeræ, and now and then a kind smile and a tune from the ever amiable *Brillante.*

B. FRANKLIN.

TO RICHARD BACHE

Passy, June 2, 1779.

—I am very easy about the efforts Messrs. Lee and Izard are using, as you tell me, to injure me on that side of the water. I trust in the justice of the Congress, that they will listen to no accusations against me, that I have not first been acquainted with, and had an opportunity of answering. I know those gentlemen have plenty of ill will to me, though I have never done to either of them the smallest injury, or given the least just cause of offence. But my too great reputation, and the general good will this people have for me, and the respect they show me, and even the compliments they make me, all grieve those unhappy gentlemen; unhappy indeed in their tempers, and in the dark, uncomfortable passions of jealousy, anger, suspicion, envy, and malice. It is enough for good minds to be affected at other people's misfortunes; but they, that are vexed at every-body's good luck, can never be happy. I take no other revenge of such enemies, than to let them remain in the miserable situation in which their malignant natures have placed them, by endeavouring to support an estimable character; and thus, by continuing the reputation the world has hitherto indulged me with, I shall continue them in their present state of damnation; and I am not disposed to reverse my conduct for the alleviation of their torments.

I am surprised to hear, that my grandson, Temple Franklin, being with me, should be an objection against me, and that there is a cabal for removing him.[96] Methinks it is rather some merit, that I have rescued a valuable young man from the danger of being a Tory, and fixed him in honest republican Whig principles; as I think, from the integrity of his disposition, his industry, his early sagacity, and uncommon abilities for business, he may in time become of great service to his country. It is enough that I have lost my *son;* would they add my *grandson?* An old man of seventy, I undertook a winter voyage at the command of the Congress, and for the public service, with no other attendant to take care of me. I am continued here in a foreign country, where, if I am sick, his filial attention comforts me, and, if I die, I have a child to close my eyes and take care of my remains. His dutiful behaviour towards me, and his diligence and fidelity in business, are both pleasing and useful to me. His conduct, as my private secretary, has been unexceptionable, and I am confident the Congress will never think of separating us.

I have had a great deal of pleasure in Ben too.[97] He is a good, honest lad, and will make, I think, a valuable man. He had made as much proficiency in his learning, as the boarding school he was at could well afford him; and, after some consideration where to find a better for him, I at length fixed on sending him to Geneva. I had a good opportunity by a gentleman of that city; who had a place for him in his chaise, and has a son about the same age at the same school. He promised to take care of him, and enclosed I send you the letters I have since received relating to him and from him. He went very cheerfully, and I understand is very happy. I miss his company on Sundays at dinner. But, if I live, and I can find a little leisure, I shall make

the journey next spring to see him, and to see at the same time
the old thirteen United States of Switzerland.

Thanks be to God, I continue well and hearty. Undoubtedly
I grow older, but I think the last ten years have made no great
difference. I have sometimes the gout, but they say that is not
so much a disease as a remedy. God bless you. I am your
affectionate father,

B. FRANKLIN.

MORALS OF CHESS [98]

[1779]

[Playing at chess is the most ancient and most universal game
known among men; for its original is beyond the memory of
history, and it has, for numberless ages, been the amusement of
all the civilised nations of Asia, the Persians, the Indians, and
the Chinese. Europe has had it above a thousand years; the
Spaniards have spread it over their part of America; and it has
lately begun to make its appearance in the United States. It is
so interesting in itself, as not to need the view of gain to induce
engaging in it; and thence it is seldom played for money. Those
therefore who have leisure for such diversions, cannot find one
that is more innocent: and the following piece, written with a
view to correct (among a few young friends) some little improprieties in the practice of it, shows at the same time that it
may, in its effects on the mind, be not merely innocent, but advantageous, to the vanquished as well as the victor.]

The Game of Chess is not merely an idle Amusement. Several
very valuable qualities of the Mind, useful in the course of human Life, are to be acquir'd or strengthened by it, so as to become habits, ready on all occasions. For Life is a kind of Chess,
in which we often have Points to gain, & Competitors or Adversaries to contend with; and in which there is a vast variety of
good and ill Events, that are in some degree the Effects of
Prudence or the want of it. By playing at Chess, then, we may
learn,

I. *Foresight*, which looks a little into futurity, and considers the Consequences that may attend an action; for it is continually occurring to the Player, "If I move this piece, what will be the advantages or disadvantages of my new situation? What Use can my Adversary make of it to annoy me? What other moves can I make to support it, and to defend myself from his attacks?"

II. *Circumspection*, which surveys the whole Chessboard, or scene of action; the relations of the several pieces and situations, the Dangers they are respectively exposed to, the several possibilities of their aiding each other, the probabilities that the Adversary may make this or that move, and attack this or the other Piece, and what different Means can be used to avoid his stroke, or turn its consequences against him.

III. *Caution*, not to make our moves too hastily. This habit is best acquired, by observing strictly the laws of the Game; such as, *If you touch a Piece, you must move it somewhere; if you set it down, you must let it stand.* And it is therefore best that these rules should be observed, as the Game becomes thereby more the image of human Life, and particularly of War; in which, if you have incautiously put yourself into a bad and dangerous position, you cannot obtain your Enemy's Leave to withdraw your Troops, and place them more securely, but you must abide all the consequences of your rashness.

And *lastly*, we learn by Chess the habit of not being discouraged by present appearances in the state of our affairs, the habit of hoping for a favourable Change, and that of persevering in the search of resources. The Game is so full of Events, there is such a variety of turns in it, the Fortune of it is so subject to sudden Vicissitudes, and one so frequently, after long contemplation, discovers the means of extricating one's self from a supposed insurmountable Difficulty, that one is encouraged to continue the Contest to the last, in hopes of Victory from our own skill, or at least [of getting a stale mate] from the Negligence of our Adversary. And whoever considers, what in Chess he often sees instances of, that [particular pieces of] success is [are] apt to produce Presumption, & its consequent Inattention, by which more is afterwards lost than was gain'd by the preceding Advantage, while misfortunes produce more care and attention, by which the loss may be recovered, will learn not to be too much discouraged by any present success of his Adversary, nor to despair of final good fortune upon every little Check he receives in the pursuit of it.

That we may therefore be induced more frequently to chuse this beneficial amusement, in preference to others which are not attended with the same advantages, every Circumstance that may increase the pleasure of it should be regarded; and every action or word that is unfair, disrespectful, or that in any way may give uneasiness, should be avoided, as contrary to the immediate intention of both the Players, which is to pass the Time agreably.

Therefore, first, if it is agreed to play according to the strict rules, then those rules are to be exactly observed by both parties, and should not be insisted on for one side, while deviated from by the other—for this is not equitable.

Secondly, if it is agreed not to observe the rules exactly, but one party demands indulgencies, he should then be as willing to allow them to the other.

Thirdly, no false move should ever be made to extricate yourself out of difficulty, or to gain an advantage. There can be no pleasure in playing with a person once detected in such unfair practice.

Fourthly, if your adversary is long in playing, you ought not to hurry him, or express any uneasiness at his delay. You should not sing, nor whistle, nor look at your watch, nor take up a book to read, nor make a tapping with your feet on the floor, or with your fingers on the table, nor do any thing that may disturb his attention. For all these things displease; and they do not show your skill in playing, but your craftiness or your rudeness.

Fifthly, you ought not to endeavour to amuse and deceive your adversary, by pretending to have made bad moves, and saying that you have now lost the game, in order to make him secure and careless, and inattentive to your schemes: for this is fraud and deceit, not skill in the game.

Sixthly, you must not, when you have gained a victory, use

any triumphing or insulting expression, nor show too much pleasure; but endeavour to console your adversary, and make him less dissatisfied with himself, by every kind of civil expression that may be used with truth, such as, "you understand the game better than I, but you are a little inattentive;" or, "you play too fast;" or, "you had the best of the game, but something happened to divert your thoughts, and that turned it in my favour."

Seventhly, if you are a spectator while others play, observe the most perfect silence. For, if you give advice, you offend both parties, him against whom you give it, because it may cause the loss of his game, him in whose favour you give it, because, though it be good, and he follows it, he loses the pleasure he might have had, if you had permitted him to think until it had occurred to himself. Even after a move or moves, you must not, by replacing the pieces, show how they might have been placed better; for that displeases, and may occasion disputes and doubts about their true situation. All talking to the players lessens or diverts their attention, and is therefore unpleasing. Nor should you give the least hint to either party, by any kind of noise or motion. If you do, you are unworthy to be a spectator. If you have a mind to exercise or show your judgment, do it in playing your own game, when you have an opportunity, not in criticizing, or meddling with, or counselling the play of others.

Lastly, if the game is not to be played rigorously, according to the rules above mentioned, then moderate your desire of victory over your adversary, and be pleased with one over yourself. Snatch not eagerly at every advantage offered by his unskilfulness or inattention; but point out to him kindly, that by such a move he places or leaves a piece in danger and unsupported; that by another he will put his king in a perilous situation, &c. By this generous civility (so opposite to the unfairness above forbidden) you may, indeed, happen to lose the game to your opponent; but you will win what is better, his esteem, his respect, and his affection, together with the silent approbation and good-will of impartial spectators.

TO BENJAMIN VAUGHAN

Passy, Nov. 9, 1779.

DEAR SIR,

I have received several kind Letters from you, which I have not regularly answered. They gave me however great Pleasure, as they acquainted me with your Welfare, and that of your Family and other Friends; and I hope you will continue writing to me as often as you can do it conveniently.

I thank you much for the great Care and Pains you have taken in regulating and correcting the Edition of those Papers. Your Friendship for me appears in almost every Page; and if the Preservation of any of them should prove of Use to the Publick, it is to you that the Publick will owe the Obligation. In looking them over, I have noted some Faults of Impression that hurt the Sense, and some other little Matters, which you will find all in a Sheet under the title of *Errata*. You can best judge whether it may be worth while to add any of them to the Errata already printed, or whether it may not be as well to reserve the whole for Correction in another Edition, if such should ever be. Inclos'd I send a more perfect copy of the *Chapter*.[99]

If I should ever recover the Pieces that were in the Hands of my Son, and those I left among my Papers in America, I think there may be enough to make three more such Volumes, of which a great part would be more interesting.

As to the *Time* of publishing, of which you ask my Opinion I am not furnish'd with any Reasons, or Ideas of Reasons, on which to form any Opinion. Naturally I should suppose the Bookseller to be from Experience the best Judge, and I should be for leaving it to him.

I did not write the Pamphlet you mention. I know nothing of it. I suppose it is the same, concerning which Dr. Priestley formerly asked me the same Question. That for which he took it was intitled, *A Dissertation on Liberty and Necessity, Pleasure and Pain*, with these Lines in the TitlePage.

"Whatever is, is right. But purblind Man
Sees but a part o' the Chain, the nearest Link;

> His Eye not carrying to that equal Beam,
> That poises all above."
>
> DRYDEN.

London, Printed M. D. C. C. X. X. V.

It was addressed to Mr. J. R., that is, James Ralph, then a youth of about my age, and my intimate friend; afterwards a political writer and historian. The purport of it was to prove the doctrine of fate, from the supposed attributes of God; in some such manner as this: that in erecting and governing the world, as he was infinitely wise, he knew what would be best; infinitely good, he must be disposed, and infinitely powerful, he must be able to execute it: consequently all is right. There were only an hundred copies printed, of which I gave a few to friends, and afterwards disliking the piece, as conceiving it might have an ill tendency, I burnt the rest, except one copy, the margin of which was filled with manuscript notes by Lyons, author of the Infallibility of Human Judgment, who was at that time another of my acquaintance in London. I was not nineteen years of age when it was written. In 1730, I wrote a piece on the other side of the question, which began with laying for its foundation this fact: "That almost all men in all ages and countries, have at times made use of prayer." Thence I reasoned, that if all things are ordained, prayer must among the rest be ordained. But as prayer can produce no change in things that are ordained, praying must then be useless and an absurdity. God would therefore not ordain praying if everything else was ordained. But praying exists, therefore all things are not ordained, etc. This pamphlet was never printed, and the manuscript has been long lost. The great uncertainty I found in metaphysical reasonings disgusted me, and I quitted that kind of reading and study for others more satisfactory.

I return the Manuscripts you were so obliging as to send me; I am concern'd at your having no other copys, I hope these will get safe to your hands. I do not remember the Duke de Chaulnes showing me the Letter you mention. I have received Dr. Crawford's book, but not your Abstract, which I wait for as you desire.

I send you also M. Dupont's *Table Economique*, which I think an excellent Thing, as it contains in a clear Method all the principles of that new sect, called here *les Economistes*.

Poor Henley's dying in that manner is inconceivable to me. Is any Reason given to account for it, besides insanity?

Remember me affectionately to all your good Family, and believe me, with great Esteem, my dear Friend, yours, most sincerely,

B. FRANKLIN.

THE WHISTLE[100]

TO MADAME BRILLON

Passy, November 10, 1779.

I received my dear friend's two letters, one for Wednesday and one for Saturday. This is again Wednesday. I do not deserve one for to-day, because I have not answered the former. But, indolent as I am, and averse to writing, the fear of having no more of your pleasing epistles, if I do not contribute to the correspondence, obliges me to take up my pen; and as Mr. B. has kindly sent me word, that he sets out to-morrow to see you, instead of spending this Wednesday evening as I have done its namesakes, in your delightful company, I sit down to spend it in thinking of you, in writing to you, and in reading over and over again your letters.

I am charmed with your description of Paradise, and with your plan of living there; and I approve much of your conclusion, that, in the mean time, we should draw all the good we can from this world. In my opinion, we might all draw more good from it than we do, and suffer less evil, if we would take care not to give too much for *whistles*. For to me it seems, that most of the unhappy people we meet with, are become so by neglect of that caution.

You ask what I mean? You love stories, and will excuse my telling one of myself.

When I was a child of seven years old, my friends, on a holiday, filled my pocket with coppers. I went directly to a shop where they sold toys for children; and, being charmed with the sound of a *whistle*, that I met by the way in the hands of another boy, I voluntarily offered and gave all my money for one. I then came home, and went whistling all over the house, much pleased with my *whistle*, but disturbing all the family. My brothers, and sisters, and cousins, understanding the bargain I had made, told me I had given four times as much for it as it was worth; put me in mind what good things I might have bought with the rest of the money; and laughed at me so much for my folly, that I cried with vexation; and the reflection gave me more chagrin than the *whistle* gave me pleasure.

This however was afterwards of use to me, the impression continuing on my mind; so that often, when I was tempted to buy some unnecessary thing, I said to myself, *Don't give too much for the whistle;* and I saved my money.

As I grew up, came into the world, and observed the actions of men, I thought I met with many, very many, who *gave too much for the whistle.*

When I saw one too ambitious of court favour, sacrificing his time in attendance on levees, his repose, his liberty, his virtue, and perhaps his friends, to attain it, I have said to myself, *This man gives too much for his whistle.*

When I saw another fond of popularity, constantly employing himself in political bustles, neglecting his own affairs, and ruining them by that neglect, *He pays, indeed,* said I, *too much for his whistle.*

If I knew a miser, who gave up every kind of comfortable living, all the pleasure of doing good to others, all the esteem of his fellow-citizens, and the joys of benevolent friendship, for the sake of accumulating wealth, *Poor man,* said I, *you pay too much for your whistle.*

When I met with a man of pleasure, sacrificing every laudable improvement of the mind, or of his fortune, to mere corporeal sensations, and ruining his health in their pursuit, *Mistaken man,* said I, *you are providing pain for yourself, instead of pleasure; you give too much for your whistle.*

If I see one fond of appearance, or fine clothes, fine houses, fine furniture, fine equipages, all above his fortune, for which he contracts debts, and ends his career in a prison, *Alas!* say I, *he has paid dear, very dear, for his whistle.*

When I see a beautiful, sweet-tempered girl married to an ill-natured brute of a husband, *What a pity*, say I, *that she should pay so much for a whistle!*

In short, I conceive that great part of the miseries of mankind are brought upon them by the false estimates they have made of the value of things, and by their *giving too much for their whistles.*

Yet I ought to have charity for these unhappy people, when I consider, that, with all this wisdom of which I am boasting, there are certain things in the world so tempting, for example, the apples of King John, which happily are not to be bought; for if they were put to sale by auction, I might very easily be led to ruin myself in the purchase, and find that I had once more given too much for the *whistle.*

Adieu, my dear friend, and believe me ever yours very sincerely and with unalterable affection,

B. FRANKLIN.

THE LORD'S PRAYER
[1779?]

OLD VERSION

1. Our Father which art in Heaven,
2. Hallowed be thy Name.
3. Thy Kingdom come.
4. Thy will be done on Earth as it is in Heaven.
5. Give us this Day our daily Bread.
6. Forgive us our Debts as we forgive our Debtors.
   And lead us not into Temptation, but deliver us from Evil.

NEW VERSION BY B. F.

1. Heavenly Father,
2. May all revere thee,
3. And become thy dutiful Children and faithful Subjects.

4. May thy Laws be obeyed on Earth as perfectly as they are in Heaven.
5. Provide for us this Day as thou hast hitherto daily done.
6. Forgive us our Trespasses and enable us likewise to forgive those that offend us.
7. Keep us out of Temptation, and deliver us from Evil.—

Reasons for the Change of Expression

Old Version. *Our Father which art in Heaven.*

New V.—*Heavenly Father*, is more concise, equally expressive, and better modern English.—

Old V.—*Hallowed be thy Name.* This seems to relate to an Observance among the Jews not to pronounce the proper or peculiar Name of God, they deeming it a Profanation so to do. We have in our Language no *proper Name* for God; the Word *God* being a common or general Name, expressing all chief Objects of Worship, true or false. The Word *hallowed* is almost obsolete. People now have but an imperfect Conception of the Meaning of the Petition. It is therefore proposed to change the expression into

New V.—*May all revere thee.*

Old V.—*Thy Kingdom come.* This Petition seems suited to the then Condition of the Jewish Nation. Originally their State was a Theocracy. God was their King. Dissatisfied with that kind of Government, they desired a visible earthly King in the manner of the Nations round them. They had such Kings accordingly; but their Offerings were *due* to God on many Occasions by the Jewish Law, which when People could not pay, or had forgotten as Debtors are apt to do, it was proper to pray that those Debts might be forgiven. Our Liturgy uses neither the *Debtors* of Matthew, nor the *indebted* of Luke, but instead of them speaks of *those that trespass against us.* Perhaps the Considering it as a Christian Duty to forgive Debtors, was by the Compilers thought an inconvenient Idea in a trading Nation.—There seems however something presumptuous in this Mode of Expression, which has the Air of proposing ourselves as an Example of Goodness fit for God to imitate. *We hope you will at least be as good as we are;* you see we forgive one another, and therefore we pray that you would forgive us. Some have considered it in another sense, *Forgive us as we forgive others;* i.e. If we do not forgive others we pray that thou wouldst not forgive us. But this being a kind of conditional *Imprecation* against ourselves, seems improper in such a Prayer; and therefore it may be better to say humbly & modestly

New V.—*Forgive us our Trespasses, and enable us likewise to forgive those that offend us.* This instead of assuming that we have already in & of ourselves the Grace of Forgiveness, acknowledges our Dependance on God, the Fountain of Mercy for any Share we may have in it, praying that he would communicate of it to us.—

Old V.—*And lead us not into Temptation.* The Jews had a Notion, that God sometimes tempted, or directed or permitted the Tempting of People. Thus it was said he tempted Pharaoh; directed Satan to tempt Job; and a false Prophet to tempt Ahab, &c. Under this Persuasion it was natural for them to pray that he would not put them to such severe Trials. We now suppose that Temptation, so far as it is supernatural, comes from the Devil only, and this Petition continued conveys a Suspicion which in our present Conception seems unworthy of God, therefore might be altered to

New V.—*Keep us out of Temptation.* Happiness was not increas'd by the Change, and they had reason to wish and pray for a Return of the Theocracy, or Government of God. Christians in these Times have other Ideas when they speak of the Kingdom of God, such as are perhaps more adequately express'd by

New V.—*And become thy dutiful Children & faithful Subjects.*

Old V.—*Thy Will be done on Earth as it is in Heaven.*

New V.—*May thy Laws be obeyed on Earth as perfectly as they are in Heaven.*

Old V.—*Give us this Day our daily Bread.* Give us what is *ours,* seems to put us in a Claim of Right, and to contain too little of the grateful Acknowledgment and Sense of Dependance that becomes Creatures who live on the daily Bounty of their Creator. Therefore it is changed to

New V.—*Provide for us this Day, as thou hast hitherto daily done.*

Old V.—*Forgive us our Debts as we forgive our Debtors.* Matthew.

Forgive us our Sins, for we also forgive every one that is indebted to us. Luke.

THE LEVÉE
[1779?]

In the first chapter of Job we have an account of a transaction said to have arisen in the court, or at the *levée*, of the best of all possible princes, or of governments by a single person, viz. that of God himself.

At this *levée*, in which the sons of God were assembled, Satan also appeared.

It is probable the writer of that ancient book took his idea of this *levée* from those of the eastern monarchs of the age he lived in.

It is to this day usual at the *levées* of princes, to have persons assembled who are enemies to each other, who seek to obtain favor by whispering calumny and detraction, and thereby ruining those that distinguish themselves by their virtue and merit. And kings frequently ask a familiar question or two, of every one in the circle, merely to show their benignity. These circumstances are particularly exemplified in this relation.

If a modern king, for instance, finds a person in the circle who has not lately been there, he naturally asks him how he has passed his time since he last had the pleasure of seeing him? the gentleman perhaps replies that he has been in the country to view his estates, and visit some friends. Thus Satan being asked whence he cometh? answers, "From going to and fro in the earth, and walking up and down in it." And being further asked, whether he had considered the uprightness and fidelity of the prince's servant Job, he immediately displays all the malignance of the designing courtier, by answering with another question: "Doth Job serve God for naught? Hast thou not given him immense wealth, and protected him in the possession of it? Deprive him of that, and he will curse thee to thy face." In modern phrase, Take away his places and his pensions, and your Majesty will soon find him in the opposition.

This whisper against Job had its effect. He was delivered into the power of his adversary, who deprived him of his fortune, destroyed his family, and completely ruined him.

The book of Job is called by divines a sacred poem, and, with the rest of the Holy Scriptures, is understood to be written for our instruction.

What then is the instruction to be gathered from this supposed transaction?

Trust not a single person with the government of your state. For if the Deity himself, being the monarch may for a time give way to calumny, and suffer it to operate the destruction of the best of subjects; what mischief may you not expect from such power in a mere man, though the best of men, from whom the truth is often industriously hidden, and to whom falsehood is often presented in its place, by artful, interested, and malicious courtiers?

And be cautious in trusting him even with limited powers, lest sooner or later he sap and destroy those limits, and render himself absolute.

For by the disposal of places, he attaches to himself all the placeholders, with their numerous connexions, and also all the expecters and hopers of places, which will form a strong party in promoting his views. By various political engagements for the interest of neighbouring states or princes, he procures their aid in establishing his own personal power. So that, through the hopes of emolument in one part of his subjects, and the fear of his resentment in the other, all opposition falls before him.

PROPOSED NEW VERSION OF THE BIBLE[101]

[1779?]

To the Printer of ***

Sir,

It is now more than one hundred and seventy years since the translation of our common English Bible. The language in that time is much changed, and the style, being obsolete, and thence less agreeable, is perhaps one reason why the reading of that excellent book is of late so much neglected. I have therefore thought it would be well to procure a new version, in which, preserving the sense, the turn of phrase and manner of expression should be modern. I do not pretend to have the necessary abilities for such a work myself; I throw out the hint for the consideration of the learned; and only venture to send you a few verses of the first chapter of Job, which may serve as a sample of the kind of version I would recommend.

A. B.

PART OF THE FIRST CHAPTER OF JOB MODERNIZED

Old Text	New Version
Verse 6. Now there was a day when the sons of God came to present themselves before the Lord, and Satan came also amongst them.	Verse 6. And it being *levée* day in heaven, all God's nobility came to court, to present themselves before him; and Satan also appeared in the circle, as one of the ministry.
7. And the Lord said unto Satan, Whence comest thou? Then Satan answered the Lord, and said, From going to and fro in the earth, and from walking up and down in it.	7. And God said to Satan, You have been some time absent; where were you? And Satan answered [,] I have been at my country-seat, and in different places visiting my friends.
8. And the Lord said unto Satan, Hast thou considered my servant Job, that there is	8. And God said, Well, what think you of Lord Job? You see he is my best friend,

none like him in the earth, a perfect and an upright man, one that feareth God, and escheweth evil?

9. Then Satan answered the Lord, and said, Doth Job fear God for naught?

10. Hast thou not made an hedge about his house, and about all that he hath on every side? Thou hast blessed the work of his hands, and his substance is increased in the land.

11. But put forth thine hand now, and touch all that he hath, and he will curse thee to thy face.

a perfectly honest man, full of respect for me, and avoiding every thing that might offend me.

9. And Satan answered, Does your Majesty imagine that his good conduct is the effect of mere personal attachment and affection?

10. Have you not protected him, and heaped your benefits upon him, till he is grown enormously rich?

11. Try him;—only withdraw your favor, turn him out of his places, and withhold his pensions, and you will soon find him in the opposition.

TO JOSEPH PRIESTLEY

Passy, Feb. 8, 1780.

DEAR SIR,

Your kind Letter of September 27 came to hand but very lately, the Bearer having staied long in Holland. I always rejoice to hear of your being still employ'd in experimental Researches into Nature, and of the Success you meet with. The rapid Progress *true* Science now makes, occasions my regretting sometimes that I was born so soon. It is impossible to imagine the Height to which may be carried, in a thousand years, the Power of Man over Matter. We may perhaps learn to deprive large Masses of their Gravity, and give them absolute Levity, for the sake of easy Transport. Agriculture may diminish its Labour and double its Produce; all Diseases may by sure means be prevented or cured, not excepting even that of Old Age, and our Lives lengthened at pleasure even beyond the antediluvian

Standard. O that moral Science were in as fair a way of Improvement, that Men would cease to be Wolves to one another, and that human Beings would at length learn what they now improperly call Humanity![102]

I am glad my little Paper on the *Aurora Borealis* pleased. If it should occasion further Enquiry, and so produce a better Hypothesis, it will not be wholly useless. I am ever, with the greatest and most sincere Esteem, dear Sir, yours very affectionately

B. FRANKLIN.

TO GEORGE WASHINGTON

Passy, March 5, 1780.

SIR,

I have received but lately the Letter your Excellency did me the honour of writing to me in Recommendation of the Marquis de la Fayette. His modesty detained it long in his own Hands. We became acquainted, however, from the time of his Arrival at Paris; and his Zeal for the Honour of our Country, his Activity in our Affairs here, and his firm Attachment to our Cause and to you, impress'd me with the same Regard and Esteem for him that your Excellency's Letter would have done, had it been immediately delivered to me.

Should peace arrive after another Campaign or two, and afford us a little Leisure, I should be happy to see your Excellency in Europe, and to accompany you, if my Age and Strength would permit, in visiting some of its ancient and most famous Kingdoms. You would, on this side of the Sea, enjoy the great Reputation you have acquir'd, pure and free from those little Shades that the Jealousy and Envy of a Man's Countrymen and Cotemporaries are ever endeavouring to cast over living Merit. Here you would know, and enjoy, what Posterity will say of Washington. For 1000 Leagues have nearly the same Effect with 1000 Years. The feeble Voice of those grovelling Passions cannot extend so far either in Time or Distance. At present I enjoy that Pleasure for you, as I frequently hear the old Generals of this martial Country, (who study the Maps of America, and mark upon them all your Operations,) speak with sincere Approbation and great Applause of your conduct; and join in giving you the Character of one of the greatest Captains of the Age.

I must soon quit the Scene, but you may live to see our Country flourish, as it will amazingly and rapidly after the War is over. Like a Field of young Indian Corn, which long Fair weather and Sunshine had enfeebled and discolored, and which in that weak State, by a Thunder Gust, of violent Wind, Hail, and Rain, seem'd to be threaten'd with absolute Destruction; yet the Storm being past, it recovers fresh Verdure, shoots up with double Vigour, and delights the Eye, not of its Owner only, but of every observing Traveller.[103]

The best Wishes that can be form'd for your Health, Honour, and Happiness, ever attend you from your Excellency's most obedient and most humble servant

                                                    B. F.

TO MISS GEORGIANA SHIPLEY

                                          Passy, Oct. 8, 1780.

It is long, very long, my dear Friend, since I had the great Pleasure of hearing from you, and receiving any of your very pleasing Letters. But it is my fault. I have long omitted my Part of the Correspondence. Those who love to receive Letters should write Letters. I wish I could safely promise an Amendment of that Fault. But, besides the Indolence attending Age, and growing upon us with it, my Time is engross'd by too much Business; and I have too many Inducements to postpone doing, what I feel I ought to do for my own Sake, and what I can never resolve to omit entirely.

Your Translations from Horace, as far as I can judge of Poetry and Translations, are very good. That of the *Quò, quò ruitis?* is so suitable to the Times, that the Conclusion, (in your Version,) seems to threaten like a Prophecy; and methinks there is at least some Appearance of Danger that it may be fulfilled. I am unhappily an Enemy, yet I think there has been enough of

Blood spilt, and I wish what is left in the Veins of that once lov'd People, may be spared by a Peace solid and everlasting.

It is a great while since I have heard any thing of the *good Bishop*. Strange, that so simple a Character should sufficiently distinguish one of that sacred Body! *Donnez-moi de ses Nouvelles*. I have been some time flatter'd with the Expectation of seeing the Countenance of that most honoured and ever beloved Friend, delineated by your Pencil. The Portrait is said to have been long on the way, but is not yet arriv'd; nor can I hear where it is.

Indolent as I have confess'd myself to be, I could not, you see, miss this good and safe Opportunity of sending you a few Lines, with my best Wishes for your Happiness, and that of the whole dear and amiable Family in whose sweet Society I have spent so many happy Hours. Mr. Jones[104] tells me, he shall have a Pleasure in being the Bearer of my Letter, of which I make no doubt. I learn from him, that to your Drawing, and Music, and Painting, and Poetry, and Latin, you have added a Proficiency in Chess; so that you are, as the French say, *tout plein de talens*. May they and you fall to the Lot of one, that shall duly value them, and love you as much as I do. Adieu.

B. F[RANKLIN].

TO RICHARD PRICE

Passy, Oct. 9, 1780.

DEAR SIR,

Besides the Pleasure of their Company, I had the great Satisfaction of hearing by your two valuable Friends, and learning from your Letter, that you enjoy a good State of Health. May God continue it, as well for the Good of Mankind as for your Comfort. I thank you much for the second Edition of your excellent Pamphlet.[105] I forwarded that you sent to Mr. Dana, he being in Holland. I wish also to see the Piece you have written (as Mr. Jones tells me) on Toleration. I do not expect that your new Parliament will be either wiser or honester than the last. All Projects to procure an honest one, by Place Bills, &c.; appear to me vain and Impracticable. The true Cure, I imagine, is to be found only in rendring all Places unprofitable, and the King too poor to give Bribes and Pensions. Till this is done, which can only be by a Revolution (and I think you have not Virtue enough left to procure one), your Nation will always be plundered, and obliged to pay by Taxes the Plunderers for Plundering and Ruining. Liberty and Virtue therefore join in the call, COME OUT OF HER, MY PEOPLE!

I am fully of your Opinion respecting religious Tests; but, tho' the People of Massachusetts have not in their new Constitution kept quite clear of them, yet, if we consider what that People were 100 Years ago, we must allow they have gone great Lengths in Liberality of Sentiment on religious Subjects; and we may hope for greater Degrees of Perfection, when their Constitution, some years hence, shall be revised. If Christian Preachers had continued to teach as Christ and his Apostles did, without Salaries, and as the Quakers now do, I imagine Tests would never have existed; for I think they were invented, not so much to secure Religion itself, as the Emoluments of it. When a Religion is good, I conceive that it will support itself; and, when it cannot support itself, and God does not take care to support, so that its Professors are oblig'd to call for the help of the Civil Power, it is a sign, I apprehend, of its being a bad one. But I shall be out of my Depth, if I wade any deeper in Theology, and I will not trouble you with Politicks, nor with News which are almost as uncertain; but conclude with a heartfelt Wish to embrace you once more, and enjoy your sweet Society in Peace, among our honest, worthy, ingenious Friends at the *London*.[106] Adieu,

                                                              B. FRANKLIN.

DIALOGUE BETWEEN FRANKLIN AND THE GOUT

Midnight, October 22, 1780.

FRANKLIN. Eh! Oh! Eh! What have I done to merit these cruel sufferings?

GOUT. Many things; you have ate and drank too freely, and too much indulged those legs of yours in their indolence.

FRANKLIN. Who is it that accuses me?

GOUT. It is I, even I, the Gout.

FRANKLIN. What! my enemy in person?

GOUT. No, not your enemy.

FRANKLIN. I repeat it; my enemy; for you would not only torment my body to death, but ruin my good name; you reproach me as a glutton and a tippler; now all the world, that knows me, will allow that I am neither the one nor the other.

GOUT. The world may think as it pleases; it is always very complaisant to itself, and sometimes to its friends; but I very well know that the quantity of meat and drink proper for a man, who takes a reasonable degree of exercise, would be too much for another, who never takes any.

FRANKLIN. I take—Eh! Oh!—as much exercise—Eh!—as I can, Madam Gout. You know my sedentary state, and on that account, it would seem, Madam Gout, as if you might spare me a little, seeing it is not altogether my own fault.

GOUT. Not a jot; your rhetoric and your politeness are thrown away; your apology avails nothing. If your situation in life is a sedentary one, your amusements, your recreations, at least, should be active. You ought to walk or ride; or, if the weather prevents that play at billiards. But let us examine your course of life. While the mornings are long, and you have leisure to go abroad, what do you do? Why, instead of gaining an appetite for breakfast, by salutary exercise, you amuse yourself, with books, pamphlets, or newspapers, which commonly are not worth the reading. Yet you eat an inordinate breakfast, four dishes of tea, with cream, and one or two buttered toasts, with slices of hung beef, which I fancy are not things the most easily digested. Immediately afterward you sit down to write at your desk, or converse with persons who apply to you on business. Thus the time passes till one, without any kind of bodily exercise. But all this I could pardon, in regard, as you say, to your sedentary condition. But what is your practice after dinner? Walking in the beautiful gardens of those friends, with whom you have dined, would be the choice of men of sense; yours is to be fixed down to chess, where you are found engaged for two

or three hours! This is your perpetual recreation, which is the
least eligible of any for a sedentary man, because, instead of
accelerating the motion of the fluids, the rigid attention it requires helps to retard the circulation and obstruct internal secretions. Wrapt in the speculations of this wretched game, you
destroy your constitution. What can be expected from such a
course of living, but a body replete with stagnant humours,
ready to fall a prey to all kinds of dangerous maladies, if I, the
Gout, did not occasionally bring you relief by agitating those
humours, and so purifying or dissipating them? If it was in
some nook or alley in Paris, deprived of walks, that you played
awhile at chess after dinner, this might be excusable; but the
same taste prevails with you in Passy, Auteuil, Montmartre, or
Sanoy, places where there are the finest gardens and walks, a
pure air, beautiful women, and most agreeable and instructive
conversation; all which you might enjoy by frequenting the
walks. But these are rejected for this abominable game of chess.
Fie, then Mr. Franklin! But amidst my instructions, I had almost forgot to administer my wholesome corrections; so take
that twinge,—and that.

FRANKLIN. Oh! Eh! Oh! Ohhh! As much instruction as you
please, Madam Gout, and as many reproaches; but pray, Madam,
a truce with your corrections!

GOUT. No, Sir, no,—I will not abate a particle of what is so
much for your good,—therefore—

FRANKLIN. Oh! Ehhh!—It is not fair to say I take no exercise, when I do very often, going out to dine and returning in
my carriage.

GOUT. That, of all imaginable exercises, is the most slight and
insignificant, if you allude to the motion of a carriage suspended
on springs. By observing the degree of heat obtained by different kinds of motion, we may form an estimate of the quantity
of exercise given by each. Thus, for example, if you turn out to
walk in winter with cold feet, in an hour's time you will be in a
glow all over; ride on horseback, the same effect will scarcely be
perceived by four hours' round trotting; but if you loll in a carriage, such as you have mentioned, you may travel all day, and

gladly enter the last inn to warm your feet by a fire. Flatter yourself then no longer, that half an hour's airing in your carriage deserves the name of exercise. Providence has appointed few to roll in carriages, while he has given to all a pair of legs, which are machines infinitely more commodious and serviceable. Be grateful, then, and make a proper use of yours. Would you know how they forward the circulation of your fluids, in the very action of transporting you from place to place; observe when you walk, that all your weight is alternately thrown from one leg to the other; this occasions a great pressure on the vessels of the foot, and repels their contents; when relieved, by the weight being thrown on the other foot, the vessels of the first are allowed to replenish, and, by a return of this weight, this repulsion again succeeds; thus accelerating the circulation of the blood. The heat produced in any given time, depends on the degree of this acceleration; the fluids are shaken, the humours attenuated, the secretions facilitated, and all goes well; the cheeks are ruddy, and health is established. Behold your fair friend at Auteuil;[107] a lady who received from bounteous nature more really useful science, than half a dozen such pretenders to philosophy as you have been able to extract from all your books. When she honours you with a visit, it is on foot. She walks all hours of the day, and leaves indolence, and its concomitant maladies, to be endured by her horses. In this see at once the preservative of her health and personal charms. But when you go to Auteuil, you must have your carriage, though it is no further from Passy to Auteuil than from Auteuil to Passy.

FRANKLIN. Your reasonings grow very tiresome.

GOUT. I stand corrected. I will be silent and continue my office; take that, and that.

FRANKLIN. Oh! Ohh! Talk on, I pray you!

GOUT. No, no; I have a good number of twinges for you to-night, and you may be sure of some more to-morrow.

FRANKLIN. What, with such a fever! I shall go distracted. Oh! Eh! Can no one bear it for me?

GOUT. Ask that of your horses; they have served you faithfully.

FRANKLIN. How can you so cruelly sport with my torments?

GOUT. Sport! I am very serious. I have here a list of offences against your own health distinctly written, and can justify every stroke inflicted on you.

FRANKLIN. Read it then.

GOUT. It is too long a detail; but I will briefly mention some particulars.

FRANKLIN. Proceed. I am all attention.

GOUT. Do you remember how often you have promised yourself, the following morning, a walk in the grove of Boulogne, in the garden de la Muette, or in your own garden, and have violated your promise, alleging, at one time, it was too cold, at another too warm, too windy, too moist, or what else you pleased; when in truth it was too nothing, but your insuperable love of ease?

FRANKLIN. That I confess may have happened occasionally, probably ten times in a year.

GOUT. Your confession is very far short of the truth; the gross amount is one hundred and ninety-nine times.

FRANKLIN. Is it possible?

GOUT. So possible, that it is fact; you may rely on the accuracy of my statement. You know M. Brillon's gardens, and what fine walks they contain; you know the handsome flight of an hundred steps, which lead from the terrace above to the lawn below. You have been in the practice of visiting this amiable family twice a week, after dinner, and it is a maxim of your own, that "a man may take as much exercise in walking a mile, up and down stairs, as in ten on level ground." What an opportunity was here for you to have had exercise in both these ways! Did you embrace it, and how often?

FRANKLIN. I cannot immediately answer that question.

GOUT. I will do it for you; not once.

FRANKLIN. Not once?

GOUT. Even so. During the summer you went there at six o'clock. You found the charming lady, with her lovely children and friends, eager to walk with you, and entertain you with their agreeable conversation; and what has been your choice? Why to sit on the terrace, satisfying yourself with the fine prospect, and passing your eye over the beauties of the garden below, without taking one step to descend and walk about in them. On the contrary, you call for tea and the chess-board; and lo! you are occupied in your seat till nine o'clock, and that besides two hours' play after dinner; and then, instead of walking home, which would have bestirred you a little, you step into your carriage. How absurd to suppose that all this carelessness can be reconcilable with health, without my interposition!

FRANKLIN. I am convinced now of the justness of poor Richard's remark, that "Our debts and our sins are always greater than we think for."

GOUT. So it is. You philosophers are sages in your maxims, and fools in your conduct.

FRANKLIN. But do you charge among my crimes, that I return in a carriage from Mr. Brillon's?

GOUT. Certainly; for, having been seated all the while, you cannot object the fatigue of the day, and cannot want therefore the relief of a carriage.

FRANKLIN. What then would you have me do with my carriage?

GOUT. Burn it if you choose; you would at least get heat out of it once in this way; or, if you dislike that proposal, here's another for you; observe the poor peasants, who work in the vineyards and grounds about the villages of Passy, Auteuil, Chaillot, &c.; you may find every day, among these deserving creatures, four or five old men and women, bent and perhaps crippled by weight of years, and too long and too great labour. After a most fatiguing day, these people have to trudge a mile or two to their smoky huts. Order your coachman to set them down. This is an act that will be good for your soul; and, at the same time, after your visit to the Brillons, if you return on foot, that will be good for your body.

FRANKLIN. Ah! how tiresome you are!

GOUT. Well, then, to my office; it should not be forgotten that I am your physician. There.

FRANKLIN. Ohhh! what a devil of a physician!

GOUT. How ungrateful you are to say so! Is it not I who, in the character of your physician, have saved you from the palsy, dropsy, and apoplexy? one or other of which would have done for you long ago, but for me.

FRANKLIN. I submit, and thank you for the past, but entreat the discontinuance of your visits for the future; for, in my mind, one had better die than be cured so dolefully. Permit me just to hint, that I have also not been unfriendly to *you*. I never feed physician or quack of any kind, to enter the list against you; if then you do not leave me to my repose, it may be said you are ungrateful too.

GOUT. I can scarcely acknowledge that as any objection. As to quacks, I despise them; they may kill you indeed, but cannot injure me. And, as to regular physicians, they are at last convinced that the gout, in such a subject as you are, is no disease, but a remedy; and wherefore cure a remedy?—but to our business,—there.

FRANKLIN. Oh! oh!—for Heaven's sake leave me! and I promise faithfully never more to play at chess, but to take exercise daily, and live temperately.

GOUT. I know you too well. You promise fair; but, after a few months of good health, you will return to your old habits; your fine promises will be forgotten like the forms of last year's clouds. Let us then finish the account, and I will go. But I leave you with an assurance of visiting you again at a proper time and place; for my object is your good, and you are sensible now that I am your *real friend*.

THE HANDSOME AND DEFORMED LEG [108]

[1780?]

There are two Sorts of People in the World, who with equal Degrees of Health, & Wealth, and the other Comforts of Life, become, the one happy, and the other miserable. This arises very much from the different Views in which they consider Things, Persons, and Events; and the Effect of those different Views upon their own Minds.

In whatever Situation Men can be plac'd, they may find Conveniencies & Inconveniencies: In whatever Company; they may find Persons & Conversation more or less pleasing. At whatever Table, they may meet with Meats & Drinks of better and worse Taste, Dishes better & worse dress'd: In whatever Climate they will find good and bad Weather: Under whatever Government, they may find good & bad Laws, and good & bad Administration of those Laws. In every Poem or Work of Genius they may see Faults and Beauties. In almost every Face & every Person, they may discover fine Features & Defects, good & bad Qualities.

Under these Circumstances, the two Sorts of People above mention'd fix their Attention, those who are to be happy, on the Conveniencies of Things, the pleasant Parts of Conversation, the well-dress'd Dishes, the Goodness of the Wines, the fine Weather; &c., and enjoy all with Chearfulness. Those who are to be unhappy, think & speak only of the contraries. Hence they are continually discontented themselves, and by their Remarks sour the Pleasures of Society, offend personally many People, and make themselves everywhere disagreable. If this Turn of Mind was founded in Nature, such unhappy Persons would be the more to be pitied. But as the Disposition to criticise, & be disgusted, is perhaps taken up originally by Imitation, and is unawares grown into a Habit, which tho' at present strong may nevertheless be cured when those who have it are convinc'd of its bad Effects on their Felicity; I hope this little Admonition may be of Service to them, and put them on changing a Habit, which tho' in the Exercise it is chiefly an Act of Imagination yet has serious Consequences in Life, as it brings on real Griefs and Misfortunes. For as many are offended by, & nobody well loves this Sort of People, no one shows them more than the most common [civility and respect, and scarcely that; and this frequently puts them out of humour, and draws them into disputes and contentions. If they aim at obtaining some advantage in rank or fortune, nobody wishes them success, or will stir a step, or speak a word, to favour their pretensions. If they incur public censure or disgrace, no one will defend or excuse, and many join to

aggravate their misconduct, and render them completely odious.
If these people will not change this bad habit, and condescend to
be pleased with what is pleasing, without fretting themselves
and others about the contraries, it is good for others to avoid an
acquaintance with them; which is always disagreeable, and sometimes very inconvenient, especially when one finds one's self
entangled in their quarrels.

An old philosophical friend of mine was grown, from experience, very cautious in this particular, and carefully avoided any
intimacy with such people. He had, like other philosophers, a
thermometer to show him the heat of the weather, and a barometer to mark when it was likely to prove good or bad; but,
there being no instrument invented to discover, at first sight, this
unpleasing disposition in a person, he for that purpose made use
of his legs; one of which was remarkably handsome, the other,
by some accident, crooked and] deformed. If a Stranger, at the
first interview, regarded his ugly Leg more than his handsome
one, he doubted him. If he spoke of it, & took no notice of the
handsome Leg, that was sufficient to determine my Philosopher
to have no further Acquaintance with him. Every body has not
this two-legged Instrument, but every one with a little Attention, may observe Signs of that carping, fault-finding Disposition, & take the same Resolution of avoiding the Acquaintance
of those infected with it. I therefore advise those critical, queru-
lous, discontented, unhappy People, that if they wish to be respected and belov'd by others, & happy in themselves they
should *leave off looking at the ugly Leg*.

TO MISS GEORGIANA SHIPLEY [109]

... Must now be next its End, as I have compleated my 75th
Year I could wish to see my dear Friends of your Family once
more before I withdraw, but I see no Prospect of enjoying
that Felicity. Let me at least have that of hearing from you a
little oftener.

I do not understand the Coldness you mention of the Nights
in the Desert. I never before heard of such an Observation. If

you have learnt what was the Degree of cold and how it was observed, and what Difference between the Night and the Day, you will oblige me by communicating it. I like to see that you retain a Taste for Philosophical Enquiries.

I rec^d also your very kind Letter by Mad^e —— [*illegible in MS*], with whom and the Princess, her Mother, I am much pleased; tho' I have not seen them so often as I wished, living as I do out of Paris.

I am glad to hear that you all pass'd the summer so agreably in Wales, and I felicitate you as the French say, on the Increase of your Brother's Family.

Accept my Thanks for your Friendly Verses and good Wishes. How many Talents you possess! Painting, Poetry, Languages, etc., etc. All valuable, but your good Heart is worth the whole.

Your mention of the Summer House brings fresh to my mind all the Pleasures I enjoyed in the sweet Retreat at Twyford: the Hours of agreable and instructive Conversation with the amiable Family at Table; with its Father alone; the delightful Walks in the Gardens and neighbouring Grounds. Pleasures past and gone forever! Since I have had your Father's Picture I am grown more covetous of the rest; every time I look at your second Drawing I have regretted that you have not given to your Juno the Face of Anna Maria, to Venus that of Emily or Betsey, and to Cupid that of Emily's Child, as it would have cost you but little more Trouble. I must, however, beg that you will make me up a compleat Set of your little Profiles, which are more easily done. You formerly obliged me with that of the Father, an excellent one. Let me also have that of the good Mother, and of all the Children. It will help me to fancy myself among you, and to enjoy more perfectly in Idea, the Pleasure of your Society. My little Fellow-Traveller, the sprightly Hetty, with whose sensible Prattle I was so much entertained, why does she not write to me? If Paris affords any thing that any of you wish to have, mention it. You will oblige me. It affords everything but *Peace!* Ah! when shall we again enjoy that Blessing!

Next to seeing our Friends is the Pleasure of hearing from them, and learning how they live. Your Accounts of your Journies and how you pass your Summers please me much. I flatter myself you will like to know something of the same kind relating to me. I inhabit, a clean, well-built Village situate on a Hill, in a fine Air, with a beautiful Prospect, about 2 Miles [*Incomplete.*]

TO DAVID HARTLEY

Passy, December 15, 1781.

MY DEAR FRIEND,

I received your favour of September 26th,[110] containing your very judicious proposition of securing the spectators in the opera and play houses from the danger of fire. I communicated it where I thought it might be useful. You will see by the enclosed, that the subject has been under consideration here. Your concern for the security of life, even the lives of your enemies, does honour to your heart and your humanity. But what are the lives of a few idle haunters of play houses, compared with the many thousands of worthy men, and honest industrious families, butchered and destroyed by this devilish war? Oh that we could find some happy invention to stop the spreading of the flames, and put an end to so horrid a conflagration! Adieu, I am ever yours most affectionately,

B. FRANKLIN.

SUPPLEMENT TO THE BOSTON
INDEPENDENT CHRONICLE[111]

Numb. 705

Boston, March 12, 1782.

Extract of a Letter from Captain Gerrish, of the New England Militia, dated Albany, March 7.

The Peltry taken in the Expedition [see the Account of the Expedition to Oswegatchie, on the River St. Laurence, in our Paper of the 1st Instant,] will, as you see, amount to a good deal of Money. The Possession of this Booty at first gave us

Pleasure; but we were struck with Horror to find among the Packages 8 large ones, containing SCALPS of our unhappy Country-folks, taken in the three last Years by the Senneka Indians from the Inhabitants of the Frontiers of New York, New Jersey, Pennsylvania, and Virginia, and sent by them as a Present to Col. Haldimand, governor of Canada, in order to be by him transmitted to England. They were accompanied by the following curious Letter to that Gentleman.

"Teoga, Jan. 3d, 1782.

"May it please your Excellency,

"At the Request of the Senneka chiefs, I send herewith to your Excellency, under the Care of James Boyd, eight Packs of Scalps, cured, dried, hooped, and painted, with all the Indian triumphal Marks, of which the following is Invoice and Explanation.

"No. 1. Containing 43 Scalps of Congress Soldiers, killed in different Skirmishes; these are Stretched on black Hoops, 4 Inches diameter; the Inside of the Skin painted red, with a small black Spot to note their being killed with Bullets. Also 62 of Farmers killed in their Houses; the Hoops red; the Skin painted brown, and marked with a Hoe; a black Circle all round, to denote their being surprised in the Night; and a black Hatchet in the Middle, signifying their being killed with that Weapon.

"No. 2. Containing 98 of Farmers killed in their Houses; Hoops red; Figure of a Hoe, to mark their Profession; great white Circle and Sun, to show they were surprised in the Daytime; a little red Foot, to show they stood upon their Defence, and died fighting for their Lives and Families.

"No. 3. Containing 97 of Farmers; Hoops green, to shew they were killed in their Fields; a large white Circle with a little round Mark on it for the Sun, to shew that it was in the Daytime; black Bullet-mark on some, Hatchet on others.

"No. 4. Containing 102 of Farmers, mixed of the several Marks above; only 18 marked with a little yellow Flame, to denote their being of Prisoners burnt alive, after being scalped, their Nails pulled out by the Roots, and other Torments; one of these latter supposed to be a rebel Clergyman, his Band being fixed to the Hoop of his Scalp. Most of the Farmers appear by the Hair to have been young or middle-aged Men; there being but 67 very grey Heads among them all; which makes the Service more essential.

"No. 5. Containing 88 Scalps of Women; hair long, braided in the Indian Fashion, to shew they were Mothers; Hoops blue; Skin yellow Ground, with little red Tadpoles, to represent, by way of Triumph, the Tears of Grief occasioned to their Relations; a black scalping-Knife or Hatchet at the Bottom, to mark their being killed with those Instruments. 17 others, Hair very grey; black Hoops; plain brown Colour; no Mark, but the short Club or *Casse-tête*, to shew they were knocked down dead, or had their Brains beat out.

"No. 6. Containing 193 Boys' Scalps, of various Ages; small green Hoops; whitish Ground on the Skin, with red Tears in the Middle, and black Bullet-marks, Knife, Hatchet, or Club, as their Deaths happened.

"No. 7. 211 Girls' Scalps, big and little; small yellow Hoops; white Ground, Tears; Hatchet, Club, scalping-Knife, &c.

"No. 8. This Package is a Mixture of all the Varieties above-mentioned; to the number of 122; with a Box of Birch Bark, containing 29 little Infants' Scalps of various Sizes; small white Hoops; white Ground; no Tears; and only a little black Knife in the Middle, to shew they were ript out of their Mothers' Bellies.

"With these Packs, the Chiefs send to your Excellency the following Speech, delivered by Conejogatchie in Council, interpreted by the elder Moore, the Trader, and taken down by me in Writing.

Father,

We send you herewith many Scalps, that you may see we are not idle Friends.

A blue Belt.

Father,

We wish you to send these Scalps over the Water to the great

King, that he may regard them and be refreshed; and that he may see our faithfulness in destroying his Enemies, and be convinced that his Presents have not been made to ungrateful people.

A blue and white Belt with red Tassels.

Father,

Attend to what I am now going to say; it is a Matter of much Weight. The great King's Enemies are many, and they grow fast in Number. They were formerly like young Panthers; they could neither bite nor scratch; we could play with them safely; we feared nothing they could do to us. But now their Bodies are become big as the Elk, and strong as the Buffalo; they have also got great and sharp Claws. They have driven us out of our Country for taking part in your Quarrel. We expect the great King will give us another Country, that our Children may live after us, and be his Friends and Children, as we are. Say this for us to the great King. To enforce it, we give this Belt.

A great white Belt with blue Tassels.

Father,

We have only to say farther, that your Traders exact more than ever for their Goods; and our hunting is lessened by the War, so that we have fewer Skins to give for them. This ruins us. Think of some Remedy. We are poor; and you have Plenty of every Thing. We know you will send us Powder and Guns, and Knives and Hatchets; but we also want Shirts and Blankets.

A little white Belt.

"I do not doubt but that your Excellency will think it proper to give some farther Encouragement to those honest People. The high Prices they complain of are the necessary Effect of the War. Whatever Presents may be sent for them, through my Hands, shall be distributed with Prudence and Fidelity. I have the Honour of being your Excellency's most obedient

"And most humble Servant,

JAMES CRAUFURD."

It was at first proposed to bury these Scalps; but Lieutenant Fitzgerald, who, you know, has got Leave of Absence to go to Ireland on his private Affairs, said he thought it better they should proceed to their Destination; and if they were given to him, he would undertake to carry them to England, and hang them all up in some dark Night on the Trees in St. James's Park, where they could be seen from the King and Queen's Palaces in the Morning; for that the Sight of them might perhaps strike Muley Ishmael (as he called him) with some Compunction of Conscience. They were accordingly delivered to Fitz, and he has brought them safe hither. To-morrow they go with his Baggage in a Waggon for Boston, and will probably be there in a few Days after this Letter.

I am, &c.

SAMUEL GERRISH.

Boston, March 20.

Monday last arrived here Lieutenant Fitzgerald above mentioned, and Yesterday the Waggon with the Scalps. Thousands of People are flocking to see them this Morning, and all Mouths are full of Execrations. Fixing them to the Trees is not approved. It is now proposed to make them up in decent little Packets, seal and direct them; one to the King, containing a Sample of every Sort for his Museum; one to the Queen, with some of Women and little Children; the Rest to be distributed among both Houses of Parliament; a double Quantity to the Bishops.

[The following part appeared in a second edition from which certain advertisements which had been published in the first edition were omitted.]

MR. WILLIS,

Please to insert in your useful Paper the following Copy of a Letter from Commodore Jones, directed

TO SIR JOSEPH YORK, AMBASSADOR FROM THE KING OF ENGLAND
TO THE STATES-GENERAL OF THE UNITED PROVINCES

"Ipswich, New England, March 7, 1781.

"SIR,

"I have lately seen a memorial, said to have been presented by your Excellency to their High Mightinesses the States-general, in which you are pleased to qualify me with the title of *pirate*.

"A pirate is defined to be *hostis humani generis* [an enemy to all mankind]. It happens, Sir, that I am an enemy to no part of mankind, except your nation, the English; which nation at the same time comes much more within the definition, being actually an enemy to, and at war with, one whole quarter of the world, America, considerable part of Asia and Africa, a great part of Europe, and in a fair way of being at war with the rest.

"A pirate makes war for the sake of *rapine*. This is not the kind of war I am engaged in against England. Ours is a war in defence of *liberty* . . . the most just of all wars; and of our *properties*, which your nation would have taken from us, without our consent, in violation of our rights, and by an armed force. Yours, therefore is a war of *rapine;* of course, a piratical war; and those who approve of it, and are engaged in it, more justly deserve the name of *pirates*, which you bestow on me. It is, indeed, a war that coincides with the general spirit of your nation. Your common people in their ale-houses sing the twenty-four songs of Robin Hood, and applaud his deer-stealing and his robberies on the highway: those, who have just learning enough to read, are delighted with your histories of the pirates and of the buccaniers; and even your scholars in the universities study Quintus Curtius, and are taught to admire Alexander for what they call 'his conquests in the Indies.' Severe laws and the hangmen keep down the effects of this spirit somewhat among yourselves (though in your little Island you have nevertheless more highway robberies than there are in all the rest of Europe put together); but a foreign war gives it full scope. It is then that, with infinite pleasure, it lets itself loose to strip of their property honest merchants, employed in the innocent and useful occupation of supplying the mutual wants of mankind. Hence, having lately no war with your ancient enemies, rather than be without a war, you chose to make one upon your friends. In this your piratical war with America, the mariners of your fleets and the owners of your privateers were animated against us by the act of your Parliament, which repealed the law of God, 'Thou shalt not steal,' by declaring it lawful for them to rob us of all our property that they could meet with on the ocean. This act, too, had a retrospect, and, going beyond bulls of pardon, declared that all the robberies you *had committed* previous to the act should be *deemed just and lawful.* Your soldiers, too, were promised the plunder of our cities; and your officers were flattered with the division of our lands. You had even the baseness to corrupt our servants, the sailors employed by us, and encourage them to rob their masters and bring to you the ships and goods they were entrusted with. Is there any society of pirates on the sea or land, who, in declaring wrong to be right, and right wrong, have less authority than your parliament? Do any of them more justly than your parliament deserve the *title* you bestow on me?

"You will tell me that we forfeited all our estates by our refusal to pay the taxes your nation would have imposed on us without the consent of our colony parliaments. Have you then forgotten the incontestable principle, which was the foundation of Hambden's glorious lawsuit with Charles the first, that 'what an English king has no right to demand, an English subject has a right to refuse'? But you cannot so soon have forgotten the instructions of your late honorable father, who, being himself a sound Whig, taught you certainly the principles of the Revolution, and that, 'if subjects might in some cases forfeit their property, kings also might forfeit their title, and all claim to the allegiance of their subjects.' I must then suppose you well acquainted with those Whig principles; on which permit me, Sir, to ask a few questions.

"Is not protection as justly due from a king to his people, as obedience from the people to their king?

"If then a king declares his people to be out of his protection:

"If he violates and deprives them of their constitutional rights:

"If he wages war against them:

"If he plunders their merchants, ravages their coasts, burns their towns, and destroys their lives:

"If he hires foreign mercenaries to help him in their destruction:

"If he engages savages to murder their defenceless farmers, women, and children:

"If he cruelly forces such of his subjects as fall into his hands, to bear arms against their country, and become executioners of their friends and brethren:

"If he sells others of them into bondage, in Africa and the East Indies:

"If he excites domestic insurrections among their servants, and encourages servants to murder their masters:—

"Does not so atrocious a conduct towards his subjects dissolve their allegiance?

"If not, please to say how or by what means it can possibly be dissolved?

"All this horrible wickedness and barbarity has been and daily is practised by the King, *your master*, (as you call him in your memorial,) upon the Americans, whom he is still pleased to claim as his subjects.

"During these six years past, he has destroyed not less than forty thousand of those subjects, by battles on land or sea, or by starving them, or poisoning them to death, in the unwholesome air, with the unwholesome food of his prisons. And he has wasted the lives of at least an equal number of his own soldiers and sailors: many of whom have been *forced* into this odious service, and *dragged* from their families and friends, by the outrageous violence of his illegal press-gangs. You are a gentleman of letters, and have read history: do you recollect any instance of any tyrant, since the beginning of the world, who, in the course of so few years, had done so much mischief, by murdering so many of his own people? Let us view one of the worst and blackest of them, Nero. He put to death a few of his courtiers, placemen, and pensioners, and among the rest his *tutor*. Had George the Third done the same, and no more, his crime, though detestable, as an act of lawless power, might have been as useful to his nation, as that of Nero was hurtful to Rome; considering the different characters and merits of the sufferers. Nero indeed wished that the people of Rome had but one neck, that he might behead them all by one stroke; but this was a simple wish. George is carrying the wish as fast as he can into execution; and, by continuing in his present course a few years longer, will have destroyed more of the British people than Nero could have found inhabitants in Rome. Hence the expression of Milton, in speaking of Charles the First, that he was '*Nerone Neronior*,' is still more applicable to George the third. Like Nero, and all other tyrants, while they lived, he indeed has his flatterers, his addressers, his applauders. Pensions, places, and hopes of preferment can bribe even bishops to approve his conduct: but when those fulsome, purchased addresses and panegyrics are sunk and lost in oblivion or contempt, impartial history will step forth, speak honest truth, and rank him among public calamities. The only difference will be, that plagues, pestilences, and famines are of this world, and arise from the nature of things; but voluntary malice, mischief, and murder, are from hell; and this King will, therefore, stand foremost in the list of diabolical, bloody, and execrable tyrants. His base-bought parliaments too, who sell him their souls, and extort from the people the money with which they aid his destructive purposes, as they share his guilt, will share his infamy,—parliaments, who, to please him, have repeatedly, by different votes year after year, dipped their hands in human blood, insomuch that methinks I see it dried and caked so thick upon them, that, if they could wash it off in the Thames, which flows under their windows, the whole river would run red to the ocean.

"One is provoked by enormous wickedness: but one is ashamed and humiliated at the view of human baseness. It afflicts me, therefore, to see a gentleman of Sir Joseph York's education and talents, for the sake of a red riband and a paltry stipend, mean enough to style such a monster *his master,* wear his livery, and hold himself ready at his command even to cut the throats of fellow subjects. This makes it impossible for me to end my letter with the civility of a compliment, and obliges me to subscribe myself simply,

"JOHN PAUL JONES,

"Whom you are pleased to style a *pirate.*"

TO JOHN THORNTON

Passy, May 8, 1782.

SIR,

I received the letter you did me the honour of writing to me, and am much obliged by your kind present of a book. The relish for reading of poetry had long since left me, but there is something so new in the manner, so easy, and yet so correct in the language, so clear in the expression, yet concise, and so just in the sentiments, that I have read the whole with great pleasure, and some of the pieces more than once. I beg you to accept my thankful acknowledgments, and to present my respects to the author.[112]

I shall take care to forward the letters to America, and shall be glad of any other opportunity of doing what may be agreeable to you, being with great respect for your character,— Your most obedient humble servant,

B. FRANKLIN.

TO JOSEPH PRIESTLEY

Passy near Paris, June 7, 1782.

DEAR SIR,

I received your kind Letter of the 7th of April, also one of the 3d of May. I have always great Pleasure in hearing from you, in learning that you are well, and that you continue your Experiments. I should rejoice much, if I could once more recover the Leisure to search with you into the Works of Nature; I mean the *inanimate*, not the *animate* or moral part of them, the more I discover'd of the former, the more I admir'd them; the more I know of the latter, the more I am disgusted with them. Men I find to be a Sort of Beings very badly constructed, as they are generally more easily provok'd than reconcil'd, more disposed to do Mischief to each other than to make Reparation, much more easily deceiv'd than undeceiv'd, and having more Pride and even Pleasure in killing than in begetting one another; for without a Blush they assemble in great armies at NoonDay to destroy, and when they have kill'd as many as they can, they exaggerate the Number to augment the fancied Glory; but they creep into Corners, or cover themselves with the Darkness of night, when they mean to beget, as being asham'd of a virtuous Action. A virtuous Action it would be, and a vicious one the killing of them, if the Species were really worth producing or preserving; but of this I begin to doubt.

I know you have no such Doubts, because, in your zeal for their welfare, you are taking a great deal of pains to save their Souls. Perhaps as you grow older, you may look upon this as a hopeless Project, or an idle Amusement, repent of having murdered in mephitic air so many honest, harmless mice, and wish that to prevent mischief, you had used Boys and Girls instead of them. In what Light we are viewed by superior Beings, may be gathered from a Piece of late West India News, which possibly has not yet reached you. A young Angel of Distinction being sent down to this world on some Business, for the first time, had an old courier-spirit assigned him as a Guide. They arriv'd over the Seas of Martinico, in the middle of the long Day of obstinate Fight between the Fleets of Rodney and De Grasse. When, thro' the Clouds of smoke, he saw the Fire of the Guns, the Decks covered with mangled Limbs, and Bodies dead or dying; the ships sinking, burning, or blown into the Air; and the Quantity of Pain, Misery, and Destruction, the Crews yet alive were thus with so much Eagerness dealing round to one another; he turn'd angrily to his Guide, and said, "You blundering Blockhead, you are ignorant of your Business;

you undertook to conduct me to the Earth, and you have brought me into Hell!" "No, Sir," says the Guide, "I have made no mistake; this is really the Earth, and these are men. Devils never treat one another in this cruel manner; they have more Sense, and more of what Men (vainly) call *Humanity*."

But to be serious, my dear old Friend, I love you as much as ever, and I love all the honest Souls that meet at the London Coffee House. I only wonder how it happen'd, that they and my other Friends in England came to be such good Creatures in the midst of so perverse a Generation. I long to see them and you once more, and I labour for Peace with more Earnestness, that I may again be happy in your sweet society.

I show'd your letter to the Duke de Larochefoucault, who thinks with me, the new Experiments you have made are extremely curious; and he has given me thereupon a Note, which I inclose, and I request you would furnish me with the answer desired.

Yesterday the Count du Nord was at the Academy of Sciences, when sundry Experiments were exhibited for his Entertainment; among them, one by M. Lavoisier, to show that the strongest Fire we yet know, is made in a Charcoal blown upon with dephlogisticated air. In a Heat so produced, he melted Platina presently, the Fire being much more powerful than that of the strongest burning mirror. Adieu, and believe me ever, yours most affectionately,

B. FRANKLIN.

TO JONATHAN SHIPLEY

Passy, June 10, 1782.

I received and read the Letter from my dear and much respected Friend with infinite Pleasure. After so long a Silence, and the long Continuance of its unfortunate Causes, a Line from you was a Prognostic of happier Times approaching, when we may converse and communicate freely, without Danger from the malevolence of Men enrag'd by the ill success of their distracted Projects.

I long with you for the Return of Peace, on the general Principles of Humanity. The Hope of being able to pass a few more of my last Days happily in the sweet Conversations and Company I once enjoy'd at Twyford, is a particular Motive that adds Strength to the general Wish, and quickens my Industry to procure that best of Blessings. After much Occasion to consider the Folly and Mischiefs of a State of Warfare, and the little or no Advantage obtain'd even by those Nations, who have conducted it with the most Success, I have been apt to think, that there has never been, nor ever will be, any such thing as a *good* War, or a *bad* Peace.

You ask if I still relish my old Studies. I relish them, but I cannot pursue them. My Time is engross'd unhappily with other Concerns. I requested of the Congress last Year my Discharge from this publick Station, that I might enjoy a little Leisure in the Evening of a long Life of Business; but it was refus'd me, and I have been obliged to drudge on a little longer.

You are happy as your Years come on, in having that dear and most amiable Family about you. Four Daughters! how rich! I have but one, and she, necessarily detain'd from me at 1000 leagues distance. I feel the Want of that tender Care of me, which might be expected from a Daughter, and would give the World for one. Your Shades are all plac'd in a Row over my Fireplace, so that I not only have you always in my Mind, but constantly before my Eyes.

The Cause of Liberty and America has been greatly oblig'd to you. I hope you will live long to see that Country flourish under its new Constitution, which I am sure will give you great Pleasure. Will you permit me to express another Hope, that, now your Friends are in Power, they will take the first Opportunity of showing the sense they ought to have of your Virtues and your Merit?

Please to make my best Respects acceptable to Mrs. Shipley, and embrace for me tenderly all our dear Children. With the utmost Esteem, Respect, and Veneration, I am ever, my dear Friend, yours most affectionately,

B. FRANKLIN.

TO JAMES HUTTON

Passy, July 7, 1782.

MY OLD AND DEAR FRIEND,

A Letter written by you to M. Bertin,[113] *Ministre d'Etat*, containing an Account of the abominable Murders committed by some of the frontier People on the poor Moravian Indians, has given me infinite Pain and Vexation. The Dispensations of Providence in this World puzzle my weak Reason. I cannot comprehend why cruel Men should have been permitted thus to destroy their Fellow Creatures. Some of the Indians may be suppos'd to have committed Sins, but one cannot think the little Children had committed any worthy of Death. Why has a single Man in England, who happens to love Blood and to hate Americans, been permitted to gratify that bad Temper by hiring German Murderers, and joining them with his own, to destroy in a continued Course of bloody Years near 100,000 human Creatures, many of them possessed of useful Talents, Virtues and Abilities to which he has no Pretension! It is he who has furnished the Savages with Hatchets and Scalping Knives, and engages them to fall upon our defenceless Farmers, and murder them with their Wives and Children, paying for their Scalps, of which the account kept in America already amounts, as I have heard, to near *two Thousand!*

Perhaps the people of the frontiers, exasperated by the Cruelties of the Indians, have been induced to kill all Indians that fall into their Hands without Distinction; so that even these horrid Murders of our poor Moravians may be laid to his Charge. And yet this Man lives, enjoys all the good Things this World can afford, and is surrounded by Flatterers, who keep even his Conscience quiet by telling him he is the best of Princes! I wonder at this, but I cannot therefore part with the comfortable Belief of a Divine Providence; and the more I see the Impossibility, from the number & extent of his Crimes, of giving equivalent Punishment to a wicked Man in this Life, the more I am convinc'd of a future State, in which all that here appears to be wrong shall be set right, all that is crooked made straight. In this Faith let you & I, my dear Friend, comfort ourselves; it is the only Comfort, in the present dark Scene of Things, that is allow'd us.

I shall not fail to write to the Government of America, urging that effectual Care may be taken to protect & save the Remainder of those unhappy People.

Since writing the above, I have received a Philadelphia Paper, containing some Account of the same horrid Transaction, a little different, and some Circumstances alledged as Excuses or Palliations, but extreamly weak & insufficient. I send it to you inclos'd. With great and sincere Esteem, I am ever, my dear Friend, yours most affectionately,

B. FRANKLIN.

TO SIR JOSEPH BANKS[114]

Passy, Sept. 9, 1782.

DEAR SIR,

I have just received the very kind friendly Letter you were so good as to write to me by Dr. Broussonnet.[115] Be assured, that I long earnestly for a Return of those peaceful Times, when I could sit down in sweet Society with my English philosophic Friends, communicating to each other new Discoveries, and proposing Improvements of old ones; all tending to extend the Power of Man over Matter, avert or diminish the Evils he is subject to, or augment the Number of his Enjoyments. Much more happy should I be thus employ'd in your most desirable Company, than in that of all the Grandees of the Earth projecting Plans of Mischief, however necessary they may be supposed for obtaining greater Good.

I am glad to learn by the D^r that your great Work goes on. I admire your Magnanimity in the Undertaking, and the Perseverance with which you have prosecuted it.

I join with you most perfectly in the charming Wish you so well express, "that such Measures may be taken by both Parties as may tend to the Elevation of both, rather than the Destruction of either." If any thing has happened endangering one of them, my Comfort is, that I endeavour'd earnestly to prevent it, and gave honest, faithful Advice, which, if it had been regarded, would have been effectual. And still, if proper Means are us'd to produce, not only a Peace, but what is much more interesting, a thorough Reconciliation, a few Years may heal the Wounds that have been made in our Happiness, and produce a Degree of Prosperity of which at present we can hardly form a Conception. With great and sincere Esteem and Respect, I am, dear Sir, &c.

B. FRANKLIN.

INFORMATION
TO THOSE WHO WOULD REMOVE TO AMERICA[116]

[1782?]

Many Persons in Europe, having directly or by Letters, express'd to the Writer of this, who is well acquainted with North America, their Desire of transporting and establishing themselves in that Country; but who appear to have formed, thro' Ignorance, mistaken Ideas and Expectations of what is to be obtained there; he thinks it may be useful, and prevent inconvenient, expensive, and fruitless Removals and Voyages of improper Persons, if he gives some clearer and truer Notions of that part of the World, than appear to have hitherto prevailed.

He finds it is imagined by Numbers, that the Inhabitants of North America are rich, capable of rewarding, and dispos'd to reward, all sorts of Ingenuity; that they are at the same time ignorant of all the Sciences, and, consequently, that Strangers, possessing Talents in the Belles-Lettres, fine Arts, &c., must be highly esteemed, and so well paid, as to become easily rich themselves; that there are also abundance of profitable Offices to be disposed of, which the Natives are not qualified to fill; and that, having few Persons of Family among them, Strangers of Birth must be greatly respected, and of course easily obtain the best of those Offices, which will make all their Fortunes; that the Governments too, to encourage Emigrations from

Europe, not only pay the Expence of personal Transportation, but give Lands gratis to Strangers, with Negroes to work for them, Utensils of Husbandry, and Stocks of Cattle. These are all wild Imaginations; and those who go to America with Expectations founded upon them will surely find themselves disappointed.

The Truth is, that though there are in that Country few People so miserable as the Poor of Europe, there are also very few that in Europe would be called rich; it is rather a general happy Mediocrity that prevails. There are few great Proprietors of the Soil, and few Tenants; most People cultivate their own Lands, or follow some Handicraft or Merchandise; very few rich enough to live idly upon their Rents or Incomes, or to pay the high Prices given in Europe for Paintings, Statues, Architecture, and the other Works of Art, that are more curious than useful. Hence the natural Geniuses, that have arisen in America with such Talents, have uniformly quitted that Country for Europe, where they can be more suitably rewarded. It is true, that Letters and Mathematical Knowledge are in Esteem there, but they are at the same time more common than is apprehended; there being already existing nine Colleges or Universities, viz. four in New England, and one in each of the Provinces of New York, New Jersey, Pensilvania, Maryland, and Virginia, all furnish'd with learned Professors; besides a number of smaller Academies; these educate many of their Youth in the Languages, and those Sciences that qualify men for the Professions of Divinity, Law, or Physick. Strangers indeed are by no means excluded from exercising those Professions; and the quick Increase of Inhabitants everywhere gives them a Chance of Employ, which they have in common with the Natives. Of civil Offices, or Employments, there are few; no superfluous Ones, as in Europe; and it is a Rule establish'd in some of the States, that no Office should be so profitable as to make it desirable. The 36th Article of the Constitution of Pennsilvania, runs expressly in these Words; "As every Freeman, to preserve his Independence, (if he has not a sufficient Estate) ought to have some Profession, Calling, Trade, or Farm, whereby he may honestly subsist, there can be no Necessity for, nor Use in, establishing Offices of Profit; the usual Effects of which are Dependance and Servility, unbecoming Freemen, in the Possessors and Expectants; Faction, Contention, Corruption, and Disorder among the People. Wherefore, whenever an Office, thro' Increase of Fees or otherwise, becomes so profitable, as to occasion many to apply for it, the Profits ought to be lessened by the Legislature."

These Ideas prevailing more or less in all the United States, it cannot be worth any Man's while, who has a means of Living at home, to expatriate himself, in hopes of obtaining a profitable civil Office in America; and, as to military Offices, they are at an End with the War, the Armies being disbanded. Much less is it adviseable for a Person to go thither, who has no other Quality to recommend him but his Birth. In Europe it has indeed its Value; but it is a Commodity that cannot be carried to a worse Market than that of America, where people do not inquire concerning a Stranger, *What is he?* but, *What can he do?* If he has any useful Art, he is welcome; and if he exercises it, and behaves well, he will be respected by all that know him; but a mere Man of Quality, who, on that Account, wants to live upon the Public, by some Office or Salary, will be despis'd and disregarded. The Husbandman is in honor there, and even the Mechanic, because their Employments are useful. The People have a saying, that God Almighty is himself a Mechanic, the greatest in the Univers; and he is respected and admired more for the Variety, Ingenuity, and Utility of his Handyworks, than for the Antiquity of his Family. They are pleas'd with the Observation of a Negro, and frequently mention it, that *Boccarorra* (meaning the White men) *make de black man workee, make de Horse workee, make de Ox workee, make ebery ting workee; only de Hog. He, de hog, no workee; he eat, he drink, he walk about, he go to sleep when he please, he libb like a Gentleman.* According to these Opinions of the Americans, one of them would think himself more oblig'd to a Genealogist, who could prove for him that his Ancestors and Relations for ten Generations had been Ploughmen, Smiths, Carpenters, Turners,

Weavers, Tanners, or even Shoemakers, and consequently that they were useful Members of Society; than if he could only prove that they were Gentlemen, doing nothing of Value, but living idly on the Labour of others, mere *fruges consumere nati*,* and otherwise *good for nothing*, till by their Death their Estates, like the Carcass of the Negro's Gentleman-Hog, come to be *cut up*.

With regard to Encouragements for Strangers from Government, they are really only what are derived from good Laws and Liberty. Strangers are welcome, because there is room enough for them all, and therefore the old Inhabitants are not jealous of them; the Laws protect them sufficiently, so that they have no need of the Patronage of Great Men; and every one will enjoy securely the Profits of his Industry. But, if he does not bring a Fortune with him, he must work and be industrious to live. One or two Years' residence gives him all the Rights of a Citizen; but the government does not at present, whatever it may have done in former times, hire People to become Settlers, by Paying their Passages, giving Land, Negroes, Utensils, Stock, or any other kind of Emolument whatsoever. In short, America is the Land of Labour, and by no means what the English call *Lubberland*, and the French *Pays de Cocagne*, where the streets are said to be pav'd with half-peck Loaves, the Houses til'd with Pancakes, and where the Fowls fly about ready roasted, crying, *Come eat me!*

Who then are the kind of Persons to whom an Emigration to America may be advantageous? And what are the Advantages they may reasonably expect?

Land being cheap in that Country, from the vast Forests still void of Inhabitants, and not likely to be occupied in an Age to come, insomuch that the Propriety of an hundred Acres of fertile Soil full of Wood may be obtained near the Frontiers, in many Places, for Eight or Ten Guineas, hearty young Labouring Men, who understand the Husbandry of Corn and Cattle, which is nearly the same in that Country as in Europe, may easily establish themselves there. A little Money sav'd of the

*". . . born merely to eat up the corn."—WATTS. [*Franklin's note.*]

good Wages they receive there, while they work for others, enables them to buy the Land and begin their Plantation, in which they are assisted by the Good-Will of their Neighbours, and some Credit. Multitudes of poor People from England, Ireland, Scotland, and Germany, have by this means in a few years become wealthy Farmers, who, in their own Countries, where all the Lands are fully occupied, and the Wages of Labour low, could never have emerged from the poor Condition wherein they were born.

From the salubrity of the Air, the healthiness of the Climate, the plenty of good Provisions, and the Encouragement to early Marriages by the certainty of Subsistence in cultivating the Earth, the Increase of Inhabitants by natural Generation is very rapid in America, and becomes still more so by the Accession of Strangers; hence there is a continual Demand for more Artisans of all the necessary and useful kinds, to supply those Cultivators of the Earth with Houses, and with Furniture and Utensils of the grosser sorts, which cannot so well be brought from Europe. Tolerably good Workmen in any of those mechanic Arts are sure to find Employ, and to be well paid for their Work, there being no Restraints preventing Strangers from exercising any Art they understand, nor any Permission necessary. If they are poor, they begin first as Servants or Journeymen; and if they are sober, industrious, and frugal, they soon become Masters, establish themselves in Business, marry, raise Families, and become respectable Citizens.

Also, Persons of moderate Fortunes and Capitals, who, having a Number of Children to provide for, are desirous of bringing them up to Industry, and to secure Estates for their Posterity, have Opportunities of doing it in America, which Europe does not afford. There they may be taught and practise profitable mechanic Arts, without incurring Disgrace on that Account, but on the contrary acquiring Respect by such Abilities. There small Capitals laid out in Lands, which daily become more valuable by the Increase of People, afford a solid Prospect of ample Fortunes thereafter for those Children. The writer of this has known several Instances of large Tracts of

Land, bought, on what was then the Frontier of Pensilvania, for Ten Pounds per hundred Acres, which after 20 years, when the Settlements had been extended far beyond them, sold readily, without any Improvement made upon them, for three Pounds per Acre. The Acre in America is the same with the English Acre, or the Acre of Normandy.

Those, who desire to understand the State of Government in America, would do well to read the Constitutions of the several States, and the Articles of Confederation that bind the whole together for general Purposes, under the Direction of one Assembly, called the Congress. These Constitutions have been printed, by order of Congress, in America; two Editions of them have also been printed in London; and a good Translation of them into French has lately been published at Paris.

Several of the Princes of Europe having of late years, from an Opinion of Advantage to arise by producing all Commodities and Manufactures within their own Dominions, so as to diminish or render useless their Importations, have endeavoured to entice Workmen from other Countries by high Salaries, Privileges, &c. Many Persons, pretending to be skilled in various great Manufactures, imagining that America must be in Want of them, and that the Congress would probably be dispos'd to imitate the Princes above mentioned, have proposed to go over, on Condition of having their Passages paid, Lands given, Salaries appointed, exclusive Privileges for Terms of years, &c. Such Persons, on reading the Articles of Confederation, will find, that the Congress have no Power committed to them, or Money put into their Hands, for such purposes; and that if any such Encouragement is given, it must be by the Government of some separate State. This, however, has rarely been done in America; and, when it has been done, it has rarely succeeded, so as to establish a Manufacture, which the Country was not yet so ripe for as to encourage private Persons to set it up; Labour being generally too dear there, and Hands difficult to be kept together, every one desiring to be a Master, and the Cheapness of Lands inclining many to leave Trades for Agriculture. Some indeed have met with Success, and are carried on to Advantage;

but they are generally such as require only a few Hands, or wherein great Part of the Work is performed by Machines. Things that are bulky, and of so small Value as not well to bear the Expence of Freight, may often be made cheaper in the Country than they can be imported; and the Manufacture of such Things will be profitable wherever there is a sufficient Demand. The Farmers in America produce indeed a good deal of Wool and Flax; and none is exported, it is all work'd up; but it is in the Way of domestic Manufacture, for the Use of the Family. The buying up Quantities of Wool and Flax, with the Design to employ Spinners, Weavers, &c., and form great Establishments, producing Quantities of Linen and Woollen Goods for Sale, has been several times attempted in different Provinces; but those Projects have generally failed, goods of equal Value being imported cheaper. And when the Governments have been solicited to support such Schemes by Encouragements, in Money, or by imposing Duties on Importation of such Goods, it has been generally refused, on this Principle, that, if the Country is ripe for the Manufacture, it may be carried on by private Persons to Advantage; and if not, it is a Folly to think of forcing Nature. Great Establishments of Manufacture require great Numbers of Poor to do the Work for small Wages; these Poor are to be found in Europe, but will not be found in America, till the Lands are all taken up and cultivated, and the Excess of People, who cannot get Land, want Employment. The Manufacture of Silk, they say, is natural in France, as that of Cloth in England, because each Country produces in Plenty the first Material; but if England will have a Manufacture of Silk as well as that of Cloth, and France one of Cloth as well as that of Silk, these unnatural Operations must be supported by mutual Prohibitions, or high Duties on the Importation of each other's Goods; by which means the Workmen are enabled to tax the home Consumer by greater Prices, while the higher Wages they receive makes them neither happier nor richer, since they only drink more and work less. Therefore the Governments in America do nothing to encourage such Projects. The People, by this Means, are not impos'd on, either by the

Merchant or Mechanic. If the Merchant demands too much Profit on imported Shoes, they buy of the Shoemaker; and if he asks too high a Price, they take them of the Merchant; thus the two Professions are checks on each other. The Shoemaker, however, has, on the whole, a considerable Profit upon his Labour in America, beyond what he had in Europe, as he can add to his Price a Sum nearly equal to all the Expences of Freight and Commission, Risque or Insurance, &c., necessarily charged by the Merchant. And the Case is the same with the Workmen in every other Mechanic Art. Hence it is, that Artisans generally live better and more easily in America than in Europe; and such as are good Œconomists make a comfortable Provision for Age, and for their Children. Such may, therefore, remove with Advantage to America.

In the long-settled Countries of Europe, all Arts, Trades, Professions, Farms, &c., are so full, that it is difficult for a poor Man, who has Children, to place them where they may gain, or learn to gain, a decent Livelihood. The Artisans, who fear creating future Rivals in Business, refuse to take Apprentices, but upon Conditions of Money, Maintenance, or the like, which the Parents are unable to comply with. Hence the Youth are dragg'd up in Ignorance of every gainful Art, and oblig'd to become Soldiers, or Servants, or Thieves, for a Subsistence. In America, the rapid Increase of Inhabitants takes away that Fear of Rivalship, and Artisans willingly receive Apprentices from the hope of Profit by their Labour, during the Remainder of the Time stipulated, after they shall be instructed. Hence it is easy for poor Families to get their Children instructed; for the Artisans are so desirous of Apprentices, that many of them will even give Money to the Parents, to have Boys from Ten to Fifteen Years of Age bound Apprentices to them till the Age of Twenty-one; and many poor Parents have, by that means, on their Arrival in the Country, raised Money enough to buy Land sufficient to establish themselves, and to subsist the rest of their Family by Agriculture. These Contracts for Apprentices are made before a Magistrate, who regulates the Agreement according to Reason and Justice, and, having in view the Formation of a future useful Citizen, obliges the Master to engage by a written Indenture, not only that, during the time of Service stipulated, the Apprentice shall be duly provided with Meat, Drink, Apparel, washing, and Lodging, and, at its Expiration, with a compleat new Suit of Cloaths, but also that he shall be taught to read, write, and cast Accompts; and that he shall be well instructed in the Art or Profession of his Master, or some other, by which he may afterwards gain a Livelihood, and be able in his turn to raise a Family. A Copy of this Indenture is given to the Apprentice or his Friends, and the Magistrate keeps a Record of it, to which recourse may be had, in case of Failure by the Master in any Point of Performance. This desire among the Masters, to have more Hands employ'd in working for them, induces them to pay the Passages of young Persons, of both Sexes, who, on their Arrival, agree to serve them one, two, three, or four Years; those, who have already learnt a Trade, agreeing for a shorter Term, in proportion to their Skill, and the consequent immediate Value of their Service; and those, who have none, agreeing for a longer Term, in consideration of being taught an Art their Poverty would not permit them to acquire in their own Country.

The almost general Mediocrity of Fortune that prevails in America obliging its People to follow some Business for subsistence, those Vices, that arise usually from Idleness, are in a great measure prevented. Industry and constant Employment are great preservatives of the Morals and Virtue of a Nation. Hence bad Examples to Youth are more rare in America, which must be a comfortable Consideration to Parents. To this may be truly added, that serious Religion, under its various Denominations, is not only tolerated, but respected and practised. Atheism is unknown there; Infidelity rare and secret; so that persons may live to a great Age in that Country, without having their Piety shocked by meeting with either an Atheist or an Infidel. And the Divine Being seems to have manifested his Approbation of the mutual Forbearance and Kindness with which the different Sects treat each other, by the remarkable Prosperity with which He has been pleased to favour the whole Country.

APOLOGUE[117]

[1783?]

Lion, king of a certain forest, had among his subjects a body of faithful dogs, in principle and affection strongly attached to his person and government, but through whose assistance he had extended his dominions, and had become the terror of his enemies.

Lion, however, influenced by evil counsellors, took an aversion to the dogs, condemned them unheard, and ordered his tigers, leopards, and panthers to attack and destroy them.

The dogs petitioned humbly, but their petitions were rejected haughtily; and they were forced to defend themselves, which they did with bravery.

A few among them, of a mongrel race, derived from a mixture with wolves and foxes, corrupted by royal promises of great rewards, deserted the honest dogs and joined their enemies.

The dogs were finally victorious: a treaty of peace was made, in which Lion acknowledged them to be free, and disclaimed all future authority over them.

The mongrels not being permitted to return among them, claimed of the royalists the reward that had been promised.

A council of the beasts was held to consider their demand.

The wolves and the foxes agreed unanimously that the demand was just, that royal promises ought to be kept, and that every loyal subject should contribute freely to enable his majesty to fulfil them.

The horse alone, with a boldness and freedom that became the nobleness of his nature, delivered a contrary opinion.

"The King," said he, "has been misled, by bad ministers, to war unjustly upon his faithful subjects. Royal promises, when made to encourage us to act for the public good, should indeed be honourably acquitted; but if to encourage us to betray and destroy each other, they are wicked and void from the beginning. The advisers of such promises, and those who murdered in consequence of them, instead of being recompensed, should be severely punished. Consider how greatly our common strength is already diminished by our loss of the dogs. If you enable the King to reward those fratricides, you will establish a precedent that may justify a future tyrant to make like promises; and every example of such an unnatural brute rewarded will give them additional weight. Horses and bulls, as well as dogs, may thus be divided against their own kind, and civil wars produced at pleasure, till we are so weakened that neither liberty nor safety is any longer to be found in the forest, and nothing remains but abject submission to the will of a despot, who may devour us as he pleases."

The council had sense enough to resolve—that the demand be rejected.

TO SIR JOSEPH BANKS

Passy, July 27, 1783.

DEAR SIR,

I received your very kind letter by Dr. Blagden,[118] and esteem myself much honoured by your friendly Remembrance. I have been too much and too closely engaged in public Affairs, since his being here, to enjoy all the Benefit of his Conversation you were so good as to intend me. I hope soon to have more Leisure, and to spend a part of it in those Studies, that are much more agreable to me than political Operations.

I join with you most cordially in rejoicing at the return of Peace. I hope it will be lasting, and that Mankind will at length, as they call themselves reasonable Creatures, have Reason and Sense enough to settle their Differences without cutting Throats; for, in my opinion, *there never was a good War, or a bad Peace.* What vast additions to the Conveniences and Comforts of Living might Mankind have acquired, if the Money spent in Wars had been employed in Works of public utility! What an extension of Agriculture, even to the Tops of our Mountains: what Rivers rendered navigable, or joined by Canals: what Bridges, Aqueducts, new Roads, and other public Works, Edifices, and Improvements, rendering England a compleat Paradise, might have been obtained by spending those Millions in doing good, which in the last War have been spent in doing Mischief; in bringing Misery into thousands of Families, and destroying the Lives of so many thousands of working people, who might have performed the useful labour!

I am pleased with the late astronomical Discoveries made by our Society [the Royal—Eds.]. Furnished as all Europe now is with Academies of Science, with nice Instruments and the Spirit of Experiment, the progress of human knowledge will be rapid, and discoveries made, of which we have at present no Conception. I begin to be almost sorry I was born so soon, since I cannot have the happiness of knowing what will be known 100 years hence.

I wish continued success to the Labours of the Royal Society, and that you may long adorn their Chair; being, with the highest esteem, dear Sir, &c.

B. FRANKLIN.

P. S. Dr. Blagden will acquaint you with the experiment of a vast Globe sent up into the Air, much talked of here, and which, if prosecuted, may furnish means of new knowledge.

TO MRS. SARAH BACHE[119]

Passy, Jan. 26, 1784.

MY DEAR CHILD,

Your Care in sending me the Newspapers is very agreable to me. I received by Capt. Barney those relating to the *Cincinnati*. My Opinion of the Institution cannot be of much Importance; I only wonder that, when the united Wisdom of our Nation had, in the Articles of Confederation, manifested their Dislike of establishing Ranks of Nobility, by Authority either of the Congress or of any particular State, a Number of private Persons should think proper to distinguish themselves and their Posterity, from their fellow Citizens, and form an Order of *hereditary Knights*, in direct Opposition to the solemnly declared Sense of their Country! I imagine it must be likewise contrary to the Good Sense of most of those drawn into it by the Persuasion of its Projectors, who have been too much struck with the Ribbands and Crosses they have seen among them hanging to the Buttonholes of Foreign Officers. And I suppose those, who disapprove of it, have not hitherto given it much Opposition, from a Principle somewhat like that of your good Mother, relating to punctilious Persons, who are always exacting little Observances of Respect; that, *"if People can be pleased with small Matters, it is a pity but they should have them."*

In this View, perhaps, I should not myself, if my Advice had been ask'd, have objected to their wearing their Ribband and Badge according to their Fancy, tho' I certainly should to the entailing it as an Honour on their Posterity. For Honour, worthily obtain'd (as for Example that of our Officers), is in its Nature a *personal* Thing, and incommunicable to any but those who had some Share in obtaining it. Thus among the Chinese, the most ancient, and from long Experience the wisest of Nations, honour does not *descend*, but *ascends*. If a man from his Learning, his Wisdom, or his Valour, is promoted by the Emperor to the Rank of Mandarin, his Parents are immediately entitled to all the same Ceremonies of Respect from the People, that are establish'd as due to the Mandarin himself; on the supposition that it must have been owing to the Education, Instruction, and good Example afforded him by his Parents, that he was rendered capable of serving the Publick.

This *ascending* Honour is therefore useful to the State, as it encourages Parents to give their Children a good and virtuous Education. But the *descending Honour*, to Posterity who could have no Share in obtaining it, is not only groundless and absurd, but often hurtful to that Posterity, since it is apt to make them proud, disdaining to be employ'd in useful Arts, and thence falling into Poverty, and all the Meannesses, Servility, and Wretchedness attending it; which is the present case with much of what is called the *Noblesse* in Europe. Or if, to keep up the Dignity of the Family, Estates are entailed entire on the Eldest male heir, another Pest to Industry and Improvement of the Country is introduc'd, which will be followed by all the odious mixture of pride and Beggary, and idleness, that have half depopulated [and *decultivated*] Spain; occasioning continual Extinction of Families by the Discouragements of Marriage [and neglect in the improvement of estates].

I wish, therefore, that the Cincinnati, if they must go on with their Project, would direct the Badges of their Order to be worn by their Parents, instead of handing them down to their Children. It would be a good Precedent, and might have good Effects. It would also be a kind of Obedience to the Fourth Commandment, in which God enjoins us to *honour* our Father and Mother, but has nowhere directed us to honour our Children. And certainly no mode of honouring those immediate Authors of our Being can be more effectual, than that of doing praiseworthy Actions, which reflect Honour on those who gave us our Education; or more becoming, than that of manifesting, by some public Expression or Token, that it is to their Instruction and Example we ascribe the Merit of those Actions.

But the Absurdity of *descending Honours* is not a mere Matter of philosophical Opinion; it is capable of mathematical Demonstration. A Man's Son, for instance, is but half of his Family, the other half belonging to the Family of his Wife. His Son, too, marrying into another Family, his Share in the Grandson is but a fourth; in the Great Grandson, by the same Process, it is but an Eighth; in the next Generation a Sixteenth; the next a Thirty-second; the next a Sixty-fourth; the next an Hundred and twenty-eighth; the next a Two hundred and Fifty-sixth; and the next a Five hundred and twelfth; thus in nine Generations, which will not require more than 300 years (no very great Antiquity for a Family), our present Chevalier of the Order of Cincinnatus's Share in the then existing Knight, will be but a 512th part; which, allowing the present certain Fidelity of American Wives to be insur'd down through all those Nine Generations, is so small a Consideration, that methinks no reasonable Man would hazard for the sake of it the disagreable Consequences of the Jealousy, Envy, and Ill will of his Countrymen.

Let us go back with our Calculation from this young Noble, the 512th part of the present Knight, thro' his nine Generations, till we return to the year of the Institution. He must have had a Father and Mother, they are two. Each of them had a father and Mother, they are four. Those of the next preceding Generation will be eight, the next Sixteen, the next thirty-two, the next sixty-four, the next one hundred and Twenty-eight, the next Two hundred and fifty-six, and the ninth in this Retrocession Five hundred and twelve, who must be now existing, and all contribute their Proportion of this future *Chevalier de Cincinnatus*. These, with the rest, make together as follows:

$$
\begin{array}{r}
2 \\
4 \\
8 \\
16 \\
32 \\
64 \\
128 \\
256 \\
512 \\
\hline
\end{array}
$$

Total 1022

One Thousand and Twenty-two Men and Women, contributors to the formation of one Knight. And, if we are to have a Thousand of these future knights, there must be now and hereafter existing One million and Twenty-two Thousand Fathers and Mothers, who are to contribute to their Production, unless a Part of the Number are employ'd in making more Knights than One. Let us strike off then the 22,000, on the Supposition of this double Employ, and then consider whether, after a reasonable Estimation of the Number of Rogues, and Fools, and Royalists and Scoundrels and Prostitutes, that are mix'd with, and help to make up necessarily their Million of Predecessors, Posterity will have much reason to boast of the noble Blood of the then existing Set of Chevaliers de Cincinnatus. [The future genealogists, too, of these Chevaliers, in proving the lineal descent of their honour through so many generations (even supposing honour capable in its nature of descending), will only prove the small share of this honour, which can be justly claimed by any one of them; since the above simple process in arithmetic makes it quite plain and clear that, in proportion as the antiquity of the family shall augment, the right to the honour of the ancestor will diminish; and a few generations more would reduce it to something so small as to be very near an absolute nullity.] I hope, therefore, that the Order will drop this part of their project, and content themselves, as the Knights of the Garter, Bath, Thistle, St. Louis, and other Orders of Europe do, with a Life Enjoyment of their little Badge and Ribband, and let the Distinction die with those who have merited it. This I imagine will give no offence. For my own part, I shall think it a Convenience, when I go into a Company where there may be Faces unknown to me, if I discover, by this Badge, the Persons who merit some particular Expression of my Respect; and it will save modest Virtue the Trouble of calling for our Regard, by awkward roundabout Intimations of having been heretofore employ'd in the Continental Service.

The Gentleman, who made the Voyage to France to provide the Ribands and Medals, has executed his Commission. To me they seem tolerably done; but all such Things are criticis'd. Some find Fault with the Latin, as wanting classic Elegance and Correctness; and, since our Nine Universities were not able to furnish better Latin, it was pity, they say, that the Mottos had not been in English. Others object to the Title, as not properly assumable by any but Gen. Washington, [and a few others] who serv'd without Pay. Others object to the *Bald Eagle* as looking too much like a *Dindon*, or Turkey. For my own part, I wish the Bald Eagle had not been chosen as the Representative of our Country; he is a Bird of bad moral Character; he does not get his living honestly; you may have seen him perch'd on some dead Tree, near the River where, too lazy to fish for himself, he watches the Labour of the Fishing-Hawk; and, when that diligent Bird has at length taken a Fish, and is bearing it to his Nest for the support of his Mate and young ones, the Bald Eagle pursues him, and takes it from him. With all this Injustice he is never in good Case; but, like those among Men who live by Sharping and Robbing, he is generally poor, and often very lousy. Besides, he is a rank Coward; the little *King Bird*, not bigger than a sparrow, attacks him boldly and drives him out of the District. He is therefore by no means a proper emblem for the brave and honest Cincinnati of America, who have driven all the *Kingbirds* from our Country; though exactly fit for that Order of Knights, which the French call *Chevaliers d'Industrie*.

I am, on this account, not displeas'd that the Figure is not known as a Bald Eagle, but looks more like a Turk'y. For in Truth, the Turk'y is in comparison a much more respectable Bird, and withal a true original Native of America. Eagles have been found in all Countries, but the Turk'y was peculiar to ours; the first of the Species seen in Europe being brought to France by the Jesuits from Canada, and serv'd up at the Wedding Table of Charles the Ninth. He is, [though a little vain and silly, it is true, but not the worse emblem for that,] a Bird of Courage, and would not hesitate to attack a Grenadier of the British Guards, who should presume to invade his Farm Yard with a *red* Coat on.

I shall not enter into the Criticisms made upon their Latin. The gallant officers of America may [not have the merit of being] be no great scholars, but they undoubtedly merit much, [as brave soldiers,] from their Country, which should therefore not leave them merely to *Fame* for their "*Virtutis Premium*," which is one of their Latin Mottos. Their "*Esto perpetua*," another, is an excellent Wish, if they meant it for their Country; bad, if intended for their Order. The States should not only restore to them the *Omnia* of their first Motto, which many of them have left and lost, but pay them justly, and reward them generously. They should not be suffered to remain, with [all] their new-created Chivalry, *entirely* in the Situation of the Gentleman in the Story, which their *omnia reliquit* reminds me of. You know every thing makes me recollect some Story. He had built a very fine House, and thereby much impair'd his Fortune. He had a Pride, however, in showing it to his Acquaintance. One of them, after viewing it all, remark'd a Motto over the Door, "Ōia Vanitas." "What," says he, "is the Meaning of this Ō͞IA? it is a word I don't understand." "I will tell you," said the Gentleman; "I had a mind to have the Motto cut on a Piece of smooth Marble, but there was not room for it between the Ornaments, to be put in Characters large enough to be read. I therefore made use of a Contraction antiently very common in Latin Manuscripts, by which the *m*'s and *n*'s in Words are omitted, and the Omission noted by a little Dash above, which you may see there; so that the Word is *omnia*, OMNIA VANITAS." "O," says his Friend, "I now comprehend the Meaning of your motto, it relates to your Edifice; and signifies, that, if you have abridged your *Omnia*, you have, nevertheless, left your VANITAS legible at full length." I am, as ever, your affectionate father,

B. FRANKLIN.

AN ECONOMICAL PROJECT

TO THE AUTHORS OF THE JOURNAL OF PARIS

[March 20, 1784? [120]]

MESSIEURS,

You often entertain us with accounts of new discoveries. Permit me to communicate to the public, through your paper, one that has lately been made by myself, and which I conceive may be of great utility.

I was the other evening in a grand company, where the new lamp of Messrs. Quinquet and Lange was introduced, and much admired for its splendour; but a general inquiry was made, whether the oil it consumed was not in proportion to the light it afforded, in which case there would be no saving in the use of it. No one present could satisfy us in that point, which all agreed ought to be known, it being a very desirable thing to lessen, if possible, the expense of lighting our apartments, when every other article of family expense was so much augmented.

I was pleased to see this general concern for economy, for I love economy exceedingly.

I went home, and to bed, three or four hours after midnight, with my head full of the subject. An accidental sudden noise waked me about six in the morning, when I was surprised to find my room filled with light; and I imagined at first, that a number of those lamps had been brought into it; but, rubbing my eyes, I perceived the light came in at the windows. I got up and looked out to see what might be the occasion of it, when I saw the sun just rising above the horizon, from whence he poured his rays plentifully into my chamber, my domestic having negligently omitted, the preceding evening, to close the shutters.

I looked at my watch, which goes very well, and found that it was but six o'clock; and still thinking it something extraordinary that the sun should rise so early, I looked into the almanac, where I found it to be the hour given for his rising on that day. I looked forward, too, and found he was to rise still earlier every day till towards the end of June; and that at no time in the year he retarded his rising so long as till eight o'clock. Your readers, who with me have never seen any signs of sunshine before noon, and seldom regard the astronomical part of the almanac, will be as much astonished as I was, when they hear of his rising so early; and especially when I assure them, *that he gives light as soon as he rises*. I am convinced of this. I am certain of my fact. One cannot be more certain of any fact. I saw it with my own eyes. And, having repeated this observation the three following mornings, I found always precisely the same result.

Yet it so happens, that when I speak of this discovery to others, I can easily perceive by their countenances, though they forbear expressing it in words, that they do not quite believe me. One, indeed, who is a learned natural philosopher, has assured me that I must certainly be mistaken as to the circumstance of the light coming into my room; for it being well known, as he says, that there could be no light abroad at that hour, it follows that none could enter from without; and that of consequence, my windows being accidentally left open, instead of letting in the light, had only served to let out the

darkness; and he used many ingenious arguments to show me
how I might, by that means, have been deceived. I owned that
he puzzled me a little, but he did not satisfy me; and the subsequent observations I made, as above mentioned, confirmed me
in my first opinion.

This event has given rise in my mind to several serious and
important reflections. I considered that, if I had not been
awakened so early in the morning, I should have slept six hours
longer by the light of the sun, and in exchange have lived six
hours the following night by candle-light; and, the latter being
a much more expensive light than the former, my love of
economy induced me to muster up what little arithmetic I was
master of, and to make some calculations, which I shall give
you, after observing that utility is, in my opinion the test of
value in matters of invention, and that a discovery which can
be applied to no use, or is not good for something, is good for
nothing.

I took for the basis of my calculation the supposition that
there are one hundred thousand families in Paris, and that these
families consume in the night half a pound of bougies, or
candles, per hour. I think this is a moderate allowance, taking
one family with another; for though I believe some consume
less, I know that many consume a great deal more. Then
estimating seven hours per day as a medium quantity between
the time of the sun's rising and ours, he rising during the six
following months from six to eight hours before noon, and
there being seven hours of course per night in which we burn
candles, the account will stand thus;—

In the six months between the 20th of March and the 20th of
September, there are

Nights	183
Hours of each night in which we burn candles .	7
Multiplication gives for the total number of hours	1,281
These 1,281 hours multiplied by 100,000, the number of inhabitants, give	128,100,000

One hundred twenty-eight millions and one
hundred thousand hours, spent at Paris by
candle-light, which, at half a pound of wax
and tallow per hour, gives the weight of .   64,050,000

Sixty-four millions and fifty thousand of pounds,
which, estimating the whole at the medium
price of thirty sols the pound, makes the sum
of ninety-six millions and seventy-five thousand livres tournois   96,075,000

An immense sum! that the city of Paris might save every
year, by the economy of using sunshine instead of candles.

If it should be said, that people are apt to be obstinately
attached to old customs, and that it will be difficult to induce
them to rise before noon, consequently my discovery can be
of little use; I answer, *Nil desperandum*. I believe all who have
common sense, as soon as they have learnt from this paper
that it is daylight when the sun rises, will contrive to rise with
him; and, to compel the rest, I would propose the following
regulations;

First. Let a tax be laid of a louis per window, on every
window that is provided with shutters to keep out the light of
the sun.

Second. Let the same salutary operation of police be made
use of, to prevent our burning candles, that inclined us last
winter to be more economical in burning wood; that is, let
guards be placed in the shops of the wax and tallow chandlers,
and no family be permitted to be supplied with more than one
pound of candles per week.

Third. Let guards also be posted to stop all the coaches, &c.
that would pass the streets after sun-set, except those of physicians, surgeons, and midwives.

Fourth. Every morning, as soon as the sun rises, let all the
bells in every church be set ringing; and if that is not sufficient,
let cannon be fired in every street, to wake the sluggards effectually, and make them open their eyes to see their true
interest.

All the difficulty will be in the first two or three days; after which the reformation will be as natural and easy as the present irregularity; for, *ce n'est que le premier pas qui coûte*. Oblige a man to rise at four in the morning, and it is more than probable he will go willingly to bed at eight in the evening; and, having had eight hours sleep, he will rise more willingly at four in the morning following. But this sum of ninety-six millions and seventy-five thousand livres is not the whole of what may be saved by my economical project. You may observe, that I have calculated upon only one half of the year, and much may be saved in the other, though the days are shorter. Besides, the immense stock of wax and tallow left unconsumed during the summer, will probably make candles much cheaper for the ensuing winter, and continue them cheaper as long as the proposed reformation shall be supported.

For the great benefit of this discovery, thus freely communicated and bestowed by me on the public, I demand neither place, pension, exclusive privilege, nor any other reward whatever. I expect only to have the honour of it. And yet I know there are little, envious minds, who will, as usual, deny me this, and say, that my invention was known to the ancients, and perhaps they may bring passages out of the old books in proof of it. I will not dispute with these people, that the ancients knew not the sun would rise at certain hours; they possibly had, as we have, almanacs that predicted it; but it does not follow thence, that they knew *he gave light as soon as he rose*. This is what I claim as my discovery. If the ancients knew it, it might have been long since forgotten; for it certainly was unknown to the moderns, at least to the Parisians, which to prove, I need use but one plain simple argument. They are as well instructed, judicious, and prudent a people as exist anywhere in the world, all professing, like myself, to be lovers of economy; and, from the many heavy taxes required from them by the necessities of the state, have surely an abundant reason to be economical. I say it is impossible that so sensible a people, under such circumstances, should have lived so long by the smoky, unwholesome, and enormously expensive light of candles, if they had really known, that they might have had as much pure light of the sun for nothing. I am, &c.

A Subscriber.

TO SAMUEL MATHER [121]

Passy, May 12, 1784.

Rev^D Sir,

I received your kind letter, with your excellent advice to the people of the United States, which I read with great pleasure, and hope it will be duly regarded. Such writings, though they may be lightly passed over by many readers, yet, if they make a deep impression on one active mind in a hundred, the effects may be considerable. Permit me to mention one little instance, which, though it relates to myself, will not be quite uninteresting to you. When I was a boy, I met with a book, entitled "*Essays to do Good*," which I think was written by your father. It had been so little regarded by a former possessor, that several leaves of it were torn out; but the remainder gave me such a turn of thinking, as to have an influence on my conduct through life; for I have always set a greater value on the character of a *doer of good*, than on any other kind of reputation; and if I have been, as you seem to think, a useful citizen, the public owes the advantage of it to that book.

You mention your being in your 78th year; I am in my 79th; we are grown old together. It is now more than 60 years since I left Boston, but I remember well both your father and grandfather, having heard them both in the pulpit, and seen them in their houses. The last time I saw your father was in the beginning of 1724, when I visited him after my first trip to Pennsylvania. He received me in his library, and on my taking leave showed me a shorter way out of the house through a narrow passage, which was crossed by a beam over head. We were still talking as I withdrew, he accompanying me behind, and I turning partly towards him, when he said hastily, "*Stoop, stoop!*" I did not understand him, till I felt my head hit against the beam. He was a man that never missed any occasion of giving instruction, and upon this he said to me, "*You are young, and have the world before you;* STOOP *as you go through it, and you will miss many hard thumps.*" This advice, thus beat into my head, has frequently been of use to me; and I often think of it, when I see pride mortified, and misfortunes brought upon people by their carrying their heads too high.

I long much to see again my native place, and to lay my bones there. I left it in 1723; I visited it in 1733, 1743, 1753, and 1763. In 1773 I was in England; in 1775 I had a sight of it, but could not enter, it being in possession of the enemy. I did hope to have been there in 1783, but could not obtain my dismission from this employment here; and now I fear I shall never have that happiness. My best wishes however attend my dear country. *Esto perpetua.* It is now blest with an excellent constitution; may it last for ever!

This powerful monarchy continues its friendship for the United States. It is a friendship of the utmost importance to our security, and should be carefully cultivated. Britain has not yet well digested the loss of its dominion over us, and has still at times some flattering hopes of recovering it. Accidents may increase those hopes, and encourage dangerous attempts. A breach between us and France would infallibly bring the English again upon our backs; and yet we have some wild heads among our countrymen, who are endeavouring to weaken that connexion! Let us preserve our reputation by performing our engagements; our credit by fulfilling our contracts; and friends by gratitude and kindness; for we know not how soon we may again have occasion for all of them. With great and sincere esteem, I have the honour to be, &c.

B. FRANKLIN.

TO BENJAMIN VAUGHAN[122]

Passy, July 26th, 1784.

DEAR FRIEND,

I have received several Letters from you lately, dated June 16, June 30, and July 13. I thank you for the Information respecting the Proceedings of your West India Merchants, or rather Planters. The Restraints what ever they may be upon our Commerce with your Islands, will prejudice their Inhabitants, I apprehend, more than us.

It is wonderful how preposterously the affairs of this world are managed. Naturally one would imagine, that the interest of a few individuals should give way to general interest; but individuals manage their affairs with so much more application, industry, and address, than the public do theirs, that general interest most commonly gives way to particular. We assemble parliaments and councils, to have the benefit of their collected wisdom; but we necessarily have, at the same time, the inconvenience of their collected passions, prejudices, and private interest. By the help of these, artful men overpower their wisdom, and dupe its possessors; and if we may judge by the acts, *arrêts*, and edicts, all the world over, for regulating commerce, an assembly of great men is the greatest fool upon earth.

I have received Cook's *Voyages*, which you put Mr. Oswald in the way of sending to me. By some Mistake the first Volume was omitted, and instead of it a Duplicate sent of the third. If there is a good Print of Cook, I should be glad to have it, being personally acquainted with him. I thank you for the Pamphlets by Mr. Estlin. Every thing you send me gives me Pleasure; to receive your Account would give me more than all.

I am told, that the little Pamphlet of *Advice to such as would remove to America*, is reprinted in London, with my Name to it, which I would rather had been omitted; but wish to see a Copy, when you have an Opportunity of sending it.

Mr. H. has long continued here in Expectation of Instructions for making a Treaty of Commerce, but they do not come, and I begin to suspect none are intended; tho' perhaps the Delay is only occasioned by the over great Burthen of Business at present on the Shoulders of your Ministers. We do not press the Matter, but are content to wait till they can see their Interest respecting America more clearly, being certain that we can shift as well as you without a Treaty.

The Conjectures I sent you concerning the cold of last Winter still appear to me probable. The moderate Season in Russia and Canada, do not weaken them. I think our Frost here began about the 24th of December; in America, the 12 of January. I thank you for recommending to me Mr. Arbuthnot; I have had Pleasure in his Conversation. I wish much to see the new Pieces you had in hand. I congratulate you on the Return of your Wedding-day, and wish for your Sake and Mrs. Vaughan's, that you may see a great many of them, all as happy as the first.

I like the young stranger very much. He seems sensible, ingenious, and modest, has a good deal of Instruction, and makes judicious Observations. He will probably distinguish himself advantageously. I have not yet heard from Mr. Nairne.

Dr. Price's Pamphlet of Advice to America is a good one, and will do Good. You ask, "what Remedy I have for the growing Luxury of my Country, which gives so much *Offence* to all *English travellers* without exception." I answer, that I think it exaggerated, and that Travellers are no good Judges whether our Luxury is growing or diminishing. Our People are hospitable, and have indeed too much Pride in displaying upon their Tables before Strangers the Plenty and Variety that our Country affords. They have the Vanity, too, of sometimes borrowing one another's Plate to entertain more splendidly. Strangers being invited from House to House, and meeting every Day with a Feast, imagine what they see is the ordinary Way of living of all the Families where they dine; when perhaps each Family lives a Week after upon the Remains of the Dinner given. It is, I own, a Folly in our People to give *such Offence* to *English Travellers*. The first part of the Proverb is thereby verified, that *Fools make Feasts*. I wish in this Case the other were as true, *and wise Men eat them*. These Travellers might, one would think, find some Fault they could more decently reproach us with, than that of our excessive Civility to them as Strangers.

I have not, indeed yet thought of a Remedy for Luxury. I am not sure, that in a great State it is capable of a Remedy. Nor that the Evil is in itself always so great as it is represented. Suppose we include in the Definition of Luxury all unnecessary Expence, and then let us consider whether Laws to prevent such Expence are possible to be executed in a great Country, and whether, if they could be executed, our People generally would be happier, or even richer. Is not the Hope of one day being able to purchase and enjoy Luxuries a great Spur to Labour and Industry? May not Luxury, therefore, produce more than it consumes, if without such a Spur People would be, as they are naturally enough inclined to be, lazy and indolent? To this purpose I remember a Circumstance. The Skipper of a Shallop, employed between Cape May and Philadelphia, had done us some small Service, for which he refused Pay. My Wife, understanding that he had a Daughter, sent her as a Present a new-fashioned Cap. Three Years After, this Skipper being at my House with an old Farmer of Cape May, his Passenger, he mentioned the Cap, and how much his Daughter had been pleased with it. "But," says he, "it proved a dear Cap to our Congregation." "How so?" "When my Daughter appeared in it at Meeting, it was so much admired, that all the Girls resolved to get such Caps from Philadelphia; and my Wife and I computed, that the whole could not have cost less than a hundred Pound." "True," says the Farmer, "but you do not tell all the Story. I think the Cap was nevertheless an Advantage to us, for it was the first thing that put our Girls upon Knitting worsted Mittens for Sale at Philadelphia, that they might have wherewithal to buy Caps and Ribbands there; and you know that that Industry has continued, and is likely to continue and increase to a much greater Value, and answer better Purposes." Upon the whole, I was more reconciled to this little Piece of Luxury, since not only the Girls were made happier by having fine Caps, but the Philadelphians by the Supply of warm Mittens.

In our Commercial Towns upon the Seacoast, Fortunes will occasionally be made. Some of those who grow rich will be prudent, live within Bounds, and preserve what they have gained for their Posterity; others, fond of showing their Wealth, will

be extravagant and ruin themselves. Laws cannot prevent this;
and perhaps it is not always an evil to the Publick. A Shilling
spent idly by a Fool, may be picked up by a Wiser Person,
who knows better what to do with it. It is therefore not lost.
A vain, silly Fellow builds a fine House, furnishes it richly,
lives in it expensively, and in few years ruins himself; but the
Masons, Carpenters, Smiths, and other honest Tradesmen have
been by his Employ assisted in maintaining and raising their
Families; the Farmer has been paid for his labour, and encouraged, and the Estate is now in better Hands. In some
Cases, indeed, certain Modes of Luxury may be a publick Evil,
in the same Manner as it is a Private one. If there be a Nation,
for Instance, that exports its Beef and Linnen, to pay for its
Importation of Claret and Porter, while a great Part of its
People live upon Potatoes, and wear no Shirts, wherein does
it differ from the Sot, who lets his Family starve, and sells his
Clothes to buy Drink? Our American Commerce is, I confess,
a little in this way. We sell our Victuals to your Islands for
Rum and Sugar; the substantial Necessaries of Life for Superfluities. But we have Plenty, and live well nevertheless, tho'
by being soberer, we might be richer.

By the by, here is just issued an *arrêt* of Council taking off
all the Duties upon the exportation of Brandies, which, it is
said, will render them cheaper in America than your Rum;
in which case there is no doubt but they will be preferr'd, and
we shall be better able to bear your Restrictions on our Commerce. There are Views here, by augmenting their Settlements,
of being able to supply the growing People of America with
the Sugar that may be wanted there. On the whole, I guess
England will get as little by the Commercial War she has begun
with us, as she did by the Military. But to return to Luxury.

The vast Quantity of Forest Lands we have yet to clear, and
put in order for Cultivation, will for a long time keep the Body
of our Nation laborious and frugal. Forming an Opinion of
our People and their Manners by what is seen among the Inhabitants of the Seaports, is judging from an improper Sample.
The People of the Trading Towns may be rich and luxurious,

while the Country possesses all the Virtues, that tend to private Happiness and publick Prosperity. Those Towns are not much regarded by the Country; they are hardly considered as an essential Part of the States; and the Experience of the last War has shown, that their being in the Possession of the Enemy did not necessarily draw on the Subjection of the Country, which bravely continued to maintain its Freedom and Independence notwithstanding.

It has been computed by some Political Arithmetician, that, if every Man and Woman would work for four Hours each Day on something useful, that Labour would produce sufficient to procure all the Necessaries and Comforts of Life, Want and Misery would be banished out of the World, and the rest of the 24 hours might be Leisure and Pleasure.

What occasions then so much Want and Misery? It is the Employment of Men and Women in Works, that produce neither the Necessaries nor Conveniences of Life, who, with those who do nothing, consume the Necessaries raised by the Laborious. To explain this.

The first Elements of Wealth are obtained by Labour, from the Earth and Waters. I have Land, and raise Corn. With this, if I feed a Family that does nothing, my Corn will be consum'd, and at the end of the Year I shall be no richer than I was at the beginning. But if, while I feed them, I employ them, some in Spinning, others in hewing Timber and sawing Boards, others in making Bricks, &c. for Building, the Value of my Corn will be arrested and remain with me, and at the end of the Year we may all be better clothed and better lodged. And if, instead of employing a Man I feed in making Bricks, I employ him in fiddling for me, the Corn he eats is gone, and no Part of his Manufacture remains to augment the Wealth and Convenience of the family; I shall therefore be the poorer for this fiddling Man, unless the rest of my Family work more, or eat less, to make up the Deficiency he occasions.

Look round the World and see the Millions employ'd in doing nothing, or in something that amounts to nothing, when the Necessaries and Conveniences of Life are in question.

What is the Bulk of Commerce, for which we fight and destroy each other, but the Toil of Millions for Superfluities, to the great Hazard and Loss of many Lives by the constant Dangers of the Sea? How much labour is spent in Building and fitting great Ships, to go to China and Arabia for Tea and Coffee, to the West Indies for Sugar, to America for Tobacco! These things cannot be called the Necessaries of Life, for our Ancestors lived very comfortably without them.

A Question may be asked; Could all these People, now employed in raising, making, or carrying Superfluities, be subsisted by raising Necessaries? I think they might. The World is large, and a great Part of it still uncultivated. Many hundred Millions of Acres in Asia, Africa, and America are still Forest, and a great Deal even in Europe. On 100 Acres of this Forest a Man might become a substantial Farmer, and 100,000 Men, employed in clearing each his 100 Acres, would hardly brighten a Spot big enough to be Visible from the Moon, unless with Herschell's Telescope; so vast are the Regions still in Wood unimproved.

'Tis however, some Comfort to reflect, that, upon the whole, the Quantity of Industry and Prudence among Mankind exceeds the Quantity of Idleness and Folly. Hence the Increase of good Buildings, Farms cultivated, and populous Cities filled with Wealth, all over Europe, which a few Ages since were only to be found on the Coasts of the Mediterranean; and this, notwithstanding the mad Wars continually raging, by which are often destroyed in one year the Works of many Years' Peace. So that we may hope the Luxury of a few Merchants on the Seacoast will not be the Ruin of America.

One reflection more, and I well end this long, rambling Letter. Almost all the Parts of our Bodies require some Expence. The Feet demand Shoes; the Legs, Stockings; the rest of the Body, Clothing; and the Belly, a good deal of Victuals. *Our* Eyes, tho' exceedingly useful, ask, when reasonable, only the cheap Assistance of Spectacles, which could not much impair our Finances. But *the Eyes of other People* are the Eyes that ruin us. If all but myself were blind, I should want neither fine Clothes, fine Houses, nor fine Furniture. Adieu, my dear Friend, I am

Yours ever

B. FRANKLIN.

P. S. This will be delivered to you by my Grandson. I am persuaded you will afford him your Civilities and Counsels. Please to accept a little Present of Books, I send by him, curious for the Beauty of the Impression.

TO GEORGE WHATELY[123]

Passy, May 23, 1785.

DEAR OLD FRIEND,

. . . I must agree with you, that the Gout is bad, and that the Stone is worse. I am happy in not having them both together, and I join in your Prayer, that you may live till you die without either. But I doubt the Author of the Epitaph you send me was a little mistaken, when he, speaking of the World, says, that

"he ne'er car'd a pin
What they said or may say of the Mortal within."

It is so natural to wish to be well spoken of, whether alive or dead, that I imagine he could not be quite exempt from that Desire; and that at least he wish'd to be thought a Wit, or he would not have given himself the Trouble of writing so good an Epitaph to leave behind him. Was it not as worthy of his Care, that the World should say he was an honest and a good Man? I like better the concluding Sentiment in the old Song, call'd *The Old Man's Wish*, wherein, after wishing for a warm House in a country Town, an easy Horse, some good old authors, ingenious and cheerful Companions, a Pudding on Sundays, with stout Ale, and a bottle of Burgundy, &c. &c., in separate Stanzas, each ending with this burthen,

"May I govern my Passions with an absolute sway,
Grow wiser and better as my Strength wears away,
Without Gout or Stone, by a gentle Decay;"

he adds,

> "With a Courage undaunted may I face my last day,
>   And, when I am gone, may the better Sort say,
>   'In the Morning when sober, in the Evening when mellow,
>   He's gone, and has not left behind him his Fellow;
>   For he governed his Passions, &c.'"

But what signifies our Wishing? Things happen, after all, as they will happen. I have sung that *wishing Song* a thousand times, when I was young, and now find, at Fourscore, that the three Contraries have befallen me, being subject to the Gout and the Stone, and not being yet Master of all my Passions. Like the proud Girl in my Country, who wished and resolv'd not to marry a Parson, nor a Presbyterian, nor an Irishman; and at length found herself married to an Irish Presbyterian Parson.

You see I have some reason to wish, that, in a future State, I may not only be *as well as I was*, but a little better. And I hope it; for I, too, with your Poet, *trust in God*. And when I observe, that there is great Frugality, as well as Wisdom, in his Works, since he has been evidently sparing both of Labour and Materials; for by the various wonderful Inventions of Propagation, he has provided for the continual peopling his World with Plants and Animals, without being at the Trouble of repeated new Creations; and by the natural Reduction of compound Substances to their original Elements, capable of being employ'd in new Compositions, he has prevented the Necessity of creating new Matter; so that the Earth, Water, Air, and perhaps Fire, which being compounded form Wood, do, when the Wood is dissolved, return, and again become Air, Earth, Fire, and Water; I say, that, when I see nothing annihilated, and not even a Drop of Water wasted, I cannot suspect the Annihilation of Souls, or believe, that he will suffer the daily Waste of Millions of Minds ready made that now exist, and put himself to the continual Trouble of making new ones. Thus finding myself to exist in the World, I believe I shall, in some Shape or other, always exist; and, with all the inconveniencies human Life is liable to, I shall not object to a new Edition of mine; hoping, however, that the *Errata* of the last may be corrected.

. . . Adieu, my dear Friend, and believe me ever yours very affectionately,

B. FRANKLIN.

TO JOHN BARD AND MRS. BARD

Philadelphia, November 14, 1785.

DEAR FRIENDS,

I received your kind letter, which gave me great pleasure, as it informed me of your welfare. Your friendly congratulations are very obliging. I had on my return some right, as you observe, to expect repose; and it was my intention to avoid all public business. But I had not firmness enough to resist the unanimous desire of my country folks; and I find myself harnessed again in their service for another year. They engrossed the prime of my life. They have eaten my flesh, and seem resolved now to pick my bones. You are right in supposing, that I interest myself in every thing that affects you and yours, sympathizing in your afflictions, and rejoicing in your felicities; for our friendship is ancient, and was never obscured by the least cloud.

I thank you for your civilities to my grandson, and am ever, with sincere and great esteem and regard, my dear friends, yours most affectionately,

B. FRANKLIN.

TO JONATHAN SHIPLEY

Philadelphia, Feb. 24th, 1786.

DEAR FRIEND,

I received lately your kind letter of Nov. 27th. My Reception here was, as you have heard, very honourable indeed; but I was betray'd by it, and by some Remains of Ambition, from which I had imagined myself free, to accept of the Chair of Government for the State of Pennsylvania, when the proper thing for me was Repose and a private Life. I hope, however, to be able to bear the Fatigue for one Year, and then to retire.

I have much regretted our having so little Opportunity for Conversation when we last met. You could have given me Informations and Counsels that I wanted, but we were scarce a Minute together without being broke in upon. I am to thank you, however, for the Pleasure I had after our Parting, in reading the new Book [124] you gave me, which I think generally well written and likely to do good; tho' the Reading Time of most People is of late so taken up with News Papers and little periodical Pamphlets, that few now-a-days venture to attempt reading a Quarto Volume. I have admir'd to see, that, in the last Century, a Folio, *Burton on Melancholly*, went through Six Editions in about Twenty Years. We have, I believe, more Readers now, but not of such large Books.

You seem desirous of knowing what Progress we make here in improving our Governments. We are, I think, in the right Road of Improvement, for we are making Experiments. I do not oppose all that seem wrong, for the Multitude are more effectually set right by Experience, than kept from going wrong by Reasoning with them. And I think we are daily more and more enlightened; so that I have no doubt of our obtaining in a few Years as much public Felicity, as good Government is capable of affording.

Your NewsPapers are fill'd with fictitious Accounts of Anarchy, Confusion, Distresses, and Miseries, we are suppos'd to be involv'd in, as Consequences of the Revolution; and the few remaining Friends of the old Government among us take pains to magnify every little Inconvenience a Change in the Course of Commerce may have occasion'd. To obviate the Complaints they endeavour to excite, was written the enclos'd little Piece, [125] from which you may form a truer Idea of our Situation, than your own public Prints would give you. And I can assure you, that the great Body of our Nation find themselves happy in the Change, and have not the smallest Inclination to return to the Domination of Britain. There could not be a stronger Proof of the general Approbation of the Measures, that promoted the Change, and of the Change itself, than has been given by the Assembly and Council of this State, in the nearly unanimous Choice for their Governor, of one who had been so much concern'd in those Measures; the Assembly being themselves the unbrib'd Choice of the People, and therefore may be truly suppos'd of the same Sentiments. I say nearly unanimous, because, of between 70 and 80 Votes, there were only my own and one other in the negative.

As to my Domestic Circumstances, of which you kindly desire to hear something, they are at present as happy as I could wish them. I am surrounded by my Offspring, a Dutiful and Affectionate Daughter in my House, with Six Grandchildren, the eldest of which you have seen, who is now at a College in the next Street, finishing the learned Part of his Education; the others promising, both for Parts and good Dispositions. What their Conduct may be, when they grow up and enter the important Scenes of Life, I shall not live to *see*, and I cannot *foresee*. I therefore enjoy among them the present Hour, and leave the future to Providence.

He that raises a large Family does, indeed, while he lives to observe them, *stand*, as Watts says, *a broader Mark for Sorrow;* but then he stands a broader Mark for Pleasure too. When we launch our little Fleet of Barques into the Ocean, bound to different Ports, we hope for each a prosperous Voyage; but contrary Winds, hidden Shoals, Storms, and Enemies come in for a Share in the Disposition of Events; and though these occasion a Mixture of Disappointment, yet, considering the Risque where we can make no Insurance, we should think ourselves happy if some return with Success. My Son's Son, Temple Franklin, whom you have also seen, having had a fine Farm of 600 Acres [126] convey'd to him by his Father when we were at Southampton, has drop'd for the present his Views of acting in the political Line, and applies himself ardently to the Study and Practice of Agriculture. This is much more agreable to me, who esteem it the most useful, the most independent, and therefore the noblest of Employments. His Lands are on navigable water, communicating with the Delaware, and but about 16 Miles from this City. He has associated to himself a very skillful English Farmer lately arrived here, who is to instruct him in the Business, and partakes for a Term of the Profits; so that there is a great apparent Probability of their Success.

You will kindly expect a Word or two concerning myself. My Health and Spirits continue, Thanks to God, as when you saw me. The only complaint I then had, does not grow worse, and is tolerable. I still have Enjoyment in the Company of my Friends; and, being easy in my Circumstances, have many Reasons to like Living. But the Course of Nature must soon put a period to my present Mode of Existence. This I shall submit to with less Regret, as, having seen during a long Life a good deal of this World, I feel a growing Curiosity to be acquainted with some other; and can chearfully, with filial Confidence, resign my Spirit to the conduct of that great and good Parent of Mankind, who created it, and who has so graciously protected and prospered me from my Birth to the present Hour. Wherever I am, I hope always to retain the pleasing remembrance of your Friendship, being with sincere and great Esteem, my dear Friend, yours most affectionately,

B. FRANKLIN.

P. S. We all join in Respects to Mrs. Shipley, and best wishes for the whole amiable Family.

TO  127

Phila. July 3, 1786 [?].

DEAR SIR,

I have read your Manuscript with some Attention. By the Argument it contains against the Doctrines of a particular Providence, tho' you allow a general Providence, you strike at the Foundation of all Religion. For without the Belief of a Providence, that takes Cognizance of, guards, and guides, and may favour particular Persons, there is no Motive to Worship a Deity, to fear its Displeasure, or to pray for its Protection. I will not enter into any Discussion of your Principles, tho' you seem to desire it. At present I shall only give you my Opinion, that, though your Reasonings are subtile, and may prevail with some Readers, you will not succeed so as to change the general Sentiments of Mankind on that Subject, and the Consequence of printing this Piece will be, a great deal of Odium drawn upon yourself, Mischief to you, and no Benefit to others. He that spits against the Wind, spits in his own Face.[128]

But, were you to succeed, do you imagine any Good would be done by it? You yourself may find it easy to live a virtuous Life, without the Assistance afforded by Religion; you having a clear Perception of the Advantages of Virtue, and the Disadvantages of Vice, and possessing a Strength of Resolution sufficient to enable you to resist common Temptations. But think how great a Proportion of Mankind consists of weak and ignorant Men and Women, and of inexperienc'd, and inconsiderate Youth of both Sexes, who have need of the Motives of Religion to restrain them from Vice, to support their Virtue, and retain them in the Practice of it till it becomes *habitual*, which is the great Point for its Security. And perhaps you are indebted to her originally, that is, to your Religious Education, for the Habits of Virtue upon which you now justly value yourself. You might easily display your excellent Talents of reasoning upon a less hazardous subject, and thereby obtain a Rank with our most distinguish'd Authors. For among us it is not necessary, as among the Hottentots, that a Youth, to be receiv'd into the Company of men, should prove his Manhood by beating his Mother.

I would advise you, therefore, not to attempt unchaining the Tyger, but to burn this Piece before it is seen by any other Person; whereby you will save yourself a great deal of Mortification from the Enemies it may raise against you, and perhaps a good deal of Regret and Repentance. If men are so wicked as we now see them *with religion*, what would they be *if without it*. I intend this Letter itself as a *Proof* of my Friendship, and therefore add no *Professions* to it; but subscribe simply yours,

B. F.

SPEECH IN THE CONVENTION;
ON THE SUBJECT OF SALARIES [129]

[Delivered June 2, 1787]

SIR,

It is with Reluctance that I rise to express a Disapprobation
of any one Article of the Plan, for which we are so much obliged
to the honourable Gentleman who laid it before us. From its
first Reading, I have borne a good Will to it, and, in general,
wish'd it Success. In this Particular of Salaries to the Executive
Branch, I happen to differ; and, as my Opinion may appear
new and chimerical, it is only from a Persuasion that it is right,
and from a Sense of Duty, that I hazard it. The Committee will
judge of my Reasons when they have heard them, and their
judgment may possibly change mine. I think I see Inconveniences in the Appointment of Salaries; I see none in refusing
them, but on the contrary great Advantages.

Sir, there are two Passions which have a powerful Influence
in the Affairs of Men. These are *Ambition* and *Avarice;* the Love
of Power and the Love of Money. Separately, each of these has
great Force in prompting Men to Action; but when united in
View of the same Object, they have in many Minds the most
violent Effects. Place before the Eyes of such Men a Post of
Honour, that shall at the same time be a Place of *Profit*, and
they will move Heaven and Earth to obtain it. The vast Number of such Places it is that renders the British Government so
tempestuous. The Struggles for them are the true Source of
all those Factions which are perpetually dividing the Nation,
distracting its Councils, hurrying it sometimes into fruitless
and mischievous Wars, and often compelling a Submission
to dishonourable Terms of Peace.

And of what kind are the men that will strive for this profitable Preëminence, thro' all the Bustle of Cabal, the Heat of
Contention, the infinite mutual Abuse of Parties, tearing to
Pieces the best of Characters? It will not be the wise and
moderate, the Lovers of Peace and good Order, the men fittest

for the Trust. It will be the Bold and the Violent, the men of strong Passions and indefatigable Activity in their selfish Pursuits. These will thrust themselves into your Government, and be your Rulers. And these, too, will be mistaken in the expected Happiness of their Situation; for their vanquish'd competitors, of the same Spirit, and from the same Motives, will perpetually be endeavouring to distress their Administration, thwart their Measures, and render them odious to the People.

Besides these Evils, Sir, tho' we may set out in the Beginning with moderate Salaries, we shall find, that such will not be of long Continuance. Reasons will never be wanting for propos'd Augmentations, and there will always be a Party for giving more to the Rulers, that the Rulers may be able in Return to give more to them. Hence, as all History informs us, there has been in every State and Kingdom a constant kind of Warfare between the Governing and the Governed; the one striving to obtain more for its Support, and the other to pay less. And this has alone occasion'd great Convulsions, actual Civil Wars, ending either in dethroning of the Princes or enslaving of the People. Generally, indeed, the Ruling Power carries its Point, and we see the Revenues of Princes constantly increasing, and we see that they are never satisfied, but always in want of more. The more the People are discontented with the Oppression of Taxes, the greater Need the Prince has of Money to distribute among his Partisans, and pay the Troops that are to suppress all Resistance, and enable him to plunder at Pleasure. There is scarce a King in a hundred, who would not, if he could, follow the Example of Pharaoh,—get first all the People's Money, then all their Lands, and then make them and their Children Servants for ever. It will be said, that we do not propose to establish Kings. I know it. But there is a natural Inclination in Mankind to kingly Government. It sometimes relieves them from Aristocratic Domination. They had rather have one Tyrant than 500. It gives more of the Appearance of Equality among Citizens; and that they like. I am apprehensive, therefore,—perhaps too apprehensive,—that the Government of these States may in future times end in a Monarchy. But this Catastrophe, I think, may be long delay'd, if in our propos'd System we do not sow the Seeds of Contention, Faction, and Tumult, by making our Posts of Honour Places of Profit. If we do, I fear, that, tho' we employ at first a Number and not a single Person, the Number will in time be set aside; it will only nourish the Fœtus of a King (as the honourable Gentleman from Virg^a very aptly express'd it), and a King will the sooner be set over us.

It may be imagined by some, that this is an Utopian Idea, and that we can never find Men to serve us in the Executive Department, without paying them well for their Services. I conceive this to be a Mistake. Some existing Facts present themselves to me, which incline me to a contrary Opinion. The High Sheriff of a County in England is an honourable Office, but it is not a profitable one. It is rather expensive, and therefore not sought for. But yet it is executed, and well executed, and usually by some of the principal Gentlemen of the County. In France, the Office of Counsellor, or Member of their judiciary Parliaments, is more honourable. It is therefore purchas'd at a High Price; there are indeed Fees on the Law Proceedings, which are divided among them, but these Fees do not amount to more than three per cent on the Sum paid for the Place. Therefore, as legal Interest is there at five per cent, they in fact pay two per cent for being allow'd to do the Judiciary Business of the Nation, which is at the same time entirely exempt from the Burthen of paying them any Salaries for their Services. I do not, however, mean to recommend this as an eligible Mode for our judiciary Department. I only bring the Instance to show, that the Pleasure of doing Good and serving their Country, and the Respect such Conduct entitles them to, are sufficient Motives with some Minds, to give up a great Portion of their Time to the Public, without the mean Inducement of pecuniary Satisfaction.

Another Instance is that of a respectable Society, who have made the Experiment, and practis'd it with Success, now more than a hundred years. I mean the Quakers. It is an establish'd Rule with them that they are not to go to law, but in their Controversies they must apply to their Monthly, Quarterly, and

Yearly Meetings. Committees of these sit with Patience to hear the Parties, and spend much time in composing their Differences. In doing this, they are supported by a Sense of Duty, and the Respect paid to Usefulness. It is honourable to be so employ'd, but it was never made profitable by Salaries, Fees, or Perquisites. And indeed, in all Cases of public Service, the less the Profit the greater the Honour.

To bring the Matter nearer home, have we not seen the greatest and most important of our Offices, that of General of our Armies, executed for Eight Years together, without the smallest Salary, by a patriot whom I will not now offend by any other Praise; and this, thro' Fatigues and Distresses, in common with the other brave Men, his military Friends and Companions, and the constant Anxieties peculiar to his Station? And shall we doubt finding three or four Men in all the United States, with public Spirit enough to bear sitting in peaceful Council, for perhaps an equal Term, merely to preside over our civil Concerns, and see that our Laws are duly executed? Sir, I have a better opinion of our Country. I think we shall never be without a sufficient Number of wise and good Men to undertake, and execute well and faithfully, the Office in question.

Sir, the Saving of the Salaries, that may at first be propos'd, is not an object with me. The subsequent Mischiefs of proposing them are what I apprehend. And therefore it is that I move the Amendment. If it is not seconded or accepted, I must be contented with the Satisfaction of having delivered my Opinion frankly, and done my Duty.

MOTION FOR PRAYERS IN THE CONVENTION

[Motion made June 28, 1787]

MR. PRESIDENT,

The small Progress we have made, after 4 or 5 Weeks' close Attendance and continual Reasonings with each other, our different Sentiments on almost every Question, several of the last producing as many *Noes* as *Ayes*, is, methinks, a melancholy Proof of the Imperfection of the Human Understanding. We indeed seem to *feel* our own want of political Wisdom, since we have been running all about in Search of it. We have gone back to ancient History for Models of Government, and examin'd the different Forms of those Republics, which, having been orig[i]- nally form'd with the Seeds of their own Dissolution, now no longer exist; and we have view'd modern States all round Europe, but find none of their Constitutions suitable to our Circumstances.

In this Situation of this Assembly, groping, as it were, in the dark to find Political Truth, and scarce able to distinguish it when presented to us, how has it happened, Sir, that we have not hitherto once thought of humbly applying to the Father of Lights to illuminate our Understandings? In the Beginning of the Contest with Britain, when we were sensible of Danger, we had daily Prayers in this Room for the Divine Protection. Our Prayers, Sir, were heard;—and they were graciously answered. All of us, who were engag'd in the Struggle, must have observed frequent Instances of a superintending Providence in our Favour. To that kind Providence we owe this happy Opportunity of Consulting in Peace on the Means of establishing our future national Felicity. And have we now forgotten that powerful Friend? or do we imagine we no longer need its assistance? I have lived, Sir, a long time; and the longer I live, the more convincing proofs I see of this Truth, *that* GOD *governs in the Affairs of Men*. And if a Sparrow cannot fall to the Ground without His Notice, is it probable that an Empire can rise without His Aid? We have been assured, Sir, in the Sacred Writings, that "except the Lord build the House, they labour in vain that build it." I firmly believe this; and I also believe, that, without his concurring Aid, we shall succeed in this political Building no better than the Builders of Babel; we shall be divided by our little, partial, local Interests, our Projects will be confounded, and we ourselves shall become a Reproach and a Bye-word down to future Ages. And, what is worse, Mankind may hereafter, from this unfortunate Instance, despair of establishing Government by human Wisdom, and leave it to Chance, War, and Conquest.

I therefore beg leave to move,

That henceforth Prayers, imploring the Assistance of Heaven and its Blessing on our Deliberations, be held in this Assembly every morning before we proceed to Business; and that one or more of the Clergy of this city be requested to officiate in that Service.*

SPEECH IN THE CONVENTION

At the Conclusion of its Deliberations [130]

[September 17, 1787]

MR. PRESIDENT,

I confess, that I do not entirely approve of this Constitution at present; but, Sir, I am not sure I shall never approve it; for, having lived long, I have experienced many instances of being obliged, by better information or fuller consideration, to change my opinions even on important subjects, which I once thought right, but found to be otherwise. It is therefore that, the older I grow, the more apt I am to doubt my own judgment of others. Most men, indeed, as well as most sects in religion, think themselves in possession of all truth, and that wherever others differ from them, it is so far error. Steele, a Protestant, in a dedication, tells the Pope, that the only difference between our two churches in their opinions of the certainty of their doctrine, is, the Romish Church is *infallible*, and the Church of England is *never in the wrong*. But, though many private Persons think almost as highly of their own infallibility as of that of their Sect, few express it so naturally as a certain French Lady, who, in a little dispute with her sister, said, "But I meet with nobody but myself that is *always* in the right." "*Je ne trouve que moi qui aie toujours raison.*"

In these sentiments, Sir, I agree to this Constitution, with all its faults,—if they are such; because I think a general Government necessary for us, and there is no *form* of government but what may be a blessing to the people, if well administered; and

*"The convention, except three or four persons, thought prayers unnecessary!" [*Franklin's note.*]

I believe, farther, that this is likely to be well administered for a course of years, and can only end in despotism, as other forms have done before it, when the people shall become so corrupted as to need despotic government, being incapable of any other. I doubt, too, whether any other Convention we can obtain, may be able to make a better constitution; for, when you assemble a number of men, to have the advantage of their joint wisdom, you inevitably assemble with those men all their prejudices, their passions, their errors of opinion, their local interests, and their selfish views. From such an assembly can a *perfect* production be expected? It therefore astonishes me, Sir, to find this system approaching so near to perfection as it does; and I think it will astonish our enemies, who are waiting with confidence to hear, that our councils are confounded like those of the builders of Babel, and that our States are on the point of separation, only to meet hereafter for the purpose of cutting one another's throats. Thus I consent, Sir, to this Constitution, because I expect no better, and because I am not sure that it is not the best. The opinions I have had of its *errors* I sacrifice to the public good. I have never whispered a syllable of them abroad. Within these walls they were born, and here they shall die. If every one of us, in returning to our Constituents, were to report the objections he has had to it, and endeavour to gain Partisans in support of them, we might prevent its being generally received, and thereby lose all the salutary effects and great advantages resulting naturally in our favour among foreign nations, as well as among ourselves, from our real or apparent unanimity. Much of the strength and efficiency of any government, in procuring and securing happiness to the people, depends on *opinion*, on the general opinion of the goodness of that government, as well as of the wisdom and integrity of its governors. I hope, therefore, for our own sakes, as a part of the people, and for the sake of our posterity, that we shall act heartily and unanimously in recommending this Constitution, wherever our Influence may extend, and turn our future thoughts and endeavours to the means of having it *well administered.*

On the whole, Sir, I cannot help expressing a wish, that every member of the Convention who may still have objections to it, would with me on this occasion doubt a little of his own infallibility, and, to make *manifest* our *unanimity*, put his name to this Instrument.

[Then the motion was made for adding the last formula, viz. "Done in convention by the Unanimous Consent," &c.; which was agreed to and added accordingly.]

TO THE EDITORS OF THE PENNSYLVANIA GAZETTE

On the Abuse of the Press

[1788]

MESSRS. HALL AND SELLERS,

I lately heard a remark, that on examination of *The Pennsylvania Gazette* for fifty years, from its commencement, it appeared, that, during that long period, scarce one libellous piece had ever appeared in it. This generally chaste conduct of your paper is much to its reputation; for it has long been the opinion of sober, judicious people, that nothing is more likely to endanger the liberty of the press, than the abuse of that liberty, by employing it in personal accusation, detraction, and calumny. The excesses some of our papers have been guilty of in this particular, have set this State in a bad light abroad, as appears by the following letter, which I wish you to publish, not merely to show your own disapprobation of the practice, but as a caution to others of the profession throughout the United States. For I have seen a European newspaper, in which the editor, who had been charged with frequently calumniating the Americans, justifies himself by saying, "that he had published nothing disgraceful to us, which he had not taken from our own printed papers." I am, &c.   A. B.

"New York, March 30, 1788.

"DEAR FRIEND,

"My Gout has at length left me, after five Months' painful

Confinement. It afforded me, however, the Leisure to read, or hear read, all the Packets of your various Newspapers, which you so kindly sent for my Amusement.

"Mrs. W. has partaken of it; she likes to read the Advertisements; but she remarks some kind of Inconsistency in the announcing so many Diversions for almost every Evening of the Week, and such Quantities to be sold of expensive Superfluities, Fineries, and Luxuries *just imported*, in a Country, that at the same time fills its Papers with Complaints of *Hard Times*, and Want of Money. I tell her, that such Complaints are common to all Times and all Countries, and were made even in Solomon's Time; when, as we are told, Silver was as plenty in Jerusalem as the Stones in the Street; and yet, even then, there were People who grumbled, so as to incur this Censure from that knowing Prince. *'Say not thou that the former Times were better than these; for thou dost not enquire rightly concerning that matter.'*

"But the Inconsistence that strikes me the most is, that between the Name of your City, Philadelphia, *(Brotherly Love,)* and the Spirit of Rancour, Malice, and *Hatred* that breathes in its NewsPapers. For I learn from those Papers, that your State is divided into Parties, that each Party ascribes all the public Operations of the other to vicious Motives; that they do not even suspect one another of the smallest Degree of Honesty; that the antifederalists are such, merely from the Fear of losing Power, Places, or Emoluments, which they have in Possession or in Expectation; that the Federalists are a set of *Conspirators*, who aim at establishing a Tyranny over the Persons and Property of their Countrymen, and to live in Splendor on the Plunder of the People. I learn, too, that your Justices of the Peace, tho' chosen by their Neighbours, make a villainous Trade of their Office, and promote Discord to augment Fees, and fleece their Electors; and that this would not be mended by placing the Choice in the Executive Council, who, with interested or party Views, are continually making as improper Appointments; witness a *'petty Fidler, Sycophant, and Scoundrel,'* appointed Judge of the Admiralty; '*an old Woman and Fomenter of Sedition*' to be another of the Judges, and '*a Jeffries*' Chief Justice, &c. &c.; with '*two Harpies*' the Comptroller and Naval Officers, to prey upon the Merchants and deprive them of their Property by Force of Arms, &c.

"I am inform'd also by these Papers, that your General Assembly, tho' the annual choice of the People, shows no Regard to their Rights, but from sinister Views or Ignorance makes Laws in direct Violation of the Constitution, to divest the Inhabitants of their Property and give it to Strangers and Intruders; and that the Council, either fearing the Resentment of their Constituents, or plotting to enslave them, had projected to disarm them, and given Orders for that purpose; and finally, that your President, the unanimous joint choice of the Council and Assembly, is '*an old Rogue*,' who gave his Assent to the federal Constitution merely to avoid refunding Money he had purloin'd from the United States.

"There is, indeed, a good deal of manifest *Inconsistency* in all this, and yet a Stranger, seeing it in your own Prints, tho' he does not believe it all, may probably believe enough of it to conclude, that Pennsylvania is peopled by a Set of the most unprincipled, wicked, rascally, and quarrelsome Scoundrels upon the Face of the Globe. I have sometimes, indeed, suspected, that those Papers are the Manufacture of foreign Enemies among you, who write with a view of disgracing your Country, and making you appear contemptible and detestable all the World over; but then I wonder at the Indiscretion of your Printers in publishing such Writings! There is, however, one of your *Inconsistencies* that consoles me a little, which is, that tho' *living*, you give one another the characters of Devils; *dead*, you are all Angels! It is delightful, when any of you die, to read what good Husbands, good Fathers, good Friends, good Citizens, and good Christians you were, concluding with a Scrap of Poetry that places you, with certainty, every one in Heaven. So that I think Pennsylvania a good country *to dye in*, though a very bad one to *live in*."

TO REV. JOHN LATHROP[131]

Philad[a], May 31, 1788.

REVEREND SIR,

. . . I have been long impressed with the same sentiments you so well express, of the growing felicity of mankind, from the improvements in philosophy, morals, politics, and even the conveniences of common living, by the invention and acquisition of new and useful utensils and instruments, that I have sometimes almost wished it had been my destiny to be born two or three centuries hence. For invention and improvement are prolific, and beget more of their kind. The present progress is rapid. Many of great importance, now unthought of, will before that period be produced; and then I might not only enjoy their advantages, but have my curiosity gratified in knowing what they are to be. I see a little absurdity in what I have just written, but it is to a friend, who will wink and let it pass, while I mention one reason more for such a wish, which is, that, if the art of physic shall be improved in proportion with other arts, we may then be able to avoid diseases, and live as long as the patriarchs in Genesis; to which I suppose we should make little objection. . . .

B. FRANKLIN.

TO THE EDITOR OF THE FEDERAL GAZETTE

A COMPARISON OF THE CONDUCT OF THE ANCIENT JEWS AND OF THE ANTI-FEDERALISTS IN THE UNITED STATES OF AMERICA

[1788?]

A zealous Advocate for the propos'd Federal Constitution, in a certain public Assembly, said, that "the Repugnance of a great part of Mankind to good Government was such, that he believed, that, if an angel from Heaven was to bring down a Constitution form'd there for our Use, it would nevertheless meet with violent Opposition." He was reprov'd for the suppos'd Extravagance of the Sentiment; and he did not justify it. Probably it might not have immediately occur'd to him, that the Experiment had been try'd, and that the Event was recorded in the most faithful of all Histories, the Holy Bible; otherwise he might, as it seems to me, have supported his Opinion by that unexceptionable Authority.

The Supreme Being had been pleased to nourish up a single Family, by continued Acts of his attentive Providence, till it became a great People; and, having rescued them from Bondage by many Miracles, performed by his Servant Moses, he personally deliver'd to that chosen Servant, in the presence of the whole Nation, a Constitution and Code of Laws for their Observance; accompanied and sanction'd with Promises of great Rewards, and Threats of severe Punishments, as the Consequence of their Obedience or Disobedience.

This Constitution, tho' the Deity himself was to be at its Head (and it is therefore call'd by Political Writers a *Theocracy*), could not be carried into Execution but by the Means of his Ministers; Aaron and his Sons were therefore commission'd to be, with Moses, the first establish'd Ministry of the new Government.

One would have thought, that this Appointment of Men, who had distinguish'd themselves in procuring the Liberty of their Nation, and had hazarded their Lives in openly opposing the Will of a powerful Monarch, who would have retain'd that Nation in Slavery, might have been an Appointment acceptable to a grateful People; and that a Constitution fram'd for them by the Deity himself might, on that Account, have been secure of a universal welcome Reception. Yet there were in every one of the *thirteen Tribes* some discontented, restless Spirits, who were continually exciting them to reject the propos'd new Government, and this from various Motives.

Many still retained an Affection for Egypt, the Land of their Nativity; and these, whenever they felt any Inconvenience or Hardship, tho' the natural and unavoidable Effect of their Change of Situation, exclaim'd against their Leaders as the Authors of their Trouble; and were not only for returning into Egypt, but for stoning their deliverers.* Those inclin'd to idola-

*Numbers, ch. xiv. [*Franklin's note.*]

try were displeas'd that their *Golden Calf* was destroy'd. Many
of the Chiefs thought the new Constitution might be injurious
to their particular Interests, that the *profitable Places* would be
engrossed by the Families and Friends of Moses and Aaron, and
others equally well-born excluded.* In Josephus and the Tal-
mud, we learn some Particulars, not so fully narrated in the
Scripture. We are there told, "That Corah was ambitious of
the Priesthood, and offended that it was conferred on Aaron;
and this, as he said, by the Authority of Moses only, *without the
Consent of the People.* He accus'd Moses of having, by various
Artifices, fraudulently obtain'd the Government, and depriv'd
the People of their Liberties; and of *conspiring* with Aaron to
perpetuate the Tyranny in their Family. Thus, tho' Corah's
real Motive was the Supplanting of Aaron, he persuaded the
People that he meant only the *Public Good;* and they, moved by
his Insinuations, began to cry out, 'Let us maintain the Common
Liberty of our *respective Tribes;* we have freed ourselves from
the Slavery impos'd on us by the Egyptians, and shall we now
suffer ourselves to be made Slaves by Moses? If we must have
a Master, it were better to return to Pharaoh, who at least fed
us with Bread and Onions, than to serve this new Tyrant, who
by his Operations has brought us into Danger of Famine.' Then
they called in question the *Reality of his Conference* with God;
and objected the *Privacy of the Meetings*, and the *preventing any
of the People from being present* at the Colloquies, or even approaching the Place, as Grounds of great Suspicion. They
accused Moses also of *Peculation;* as embezzling part of the
Golden Spoons and the Silver Chargers, that the Princes had
offer'd at the Dedication of the Altar,† and the Offerings of
Gold by the common People,‡ as well as most of the Poll-Tax;§
and Aaron they accus'd of pocketing much of the Gold of which

*Numbers, ch. xiv, verse 3. "And they gathered themselves together
against Moses and Aaron, and said unto them, 'Ye take too much upon you,
seeing all the congregation are holy, *every one of them;* wherefore, then, lift
ye up yourselves above the congregation?' "
† Numbers, ch. vii.
‡ Exodus, ch. xxxv, verse 22.
§ Numbers, ch. iii, and Exodus, ch. xxx.   [*Franklin's notes.*]

he pretended to have made a molten Calf. Besides *Peculation*, they charg'd Moses with *Ambition;* to gratify which Passion he had, they said, deceiv'd the People, by promising to bring them *to* a land flowing with Milk and Honey; instead of doing which, he had brought them *from* such a Land; and that he thought light of all this mischief, provided he could make himself an *absolute Prince*.* That, to support the new Dignity with Splendor in his Family, the partial Poll-Tax already levied and given to Aaron† was to be follow'd by a general one, ‡ which would probably be augmented from time to time, if he were suffered to go on promulgating new Laws, on pretence of new occasional Revelations of the divine Will, till their whole Fortunes were devour'd by that Aristocracy."

Moses deny'd the Charge of Peculation; and his Accusers were destitute of Proofs to support it; tho' *Facts*, if real, are in their Nature capable of Proof. "I have not," said he (with holy Confidence in the Presence of his God), "I have not taken from this People the value of an Ass, nor done them any other Injury." But his Enemies had made the Charge, and with some Success among the Populace; for no kind of Accusation is so readily made, or easily believ'd, by Knaves as the Accusation of Knavery.

In fine, no less than two hundred and fifty of the principal Men, "famous in the Congregation, Men of Renown,"§ heading and exciting the Mob, worked them up to such a pitch of Frenzy, that they called out, "Stone 'em, stone 'em, and thereby *secure our Liberties;* and let us chuse other Captains, that may lead us back into Egypt, in case we do not succeed in reducing the Canaanites!"

On the whole, it appears, that the Israelites were a People jealous of their newly-acquired Liberty, which Jealousy was in itself no Fault; but, when they suffer'd it to be work'd upon by

* Numbers, ch. xvi, verse 13. "Is it a small thing that thou hast brought us up out of a land that floweth with milk and honey, to kill us in the wilderness, except thou make thyself altogether a prince over us?"

† Numbers, ch. iii.
‡ Exodus, ch. xxx.
§ Numbers, ch. xvi. [*Franklin's notes.*]

artful Men, pretending Public Good, with nothing really in view but private Interest, they were led to oppose the Establishment of the *New Constitution*, whereby they brought upon themselves much Inconvenience and Misfortune. It appears further, from the same inestimable History, that, when after many Ages that Constitution was become old and much abus'd, and an Amendment of it was propos'd, the populace, as they had accus'd Moses of the Ambition of making himself a *Prince*, and cried out, "Stone him, stone him;" so, excited by their High Priests and SCRIBES, they exclaim'd against the Messiah, that he aim'd at becoming King of the Jews, and cry'd out, "*Crucify him, Crucify him.*" From all which we may gather, that popular Opposition to a public Measure is no Proof of its Impropriety, even tho' the Opposition be excited and headed by Men of Distinction.

To conclude, I beg I may not be understood to infer, that our General Convention was divinely inspired, when it form'd the new federal Constitution, merely because that Constitution has been unreasonably and vehemently opposed; yet I must own I have so much Faith in the general Government of the world by *Providence*, that I can hardly conceive a Transaction of such momentous Importance to the Welfare of Millions now existing, and to exist in the Posterity of a great Nation, should be suffered to pass without being in some degree influenc'd, guided, and governed by that omnipotent, omnipresent, and beneficent Ruler, in whom all inferior Spirits live, and move, and have their Being.   B. F.

TO CHARLES CARROLL [132]

Philadelphia, May 25, 1789.

DEAR FRIEND,

I am glad to see by the papers, that our grand machine has at length begun to work. I pray God to bless and guide its operations. If any form of government is capable of making a nation happy, ours I think bids fair now for producing that effect. But, after all, much depends upon the people who are to be governed. We have been guarding against an evil that old States are most liable to, *excess of power* in the rulers; but our present danger seems to be *defect of obedience* in the subjects.[133] There is hope, however, from the enlightened state of this age and country, we may guard effectually against that evil as well as the rest.

My grandson, William Temple Franklin, will have the honour of presenting this line. He accompanied me to France, and remained with me during my mission. I beg leave to recommend him to your notice, and that you would believe me, my dear friend, yours most affectionately,

B. FRANKLIN.

AN ACCOUNT OF THE SUPREMEST COURT OF JUDICATURE IN PENNSYLVANIA, VIZ. THE COURT OF THE PRESS

[From the *Federal Gazette*, September 12, 1789.]

Power of this Court.

It may receive and promulgate accusations of all kinds, against all persons and characters among the citizens of the State, and even against all inferior courts; and may judge, sentence, and condemn to infamy, not only private individuals, but public bodies, &c., with or without inquiry or hearing, *at the court's discretion.*

In whose Favour and for whose Emolument this Court is established.

In favour of about one citizen in five hundred, who, by education or practice in scribbling, has acquired a tolerable style as to grammar and construction, so as to bear printing; or who is possessed of a press and a few types. This five hundredth part of the citizens have the privilege of accusing and abusing the other four hundred and ninety-nine parts at their pleasure; or they may hire out their pens and press to others for that purpose.

Practice of the Court.

It is not governed by any of the rules of common courts of law. The accused is allowed no grand jury to judge of the truth of the accusation before it is publicly made, nor is the Name of the Accuser made known to him, nor has he an Opportunity of confronting the Witnesses against him; for they are kept in the dark, as in the Spanish Court of Inquisition. Nor is there any petty Jury of his Peers, sworn to try the Truth of the Charges. The Proceedings are also sometimes so rapid, that an honest, good Citizen may find himself suddenly and unexpectedly accus'd, and in the same Morning judg'd and condemn'd, and sentence pronounc'd against him, that he is a *Rogue* and a *Villain*. Yet, if an officer of this court receives the slightest check for misconduct in this his office, he claims immediately the rights of a free citizen by the constitution, and demands to know his accuser, to confront the witnesses, and to have a fair trial by a jury of his peers.

The Foundation of its Authority.

It is said to be founded on an Article of the Constitution of the State, which establishes *the Liberty of the Press;* a Liberty which every Pennsylvanian would fight and die for; tho' few of us, I believe, have distinct Ideas of its Nature and Extent. It seems indeed somewhat like the *Liberty of the Press* that Felons have, by the Common Law of England, before Conviction, that is, to be *press'd* to death or hanged. If by the *Liberty of the Press* were understood merely the Liberty of discussing the Propriety of Public Measures and political opinions, let us have as much of it as you please: But if it means the Liberty of affronting, calumniating, and defaming one another, I, for my part, own myself willing to part with my Share of it when our Legislators shall please so to alter the Law, and shall cheerfully consent to exchange my *Liberty* of Abusing others for the *Privilege* of not being abus'd myself.

By whom this Court is commissioned or constituted.

It is not by any Commission from the Supreme Executive Council, who might previously judge of the Abilities, Integrity, Knowledge, &c. of the Persons to be appointed to this great Trust, of deciding upon the Characters and good Fame of the Citizens; for this Court is above that Council, and may *accuse*, *judge*, and *condemn* it, at pleasure. Nor is it hereditary, as in the Court of *dernier Resort*, in the Peerage of England. But any Man who can procure Pen, Ink, and Paper, with a Press, and a huge pair of BLACKING Balls, may commissionate himself; and his court is immediately established in the plenary Possession and exercise of its rights. For, if you make the least complaint of the *judge's* conduct, he daubs his blacking balls in your face wherever he meets you; and, besides tearing your private character to flitters, marks you out for the odium of the public, as an *enemy to the liberty of the press.*

Of the natural Support of these Courts.

Their support is founded in the depravity of such minds, as have not been mended by religion, nor improved by good education;

> "There is a Lust in Man no Charm can tame,
> Of loudly publishing his Neighbour's Shame."

Hence;

> "On Eagle's Wings immortal Scandals fly,
> While virtuous Actions are but born and die."
> DRYDEN.

Whoever feels pain in hearing a good character of his neighbour, will feel a pleasure in the reverse. And of those who, despairing to rise into distinction by their virtues, are happy if others can be depressed to a level with themselves, there are a number sufficient in every great town to maintain one of these courts by their subscriptions. A shrewd observer once said, that, in walking the streets in a slippery morning, one might see where the good-natured people lived by the ashes thrown on the ice before their doors; probably he would have formed a different conjecture of the temper of those whom he might find engaged in such a subscription.

Of the Checks proper to be established against the Abuse of Power in these Courts.

Hitherto there are none. But since so much has been written and published on the federal Constitution, and the necessity of checks in all other parts of good government has been so clearly and learnedly explained, I find myself so far enlightened as to suspect some check may be proper in this part also; but I have been at a loss to imagine any that may not be construed an infringement of the sacred *liberty of the press*. At length, however, I think I have found one that, instead of diminishing general liberty, shall augment it; which is, by restoring to the people a species of liberty, of which they have been deprived by our laws, I mean the *liberty of the cudgel*. In the rude state of society prior to the existence of laws, if one man gave another ill language, the affronted person would return it by a box on the ear, and, if repeated, by a good drubbing; and this without offending against any law. But now the right of making such returns is denied, and they are punished as breaches of the peace; while the right of abusing seems to remain in full force, the laws made against it being rendered ineffectual by the *liberty of the press*.

My proposal then is, to leave the liberty of the press untouched, to be exercised in its full extent, force, and vigor; but to permit the *liberty of the cudgel* to go with it *pari passu*. Thus, my fellow-citizens, if an impudent writer attacks your reputation, dearer to you perhaps than your life, and puts his name to the charge, you may go to him as openly and break his head. If he conceals himself behind the printer, and you can nevertheless discover who he is, you may in like manner way-lay him in the night, attack him behind, and give him a good drubbing. Thus far goes my project as to *private* resentment and retribution. But if the public should ever happen to be affronted, *as it ought to be*, with the conduct of such writers, I would not advise proceeding immediately to these extremities; but that we should in moderation content ourselves with tarring and feathering, and tossing them in a blanket.

If, however, it should be thought that this proposal of mine may disturb the public peace, I would then humbly recommend to our legislators to take up the consideration of both liberties, that of the *press*, and that of the *cudgel*, and by an explicit law mark their extent and limits; and, at the same time that they secure the person of a citizen from *assaults*, they would likewise provide for the security of his *reputation*.

AN ADDRESS TO THE PUBLIC

From the Pennsylvania Society for Promoting the Abolition
of Slavery, and the Relief of Free Negroes
Unlawfully Held in Bondage. [134]

It is with peculiar satisfaction we assure the friends of humanity, that, in prosecuting the design of our association, our endeavours have proved successful, far beyond our most sanguine expectations.

Encouraged by this success, and by the daily progress of that luminous and benign spirit of liberty, which is diffusing itself throughout the world, and humbly hoping for the continuance of the divine blessing on our labours, we have ventured to make an important addition to our original plan, and do therefore earnestly solicit the support and assistance of all who can feel the tender emotions of sympathy and compassion, or relish the exalted pleasure of beneficence.

Slavery is such an atrocious debasement of human nature, that its very extirpation, if not performed with solicitous care, may sometimes open a source of serious evils.

The unhappy man, who has long been treated as a brute animal, too frequently sinks beneath the common standard of the human species. The galling chains, that bind his body, do also fetter his intellectual faculties, and impair the social affections of his heart. Accustomed to move like a mere machine, by the will of a master, reflection is suspended; he has not the power of choice; and reason and conscience have but little influence over his conduct, because he is chiefly governed by the passion of fear. He is poor and friendless; perhaps worn out by extreme labour, age, and disease.

Under such circumstances, freedom may often prove a misfortune to himself, and prejudicial to society.

Attention to emancipated black people, it is therefore to be hoped, will become a branch of our national policy; but, as far as we contribute to promote this emancipation, so far that attention is evidently a serious duty incumbent on us, and which we mean to discharge to the best of our judgment and abilities.

To instruct, to advise, to qualify those, who have been restored to freedom, for the exercise and enjoyment of civil liberty, to promote in them habits of industry, to furnish them with employments suited to their age, sex, talents, and other circumstances, and to procure their children an education calculated for their future situation in life; these are the great outlines of the annexed plan, which we have adopted, and which we conceive will essentially promote the public good, and the happiness of these our hitherto too much neglected fellow-creatures.

A plan so extensive cannot be carried into execution without considerable pecuniary resources, beyond the present ordinary funds of the Society. We hope much from the generosity of enlightened and benevolent freemen, and will gratefully receive any donations or subscriptions for this purpose, which may be made to our treasurer, James Starr, or to James Pemberton, chairman of our committee of correspondence.

Signed, by order of the Society,

B. FRANKLIN, *President.*

Philadelphia, 9th of
    November, 1789.

TO DAVID HARTLEY

Philadᵃ, Decʳ 4, 1789.

MY VERY DEAR FRIEND,

I received your Favor of August last. Your kind Condolences on the painful State of my Health are very obliging. I am thankful to God, however, that, among the numerous Ills human Life is subject to, one only of any Importance is fallen to my Lot; and that so late as almost to insure that it can be but of short Duration.

The Convulsions in France are attended with some disagreable Circumstances; but if by the Struggle she obtains and secures for the Nation its future Liberty, and a good Constitution, a few Years' Enjoyment of those Blessings will amply repair all the Damages their Acquisition may have occasioned.[135] God grant, that not only the Love of Liberty, but a thorough Knowledge of the Rights of Man, may pervade all the Nations of the Earth, so that a Philosopher may set his Foot anywhere on its Surface, and say, "This is my Country."

Your Wishes for a cordial and perpetual Friendship between Britain and her ancient Colonies are manifested continually in every one of your Letters to me; something of my Disposition on the same Subject may appear to you in casting your Eye over the enclosed Paper. I do not by this Opportunity send you any of our Gazettes, because the Postage from Liverpool would be more than they are worth. I can now only add my best Wishes of every kind of Felicity for the three amiable Hartleys, to whom I have the honor of being an affectionate friend and most obedient humble servant,

[B. FRANKLIN.]

TO EZRA STILES[136]

Philadᵃ, March 9, 1790.

REVEREND AND DEAR SIR,

I received your kind Letter of Jan'y 28, and am glad you have at length received the portrait of Gov'r Yale from his Family, and deposited it in the College Library. He was a great and good Man, and had the Merit of doing infinite Service to your Country by his Munificence to that Institution. The Honour you propose doing me by placing mine in the same Room with his, is much too great for my Deserts; but you always had a Partiality for me, and to that it must be ascribed. I am however

too much obliged to Yale College, the first learned Society that
took Notice of me and adorned me with its Honours, to refuse
a Request that comes from it thro' so esteemed a Friend. But
I do not think any one of the Portraits you mention, as in my
Possession, worthy of the Place and Company you propose to
place it in. You have an excellent Artist lately arrived. If he
will undertake to make one for you, I shall cheerfully pay the
Expence; but he must not delay setting about it, or I may slip
thro' his fingers, for I am now in my eighty-fifth year, and very
infirm.

I send with this a very learned Work, as it seems to me, on
the antient Samaritan Coins, lately printed in Spain, and at
least curious for the Beauty of the Impression. Please to accept
it for your College Library. I have subscribed for the Encyclo-
pædia now printing here, with the Intention of presenting it to
the College. I shall probably depart before the Work is finished,
but shall leave Directions for its Continuance to the End. With
this you will receive some of the first numbers.

You desire to know something of my Religion. It is the first
time I have been questioned upon it. But I cannot take your
Curiosity amiss, and shall endeavour in a few Words to gratify
it. Here is my Creed. I believe in one God, Creator of the Universe. That he governs it by his Providence. That he ought to
be worshipped. That the most acceptable Service we render to
him is doing good to his other Children. That the soul of Man
is immortal, and will be treated with Justice in another Life respecting its Conduct in this. These I take to be the fundamental Principles of all sound Religion, and I regard them as
you do in whatever Sect I meet with them.

As to Jesus of Nazareth, my Opinion of whom you particularly desire, I think the System of Morals and his Religion, as
he left them to us, the best the World ever saw or is likely to
see; but I apprehend it has received various corrupting Changes,
and I have, with most of the present Dissenters in England,
some Doubts as to his Divinity; tho' it is a question I do not
dogmatize upon, having never studied it, and think it needless
to busy myself with it now, when I expect soon an Opportunity

of knowing the Truth with less Trouble. I see no harm, however, in its being believed, if that Belief has the good Consequence, as probably it has, of making his Doctrines more respected and better observed; especially as I do not perceive, that the Supreme takes it amiss, by distinguishing the Unbelievers in his Government of the World with any peculiar Marks of his Displeasure.

I shall only add, respecting myself, that, having experienced the Goodness of that Being in conducting me prosperously thro' a long life, I have no doubt of its Continuance in the next, though without the smallest Conceit of meriting such Goodness. My Sentiments on this Head you will see in the Copy of an old Letter enclosed, which I wrote in answer to one from a zealous Religionist, whom I had relieved in a paralytic case by electricity, and who, being afraid I should grow proud upon it, sent me his serious though rather impertinent Caution. I send you also the Copy of another Letter, which will shew something of my Disposition relating to Religion. With great and sincere Esteem and Affection, I am, Your obliged old Friend and most obedient humble Servant

B. FRANKLIN.

P. S. Had not your College some Present of Books from the King of France? Please to let me know, if you had an Expectation given you of more, and the Nature of that Expectation? I have a Reason for the Enquiry.

I confide, that you will not expose me to Criticism and censure by publishing any part of this Communication to you. I have ever let others enjoy their religious Sentiments, without reflecting on them for those that appeared to me unsupportable and even absurd. All Sects here, and we have a great Variety, have experienced my good will in assisting them with Subscriptions for building their new Places of Worship; and, as I have never opposed any of their Doctrines, I hope to go out of the World in Peace with them all.

ON THE SLAVE-TRADE

TO THE EDITOR OF THE FEDERAL GAZETTE [137]

March 23d, 1790.

SIR,

Reading last night in your excellent Paper the speech of Mr. Jackson in Congress against their meddling with the Affair of Slavery, or attempting to mend the Condition of the Slaves, it put me in mind of a similar One made about 100 Years since by Sidi Mehemet Ibrahim, a member of the Divan of Algiers, which may be seen in Martin's Account of his Consulship, anno 1687. It was against granting the Petition of the Sect called *Erika*, or Purists, who pray'd for the Abolition of Piracy and Slavery as being unjust. Mr. Jackson does not quote it; perhaps he has not seen it. If, therefore, some of its Reasonings are to be found in his eloquent Speech, it may only show that men's Interests and Intellects operate and are operated on with surprising similarity in all Countries and Climates, when under similar Circumstances. The African's Speech, as translated, is as follows.

"*Allah Bismillah, &c. God is great, and Mahomet is his Prophet.*

"Have these *Erika* considered the Consequences of granting their Petition? If we cease our Cruises against the Christians, how shall we be furnished with the Commodities their Countries produce, and which are so necessary for us? If we forbear to make Slaves of their People, who in this hot Climate are to cultivate our Lands? Who are to perform the common Labours of our City, and in our Families? Must we not then be our own Slaves? And is there not more Compassion and more Favour due to us as Mussulmen, than to these Christian Dogs? We have now above 50,000 Slaves in and near Algiers. This Number, if not kept up by fresh Supplies, will soon diminish, and be gradually annihilated. If we then cease taking and plundering the Infidel Ships, and making Slaves of the Seamen and Passengers, our Lands will become of no Value for want of Cultivation; the Rents of Houses in the City will sink one half; and the Revenues of Government arising from its Share of Prizes be totally destroy'd! And for what? To gratify the whims of a whimsical Sect, who would have us, not only forbear making more Slaves, but even to manumit those we have.

"But who is to indemnify their Masters for the Loss? Will the State do it? Is our Treasury sufficient? Will the *Erika* do it? Can they do it? Or would they, to do what they think Justice to the Slaves, do a greater Injustice to the Owners? And if we set our Slaves free, what is to be done with them? Few of them will return to their Countries; they know too well the greater Hardships they must there be subject to; they will not embrace our holy Religion; they will not adopt our Manners; our People will not pollute themselves by intermarrying with them. Must we maintain them as Beggars in our Streets, or suffer our Properties to be the Prey of their Pillage? For Men long accustom'd to Slavery will not work for a Livelihood when not compell'd. And what is there so pitiable in their present Condition? Were they not Slaves in their own Countries?

"Are not Spain, Portugal, France, and the Italian states govern'd by Despots, who hold all their Subjects in Slavery, without Exception? Even England treats its Sailors as Slaves; for they are, whenever the Government pleases, seiz'd, and confin'd in Ships of War, condemn'd not only to work, but to fight, for small Wages, or a mere Subsistence, not better than our Slaves are allow'd by us. Is their Condition then made worse by their falling into our Hands? No; they have only exchanged one Slavery for another, and I may say a better; for here they are brought into a Land where the Sun of Islamism gives forth its Light, and shines in full Splendor, and they have an Opportunity of making themselves acquainted with the true Doctrine, and thereby saving their immortal Souls. Those who remain at home have not that Happiness. Sending the Slaves home then would be sending them out of Light into Darkness.

"I repeat the Question, What is to be done with them? I have heard it suggested, that they may be planted in the Wilderness, where there is plenty of Land for them to subsist on, and where they may flourish as a free State; but they are, I doubt, too little dispos'd to labour without Compulsion, as well as too ignorant to establish a good government, and the wild Arabs would soon molest and destroy or again enslave them. While serving us, we take care to provide them with every thing, and they are treated with Humanity. The Labourers in their own Country are, as I am well informed, worse fed, lodged, and cloathed. The Condition of most of them is therefore already mended, and requires no further Improvement. Here their Lives are in Safety. They are not liable to be impress'd for Soldiers, and forc'd to cut one another's Christian Throats, as in the Wars of their own Countries. If some of the religious mad Bigots, who now teaze us with their silly Petitions, have in a Fit of blind Zeal freed their Slaves, it was not Generosity, it was not Humanity, that mov'd them to the Action; it was from the conscious Burthen of a Load of Sins, and Hope, from the supposed Merits of so good a Work, to be excus'd Damnation.

"How grossly are they mistaken in imagining Slavery to be disallow'd by the Alcoran! Are not the two Precepts, to quote no more, '*Masters, treat your Slaves with kindness; Slaves, serve your Masters with Cheerfulness and Fidelity*,' clear Proofs to the contrary? Nor can the Plundering of Infidels be in that sacred Book forbidden, since it is well known from it, that God has given the World, and all that it contains, to his faithful Mussulmen, who are to enjoy it of Right as fast as they conquer it. Let us then hear no more of this detestable Proposition, the Manumission of Christian Slaves, the Adoption of which would, by depreciating our Lands and Houses, and thereby depriving so many good Citizens of their Properties, create universal Discontent, and provoke Insurrections, to the endangering of Government and producing general Confusion. I have therefore no doubt, but this wise Council will prefer the Comfort and Happiness of a whole Nation of true Believers to the Whim of a few *Erika*, and dismiss their Petition."

The Result was, as Martin tells us, that the Divan came to this Resolution; "The Doctrine, that Plundering and Enslaving the Christians is unjust, is at best *problematical;* but that it is the

Interest of this State to continue the Practice, is clear; therefore let the Petition be rejected."

And it was rejected accordingly.

And since like Motives are apt to produce in the Minds of Men like Opinions and Resolutions, may we not, Mr. Brown, venture to predict, from this Account, that the Petitions to the Parliament of England for abolishing the Slave-Trade, to say nothing of other Legislatures, and the Debates upon them, will have a similar Conclusion? I am, Sir, your constant Reader and humble Servant,

HISTORICUS.

REMARKS CONCERNING THE SAVAGES
OF NORTH AMERICA[138]

Savages we call them, because their Manners differ from ours, which we think the Perfection of Civility; they think the same of theirs.

Perhaps, if we could examine the Manners of different Nations with Impartiality, we should find no People so rude, as to be without any Rules of Politeness; nor any so polite, as not to have some Remains of Rudeness.

The Indian Men, when young, are Hunters and Warriors; when old, Counsellors; for all their Government is by Counsel of the Sages; there is no Force, there are no Prisons, no Officers to compel Obedience, or inflict Punishment. Hence they generally study Oratory, the best Speaker having the most Influence. The Indian Women till the Ground, dress the Food, nurse and bring up the Children, and preserve and hand down to Posterity the Memory of public Transactions. These Employments of Men and Women are accounted natural and honourable. Having few artificial Wants, they have abundance of Leisure for Improvement by Conversation. Our laborious Manner of Life, compared with theirs, they esteem slavish and base; and the Learning, on which we value ourselves, they regard as frivolous and useless. An Instance of this occurred at the Treaty of Lancaster, in Pennsylvania, *anno* 1744, between the Government of Virginia and the Six Nations. After the principal Business was settled, the Commissioners from Virginia acquainted the Indians by a Speech, that there was at Williamsburg a College, with a Fund for Educating Indian youth; and that, if the Six Nations would send down half a dozen of their young Lads to that College, the Government would take care that they should be well provided for, and instructed in all the Learning of the White People. It is one of the Indian Rules of Politeness not to answer a public Proposition the same day that it is made; they think it would be treating it as a light matter, and that they show it Respect by taking time to consider it, as of a Matter important. They therefore deferr'd their Answer till the Day following; when their Speaker began, by expressing their deep Sense of the kindness of the Virginia Government, in making them that Offer; "for we know," says he, "that you highly esteem the kind of Learning taught in those Colleges, and that the Maintenance of our young Men, while with you, would be very expensive to you. We are convinc'd, therefore, that you mean to do us Good by your Proposal; and we thank you heartily. But you, who are wise, must know that different Nations have different Conceptions of things; and you will therefore not take it amiss, if our Ideas of this kind of Education happen not to be the same with yours. We have had some Experience of it; Several of our young People were formerly brought up at the Colleges of the Northern Provinces; they were instructed in all your Sciences; but, when they came back to us, they were bad Runners, ignorant of every means of living in the Woods, unable to bear either Cold or Hunger, knew neither how to build a Cabin, take a Deer, or kill an Enemy, spoke our Language imperfectly, were therefore neither fit for Hunters, Warriors, nor Counsellors; they were totally good for nothing. We are however not the less oblig'd by your kind Offer, tho' we decline accepting it; and, to show our grateful Sense of it, if the Gentlemen of Virginia will send us a Dozen of their Sons, we will take great Care of their Education, instruct them in all we know, and make *Men* of them."

Having frequent Occasions to hold public Councils, they have acquired great Order and Decency in conducting them. The old Men sit in the foremost Ranks, the Warriors in the next, and the Women and Children in the hindmost. The Business of the Women is to take exact Notice of what passes, imprint it in their Memories (for they have no Writing), and communicate it to their Children. They are the Records of the Council, and they preserve Traditions of the Stipulations in Treaties 100 Years back; which, when we compare with our Writings, we always find exact. He that would speak, rises. The rest observe a profound Silence. When he has finish'd and sits down, they leave him 5 or 6 Minutes to recollect, that, if he has omitted any thing he intended to say, or has any thing to add, he may rise again and deliver it. To interrupt another, even in common Conversation, is reckon'd highly indecent. How different this is from the conduct of a polite British House of Commons, where scarce a day passes without some Confusion, that makes the Speaker hoarse in calling *to Order;* and how different from the Mode of Conversation in many polite Companies of Europe, where, if you do not deliver your Sentence with great Rapidity, you are cut off in the middle of it by the Impatient Loquacity of those you converse with, and never suffer'd to finish it!

The Politeness of these Savages in Conversation is indeed carried to Excess, since it does not permit them to contradict or deny the Truth of what is asserted in their Presence. By this means they indeed avoid Disputes; but then it becomes difficult to know their Minds, or what Impression you make upon them. The Missionaries who have attempted to convert them to Christianity, all complain of this as one of the great Difficulties of their Mission. The Indians hear with Patience the Truths of the Gospel explain'd to them, and give their usual Tokens of Assent and Approbation; you would think they were convinc'd. No such matter. It is mere Civility.

A Swedish Minister, having assembled the chiefs of the Susquehanah Indians, made a Sermon to them, acquainting them with the principal historical Facts on which our Religion is founded; such as the Fall of our first Parents by eating an Apple, the coming of Christ to repair the Mischief, his Miracles and Suffering, &c. When he had finished, an Indian Orator stood up to thank him. "What you have told us," says he, "is all very good. It is indeed bad to eat Apples. It is better to make them all into Cyder. We are much oblig'd by your kindness in coming so far, to tell us these Things which you have heard from your Mothers. In return, I will tell you some of those we have heard from ours. In the Beginning, our Fathers had only the Flesh of Animals to subsist on; and if their Hunting was unsuccessful, they were starving. Two of our young Hunters, having kill'd a Deer, made a Fire in the Woods to broil some Part of it. When they were about to satisfy their Hunger, they beheld a beautiful young Woman descend from the Clouds, and seat herself on that Hill, which you see yonder among the Blue Mountains. They said to each other, it is a Spirit that has smelt our broiling Venison, and wishes to eat of it; let us offer some to her. They presented her with the Tongue; she was pleas'd with the Taste of it, and said, 'Your kindness shall be rewarded; come to this Place after thirteen Moons, and you shall find something that will be of great Benefit in nourishing you and your Children to the latest Generation.' They did so, and, to their Surprise, found Plants they had never seen before; but which, from that ancient time, have been constantly cultivated among us, to our great Advantage. Where her right Hand had touched the Ground, they found Maize; where her left hand had touch'd it, they found Kidney-Beans; and where her Backside had sat on it, they found Tobacco." The good Missionary, disgusted with this idle Tale, said, "What I delivered to you were sacred Truths; but what you tell me is mere Fable, Fiction, and Falshood." The Indian, offended, reply'd, "My brother, it seems your Friends have not done you Justice in your Education; they have not well instructed you in the Rules of Common Civility. You saw that we, who understand and practise those Rules, believ'd all your stories; why do you refuse to believe ours?"

When any of them come into our Towns, our People are apt

to crowd round them, gaze upon them, and incommode them, where they desire to be private; this they esteem great Rudeness, and the Effect of the Want of Instruction in the Rules of Civility and good Manners. "We have," say they, "as much Curiosity as you, and when you come into our Towns, we wish for Opportunities of looking at you; but for this purpose we hide ourselves behind Bushes, where you are to pass, and never intrude ourselves into your Company."

Their Manner of entring one another's village has likewise its Rules. It is reckon'd uncivil in travelling Strangers to enter a Village abruptly, without giving Notice of their Approach. Therefore, as soon as they arrive within hearing, they stop and hollow, remaining there till invited to enter. Two old Men usually come out to them, and lead them in. There is in every Village a vacant Dwelling, called *the Strangers' House.* Here they are plac'd, while the old Men go round from Hut to Hut, acquainting the Inhabitants, that Strangers are arriv'd, who are probably hungry and weary; and every one sends them what he can spare of Victuals, and Skins to repose on. When the Strangers are refresh'd, Pipes and Tobacco are brought; and then, but not before, Conversation begins, with Enquiries who they are, whither bound, what News, &c.; and it usually ends with offers of Service, if the Strangers have occasion of Guides, or any Necessaries for continuing their Journey; and nothing is exacted for the Entertainment.

The same Hospitality, esteem'd among them as a principal Virtue, is practis'd by private Persons; of which Conrad Weiser, our Interpreter, gave me the following Instance. He had been naturaliz'd among the Six Nations, and spoke well the Mohock Language. In going thro' the Indian Country, to carry a Message from our Governor to the Council at Onondaga, he call'd at the Habitation of Canassatego, an old Acquaintance, who embrac'd him, spread Furs for him to sit on, plac'd before him some boil'd Beans and Venison, and mix'd some Rum and Water for his Drink. When he was well refresh'd, and had lit his Pipe, Canassatego began to converse with him; ask'd how he had far'd the many Years since they had seen each other;

whence he then came; what occasion'd the Journey, &c. Conrad answered all his Questions; and when the Discourse began to flag, the Indian, to continue it, said, "Conrad, you have lived long among the white People, and know something of their Customs; I have been sometimes at Albany, and have observed, that once in Seven Days they shut up their Shops, and assemble all in the great House; tell me what it is for? What do they do there?" "They meet there," says Conrad, "to hear and learn *good Things*." "I do not doubt," says the Indian, "that they tell you so; they have told me the same; but I doubt the Truth of what they say, and I will tell you my Reasons. I went lately to Albany to sell my Skins and buy Blankets, Knives, Powder, Rum, &c. You know I us'd generally to deal with Hans Hanson; but I was a little inclin'd this time to try some other Merchant. However, I call'd first upon Hans, and asked him what he would give for Beaver. He said he could not give any more than four Shillings a Pound; 'but,' says he, 'I cannot talk on Business now; this is the Day when we meet together to learn *Good Things*, and I am going to the Meeting.' So I thought to myself, 'Since we cannot do any Business to-day, I may as well go to the meeting too,' and I went with him. There stood up a Man in Black, and began to talk to the People very angrily. I did not understand what he said; but, perceiving that he look'd much at me and at Hanson, I imagin'd he was angry at seeing me there; so I went out, sat down near the House, struck Fire, and lit my Pipe, waiting till the Meeting should break up. I thought too, that the Man had mention'd something of Beaver, and I suspected it might be the Subject of their Meeting. So, when they came out, I accosted my Merchant. 'Well, Hans,' says I, 'I hope you have agreed to give more than four Shillings a Pound.' 'No,' says he, 'I cannot give so much; I cannot give more than three shillings and sixpence.' I then spoke to several other Dealers, but they all sung the same song, —Three and sixpence,—Three and sixpence. This made it clear to me, that my Suspicion was right; and, that whatever they pretended of meeting to learn *good Things*, the real purpose was to consult how to cheat Indians in the Price of Beaver.

Consider but a little, Conrad, and you must be of my Opinion. If they met so often to learn *good Things*, they would certainly have learnt some before this time. But they are still ignorant. You know our Practice. If a white Man, in travelling thro' our Country, enters one of our Cabins, we all treat him as I treat you; we dry him if he is wet, we warm him if he is cold, we give him Meat and Drink, that he may allay his Thirst and Hunger; and we spread soft Furs for him to rest and sleep on; we demand nothing in return. But, if I go into a white Man's House at Albany, and ask for Victuals and Drink, they say, 'Where is your Money?' and if I have none, they say, 'Get out, you Indian Dog.' You see they have not yet learned those little *Good Things*, that we need no Meetings to be instructed in, because our Mothers taught them to us when we were Children; and therefore it is impossible their Meetings should be, as they say, for any such purpose, or have any such Effect; they are only to contrive *the Cheating of Indians in the Price of Beaver*."

NOTE.—It is remarkable that in all Ages and Countries Hospitality has been allow'd as the Virtue of those whom the civiliz'd were pleas'd to call Barbarians. The Greeks celebrated the Scythians for it. The Saracens possess'd it eminently, and it is to this day the reigning Virtue of the wild Arabs. St. Paul, too, in the Relation of his Voyage and Shipwreck on the Island of Melita says the Barbarous People shewed us no little kindness; for they kindled a fire, and received us every one, because of the present Rain, and because of the Cold. [*Franklin's note.*]

AN ARABIAN TALE[139]

Albumazar, the good magician, retired in his old age to the top of the lofty mountain Calabut; avoided the society of men, but was visited nightly by genii and spirits of the first rank, who loved him, and amused him with their instructive conversation.

Belubel, the strong, came one evening to see Albumazar; his height was seven leagues, and his wings when spread might overshadow a kingdom. He laid himself gently down between the long ridges of Elluem; the tops of the trees in the valley were his couch; his head rested on Calabut as on a pillow, and his face shone on the tent of Albumazar.

The magician spoke to him with rapturous piety of the wisdom and goodness of the Most High; but expressed his wonder at the existence of evil in the world, which he said he could not account for by all the efforts of his reason.

"Value not thyself, my friend," said Belubel, "on that quality which thou callest reason. If thou knewest its origin and its weakness, it would rather be matter of humiliation."

"Tell me then," said Albumazar, "what I do not know; inform my ignorance, and enlighten my understanding." "Contemplate," said Albumazar [*sic.* Belubel], "the scale of beings, from an elephant down to an oyster. Thou seest a gradual diminution of faculties and powers, so small in each step that the difference is scarce perceptible. There is no gap, but the gradation is complete. Men in general do not know, but thou knowest, that in ascending from an elephant to the infinitely Great, Good, and Wise, there is also a long gradation of beings, who possess powers and faculties of which thou canst yet have no conception."

A PETITION OF THE LEFT HAND

TO THOSE WHO HAVE THE SUPERINTENDENCY OF EDUCATION

[Date unknown]

I address myself to all the friends of youth, and conjure them to direct their compassionate regards to my unhappy fate, in order to remove the prejudices of which I am the victim. There are twin sisters of us; and the two eyes of man do not more resemble, nor are capable of being upon better terms with each other, than my sister and myself, were it not for the partiality of our parents, who make the most injurious distinctions between us. From my infancy, I have been led to consider my sister as a being of a more elevated rank. I was suffered to grow up without the least instruction, while nothing was spared in her education. She had masters to teach her writing, drawing, music, and other accomplishments; but if by chance I touched a pencil, a pen, or a needle, I was bitterly rebuked; and more than once I have been beaten for being awkward, and wanting a graceful manner. It is true, my sister associated me with her upon some occasions; but she always made a point of taking the lead, calling upon me only from necessity, or to figure by her side.

But conceive not, Sirs, that my complaints are instigated merely by vanity. No; my uneasiness is occasioned by an object much more serious. It is the practice in our family, that the whole business of providing for its subsistence falls upon my sister and myself. If any indisposition should attack my sister,—and I mention it in confidence upon this occasion, that she is subject to the gout, the rheumatism, and cramp, without making mention of other accidents,—what would be the fate of our poor family? Must not the regret of our parents be excessive, at having placed so great a difference between sisters who are so perfectly equal? Alas! we must perish from distress; for it would not be in my power even to scrawl a suppliant petition for relief, having been obliged to employ the hand of another in transcribing the request which I have now the honour to prefer to you.

Condescend, Sirs, to make my parents sensible of the injustice of an exclusive tenderness, and of the necessity of distributing their care and affection among all their children equally. I am, with a profound respect, Sirs, your obedient servant,

THE LEFT HAND.

SOME GOOD WHIG PRINCIPLES

[Date unknown]

DECLARATION of those RIGHTS of the Commonalty of Great Britain, *without which they cannot be* FREE.

It is declared,

First, That the government of this realm, and the making of laws for the same, ought to be lodged in the hands of King, Lords of Parliament, and Representatives of *the whole body* of the freemen of this realm.

Secondly, That *every man* of the commonalty (excepting

infants, insane persons, and criminals) is, of common right, and by the laws of God, a *freeman*, and entitled to the free enjoyment of *liberty*.

Thirdly, That liberty, or freedom, consists in having *an actual share* in the appointment of those who frame the laws, and who are to be the guardians of every man's life, property, and peace; for the *all* of one man is as dear to him as the *all* of another; and the poor man has an *equal* right, but *more* need, to have representatives in the legislature than the rich one.

Fourthly, That they who have *no* voice nor vote in the electing of representatives, *do not enjoy* liberty; but are absolutely *enslaved* to those who *have* votes, and to their representatives; for to be enslaved is to have governors whom *other men have set over us*, and be subject to laws *made by the representatives of others*, without having had representatives of our own to give consent in *our* behalf.

Fifthly, That *a very great majority* of the commonalty of this realm are denied the privilege of voting for representatives in Parliament; and, consequently, they are enslaved to a *small number*, who do now enjoy the privilege exclusively to themselves; but who, it may be presumed, are far from wishing to continue in the exclusive possession of a privilege, by which their fellow-subjects are deprived of *common right*, of *justice*, of *liberty;* and which, if not communicated to all, must speedily cause *the certain overthrow of our happy constitution*, and enslave us *all*.

And, sixthly and lastly, We also say and do assert, that it is *the right* of the commonalty of this realm to elect a *new* House of Commons once in *every year*, according to the ancient and sacred laws of the land; because, whenever a Parliament continues in being for *a longer term*, very great numbers of the commonalty, who have arrived at years of manhood since the last election, and *therefore* have a right to be actually represented in the House of Commons, are then *unjustly deprived* of that right.

THE ART OF PROCURING PLEASANT DREAMS

INSCRIBED TO MISS [SHIPLEY], BEING WRITTEN AT HER REQUEST[140]

As a great part of our life is spent in sleep during which we have sometimes pleasant and sometimes painful dreams, it becomes of some consequence to obtain the one kind and avoid the other; for whether real or imaginary, pain is pain and pleasure is pleasure. If we can sleep without dreaming, it is well that painful dreams are avoided. If while we sleep we can have any pleasing dream, it is, as the French say, *autant de gagné*, so much added to the pleasure of life.

To this end it is, in the first place, necessary to be careful in preserving health, by due exercise and great temperance; for, in sickness, the imagination is disturbed, and disagreeable, sometimes terrible, ideas are apt to present themselves. Exercise should precede meals, not immediately follow them; the first promotes, the latter, unless moderate, obstructs digestion. If, after exercise, we feed sparingly, the digestion will be easy and good, the body lightsome, the temper cheerful, and all the animal functions performed agreeably. Sleep, when it follows, will be natural and undisturbed; while indolence, with full feeding, occasions nightmares and horrors inexpressible; we fall from precipices, are assaulted by wild beasts, murderers, and demons, and experience every variety of distress. Observe, however, that the quantities of food and exercise are relative things; those who move much may, and indeed ought to eat more; those who use little exercise should eat little. In general, mankind, since the improvement of cookery, eat about twice as much as nature requires. Suppers are not bad, if we have not dined; but restless nights naturally follow hearty suppers after full dinners. Indeed, as there is a difference in constitutions, some rest well after these meals; it costs them only a frightful dream and an apoplexy, after which they sleep till doomsday. Nothing is more common in the newspapers, than instances of people who, after eating a hearty supper, are found dead abed in the morning.

Another means of preserving health, to be attended to, is the having a constant supply of fresh air in your bed-chamber. It has been a great mistake, the sleeping in rooms exactly closed, and in beds surrounded by curtains. No outward air that may come in to you is so unwholesome as the unchanged air, often breathed, of a close chamber. As boiling water does not grow hotter by longer boiling, if the particles that receive greater heat can escape; so living bodies do not putrefy, if the particles, so fast as they become putrid, can be thrown off. Nature expels them by the pores of the skin and the lungs, and in a free, open air they are carried off; but in a close room we receive them again and again, though they become more and more corrupt. A number of persons crowded into a small room thus spoil the air in a few minutes, and even render it mortal, as in the Black Hole at Calcutta. A single person is said to spoil only a gallon of air per minute, and therefore requires a longer time to spoil a chamber-full; but it is done, however, in proportion, and many putrid disorders hence have their origin. It is recorded of Methusalem, who, being the longest liver, may be supposed to have best preserved his health, that he slept always in the open air; for, when he had lived five hundred years, an angel said to him; "Arise, Methusalem, and build thee an house, for thou shalt live yet five hundred years longer." But Methusalem answered, and said, "If I am to live but five hundred years longer, it is not worth while to build me an house; I will sleep in the air, as I have been used to do." Physicians, after having for ages contended that the sick should not be indulged with fresh air, have at length discovered that it may do them good. It is therefore to be hoped, that they may in time discover likewise, that it is not hurtful to those who are in health, and that we may be then cured of the *aërophobia*, that at present distresses weak minds, and makes them choose to be stifled and poisoned, rather than leave open the window of a bed-chamber, or put down the glass of a coach.

Confined air, when saturated with perspirable matter, will not receive more; and that matter must remain in our bodies, and occasion diseases; but it gives some previous notice of its being about to be hurtful, by producing certain uneasiness, slight indeed at first, which as with regard to the lungs is a trifling sensation, and to the pores of the skin a kind of restlessness, which is difficult to describe, and few that feel it know the cause of it. But we may recollect, that sometimes on waking in the night, we have, if warmly covered, found it difficult to get asleep again. We turn often without finding repose in any position. This fidgettiness (to use a vulgar expression for want of a better) is occasioned wholly by an uneasiness in the skin, owing to the retention of the perspirable matter—the bed-clothes having received their quantity, and, being saturated, refusing to take any more. To become sensible of this by an experiment, let a person keep his position in the bed, but throw off the bed-clothes, and suffer fresh air to approach the part uncovered of his body; he will then feel that part suddenly refreshed; for the air will immediately relieve the skin, by receiving, licking up, and carrying off, the load of perspirable matter that incommoded it. For every portion of cool air that approaches the warm skin, in receiving its part of that vapour, receives therewith a degree of heat that rarefies and renders it lighter, when it will be pushed away with its burthen, by cooler and therefore heavier fresh air, which for a moment supplies its place, and then, being likewise changed and warmed, gives way to a succeeding quantity. This is the order of nature, to prevent animals being infected by their own perspiration. He will now be sensible of the difference between the part exposed to the air and that which, remaining sunk in the bed, denies the air access: for this part now manifests its uneasiness more distinctly by the comparison, and the seat of the uneasiness is more plainly perceived than when the whole surface of the body was affected by it.

Here, then, is one great and general cause of unpleasing dreams. For when the body is uneasy, the mind will be disturbed by it, and disagreeable ideas of various kinds will in sleep be the natural consequences. The remedies, preventive and curative, follow:

1. By eating moderately (as before advised for health's sake)

less perspirable matter is produced in a given time; hence the bed-clothes receive it longer before they are saturated, and we may therefore sleep longer before we are made uneasy by their refusing to receive any more.

2. By using thinner and more porous bed-clothes, which will suffer the perspirable matter more easily to pass through them, we are less incommoded, such being longer tolerable.

3. When you are awakened by this uneasiness, and find you cannot easily sleep again, get out of bed, beat up and turn your pillow, shake the bed-clothes well, with at least twenty shakes, then throw the bed open and leave it to cool; in the meanwhile, continuing undrest, walk about your chamber till your skin has had time to discharge its load, which it will do sooner as the air may be dried and colder. When you begin to feel the cold air unpleasant, then return to your bed, and you will soon fall asleep, and your sleep will be sweet and pleasant. All the scenes presented to your fancy will be too of the pleasing kind. I am often as agreeably entertained with them, as by the scenery of an opera. If you happen to be too indolent to get out of bed, you may, instead of it, lift up your bed-clothes with one arm and leg, so as to draw in a good deal of fresh air, and by letting them fall force it out again. This, repeated twenty times, will so clear them of the perspirable matter they have imbibed, as to permit your sleeping well for some time afterwards. But this latter method is not equal to the former.

Those who do not love trouble, and can afford to have two beds, will find great luxury in rising, when they wake in a hot bed, and going into the cool one. Such shifting of beds would also be of great service to persons ill of a fever, as it refreshes and frequently procures sleep. A very large bed, that will admit a removal so distant from the first situation as to be cool and sweet, may in a degree answer the same end.

One or two observations more will conclude this little piece. Care must be taken, when you lie down, to dispose your pillow so as to suit your manner of placing your head, and to be perfectly easy; then place your limbs so as not to bear inconveniently hard upon one another, as, for instance, the joints of

your ankles; for, though a bad position may at first give but
little pain and be hardly noticed, yet a continuance will render
it less tolerable, and the uneasiness may come on while you are
asleep, and disturb your imagination. These are the rules of the
art. But, though they will generally prove effectual in producing
the end intended, there is a case in which the most punctual
observance of them will be totally fruitless. I need not mention
the case to you, my dear friend, but my account of the art would
be imperfect without it. The case is, when the person who
desires to have pleasant dreams has not taken care to preserve,
what is necessary above all things,

A Good Conscience.

NOTES

References are to Franklin's *Writings*, edited by A. H. Smyth, 10 vols., 1905–1907.

1. In addition to John Bigelow's "Historical Sketch of the Fortunes and Misfortunes of the Autograph Manuscript of Franklin's Memoirs of His Own Life," see Franklin's references to the *Autobiography*, in *Writings*, IX, 550–51, 559, 665, 675, 688; X, 50.

2. The *New England Courant*, begun Aug. 21, 1721 (fourth American newspaper), was preceded by *Boston News-Letter*, April 24, 1704, *Boston Gazette*, Dec. 21, 1719, *American Weekly Mercury*, Dec. 22, 1719 (Philadelphia).

3. Sir Wm. Keith (1680–1749), governor of Pennsylvania 1717–1726. He was dismissed by the Proprietaries in 1726; after casting his lot with the provincial assembly, he became "a tribune of the people" (*Dictionary of American Biography*, X, 292–3). It is not improbable that Franklin's antipathy for the Proprietaries was quickened by his contacts with Keith (even though he was the victim of the governor's gulling). See note 65 for "James Ralph."

4. Sir Hans Sloane (1660–1753), botanist and physician, friend of Sydenham, Newton, Ray, and Boyle, made President of the Royal Society in 1727 (until 1741). See *Dictionary of National Biography*, LII, 379–80, and Franklin's letter to Sir Hans Sloane (London, June 2, 1725) in *Writings*, II, 52–3.

5. Sir Hans Sloane contributed curiosities to Don Saltero's place, Cheyne Walk, Chelsea. Steele dedicated a *Tatler* to this collector of gimcracks who wrote of his oddities:

> "Monsters of all sorts here are seen
> Strange things in nature as they grew so;
> Some relicks of the Sheba queen,
> And fragments of the fam'd Bob Crusoe."

6. See note 22.

7. For an account of this sturdy colonial who learned Latin in order to read Newton's *Principia*, see E. P. Oberholtzer's *A Literary History of Philadelphia*, 57 ff.

8. James Parton's *Life and Times of Benjamin Franklin*, I, 154–67 (chap. XIII) contains a good account of this junto of friends.

9. See C. E. Jorgenson's "A Brand Flung at Colonial Orthodoxy" (in Bibliography, p. clxv above), for the deistic patterns of thought found in Keimer's newspaper.

10. Consult C. H. Hart, "Who Was the Mother of Franklin's Son? An Inquiry Demonstrating that She Was Deborah Read, Wife of Benjamin

Franklin." (See Bibliography, p. clxiv above.) Also see *Who Was the Mother of Franklin's Son? An Historical Conundrum, hitherto given up, now partly answered by Paul Leicester Ford.* With an afterword by John Clyde Oswald (New Rochelle, N. Y.: 1932).

11. End of reprint of the original MS in the Henry E. Huntington Library. The selections that follow are from *Writings*, in which A. H. Smyth reprints the Bigelow transcript with indifferent accuracy. "Continuation of the Account of my Life, begun at Passy, near Paris, 1784." Abel James and Benjamin Vaughan urge Franklin to continue his life beyond 1730 (see *Writings*, I, 313–20). Vaughan promises that when finished "it will be worth all Plutarch's Lives put together" (p. 318).

12. Dated July 1, 1733.

13. "Thus far written at Passy, 1784." He continues his *Autobiography* in Philadelphia in August, 1788.

14. Consult C. E. Jorgenson's "The New Science in the Almanacs of Ames and Franklin" (see Bibliography, p. clxv, above).

15. "Self-Denial Not the Essence of Virtue," *Pennsylvania Gazette*, No. 324, Feb. 18, 1735; printed in W. T. Franklin's edition, III, 233–5. "On True Happiness," *Pennsylvania Gazette*, No. 363, Nov. 20, 1735; printed in W. T. Franklin's edition, III, 238–9.

16. Chosen Clerk of Pennsylvania General Assembly in 1736.

17. See their correspondence in L. Tyerman's *Life of the Rev. George Whitefield* (2 vols., London, 1876).

18. J. Parton observes that this list may have been suggested by the word-catalogs in the *Gargantua* (*Life and Times of Benjamin Franklin*, I, 221). This mildly Rabelaisian series is later elaborated into "The Drinker's Dictionary" found in the *Pennsylvania Gazette*, No. 494, May 25, 1738; and reprinted by Parton, I, 222–5.

19. When James Franklin was accused of mocking the clergy and unsettling the peace, he was refused license to print the *New England Courant*. So Benjamin, his apprenticeship indentures cancelled (though new ones were privately signed), became nominal editor. Consult C. A. Duniway, *The Development of Freedom of the Press in Massachusetts*, 97–103; W. G. Bleyer, *Main Currents in the History of American Journalism*, chaps. I–II.

20. Rules for his famous Junto, begun in 1727.

21. No Part II has ever been found. A. H. Smyth suggests that this creed and liturgy was "Franklin's daily companion to the end of his life" (*Writings*, II, 92 note).

22. When Samuel Keimer discovered that Franklin and Meredith were about to launch a newspaper, he began his *Universal Instructor in all Arts and Sciences: and Pennsylvania Gazette* (first issue, Dec. 28, 1728). Franklin and Joseph Breintnall wrote the *Busy-Body* series for Bradford's *American Weekly Mercury*. Nos. I–V and VIII are by Franklin. See S. Bloore's "Joseph Breintnall, First Secretary of the Library Company" (in Bib-

liography). That Keimer became infuriated, one can see in issues X, XII, and XVI of the *Universal Instructor* . . . , in which *Busy-Body* is scourged with both prose and poetry.

23. Franklin purchases Keimer's *Universal Instructor* . . . , deleting the first half of the title, which had appeared in small italic type.

24. See *Autobiography*, *Writings*, I, 343.

25. The use of scales suggests that Franklin probably knew Aristophanes' *The Frogs*. It is more likely, however that he was acquainted with the use of scales in contemporary witch trials. In the *Gentleman's Magazine* for Jan., 1731, there is an account of a witch trial at "Burlington, in Pensilvania," in the course of which scales and the Bible were used. (See Brand's *Popular Antiquities* [H. Ellis, ed., London, 1888], III, 35.) In the same magazine for Feb., 1759, is an account of a similar trial which took place in England (*ibid.*, III, 22).

26. In his 1734 issue of the *American Almanack* Leeds observed that the account of his death was grossly exaggerated. Doubtless Franklin had read (Swift's) Bickerstaff's predictions of the death of Partridge.

27. Compare Swift's *A Meditation upon a Broomstick*. Mug and broomstick are alike obliged to undergo the indignities of a "dirty wench." But more conclusively, the rhetoric and the ethical application to human affairs suggest Franklin's indebtedness to Swift.

28. His parents' response is learned from a letter (not in Smyth) to his father: "Hon. Father, I received your kind letter of the 4th of May in answer to mine of April 13th. I wrote that of mine with design to remove or lessen the uneasiness you and my Mother appear'd to be under on account of my Principles, and it gave me great Pleasure when she declar'd in her next to me that she approved of my Letter and was satisfy'd with me." (Cited in J. F. Sachse, *Benjamin Franklin as a Free Mason*, 75.)

29. Rev. George Whitefield, whom Franklin met in 1739.

30. *M. T. Cicero's Cato Major, or his Discourse of Old-Age: With Explanatory Notes*. Philadelphia. Printed and Sold by B. Franklin, 1744.

31. "This letter is undated, but from Franklin's ecclesiastical mathematics it would appear to have been written on the tenth of March" (A. H. Smyth, *Writings*, II, 283 note).

32. Excellent note in *Writings*, II, 463–4. Abbé Raynal published *Polly Baker* in his *Histoire* . . . as an authentic document. Also Peter Annet printed this *jeu d'esprit* in his *Social Bliss* (1749). See N. L. Torrey, *Voltaire and the English Deists*, 187. A. H. Smyth confesses: "The mystery surrounding the authorship and first publication of the 'Speech' remains an impenetrable mystery. The style is altogether Franklinian, and the story seems unquestionably to have been written by him, but I have searched *The Pennsylvania Gazette* in vain for it. It is not there."

33. See "Introduction" in Wm. Pepper's Facsimile Reprint of the *Proposals* (Philadelphia, 1931), vii–xvii. Although A. H. Smyth prints "Authors quoted in this Paper," he does not print the copious documen-

tation Franklin included. The "Authors" listed are: Milton, Locke, Hutcheson, Obadiah Walker, M. Rollin, George Turnbull, "with some others."

34. Printed as Appendix to Rev. R. Peters's *A Sermon on Education . . .*, Philadelphia, Printed and Sold by B. Franklin and D. Hall, 1751.

35. Samuel Croxall's (d. 1752) *Fables of Æsop and Others*, 1722. "The remarkable popularity of these fables, of which editions are still published, is to be accounted for by their admirable style. They are excellent examples of naïve, clear, and forcible English" (*Dictionary of National Biography*, XIII, 246–8).

36. A part of Johnson's *Elementa Philosophica*, printed by Franklin in 1752. See H. and C. Schneider, eds., *Samuel Johnson, President of King's College. His Career and Writings*. 4 vols., New York, 1929.

37. Fénelon's *Telemachus*. Chevalier de Ramsay's *Travels of Cyrus*. 2 vols. London, 1727 (2d ed.).

38. For Franklin's awareness of Rabelais, see C. E. Jorgenson's "Benjamin Franklin and Rabelais," *Classical Journal*, XXIX, 538–40 (April, 1934).

39. First published in [Clarke, Wm.] *Observations on the Late and present Conduct of the French, with Regard to their Encroachments upon the British Colonies in North America . . . To which is added, wrote by another Hand; Observations concerning the Increase of Mankind, Peopling of Countries, Etc.* Boston, 1755. See L. J. Carey's *Franklin's Economic Views*, 46–60, for able survey of Franklin's theory of population and its relation to Malthus and Adam Smith. Also see L. C. Wroth, *An American Bookshelf, 1755* (Philadelphia, 1934), 25–7.

40. Hume having objected to the use of "pejorate" and "colonize," Franklin yields to him. "Since they are not in common use here [England], I give up as bad; for certainly in writings intended for persuasion and for general information, one cannot be too clear; and every expression in the least obscure is a fault" (*Writings*, IV, 82–4; Sept. 27, 1760).

41. On complaint of John Bartram and Cadwallader Colden, Franklin deleted the concluding paragraphs in subsequent editions.

42. Read before the Royal Society on Dec. 21, 1752. It was printed in the *Gentleman's Magazine*, December, 1752. Essentially because of his identification of electricity with lightning, Franklin in 1753 received the Copley medal and was in 1756 elected F. R. S.

43. Mr. George S. Eddy has compiled a "Catalogue of Pamphlets, Once a Part of the Library of Benjamin Franklin, and now owned by the Historical Society of Pennsylvania," which one of the editors was permitted to use in MS form in the W. S. Mason Collection. One of the pamphlets is: *An Hymn to the Creator of the World, The Thoughts taken chiefly from Psal. CIV. To which is added in Prose An Idea of the Creator From His Works . . .* London, MDCCL. James Burgh. If most of the material in this issue (it is equally true of many of the other issues) is

"borrowed," it none the less shows toward what ideas Franklin was sympathetic. Almanac makers on the whole were not characterized by a vast display of originality.

44. Brackets in this letter are the result of A. H. Smyth's collation of two MSS.

45. "These letters first appeared in *The London Chronicle*, February 6 and 8, 1766. They were published again in *The London Magazine*, February, 1766, and in *The Pennsylvania Chronicle*, January 16, 1769. They were republished in Almon's 'Remembrancer' in 1766." (A. H. Smyth, *Writings*, III, 231 note.)

After the failure of his *Albany Plan* (for text see *Writings*, III, 197–226), Franklin, visiting Governor Shirley in Boston, was shown an English plan: it "was, that the governors of all the colonies, each attended by one or two members of his council, should assemble at some central town, and there concert measures of defense, raise troops, order the construction of forts, and draw on the British treasury for the whole expense; the treasury to be afterwards reimbursed *by a tax laid on the colonies by an act of Parliament*" (Parton, I, 340). The letters are a protest against this plan, a protest marking the first stages of the revolution.

46. The second cousin and in 1758 the wife of William Greene, the second governor of the state of Rhode Island. See *Dictionary of American Biography*, VII, 576–7.

47. Had made a tour inspecting post offices.

48. Daughter of Samuel Ward, governor of Rhode Island.

49. Franklin's daughter, born 1744.

50. John Franklin died in Boston, January, 1756, age sixty-five.

51. Daughter of John Franklin's second wife by a former marriage.

52. See discussion (including bibliographical note) of Rev. Wm. Smith in Introduction, section on "Franklin's Theories of Education."

53. From an exact reprint made by W. S. Mason from a copy of *Poor Richard* (1758) in his collection. Lindsay Swift, in *Benjamin Franklin*, notes: "It may safely be said that it is the American classic *par excellence*, and shares with Mrs. Stowe's *Uncle Tom's Cabin* the honour of having passed by translation into more other tongues than anything else thus far bearing the stamp of our national spirit" (pp. 33–4). A glance at Ford's *Franklin Bibliography*, 53–111, will suggest the vogue of this classic. See L. L. L.'s "The Way to Wealth: History and Editions," *Nation*, XCVI, 494–6 (May 15, 1913).

William Temple Franklin observes that *The Way to Wealth* "is supposed to have greatly contributed to the formation of that *national character* they [people of America] have since exhibited" (1818 ed. of Franklin's *Works*, III, 248).

54. Stephen Potts and William Parsons were among the original members of the Junto (*Writings*, I, 299–300). See note on Parsons in *Pennsylvania Magazine of History and Biography*, XXXIII, 340 (1909).

55. Henry Home, Lord Kames (1696–1782). See *Dictionary of National Biography*, XXVII, 232–4; A. F. Tytler's *Memoirs* of Lord Kames, 3 vols., Edinburgh, 1814 (2d ed.). Franklin writes an interesting letter to Kames (London, Jan. 3, 1760) affirming that he rejoices "on the reduction of Canada; and this is not merely as I am a colonist, but as I am a Briton. I have long been of opinion, that the *foundations of the future grandeur and stability of the British empire lie in America;* and though, like other foundations, they are low and little seen, they are, nevertheless, broad and strong enough to support the greatest political structure human wisdom ever yet erected." Concerning his recent visit to Kames in Scotland he writes, "On the whole, I must say, I think the time we spent there, was six weeks of the *densest* happiness I have met with in any part of my life . . ." (*Writings*, IV, 3–7). In a letter (London, Nov., 1761) he praises Kames's *Introduction to the Art of Thinking* and inquires "after your *Elements of Criticism.*" He also tells Kames about his plans to write an *Art of Virtue* (*ibid.*, IV, 120–3). From Portsmouth, Aug. 17, 1762, he sends his farewell: "I am going from the old world to the new; and I fancy I feel like those, who are leaving this world for the next: grief at the parting; fear of the passage; hope of the future" (*ibid.*, IV, 174).

56. *The Interest of Great Britain Considered?*

57. If ever written, not extant.

58. Daughter of Mrs. Margaret Stevenson, Franklin's landlady at Number Seven, Craven Street, Strand, London. Miss Mary later married Dr. Hewson (see note 77, below).

59. Dr. Thomas Bray's philanthropic schemes for education of Negroes is here referred to. See E. L. Pennington's "The Work of the Bray Associates in Pennsylvania" for Franklin's connection with this work. Mr. Wm. Strahan wished to prevail on Franklin to remove permanently to England. Franklin writes to Deborah, March 5, 1760 (*Writings*, IV, 9–10), offering two reasons for his veto of Strahan's plan: "One, my Affection to Pensilvania, and long established Friendships and other connections there: The other, your invincible Aversion to Crossing the Seas." The remainder of the letter indicates, however, that he was not dead to the hope that his wife would relent.

60. For Franklin's friendship with Ingersoll consult L. H. Gipson's *Jared Ingersoll. A Study of American Loyalism in Relation to British Colonial Government* (New Haven, 1920).

61. Richard ("Omniscient") Jackson (d. 1787), member of Parliament, friend of the colonial cause. See *Dictionary of National Biography*, XXIX, 104–5.

62. John Hawkesworth (1715?–1773). From 1752 to 1754 he edited the *Adventurer*, aided by Johnson, Bathurst, and Wharton. Edited Swift's writings in 1755, Swift's letters in 1766, and Cook's, Byron's, Carteret's, and Wallis's *Voyages* in 1773. (*Dictionary of National Biography*, XXV, 203–5.)

63. John Stanley (1714–1786). Blind organist who composed the music for Hawkesworth's oratorio, *Zimri* (1760); and for his *The Fall of Egypt* (1774). (*Dictionary of National Biography*, LIV, 74–5.)

64. Benjamin West (1738–1820).

65. James Ralph (d. 1762); see *Dictionary of National Biography*, XLVII, 221–4. His *Night: A Poem* (London, 1728), dedicated to the Earl of Chesterfield, is a jejune imitation of Thomson's *Seasons*. He professes himself "a bigotted Admirer of the Antients, and all their Performances" (p. 197) in *The Touch-Stone* . . . (London, 1728): "My Design was, to animadvert upon the Standard Entertainments of the present Age, in Comparison with those of Antiquity" (p. 237). He aided Fielding in bringing out *The Champion* (1741 ff.). Hallam characterized his *History of England* (1744–1746) as one of the best accounts of the time of Charles II. Succinct survey of Ralph in M. K. Jackson's *Outlines of the Literary History of Colonial Pennsylvania*, 37–42.

66. John Fothergill (1712–1780). See *Dictionary of National Biography* XX, 66–8. See J. C. Lettsom's *Memoirs of John Fothergill* (4th ed., London, 1786) for a full treatment of his friendship with Franklin. J. J. Abraham's *Lettsom, His Life, Times, Friends and Descendants* (London, 1933, chap. XVIII), contains an account of the "conciliation negotiations" between Hyde and Dartmouth (representing Lord North) and Barclay and Fothergill (representing Franklin and the colonial cause). Only George III could not be persuaded. Also see R. H. Fox, *Dr. John Fothergill and His Friends* . . . (London, 1919).

For Franklin's quarrel with the Proprietors see *Cool Thoughts on the Present Situation of Our Public Affairs* (April 12, 1764, *Writings*, IV, 226–41). A month later he writes to Wm. Strahan: "Our petty publick affairs here are in the greatest confusion, and will never, in my opinion, be composed, while the Proprietary Government subsists" (*ibid.*, IV, 246).

67. His son William Franklin (1731–1813), governor of New Jersey, and wife. See *Dictionary of American Biography*, VI, 600–1.

68. The barbarities of the "Paxton boys" virtually "threatened a civil war, which Franklin and others averted. This episode marks the beginnings of the predominance of the Ulster Scotch and other Calvinists in Pennsylvania affairs, replacing the old Quaker supremacy." (A. Nevins, *The American States During and After the Revolution, 1775–1789*, New York, 1924, 12.) This uprising, suggests Mr. Nevins, may be viewed as a fragment of that "struggle between East and West, Tidewater and Uplands" which "cut in the later Colonial period across the alignment between people and Crown" (*ibid.*, 11).

69. Pope's translation. Franklin omits lines not essential to the thought in a particular sequence.

70. From Herodotus refracted through Rabelais? See C. E. Jorgenson's "Benjamin Franklin and Rabelais."

71. For Franklin's activities in behalf of the repeal of the Stamp Act

see especially *The Examination of Dr. B. F. Etc. in the British House of Commons, Relative to the Repeal of the American Stamp Act, in 1766* (*Writings*, IV, 412–48).

72. A. F. Tytler, in *Memoirs of the Life and Writings of the Honourable Henry Home of Kames* . . . (2d ed., Edinburgh, 1814, II, 99, 112), suggests that this letter never reached its destination, but "was in all probability intercepted." Brackets in excerpt from letter to Lord Kames, June 2, 1765, pp. 318–21 above, are the result of Smyth's collation of Tytler's and Sparks's versions.

73. Sir John Pringle (1707–1782). Physician (student of Albinus and Boerhaave) whose "great work in life was the reform of military medicine and sanitation" (*Dictionary of National Biography*, XLVI, 386–8). From 1772 to 1778 he was President of the Royal Society. In 1778 he was made one of the eight foreign members of the Academy of Sciences at Paris. Since Pringle was physician to the queen, Parton thinks it probable that he was used by Franklin "to forward to the king such papers and documents as tended to show how loyal to his person and his throne were the vast majority of the American colonists" (*op. cit.*, I, 506). George III, having sided with Dr. Wilson who championed *blunt* lightning rods, asked Pringle to use his influence to have the Royal Society rescind its opinion in favor of *pointed* ones. Pringle's answer "was to the effect that duty as well as inclination would always induce him to execute his majesty's wishes to the utmost of his power: but 'Sire,' said he, 'I cannot reverse the laws and operations of nature' " (*ibid.*, II, 217 note).

74. The full title of Dupont de Nemours's work is *Physiocratie, ou constitution naturelle du gouvernement le plus avantageux au genre humain.* 2 vols. Leyden and Paris, 1767, 1768. Peter Templeman (1711–1769) was Secretary of the London Society of Arts, Manufactures, and Commerce and in 1762 corresponding member of the Royal Academy of Sciences at Paris (*Dictionary of National Biography*, LVI, 53–4). "Ami des hommes" is the Marquis de Mirabeau (1715–1789) who wrote *L'Ami des hommes, ou traité de la population.* [1756] 5th ed., Hamburg, 1760, 4 vols. The "crowning work" of the Physiocrats is François Quesnay's *Tableau économique.* Published by the British Economic Association, London, 1894.

Dupont's letter of May 10, 1768, to which Franklin's is an answer, is printed in *Writings*, V, 153–4. From London (Oct. 2, 1770) Franklin writes to Dupont: "Would to God I could take with me [to America] Messrs. du Pont, du Bourg, and some other French Friends with their good Ladies! I might then, by mixing them with my Friends in Philadelphia, form a little happy Society that would prevent my ever wishing again to visit Europe" (*Writings*, V, 282). Elision marks in letter of July 28 are Franklin's own.

75. John Alleyne. See his *The Legal Degrees of Marriage Stated and Considered* . . . , London, 1774. The second edition (London, 1775) includes Franklin's letter to Alleyne, Appendix, pp. 1–2.

76. Compare *To the Printer of the London Public Advertiser* (August 25, 1768; *Writings*, V, 162–5): "And what are we to gain by this war, by which our trade and manufactures are to be ruined, our strength divided and diminished, our debt increased, and our reputation, as a generous nation, and lovers of liberty, given up and lost? Why, we are to convert millions of the King's loyal subjects into rebels, for the sake of establishing a new claimed power in P—— to tax a distant people, whose abilities and circumstances they cannot be acquainted with, who have a constitutional power of taxing themselves; who have never refused to give us voluntarily more than we can ever expect to wrest from them by force; and by our trade with whom we gain millions a year!" (*Ibid.*, 164–5.)

77. William Hewson (1739–1774). He was married to Miss Stevenson in 1770. Hewson received the Copley medal in 1769 and was made a Fellow of the Royal Society in 1770. (*Dictionary of National Biography*, XXVI, 312–3.)

78. Daughter of Jonathan Shipley, Bishop of St. Asaph, who wrote *A Speech Intended to have been Spoken on the Bill for Altering the Charters of the Colony of the Massachusetts Bay*. New York. Ed. 1774. (Cf. *Writings*, I, 164–6.) Urging that "the true art of government consists in NOT GOVERNING TOO MUCH" (cited in Parton, *op. cit.*, I, 549), Shipley lent sanction to colonial resistance. Franklin writes to Thomas Cushing (London, Oct. 6, 1774): "The Bishop of St. Asaph's intended speech, several Copies of which I send you, and of which many Thousands have been printed and distributed here has had an extraordinary Effect, in changing the Sentiments of Multitudes with regard to America" (*Writings*, VI, 250).

Mungo was a "fine large grey Squirrel" which Deborah sent to her husband (*ibid.*, VI, 16).

79. Printed in *Experiments and Observations on Electricity*. London, 1769.

80. Printed in *Éphémérides du Citoyen* (edited by Dupont after 1767), periodical of the French Physiocrats; and in the *London Chronicle* in 1766.

81. J. Parton observes that this brilliant illustration of Franklin's use of Swiftian hoax and irony "was the nine-days' talk of the kingdom" (*op. cit.*, I, 518).

82. See R. M. Bache, in Bibliography. In addition, article in New York *Times*, Dec. 3, 1896, and notes in E. P. Buckley's "The Library of a Philadelphia Antiquarian," *Magazine of American History*, XXIV, 388–98 (1890). Mr. Buckley reviews the making of the prayer book: "Column after column of the calendar disappeared with a single stroke of the pen— nearly the whole of the Exhortation, a portion of the Confession, all the Absolution, nearly all the Venite, exultemus Domino. Likewise, the Te Deum, and all the Canticle. Of the Creed all he retained was the following: 'I believe in God the Father Almighty, maker of Heaven and Earth, and in Jesus Christ His Son our Lord. I believe in the Holy Ghost,

the forgiveness of sins, and the life everlasting, Amen'" (*ibid.*, 393). Franklin collaborated with Lord Le Despencer in this work. For Franklin's own comments see *Writings*, IX, 358–9, 556. Smyth brackets parts of the *Preface* found in an incomplete MS draft.

83. Date unknown. For history of this hoax see *Writings*, I, 179–81, and L. S. Livingston, *Benjamin Franklin's Parable against Persecution. With an Account of the Early Editions* (Cambridge, Mass., 1916).

84. Date unknown.

85. This letter was never sent.

86. A. H. Smyth thinks that the friend might have been David Hartley.

87. A photostat in the W. S. Mason Collection from the Huntington Library gives the date as July 20, 1776.

88. Time and place of first publication unknown. For an interesting discussion of this piece, see M. C. Tyler's *Literary History of the American Revolution*, II, 367–80. "A British magazine of 1786, says that there was then a transfer made at the Bank of England of £471,000 to Mr. Van Otten on account of the Landgrave of Hesse, for so much due for Hessian soldiers lost in the American war, at £30 a head, thus making the total number lost to be 15,700 men." (Cited in J. F. Watson, *Annals of Philadelphia and Pennsylvania*, Philadelphia, 1857, II, 294.)

89. He writes to M. Lith (April 6, 1777): "If I were to practise giving Letters of Recommendation to Persons of whose Character I knew no more than I do of yours, my Recommendations would soon be of no Authority at all" (*Writings*, VII, 39); and to George Washington (June 13, 1777), apropos of foreign applicants for American posts: "I promise nothing" (VII, 59). In another letter (Oct. 7, 1777) he admitted that "the Numbers we refuse" are "incredible" (VII, 66). Elsewhere he confesses that "These Applications are my perpetual Torment" (VII, 81). Consult E. Repplier, "Franklin's Trials as a Benefactor" (in Bibliography).

90. This controversy evoked the following verse:

> "While you, great George, for safety hunt,
>   And sharp conductors change for blunt,
>   The Empire's out of joint.
>   Franklin a wiser course pursues,
>   And all your thunder fearless views,
>   By keeping to the *point*."

(Cited in Parton, *op. cit.*, II, 217.)

91. Son of the philosopher, David Hartley. Hartley the younger (1732–1813) met Franklin about 1759. A Lord Rockingham man, he opposed the war with the colonies. He and Franklin drew up the Peace Treaty of 1783. See *Dictionary of National Biography*, XXV, 68–9.

92. A. H. Smyth thinks that this dialogue was "written soon after Franklin's arrival in France" (*Writings*, VII, 82 note).

93. A Charles de Weissenstein included in his letter from Brussels, June 16, 1778, a "Plan of Reconciliation," plans for a future American govern-

ment: he wished to have a secret conference with Franklin (*Writings*, VII, 166; Smyth note).

94. *Arcana imperii detecta: or, divers select cases in Government*, London, 1701. [A trans. of *Disquisitiones politicae* by Mark Zuirius Boxhorn.] (A. H. Smyth note, *Writings*, VII, 169.)

95. Franklin writes to William Carmichael (Passy, June 17, 1780): "The Moulin Joli is a little island in the Seine about two leagues hence, part of the country-seat of another friend [Claude-Henri Watelet], where we visit every summer, and spend a day in the pleasing society of the ingenious, learned, and very polite persons who inhabit it. At the time when the letter was written, all conversations at Paris were filled with disputes about the music of Gluck and Picini, a German and Italian musician, who divided the town into violent parties. A friend of this lady [Madame Brillon] having obtained a copy of it, under a promise not to give another, did not observe that promise; so that many have been taken, and it is become as public as such a thing can well be, that is not printed; but I could not dream of its being heard of at Madrid! The thought was partly taken from a little piece of some unknown writer, which I met with fifty years since in a newspaper, and which the sight of the Ephemera brought to my recollection" (*Writings*, VIII, 100). A. H. Smyth observes that it is generally thought that the Ephemera is a reworking of an essay on "Human Vanity" which appeared in the *Pennsylvania Gazette*, Dec. 4, 1735. Also see M. K. Jackson, *op. cit.*, 75; and L. S. Livingston, *Franklin and His Press at Passy* (New York, 1914), 30. Compare Wm. Bartram's similar description of Ephemera in his *Travels* ed. by M. Van Doren (An American Bookshelf), New York, 1928, 88–9. See H. H. Clark's Introduction to *Poems of Freneau* (New York, 1929), xlvii-lviii, for provocative discussion of the degree to which naturalism may motivate an obsession with transience, mutability, and death.

96. On Oct. 22, 1779, Bache wrote to Franklin explaining that Lee and Izard objected to his employing William Temple Franklin, his grandson.

97. Benjamin Franklin Bache (1769–1798), son of Richard Bache, Franklin's son-in-law. See B. Faÿ, *The Two Franklins: Fathers of American Democracy* (Boston, 1933). See *The Diary of B. F. B. Aug. 1, 1782, to Sept. 14, 1785. Trans. from the French by William Duane*, 1865 (in W. S. Mason Collection). A charming self-portrait of a precocious lad who is grief-stricken when rain prevents him from going to the mountains to witness M. du Villard's experiments, who follows avidly the ascensions of "aërostatic globes," who takes M. Charles's course in natural philosophy. Franklin had Didot, the master type founder, come to Passy to teach Ben how "to cast printing types." On July 12, 1785, he records the patriarch's exodus from Passy: "A mournful silence reigned around him and was only interrupted by sobs."

98. Barbeu Dubourg (June 28, Paris) wrote to Franklin, "sending Franklin's manuscript on 'The Morals of Chess,' of which he has retained

a copy; expects to have it printed shortly in *le Journal de Paris;* hopes to follow it with a few reflections of his own on the subject." (*Calendar of the Papers of Benjamin Franklin in the Library of the American Philosophical Society,* III, 102.) [XIV, 218.] Brackets in selection indicate Smyth's collation of incomplete MS copy and printed version.

99. *The Parable against Persecution.*

100. Consult *Benjamin Franklin's Story of the Whistle, with an Introductory Note* by L. S. Livingston, and *A Bibliography to 1820* (Cambridge, Mass., 1922).

101. Matthew Arnold in *Sweetness and Light* appraises Franklin as "a man the most considerable, . . . whom America has yet produced." Missing the irony of Franklin's burlesque, however, Arnold exclaimed after reading the *Proposed Version:* "After all, there is a stretch of humanity beyond Franklin's victorious good sense!"

102. Two days before, he wrote to Richard Price: "We make daily great Improvements in *Natural,* there is one I wish to see in *Moral* Philosophy; the Discovery of a Plan, that would induce and oblige Nations to settle their Disputes without first Cutting one another's Throats" (*Writings,* VIII, 9). One remembers Franklin's classic utterance (in a letter to David Hartley, Passy, Feb. 2, 1780): "There hardly ever existed such a thing as a bad Peace, or, a good War" (*ibid.,* VIII, 5; also see VIII, 506). An interesting comment on Franklin's devotion to peace may be found in *A Project of Universal and Perpetual Peace.* Written by Pierre-André Gargaz, a former Galley-Slave, and printed by Benjamin Franklin at Passy in the Year 1782. Here reprinted, together with an English Version, Introduction, and Typographical Note by George Simpson Eddy, New York, 1922.

103. Sainte-Beuve asks, "Is not that a comparison which, by the sweetness of its inspiration and the breadth of its imagery, recalls the Homeric comparisons of the Odyssey?" (*Portraits of the Eighteenth Century, Historic and Literary,* 366.)

104. The famous Orientalist, later Sir William Jones. Married Georgiana Shipley. In 1779 Jones attempted unofficially to bring about a reconciliation between the colonies and England. See Parton, *op. cit.,* II, 333–4.

105. *Essay on the Population of England,* 2d ed., 1780.

106. London Coffee House.

107. Madame Helvétius.   Consult A. Guillois, *Le salon de Madame Helvétius* (Paris, 1894).

108. Georgiana Shipley (in a letter, May 6, 1781) acknowledges his *Dialogue with the Gout* and this piece. See *Calendar of the Papers of Benjamin Franklin in the Library of the American Philosophical Society,* III, 371 (XXII, 8). This delightful letter is printed in Sparks, IX, 25; Bigelow, VII, 230; and Stifler, *"My Dear Girl"* . . . (New York, 1927). Smyth brackets a passage, not in the MS draft, which is printed in the W. T. Franklin edition.

109. Date uncertain. A. H. Smyth notes that since Miss Shipley replied May 6, 1781 (cf. note 108), it was probably written between January and May, 1781. MS incomplete at both beginning and end.

110. For Hartley's letter see *Calendar of the Papers of Benjamin Franklin in the Library of the American Philosophical Society*, III, 398 (XXII, 162), Sept. 26, 1781. From Passy (Jan. 15, 1782) Franklin writes to Hartley: "Whatever may be the Fate of our poor Countries, let you and I die as we have lived, in Peace with each other" (*Writings*, VIII, 361).

111. Excellent summary of the effect of this hoax may be found in L. S. Livingston, *Franklin and His Press at Passy*, 59–67. Walpole wrote to the Countess of Ossory, Oct. 1, 1782: "Have you seen in the papers an excellent letter of Paul Jones to Sir Joseph York? *Elle nous dit bien des verités!* I doubt poor Sir Joseph cannot answer them! Dr. Franklin himself, I should think, was the author. It is certainly written by a first-rate pen, and not by a common man-of-war" (*ibid.*, 62). A. H. Smyth quotes Wm. Temple Franklin's note: "The deception intended by this supposed 'Supplement,' (which was very accurately imitated with respect to printing, paper, the insertion of advertisements, etc.,) was, that, by transmitting it to England, it might actually be taken for what it purported to be" (*Writings*, VIII, 437). To Charles W. F. Dumas, Franklin writes (Passy, May 3, 1782): "Enclosed I send you a few copies of a paper that places in a striking light, the English barbarities in America, particularly those committed by the savages at their instigation. The *Form* may perhaps not be genuine, but the *substance* is truth; the number of our people of all kinds and ages, murdered and scalped by them being known to exceed that of the invoice. Make any use of them you may think proper to shame your Anglomanes, but do not let it be known through what hands they come" (*ibid.*, 448). Brackets are Franklin's.

112. William Cowper. See *Correspondence of William Cowper*, ed. by Thomas Wright, I, 479, for his note that Thornton, a merchant, had sent Franklin his poems.

113. Henri-Léonard-Jean-Baptiste Bertin (1719–1792).

114. President of the Royal Society (1743–1820). See *Dictionary of National Biography*, III, 129–33.

115. Dr. Pierre-Marie-Auguste Broussonet (1761–1807) met Sir Joseph Banks in 1782.

116. A. H. Smyth believes that this was "written in September, 1782" (*Writings*, VIII, 603 note). It was often translated and may well have drawn many immigrants to the colonies.

117. Probably written after signing of the peace treaty. Compare his letter to Richard Oswald, Passy, Nov. 26, 1782 (*Writings*, VIII, 621–7); and his *The Retort Courteous* (*ibid.*, X, 105–16).

118. Sir Charles Blagden (1748–1820), physician and physicist, friend to Sir Joseph Banks, F. R. S., in 1772. (*Dictionary of National Biography*, V, 155–6.)

119. B. Faÿ in "Franklin et Mirabeau collaborateurs" (see Bibliography) shows that Franklin furnished information for *Considerations on the Order of Cincinnatus . . .* (London ed., 1785). Mirabeau thunders, "Must we then own, with the enemies of freedom, that the noble ideas of Sidney, Locke, Rousseau, and others, who have indulged dreams of political happiness, may be the object of a sublime theory, but cannot possibly be reduced into practice?" (Mirabeau, *op. cit.*, 73.) The members of the order will in time become "Gothic tyrants" (*ibid.*, 14). He warns America against paralleling the decadence of Rome (*ibid.*, 25), suggesting a Rousseauistic equalitarianism. Other references to Franklin's antipathy for the Order are *Writings*, IX, 222, 269–70. Smyth observes that "passages in brackets are not found in the draft in Library of Congress."

120. The Quinquet lamp was invented in 1784. A. H. Smyth suggests that March 20, 1784, is the exact date of composition, from Franklin's sentence, "In the six months between the 20th of March and the 20th of September. . . ."

121. Son of Cotton Mather. Died June 27, 1785.

122. Benjamin Vaughan (1751–1835), unitarian, pro-colonial, and a Lord Shelburne man. He edited the first collective edition of Franklin's works in London (1779). See *Dictionary of National Biography*, LVIII, 158–9.

123. See *Writings*, IX, 264. Sparks (II, 383–426) reprints George Whately's *Principles of Trade*. Elision marks indicate that parts of this letter are omitted.

124. A. H. Smyth quotes W. T. Franklin, who observes that the book was Paley's *Moral Philosophy* (*Writings*, IX, 488 note).

125. A. H. Smyth thinks *The Retort Courteous* (*ibid.*, IX, 489 note).

126. At Rancocas, New Jersey.

127. Sparks (X, 281–2) prints this letter as to Thomas Paine. Smyth, suggesting that Paine's "deistical writings" were not done before 1786, denies that Paine is the correspondent. H. H. Clark has argued shrewdly (and with evidence) that since part of *The Age of Reason* was written before 1781 (this M. C. Conway in his *Life of Paine* admits), it is not implausible that Franklin's letter was directed to Paine. ("An Historical Interpretation of Thomas Paine's Religion," *University of California Chronicle*, XXXV, 84, 1933.)

128. Since Franklin was acquainted with John Ray's *Wisdom of God . . .*, it is not improbable that he was acquainted with his aphorisms published in 1670 (Cambridge), in which this wit occurs. It is also found in Wollaston's *Religion of Nature Delineated*, but as in Ray, in crude form: "It is as when a man spits at heaven, and the spittle falls back upon his own face" (1725 ed., 132). Remembering that Franklin helped set up this piece while working for Samuel Palmer in 1725, his use of it may not be wholly fortuitous.

129. His speech (delivered June 11, 1787) *On the Proportion of Repre-*

sentation and Votes (*Writings*, IX, 595-9) shows how with gift for compromise he helped to bring together the large and small states through his dual scheme of equal and proportional representation in the Senate and House.

130. Compare *Writings*, IX, 659. He observes to Dupont de Nemours (June 9, 1788), "The wisest must agree to some unreasonable things, that reasonable ones of more consequence may be obtained." Brackets are Franklin's.

131. Clergyman of Boston and friend of Mrs. Mecom, Franklin's sister. Elision marks indicate that parts of this letter are omitted.

132. Charles Carroll (1737-1832). He had accompanied Franklin on his Canada commission. See *Dictionary of American Biography*, III, 522-3.

133. Compare *Writings*, IX, 636-9.

134. Compare *Writings*, X, 60-3, 127-9.

135. He writes (Nov. 2, 1789) to Benjamin Vaughan: "The revolution in France is truly surprising. I sincerely wish it may end in establishing a good constitution for that country. The mischiefs and troubles it suffers in the operation, however, give me great concern" (*Writings*, X, 50). He confesses (Nov. 13, 1789) to Jean Baptiste Le Roy: "The voice of *Philosophy* I apprehend can hardly be heard among those tumults" (*ibid.*, 69).

136. Rev. Ezra Stiles (1727-1795), member of the American Philosophical Society (1768), theologian and Newtonian scientist, President of Yale (1778-1795). For the activities of this versatile clergyman, see his *Literary Diary*, ed. by F. B. Dexter (3 vols., New York, 1901), and I. M. Calder (ed.), *Letters and Papers of Ezra Stiles* (New Haven, 1933). Also see Abiel Holmes's *Life of Ezra Stiles* (Boston, 1798).

137. Dr. Stuber's note, cited in *Writings*, X, 86-7: "Dr. Franklin's name, as President of the Abolition Society, was signed to the memorial presented to the House of Representatives of the United States, on the 12th of February, 1789, praying them to exert the full extent of power vested in them by the Constitution, in discouraging the traffic of the human species. This was his last public act. In the debates to which this memorial gave rise, several attempts were made to justify the trade. In the *Federal Gazette* of March 25th, 1790, there appeared an essay, signed *Historicus*, written by Dr. Franklin, in which he communicated a Speech, said to have been delivered in the Divan of Algiers, in 1687, in opposition to the prayer of the petition of a sect called *Erika*, or Purists, for the abolition of piracy and slavery. This pretended African speech was an excellent parody of one delivered by Mr. Jackson, of Georgia. All the arguments, urged in favour of negro slavery, are applied with equal force to justify the plundering and enslaving of Europeans. It affords, at the same time, a demonstration of the futility of the arguments in defence of the slave-trade, and of the strength of mind and ingenuity of the author, at his advanced period

of life. It furnishes, too, a no less convincing proof of his power of imitating the style of other times and nations, than his *Parable against Persecution*. And as the latter led many persons to search the Scriptures with a view to find it, so the former caused many persons to search the bookstores and libraries for the work from which it was said to be extracted." According to the *Pennsylvania Magazine of History and Biography*, XX, 50, the memorial was presented in 1790.

138. Date of composition uncertain. Printed as pamphlet in 1784.

139. Date unknown.

140. A. H. Smyth dates this piece as during the summer of 1786 (*Writings*, X, 131–2 note). Sparks and Bigelow had conjecturedly dated it 1772.